SECOND EDITION

An Insider's Guide to Academic Writing

A Rhetoric and Reader

Susan Miller-Cochran
University of Arizona

Roy Stamper
North Carolina State University

Stacey Cochran
University of Arizona

D0913421

bedford/st.martin's
Macmillan Learning
Boston | New York

For Bedford/St. Martin's

Vice President, Editorial, Macmillan Learning Humanities: Edwin Hill
Executive Program Director for English: Leasa Burton
Senior Program Manager: Laura Arcari
Marketing Manager: Vivian Garcia
Director of Content Development: Jane Knetzger
Developmental Editor: Sherry Mooney
Senior Content Project Manager: Ryan Sullivan
Workflow Project Manager: Lisa McDowell
Production Supervisor: Robert Cherry
Associate Media Project Manager: Emily Brower
Media Editor: Julia Domenicucci
Editorial Services: Lumina Datamatics, Inc.
Composition: Lumina Datamatics, Inc.
Text Permissions Manager: Kalina Ingham
Text Permissions Researcher: Arthur Johnson, Lumina Datamatics, Inc.
Photo Permissions Editor: Angela Boehler
Photo Researcher: Candice Cheesman, Lumina Datamatics, Inc.
Director of Design, Content Management: Diana Blume
Text Design: Claire Seng-Niemoeller
Cover Design: William Boardman
Cover Art: Andrea Tsurumi
Printing and Binding: LSC Communications

Manufactured in the United States of America.

1   2   3   4   5   6   23   22   21   20

For information, write: Bedford/St. Martin's, 75 Arlington Street, Boston, MA 02116
ISBN   978-1-319-36175-4

Acknowledgments

Text acknowledgments and copyrights appear at the back of the book on pages 679–81, which constitute an extension of the copyright page. Art acknowledgments and copyrights appear on the same page as the art selections they cover.

Preface for Instructors

What is an "insider"? In all walks of life, insiders are the ones who know the territory, speak the language, have the skills, understand the codes, keep the secrets. With the second edition of *An Insider's Guide to Academic Writing*, we want to build on the success of the first edition and continue to help college students, new to the world of higher education, to learn the territory, language, skills, codes, and secrets of academic writing in disciplinary contexts. While no single book, or course, or teacher could train all students in all the details of scholarly writing in all disciplines, *An Insider's Guide* offers a flexible, rhetoric-based pedagogy that has helped our students, and students across the country, to navigate the reading and writing expectations of academic discourse communities across the curriculum. We have found that because the pedagogy is grounded in rhetorical principles and concepts, writing instructors who might otherwise be wary of teaching outside their scholarly expertise feel confident about the approach. Moreover, students quickly grasp the transferable benefits of the approach to their future courses, so their level of enthusiasm and personal investment is high. With this new edition, we are celebrating the success of this book in achieving its goal of bringing students into the academic fold, as it was adopted at more than seventy schools, spanning four-year and two-year institutions. We are also fine-tuning that approach based on feedback from the students and instructors who have trusted us to support their efforts. New to the second edition is additional foundational support on the writing process, critical reading, and reflection, to give students the tools they need to be confident writers in any discipline.

As a unique enhancement to its rhetoric-based pedagogy, *An Insider's Guide to Academic Writing* integrates, through video and print interviews, the writing advice of scholars and undergraduates from many disciplines; they speak from and about their own experiences as academic writers. (We conducted, filmed, and curated the interviews ourselves, and they are available as part of the LaunchPad package with the book.) Whether professor or student, these credible and compelling experts humanize and demystify disciplinary discourse, sharing their insider knowledge with academic novices.

An Insider's Guide to Academic Writing derives from the research and teaching that went into transitioning the first-year writing program at North Carolina State University to a writing-in-the-disciplines (WID) approach. This approach is gaining wider currency nationwide as calls for instruction in transferable college writing skills increase. At that time, more than a decade ago, faculty in the program (including the authors of this book) immersed themselves in scholarship on WID and WID pedagogy. We also began to seek supporting instructional materials, but did not find any existing textbooks that met our needs. While several texts focused, to varying degrees, on introducing students to writing in the academic disciplines, few texts employed a rhetorical approach to explore these kinds of writing. Fewer still employed a rhetorical approach to understanding the conventions of writing that characterize those disciplinary texts while also providing support for students' own production of disciplinary genres.

The book that emerged from these years of teaching and research, *An Insider's Guide to Academic Writing*, is a composition rhetoric with readings that distills much of the writing-in-the-disciplines approach that we and our colleagues have used with success for many years. This approach begins by applying rhetorical principles to the understanding of texts, and then shows those principles at work in various domains of academic inquiry, including the humanities, the social sciences, the natural sciences, and the applied fields. It does so mainly by (1) introducing students to rhetorical lenses through which they can view the genres and conventions they will be expected to read and produce in other courses, (2) providing examples of those genres and conventions to analyze and discuss, and (3) including carefully scaffolded writing activities and projects designed to help students explore and guide their production of those genres.

We believe that composition programs pursuing a WID-oriented approach to academic writing will find that *An Insider's Guide* provides a foundation of instruction in disciplinary thinking and writing that is flexible enough to accommodate the diverse teaching interests of individual instructors. Some faculty, for instance, use this approach to support themed courses; they examine how a particular topic or issue is explored by scholars across a range of disciplines. Other faculty situate principles of argument at the center of their course designs and explore disciplinary perspectives and writing in light of those principles. Still others organize their courses as step-by-step journeys through academic domains while attending to the similarities and distinctions in writing practices (rhetorical conventions and genres) of various fields.

The goal of each of these approaches is to foster students' understanding of the various academic communities they participate in as part of the typical undergraduate experience. With the support of *An Insider's Guide to Academic Writing*, these approaches can also foster a deepening rhetorical sensitivity in our students while providing opportunities for them to analyze and practice the kinds of genres they often encounter in college. The book encourages students to exercise rhetorical skills that are transferable from one writing situation to another and supports a rhetorical approach to understanding writing that should be at the core of any first-year writing experience.

A Closer Look at the Rhetoric

The ten chapters of the rhetoric take students inside the worlds of higher education, academic writing and research, and disciplinary writing.

- Part One, "A Guide to College and College Writing," begins by introducing students to colleges and universities, as well as to the kinds of writing expectations they will likely face in college. It introduces students to core principles of rhetoric and writing process, and reviews basic principles of argument and strategies for conducting library research.

- Part Two, "Inside Academic Writing," is an exploration of the research practices, rhetorical conventions, and genres that characterize the major academic disciplinary domains: the humanities, the social sciences, the natural sciences, as well as a number of applied fields. The first chapter in Part Two (Chapter 6) explores the role of the core principles from Part One—rhetoric, argument, and research—in the various academic disciplines. Each of the remaining chapters begins with an exploration of research practices specific to particular academic communities and employs a practical, three-part framework (SLR, or "structure, language, and reference")* for identifying and analyzing the conventions that characterize writing in each discipline.

"INSIDER" FEATURES OF THE RHETORIC

The rhetoric chapters provide a number of features that help facilitate instruction and student learning:

"Insider's View" Sidebars and Videos Linked to LaunchPad
Students hear directly from scholars in various academic fields who explore disciplinary writing expectations and reflect on their own writing practices. These unique features provide a form of personal access to the academic world that students sometimes find alien, uninviting, or intimidating. Each video is accompanied by a pair of activities within LaunchPad, one to confirm

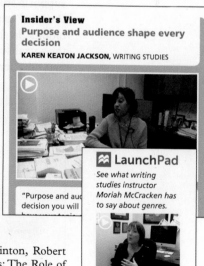

Insider's View
Purpose and audience shape every decision
KAREN KEATON JACKSON, WRITING STUDIES

LaunchPad
See what writing studies instructor Moriah McCracken has to say about genres.

"Purpose and aud
decision you will

Sidebars and video links

*For the concept of the SLR framework, we are indebted to Patricia Linton, Robert Madigan, and Susan Johnson ("Introducing Students to Disciplinary Genres: The Role of the General Composition Course," *Language and Learning across the Disciplines*, vol. 1, no. 2, October 1994, pp. 63-78).

students' understanding of the content and the second inviting them to make larger connections and provide thoughtful written responses.

"Insider Example" Readings These readings appear throughout the chapters, providing models of writing by scholars and students. Most of the readings exemplify important genres of academic and disciplinary writing; many are annotated with marginal commentary that identifies writers' rhetorical moves and/or poses questions for students' further consideration. These annotations take students "inside" the production of various disciplinary texts and, by extension, inside the academy itself.

---

simultaneously, so you'll want to consider their texts from both perspectives. Also keep in mind that their arguments are supported by evidence found in their own research. We'll explore how to conduct research in more detail in Chapter 5.

Insider Example
Professional Analysis of an Advertisement

In the following passage from "Masters of Desire: The Culture of American Advertising," Jack Solomon uses *semiotics*—a method for studying and interpreting cultural signs and symbols—to analyze the arguments made in two advertisements. As you read Solomon's argument, try to identify which elements of argument discussed in this chapter he uses in his analysis.

Excerpt from **"Masters of Desire: The Culture of American Advertising"**

JACK SOLOMON

The American dream . . . has two faces: the one communally egalitarian and the other competitively elitist. This contradiction is no accident; it is fundamental to the structure of American society. Even as America's great myth of equality celebrates the virtues of mom, apple pie, and the girl or boy next door, it also lures us to achieve social distinction, to rise above the crowd and bask alone in the glory. This land

"Insider Example" reading

"Inside Work" and "Writing Project" Activities These activities appear strategically throughout the book's chapters. They are designed to provide opportunities for students to put their learning into action, to analyze and practice the skills and moves taught in the chapters, building a scaffold that supports students' mastery of skills needed to produce the various "Writing Projects" explored throughout the book, from rhetorical analyses and interpretations (in the humanities), theory response papers and literature reviews (in the social sciences), research proposals and formal observation reports (in the natural sciences), to lesson plans and memoranda (in the applied fields).

"Inside Work" and "Writing Project" activities

INSIDE WORK **Drafting a Scene for a Literacy Narrative**

Brainstorm a list of at least five specific scenes you could choose from that best illustrate your literacy development.

Choose one and free-write for five minutes about where the scene happened (location), how long the scene took place (ideally, between a few minutes and a few hours), who was in the scene, and how the scene helped shape your identity.

WRITING PROJECT **Composing a Literacy Narrative**

The purpose of the literacy narrative is for you to reflect on and tell the story of your literacy development. Effective narratives have a beginning, middle, and end, and a literacy narrative follows a series of connected scenes (perhaps three) that illustrate points regarding how you developed your skills, identity, and views of yourself and others as a literate person.

Summary "Tip Sheets"   Each chapter in the rhetoric concludes with a "Tip Sheet" that underscores critical concepts and insights for students as they move from novices to academic insiders.

A Closer Look at the Thematic Reader

Part Three, "Entering Academic Conversations: Readings and Case Studies," is a thematic anthology that takes students inside issues of cultural and academic interest. Along with many examples of writing from non-academic venues that you would expect to find in a composition reader, *An Insider's Guide* distinguishes itself from other texts by including many full-length examples of scholarly articles that highlight the research and communication practices explored through the rhetoric. Unlike

> **tip sheet** **Writing Process and Reflection**
>
> - **You should work to achieve specific goals** related to your writing process during your writing classes:
>   - Develop a writing project through multiple drafts
>   - Develop flexible strategies for reading, drafting, reviewing, collaborating, revising, rewriting, rereading, and editing
>   - Learn to give and to act on productive feedback to works in progress
>   - Use composing processes and tools as a means to discover and reconsider ideas
>   - Reflect on the development of composing practices and how those practices influence your work
> - **Your purpose in using reflective writing is to process experiences** you've had in order to better understand how those experiences shape you and your writing.
> - **Literacy can be broadly or narrowly defined** as the ability to read, write, and communicate in a variety of contexts.
> - **A literacy narrative is a reflective writing genre** used to process the experiences you've had that shape your views of reading, writing, and how you communicate with others.
> - **The key features of a literacy narrative are**
>   - a main idea or point
>   - scenes
>   - sensory detail descriptions
>   - the "I" point of view

"Tip Sheet"

so many other texts, which often provide only excerpted portions of scholarly works of interest, our reader provides full-on "academic case studies," as we explain below.

The reader is composed of four chapters: "Love, Marriage, and Family," "Crime, Punishment, and Justice," "Food, Sustainability, and Class," and "Writing, Identity, and Technology." These are topics that claim students' attention all the time, popular issues that are real to them, newsworthy sub-jects that are staples of media coverage—and they are the kinds of topics that academic commentators are expected to weigh in on. Here are the specifics of how the chapters work:

- Each of the four thematic chapters begins with an introduction that offers a general overview of the chapter's contents, including identifica-tion of each chapter's case study focus. For example, the introduction to Chapter 11, "Love, Marriage, and Family," identifies a number of issues and perspectives offered by the popular readings, including an assess-ment of the current state of marriage in the United States, an exploration of the dynamics of control between parents and children, as well as an examination of various definitions of "family." Each chapter introduction further briefly describes the scholarly perspectives offered in the chapter's academic case study (see the next page for further description of the case studies).

- Each selection in the reader is framed by a brief introduction that provides insight into elements of the rhetorical context of each work, as well as by a series of questions that come at the end of each reading, aimed at supporting reading comprehension, fostering consideration of the text's rhetorical elements, eliciting students' personal connections, and encouraging further active knowledge-making and research.

- Each of the chapters includes a collection of engaging readings designed to highlight various aspects of the topic under consideration in the chapter. Writings are taken from such popular sources as print and online magazines (*Psychology Today*, *Marie Claire*, and the *New Yorker*, for example), as well as newspapers and sites for online news reporting (the *New York Times*, *Daily Beast*, *reason.com*), just to name a few. Collectively, these readings provide additional context for understanding the range of perspectives and approaches individuals assume in response to the topics.

- Each of the chapters in the reader also includes an academic case study that provides a scholarly perspective from the humanities, the social sciences, the natural sciences, and the applied fields on a more focused issue of inquiry related to the chapter's themes. For example, Chapter 12, "Crime, Punishment, and Justice," takes up capital punishment as its more focused case study topic and includes scholarly articles from the *Theatre Journal* (humanities), the *International Journal of Public Opinion Research* (social sciences), *PLoS Medicine* (natural sciences), and the *Journal of Criminal Law and Criminology* (applied fields) to offer readers a range of academic perspectives on the topic. These readings highlight the research focus, forms of evidence, and communication practices that define these discourse communities. Students and instructors can use these readings to learn about the topics scholars explore and the ways they explore those topics, as well as about the literate practices of scholars across the academic domains.

- Each case study contains an annotated scholarly article, each of which represents a different academic disciplinary area. Annotations help guide students' reading of the texts, but they also highlight rhetorical features of the texts and direct students to relevant sections throughout the text that might support their comprehension and analysis.

- Each chapter in the reader concludes with two suggested writing projects. In each case, the first assignment asks students, in response to the chapter's readings, to produce a genre explored in the book's rhetoric. The second assignment asks students to consider further the rhetorical features of one or more of the texts in each chapter.

An instructor can draw on the readings selectively; we have included more options than can realistically be used in a semester. Some instructors may prefer to assign entire academic casebooks; others may choose to cherry-pick them to support a specific disciplinary emphasis at certain points during a semester or quarter; still others may elect to concentrate only on excerpts from scholarly articles, where certain structure, language, or reference features may be examined closely. In any case, we hope that instructors find our selections useful; the thematic chapters do not present a reading list to be marched through over the course of a semester, but a resource to be tapped to suit the particular needs of students as they explore the byways of academic reading and writing.

Finally, the appendix, "Introduction to Documentation Styles," discusses how specific citation styles reflect disciplinary concerns and emphases while concisely explaining and exemplifying the basics of MLA, APA, and CSE documentation.

What's New in the Second Edition?

In response to instructor feedback, we have enhanced the second edition of *An Insider's Guide to Academic Writing* to include the following new features:

- A new Chapter 2, "Writing Process and Reflection," introduces students more fully to process-based writing, and it prepares them for the kinds of reflection that writing research shows us will help them develop as writers in the long term. The principles and activities in Chapter 2 will help scaffold reflection throughout a course so that students develop reflective writing habits. That reflection will further enable them to translate their skills into future coursework or writing in their eventual careers.

- In the reader, a new Chapter 14, "Writing, Identity, and Technology," brings together readings from a range of disciplines, each of which explores the importance or nature of writing in those fields. This chapter can work as a nice capstone to a course on writing in the disciplines, or it can be a useful starting point, helping students to understand that writing is valued across a range of different disciplines.

- In the reader, critical reading support for engaging with scholarly articles has been added. Annotated readings point out Insider moves and provide guidance for incorporating them into a student's own writing.

- New and updated examples throughout the text, including more extensive coverage of school types and the exploration of a community college mission statement in Chapter 1, reflect a broader range of educational experiences and career goals, attending to the needs and interests of students at community colleges as well as four-year schools.

- Expanded coverage of health fields and criminal justice has been added to Chapter 10, "Reading and Writing in the Applied Fields," broadening the scope of student career paths covered. This material, including a new Insider video, illuminates additional professional avenues and the writing conventions within them.

- **New modules on Engineering, Media, and Information Technology** show-case additional applied fields in the LaunchPad—and are available as custom options for the print text. These brief modules address the conventions and concerns of writing in these career-focused disciplines and include key writing genres for each field, such as script pages in the Media module and a problem-solution proposal in the Engineering module.

- **A full LaunchPad includes the complete e-book,** offering the most extensive resources for teaching and learning with *An Insider's Guide to Academic Writing*. Along with the e-book, the LaunchPad includes Insider videos and activities, reading comprehension quizzes for every selection in the book, and LearningCurve adaptive quizzing.

In all walks of life, not all who are invited inside become insiders. Students taking your course in writing are there because they have accepted the invitation to higher education; they've crossed the first threshold. But to become insiders, they'll need the wisdom and counsel of other insiders. We have prepared this book, with its supporting videos and ancillary materials (detailed on p. xii), to help them learn the territory, language, skills, codes, and secrets of academic writing. But a guidebook can only do so much. Students need insiders such as yourself and your colleagues to guide their understanding. We hope our *Insider's Guide* proves to be a resource you rely on as you start them on their journeys.

Acknowledgments

We are indebted to the many skilled and thoughtful instructors who have used and offered feedback on the first edition of this book. We are truly grateful to you for supporting, through your engaging advice and encouraging criticism, our efforts to make this book the best it can possibly be. Most of all, we are grateful to the student writers who shared their work with us for inclusion in this edition of the book. We are grateful for the incredible support from our team at Bedford. First and foremost among that team is Sherry Mooney, our editor, who has helped us see this project through to completion while providing insightful suggestions that have guided our approach. We are also indebted to composition publisher Leasa Burton, who understood our goals and championed this project from the beginning. We have also received outstanding support and guidance from Ryan Sullivan, who guided the book through the production process with great care and good humor. Claire Seng-Niemoeller created the superb design of the book. We thank Vivian Garcia for her marketing and market development efforts. We remain grateful to other contributors who helped in so many ways behind the scenes, including Edwin Hill, Laura Arcari, Michael Granger, Kalina Ingham, Suzanne Chouljian, and Julia Domenicucci, as well as William Boardman, who designed the cover.

We are also indebted to the students who were willing to try this approach and, in many cases, share their writing in this book. Their examples provide essential scaffolding for the book's approach, and their honest feedback helped us refine our explanation of various genres and disciplines.

We are also grateful to our colleagues in the First-Year Writing Program at North Carolina State University and the Writing Program at the University of Arizona, who have shared their expertise and ideas about teaching writing in and about disciplines over the years. Without their support and their innovation, we would not have been able to complete this project. We are also indebted to Kate Lavia-Bagley, whose experience and success with teaching this approach is showcased in the outstanding Instructor's Manual she has written to accompany the book.

We also appreciate the outstanding comments and suggestions we received from reviewers throughout the development of this second edition: Mark Blaauw-Hara, North Central Michigan College; Polina Chemishanova, University of North Carolina at Pembroke; Jonathan Cook, Durham Technical Community College; Virginia Crisco, California State University, Fresno; Kelly Giles, McDowell Technical Community College; Megan Hall, North Carolina State University; Anne Helms, Alamance Community College; Michelle Jarvis, Davidson County Community College; Kyle Jensen, University of North Texas; Brenda Kennedy, Rockingham Community College; Kevin Knight, Cape Fear Community College; Melissa Mohlere, Rowan-Cabarrus Community College; Christopher Osborne, Guilford Technical Community College; Travis Price, North Carolina State University; Paula Rash, Caldwell Community College & Technical Institute; Meg Ruggiero, Appalachian State University; Jessica Saxon, Craven Community College; Daniel Stanford, Pitt Community College; Elizabeth Terry, University of Cincinnati/Clermont; and David Townsend, Richmond Community College.

As always, we remain indebted to our friends and families, who provided a great deal of support as we worked on this edition of the book.

Susan Miller-Cochran

Roy Stamper

Stacey Cochran

We're all in. As always.

Bedford/St. Martin's is as passionately committed to the discipline of English as ever, working hard to provide support and services that make it easier for you to teach your course your way.

Find **community support** at the Bedford/St. Martin's English Community (**community.macmillan.com**), where you can follow our *Bits* blog for new teaching ideas, download titles from our professional resource series, and review projects in the pipeline.

Choose **curriculum solutions** that offer flexible custom options, combining our carefully developed print and digital resources, acclaimed works from Macmillan's trade imprints, and your own course or program materials to provide the exact resources your students need. Our approach to customization makes it possible to create a customized project uniquely suited for your students and, based on your enrollment size, return money to your department and raise your institutional profile with a high-impact author visit through the Macmillan Author Program ("MAP"). *An Insider's Guide to Academic Writing* has pre-built custom modules for Engineering, Media, and Information Technology that can be added to customize the base text.

Rely on **outstanding service** from your Bedford/St. Martin's sales representative and editorial team. Contact us or visit **macmillanlearning.com** to learn more about any of the options below.

LAUNCHPAD FOR *AN INSIDER'S GUIDE TO ACADEMIC WRITING*: WHERE STUDENTS LEARN

LaunchPad provides engaging content and new ways to get the most out of your book. Get an interactive e-book combined with assessment tools in a fully customizable course space; then assign and mix our resources with yours.

- Insider videos offer insights into how experts write in various disciplinary fields.

- Expanded coverage of the applied fields, featuring modules on Engineering, Media, and Information Technology.

- Diagnostics provide opportunities to assess areas for improvement and assign additional exercises based on students' needs. Visual reports show performance by topic, class, and student as well as improvement over time.

- Pre-built units—including readings, videos, quizzes, and more—are easy to adapt and assign by adding your own materials and mixing them with our high-quality multimedia content and ready-made assessment options, such as **LearningCurve** adaptive quizzing and Exercise Central.

- Use LaunchPad on its own or integrate it with your school's learning management system so that your class is always on the same page.

LaunchPad for *An Insider's Guide to Academic Writing* can be purchased on its own or packaged with the print book at a significant discount. An activation code is required. To order LaunchPad for *An Insider's Guide to Academic Writing* with the print book, use ISBN 978-1-319-22338-0. For more information, go to **launchpadworks.com**.

CHOOSE FROM ALTERNATIVE FORMATS OF *AN INSIDER'S GUIDE TO ACADEMIC WRITING*

Bedford/St. Martin's offers a range of formats. Choose what works best for you and your students:

- **Brief Edition**   The brief edition includes the same great content without the four-chapter reader. To order the brief edition, use ISBN 978-1-319-36173-0. To order the brief edition packaged with Launchpad, contact your local sales rep.
- **Popular e-book formats**   For details of our e-book partners, visit **macmillanlearning.com/ebooks**.

INSTRUCTOR RESOURCES

You have a lot to do in your course. We want to make it easy for you to find the support you need—and to get it quickly.

- *Resources for Teaching An Insider's Guide to Academic Writing: A Rhetoric and Reader* is available as a PDF that can be downloaded from **macmillanlearning.com**. Visit the instructor resources tab for *An Insider's Guide to Academic Writing*. In addition to chapter overviews and teaching tips, the instructor's manual includes sample syllabi, context and suggested responses for questions within the book, and suggestions for expanding activities and writing projects.
- *Resources for Teaching North Carolina English 112 with An Insider's Guide to Academic Writing* is available as a PDF that can be downloaded from the Bedford/St. Martin's online catalog at **macmillanlearning.com**. This brief resource complements *Resources for Teaching An Insider's Guide to Academic Writing*, with teaching attention to specific course outcomes and transfer requirements articulated in the 2014 Comprehensive Articulation Agreement between the University of North Carolina and the North Carolina Community College System.

How This Book Supports WPA Outcomes for First-Year Composition

Note: This chart aligns with the latest WPA Outcomes Statement, ratified in July 2014.

WPA Outcomes	Relevant Features of *An Insider's Guide to Academic Writing*
Rhetorical Knowledge	
Learn and use key rhetorical concepts through analyzing and composing a variety of texts.	*An Insider's Guide to Academic Writing* is built on a foundation of rhetorical analysis and production that commences in Chapter 3, "Reading and Writing Rhetorically" (pp. 45–58), and is extended through the rest of the book. The book uses a variety of "rhetorical lenses" to help students become academic insiders who know what conventions to expect and adapt in disciplinary writing. And it brings in, via print and video, the insights of real academic professionals to help students become insiders.
Gain experience reading and composing in several genres to understand how genre conventions shape and are shaped by readers' and writers' practices and purposes.	Each of the ten chapters in Parts One and Two provide instruction in reading and composing a variety of key academic and disciplinary genres, from a rhetorical analysis (Chapter 3, "Reading and Writing Rhetorically," pp. 52–58) to a literature review (Chapter 8, "Reading and Writing in the Social Sciences," pp. 211–26) to a research proposal (Chapter 9, "Reading and Writing in the Natural Sciences," pp. 271–79).
Develop facility in responding to a variety of situations and contexts, calling for purposeful shifts in voice, tone, level of formality, design, medium, and/or structure.	*An Insider's Guide* is predicated on the practice of situational and contextual composition, where rhetorical context and attention to conventions of structure, language, and reference determine a writer's approach to material. For example, in Chapter 6, "Reading and Writing in Academic Disciplines" (pp. 122–28), an astronomer explains how he writes for different audiences, with examples of the same scientific research written up for two different audiences. The chapter introduces the "Structure/Language/Reference" heuristic.
Understand and use a variety of technologies to address a range of audiences.	The use of "Insider's View" videos, available in LaunchPad for *An Insider's Guide to Academic Writing*, models and reinforces the principle of using different technologies to communicate to a range of audiences. The videos of academics explaining how and why they write represent a different channel of explanation, to students and instructors, than the pedagogy in the print book. See astronomer Mike Brotherton's interviews (Chapter 6, "Reading and Writing in Academic Disciplines," pp. 121, 124, 128) and "Insider's View" videos, for example.
Match the capacities of different environments (e.g., print and electronic) to varying rhetorical situations.	See the previous entry, and also the various discussions of genre and genre awareness throughout the book—for example, the opening pages of Chapter 3, "Reading and Writing Rhetorically" (pp. 46–50). See also the cluster of material in Chapter 7, "Reading and Writing in the Humanities," on interpreting images (pp. 140–43) and the Dale Jacobs essay on multimodality (pp. 145–54).

WPA Outcomes	Relevant Features of *An Insider's Guide to Academic Writing*
Critical Thinking, Reading, and Composing	
Use composing and reading for inquiry, learning, thinking, and communicating in various rhetorical contexts.	All of the discipline-specific chapters include detailed information about research and inquiry in their academic domains. See Chapter 7, "Reading and Writing in the Humanities" (pp. 142–60); Chapter 8, "Reading and Writing in the Social Sciences" (pp. 185–96); Chapter 9, "Reading and Writing in the Natural Sciences" (pp. 243–52); and Chapter 10, "Reading and Writing in the Applied Fields" (pp. 294–300).
Read a diverse range of texts, attending especially to relationships between assertion and evidence, to patterns of organization, to interplay between verbal and nonverbal elements, and how these features function for different audiences and situations.	Chapter 4, "Developing Arguments" (pp. 59–80), offers instruction in identifying claims and assertions and relating them to evidence. The genres sections of all the disciplinary chapters in Part Two, "Inside Academic Writing" (Chapters 6–10), help students pay attention to patterns of organization (e.g., the IMRaD format), with particular attention to the Structure, Language, and Reference systems in play. See, for example, "Genres of Writing in the Natural Sciences" (pp. 258–90).
Locate and evaluate primary and secondary research materials, including journal articles, essays, books, databases, and informal Internet sources.	See in particular Chapter 5, "Academic Research" (pp. 81–115), where information on locating and evaluating primary and secondary research materials—including journal articles, essays, books, databases, and informal Internet sources—can be found.
Use strategies—such as interpretation, synthesis, response, critique, and design/ redesign—to compose texts that integrate the writer's ideas with those from appropriate sources.	Chapter 5, "Academic Research" (pp. 81–115), discusses working with sources. Furthermore, Chapter 7, "Reading and Writing in the Humanities" (pp. 139–82), explores textual interpretation, response, and critique; and Chapter 8, "Reading and Writing in the Social Sciences" (pp. 183–239), pays particular attention to strategies of synthesis.
Processes	
Develop a writing project through multiple drafts.	*An Insider's Guide to Academic Writing* presents a detailed overview of the writing process in Chapter 2, "Writing Process and Reflection" (pp. 19–44), and many chapters include "Inside Work" activities that ask students to build on the previous activities to develop a paper. For example, Chapter 4, "Developing Arguments," includes a sequence of such activities on pp. 61, 64, 67, 68, and 69.
Develop flexible strategies for reading, drafting, reviewing, collaboration, revising, rewriting, rereading, and editing.	See the previous entry. Additionally, the "Writing Project" activities that generally close each chapter in the rhetoric are sequenced and scaffolded to support process writing. Throughout the book and in LaunchPad interviews, academic insiders discuss the nature of collaborative writing and working with editors.

WPA Outcomes	Relevant Features of *An Insider's Guide to Academic Writing*
Use composing processes and tools as a means to discover and reconsider ideas.	Chapter 2, "Writing Process and Reflection," includes the section "Use Composing Processes and Tools as a Means to Discover and Reconsider Ideas" (pp. 25–28). Additionally, all of the discipline-specific chapters include detailed information about research and inquiry in their academic domains, and pay attention to the notion of testing ideas with audiences. See in particular Chapter 9, "Reading and Writing in the Natural Sciences," which traces how the process of developing observation and research inevitably leads to a modification of ideas (contrast the two papers by student Kedric Lemon on pp. 260–70 and pp. 280–90).
Experience the collaborative and social aspects of writing processes.	Many of the "Inside Work" activities require collaborative work, and the ethos of collaboration comes through strongly in the chapters on social sciences (Chapter 8) and natural sciences (Chapter 9). The chapter on writing in the natural sciences explicitly discusses the importance of cooperation and collaboration in the conventions section (pp. 257–58).
Learn to give and act on productive feedback to works in progress.	See the previous rubric and Lesson 2, which includes coverage on giving and receiving productive feedback and offers a sample rough draft with a model of peer review feedback to showcase useful feedback for students.
Adapt composing processes for a variety of technologies and modalities.	*An Insider's Guide to Academic Writing*'s start-to-finish emphasis on rhetorically situated, genre-aware, and convention-informed writing underscores this point for students.
Reflect on the development of composing practices and how those practices influence their work.	Chapter 2, "Writing Process and Reflection" (pp. 19–44), introduces students to reflective writing and the benefits of considering their own processes as they develop their writing. See in particular "Reflect on the Development of Composing Practices and How Those Practices Influence Your Work" (p. 28). Additionally, many of the "Inside Work" activities throughout the book have students reflect on what they know, what they think they know, and what they learn. For example, see the "Inside Work" activities throughout Chapter 1, "Inside Colleges and Universities" (pp. 3–18), and the "Inside Work" exercise "Reflecting on Your Thought Processes" in Chapter 2 (p. 28).
Knowledge of Conventions	
Develop knowledge of linguistic structures, including grammar, punctuation, and spelling, through practice in composing and revising.	The distinctive SLR framework (Structure/Language/Reference) introduced in Part Two ("Inside Academic Writing," Chapters 6–10; see the introduction to SLR in Chapter 6, pp. 125–26) has a Language category that emphasizes the linguistic choices and conventions in disciplinary writing, and the Reference feature puts emphasis on formatting issues that include spelling and punctuation. Bedford/St. Martin's also offers a variety of writing handbooks that can be packaged inexpensively with *An Insider's Guide*. See the preface for information.

WPA Outcomes	Relevant Features of *An Insider's Guide to Academic Writing*
Understand why genre conventions for structure, paragraphing, tone, and mechanics vary.	Genre conventions across and within disciplines are emphasized throughout Part Two of the book. Beyond that, the Appendix on documentation styles (pp. 663–77) discusses disciplinary conventions in referencing, with implications for structure and mechanics.
Gain experience negotiating variations in genre conventions.	*An Insider's Guide* provides many opportunities for students to experiment and negotiate variations in disciplinary conventions. See, for example, the "Writing Projects" in Chapter 6, "Reading and Writing in Academic Disciplines," which include "Comparing Scholarly and Popular Articles" (p. 130) and "Translating a Scholarly Article for a Public Audience" (p. 134). In particular, some of the "Inside Work" activities in Chapter 10, "Reading and Writing in the Applied Fields" (pp. 304, 314, 326, 337), ask students to become professionals "for a day" and try writing important genres by extrapolating from models in the chapter.
Learn common formats and/or design features for different kinds of texts.	The design features of key genres, such as IMRaD, are highlighted (especially in Chapters 8 and 9, on the social sciences and natural sciences respectively). Chapter 5, "Academic Research," introduces different documentation formats (MLA, APA, CSE—see pp. 99–101), which is expanded upon in the Appendix on documentation styles (pp. 663–77). Furthermore, the range of multidisciplinary readings in Chapters 11–14 foregrounds a variety of formats used in the humanities, social sciences, and sciences.
Explore the concepts of intellectual property (such as fair use and copyright) that motivate documentation conventions.	The Appendix on documentation styles (MLA, APA, CSE formats) raises issues of different documentation conventions (pp. 663–77), and the discussion of plagiarism in Chapter 5, "Academic Research," raises concerns about intellectual property (pp. 98–99).
Practice applying citation conventions systematically in their own work.	The Appendix (pp. 663–77) enables students to apply citation conventions of MLA, APA, and CSE styles systematically in their own work.

Contents

LaunchPad Additional video material may be found online in LaunchPad when the ◐ icon appears.

2   Writing Process and Reflection   19

7 Reading and Writing in the Humanities 139

A Guide to College and College Writing

ANDREA TSURUMI

Inside Colleges and Universities

What Is Higher Education?

This book introduces expectations about writing you'll likely encounter in college and helps you develop a set of tools to complete writing tasks successfully. To understand those expectations, you may find it helpful to understand first how colleges and universities are structured; how your other writing experiences in high school, college, and work might compare; and what expectations about writing you might encounter in your particular college or university classes. These expectations will likely differ according to the type of college or university you attend.

As you read through the chapters in this book, certain recurring features will help expand your knowledge of college writing:

- *Insider's View* boxes contain excerpts of comments by scholars and students discussing academic writing. Several of these are gleaned from video interviews that complement the instruction in this book. The videos, which are further referenced in the page margins, can be viewed for greater insight into the processes and productions of academic writers. Video content and other helpful resources are available on LaunchPad, designed to accompany this text.

- *Inside Work* activities prompt you to reflect on what you have learned while trying out new insights and techniques.

- *Writing Projects* offer sequences of activities that will help you develop your own compositions.

- *Tip Sheets* summarize key lessons of the chapters.

Before we turn to college writing, however, we ask you to read about and reflect on some of the wider contexts of higher education—in particular, your place in it.

HOW DO COLLEGES AND UNIVERSITIES DIFFER FROM ONE ANOTHER?

As we discuss the expectations you might encounter related to writing in college, you should consider the specific context of the school you're attending. What kind of school is it? What types of students does it serve? What is the school's mission? It's important to realize that different schools have differing missions and values that influence their faculty members' expectations for students.

How did you determine where to attend college? Some prospective students send out applications to multiple schools, while others know exactly where they want to start their college careers. Some students transfer from one school to another, and they do so for a variety of reasons. If you researched potential schools, you likely realized that there are many different kinds of schools in the United States (not to mention the variety of institutions of higher education elsewhere in the world). If we just focus on the range of higher education options in the United States, we find:

- **Community Colleges:** schools that typically offer associate's degrees. Some community colleges prepare students to enter careers directly following graduation; others specialize in helping students transfer to bachelor's-granting institutions after completing most of their general education requirements or an associate's degree.

- **Liberal Arts Colleges/Universities:** schools that introduce students to a broad variety of disciplines as they pursue their bachelor's degrees. Liberal arts schools generally focus on undergraduate education, although some offer graduate degrees as well.

- **Comprehensive Colleges/Universities:** schools that emphasize undergraduate education. They offer bachelor's degrees and often some master's degrees and other graduate degree options. Comprehensive schools are frequently regional public institutions, and they can range in size. Such schools usually have a dual focus on undergraduate and graduate education, but they might not emphasize research expectations for their faculty as intensely as doctoral-granting institutions do.

- **Doctoral-Granting/Research-Intensive Universities:** schools with an emphasis on research and a focus on both undergraduate and graduate education. Doctoral-granting universities, especially those that are research-intensive, can often be quite large, and they generally have higher expectations for faculty members' research activities than other types of institutions do. As a result, students may have more opportunities for collaborative research with faculty members, and graduate students might teach some under-graduate classes.

- **Schools That Serve a Specific Population:** schools that serve specific populations or prepare students for particular careers. Such schools might be single-sex institutions, historically black colleges and universities,

Hispanic-serving institutions, or religious-affiliated schools, to name a few.

- **Schools with a Specific Vocational Focus:** schools that prepare students for careers in particular professional areas. These schools might have a focus on agricultural careers, technical careers, culinary careers, or other vocations.

- **For-Profit Institutions:** schools that operate on a business model and are privately held or publicly traded companies. Some are regionally accredited institutions; many focus on meeting the needs of students whose schedules or other commitments require a different approach from what a typical non-profit college or university provides.

What kind of school is the institution that you currently attend? Knowing how your particular college or university is structured, and how it fits into the larger context of higher education, can help you understand its institutional values and the emphasis it places on particular kinds of academic preparation. If you know these important factors, you'll be able to anticipate the expectations for your academic work and understand the reasoning behind the requirements for your degree.

INSIDE WORK) **Choosing a College**

Write brief responses to the following questions, and be prepared to discuss them with your classmates.

- What kind of institution do you attend? What characteristics of your school seem to match that category?

- What degree program or major are you most interested in? Why?

- Was your interest in a particular degree program or major a factor when you decided to go to college? Why or why not?

- What classes are you taking, and how did you choose them?

- What kinds of factors do you consider when choosing your classes? What guidance, requirements, or other influences help you make those choices? ▶

WHAT IS THE PURPOSE OF COLLEGE?

People's reasons for pursuing an undergraduate degree can differ, depending on the school and the individual student. Some schools and degree programs focus on preparing students for particular careers that they can pursue directly after graduation. Others focus more broadly on developing well-rounded, informed graduates who will be active in their communities regardless of which careers they pursue. Still others emphasize different, and sometimes quite specific, outcomes for their graduates. If you have never done so, consider taking a look at the mission or values statements for your university, college, or department. What do the faculty members and administrators value? What are their expectations of you as a student?

For example, the mission statement of Texas A&M University begins by stating:

> Texas A&M University is dedicated to the discovery, development, communication, and application of knowledge in a wide range of academic and professional fields.

This statement shows a broad commitment to a range of academic interests and professions; therefore, students at Texas A&M can expect to find a wide range of majors represented at the university. The mission statement also emphasizes that knowledge discovery is important at Texas A&M, highlighting the school's role as a research-intensive university.

As another example, the mission statement of Glendale Community College in California reads:

> Glendale Community College serves a diverse population of students by providing the opportunities and support to achieve their educational and career goals. We are committed to student learning and success through transfer preparation, certificates, associate degrees, career development, technical training, continuing education, and basic skills instruction.

This statement illustrates Glendale Community College's emphasis on preparing students for careers and serving a broad range of students with specific academic and professional goals.

A third example is the mission statement of Endicott College in Massachusetts, which begins by stating:

> Shaped by a bold entrepreneurial spirit, Endicott College offers students a vibrant academic environment that remains true to its founding principle of integrating professional and liberal arts with experiential learning including internship opportunities across disciplines.

Endicott's mission mentions an emphasis on "experiential" learning, which is evident through the connection of professional experiences with academics and the availability of internships for students. Students who enroll at Endicott College should expect a practical, hands-on application of their learning throughout their coursework.

Of course, different students have different goals and reasons for pursuing undergraduate degrees. Sometimes those goals match the institution's mission fairly closely, but not always. What is your purpose in attending your college or university? How do your personal and professional goals fit within the school's goals and values?

INSIDE WORK Writing about Your School's Mission

Find your college or university's mission statement (usually available on the school's website), and write a brief description that compares your goals for college to the mission statement. How does the mission of your school fit your goals? How might the characteristics and mission of your college or university help you achieve your goals? ▶

INSIDE WORK Writing about College

Read the following questions, and write a brief response to each.

- What goals do you hope to achieve by attending college?
- What steps should you take to maximize your opportunity to achieve your academic goals?
- What will you need to do while in college to achieve your goals?
- What have you already accomplished, and what do you still need to know and do?
- How do you feel about attending college?
- What concerns you the most about being in college?
- What do you like the most about being in college? ▶

Regardless of your purpose for attending college, the transition to college can be a challenging one. Vincent Tinto, a researcher interested in what helps students succeed as they make the transition to college, has identified and written extensively about three stages that students go through as they adapt to college: separation, transition, and incorporation.* At the separation stage, students might feel disconnected to prior communities and commitments, but successful students move through a transition stage and then find a way to connect themselves with new communities in college (incorporation). The separation stage can be very challenging, though, and knowing what resources you have available to you as you make the transition to college can be incredibly helpful.

INSIDE WORK Writing about Resources at Your Institution

Take a look at your institution's website and look for support services that are available to students. These might include academic, professional, and counseling services, to name a few. What resources are available at your school that might help you improve your transition to college? ▶

---

* Tinto discusses these stages in "Stages of Student Departure: Reflections on the Longitudinal Character of Student Leaving." *The Journal of Higher Education*, vol. 59, no. 4, 1988, pp. 438-55.

ANDREA TSURUMI

What Are Academic Disciplines?

An important structural feature of colleges and universities is the way they are divided into academic disciplines. Depending on the school, this might take the form of departments, divisions, colleges, or other groupings. **Academic disciplines** are, broadly defined, areas of teaching, research, and inquiry that academics pursue. Sometimes these disciplines are listed in broad categories, such as psychology, English, biology, physics, and engineering.

At other times, disciplines are listed in more specialized categories that demonstrate the diversity of areas encompassed within higher education: for example, adolescent psychology, abnormal psychology, sociolinguistics, second language acquisition, molecular biology, physiology, astrophysics, quantum mechanics, civil engineering, mechanical engineering, computer science, Victorian poetry, and medieval literature.

While the specific divisions may differ according to the institution, most college and university faculties are grouped into departments or divisions. Larger schools are typically further divided into colleges or schools-within-schools, which usually cluster together departments that are related to one another in some way. These groupings often, but not always, fall along common lines that divide departments into broader disciplinary areas of the humanities, social sciences, natural sciences, and applied fields. We describe these broad categories in more detail in the next section.

HOW MANY DIFFERENT ACADEMIC DISCIPLINES ARE THERE?

You might find that different faculty members give varying answers to the question, "How many different academic disciplines are there?" And those answers differ for good reason. Sometimes academic disciplines are seen as equivalent to departments. Faculty in the history department study history, right? But the subject of history can be divided into many different categories, too: antebellum U.S. history, Middle Eastern history, and African American history, for example. In addition, people in other departments might study and teach topics that are related to history, such as American religious history, medieval literature and culture, and ancient rhetoric. You can probably imagine how categorizing all these different areas of study and research would be difficult.

For the purposes of this text, we're going to explore writing in different disciplinary areas that are grouped together according to (1) the kinds of questions that scholars ask in those disciplines and (2) the research strategies, or methods of inquiry, that they use to answer those questions. As mentioned earlier, we've divided various academic disciplines into four broad disciplinary categories: humanities, social sciences, natural sciences, and applied fields. As we talk about these four areas of study and the disciplines associated with them, both here and in Part Two of the book, you'll notice some similarities and differences within the categories:

ANDREA TSURUMI

- Scholars in the **humanities** usually ask questions about the human condition. To answer these questions, they often employ methods of inquiry that are based on analysis, interpretation, and speculation. Examples of academic disciplines that are generally considered part of the humanities are history, literature, philosophy, foreign languages, religious studies, and the fine arts. For examples of the kinds of questions humanists ask, see Chapter 7.

- Scholars in the **social sciences** usually ask questions about human behavior and society. To answer these questions, they often employ methods of inquiry that are based on theory building or empirical research. Examples of academic disciplines that are generally considered part of the social sciences are communication, psychology, sociology, political science, economics, and anthropology. For examples of the kinds of questions social scientists ask, see Chapter 8.

- Scholars in the **natural sciences** usually ask questions about the natural world. To answer these questions, they often employ methods of inquiry that are based on experimentation and quantifiable data. Examples of academic disciplines that are generally considered part of the natural sciences are chemistry, biology, physics, astronomy, and mathematics. For examples of the kinds of questions natural scientists ask, see Chapter 9.

- Scholars in **applied fields** might have their foundation in any one (or more) of the disciplinary categories, but their work is generally focused on practical application. Some disciplines that could fall under the category of applied fields are criminal justice, medicine, nursing, education, business, agriculture, and engineering. Each of these fields has elements that are closely aligned with the humanities, social sciences, and/or natural sciences, but each also focuses on application of that knowledge in specific contexts. For examples of the kinds of questions scholars in applied fields ask, see Chapter 10.

These categories are not perfectly distinct, though; they sometimes overlap with one another, and they are debatable. Sometimes you'll find that different institutions categorize certain classes as part of a particular disciplinary area through their General Education requirements, for example. Another institution might list a similar class as meeting a different requirement. You'll see examples of disciplinary overlap in the chapters in Part Two and in the student writing examples there. Regardless of some of these complexities, the disciplinary categories of humanities, social sciences, natural sciences, and applied fields are useful for understanding some of the distinctions in the ways academics think and do research.

INSIDE WORK **Understanding Disciplinarity**

In your own words, write a brief description of the four academic disciplines mentioned in the previous section.

- humanities

- social sciences

- natural sciences

- applied fields

Next, look at your current course schedule. How might you classify the classes you're taking in terms of these four categories? For each class, write for a few minutes about what characteristics of the class cause it to fit into the category you've chosen. Finally, compare your answers with a classmate's. ▶

WHY DO ACADEMICS WRITE?

As you think about the writing you will do in college, keep in mind that you are learning how to participate in the kinds of discussions that scholars and faculty members engage in about topics and issues of mutual interest. In other words, you're entering into academic conversations that have been going on for a while. As you are writing, you will need to think about who your audience is (other students? teachers? an audience outside of the academic setting?), who has already been participating in the conversations of interest to you (and perhaps who hasn't), and what expectations for your writing you'll need to follow in order to contribute to those conversations. (We'll have much more to say about the concept of audience in Chapter 3.)

As we explore the kinds of writing done in various disciplinary areas, you'll notice that different disciplines have different expectations for writing. In other words, faculty members in a particular discipline might expect a piece of writing to be structured in a particular way, or they might use specific kinds of language, or they might expect you to be familiar with certain research by others and refer to it in prescribed ways. Each of these expectations is an aspect of the writing conventions of a particular discipline. **Conventions** are the customs that scholars in a particular discipline follow in their writing. Sometimes those conventions take the form of repeated patterns in structure or certain choices in language use, just to name a couple.

To prepare for writing in varied academic contexts, it might be helpful to think about why academics write. Most faculty members at institutions of higher education explain their responsibilities to the institution and their discipline in terms of three categories: their teaching, their research (which generates much of their writing), and their service (what they do outside of their research and teaching that contributes both to the school and to their discipline). Many academics' writing is related to communicating the results of their research, and it might be published or shared with academic audiences or more general audiences. In fact, a scholar might conduct a research project and then find that he or she needs to communicate the results of that project to a variety of audiences.

Imagine that a physiologist who studies diabetes has discovered a new therapy that could potentially benefit diabetic individuals. The researcher might want to publish the results of her study in an academic journal so that other scientists can read about the results, perhaps replicate the study (repeat it to confirm that the results are the same), and maybe expand on the research findings. She might also want to communicate the results of her research to doctors who work with diabetic patients but who don't necessarily read academic journals in physiology. They might read medical journals, though, so in this case the researcher would need to tailor her results to an audience that is primarily interested in the application of research results to patients. In addition, she might want to report the results of her research to the general public, in which case she might write a press release so that newspapers and magazines can develop news stories about her findings. Each of these writing situations involves reporting the same research results, but to different audiences and for different purposes. The physiologist would need to tailor her writing to meet the needs of each writing situation.

INSIDE WORK **Thinking about What Academics Write**

> Look for a published piece that has been written by one of the professors that you have for another class. Try to find something that you can access in full, either online or through your school's library. Some colleges and universities

have lists of recent publications by faculty on their websites. Additionally, some faculty members list their publications on personal websites. You might also seek help from librarians at your institution if you aren't familiar with the library's resources. Then write your responses to the following questions.

- What does the professor write about?
- Where was that work published?
- Who is the audience for your professor's work?
- What surprised you most about your professor's published work? ▶

Insider's View
Undergraduate students on academic writing

SAM STOUT, GENA LAMBRECHT, ALEXANDRIA WOODS, STUDENTS

Left to right: Sam, engineering; Gena, design; Alexandria, biology

QUESTION: How does the writing you did in high school compare to the writing you've done in college so far?

SAM: Well, in high school [teachers] mainly chose what we wrote about. And here in college they allow you to write about what you're going to be focusing on and choose something that's actually going to benefit you in the future instead of writing for an assignment grade.

GENA: Well, I thought I would be doing a lot more writing, like in my AP English classes, which was analyzing literature and poems and plays and writing to a prompt that talked a lot about specific conventions for that type of literature.

ALEXANDRIA: I expected my college writing to be science-related—doing lab reports and research proposals—rather than what I did before college, in middle school and high school, which was just doing definition papers, analysis of books, and things like that.

 **LaunchPad**

Hear more from students about college writing.

How Does Writing in College Compare with Writing in Other Contexts?

Many of your expectations for writing in college might be based on prior experiences, such as the writing you did in high school or in a work setting. Some students find that writing in college focuses less on personal experience and more on research than writing they've done in other contexts. Some students are surprised to find that writing instruction in college is not always paired with discussion of literature, as it often is in high school. While some colleges and universities use literature as a starting point for teaching writing, many other schools offer writing instruction that is focused on principles of **rhetoric**—the study of how language is used to communicate—apart from the study of literature. (Rhetoric will be discussed in detail in subsequent chapters throughout this book.) As you may have already experienced, many courses require you to write about different topics, in different forms, and for different audiences. Depending on your school, writing program, and instructor, the study of literature might be part of that approach, but you might also need to learn about the expectations of instructors in other disciplines.

When we compare the writing expectations in college with what you might have experienced in other contexts, we're making some general assumptions about your experience that may or may not be true. We're also making generalizations about colleges and universities that might differ from the school you're currently attending. One of the most important concepts we'll discuss in this book is the importance of context (see Chapter 3), so you'll need to balance the principles we talk about in this text with your firsthand experience of the context of your particular college or university. You might find that some of our assumptions are true to your particular experience and some are not. When possible, make note of the principles we discuss that are similar to your experience and the ones that are different. As you do so, you'll be learning about and applying these principles in a way that is much more useful than just memorizing information.

Although the approaches toward teaching writing at various colleges and universities differ, we can talk about some common expectations for college-level writing. The Council of Writing Program Administrators (CWPA), a professional organization of hundreds of writing program directors from across the country, published a list of common outcomes for first-year writing courses that has been adapted for use by many schools. The first list of common outcomes was published in 2000, and it has been revised twice since then, most recently in 2014. The purpose of the statement is to provide common expectations for what college students should be able to accomplish in terms of their writing after finishing a first-year course, but the details of those expectations are often revised to fit a specific institution's context. For example, the first outcome deals with "Rhetorical Knowledge" and emphasizes the importance of understanding how to shape your writing for different purposes and audiences. It states that:

> By the end of first-year composition, students should
> - Learn and use key rhetorical concepts through analyzing and composing a variety of texts

Insider's View
We're looking for students to get their own voices
KAREN KEATON JACKSON, WRITING STUDIES

"In general, the sense that I get is that in high school, writing is more focused on literature. At the college level, we're more interested in critical thinking. We're looking for students to get their own voices in place. Really getting students to think stylistically about the choices they make, really thinking about purpose and audience and the whole rhetorical context. I think that's really key at the college level. By college we're looking at the purpose, and the audience, and the style, and how all of this is determined based on the different writing situation you're in."

 **LaunchPad**

Get expert advice on transitioning to college writing.

- Gain experience reading and composing in several genres to understand how genre conventions shape and are shaped by readers' and writers' practices and purposes
- Develop facility in responding to a variety of situations and contexts calling for purposeful shifts in voice, tone, level of formality, design, medium, and/or structure
- Understand and use a variety of technologies to address a range of audiences
- Match the capacities of different environments (e.g., print and electronic) to varying rhetorical situations

http://wpacouncil.org/positions/outcomes.html

The statement introduces several specialized concepts and terms that we will describe in more detail throughout the book. You might also notice that the statement doesn't specify what kinds of writing students should do in their classes. It is left up to individual schools to determine what will be most helpful for their students.

Some institutions follow the guidelines from the Council of Writing Program Administrators explicitly, while others do not. Even at institutions that use these outcomes as a foundation for the writing curriculum, however, it's often possible to find many different approaches to teaching writing that help students achieve academic literacy. How do your institution's outcomes for writing compare and contrast with your experience in other English classes you have taken? How do the outcomes for writing compare and contrast with your writing experience outside of school (perhaps in work-related or personal settings)?

INSIDE WORK   **Understanding the Goals of Your Writing Course**

Take a look at the goals, objectives, or outcomes listed for the writing course you are currently taking. You might look for a course description on the school's website or in a course catalog, or you might find goals or learning objectives listed in the course syllabus.

- What surprised you about the goals or objectives for your writing course?
- What is similar to or different from the writing courses you have taken before?
- What is similar to or different from the expectations you had for this course?
- How do the outcomes for the course align with your goals for writing and for college?
- What does the list of goals for your course tell you about what is valued at your institution? ▶

HOW DO WRITERS LEARN TO WRITE IN NEW CONTEXTS?

In this chapter, we have discussed the goals and expectations of writing in college and how they might differ from writing you have done in other contexts. The culminating writing project in this chapter asks you to learn from another writer, someone who has more experience in the kind of writing you will be doing in your own academic or professional career, by asking how they discovered the conventions and expectations for writing in their field.

INSIDE WORK **Learning about Writing in Other Contexts**

For this activity, you will interview one of your classmates to understand the kinds of writing they have done in school and how they have learned about writing in a new context. Choose one major writing assignment for a course other than your English class and discuss the following questions:

- What was the assignment?
- What kinds of writing instruction did the instructor give you?
- Was there a writing prompt?
- Did you receive feedback?
- Did you read student samples?
- How did you feel about the instruction and the assignment?
- What are the biggest challenges you've faced regarding writing that you've done in classes other than our English course?
- What advice would you give to students who must take a writing class in order to help them succeed? ▶

Profile of a Writer

WRITING PROJECT

For this writing project, you will develop a profile of a writer in an academic field or profession of interest to you based on an interview you conduct. Under the guidance of your instructor, identify someone who is either a professor, graduate student, or upper-level student in your major (or a major that interests you); or a professional who works in a career that you could imagine for yourself. You might choose someone with whom you already have a connection, either through taking a class, having a mutual acquaintance, or enjoying a shared interest. Ask the person if you can interview him or her, either in person or through e-mail. Consider the descriptions of different disciplinary areas in this chapter, and write a profile of the writer that addresses questions about his or her writing, such as the following.

- What kinds of writing do people do in your field?
- What is the purpose of the writing you do in your field?

- What writing conventions are specific to and important to your research or work? How did you learn those conventions?
- What kinds of writing do you do most often in your work?
- What was your experience the first time you attempted to do those kinds of writing?
- What expectations do you have for students or new professionals who are learning to write in this field?

Be sure to follow up your questions by asking for specific examples if you need more information to understand your interviewee's responses. In addition, you might ask to see an example of his or her writing to use as an illustration in your profile. Don't forget to thank the person for taking the time to respond to your questions.

A profile of a writer should do two things: (1) make a point about the person being interviewed (in this case, your point should focus on the person's writing), and (2) include details about the person's experiences that help develop the point. Incorporate the person's responses into an essay that uses the interview to make a specific point about his or her development and experience as a writer.

Insider Example
Student Profile of a Business Professional

Rubbal Kumar, a sophomore at the University of Arizona, conducted an interview with Benu Badhan, a software engineer from India. Kumar is a computer science major, and he interviewed Ms. Badhan to learn more about the expectations for writing in his future profession. Through his interview with Ms. Badhan, Kumar learned that writing is very different for a software engineer than for a computer science major, but the writing he does as a computer science major will still prepare him well for his future career.

Rubbal Kumar's First Draft of Interview Questions

1. Why did you choose this specific major?
2. What is your specific area of interest in computer science and why?
3. What different types of writing are involved in this field?
4. Is there any specific set of rules for writing in the IT field? If yes, then how is it different from college writing?
5. Did you face any difficulties in understanding writing conventions of computer science?

Rubbal Kumar's Final Profile Draft

Rubbal Kumar

ENG108

May 30, 2017

Profile of a Writer: Benu Badhan

Benu Badhan is a software engineer at Infosys, an information technology consulting company. She has been working in this field for about five years and her specialty includes software testing: manual testing and automation. She has completed her Bachelors in Technology in Computer Science from the Indian Institute of Technology, Mumbai, and completed her Masters from Delhi University, New Delhi. She worked for two different IT firms, Calsoft and Wipro, before joining Infosys.

A key point of the profile, followed by examples from the interview

In an in-person interview, she told me that writing expectations in an IT firm are totally different in comparison with college writing. She said, "In college, we had to write 4-5 page essays, but in the workplace there are totally different conventions." At work, software engineers are expected to write programming codes, and along with each programming code, they have to explain the function of each line using the comment feature. Comments are the description of the logic used to write the code. Commenting on the code is necessary because a programmer may inherit the features of existing code in his or her own code. Therefore, to transfer code successfully, comments are necessary. In this way, if someone else reads the code, the comments make understanding the logic far easier. She said that comments are the heart of the code because without comments another person cannot easily understand the programming code.

Quotation that emphasizes the differences between college and IT writing

When I asked further about whether college had prepared her for writing comments clearly for her code, she replied that if there had been no college writing then she would have had difficulty. She also said that college writing prepares students to express things clearly and concisely, and this is one of the requirements in the IT field. She said that whether it is college writing or workplace writing, quality matters instead of quantity.

A second key point, which builds from the first one

Apart from writing comments in programming code, another form of writing she engages in frequently is writing email. In order to communicate effectively with colleagues, she mentioned that it is important to have good email etiquette. She said that without good communication skills, a person cannot survive in an IT company. In addition to commenting on code and writing email, there are video conference calls and PowerPoint presentations which demand good communication skills. Sometimes she has to lead projects, so leadership qualities and clear communication with a team are also important. As an example, she described working on an idea proposal with her project group and drawing on skills she had learned through college writing. She is convinced that college writing prepares students for other writing assignments in their careers.

A paragraph elaborating on the second key point with examples from the interview

I learned through my conversation with Ms. Badhan that workplace writing is different from college writing in computer science, but the academic writing we do in college prepares us well for what we will be asked to do in the workplace. The workplace is competitive, so it is important to have good writing skills, communication skills, and leadership qualities, and to be a

The central point of the profile

good problem solver. Through my interview with Ms. Badhan, I learned that in order to be successful in writing in the workplace I must also perform well in my writing in college. While the writing conventions may change in the IT industry, the foundation built in college writing is essential.

Work Cited

Badhan, Benu. Personal Interview. 22 May 2017.

Discussion Questions

1. Read through Rubbal Kumar's interview questions of Badhan. What was his purpose in interviewing Badhan? What did he want to understand?

2. Was there anything that surprised you in the profile? If so, what was it?

3. If you were going to add a question to Kumar's interview, what would it be? Why would you add that question?

tip sheet
Inside Colleges and Universities

- **Colleges and universities are not all the same.** Different kinds of colleges and universities have varying purposes, majors, and degrees, and they appeal to a variety of potential students.

- **The institution you attend has a specific focus.** You may find it helpful to identify this focus and understand how it fits with your academic and career goals.

- **Colleges and universities are divided into disciplinary areas.** You might see these areas at your school as departments, divisions, and/or colleges. In this book, we talk about four broad disciplinary areas: humanities, social sciences, natural sciences, and applied fields.

- **Academic and professional writing follow unique conventions.** When academics and professionals write, they often follow conventions specific to their writing situations and to their disciplinary and career areas.

- **Writing in college is not always the same as writing in other contexts.** In college writing courses, we focus on principles of rhetoric, or how language is used to communicate.

Writing Process and Reflection

CHAPTER

2

This chapter has two main purposes. The first purpose is to introduce and discuss the concept of a writing process. The second purpose is to support the development of your reflective writing skills in order to help you better understand the writing processes that you use. The culminating project for this chapter is a literacy narrative, a genre of reflective writing that can help you develop agency in understanding who you are, see how and why you've come to view writing the way you do (both good and bad), and discover what direction your academic and professional career might take based on what you discover about yourself. This is particularly relevant if you are trying to decide what to major in, what career to choose, or whether the major or career you're considering is the right one for you. Reflective writing emerges as a powerful tool for understanding the values and experiences that have shaped you, as well as how those values and experiences may align with the academic major you are considering.

Research study after research study across virtually every profession points to the need for excellent communication skills and development of the "whole person" in the workplace. Whether you want to become an accountant, a nurse, an attorney, an architect, or an engineer, the ability to communicate exceptionally well is a skill that supervisors look for during the hiring process and when making decisions regarding raises and promotions. Many of your communication skills are highly developed already. This chapter will help you develop your writing process and

ANDREA TSURUMI

19

reflective writing skills in order to better understand yourself and to develop a set of tools that you can take with you into new writing situations you may encounter in your major and profession.

What Is a Writing Process?

When you think about major writing assignments you have written in the past, how would you describe the steps you took to complete them? You've written a lot of things by the time you reach college, and when you're asked to write a new assignment for a new class, you may find it helpful to think about how you've written most successfully in the past. What works best for you? What doesn't? And how do you draw from the steps you've taken in the past when you're encountering new assignments? In short, what are the writing processes that you use to make your writing the absolute best it can be?

A **writing process** consists of all the steps you use when writing. Some common steps include brainstorming, freewriting, collecting evidence, drafting, outlining, revising, and receiving and applying feedback from others. How many revisions do you usually work through on a major assignment? Do you like to receive feedback from peers, an instructor, a parent, or a tutor as you are drafting? What types of feedback are most helpful to you? If you have to write an assignment that requires multiple days of drafting, or even weeks, what are the steps you use to maintain focus and consistency?

In Chapter 1, we discussed the Council of Writing Program Administrators' recommended goals for college writing classes, especially the goals related to rhetorical knowledge. Listed below are their recommended goals related to college students' writing processes, highlighting skills you need in order to develop an effective writing process and to succeed in college.

Council of Writing Program Administrators' Selected Goals for Writing Processes

By the end of first-year composition, students should:

- Develop a writing project through multiple drafts
- Develop flexible strategies for reading, drafting, reviewing, collaborating, revising, rewriting, rereading, and editing
- Learn to give and to act on productive feedback to works in progress
- Use composing processes and tools as a means to discover and reconsider ideas
- Reflect on the development of composing practices and how those practices influence their work

Let's consider these goals and reflect on the experiences you have had that demonstrate relevant skills.

DEVELOP A WRITING PROJECT THROUGH MULTIPLE DRAFTS

By now, drafting is a skill you have probably developed quite well. The hard part about drafting is just doing it. We live busy lives and sometimes put off work until the last minute. For some writing assignments, you might be able to get away with last-minute writing. For more complicated projects, however, you may need to develop your assignment over the course of several weeks or months. A lot of this time may be spent analyzing an assignment sheet, reading examples of the kinds of assignments you're asked to write, brainstorming topics, highlighting or annotating sources you've found to support your points, writing an outline, and drafting. These steps are all part of a well-developed writing process that will be discussed throughout this chapter. Just keep in mind that becoming a better writer takes hard work and practice, but developing a writing project through multiple drafts can take your work to a higher level.

Don't be too hard on yourself. Sometimes the expectations for what you have to write can overwhelm you or just aren't interesting to you, and the motivation to stay on task and do a little bit of work each day on an assignment can be hard to come by. The keys are to stay focused, to understand the purpose of the assignment, and to remain as open and engaged as possible.

INSIDE WORK **Reflecting on Your Drafting Process**

Describe the most complicated writing assignment you've written prior to this course. It could be for any class, not necessarily an English class.

- What was the class, and what topic did you write about?
- What was the purpose of the assignment?
- How many revisions did you work through before turning in a final draft of the assignment?
- What writing processes did you use to maintain your focus when drafting the assignment? If you have difficulty naming steps, this might indicate just how much work you need to do to improve your drafting process. By contrast, if you're able to name several specific steps you took to maintain your focus while remaining open to improving your drafts, chances are you've developed some good drafting skills. ▶

DEVELOP FLEXIBLE WRITING PROCESS STRATEGIES

The key word in this goal is *flexible*. In a first-year college writing class, flexibility is most important in the context of reading, drafting, reviewing, collaborating, revising, rewriting, rereading, and editing. That's a long list for sure. But each of these steps is essential to improving your success in college writing.

If you had to rate which of the items in the list you're already adept at, what would you choose? Reading and revising? How about collaborating? Equally important, right?

If you are rigid, set in your ways, and unable to adapt to a variety of demands, you're going to have trouble. By contrast, if you are flexible and adaptable in your approach to collaborating, writing, and learning more broadly, you will be much more likely to succeed. Everybody brings a different set of experiences to a classroom, and your experiences have gotten you this far, so you certainly have some successful strategies already.

Nonetheless, flexibility is essential in a writing classroom and beyond.

INSIDE WORK   **Reflecting on Flexibility**

1. Begin by defining what "flexibility" means to you as a personal character trait. Then, think of examples of people in your life who are inflexible. How does their inflexibility affect their relationships, work, and ability to succeed?

2. Describe a time when a situation demanded that you be flexible in your approach to a relationship, friendship, move, or work situation. How did the demand to be flexible affect you? Was it easy or stressful?

3. Reflect on your writing experiences. What teacher or assignment required that you be the most flexible? What was it about the teacher or a specific assignment that required a flexible approach on your part? ▶

LEARN TO GIVE AND TO ACT ON PRODUCTIVE FEEDBACK TO WORKS IN PROGRESS

Many of the skills that demand flexibility in writing are demonstrated in peer review activities. **Peer review** is the process of reviewing a peer's writing while a project is in a drafting phase in order to provide feedback to improve their work, or of having your own work reviewed by a peer. When you think of peer review, perhaps you think of fixing grammar, punctuation, and spelling issues—content we would refer to as surface-level improvements. While that kind of feedback is important, equally important is the more variable and flexible feedback that shapes the direction or ideas in a peer's writing. These might be called deeper-level revisions.

Essential too, and often overlooked, is the understanding that giving feedback is itself a skill that is developed in the peer review process, and it is also one that requires flexibility. Often we tend to focus only on the end product of the paper that will be graded, but the skill of giving effective feedback to peers is one that requires excellent social skills, generosity, and intellect. Furthermore, the ability to give constructive feedback to peers is a highly sought-after skill relevant to a variety of careers beyond college. To give effective feedback on someone else's writing, you must be able to read the writing from different perspectives and write comments that will be helpful to the author—this requires flexibility in both your reading and writing.

Below, you will see a draft of student Jack Stegner's literacy narrative project for a first-year composition class that has been peer-reviewed by one of his classmates, Nichelle Oquendo. We will discuss the literacy narrative in more detail later in this chapter as an example of reflective writing. As you read Jack's literacy narrative, you should pay attention to the comments Nichelle wrote. In what ways is she practicing flexibility in her reading of Jack's work and in the ways she writes her comments? How is she thinking about his writing from perspectives other than her own?

Insider Example
Sample Rough Draft of Student Jack Stegner's Literacy Narrative, with Peer Review Feedback from Student Nichelle Oquendo

JACK STEGNER

NICHELLE OQUENDO

Orientation to high school was a big thing for me when I was fourteen. I was at one of the best high schools in the country getting ready to start my future life. I was excited yet nervous at the same. I came from a school where I had known kids my whole life and it was different seeing these new faces. I was afraid to talk to anyone since I felt like everyone knew each other. I got my school ID photo taken as I heard a man yelling from the crowd telling freshman to get in line. I looked over and saw this lean man with dark blonde hair and eyes as blue as the sky. As a tiny freshman I was scared to get even close to this man. That was before I realized he was one of the best teachers I would ever have.

> how did ya feel about that

> that was deep

> why were you scared of this man

The next day I walked into my fourth period classroom, and the tall lean man from yesterday was there standing in front of the class. I rolled my eyes to the back of my head saying, "Great, I have to deal with this guy the entire year." The first thing he did was assign us seats, which I wasn't used to, coming from a public school to a private school. He stood in front of the class and said his name was Mr. Alumbaugh and that he was going to be teaching us for the next school year. Then he asked us to write a paper that was due the next day discussing why we decided to go to De La Salle. I left class that day wanting to transfer out. I was already depressed as well not having many friends at the school. I came home crying to my mom saying how I didn't want to go back and

> add some description of what he was wearing, etc.

> how did your mother react when you said this

how I wanted to go to the high school all my friends were going to which was Northgate. She told me at the end of the year if you still feel the same way we can transfer you out.

make a transition from the first sentence to the second

add description of what natalie and lauren looked like and describe your friendship with lauren

A few months went by. I was still at De La Salle but still depressed from not having much of a social life. My friend Lauren wanted me to go out with her friend Natalie. We went on a few dates and we started to catch feelings for each other. Although I was her boyfriend and was friends with her friends I still didn't have many male friends. Then one day in English, Natalie was texting me during class when Mr. Alumbaugh saw. He then took my phone and started texting Natalie as my whole class was laughing at me. I was so embarrassed being called out and having everyone laugh at me. After class however, my friend till this day as well, Chris came up to me and asked if I could join him and his group for lunch. I was finally invited to something and although I was embarrassed I was happy to be made an example of to get noticed.

In the Spring, I was conditioning for football and track, had to give my girlfriend attention, and had to juggle school and social life as well. I was starting to become closer with my classmates and actually making friends. I ended up forgetting about my friends at Northgate and even not wanting to go there. I was starting to become happy and realizing that people did care about me and that they did know me. In English, Mr. Alumbaugh assigned us homework to go up in front of the class and just talk about ourselves for two minutes. At first, I laughed, saying to myself "That's too easy of an assignment." When it actually came to writing about it though, I was puzzled and had no idea what to write about. I went to Mr. Alumbaugh's room one day after class ended and asked if he could help me with the assignment. He looked at me smiled and said, "Jack I can come up with a five minute speech about you and who you are. Just write how other people perceive you."

what was the office room set up like

what was he wearing

The day of the presentation came and I was calm. It felt like I wrote a pretty good speech about myself, good enough to be confident about speaking it to the class. My name was called up and as I stood there the butterflies came out of nowhere, reminding me of the beginning of the year. I started speaking "Hello my name is . . . ." I looked down at my paper when suddenly Mr. Alumbaugh yelled "Stop! Cut!" I was startled. Mr. Alumbaugh said that he could tell I was nervous but I didn't need to look down to see what my name was. The class laughed and I laughed about it, shaking off my nerves. He then said, "Go ahead and try again." I read my speech about myself and my goals in life, and I actually got the best grade in the class.

why

Ever since that day in Mr. Alumbaugh's class, I have never been nervous to give a speech to an audience or to a class. He congratulated me personally and we had a great friendship after that year.

Discussion Questions

1. How did you feel about Nichelle's peer review feedback? Which of her comments is the most helpful to Jack and why? Where is she practicing flexibility in her comments?

2. What type of feedback do you prefer to receive when drafting your own papers?

3. What are some of the skills necessary in order to give effective peer review feedback?

One of the remarkable things about Nichelle's feedback on Jack's draft is that many of the comments she makes are description-related and idea-related. She doesn't comment much about grammar, punctuation, and spelling matters, and she often phrases her feedback in the form of questions and points to things she would like to know more about. She uses humor and seems authentic and sincere in her approach. She helps Jack see his own writing through another perspective, which will help Jack develop flexibility in his own writing. This ability to give and receive effective feedback is a skill that can be developed with practice and guidance and is relevant to many careers beyond college.

USE COMPOSING PROCESSES AND TOOLS AS A MEANS TO DISCOVER AND RECONSIDER IDEAS

A robust, well-developed writing process is critical to improving the quality of your ideas and writing. It's important, too, to know how to use the processes you've developed and the tools available to you for writing. Often the best moments for discovering new ideas come when you encounter a problem and need to draw on your composing processes to solve it. Perhaps you have a page or two of your draft completed, but then you suddenly find yourself stuck and you don't know how to continue writing. You might talk with peers, family, and teachers, or you might search for a more technological solution, such as a digital bibliography generator. It's at exactly these moments when, if you possess the skills of a complex writing process, you can navigate toward the insight and discovery of ideas that will make your work outstanding.

You might already be familiar with some of the commonly discussed steps of the writing process from other classes you've taken. Often, writing teachers talk about some variation of the following elements of the writing process:

- **Prewriting/Invention** This is the point at which you gather ideas for your writing. There are a number of useful brainstorming strategies that students find helpful to the processes of gathering their thoughts and arranging them for writing. A few of the most widely used strategies are freewriting, listing, and idea mapping.

JONATHAN MORRIS AND JODY BAUMGARTNER,
POLITICAL SCIENCE

MORRIS: So often it's not about "I need to write this page." It's that "I have to spend hours and hours and hours doing the analysis. And even once I've done the analysis, taking the statistics and putting them in a way that the reader can understand and is relevant to the story will take days." Now, what I've adjusted to in this *writing process* is "Okay, I don't need to get a page a day. But I've got to have these sets of tasks for today." And it may be doing a series of statistics and then putting them into Excel to make a nice, pretty chart that'll support the story.

BAUMGARTNER: Well, sure.

MORRIS: So it's about tasks.

LaunchPad

Find additional advice on the writing process.

Freewriting, as the term implies, involves writing down your thoughts in a free-flow form, typically for a set amount of time. There's no judgment or evaluation of these ideas as they occur to you. You simply write down whatever comes to mind as you consider a topic or idea. Later, of course, you revisit what you've written to see if it contains ideas or information worth examining further.

Listing is a way of quickly highlighting important information for yourself. You start with a main idea and then just list whatever comes to mind. These lists are typically done quickly the first time, but you can return to them and rework or refine them at any point in the writing process.

Idea mapping is a brainstorming technique that is a favorite among students because it allows you to represent your ideas in an easy-to-follow map. Idea mapping is sometimes referred to as cluster mapping because as you brainstorm, you use clusters of ideas and lines to keep track of the ideas and the relationships among them.

- **Research**   Sometimes research is considered a separate step in the writing process, and sometimes it is part of prewriting/invention. Of course, depending on the nature of your project, there might be a considerable amount of research or very little research involved. We explore some strategies for conducting research in more detail in Chapter 5.

- **Drafting**   At the drafting stage, you get ideas down on paper or screen. You might already realize that these stages don't happen in isolation in most cases; drafting might occur while you're doing prewriting/invention and research, and you might go back and forth between different stages as you work.

- **Peer Review**   As we discuss above, writers often benefit from seeking the feedback of others before considering a project complete. This is only one stage in your writing process, so be sure to consider the point at which it will be the most beneficial to you.

- **Revising**   At the revision stage, a writer takes another look at his or her writing and makes content-level and organizational changes.

This is different from the final step of editing/proofreading.

- **Editing/Proofreading** Finally, the writer focuses on correcting grammatical, mechanical, stylistic, and referential problems in the text.

Depending on the rhetorical context of a writing task, these processes might shift in importance and in the order in which you do them. Imagine you get a last-minute writing assignment at work. You would progress through these stages rather quickly, and you might not have time for more than a cursory peer review. If you're writing a term paper for a class, however, you might be able to do initial prewriting, research, and drafting well before the project's deadline. As we discuss different types of scholarly writing in this text, you might also consider how the writing process for each of these types of writing can vary. For instance, when conducting an experimental study, the research stage of the process will take a significant portion of the time allocated to the project.

Increasingly, students and professionals must also learn how to use technological tools to support the writing process. No doubt you've had a great deal of experience using technologies that contribute to your writing. As you think about the more complex writing assignments you've completed, consider which technological tools have been most helpful in your writing process.

"The more formally recognized genres would be research articles or expository articles or reviews of one another's work. Sometimes you'll see technical reports, depending on what area you're working in. Statisticians will frequently write technical reports for folks for whom they're doing consulting or for government work.

"But I think the day-to-day writing, to me, is much richer and often goes overlooked. When you think about the finished product of a five- or six-page research article—I'll look back over the notes that I would've written to generate the work to end up with that article. And even if you only see five or six pages of polished writing, I look back over my notes and see a hundred or two hundred pages of just scribbles here and scribbles there."

INSIDE WORK   **Talking about Technology with a Partner**

LaunchPad
Hear more about genres of writing.

Choose a partner and talk about technologies you have both used when writing or researching. Perhaps your partner has used Google Docs, PowerPoint, Google Slides, Prezi, or some other technology to improve their writing. Perhaps you have accessed articles, videos, or audio clips from a database, mobile app, or website that represents an emerging technology.

Ask each other the following questions and take notes regarding your partner's responses:

- What technologies have you found most useful in improving the quality of your writing?

- Is there a mobile app you've used or heard about that might be helpful for developing research or writing?

- What tools do you find most useful when you're trying to gather information on a topic that interests you?

- What tools do you know about that other people may not that could be helpful in the writing and research process?

After talking with your peer, what did you learn? Did your peer's discussion of technologies give you insight into tools you already use or would like to use? ❱

We'll ask you to practice different parts of your writing process throughout this book, both through the exercises you'll participate in and the larger writing assignments that you'll complete. As you work through the exercises, think about what part of the writing process you're addressing and what tools might help you to complete that stage most effectively.

REFLECT ON THE DEVELOPMENT OF COMPOSING PRACTICES AND HOW THOSE PRACTICES INFLUENCE YOUR WORK

Reflection—and reflective writing—is a powerful tool for understanding yourself, your experiences, your strengths, your weaknesses, and your unique way of seeing the world. Understanding who you are is absolutely essential to aligning with a satisfying major and career. Scholars refer to this kind of awareness and understanding of one's own thought processes as **metacognition**.

INSIDE WORK   **Reflecting on Your Thought Processes**

Practice engaging in reflection by writing your responses to the following questions:

- If you could learn one thing about yourself that you don't already know, what would it be?

- Discuss a time when you realized your thought processes were different than someone else's and that their thought processes had value to you.

- Describe your personality in three to five sentences.

- Describe the personality of one person who is not related to you, but who contributed positively to who you are. What do you like about their personality and how is it different from your own?

- Discuss how your personality aligns with the career you'd like to have. If you're not sure what career you would like to have, discuss a dream job and explain how that job would make you happy. What kind of major would lead to the career you want? ❱

What Is Reflective Writing?

Reflective writing is writing based on an author's experience. It is often used to process events, relationships, or experiences in order to make sense of them. One of the best-known genres of reflective writing is the diary, but there are many other reflective writing genres such as memoir, exercise/workout journal, travel blog, research logbook, personal letters, and the literacy narrative.

One of the common purposes of these genres is to process experiences and to organize those experiences in a meaningful way. Diaries often feature sections organized by date, and the audience is usually limited to only the writer herself. Sometimes diaries do reach publication and a wide audience, such as *The Diary of Anne Frank*, but this is usually not their intended purpose.

By contrast, the memoir genre of reflective writing is usually written for publication and with a wider audience in mind. Famous examples of the memoir genre include Maya Angelou's *I Know Why the Caged Bird Sings*, Elie Wiesel's *Night*, and Jon Krakauer's *Into Thin Air: A Personal Account of the Mt. Everest Disaster*. Krakauer's memoir, for example, details the author's experience in the 1996 Mount Everest disaster, one of the deadliest expeditions in mountaineering history.

In academic writing classes, the literacy narrative is one of the most commonly used reflective genres. The purpose of the literacy narrative is to describe the events that contributed to development of literacy and how that literacy helped shape understanding of the world. We'll talk more about literacy narratives after exploring what we mean by the word *literacy*.

What Is Literacy?

Literacy is sometimes defined as the ability to read and write, but when we are talking about academic contexts, we'd like you to use a broader definition. Think of literacy not only as the ability to read and write, but also as the ability to function successfully in a specific context or contexts. When you consider your literacy development over the span of your life, it is easy to see marked improvement. When you were a small child, for example, you first learned the alphabet, how to hold a pencil or crayon, and how to make the shapes of letters that would later become words and sentences. What's harder to see are the subtle changes that take place over a shorter span of time, such as a single semester of college. Perhaps you only pick up a few skills: knowledge about when to ask a peer to review your writing, how to insert a direct quotation into a paper, or how to create a graph from data you've collected. Each of these small skills accumulates with others over time to prepare you for the kinds of writing and research that will serve you in a career beyond college.

Scholarship in writing studies suggests that the habits of mind most essential to transferring knowledge gained in one context (say this class) to another context (say a senior-level writing intensive course in your major) are metacognition and flexibility/adaptability. If you think about it for a moment, it makes sense. Metacognition is the awareness of one's own thought processes. If your awareness of how you think and process knowledge is highly developed, you'll be able to take knowledge you acquire and more readily draw from that knowledge in another instance. This is where reflective writing is especially helpful because reflective writing improves metacognition.

What Is a Literacy Narrative?

A **literacy narrative** is an essay that reflects on how someone has developed literacy over time. It is a form of reflective writing that draws on your memories and experiences, and as such it is non-fiction. The purpose of the genre is to reflect on your identity as a literate person, as someone who has or needs to develop a skill. When done well, the literacy narrative makes meaning from experience and helps you to better understand yourself, why you feel the way you do about the skill you gained, and how to chart a path forward in your life, drawing from the knowledge you have acquired.

A literacy narrative need not be confined to an academic setting. As we've begun to explore, literacy can mean much more than the ability to read and write, and the attitudes we bring to a classroom are informed by thousands of experiences that may have nothing to do with a classroom, teachers, or reading and writing directly. A literacy narrative might encompass the story of how you learned to speak and act as a softball player, YouTube celebrity, or employee at a movie theater. That kind of literacy narrative might explore the slang, codes of behavior, dress, or attitudes that others impressed upon you. Your instructor may have specific guidelines about the kinds of events she wants to see in your literacy narrative. The underlying theme, though, should be literacy (either narrowly or broadly defined), how you came to be literate, and what your feelings and attitudes about literacy are.

CHARACTERISTICS OF A LITERACY NARRATIVE

A literacy narrative almost always includes the following characteristics:

1. a main idea (or point) regarding your literacy development
2. scene writing (specific settings with a location and time)
3. use of sensory detail to describe the scenes (sight, sound, smell, touch, taste)
4. the "I" point of view

Effective narratives generally involve a struggle, obstacle, or challenge that you overcame. The struggle could be emotional (shame or anxiety, for example), or it could be physical or situational (perhaps you learned how to read with the help of a single mother who was working two jobs). All struggles appeal to emotions and as such can inspire readers to find persistence, passion, and perseverance, or to overcome challenges.

Main Idea

Probably the most important aspect of a literacy narrative is the guiding principle or main idea of your narrative. This should be something you have a sense of before you get far into the drafting phase of your essay, but it may well develop or change as you write. For some students, it takes writing a full draft of a paper to really begin to see what the main idea is and what point they are trying to make.

The main idea of your literacy narrative should be tied into your identity, how you view literacy, and how your views developed through experiences good and bad. One activity that helps to brainstorm ideas is to list five words that describe your personality.

Scenes

In a literacy narrative, a scene consists of a specific time and location. The bus stop on the morning of your first day of high school, the classroom where you took the SAT, an auditorium stage where you gave a speech, your kitchen table where an adult helped you learn to spell your name when you were four years old. These are specific scenes. They take place at a specific location over a fairly short amount of time (from a few minutes to a few hours). A literacy narrative written for a college class will usually be between four and ten pages. This affords you the space to select approximately three scenes from your life to describe.

If you had to select three scenes from your life that informed how you view reading, writing, language, and education, what would they be? Can you connect the scenes to the main idea you would like to convey about your identity as a student?

Sensory Details

So you decide on a scene. Then what? Writers rely on our five senses — sight, sound, touch, smell, and taste — to describe scenes vividly. To use sensory detail, you absolutely have to use your imagination and memory.

It's like painting. The key is to blend your sensory details to create an impression. Make use of as many senses as you can.

Rather than summarize huge chunks of time (your entire middle school experience, for example), decide on three specific scenes with short timespans and fixed locations that paint an impression of who you are, how your views of reading and writing were shaped in an instant of time, and then make use of all the sensory details you can to paint that scene.

"I" Point of View

One of the most commonly asked questions in a first-year writing course is "Can I use the 'I' point of view in my paper?" It seems that many college students arrive having been taught contradictory rules about using the "I" point of view for writing in a class. Let's try and clarify this rule for you once and for all.

Use or non-use of the "I" point of view in a paper for a class totally depends on the genre in which you are writing. When writing in the literacy narrative genre, you should make use of the "I" point of view. You are telling your story from your life, and the "I" point of view is the most appropriate point of view to use. In a scientific report, however, it might not always be helpful or appropriate to use the "I" point of view.

Insider Example
Professional Literacy Narrative

In the following scholarly article, "Two Vowels Together: On the Wonderfully Insufferable Experiences of Literacy," Aimee C. Mapes advocates for the use of reflective writing such as the literacy narrative as a form of resistance to the emphasis on standardized testing in school curricula over the past two decades. In making her case, Mapes draws on some of the stylistic conventions of the literacy narrative while introducing readers to the scholarly discourse surrounding the literacy narrative itself. Notice the ways that she develops a main idea through specific scenes in her narrative.

Two Vowels Together: On the Wonderfully Insufferable Experiences of Literacy

AIMEE C. MAPES

When I was four years old, I learned to write my given name using big and small letters: *A-i-m-e-e*. The problem was that I couldn't write the little *e*. For two years, every *e* turned upside down.

I could write: A
I could write: i
I could write: m
I could write: ə
Twice: ə

Despite my Irish Catholic grandmother trying her damnedest to rehabilitate this propensity, the habit formed. Even now, using tools in

Microsoft Word to recreate an upside down *e* (twice!), I transport back in time to my grandmother's small bungalow in the north valley of California, kneeling over a mocha-stained wood coffee table, issues of the *National Enquirer* and *Readers Digest* layered on the lower level. On recycled white construction paper, my unsteady hand sketched *A*, then *i*, then *m*. My pencil moved directly left, circled down right, and then circled up to the left. Upside down. *Slap.*

My hand stinging, Grammie said, "You're doing it wrong. Do it right. Like this."

Stubby pencil in hand, I moved left, circled down to the right, and circled up, to the left. Upside down. *Slap.*

With two vowels together, I was twice wrong. *Slap. Slap.*

INSUFFERABLE HABITS

When I return to four-year-old me tracing letters, what I recall is not Slap, Slap. It is shame. Myself a teacher of writing with a four-year-old son experiencing his emergent literate practices, I'm curious about what heightened my grandmother's desire to rectify this upside-down *e* habit. Doing it wrong was failing. Doing it right, "like this," was learning. Where she observed failure, many literacy scholars would describe learning (see Goodman). There's the rub. My grandmother observed only deficits. As an instructor of first-year writing and an assistant director of a university writing program, I imagine first-year students similarly positioned as not learning. I imagine how high-stakes assessments and institutional placements attach a discourse of deficit to students as a consequence of facile narratives of learning. Anxieties over college readiness come to mind. Slap. Slap. The current sociopolitical and economic juncture—where fears about a literacy crisis, socioeconomic uncertainties, and flourishing digital and information technologies coalesce into economies of an educational crisis—is precisely when literacy narratives are necessary.

THE KIDS DON'T STAND A CHANCE

At present, teachers of English know all too well claims of a literacy crisis in education. Popular and scholarly reports lament students' reading and writing habits—texting, being distracted, the five-paragraph theme, low achievement on standardized measures. Chris Gallagher writes that standardized testing, among other neoliberal agendas, "provides fodder for a continuous, manufactured education crisis" (454). Calls for education reform construct students as failing to learn. Since the early 2000s, reports contribute to manufacturing a college student crisis. Citing a 2003 National Assessment of Adult Literacy, for instance, Emory University English professor Mark Bauerlein surmises a decline in college graduates' literacy skills in the 1990s. Based on results of numerous standardized assessments of civic learning, quantitative skills, and participation in the arts, he contends that today's college students have stark knowledge deficits, as does another notable (and contested) study by Richard Arum and Josipa Roksa in *Academically Adrift*. Grand narratives about learning circulate locally and nationally that, taken together, advance an educational crisis. Amongst circulating narratives, accountability discourses, according to Chris Gallagher, reinforce a "bureaucratic-institutional model" of assessment wherein "those closest to and most involved in the central activity of the system—teaching and learning—are accorded the least primacy and authority" (463). That is, teachers and learners function as byproducts of wider systems of institutional competition. In neoliberal accountability discourse, what follows is rote pedagogy designed to support students' achievement on high-stakes assessments—or, as my grandmother would describe, doing it right, "like this." Indeed, Yancey, Robertson, and Taczak's research in *Writing across Contexts* explains that "students do bring to college what the school culture has emphasized: a test-based writing practice keyed to creating texts with simple beginning-middle-end structures, a central claim, and some evidence, producing what is called the five-paragraph theme" (13). There is no room for upside-down *e*'s.

For me, literacy narratives in first-year writing emerge as powerful tools to disentangle these economies and interject complexly lived experiences with literacy. As a writing program administrator, I champion literacy narratives knowing the genre has been/is maligned by some in the field of composition and rhetoric (see Kara Alexander; Daniel; Hall and Minnix). For instance, literacy narratives, according to Kara Poe Alexander, reinforce dominant master narratives, as simple success stories. Some personal narratives, explains Thomas Newkirk ("Transformation"), invite "students to view their self-development as a series of pivotal moments that result in qualitative changes in their value systems or identities" (264). As a genre, literacy narratives suffer from the same pitfalls: the story is at once a celebration of writing "for self-examination" and also the burden of transformation (Newkirk, *Performance*, 23). Despite this, for over twenty years, composition scholars depict benefits of pedagogies focused on students' literacy experiences prior to college and in relation to academic literacies. Elizabeth Chiseri-Strater explains that all literate practices inform students' overall literacy. Literacy narratives, according to Mary Soliday, invite students to consider the place and communities where language is acquired. Jonathan Alexander's case study of two gamers argues for composition pedagogy built around "literacies that students are already developing outside the classroom and [that] demonstrate how they can be complemented and augmented with more 'traditional' academic literacies" (53). So, too, literacy narratives allow students to identify and carefully cultivate an awareness of sponsorship in their literate lives as Deborah Brandt's research demonstrates in *Literacy in American Lives*. For the students that I teach, the benefits of tapping these enterprises are twofold: (1) Students are in a position to acknowledge themselves as legitimate readers, writers, and producers of texts and as having a history of engaging organizations much like they will or are engaging the university, and (2) The engagement can scaffold students' recognitions of intricate webs of support over a lifespan, for narrative reflections create opportunities for relationships and meaning making. Coming from the belief that students bring personal lives into the classroom, I expect first-year writing, in particular, to draw on the multiple lifeworlds of students, and literacy narratives afford legitimate opportunities to do so.

TAKE THE POWER BACK

When I reflect on being four years old and resisting standards for drawing the letter *e*, I recall feeling shame, certainly, then anger, and finally resentment about my name. I was always twice wrong. But there is more to that story. The narrative shifts. After three years in elementary school—three years of being one of two or even three Amy's to a classroom—my perspective changed. I still resented being one of a pair of girls named Amy in my third grade class, but I experienced the spelling of my name newly. The other girls spelled their name *A-m-y* and arrived in school with well-combed hair. A-m-y wore dresses. She brought lunch in Care Bear lunchboxes, sandwiches secured in orange Tupperware. My Wonderbread peanut butter sandwiches came to school in plastic wrap inside a brown paper bag, which I subsequently discarded. On rare occasions I brushed my hair for school, and usually my mom reminded me. I wore faded jeans and jersey tees. *A-i-m-e-e*, as I learned, was French. It meant beloved. It was unique. Being A-i-m-e-e undercut feelings of inferiority in school where I felt shame differently, shame for being a girl who didn't comb her hair perfectly. Shame for living in a rental duplex with a kitchen absent Tupperware. Shame for having a single mother. By contrast, A-i-m-e-e meant my parents loved me. The trouble with an upside-down *e* transformed.

Whenever I encounter cyclical reports of an American literacy crisis, I'm reminded of my own literacy crisis. Current anxieties about college readiness aren't new. They are new versions of old conflicts. Composition theorists have a history of contesting literacy crisis discourse, especially as it disproportionately harms non-dominant communities (see Lamos, Fox, Trimbur). One of the most celebrated literacy narratives in our field, Mike Rose's *Lives on the Boundary* artfully details this very pattern. Almost thirty years ago, literacy scholar Geraldine Clifford (1988) explained that "cycles of concern for an integrated holistic approach to English language instruction have periodically emerged in reaction to historical forces that are essentially fragmenting in their effects" (3), but it is misleading to perceive the pattern as endlessly repeated cycles of back to the basics because over time reversals are not as extreme as they first seemed. When situated amid historic perspectives on literacy instruction, even current research in composition and rhetoric on program assessment, transfer of knowledge, and metacognition is circumscribed by discourses of accountability. As the field explores concepts like transfer and metacognition, for example, I think about how current scholarship has the potential to default into narratives of progress that fail to characterize learning as full of regressions and resistance.

EVERYTHING IS EVERYTHING

As a mother of a four-year-old and a teacher for twenty years, I am ever grateful for upside-down *e*'s. Teaching and learning, according to Gallagher, "succeed or fail on the strength of *relationships*" (463, emphasis kept) because, Robert Yagelski explains, "language and literacy are wonderfully, insufferably complex and resist control (and human beings, the more so)" (266). In the current educational crisis, curriculum should provide a counterscript to pervasive constructions of student deficits. The power to showcase literacies rests firmly in first-year writing where narrow scripts of learning can be grappled with, explored, and resisted through effortful reflections of students' cultural histories and shared literacies. Provide students opportunities to voice their stories, and you will create meaningful reflections on the wonderfully insufferable complexities of literacy.

REMIX: THE WONDERFULLY INSUFFERABLE LITERACY PLAYLIST

"Wonderful World," Sam Cooke. *Greatest Hits: Sam Cooke*. BMG Entertainment, 1997.
"Habit," Ought. *More Than Any Other Day*. Constellation Records, 2014.
"2 Vowels Together," Miss Jenny & Friends. *Phonics Time*. Jennifer Fixman Kramer, 2013.
"The Kids Don't Stand a Chance," Vampire Weekend. *Vampire Weekend*. XL Recordings, 2008.
"School," Nirvana. *Bleach*. Sub Pop Records, 1989.
"We're Going to Be Friends," The White Stripes. *White Blood Cells*. Third Man Records, 2001.
"Take the Power Back," Rage Against the Machine. *Rage Against the Machine*. Sony Music Entertainment, 1992.
"Everything Is Everything," Lauryn Hill. *The Miseducation of Lauryn Hill*. Ruffhouse Records, 1998.

WORKS CITED

Alexander, Jonathan. "Gaming, Student Literacies, and the Composition Classroom: Some Possibilities for Transformation." *College Composition and Communication*, vol. 61, no. 1, 2009, pp. 35–63.

Alexander, Kara Poe. "Success, Victims, and Prodigies: 'Master' and 'Little' Cultural Narratives in the Literacy Narrative Genre." *College Composition and Communication*, vol. 62, no. 4, 2011, pp. 608–33.

Arum, Richard, and Josipa Roksa. *Academically Adrift: Limited Learning on College Campuses*. University of Chicago Press, 2011.

Bauerlein, Mark. *The Dumbest Generation: How the Digital Age Stupefies Young Americans and Jeopardizes Our Future.* Jeremy P. Tarcher/Penguin, 2008.

Brandt, Deborah. *Literacy in American Lives.* Cambridge UP, 2001.

Chiseri-Strater, Elizabeth. *Academic Literacies: The Public and Private Discourse of University Students.* Boynton/Cook, 1991.

Clifford, Geraldine Joncich. *A Sisyphean Task: Historical Perspectives on Writing and Reading Instruction.* National Center for the Study of Writing, 1987. Technical Report, no. 7, NWP.org. National Writing Project, 1987.

Cooke, Sam. "Wonderful World." *Greatest Hits: Sam Cooke*, BMG Entertainment, 1997.

Daniel, Beth. "Narratives of Literacy: Connecting Composition to Culture." *College Composition and Communication*, vol. 50, no. 3, 1999, pp. 393–410.

Fox, Tom. *Defending Access: A Critique of Standards in Higher Education.* Boynton/Cook, 1999.

Gallagher, Chris. "Being There: (Re)Making the Assessment Scene." *College Composition and Communication*, vol. 62, no. 3, 2011, pp. 450–76.

Goodman, Yetta. "The Development of Initial Literacy." *Perspectives on Literacy*, edited by Eugene Kintgen, Barry M. Kroll, and Mike Rose, Southern Illinois University Press, 1989, pp. 312–20.

Hall, Anne-Marie, and Christopher Minnix. "Beyond the Bridge Metaphor: Rethinking the Place of the Literacy Narrative in the Basic Writing Curriculum." *Journal of Basic Writing*, vol. 31, no. 2, 2012, pp. 57–82.

Hill, Lauryn. "Everything Is Everything." *The Miseducation of Lauryn Hill*, Ruffhouse Records LP, 1998.

Lamos, Steve. "Literacy Crisis and Color-Blindness: The Problematic Racial Dynamics of Mid-1970s Language and Literacy Instruction for 'High Risk' Minority Students." *College Composition and Communication*, vol. 61, no. 2, 2009, pp. W125-W148.

Miss Jenny & Friends. "2 Vowels Together with Miss Jenny." *Phonics Time*, Jennifer Fixman Kramer, 2013.

Newkirk, Thomas. "The Dogma of Transformation." *College Composition and Communication*, vol. 56, no. 1, 2004, pp. 251–71.

-----. *The Performance of Self in Student Writing.* Boynton/Cook, 1997.

Nirvana. "Schools." *Bleach*, Sub Pop Records, 1989.

Ought. "Habit." *More Than Any Other Day*, Constellation, 2014.

Rage Against the Machine. "Take the Power Back." *Rage Against the Machine*, Sony Music Entertainment, 1992.

Rose, Mike. *Lives on the Boundary.* Penguin, 1989.

Soliday, Mary. "Translating Self and Difference through Literacy Narratives." *College English*, vol. 56, no. 5, 1994, pp. 511–26.

Trimbur, John. "Literacy and the Discourse of Crisis." *The Politics of Writing Instruction: Postsecondary*, edited by Richard Bullock, John Trimbur, and Charles Schuster, Heinemann, 1991, pp. 277–95.

Vampire Weekend. "The Kids Don't Stand a Chance." *Vampire Weekend*, XL, 2008.

The White Stripes. "We're Going to Be Friends." *White Blood Cells*, Third Man Records, 2001.

Yagelski, Robert. "Stasis and Change: English Education and the Crisis of Sustainability." *English Education*, vol. 37, no. 4, 2005, pp. 262–71.

Yancey, Kathleen Blake, Liane Robertson, and Kara Taczak. *Writing Across Contexts: Transfer, Composition, and Sites of Writing.* Utah State University Press, 2014.

Discussion Questions

1. What do you think is the main point that Mapes is making in her literacy narrative?

2. Why does Mapes says she feels "shame" when she recalls her early literacy development with her grandmother? Why shame?

3. What scenes does Mapes develop in her narrative that demonstrate that shame?

4. How does Mapes feel about Mark Bauerline's assertion that college students' literacy skills have declined? Who do you agree with and why?

5. What does Mapes mean by "curriculum should provide a counterscript to pervasive constructions of student deficits"? How might the literacy narrative be beneficial, according to Mapes?

Finally a word or two about scene length. If the scene you're envisioning takes place over more than a few hours, it likely ceases to be a scene. Your entire freshman year of high school, for example, isn't a scene. However, one specific lunch period in the cafeteria during your freshman year when you and a friend decided to ditch school would be a scene. Scenes consist of fairly short stretches of time in a specific location. The tighter the time-line and location is in your mind, the more vivid the scene will be when you write it.

INSIDE WORK   **Drafting a Scene for a Literacy Narrative**

Brainstorm a list of at least five specific scenes you could choose from that best illustrate your literacy development.

Choose one and free-write for five minutes about where the scene happened (location), how long the scene took place (ideally, between a few minutes and a few hours), who was in the scene, and how the scene helped shape your identity.

WRITING PROJECT   ## Composing a Literacy Narrative

The purpose of the literacy narrative is for you to reflect on and tell the story of your literacy development. Effective narratives have a beginning, middle, and end, and a literacy narrative follows a series of connected scenes (perhaps three) that illustrate points regarding how you developed your skills, identity, and views of yourself and others as a literate person.

Your instructor may give you more direction about how to define literacy for the purpose of this assignment, but you could focus on the following questions:

Academic Literacy

- What are your first memories of writing in school?
- How did you learn about the expectations for writing in school?
- Can you think of a time when you struggled to meet the requirements of a school writing assignment? What happened?

Technological Literacy

- What early memories do you have of using technology?
- How do you use technology now to communicate in your daily life? What technologies are most important to you for work, for school, and/or for personal commitments?

Workplace Literacy

- What writing and communication skills are expected in the occupation you aspire to when you graduate? How will you develop those skills?
- Can you think of a time when you encountered a task at work that you didn't know how to accomplish? What did you do? How did you address the challenge?

Social and/or Cultural Literacy

- Have you ever been in a social situation where you didn't know how to act? What did you do?
- What groups do you identify with, and what expectations and shared beliefs make that group cohesive?

In a narrative essay, explore the development of your own literacy. You might do this chronologically, at least as you start writing. Be specific in identifying how you define literacy and how you developed your abilities. In your narrative and analysis, provide examples from your experience, and show how they contribute to the development of that literacy. Ultimately, your narrative should be directed to a particular audience for a particular purpose, so think of a context in which you might tell this story. For example, a student who is studying to be a teacher might write about his early literacy experiences and how they led to an interest in teaching other children to read and write. Or an applicant for a job requiring specific technological ability might include a section in an application letter that discusses her development of expertise in technological areas relevant to the job. Be imaginative if you like, but make sure that your narrative provides specific examples and makes a point about your literacy development that you believe is important.

Insider Example
Student Literacy Narrative

MICHAELA BIEDA

The following literacy narrative was written by first-year college student Michaela Bieda regarding her self-awareness that her strengths and skills did not always align well with the expectations that schools, teachers, and peers had about what a "good student" should be. In her literacy narrative, Bieda reflects on the awakening she had through learning her strengths in an academic context and how a teacher contributed to her developing self-awareness of her individuality, her strengths, and her identity. Bieda makes use of all of the aspects of the literacy narrative we've introduced so far:

1. a main idea
2. scenes (locations and a fixed period of time)
3. sensory detail to describe those scenes (sight, sound, smell, touch, taste)
4. the "I" point of view

Literacy Narrative

Michaela Bieda

My Journey to Writing

"I" point of view

As a young kid, I struggled a lot in school. I was that student who had a hard time being able to focus and maintain that focus. I was easily distracted, and my eyes and mind would wander rather than listen and watch my teacher. I even fell asleep in class at times either as a result of over-stimulation that I couldn't handle or maybe an underlying depression, knowing I just couldn't cope in a regular classroom or keep up with my fellow students who didn't seem to share my mindset. I remember many a teacher telling my parents, "Micki just doesn't apply herself. She's smart but she's lazy." I wasn't lazy, and I wasn't sure if I was smart or not. I just knew that I couldn't sit still at my desk and do what all the other kids

Michaela sets up a problem that leads to the main point.

were able to do. Nothing in school held my interest. The traditional way of presenting the three R's didn't hold my attention. I would much rather daydream, waiting to go home and work on my art projects, designing and coloring a world I created. The world of academia had already labeled me ADHD, where I thought of myself as creative. My parents were well aware of the skills I had as well as the ones I didn't have. They thought that by changing schools, I might not resent schoolwork and teachers so much. When

I was in 4th grade, I went to another school, but since it was just another private Jewish day school, nothing much was different. "Mom," I complained almost from the first day at the new school, "I've got the same books and the same schedule. All that's happened is that I have to make new friends." The change of schools didn't result in an attitude change for me or a new understanding—and possible appreciation—by my new set of teachers. As they say, "Same old, same old."

In 5th grade, I remember sitting at circular tables, waiting for the teacher to come into the classroom. The school principal walked in and announced, "Class, this is Mrs. Crincolli. Please make her feel welcome." As usual, I wasn't really paying attention to the person entering the room, but I did perk up when she had us decorate nametags and stand them up on our desks. Finally! An art project! And it had a practical application! I was thrilled. It meant so much to me to be able to perform a task I knew I could excel at. I loved my nametag, and I have kept it all these years as a tangible marker of my first school success. From that point on, I started noticing how different I felt about going to school. I had never been so excited to see what Mrs. Crincolli was going to ask us to do next. For her part as a caring teacher, she noticed my lack of success on tests yet how good my writing and art projects were. She took the time to work with me to help me find ways to understand and remember the material for tests. I was a tricky learner because, with a mind that tried to absorb a billion things at once, prioritizing one thing to concentrate on took skills I didn't innately have but had to acquire. Mrs. Crincolli helped me to believe that I could learn that skill and then apply it. I can still hear her voice in my head, encouraging me: "Give it a whirl, Micki. You can do it."

By the time I hit 8th grade, I had fallen in love with writing, whether formal essays or free-form association. Mrs. Crincolli had also introduced me to the stories and poetry of Edgar Allan Poe. His dark Gothic elements spoke to me, and I tried writing stories and poems—not just emulating him but in my own voice as well. My favorite writing in school was free thought writing. Every day in class, we students had about 10 minutes to write in our journals. We could use the teacher's prompt or just go off on a personal tangent of feeling. Thanks to Mrs. Crincolli, from 5th grade on, I grasped that writing and literature could appeal to anyone needing a creative outlet. Mrs. Crincolli had been so clever in the types of assignments she gave and the books we were assigned to read in class. I always identified something

A new scene

An important character is introduced.

Dialogue adds specific detail

in my life with what I had to write about or the characters and plots I had to follow. The lack of direction and purpose I'd felt before Mrs. Crincolli entered my school life was now replaced by the joy of expressing myself on paper . . . or a screen. I wanted to impress her and the other teachers I had in each successive grade. In each English class I had with Mrs. Crincolli, the way she presented curriculum was so different from the usual textbook approach. Everything she had us students do was interesting, encouraging, and provocative. She had us constantly thinking out of the box, which was something I never thought I could do before she became my mentor.

I became very close with Mrs. Crincolli, spending time after class to help her with her bulletin boards. Eventually during my high school years, I became her Teacher's Assistant. Throughout high school under her tutelage, I learned to appreciate English even more and felt my strength in those skills more than any other class. I remember on more than one occasion, counting pages of younger classes' writing journals. So many of those students just scribbled or wrote random words in order to get the required number of pages completed. I shook my head, sad that these youngsters hadn't yet caught on to the value of journal writing or the joy of exploring oneself through language.

When it came time to graduate from high school, I reflected on the many years I had developed a real relationship with words—using and understanding them—as well as the prize of having a friendship with Mrs. Crincolli. My school, like so many others, had the usual awards ceremony at graduation. Special to my school though was the tradition that each teacher spoke about one student who had made a real impact during high school. I was sitting far in the back of the assembly with my mom as the slide show of our senior class played. All the other students in my class and our teachers | sat together, watching this heartwarming video under twinkly lights tangled in the trees. One by one, each teacher walked up to the front of the gathering. When it was Mrs. Crincolli's turn, my mom whispered to me, "I just know she'll talk about you." I wanted that to happen so badly—for her to know and share how much she meant to me and also how much I meant to her. My heart overflowed and so did my tears as she started to talk . . . about ME! She mentioned not only how I had been her student for so many years, but one of the first friends she had at the school—someone who put herself out for

Sensory detail

a teacher with the only expectation of learning as much as she could. I was so grateful that she understood just how I felt. She was the one, the pivotal one at the pivotal point in my life who made such a difference and such a contribution to me as a person as well as a writer. I don't have to wonder whether she knows how important she is to me or whether she has done her job as a teacher. We both know, and I cherish her and the confidence she gave me to celebrate a creative mind and channel it to positive and productive ends.

The main point of the narrative: Mrs. Crincolli helped Michaela identify her own strengths.

Discussion Questions

1. What would you say Michaela learned about herself by writing her literacy narrative? What evidence suggests this?

2. What is the main idea (or ideas) of her specific story? What point is she trying to make about her literacy development?

3. What kind of major and career could you see someone with Michaela's strengths going into that would make her happy?

4. How did Michaela's teacher, Mrs. Crincolli, contribute to Michaela's development?

5. What relationships or events from your own life contributed the most to how you see yourself as a student? Who contributed the most to the vision you see of yourself in a specific career one day? How did they contribute?

tip sheet

Writing Process and Reflection

- **You should work to achieve specific goals** related to your writing process during your writing classes:
  - Develop a writing project through multiple drafts
  - Develop flexible strategies for reading, drafting, reviewing, collaborating, revising, rewriting, rereading, and editing
  - Learn to give and to act on productive feedback to works in progress
  - Use composing processes and tools as a means to discover and reconsider ideas
  - Reflect on the development of composing practices and how those practices influence your work

- **Your purpose in using reflective writing is to process experiences** you've had in order to better understand how those experiences shape you and your writing.

- **Literacy can be broadly or narrowly defined** as the ability to read, write, and communicate in a variety of contexts.

- **A literacy narrative is a reflective writing genre** used to process the experiences you've had that shape your views of reading, writing, and how you communicate with others.

- **The key features of a literacy narrative are**
  - a main idea or point
  - scenes
  - sensory detail descriptions
  - the "I" point of view

Reading and Writing Rhetorically

You read and write in many different situations: at school, at home, with your friends, and maybe at work. Perhaps there are other situations in which you read and write, too, likely through a variety of different media. You might read and write in a journal, on social media, in a word processor as you prepare a paper for school, in a text message, or in a note to a friend. You could probably name many other situations in which you read and write on a daily basis.

Have you ever considered how different the processes of reading and writing are in these situations? You're performing the same act (reading or writing a text) in many ways, but several features might change from one situation to another:

- the way the text looks
- the medium or technology you use
- the tone you use
- the words you use (or avoid using)
- the grammar and mechanics that are appropriate

Even within the more specific category of "academic writing" that we address in this book, some of these features might shift depending on the context. The structure, vocabulary, style, and documentation expectations differ from one discipline to another. If you've ever written a lab report for a physics class and a literary analysis for a literature class, then you've likely experienced some of those differences. The differences arise because of the specific demands of each of the differing writing situations.

ANDREA TSURUMI

LaunchPad

See more on considering audience as you write.

Understanding Rhetorical Context

As you read and write, we want you to consider closely the specific situation for which you are writing. In other words, you should always think about the **rhetorical context** in which your writing takes place. We introduced the importance of "rhetorical knowledge" through the Council of Writing Program Administrators' outcomes statement in Chapter 1, but we want to explore in more detail what rhetorical knowledge and rhetorical context mean. In this text, we'll define rhetorical context through four elements:

- who the author is, and what background and experience he or she brings to the text
- who the intended audience is for the text
- what issue or topic the author is addressing
- what the author's purpose is for writing

Each of these elements has an impact on the way a text is written and interpreted. Consider how you might write about your last job in a text message to a friend in comparison with how you might write about it in an application letter for a new job. Even though the author is the same (you) and the topic is the same (your last job), the audience and your purpose for writing are vastly different. These differences thus affect how you characterize your job and your choice in medium for writing the message.

Sometimes writing situations call for more than one audience as well. You might address a **primary audience**, the explicitly addressed audience for the text, but you might also have a **secondary audience**, an implied audience who also might read your text or be interested in it. Imagine you wrote a job application letter as an assignment for a business writing class. Your primary audience would likely be your instructor, but you might also write the letter as a template to use when actually sending out a job application letter in the future. So your future prospective employer might be a secondary audience.

In academic settings, these elements of rhetorical context shift depending on the disciplinary context within which you're writing as well. Consider another example: Imagine a student has decided to research the last presidential election for a school assignment. If the research assignment were given in a history class, then the student might research and write about other political elections that provide a precedent for the outcome of the recent election and the events surrounding it. The student would be approaching the topic from a historical perspective, which would be appropriate for the context of the discipline and audience (a history professor). If the student were writing for an economics class, he or she might focus on the economic impact of elections and how campaign finance laws, voter identification laws, and voters' socioeconomic statuses affected the election. Even though the author, audience, topic, and purpose seem similar at first glance (they're all academic research assignments, right?), the student would focus on different questions and aspects of the topic when examining the election from different disciplinary perspectives and for different audiences. Other elements of the student's writing would likely shift, too, and we'll discuss those differences in Part Two of this book.

Why might it be important to consider the rhetorical context when reading or writing? As you read, noticing the rhetorical context of a text can help you understand choices that the author makes in writing that might at first seem confusing or inconsistent, even in academic writing. For example, writers might use the passive voice in an experimental study report ("the data were collected by . . .") but not in a reflective essay about conducting the same experimental study ("I collected the data . . ."). Or the same scholar might write in the first person in one kind of academic text (like this textbook) but not in another (perhaps a scholarly article). In all these writing situations, the author makes choices based on the rhetorical context. In this textbook, the first person ("I" or "We") and second person ("You") help to establish a personal tone that might not be appropriate for an academic journal article. We (first person) made this choice specifically because of our audience for the textbook—students (like you, second person) who are learning to navigate academic writing. We wanted the text to have a friendlier and less academically distant tone. Such a conversational tone wouldn't always be appropriate in other rhetorical contexts, though. When you write, understanding the rhetorical context can help you be more effective in achieving your purpose and communicating with your audience because you make choices that are appropriate to the situation.

As you notice the kinds of choices a writer makes, you are analyzing the rhetorical context of the writing: that is, you are taking elements of the writing apart to understand how they work together. Analyzing rhetorical context is a key strategy we'll use throughout this book to understand how different forms of writing work and what the similarities and differences are in writing across various disciplines.

INSIDE WORK   Identifying Rhetorical Context

Think about a specific situation in the past that required you to write something. It could be any kind of text; it doesn't have to be something academic. Then create a map—by drawing a diagram, a chart, or some other visual image—of the rhetorical context of that piece of writing. Consider the following questions as you draw:

- What was your background and role as the author?
- Who was the audience?
- What was the topic?
- What was your purpose for writing? ▶

Understanding Genres

As you learn to analyze the rhetorical context of writing, keep in mind that much writing takes place within communities of people who are interested in similar subjects. They might use similar vocabulary, formats for writing, and grammatical and stylistic rules. In a sense, they speak the same "language." The common practices that they typically employ in their writing are called conventions, as we discussed in Chapter 1. As you read and analyze the writing of academic writers, we'll ask you to notice and comment on the conventions that different disciplines use in various rhetorical contexts. When you write, you'll want to keep those conventions in mind, paying attention to the ways you should shape your own writing to meet the expectations of the academic community you are participating in. We'll go into more detail about how to analyze the specific conventions of disciplinary writing in Part Two.

In addition to paying close attention to the conventions that writers employ, we'll ask you to consider the genre through which writers communicate their information. **Genres** are approaches to writing situations that share some common features, or conventions. You already write in many genres in your daily life: If you've sent an e-mail message to a friend to schedule an event, written a text message to verify directions to the event, and written a thank-you note for a gift, then you've written and read examples of three different genres that are all associated with personal writing. If you like to cook, you've probably noticed that recipes in cookbooks follow similar patterns by presenting the ingredients first and then providing step-by-step directions for preparation. The ingredients usually appear in a list, and the instructions generally read as directives (e.g., "Add the eggs one at a time and mix well"), often in more of a prose style. Recipes are a genre. If you've looked for an office job before, you've probably encountered at least three different genres in the job application process: job advertisements, application letters, and résumés. How well you follow the expected conventions of the latter two genres often affects whether or not you get the job.

You've also likely had experience producing academic genres. If you've ever written a business letter, an abstract, a mathematical proof, a poem, a book review, a research proposal, or a lab report, then you might have noticed that these kinds of academic writing tasks have certain conventions that make them unique. Lab reports, for example, typically have specific expectations for the organization of information and for the kind of language used to communicate that information. Throughout Part Two of the book, we offer examples of a number of other academic genres—a literature review, an interpretation of an artistic text, as well as a theory response, just to name a few.

We'll focus more on analyzing genres in Part Two. But because different writing situations, or rhetorical contexts, call for different approaches, we ask you to think about the genre, as well as associated conventions, that you might be reading or writing in any particular situation so that you understand the rhetorical context better. Our goal is not to have you identify a formula to follow for every type of academic writing, but rather to understand the expectations of a writing situation—and how much flexibility you have in meeting those expectations—so that you can make choices appropriate to the genre.

LaunchPad

See what writing studies instructor Moriah McCracken has to say about genres.

Reading Rhetorically

Since we're talking about paying attention to rhetorical context, we want to explain the difference between the reading you do with an eye toward rhetorical context and the reading you might do in other circumstances. Whenever you read during a typical day, you probably do so for a variety of reasons. You might read:

- **To Communicate:** reading a text message, a letter from a friend, an e-mail, a birthday card, or a post on Instagram
- **To Learn:** reading instructions, a textbook, street signs while you drive, dosage instructions on a medication bottle, or the instructor's comments at the end of a paper that you turned in for a class
- **To Be Entertained:** reading novels, stories, comics, a joke forwarded in e-mail, or a favorite website

The details that you pay attention to, and the level at which you notice those details, vary according to your purpose in reading.

In this text, however, we will ask you to read in a way that is different from reading just to communicate, learn, or be entertained. We want you to *read rhetorically*, paying close attention to the rhetorical context of whatever you are reading. When you read rhetorically, you make note of the different elements of rhetorical context that help to shape the text. You'll notice who the **author** is (or, if there are multiple authors, who each one is) and what background, experience, knowledge, and potential biases the author brings to the text. In addition, you'll notice who the intended **audience** is for the text. Is the author writing to a group of peers? To other scholars in the field? How much prior knowledge does that audience have, and how does the intended audience shape the author's approach in the text? Are there multiple audiences (primary and secondary)? You'll also notice what the **topic** is and how it influences the text. Does the author use a specific approach related to the topic choice?

Additionally, you'll notice the author's **purpose** for writing. Sometimes the purpose is stated explicitly, and sometimes it is implied. Why does the author choose to write about this topic at this point? What does the author hope to achieve? Finally, you'll want to notice how these four elements work together to shape the text. How is the choice of audience related to the author's background, topic, and purpose for writing?

Reading Visuals Rhetorically

We should stress that the strategies for understanding rhetorical context and for reading rhetorically are applicable to both verbal and visual texts. In fact, any rhetorical event, or any occasion that requires the production of a text, establishes a writing situation with a specific rhetorical context. Consider the places you might encounter visual advertisements, as one form of visual texts, over the course of a single day: in a magazine, on a website, in stores, on billboards, on television, and so on. Each encounter provides an opportunity to read the visual text rhetorically, or to consider how the four elements of author, audience, topic, and purpose work together to shape the text itself (in this case, an advertisement). This process is called **rhetorical analysis**.

In fact, noticing these elements when you read will help you become a careful and critical reader of all kinds of texts. When we use the term *critical*, we don't use it with any negative connotations. We use it in the way it works in the term *critical thinking*, meaning that you will begin to understand the relationships among author, audience, topic, and purpose by paying close attention to context.

INSIDE WORK **Reading Rhetorically**

> With the direction of your instructor, choose a text (either verbal or visual) to read and analyze. As you read the text, consider the elements of rhetorical context. Write about who the author is, who the intended audience is, what the topic is, and what the author's purpose is for writing or for creating the text. Finally, consider how these elements work together to influence the way the text is written or designed. Later in the chapter, we'll ask you to engage in this kind of *rhetorical analysis* in a more formal way to understand different kinds of texts. ▶

Writing Rhetorically

Writing is about choices. Writing is not a firm set of rules to follow. There are multiple choices available to you any time you take on a writing task, and the choices you make will help determine how effectively you communicate with your intended audience, about your topic, for your intended purpose. Some choices, of course, are more effective than others, based on the conventions expected for certain situations. And yet, sometimes you might break conventions in order to make a point or draw attention to what you are writing. In both cases, though, it's important to understand the expectations of the rhetorical context for which you are writing so that your choices will have the effect you intend.

When you write rhetorically, you'll analyze the four elements of rhetorical context, examining how those elements shape your text through the choices that you make as a writer. You'll think about the following elements:

- **What You, as the *Author*, Bring to the Writing Situation**   How do your background, experience, and position relative to the audience shape the way you write?

- **Who Your Intended *Audience* Is**   Should you address a specific audience? Has the audience already been determined for you (e.g., by your instructor)? What do you know about your audience? What does your audience value?

- **What Your *Topic* Is**   What are you writing about? Has the topic been determined for you, or do you have the freedom to focus your topic according to your interests? What is your relationship to the topic? What is your audience's relationship to it?

- **What Your *Purpose* Is for Writing**   Why are you writing about this topic, at this time? For example, are you writing to inform? To persuade? To entertain?

Outside of school contexts, we often write because we encounter a situation that calls for us to write. Imagine a parent who wants to write a note to thank her son's teacher for inviting her to assist in a class project. The audience is very specific, and the topic is determined by the occasion for writing. Depending on the relationship between the parent and the teacher, the note might be rather informal. But if the parent wants to commend the teacher and copy the school's principal, she might write a longer, more formal note that could be included in the teacher's personnel file. Understanding the rhetorical context would help the parent decide what choices to make in this writing situation.

For school assignments, thinking about the topic is typically the first step because students are often assigned to write about something specific. If your English professor asks you to write a literary interpretation of Toni Morrison's *Song of Solomon*, your topic choice is limited. Even in this situation, though, you have the freedom to determine what aspect of the text you'll focus on. Do you want to look at imagery in the novel? Would you like to examine Morrison's use of language? Would you like to analyze recurring themes, or perhaps interpret the text in the historical and cultural context in which it was written?

In this text, we would like you also to consider the other elements of rhetorical context—author, audience, and purpose—to see how they influence your topic. Considering your purpose in writing can often shape your audience and topic. Are you writing to communicate with a friend? If so, about what? Are you completing an assignment for a class? Are you writing to persuade someone to act on an issue that's important to you? If you are writing to argue for a change in a policy, to whom do you need to write in order to achieve your purpose? How will you reach that audience, and what would the audience's expectations be for your text? What information will you need to provide? Your understanding of the rhetorical context for writing will shape your writing and help you to communicate more effectively with your audience, about your topic, to meet your purpose.

INSIDE WORK **Analyzing Rhetorical Context**

Think back to the rhetorical situation you identified in the "Inside Work: Identifying Rhetorical Context" activity on page 47. Consider that situation more analytically now, using slightly revised versions of the questions from that activity as a guide. Write your responses to the following questions.

- As the *author*, how did your background, experience, and position relative to the audience shape the way you created your text?

- Were you addressing a specific *audience*? Was the audience already determined for you? What did you know about your audience? What did your audience value or desire?

- What was your text about? Was the *topic* determined for you, or did you have the freedom to focus your topic according to your interests? What was your relationship to the topic? What was your audience's relationship to it?

- What was your *purpose* for creating a text about that topic, at that time? For example, were you writing to inform? To persuade? To entertain? ❯

Writing a Rhetorical Analysis

When you read rhetorically, you analyze a text through a particular lens. Examining a text through the formal framework of author, audience, topic, and purpose can be a way of analyzing a text in a written assignment as well. Such an examination, called a rhetorical analysis, is a genre of writing that explores elements of a text's rhetorical context. We'll provide several opportunities for you to conduct rhetorical analyses in this book, since it is one of the ways you will begin to discover the features of writing across different academic contexts.

In a rhetorical analysis, the writer uses a rhetorical framework to understand how the context of the text helps to create meaning. One framework you might use involves walking through the different elements of rhetorical context to examine the piece of writing in detail:

Rhetorical Context

Author	What does the author bring to the writing situation?
Audience	Who is the author addressing, and what do they know or think about this topic?
Topic	What is the author writing about, and why did he or she choose it?
Purpose	Why is the author writing about this topic, at this time?

These four components of the rhetorical context function together dynamically. You might analyze the author's background and experience and how he or she develops credibility in the text. Or you could make assertions about the author's primary and secondary audiences based on the author's choices regarding style and language. But in reality, all four of the rhetorical context components function together to shape how someone writes or speaks.

The following text is a historic letter that George H. W. Bush, the forty-first president of the United States (and father of the forty-third president, George W. Bush), sent to Iraqi president Saddam Hussein on January 9, 1991, shortly before the United States, in cooperation with over thirty other countries, launched an assault to expel Iraqi forces from Kuwait. This action came in response to Iraq's invasion and annexation of Kuwait in 1990, and it became a part of the history that is now referred to as the First Gulf War. While the events that precipitated this letter occurred a long time ago, it is a helpful artifact for understanding the complicated power dynamics at play in the U.S. involvement in ongoing events in the Middle East. As you read the letter, pay close attention to the rhetorical moves that President Bush makes. Who are his primary and secondary audiences? Is his audience only Saddam Hussein? If not, then who else is his audience, and what in his letter suggests who the secondary audience is? What is the letter's purpose? Does Bush seem to think Saddam will leave Kuwait? How do you know?

Letter to Saddam Hussein

GEORGE H. W. BUSH

Mr. President,

We stand today at the brink of war between Iraq and the world. This is a war that began with your invasion of Kuwait; this is a war that can be ended only by Iraq's full and unconditional compliance with UN Security Council resolution 678.

I am writing to you now, directly, because what is at stake demands that no opportunity be lost to avoid what would be a certain calamity for the people of Iraq. I am writing, as well, because it is said by some that you do not understand just how isolated Iraq is and what Iraq faces as a result.

I am not in a position to judge whether this impression is correct; what I can do, though, is try in this letter to reinforce what Secretary of State James A. Baker told your foreign minister and eliminate any uncertainty or ambiguity that might exist in your mind about where we stand and what we are prepared to do.

The international community is united in its call for Iraq to leave all of Kuwait without condition and without further delay. This is not simply the policy of the United States; it is the position of the world community as expressed in no less than twelve Security Council resolutions.

We prefer a peaceful outcome. However, anything less than full compliance with UN Security Council resolution 678 and its predecessors is unacceptable. There can be no reward for aggression.

Nor will there be any negotiation. Principles cannot be compromised. However, by its full compliance, Iraq will gain the opportunity to rejoin the international community. More immediately, the Iraqi military establishment will escape destruction. But unless you withdraw from Kuwait completely and without condition, you will lose more than Kuwait. What is at issue here is not the future of Kuwait—it will be free, its government restored—but rather the future of Iraq. This choice is yours to make.

The United States will not be separated from its coalition partners. Twelve Security Council resolutions, twenty-eight countries providing military units to enforce them, more than one hundred governments complying with sanctions—all highlight the fact that it is not Iraq against the United States, but Iraq against the world. That most Arab and Muslim countries are arrayed against you as well should reinforce what I am saying. Iraq cannot and will not be able to hold on to Kuwait or exact a price for leaving. You may be tempted to find solace in the diversity of opinion that is American democracy. You should resist any such temptation. Diversity ought not to be confused with division. Nor should you underestimate, as others have before you, America's will.

Iraq is already feeling the effects of the sanctions mandated by the United Nations. Should war come, it will be a far greater tragedy for you and your country. Let me state, too, that the United States will not tolerate the use of chemical or biological weapons or the destruction of Kuwait's oil fields and installations. Further, you will be held directly responsible for terrorist actions against any member of the coalition. The American people would demand the strongest possible response. You and your country will pay a terrible price if you order unconscionable acts of this sort.

I write this letter not to threaten, but to inform. I do so with no sense of satisfaction, for the people of the United States have no quarrel with the people of Iraq. Mr. President, UN Security Council resolution 678 establishes the period before January 15 of this year as a "pause of good will" so that this crisis may end without further violence. Whether this pause is used as intended, or merely becomes a prelude to further violence, is in your hands, and yours alone.

I hope you weigh your choice carefully and choose wisely, for much will depend upon it.

Discussion Questions

1. For what purpose(s) does President Bush write this letter?
2. How does Bush establish his credibility, honesty, and resolve in the letter?
3. Who is the primary audience? Who are the secondary audiences?
4. What conventional features for this form of writing (genre) does Bush's letter exhibit?

Insider Example
Student Rhetorical Analysis

The following is a student rhetorical analysis of the letter written from George H. W. Bush to Saddam Hussein. As you read this analysis, consider how the student, Sofia Lopez, uses audience, topic, and purpose to construct meaning from Bush's letter. Additionally, pay attention to how Sofia uses evidence from the letter to support her assertions. These moves will become more important when we discuss using evidence to support claims in Chapter 4 (see pp. 65–67).

Sofia Lopez
Mr. Harris
English 100
January 2018

The Multiple Audiences of George H. W. Bush's Letter

to Saddam Hussein

President George H. W. Bush's 1991 letter to Saddam Hussein, then the president of Iraq, is anything but a simple piece of political rhetoric.

The topic of the letter is direct and confrontational. On the surface, Bush directly calls upon Hussein to withdraw from Kuwait, and he lays out the potential impact should Hussein choose not to withdraw. But when analyzed according to the rhetorical choices Bush makes in the letter, a complex rhetorical situation emerges. Bush writes to a dual audience in his letter and establishes credibility by developing a complex author position. By the conclusion of the letter, Bush accomplishes multiple purposes by creating a complex rhetorical situation.

While Bush's direct and primary audience is Saddam Hussein, Bush also calls upon a much larger secondary audience in the first sentence of the letter by identifying "the world" as the second party involved in the imminent war that the letter is written to prevent. Bush continues to write the letter directly to Hussein, using second person to address him and describe the choices before him. Bush also continues, however, to engage his secondary audience throughout the letter by referring to resolutions from the UN Security Council in five separate paragraphs (1, 4, 5, 7, and 9). The letter can even be interpreted to have tertiary audiences of the Iraqi and the American people because the letter serves to justify military action should Hussein not comply with the conditions of the letter.

Because Bush is addressing multiple audiences, he establishes a complex author position as well. He is the primary author of the letter, and he uses first person to refer to himself, arguably to emphasize the direct, personal confrontation in the letter. He constructs a more complex author position, however, by speaking for other groups in his letter and, in a sense, writing "for" them. In paragraph 4, he speaks for the international community when he writes, "The international community is united in its call for Iraq to leave all of Kuwait. . . ." He draws on the international community again in paragraph 6 and refers to his coalition partners in paragraph 7, aligning his position with the larger community. Additionally, in paragraph 7, he builds his credibility as an author by emphasizing that he is aligned with other Arab and Muslim countries in their opposition to Hussein's actions. Writing for and aligning himself with such a diverse group of political partners helps him address the multiple audiences of his letter to accomplish his purposes.

While the primary and literal purpose of the letter is to call upon Iraq to withdraw from Kuwait and to outline the consequences of noncompliance, Bush accomplishes additional purposes directly related to his additional audiences and the complex author position he has established. The primary

---

The introduction outlines the writer's approach to analyzing Bush's letter. Based on the introduction, what do you see as the writer's overall purpose for this rhetorical analysis?

In this paragraph, the writer outlines potential audiences for Bush's letter in more detail. Who are those audiences?

In this paragraph, the writer explores the ways Bush is able to align himself with multiple audiences. What evidence does the writer use to demonstrate Bush's associations with his various audiences?

The writer frequently refers to Bush's "complex author position." What do you think the writer means by this?

purpose of his letter, naturally, is addressed to his primary audience, Saddam Hussein. The construction of the letter, however, including the repeated mention of UN Security Council resolutions, the invocation of support from other Arab and Muslim countries, and the reference to other coalition partners and the international community, serves to call upon the world (and specifically the United Nations) to support military action should Hussein not comply with the conditions of the letter. The construction of a letter with a complex audience and author allows Bush to address multiple purposes that support future action.

> What other elements of the rhetorical situation might the writer explore to further analyze Bush's letter?

Discussion Questions

1. What does Sofia Lopez identify as Bush's purpose? How does she support that interpretation of Bush's purpose?

2. Whom does Sofia see as Bush's audience? How does she support that reading of the letter?

3. What might you add to the analysis, from a rhetorical perspective?

Writing a Rhetorical Analysis

WRITING PROJECT

In this paper, you will analyze the rhetorical situation of a text of your choosing. You might want to choose something publicly available (already published) that represents a piece of polished writing so that you know that the author(s) has finished making revisions and has had time to think through important rhetorical choices. Alternatively, you might choose something written for an academic, personal, work, or other context. Start by reading the text carefully and rhetorically. Use the elements of rhetorical context to analyze and understand the choices the writer has made in the text.

Rhetorical Context

- author
- audience
- topic
- purpose

In addition to describing the rhetorical features of the article, you will also explore why you believe the author made certain choices. For example, if you're analyzing a blog entry on a political website, you might discuss who the author is and review his or her background. Then you could speculate about the writing choices the author has made and how his or her background might have influenced those choices.

Consider what conclusion you can draw about the text, and highlight that as an assertion you can make in the introduction to your analysis. The body of your paper should be organized around the rhetorical features you are analyzing, demonstrating how you came to your conclusion about the text.

In your conclusion, reflect on what you have found. Are there other issues still to be addressed? What other rhetorical strategies could be explored to analyze the work further? Are there surprises in the choices the writer makes that you should mention?

Keep in mind that your essential aim is to analyze, not to evaluate.

tip sheet — Reading and Writing Rhetorically

- **It is important to consider rhetorical context as you read and write.** Think about how the following four elements have shaped or might shape a text:
  - who the *author* is, and what background and experience he or she brings to the text
  - who the intended *audience* is
  - what issue or *topic* the author is addressing
  - what the author's *purpose* is for writing

- **Genres are approaches to writing situations that share some common features, or conventional expectations.** As you read and write texts, consider the form of writing you're asked to read or produce: Is it a recognizable genre? What kinds of conventional expectations are associated with the genre? How should you shape your text in response to those expectations?

- **Reading rhetorically means reading with an eye toward how the four elements of author, audience, topic, and purpose work together** to influence the way an author shapes a text, verbal or visual or otherwise.

- **Writing rhetorically means crafting your own text based on an understanding of the four elements of your rhetorical context.** Specifically, you consider how your understanding of the rhetorical context should affect the choices you make as a writer, or how your understanding should ultimately shape your text.

- **A rhetorical analysis is a formal piece of writing that examines the different elements of the rhetorical context of a text.** It also often considers how these elements work together to explain the shape of a text targeted for analysis.

Developing Arguments

Many writing situations, both academic and non-academic, require us as writers to persuade audiences on a particular topic—that is, to develop an argument. When we refer to arguments, we don't mean heated, emotional sparring matches. Rather, we use **argument** to refer to the process of making a logical case for a particular position, interpretation, or conclusion. Of course we all experience and participate in these kinds of arguments around us every day as we decide where to eat dinner with friends, what classes to take, or which movie to download or concert to see. We are immersed in these kinds of popular arguments constantly through advertisements, marketing campaigns, social media posts, and texting with friends, and so we are adept at critically thinking about arguments and persuasion in those contexts.

In academic settings, arguments are frequently more developed and nuanced because the authors are arguing for a particular interpretation or conclusion or action based on the results of research. To make such an argument effectively, academics must develop clear, persuasive texts through which to present their research. These arguments are built on **claims**—arguable assertions—that are supported with evidence from research. The unifying element of any academic argument is its primary or central claim, and although most sustained arguments make a series of claims, there is usually one central claim that makes an argument a coherent whole. Our goal in this chapter is to introduce you to some of the basic principles of argumentation and to help you write clear central claims and develop successful arguments, especially in your academic writing.

ANDREA TSURUMI

Understanding Proofs and Appeals

Aristotle, a rhetorician in ancient Greece, developed a method of analyzing arguments that can be useful to us in our own reading and writing today. He explained that arguments are based on a set of proofs that are used as evidence to support a claim. He identified two kinds of proofs: inartistic and artistic. **Inartistic proofs** are based on factual evidence, such as statistics, raw data, or contracts. **Artistic proofs**, by contrast, are created by the writer or speaker to support an argument. Many arguments contain a combination of inartistic and artistic proofs, depending on what facts are available for support. Aristotle divided the complex category of artistic proofs into three kinds of **rhetorical appeals** that speakers and writers can rely on to develop artistic proofs in support of an argument:

- Appeals to **ethos** are based on credibility or character. An example might be a brand of motor oil that is endorsed by a celebrity NASCAR driver. Another example could be a proposal for grant money to conduct a research study that discusses the grant writer's experience in successfully completing similar research studies in the past. In both examples, the speaker's or writer's experiences (as a NASCAR driver or as an established researcher) are persuasive elements in the argument.

- Appeals to **logos** are based on elements of logic and reason. An example might be an argument for change in an attendance policy that reveals a correlation between attendance and grades. The argument relies on logic and reason because it presents a relationship between attendance and grades and draws a connection to the policy, emphasizing how a change in the policy might affect grades.

- Appeals to **pathos** are based on emotions. Emotion can be a powerful motivator to convince an audience to hear an argument. An example might include telling the story of a program that helps homeless teenagers complete high school by finding shelter, food, and social support that enables them to improve their living conditions. Perhaps the program is in need of financial assistance in order to continue helping homeless teens. A story that features one or two specific teens who have come through the program and successfully completed high school would be an example of an appeal to emotion.

These types of appeals are present in arguments in both academic and non-academic settings. Many arguments, and often the most effective ones, include elements of more than one kind of appeal, using several strategies to persuade an audience. Based on the example above about a program that helps homeless teens, imagine that there is a campaign to solicit financial donations from the public to support the program. Now consider how much more persuasive that campaign would be if other appeals were used in addition to an emotional appeal. The campaign might develop an argument that includes raw data and statistics (an inartistic proof), the advice of civic leaders or sociological experts (ethos), the demonstration of a positive cause-and-effect relationship of the program's benefits in teens' lives (logos), along with a story of one teen, describing how she became homeless and how the program helped to get her back on her feet (pathos). Understanding the structure of arguments, and knowing the potential ways you can develop your own arguments to persuade an audience, will help you to write more effectively and persuasively.

INSIDE WORK **Writing about Arguments**

> Choose a text to read that makes a claim. Consider something that interests you—perhaps an advertisement, or even your college's or university's website. Write about the kinds of rhetorical appeals you notice. Do you see evidence of ethos? Logos? Pathos? Is the argument drawing on statistics or raw data, an inartistic proof? Why do you think the author(s) or designer(s) structured the argument in this way? To answer this question, you'll also need to consider the rhetorical context. Who is the author, and who is the intended audience? What is the topic, and what is the purpose of the argument? In other words, what is the ultimate goal of the argument? ❱

Making Claims

As we mentioned earlier, the unifying element of any academic argument is its primary or central claim. In American academic settings, the central claim is often (but not always) presented near the beginning of a piece so that it can tie the elements of the argument together. A form of the central claim that you're likely familiar with is the **thesis statement**. Thesis statements, whether revealed in an argument's introduction or delayed and presented later in an argument (perhaps even in the conclusion), are central claims of arguments that are typical of writing that is primarily focused on civic concerns, as well as writing in some academic fields such as those in the humanities (see Chapter 7).

Imagine for a moment that you've been asked to write an argument taking a position on a current topic like cell phone usage, and you must decide whether or not to support legislation to limit cell phone use while driving. In this instance, the statement of your position is your claim. It might read something like this: "We should support legislation to limit the use of cell phones while driving," or "We should not support legislation to limit the use of cell phones while driving." Although there are many types of claims, the statement "We should pass legislation to limit the use of cell phones" is a claim of proposal or policy, indicating that the writer will propose some action or solution to a problem. We could also explore claims of definition

("Cheerleading is a sport") or claims of value ("Supporting a charity is a good thing to do"), just to name a few.

Literary analysis, a genre commonly taught in high school English classes, usually presents a thesis statement as part of the introduction. You may be familiar with a thesis statement that reads something like this: "Suzanne Collins's *Hunger Games* is a dystopian novel that critiques totalitarian regimes and empowers young women who are far too often marginalized and oppressed." This thesis statement makes a claim in support of a specific interpretation of the story. Regardless of the specific type of claim offered, the argument that follows it provides evidence to demonstrate why an audience should find the claim persuasive.

THESIS VERSUS HYPOTHESIS

In an academic setting, thesis statements like those typical of arguments in the humanities are not the only kind of unifying claim you might encounter. In fact, arguments in the natural and social sciences are often organized around a statement of hypothesis, which is different from a thesis statement. Unlike a thesis statement, which serves to convey a final position or conclusion on a topic or issue that a researcher has arrived at based on study, a **hypothesis** is a proposed explanation or conclusion that is usually either confirmed or denied on the basis of rigorous examination or experimentation later in a paper. This means that hypothesis statements are, in a sense, still under consideration by a writer or researcher. A hypothesis is a proposed answer to a research question. Thesis statements, in contrast, represent a writer or researcher's conclusion(s) after much consideration of the issue or topic.

Consider the following examples of a hypothesis and a thesis about the same topic:

Hypothesis	Thesis
Decreased levels of sleep will lead to decreased levels of academic performance for college freshmen.	College freshmen should get at least seven hours of sleep per night because insufficient sleep has been linked to emotional instability and poor academic performance.

The hypothesis example above includes several elements that distinguish it from the thesis statement. First, the hypothesis is written as a prediction, which indicates that the researcher will conduct a study to test the claim. Additionally, it is written in the future tense, indicating that an experiment or study will take place to prove or disprove the hypothesis. The thesis statement, however, makes a claim that indicates it is already supported by evidence gathered by the researcher. A reader would expect to find persuasive evidence from sources later in that essay.

We highlight this distinction in types of claims to underscore that there is no single formula for constructing a good argument in all academic contexts. Instead, expectations for strong arguments are bound up with the expectations of particular writing communities. If you write a lab report with the kind of thesis statement that usually appears in a literary analysis, your work would likely convey the sense that you're a novice to the community of writers and researchers who expect a hypothesis statement instead of a thesis statement. One of the goals of this text is to help you develop awareness of how the expectations for good argumentation change from one academic context to the next.

Developing Reasons

When writing an academic argument that requires a thesis statement, you can choose how detailed to make that thesis statement. When we introduced thesis statements as a type of claim, we asked you to consider two possible statements on the topic of cell phone use while driving: "We should/should not support legislation to limit the use of cell phones while driving." You can also refer to these two possible forms as **simple thesis statements** because they reveal a writer's central position on a topic but do not include any reasoning as support for that position. When reasons are included as logical support, then you can think about the thesis statement as a **complex thesis statement**:

Simple Thesis: We should support legislation to limit the use of cell phones while driving.

Reasons: They are an unnecessary distraction.
They increase the incidence of accidents and deaths.

When you combine the simple statement of position or belief with the reasons that support it, then you have a more complex, and fuller, thesis statement:

Complex Thesis: We should support legislation to limit the use of cell phones because they are an unnecessary distraction for drivers and because they increase needless accidents and deaths on our roadways.

Although constructing complex thesis statements allows you to combine your statement of position, or your central claim, with the reasons you'll use to defend that position, you may frequently encounter arguments that do not provide the reasons as part of the thesis. That is, some writers, depending on their rhetorical context, prefer to present a simple thesis and then reveal the reasons for their position throughout their argument. Others choose to write a thesis that both establishes their position and provides the reasoning for it early on. An advantage of providing a complex thesis statement is that it offers a road map to the reader for the argument that you will develop.

INSIDE WORK   **Constructing Thesis Statements**

Generate a list of six to eight current social issues that require you to take a position. Consider especially issues that are important to your local community. Choose one or two to focus on for the other parts of this activity.

Next, explore multiple positions. Consider competing positions you can take for each of the issues you identified. Write out a simple thesis statement for those positions. Be careful not to limit your positions to pros and cons, especially if you can think of alternative positions that might be reasonable for someone to argue. Often, there are multiple sides to an issue, and we miss the complexity of the issue if we only acknowledge two sides. Then, list as many reasons as you can think of to support each of those positions. It might be help-ful to connect your simple statement of thesis to your reasons using the word *because*. This activity can help you to strengthen your argument by anticipating rebuttals or counterarguments. We'll take these issues up later in the chapter. For example:

Claim: The U.S. Congress should enact legislation to prohibit animal testing for cosmetics manufactured or sold in the United States.

Reasons:

because _____.

because _____.

because _____.

Alternate Claim: The U.S. Congress should not enact legislation to prohibit animal testing for cosmetics manufactured or sold in the United States.

Reasons:

because _____.

because _____.

because _____.

Alternate Claim: The decision to prohibit animal testing for cosmetics manufactured or sold in the United States should be made at the state level and not by the federal government.

Reasons:

because _____.

because _____.

because _____.

Finally, combine your simple thesis with your reasoning to construct a complex thesis for each potential position. Write out your thesis statements. ▶

Supporting Reasons with Evidence

Reasons that support a claim are not particularly powerful unless there is evidence to back them up. Evidence that supports an argument can take the form of any of the rhetorical appeals. Let's look again at the complex thesis from the previous section: "We should support legislation to limit the use of cell phones because they are an unnecessary distraction for drivers and because they increase needless accidents and deaths on our roadways." In order to generate the reasons, the writer relied on what he already knew about the dangers of cell phone use. Perhaps the writer had recently read a newspaper article that cited statistics concerning the number of people injured or killed in accidents as a direct result of drivers using their phones instead of paying attention to the roadways. Or perhaps the writer had read an academic study that examined attention rates and variables affecting them in people using cell phones. Maybe the writer even had some personal knowledge or experience to draw upon as evidence for her or his position. Strong, persuasive arguments typically spend a great deal of time unpacking the logic that enables a writer to generate reasons in support of a particular claim, and that evidence can take many forms.

Personal Experience   You may have direct experience with a particular issue or topic that allows you to speak in support of a position on that topic. Your personal experience can be a rich resource for evidence. Additionally, you may know others who can provide evidence based on their experiences with an issue. Stories of personal experience often appeal to either ethos (drawing on the credibility of the writer's personal experience) or pathos (drawing on readers' emotions for impact). Sometimes these stories appeal to both ethos and pathos at the same time. Imagine the power of telling the story of someone you know who has been needlessly injured in an accident because another driver was distracted by talking on the phone.

Expert Testimony   Establishing an individual as an expert on a topic and using that person's words or ideas in support of your own position can be an effective way of bolstering your own ethos while supporting your central claim. However, the use of expert testimony can be tricky, as you need to carefully establish what makes the person you're relying on for evidence an actual expert on the topic or issue at hand. You must also consider your audience—whom would your audience consider to be an expert? How would you determine the expert's reputation within that community? The use of expert testimony is quite common in academic argumentation. Researchers often summarize, paraphrase, or cite experts in their own discipline, as well as from others, to support their reasoning. If you've ever taken a class in which your instructor asked you to use reputable

Insider's View
Figuring out who the experts are
MORIAH McCRACKEN, WRITING STUDIES

"When you jump into a scholarly text, the conversation is so implicit. . . . For me, the biggest thing that can be kind of disconcerting is that you have to figure out, what are people even talking about? And then you have to figure out, who are the voices that are most popular? Who are the voices that people turn to when they're trying to resolve this issue?"

Learn more about entering academic conversations.

Hear criminologist Michelle Richter comment on types of research in her field.

sources to support your argument, then you've probably relied on expert testimony to support a claim or reason already. As evidence for our complex thesis, imagine the effectiveness of citing experts who work for the National Transportation and Safety Board about their experiences investigating accidents that resulted from inattentive driving due to cell phone use.

Statistical Data and Research Findings   Statistics frequently serve as support in both popular and academic argumentation. Readers tend to like numbers, partly because they seem so absolute and scientific. However, it is important, as with all evidence, to evaluate statistical data for bias. Consider where statistics come from and how they are produced, if you plan to use them in support of an argument. Additionally, and perhaps most important, consider how those statistics were interpreted in the context of the original research reported. What were the study's conclusions? Imagine the effectiveness of citing recently produced statistics (rates of accidents) on the highways in your state from materials provided by your state's Department of Transportation.

Writers also often present the findings, or conclusions, of a research study as support for their reasons and claims. These findings may sometimes appear as qualitative, rather than just statistical, results or outcomes.

When selecting the types and amounts of evidence to use in support of your reasons, be sure to study your rhetorical context and pay particular attention to the expectations of your intended audience. Some audiences, especially academic ones, are less likely to be convinced if you only provide evidence that draws on their emotions. Other audiences may be completely turned off by an argument that relies only on statistical data for support.

So far, we've discussed several types of evidence that are typically used in the construction of arguments—personal experience, expert testimony, statistical data and research findings. Collecting the data you need to make a strong argument can seem like a daunting task at times. It's important to keep in mind, though, that the amount of evidence you provide and the types of data your argument requires will depend entirely on the kind of argument you are constructing, as well as on the potential audience you want to persuade. Therefore, it's essential that you analyze and understand your audience's expectations when selecting support for your argument. Above all, select support that your audience will find credible, reliable, and relevant to your argument.

INSIDE WORK **Analyzing Audience Expectations**

Choose any one of the complex thesis statements you constructed in the "Inside Work" activity on pages 64–65. Then identify two potential target audiences for your arguments. Freewrite for five to ten minutes in response to the following questions about these audiences' likely expectations for evidence.

- What does each audience already know about your topic? That is, what aspects of it can you assume they already have knowledge about?

- What does each audience need to know? What information do you need to make sure to include?

- What does each audience value in relation to your topic? What kinds of information will motivate them, interest them, or persuade them? How do you know?

- What sources of information about your topic might your audiences find reliable, and what sources would they question? Why? ❯

Understanding Assumptions

Any time you stake a claim and provide a reason, or provide evidence to support a reason, you are assuming something about your audience's beliefs and values, and it is important to examine your own assumptions very carefully as you construct arguments. Though assumptions are often unstated, they function to link together the ideas of two claims.

Let's consider a version of the claim and reason we've been looking at throughout this section to examine the role of assumptions: "We should support legislation to limit the use of cell phones while driving because they increase needless accidents and deaths on our roadways." In this instance, the claim and the reason appear logically connected, but let's identify the implied assumptions that the reader must accept in order to be persuaded by the argument:

Claim:	We should support legislation to limit the use of cell phones while driving.
Reason:	They increase needless accidents and deaths on our highways.
Implied Assumptions:	We should do whatever we can to limit accidents and deaths.
	Legislation can reduce accidents and deaths.

Many audiences would agree with these implied assumptions. As a result, it would likely be unnecessary to make the assumptions explicit or provide support for them. However, you can probably imagine an instance when a given audience would argue that legislating people's behavior does not affect how people actually behave. To such an audience, passing laws to regulate the use of cell phones while driving might seem ineffective. As a result, the audience might actually challenge the assumption(s) upon which your argument rests, and you may need to provide evidence to support the implied assumption that "legislation can reduce accidents and deaths."

A writer who is concerned that an audience may attack his argument by pointing to problematic assumptions might choose to explicitly state the assumption and provide support for it. In this instance, he might consider whether precedents exist (e.g., the effect of implementing seat belt laws, or statistical data from other states that have passed cell phone use laws) that could support his assumption that "legislation can reduce accidents and deaths."

INSIDE WORK **Considering Assumptions and Audience**

In the previous activity, you considered the most appropriate kinds of evidence for supporting thesis statements for differing audiences. This time, we ask you to identify the assumptions in your arguments and to consider whether or not those assumptions would require backing or additional support for varying audiences.

Begin by identifying the assumption(s) for each of your thesis statements. Then consider whether or not those assumptions need backing as the intended audience for your argument changes to the following:

- a friend or relative

- a state legislator

- an opinion column editor

- a professional academic in a field related to your topic ❱

Anticipating Counterarguments

Initially, it may strike you as odd to think of counterarguments as a strategy to consider when constructing an argument. However, anticipating **counterarguments**—the objections of those who might disagree with you—may actually strengthen your argument by forcing you to consider competing chains of reasoning and evidence. In fact, many writers actually choose to present counterarguments, or rebuttals of their own arguments, as part of the design of their arguments.

Why would anyone do this? Consider for a moment that your argument is like a debate. If you are able to adopt your opponent's position and then explain why that position is wrong, or why her reasoning is flawed, or in what ways her evidence is insufficient to support her own claim, then you support your own position. This is what it means to offer a **rebuttal** to potential counterarguments. Of course, when you provide rebuttals, you must have appropriate evidence to justify dismissing part or all of the counterargument. By anticipating and responding to counterarguments, you also strengthen your own ethos as a writer on the topic. Engaging counterarguments demonstrates that you have considered multiple positions and are knowledgeable about your subject.

You can also address possible counterarguments by actually conceding to an opposing position on a particular point or in a limited instance. Now, you're probably wondering: Why would anyone do this? Doesn't this mean losing your argument? Not necessarily. Often, such a concession reveals that you're developing a more complex argument and moving past the pro/con positions that can limit productive debate.

Imagine that you're debating an opponent on a highly controversial issue like free college tuition. You're arguing that tuition should be free, and your opponent makes the point that free tuition could have the effect of lowering the quality of education an institution is able to offer. You might choose to concede this possibility, but counter it by explaining how varying tuition costs among different kinds of universities contribute to socioeconomic stratification. Though you acknowledge the validity of your opponent's concerns, you are able to make a case that the social damage caused by the current system makes that risk acceptable. That is, you could **qualify** your position by acknowledging your opponent's concerns and explaining why you feel that your argument is still valid. In this case, your opponents' points are used to adjust or to qualify your own position, but this doesn't negate your argument. Your position may appear even stronger precisely because you've acknowledged the opponent's points and refined the scope of your argument as a result.

Insider's View
Figuring out the "right" side
MIKE BROTHERTON, ASTRONOMY

"In science, we're really worried about which side is right, and you discuss both sides only to the extent of figuring out which one's right. It's not one opinion versus another. It's one set of ideas supported by a certain set of observations against another set of ideas supported, or not supported, by the same set of observations, and trying to figure out which one is a better explanation for how things work."

LaunchPad

Hear more about writing to solve problems.

INSIDE WORK   **Dealing with Counterarguments**

Throughout this section, you've been working with a series of claims that you constructed. You've linked those claims to reasons as support, and you've considered the kinds of evidence most appropriate for your theses in light of particular audiences. You've also considered the likely acceptability of your assumptions, according to various potential audiences. This time, consider possible counterarguments for your thesis statements.

- Who might argue against you?
- What might their arguments be?

- What will their arguments be based on?
- How might you use a counterargument to actually support your own claim?

Brainstorm a list of instances in which you might want to concede a point or two as a means of strengthening your own position. ▶

Analyzing Arguments

One way to understand the process of developing a persuasive argument is to study how others structure theirs. If you'll recall, in Chapter 3 we discussed how visual texts, like verbal ones, construct rhetorical situations. In the same way, visual texts may also seek to persuade an audience, and they may use many of the techniques explored throughout this chapter.

The following papers present arguments about visual texts. In the first, Jack Solomon, a professional writer, explores how advertisements reflect what he sees as contradictory impulses in the American character. In the second, Timothy Holtzhauser, a student writer, examines the argument strategies employed in a 1943 ad for American war bonds. As you engage with their arguments, keep in mind that each writer is both making an argument and analyzing an argument simultaneously, so you'll want to consider their texts from both perspectives. Also keep in mind that their arguments are supported by evidence found in their own research. We'll explore how to conduct research in more detail in Chapter 5.

Insider Example
Professional Analysis of an Advertisement

In the following passage from "Masters of Desire: The Culture of American Advertising," Jack Solomon uses *semiotics*—a method for studying and interpreting cultural signs and symbols—to analyze the arguments made in two advertisements. As you read Solomon's argument, try to identify which elements of argument discussed in this chapter he uses in his analysis.

Excerpt from "Masters of Desire: The Culture of American Advertising"

JACK SOLOMON

The American dream . . . has two faces: the one communally egalitarian and the other competitively elitist. This contradiction is no accident; it is fundamental to the structure of American society. Even as America's great myth of equality celebrates the virtues of mom, apple pie, and the girl or boy next door, it also lures us to achieve social distinction, to rise above the crowd and bask alone in the glory. This land is your land and this land is my land, Woody Guthrie's populist anthem tells us, but we keep trying to increase the "my" at the expense of the "your." Rather than fostering contentment, the American dream breeds desire, a longing for a greater share of the pie. It is as if our society were a vast high-school football game, with the bulk of the participants noisily rooting in the stands while, deep down, each of them is wishing he or she could be the star quarterback or head cheerleader.

For the semiotician, the contradictory nature of the American myth of equality is nowhere written so clearly as in the signs that American advertisers use to manipulate us into buying their wares. "Manipulate" is the word here, not "persuade"; for advertising campaigns are not sources of product information, they are exercises in behavior modification. Appealing to our subconscious emotions rather than to our conscious intellects, advertisements are designed to exploit the discontentments fostered by the American dream, the constant desire for social success and the material rewards that accompany it. America's consumer economy runs on desire, and advertising stokes the engines by transforming common objects—from peanut butter to political candidates—into signs of all the things that Americans covet most.

But by semiotically reading the signs that advertising agencies manufacture to stimulate consumption, we can plot the precise state of desire in the audiences to which they are addressed. In this chapter, we'll look at a representative sample of ads and what they say about the emotional climate of the country and the fast-changing trends of American life. Because ours is a highly diverse, pluralistic society, various advertisements may say different things depending on their intended audiences, but in every case they say something about America, about the status of our hopes, fears, desires, and beliefs.

Let's begin with two ad campaigns conducted by the same company that bear out Alexis de Tocqueville's observations about the contradictory nature of American society: General Motors' campaigns for its Cadillac and Chevrolet lines. First, consider an early magazine ad for the Cadillac Allanté. Appearing as a full-color, four-page insert in *Time*, the ad seems to say "I'm special—and so is this car" even before we've begun to read it. Rather than being printed on the ordinary, flimsy pages of the magazine, the Allanté spread appears on glossy coated stock. The unwritten message

Allanté Specifications

Conceived and Commissioned by America's Luxury Car Leader—Cadillac.

Designed and Handcrafted by Europe's Renowned Design Leader—Pininfarina, SpA, of Turin, Italy.

The New Spirit of Cadillac.

here is that an extraordinary car deserves an extraordinary advertisement, and that both car and ad are aimed at an extraordinary consumer, or at least one who wishes to appear extraordinary compared to his more ordinary fellow citizens.

Ads of this kind work by creating symbolic associations between their product and what is most coveted by the consumers to whom they are addressed. It is significant, then, that this ad insists that the Allanté is virtually an Italian rather than an American car—an automobile, as its copy runs, "Conceived and Commissioned by America's Luxury Car Leader—Cadillac" but "Designed and Handcrafted by Europe's Renowned Design Leader—Pininfarina, SpA, of Turin, Italy." This is not simply a piece of product information; it's a sign of the prestige that European luxury cars enjoy in today's automotive marketplace. Once the luxury car of choice for America's status drivers, Cadillac has fallen far behind its European competitors in the race for the prestige market. So the Allanté essentially represents Cadillac's decision, after years of resisting the trend toward European cars, to introduce its own European import—whose high cost is clearly printed on the last page of the ad. Although $54,700 is a lot of money to pay for a Cadillac, it's about what you'd expect to pay for a top-of-the-line Mercedes-Benz. That's precisely the point the ad is trying to make: the Allanté is no mere car. It's a potent status symbol you can associate with the other major status symbols of the 1980s.

American companies manufacture status symbols because American consumers want them. As Alexis de Tocqueville recognized a century and a half ago, the competitive nature of democratic societies breeds a desire for social distinction, a yearning to rise above the crowd. But given the fact that those who do make it to the top in socially mobile societies have often risen from the lower ranks, they still look like everyone else. In the socially immobile societies of aristocratic Europe, generations of fixed social conditions produced subtle class signals. The accent of one's voice, the shape of one's nose, or even the set of one's chin immediately communicated social status. Aside from the nasal bray and uptilted head of the Boston Brahmin, Americans do not have any native sets of personal status signals. If it weren't for his Mercedes-Benz and Manhattan townhouse, the parvenu Wall Street millionaire often couldn't be distinguished from the man who tailors his suits. Hence, the demand for status symbols, for the objects that mark one off as a social success, is particularly strong in democratic nations—stronger even than in aristocratic societies, where the aristocrat so often looks and sounds different from everyone else.

Status symbols, then, are signs that identify their possessors' place in a social hierarchy, markers of rank and prestige. We can all think of any number of status symbols—Rolls-Royces, Beverly Hills mansions, even Shar Pei puppies (whose rareness has rocketed them beyond Russian wolfhounds as status pets and has inspired whole lines of wrinkle-faced stuffed toys)—but how do we know that something is a status symbol? The explanation is quite simple: when an object (or puppy!) either costs a lot of money or requires influential connections to possess, anyone who possesses it must also possess the necessary means and influence to acquire it. The object itself really doesn't matter, since it ultimately disappears behind the presumed social potency of its owner. Semiotically, what matters is the signal it sends, its value as a sign of power. One traditional sign of social distinction is owning a country estate and enjoying the peace and privacy that attend it. Advertisements for Mercedes-Benz, Jaguar, and Audi automobiles thus frequently feature drivers motoring quietly along a country road, presumably on their way to or from their country houses.

Advertisers have been quick to exploit the status signals that belong to body language as well. As Hegel observed in the early nineteenth century, it is an ancient aristocratic prerogative to be seen by the lower orders without having to look at them in return. Tilting his chin high in the air and gazing down at the world under hooded eyelids, the aristocrat invites observation while refusing to look back. We can find such a pose exploited in an advertisement for Cadillac Seville in which an elegantly dressed woman goes out for a drive with her husband in their new Cadillac. If we look closely at the woman's body language, we see her glance inwardly with a satisfied smile on her face but not outward toward the camera that represents our gaze. She is glad to be seen by us in her Seville, but she isn't interested in looking at us!

Ads that are aimed at a broader market take the opposite approach. If the American dream encourages the desire to arrive, to vault above the mass, it also fosters a desire to be popular, to "belong." Populist commercials accordingly transform products into signs of belonging, utilizing such common icons as country music, small-town life, family picnics, and farmyards. All of these icons are incorporated in GM's "Heartbeat of America" campaign for its Chevrolet line. Unlike the Seville commercial, the faces in the Chevy ads look straight at us and smile. Dress is casual, the mood upbeat. Quick camera cuts take us from rustic to suburban to urban scenes, creating an American montage filmed from sea to shining sea. We all "belong" in a Chevy.

Discussion Questions

1. Jack Solomon sets up an interesting contrast between "manipulate" and "persuade" at the beginning of this excerpt. How does his description of these ads mirror our understanding of arguments? In your own words, how would you describe the differences he establishes between manipulating and persuading?

2. In Solomon's analysis of the Cadillac and Chevrolet ads, where does he address the claims and reasons given by the advertisers to buy their products? Do the ads address assumptions?

3. How does Solomon characterize the appeals made by both advertisements? Where does he describe appeals to ethos? Logos? Pathos?

Insider Example
Student Analysis of an Advertisement

Timothy Holtzhauser, a student in a first-year writing class, wrote the following analysis of an advertisement as a course assignment. He used elements of rhetorical analysis and argument analysis to understand the persuasive effects of the advertisement he chose. Notice, also, that he followed Modern Language Association (MLA) style conventions, especially when citing sources within his paper and documenting them at the end of the paper. (See Chapter 5 and the Appendix for additional information on documentation styles.)

Timothy Holtzhauser

ENG 101-79

February 13, 2018

Rhetoric of a 1943 War Bonds Ad

From the front covers of magazines at the store, to the ads by Google on sidebars of websites, to the incessant commercials on television, advertisements are visible everywhere. Whether the advertisement announces or insinuates its purpose, all advertisements attempt to change the audience's manner of thinking or acting. In "Masters of Desire: The Culture of American Advertising," Jack Solomon describes the motive behind advertising as pure and simple manipulation: "'Manipulate' is the word here, not 'persuade'; for advertising campaigns are not sources of product information, they are exercises in behavior modification" (60). Even the most innocent advertisement performs this maneuver, and the "Death Warrant . . . US War Bonds" advertisement drawn by S. J. Woolf is no different. This 1943 ad, printed in the *New York Daily News* for Bloomingdale's department store, not only encourages the purchase of U.S. war bonds by exaggerating Hitler's negative aspects, but also depicts the growing influence and activism of the United States during this era.

> The main claim, or thesis

When this advertisement appeared, the United States was rapidly becoming more involved in the hostilities of World War II. While not yet engaged in the war in Europe, the United States was providing supplies and manpower for the war in the Pacific, and the government was in serious need of funds to keep the war machine rolling. The main method that the government used to obtain these funds was selling war bonds and advertising, to push the sale of these bonds. War bonds were used as a tool to raise money for the government by selling certificates that promised a return on the investment after a period of time in exchange for the investment. In New York City, publishing city of the *New York Daily*

> The next two paragraphs provide the reader with historical context for the ad and its publication. This information clarifies the rhetorical situation for readers and sets the stage for the analyses of the ad's elements that follow.

News and home of Bloomingdale's main store, there was tremendous outrage at the atrocities being committed as a result of the war. Due to this, the general public showed interest in ending the war, especially the war in the Pacific. For the most part, the city trended toward the progressive democratic mind-set and agreed with the mostly Democrat-controlled government of the era (Duranti 666). While factors such as these propelled the citizens to purchase bonds as the advertisement suggests, there were other factors resisting this push as well. Particularly important was the ever-present aftermath of the Great Depression. The combination of these factors created a mixed feeling about the purchase of war bonds, but the fear of Hitler's reign continuing tended to bias the populace toward purchasing the bonds.

At the time of the release of this ad, the *New York Daily News* was a fairly new newspaper in New York City, as it had been initially released about twenty years beforehand. Even as a new publication, it had an extremely wide readership due to its tabloid format, which focused on images, unlike other New York papers. At the time of the printing of this ad, the *Daily News* was known to be slightly biased toward the democratic mind-set common among the citizens of the city ("New York Daily News"). The publishing of this advertisement at this time could be viewed as an appeal to ethos in order to push the patriotic sense of the paper. The advertisement can also be seen as an appeal to ethos by Bloomingdale's, as the company was seeking to portray itself as a patriotic firm. With that context in mind, several components of the advertisement make more sense and can be more effectively analyzed.

The most prominent feature in the advertisement is Hitler's face, and ——— in particular, his facial expression. Woolf's image here uses two primary components to make the facial expression stand out: the humorously exaggerated bug-eyed stare and the dropped jaw. The effect created by these two factors is compounded by the addition of the buck teeth and

Drawing courtesy of S. J. Woolf

TO BRING CLOSER THE HAPPY DAY SHOWN
ABOVE—BUY MORE AND MORE WAR BONDS

BLOOMINGDALE'S
Lexington Avenue and 59th Street

The analysis now focuses on specific elements of the ad. In this paragraph, the student analyzes features of Hitler's face: the bug eyes, the dropped jaw, the tufts of hair. These, he suggests, express Hitler's fear of American strength, which stems at least partially from the selling and purchasing of war bonds.

the protruding ears. The bug eyes commonly serve in American imagery to express shock, and they perform that role excellently here in this advertisement. The dropped jaw is used very frequently as well, especially in cartoons, and here it strengthens the shocked expression. The buck teeth and protruding ears are two images that are used in American culture to convey the idea of a buffoon. In addition to these features, Woolf comically adds in two tufts of hair in imitation of devil horns to further enhance Hitler's evil image. When these two are added to the previous facets, it creates an image of a completely dumbfounded and baffled Hitler. The image was designed in this manner to enhance the feeling that purchasing U.S. war bonds would benefit society by eliminating the severe hindrance known as Hitler.

The next feature that stands out is the death warrant and war bond itself and Hitler's hands clutching it. Woolf draws Hitler's hands in a manner that makes them appear to be tightly gripping the paper as in anger. The paper itself shows only the words "death warrant" and "U.S. War Bonds," but one can infer from the context that the warrant is for Hitler. The fact that the warrant is printed on a war bond suggests that the U.S. government completely backs the killing of Hitler and will take action to see it through. The document appeals to the viewer's logos through the suggestion that war bonds will end the war sooner and save countless lives in the process. There is also an inherent appeal to ethos in the suggestion of the character of Bloomingdale's as a firm that strongly opposes the horrors committed by Hitler and his followers. In addition, there is an appeal to pathos, with the ad attempting to home in on the audience's moral code. This apparent encouragement of killing Hitler, coupled with the text at the bottom of the advertisement, creates a mood of vengeance directed toward Hitler.

The next major feature of the advertisement is the caption at the bottom of the image, which reads, "To bring closer the happy day shown above—buy more and more war bonds." The image shown above the text in most scenarios would not be considered a happy day for most people. The thought of death is normally enough to ruin anyone's day, but this image banks on the public having a burning vengeance that justifies the end of Hitler. The idea of vengeance is generally viewed as having serious negative repercussions, but this ad portrays the idea in a positive manner by making an appeal to the audience's logos. The appeal here could best be described as sacrificing one to save millions. The caption also makes an appeal to

The writer shifts focus to analyze the ad's caption.

pathos in the manner that it tries to connect with the viewer's sense of morals that Hitler has almost definitely broken in numerous ways.

The next aspect of the advertisement that stands out is the use of shading. Woolf's decision here may have been influenced by requirements of the *Daily News* at the time, but even viewed in that light it has a rhetorical effect on the advertisement. The usage of shading here creates the appearance of an unfinished image, further enhancing the idea that Hitler has just been served his death warrant hot off the press by the United States and its war bonds. It also creates a worried cast to Hitler's face through the heavy shading in the creases along his jawline. The overall image of Hitler created through the use of shading comes off as dark and sinister, representative of the common American's view on Hitler's character. In contrast, the war bond is virtually untouched by shading, leaving it nearly white. This creates the image of a beacon of hope shining through the darkness that provides a means to eliminate this terror. Additionally, the presence of a heavily shaded advertisement among the more crisp images, popular among tabloids, accents this advertisement and its message.

The final aspect of the advertisement that draws major attention is the overall construction of the image. The layout emphasizes the two key components of the advertisement: Hitler's face and the war bond. Not only does this accentuate the relationship between buying war bonds and bringing the hammer down on Hitler, but it also provides further depth to the image's rhetorical context. Hitler is posed hunched over as if to imply a deformity in his body and represent a deformity of his mind. The statement here runs on the classic American stereotype that a malformed person is either inferior or evil, a stereotype popularly used in comical representations such as this one. In addition, the hunched posture can be interpreted as the weight of the American war machine, fueled by the war bond purchases, dragging Hitler down to end his reign of terror.

With each of these analyzed aspects in mind, the advertisement can serve as an effective description of the period similar to what Jack Solomon suggests is possible in "Masters of Desire." He uses the following statement to show how advertisements are indicative of the culture of their audiences: "But by semiotically reading the signs that advertising agencies manufacture to stimulate consumption, we can plot the precise state of desire in the audiences to which they are addressed" (61). Based upon the patriotic push shown through this advertisement's attack on Hitler and visualization of

Notice how the ending addresses elements of the paper's thesis statement, or how the ad "depicts the growing influence and activism of the United States during this era."

handing him a death warrant, the advertisement shows the general patriotic mood of America at the time. Given the war footing of the country during this era, this patriotic pride fits well into the time frame. It also shows the growing influence of the United States across the world. Up until this point in time, America was not taken very seriously, and U.S. foreign policy was mostly designed to ignore the rest of the world and preserve America. With the serving of the death warrant to Hitler shown in this advertisement, the change in ideology is starkly apparent. Instead of the wait-and-see mentality common in America before World War II, the highly proactive and aggressive nature of America today begins to show. For a small snippet in a tabloid newspaper, this advertisement packs quite a rhetorical punch.

Taking into account all the elements of this advertisement, rhetorical and otherwise, the advertisement creates an astounding patriotic push for the purchase of war bonds through exaggeration and establishes the United States as a globally significant force through the implications of the death warrant for a foreign citizen. All aspects used in this advertisement work well to cleverly goad readers of the paper to purchase war bonds from Bloomingdale's, holding true to Jack Solomon's statement about advertisements not seeking to provide information, but to manipulate the audience. In the end, however, this advertisement does not convey the negative connotation often associated with manipulative advertising; rather, it uses manipulative elements to try to create a better future for the readers.

Works Cited

Bloomingdale's. Advertisement. *New York Daily News*. 1943.

Duranti, Marco. "Utopia, Nostalgia, and World War at the 1939–40 New York
World's Fair." *Journal of Contemporary History,* vol. 41, no. 4, 2006,
pp. 663–83.

"New York Daily News." *Encyclopaedia Britannica Online*, 2016. www
.britannica.com/topic/New-York-Daily-News.

Solomon, Jack. "Masters of Desire: The Culture of American Advertising."
*The Signs of Our Time: Semiotics: The Hidden Messages of Environments,
Objects, and Cultural Images*. Jeremy P. Tarcher, 1988, pp. 59–76.

Discussion Questions

1. Where does Timothy Holtzhauser state his thesis? Why do you think he phrases his thesis in the way that he does?

2. How does Timothy use logos in his own argument? Why do you think he relies on logos to support his claim?

3. Who is the intended audience for this argument?

4. What scholarly or popular conversation(s) is Timothy joining in?

5. Which claim(s) do you find most convincing and least convincing for Timothy's rhetorical situation? Why?

Composing a Rhetorical Analysis of an Advertisement

WRITING PROJECT

For this project, we ask you to consider the ways in which rhetorical context and appeals work together in an advertisement to create an argument.

- To begin, choose a print or online advertisement that you can analyze based on its rhetorical context and the appeals it uses to persuade the intended audience.

- Then, drawing on the principles of rhetorical analysis from Chapter 3 and the discussion of developing arguments in this chapter, compose an analysis examining the ad's use of appeals in light of the rhetorical situation the ad constructs.

RHETORICAL CONTEXT (SEE CHAPTER 3)
Central Question: How do the elements of the rhetorical context affect the way the advertisement is structured?

Author _____

Audience _____

Topic _____

Purpose _____

RHETORICAL APPEALS
Central Question: What appeals does the advertisement use, and why?

Ethos _____

Logos _____

Pathos _____

Keep in mind that a rhetorical analysis makes an argument, so your analysis should have a central claim that you develop based on what you observed, through the frameworks of rhetorical context and rhetorical appeals, in the advertisement. Make your claim clear, and then support it with reasons and evidence from the advertisement.

- **Presenting an argument is different from merely stating an opinion.** Presenting and supporting an argument mean establishing a claim that is backed by reasons and evidence.

- **The unifying element of any academic argument is its primary or central claim.** A unifying claim may take the form of a thesis, a hypothesis, or a more general statement of purpose. There are numerous kinds of claims, including claims of value, definition, and policy.

- **Reasons are generated from and supported by evidence.** Evidence may take the form of inartistic proofs (including statistics and raw data) or artistic proofs, including the rhetorical appeals of ethos (appeal to credibility), logos (appeal to reason and logic), and pathos (appeal to emotion).

- **Claims presented as part of a chain of reasoning are linked by (often) unstated assumptions.** Assumptions should be analyzed carefully for their appropriateness (acceptability, believability) in a particular rhetorical context.

- **Considering and/or incorporating counterarguments is an excellent way to strengthen your own arguments.** You may rebut counterarguments, or you may concede (or partially concede) to them and qualify your own arguments in response.

- **Analyzing others' arguments is a good way to develop your skills at arguing,** particularly in an academic context.

Academic Research

Conducting Research

Research projects have all kinds of starting points. Sometimes we start them because a course instructor or an employer asks us to. At other times, we embark on research projects because we want to learn about something on our own. In all these cases, though, the research we undertake typically responds to a question or to a set of questions that we need to answer. These are called **research questions**. Constructing research questions and narrowing them to focus specifically on the relevant information needed to answer them is usually the first step in any research project, especially in an academic context.

DEVELOPING A RESEARCH QUESTION

For many students, choosing a subject to research can be incredibly difficult. Whenever you have free rein to choose the topic of a research project, one way to start is by thinking about issues that really matter to you. Writers tend to do their best work when writing about issues in which they have a personal investment. Even if you're conducting research in a course with a topic that has been assigned, you should always consider how you might approach the topic from an angle that matters to you or that brings in your unique point of view. Your personal investment and level of interest in the topic of your research can greatly impact the kinds of questions you ask of that topic, but they may also influence your level of commitment to, and the quality of, your research.

Another challenge many students face is narrowing down a solid research question once they've selected an issue of interest. If a research question is too broad, then it may not be feasible to respond to it adequately in the scope of your research assignment. If it's too narrow, though, it

ANDREA TSURUMI

might not be researchable; in other words, you might not be able to find enough sources to support a solid position on the issue. A good research question has an appropriately narrow scope and can be answered with available resources in the space and time allowed to do so.

A focused question sometimes comes from reading previously published materials on a topic or issue. If you are able to review what others have already written on a topic before conducting a study or making an argument of your own on that topic, then you will know what still needs to be understood, explained, or debated. In this way, you may identify a gap in what is already known or understood about a topic in order to build a research question that, when answered, could help fill that gap. This is how researchers continue to contribute to ongoing conversations.

As you work on drafting a research question, keep these five criteria in mind:

- **Personal Investment**   Is this an issue you care about? If the issue is too broad, is there a way you can narrow down the topic to an aspect of the issue that is of the most importance to you?

- **Debatable Subject**   Could two reasonable people looking at evidence about this issue come to different conclusions?

- **Researchable Issue**   Can you locate or collect adequate evidence to support a position on this issue?

- **Feasibility**   Is the scope of the research question manageable, given the amount of time you have to research the issue and the amount of space in which you will make your argument?

- **Contribution**   Will your response to your question contribute to the ongoing conversation about the issue?

INSIDE WORK   **Writing a Research Question**

As you begin your research project, you should identify a research question that will guide your research and keep you on track. Start by brainstorming a list of possible research questions for ten minutes, and then use the five criteria above to narrow down your list to a research question that might work for you. If your answer to any of the questions is a definitive "No," then the research question might not be a good choice, or you might need to revise it to make it work for your research project. ❭

LaunchPad

A political scientist emphasizes the importance of supporting evidence.

CHOOSING PRIMARY AND SECONDARY SOURCES

You can gather several different types of sources to respond to a research question. When considering sources to gather, you should look for those that provide specific evidence to address aspects of your research question.

Remember to keep your target audience in mind as you select evidence, taking into account the kinds of evidence that would likely be most convincing to your audience.

To respond to any research question, you must collect evidence to prove or disprove a hypothesis or to support or refute a claim. Once you have identified a solid research question, then you must decide whether you need to collect primary and/or secondary sources to support your research aims.

Primary sources include the results of data that researchers might collect on their own. If you're making a claim about how to interpret a work of art and you've studied the piece carefully for images and symbols that you discuss in your argument, for instance, then the work of art is your primary source. Or perhaps you've designed and conducted a survey of people's experiences with a particular social phenomenon, like culture shock. In this case, the results you've gathered from your survey are a primary source from which you can provide evidence to answer a research question or support an argument about the experience of culture shock. Other forms of primary sources include original historical documents and responses from interviews you may have conducted.

Insider's View
Primary research in writing studies
MORIAH McCRACKEN, WRITING STUDIES

"I like to try to introduce my students to qualitative research in their first year, when our students have to interview a professor. Sometimes I'll help them develop survey questions and questionnaires so they can have that kind of experience, and I'll teach them about double-entry notebooks so they can do some observations in the classroom. I like to bring in qualitative methods so that students realize there are different kinds of questions to ask, and depending on my question, I'm going to have to try something a little bit different and learn how to do this kind of research in my discipline."

 **LaunchPad**
Find additional advice on doing primary research.

INSIDE WORK **Collecting Primary Evidence**

Freewrite for five to ten minutes about a time in the past when you had to collect data on your own to answer a research question.

- Why were you collecting the data? What question were you trying to answer?

- What data did you collect, and how did you collect it? Did you observe something? Conduct a survey? Interview someone?

- If you were to try to answer that research question now, what data would you collect? Would you do anything differently? Why or why not? ▶

Based on the scope of your argument and the expectations of your audience, you may also need to engage **secondary sources,** or research collected by and/or commented on by others. Let's say that your literature professor wants you to offer an interpretation of a poem. You study the poem carefully as your primary source and arrive at a conclusion or claim about the work. But imagine that the assignment also requires you to use scholarly opinions to support your own position or interpretation. As a result, you spend time in the library or searching online databases to locate articles or books by scholars who provide their own interpretations or perspectives on the poem. The articles or books you rely on to support your interpretation are secondary sources because the interpretations were developed by others, commenting on the poem. Likewise, if you cite as part of your own argument the results of a survey published in an academic article, then that article serves as a secondary source of information to you. Other secondary sources include newspapers and magazines, textbooks, and encyclopedias. Many of the researched arguments you'll produce in college will require you to use both primary and secondary sources as support.

INSIDE WORK   **Using Primary and Secondary Sources**

Read Timothy Holtzhauser's ad analysis on pages 74–78 of Chapter 4. After reviewing his analysis, look at the list of works cited at the end of his essay. Then answer the following questions.

- What primary source(s) does Timothy use to support his argument? Why do you think he chooses the primary source(s) he does?

- What would the impact be if Timothy didn't use primary sources in his argument? Would his argument be more or less persuasive to his audience?

- What secondary sources does Timothy use to support his argument?

- Why do you think he chooses these particular secondary sources? What impact do they have on the development of his argument?

- If Timothy had only used primary sources and no secondary sources, what would the impact have been on the persuasiveness of his argument? ▶

SEARCHING FOR SOURCES

In Part Two, we discuss collecting primary sources to support claims in specific disciplinary areas or genres in more detail. In the rest of this chapter, though, we provide support for collecting secondary sources, which build a foundation for research and writing in academic contexts. Even if the main evidence used to support an academic research project comes from primary sources, secondary sources can provide an overview of what other scholars have already argued with regard to a particular issue or topic. Keep in mind that academic writing and research essentially comprise a series of extended conversations about different issues, and secondary sources help you understand what part of the conversation has already happened before you start researching a topic on your own, or before you consider entering an established conversation on a topic or issue.

Identifying Search Terms

The school, college, or university you attend likely offers many avenues to help navigate the processes for conducting library research at your institution. Most of these processes include searching for source materials online. When you search for secondary sources online to support the development of a research study or to support a claim in an argument, it's important to consider your **search terms**, the key words and phrases you'll use while you're searching. Let's say that you're interested in understanding the effects of using cell phones while driving, a topic we explored in Chapter 4. In such a case, you might begin your research with a question that reads something like this:

What are the effects of using cell phones while driving?

The first step in your research process would likely be to find out what others have already written about this issue. To start, then, you might temporarily rephrase your research question to ask:

What have others written or argued about the effects of using cell phones while driving?

To respond, you'll need to identify the key terms of your question that will focus your search for secondary sources about the subject. You might highlight some of the key terms in the question:

What have others written or argued about the effects of using **cell phones** while **driving**?

If you started your search by typing "cell phones and driving" into Google, your search would return millions of results:

These results include links to images of people on cell phones in their cars, to news articles, and to statistics from insurance companies, to name a few. In the figure above, the first three items in the list and the ones in the sidebar are all sponsored advertisements. You might want to seek out non-sponsored links in the list. After careful evaluation, you may decide that some of these sources of data would be useful for your research, but you can also see that the results produce far too many hits to manage. There's simply no way you can comb through the millions of hits to find information that is appropriate for your purposes. As a result, you may choose to narrow your search to something that emerges as a specific issue, like "reaction time." If you narrowed your search to "cell phones and reaction time," you would see results like this:

Focusing your research terms in this way narrows the scope of your search somewhat further, but you still have far too many results to review. One concern to keep in mind, then, is that basic Google searches are not very useful in helping to locate the kinds of sources you might rely on for your research, especially in an academic context. If you want to understand, more specifically, what scholars have written about your topic, then you need to find scholarly or academic sources as support. A basic Google search doesn't filter different kinds of sources, so it's not generally very helpful.

Instead, you might choose to search Google Scholar to understand the ongoing conversation among scholars about your topic. Conducting a search for "cell phones and driving accidents and reaction time" in Google Scholar returns tens of thousands of results:

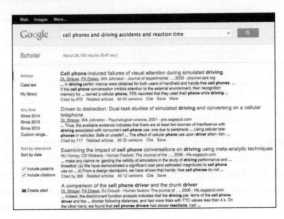

If you take a close look at the left-hand side of the screen, however, you'll notice that you can limit your search in several additional ways. By limiting the search to sources published since 2014, you can reduce your results significantly:

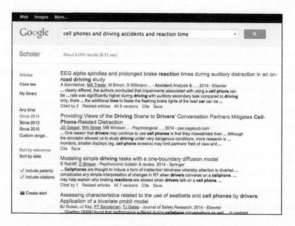

You can continue refining your search until you end up with a more manageable number of hits to comb through. Although the number is still large, thousands of results are more manageable than millions. Of course, you would likely need to continue narrowing your results. As you conduct this narrowing process, you are simultaneously focusing in on the conversation you originally wanted to understand: what scholars have written about your topic. Consider the criteria that would be most meaningful for your project as you refine your search by revising your search terms.

INSIDE WORK   **Generating Search Terms**

Think of a controversial social issue that interests you. We chose driving while using a cell phone, but you should choose something you would potentially be interested in learning more about. Then follow these instructions, preferably working with classmates.

- Brainstorm the search terms you would use for that topic. What terms would you enter into a web search engine?

- List your search terms in the box for Round 1 below, and then try doing a search using your preferred web search engine.

- How many hits did you get? Write the number in the box for Round 1.

- Switch seats with a classmate so that you can look at someone else's search terms. Should the search be narrowed? If so, revise your classmate's search terms to narrow them slightly. Write those in the box for Round 2. Try the search, and record the number of hits.

- Follow the instructions again for Rounds 3 and 4.

	Search Terms	Number of Hits
Round 1		
Round 2		
Round 3		
Round 4		

After you have finished the exercise, reflect on the following questions.

- How did your classmates narrow your search terms? What changes worked well, and what changes didn't work as well?
- If you were going to write advice for students using web search engines for research, what advice would you give about search terms? ▶

Keep in mind that general search engines such as Google are not always the best places to conduct academic research, although they can often be useful starting points. Experienced researchers generally rely on more specialized databases to find the kinds of sources that will support their research most effectively.

Using Journal Databases

If you are conducting academic research, then one of the first types of sources you should look for is peer-reviewed journal articles. You may wonder why we don't recommend beginning your search by scouring your library's catalog for books. The answer is that academic books, which are often an excellent source of information, generally take much longer to make their way through the publishing process before they appear in libraries. Publishing the results of research in academic journal articles, however, is a faster method for academics to share their work with their scholarly communities. Academic journals, therefore, are a valuable resource precisely because they offer insight into the most current research being conducted in a field.

Additionally, like other scholarly work, most academic journals publish research only after it has undergone rigorous scrutiny through a peer-review process by other scholars in the relevant academic field. Work that has gone through the academic peer-review process has been sent out, with the authors' identifying information removed, and reviewed by other scholars who determine whether it makes a sufficiently significant contribution to the field to be published. Work published in a peer-reviewed academic journal has been approved not only by the journal's editor but also by other scholars in the field.

If you've ever browsed through your school's library, you've probably noticed that there are thousands of academic journals, and many are available online and easy to locate via the Internet. If you're associated with a college or university, you likely have access to a wide array of online academic journals that can be explored through databases via the library's website. You can search general library databases by refining search terms, as we discussed in the examples of using Google, but you can also find relevant resources by searching in specific disciplinary databases.

Searching for Journal Articles by Discipline

One way of searching for journal articles through your school's library is to explore the academic databases by subject or discipline. These databases usually break down the major fields of study into the many subfields that make up smaller disciplinary communities. Individual schools, colleges, and universities choose which databases they subscribe to. In the following image from the North Carolina State University's library website, you can see that agriculture is divided into various subfields: agricultural economics, animal science, crop science, and so on.

Let's say you need to find information on post-traumatic stress disorder (PTSD) among veterans of the Iraq War that began in March 2003. You spend some time considering the subfields of the social sciences where you're most likely to find research on PTSD: history, sociology, political science, and psychology, for instance. If you choose to focus on the psychological aspects of PTSD, then you would likely select "Social Sciences" and then "Psychology." When you select "Psychology" from the list of available disciplines, typically you'll see a screen that identifies major research databases in psychology, along with some related databases. Choosing the database at the top of the page, "PsycINFO," gains you access to one of the most comprehensive databases in that field of study.

Selecting "PsycINFO" grants access to the PsycINFO database via a search engine — in this case, EbscoHOST. You can now input search terms such as "PTSD and Iraq War veterans" to see your results.

Notice that the search engine allows you to refine your search in a number of ways, very similar to the criteria that you can use in Google Scholar: you can limit the years of publication for research articles, you can limit the search to sources that are available full-text online, you can limit the search to peer-reviewed journal articles, and more. If you limit your search for "PTSD and Iraq War veterans" to peer-reviewed journal articles available in full-text form online, then the results look something like this:

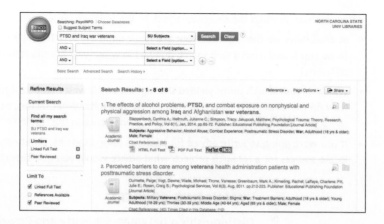

You can now access the texts of journal articles that you find interesting or that might be most relevant to your research purposes. Depending on the number and content of the results, you may choose to revise your search terms and run the search again.

INSIDE WORK **Generating Sources from an Academic Database**

For this activity, use the same controversial social issue you relied on to complete the previous Inside Work activity, for which you generated and refined possible search terms to assess the number of hits, as possible sources, you could locate. This time, however, you should conduct your search using a more specialized academic database that is appropriate to your topic, such as PsycINFO or Sociological Abstracts. If you do not have access to such a database, then you may choose to use Google Scholar as an alternative.

Input each of the four sets of search terms generated in your previous Inside Work activity into the database and record the number of hits yielded. As you conduct your search, using each of the search terms, take a few minutes to peruse the kinds of results that are generated by each search.

	Search Terms	Number of Hits
Round 1		
Round 2		
Round 3		
Round 4		

After you have finished the exercise, reflect on the following questions:

- In what ways are the results of your academic database search similar to those you found from a web search engine? In what ways are the results different?

- Which of your search terms yielded the highest and lowest number of hits? How do these results compare to your previous results? What factors, besides using different terms, could account for any difference in the results?

- If you were going to write advice for students using academic databases to locate sources for a research project, what advice would you give them? ▶

EVALUATING SOURCES

Distinguishing between Scholarly and Popular Sources

Using search engines to find relevant sources is fairly easy. The difficult part is deciding which sources are worth your time. If you are working on an academic paper, it is particularly useful to be able to distinguish between popular and scholarly sources.

Depending on your research and writing context, you might be able to use both scholarly and popular sources to support your research. However, in some writing situations it is most appropriate to rely primarily on scholarly sources. For this reason, you should understand the difference between scholarly and popular sources, which comes down to a matter of audience and the publication process. **Scholarly sources** are produced for an audience of other scholars, and **popular sources** are produced for a general audience. Scholarly sources have undergone a peer-review process prior to publication, while popular sources typically have been vetted only by an editor. Generally speaking, popular sources are not very useful for supporting academic research. Let's examine a number of publication types in terms of the kind of information, scholarly or popular, they most often provide:

Examples of Scholarly Sources

- **Academic Journals**   Most journal articles are produced for an audience of other scholars, and the vast majority are peer-reviewed before they are published in academic journals.

Insider's View
On distinguishing scholarly sources
JONATHAN MORRIS, POLITICAL SCIENCE

"We have to teach our students what's scholarly literature and what isn't. Peer-review journal articles, books — that's scholarly literature. When you pull things off of Wikipedia, when you go even to newspaper articles from the *New York Times* — that's not scholarly research. They need to know that differentiation."

 **LaunchPad**

Get expert advice on finding scholarly sources.

- **Books Published by Academic Presses**   Academic presses publish books that also go through the peer-review process. You can sometimes identify academic presses by their names (e.g., a university press), but sometimes you need to dig deeper to find out whether a press generally publishes scholarly or popular sources. Looking at the press's website can often help answer that question.

Examples of Popular Sources

- **Newspapers**   Most newspaper articles are reviewed by editors for accuracy and reliability. However, they typically provide only information that would be of interest to a general audience. They are not specifically intended for an academic audience. A newspaper might report the results of a study published in an academic journal, but it will generally not publish original academic research.

- **Magazines**   Like newspaper articles, magazine articles are typically reviewed by editors and are intended for a general reading audience, not an academic one.

Although it may seem easy to classify sources into one of these two categories, in fact it is often difficult to determine if a source is scholarly or not. Understanding the nature of scholarly and popular sources and recognizing their differences as you conduct your research will help you develop more effective arguments.

Scholarly works, for instance, are typically built on other sources, so they generally include references to other works that are documented in the text and listed in a complete bibliography at the end. Imagine for a moment, though, that you locate a study published on the Internet that you think would be a really good source for your research. It looks just like an article that might appear in a journal, and it has a bibliography that includes other academic sources. However, as part of your analysis of the source, you discover that the article, published only on a website, has never been published by a journal. Is this a scholarly work? It might be. Could this still be a useful scholarly work for your purposes? Perhaps. Still, as a writer and researcher, you would need to know that the article you're using as part of your own research has never been peer-reviewed or published by a journal or an academic press. This means that the validity of the work has never been assessed by other experts in the field. If you use the source in your own work, you would probably want to indicate that it has never been peer-reviewed or published in an academic journal as part of your discussion of that source.

Answering the following questions about your sources can help you evaluate their credibility and reliability:

1. Who are the authors?
2. Who is the intended audience?

3. Where is the work published?

4. Does the work rely on other reputable sources for information?

5. Does the work seem biased?

As a writer, you must ultimately make the decisions about what is or is not an appropriate source, based on your goals and an analysis of your audience. Answering the questions above can help you assess the appropriateness of sources.

INSIDE WORK **Evaluating Sources**

For this exercise, either look at the sample essay from Timothy Holtzhauser on pages 74–78 of Chapter 4 or look at an essay that you wrote for a class in the past. Choose one of the references listed in the essay's bibliography, and write answers to the following questions.

- Who are the authors? Do they possess any particular credentials that make them experts on the topic? With what institutions or organizations are the authors associated?

- Who is the intended audience — the general public or a group of scholars? How do you know?

- Where is the work published? Do works published there undergo a peer-review process?

- Does the work rely on other reputable sources for information? What are those sources, and how do you know they are reputable?

- Does the work seem biased? How do you know this? Is the work funded or supported by individuals or parties who might have a vested interest in the results? If so, is there a potential conflict of interest? ▶

SUMMARIZING, PARAPHRASING, AND QUOTING FROM SOURCES

Once you've located and studied the sources you want to use in a research paper, then you're ready to begin considering ways to integrate that material into your own work. There are a number of ways to integrate the words and ideas of others into your research, and you've likely already had experience summarizing, paraphrasing, and quoting from sources as part of an academic writing assignment. For many students, though, the specifics of how to summarize, paraphrase, and quote accurately are often unclear, so we'll walk through these processes in some detail.

Summarizing

Summarizing a text is a way of condensing the work to its main ideas. A summary therefore requires you to choose the most important elements of a text and to answer these questions: *What* is this work really trying to say, and *how* does it say it? Composing a summary of a source can be valuable for a number of reasons. Writing a summary can help you carefully analyze the content of a text and understand it better, but a summary can also help you identify and keep track of the sources you want to use in the various parts of your research. You may sometimes be able to summarize a source in only a sentence or two. We suggest a simple method for analyzing a source and composing a summary:

1. Read the source carefully, noting the **rhetorical context**. Who composed the source? For whom is the source intended? Where was it published? Identify the source and provide answers to these questions at the beginning of your summary, as appropriate.

2. Identify the **main points**. Pay close attention to topic sentences at the beginnings of paragraphs, as they often highlight central ideas in the overall structure of an argument. Organize your summary around the main ideas you identify.

3. Identify **examples**. You will want to be able to summarize the ways the writer illustrates, exemplifies, or argues the main points. Though you will likely not discuss all of the examples or forms of evidence you identify in detail as part of your summary, you will want to comment on one or two, or offer some indication of how the writer supports his or her main points.

The following excerpt is taken from the text of Jack Solomon's "Masters of Desire: The Culture of American Advertising," which appears on pages 70–73 in Chapter 4:

> Status symbols, then, are signs that identify their possessors' place in a social hierarchy, markers of rank and prestige. We can all think of any number of status symbols — Rolls-Royces, Beverly Hills mansions, even Shar Pei puppies (whose rareness and expense has rocketed them beyond Russian wolfhounds as status pets and has even inspired whole lines of wrinkle-faced stuffed toys) — but how do we know that something is a status symbol? The explanation is quite simple: when an object (or puppy!) either costs a lot of money or requires influential connections to possess, anyone who possesses it must also possess the necessary means and influence to acquire it. The object itself really doesn't matter, since it ultimately disappears behind the presumed social potency of its owner. Semiotically, what matters is the signal it sends, its value as a sign of power. One traditional sign of social distinction is owning a country estate and enjoying the peace and privacy that attend it. Advertisements for Mercedes-Benz, Jaguar, and Audi automobiles thus frequently feature drivers motoring quietly along a country road, presumably on their way to or from their country houses.

A summary of this part of Solomon's text might read something like this:

> In "Masters of Desire: The Culture of American Advertising," Jack Solomon acknowledges that certain material possessions may be understood as representations of an individual's rank or status. He illustrates this point by identifying a number of luxury automobiles that, when observed, cause us to consider the elevated economic status of the vehicles' owners (63).

You'll notice that this summary eliminates discussion of the specific examples Solomon provides. Further, it removes any discussion of the concept of semiotics. Though Solomon's ideas are clearly condensed and the writer of this summary has carefully selected the ideas to be summarized in order to further his or her own aims, the core of Solomon's idea is accurately represented.

Paraphrasing

Sometimes a writer doesn't want to summarize a source because condensing its ideas risks losing part of its importance. In such a case, the writer has to choose whether to paraphrase or quote directly from the source. **Paraphrasing** means translating the author's words and sentence structure into your own for the purpose of making the ideas clear for your audience. A paraphrase may be the same length or even longer than the part of a text being paraphrased, so the purpose of paraphrase is not really to condense a passage, as is the case for summary.

Often, writers prefer to paraphrase sources rather than to quote from them, especially if the exact language from the source isn't important, but the ideas are. Depending on your audience, you might want to rephrase highly technical language from a scientific source, for example, and put it in your own words. Or you might want to emphasize a point the author makes in a way that isn't as clear in the original language. Many social scientists and most scientists routinely paraphrase sources as part of the presentation of their own research because the results they're reporting from secondary sources are more important than the exact language used to explain the results. Quotations should be reserved for instances when the exact language of the original source is important to the point being made. Remember that paraphrasing requires you to restate the passage in your own words and in your own sentence structure. Even if you are putting the source's ideas in your own words, you must acknowledge where the information came from by providing an appropriate citation.

The following paragraph was taken from William Thierfelder's article "Twain's *Huckleberry Finn*," published in *The Explicator*, a journal of literary criticism.

> An often-noted biblical allusion in *Huckleberry Finn* is that comparing Huck to the prophet Moses. Like Moses, whom Huck learns about from the Widow Douglas, Huck sets out, an orphan on his raft, down the river. In the biblical story, it is Moses's mother who puts him in his little "raft," hoping he will be found. In the novel, Huck/Moses takes charge of his own travels. . . .

Inappropriate Paraphrase

William Thierfelder suggests that Huckleberry is often compared to the prophet Moses. Huck, an orphan like Moses, travels down a river on a raft (194).

Although some of the language has been changed and the paraphrase includes documentation, this paraphrase of the first two sentences of Thierfelder's passage is inappropriate because it relies on the language of the original text and employs the author's sentence structure. An appropriate paraphrase that uses new language and sentence structure might look like this:

> William Thierfelder notes that numerous readers have linked the character of Huckleberry Finn and the biblical figure of Moses. They are both orphans who take a water journey, Thierfelder argues. However, Moses's journey begins because of the actions of his mother, while Huck's journey is undertaken by himself (194).

Quoting

Depending on your rhetorical context, you may find that **quoting** the exact words of a source as part of your argument is the most effective strategy. The use of quotations is much more common in some academic fields than in others. Writers in the humanities, for example, often quote texts directly because the precise language of the original is important to the argument. You'll find, for instance, that literary scholars often quote a short story or poem (a primary source) for evidence. You may also find that a secondary source contains powerful or interesting language that would lose its impact if you paraphrased it. In such circumstances, it is entirely appropriate to quote the text. Keep in mind that your reader should always be able to understand why the quotation is important to your argument. We recommend three methods for integrating quotations into your writing. (The examples below follow American Psychological Association style conventions; see "Understanding Documentation Systems" on pages 99–101 and the Appendix for more information about documentation styles.)

1. **Attributive Tags**   Introduce the quotation with a tag (with words like *notes*, *argues*, *suggests*, *posits*, *maintains*, etc.) that attributes the language and ideas to its author. Notice that different tags suggest different relationships between the author and the idea being cited. For example:

   > De Niet, Tiemens, Lendemeijer, Lendemei, and Hutschemaekers (2009) argued, "Music-assisted relaxation is an effective aid for improving sleep quality in patients with various conditions" (p. 1362).

2. **Further Grammatical Integration**   You may also fully integrate a quotation into the grammar of your own sentences. For example:

   > Their review of the research revealed "scientific support for the effectiveness of the systematic use of music-assisted

relaxation to promote sleep quality" in patients (De Niet et al., 2009, p. 1362).

3. **Introduce with Full Sentence + Punctuation** You can also introduce a quotation with a full sentence and create a transitional link to the quotation with punctuation, like the colon. For example:

The study reached a final conclusion about music-assisted relaxation: "It is a safe and cheap intervention which may be used to treat sleep problems in various populations" (De Niet et al., 2009, p. 1362).

INSIDE WORK **Summarizing, Paraphrasing, and Quoting from Sources**

Choose a source you have found on a topic of interest to you, and find a short passage (only one or two sentences) from the source that provides information that might be useful in your own research. Then complete the following steps and write down your responses.

1. Summarize the passage. It might help to look at the larger context in which the passage appears.

2. Paraphrase the passage, using your own words and sentence structure.

3. Quote the passage, using the following three ways to integrate the passage into your own text:
   – attributive tags
   – grammatical integration
   – full sentence + punctuation

For your own research, which approach (summarizing, paraphrasing, quoting) do you think would be most useful? Consider your writing context and how you would use the source. ❱

AVOIDING PLAGIARISM

Any language and ideas used in your own writing that belong to others must be fully acknowledged and carefully documented, with both in-text citations and full bibliographic documentation. Failure to include either of these when source materials are employed could lead to a charge of **plagiarism**, perhaps the most serious of academic integrity offenses. The procedures for document-ing cited sources vary from one rhetorical and disciplinary context to another, so you'll always want to clarify the expectations for documentation with your instructor when responding to an assigned writing task. Regardless, you should always acknowledge your sources when you summarize, paraphrase, or quote, and be sure to include the full information for your sources in the bibliography of your project.

Understanding Plagiarism

Most schools, colleges, and universities have established definitions of plagiarism and penalties or sanctions that may be imposed on students found guilty of plagiarism. You should become familiar with the definitions of plagiarism used by your institution as well as by your individual instructors.

- Locate a resource on campus (e.g., a student handbook or the website of your institution's Office of Student Conduct) that provides a definition of plagiarism from the perspective of your institution. You may discover that in addition to defining plagiarism, your institution provides avenues of support to foster academic integrity and/or presents explanations of the consequences or penalties for violating rules of academic integrity.

- Locate a resource from one of your classes (e.g., a course website, a course syllabus) that provides a definition of plagiarism from the perspective of one of your instructors.

- Consider what is similar about the two definitions. Consider the differences between them. What do these similarities and differences reveal about your instructor's expectations and those of the larger academic community in which you participate? ▶

Insider's View
On accidental plagiarism
KAREN KEATON JACKSON, WRITING STUDIES

"Many students come in who are already familiar with using direct quotations. But when it comes to paraphrasing and summarizing, that's when I see a lot of accidental plagiarism. So it's really important for students to understand that if you don't do the research yourself, or if you weren't there in the field or doing the survey, then it's not your own idea and you have to give credit."

 **LaunchPad**
Hear more on avoiding plagiarism.

UNDERSTANDING DOCUMENTATION SYSTEMS

Documentation systems are often discipline-specific, and their conventions reflect the needs and values of researchers and readers in those particular disciplines. For these reasons, you should carefully analyze any writing situation to determine which documentation style to follow. You'll find examples of specific documentation systems in the disciplinary chapters in Part Two. Here are some of the most common ones:

Modern Language Association (MLA)

MLA documentation procedures are generally followed by researchers in the humanities. One of the most important elements of the in-text citation requirements for the MLA documentation system is the inclusion of page numbers in a parenthetical reference. Though page numbers are used in other documentation systems for some in-text citations (as in the APA system when quoting a passage directly), page numbers in MLA are especially important because they serve as a means for readers to assess your use of sources, both primary and secondary, and are used whether you are quoting, paraphrasing, or summarizing a passage. Page numbers enable readers to quickly identify cited passages and evaluate the evidence: readers may verify that you've accurately represented a source's intent when citing the author's words, or that you've fully examined all the elements at play in your analysis of a photograph or poem. Of course, this kind of examination is important in all disciplines, but it is especially the case in the humanities, where evidence typically takes the form of words and images. Unlike some other documentation systems, the MLA system does not require dates for in-text citations, because scholars in this field often find that past discoveries or arguments are just as useful today as when they were first observed or published. Interpretations don't really expire; their usefulness remains valid across exceptionally long periods of time. Learn more about the style guides published by the Modern Language Association, including the *MLA Handbook*, along with more information about the MLA itself, at www.mla.org.

American Psychological Association (APA)

APA documentation procedures are followed by researchers in many areas of the social sciences and related fields. Although you will encounter page numbers in the in-text citations for direct quotations in APA documents, you're much less likely to find direct quotations overall. Generally, researchers in the social sciences are less interested in the specific language or words used to report research findings than they are in the results or conclusions. Therefore, social science researchers are more likely to paraphrase information than to quote information. Additionally, in-text documentation in the APA system requires the date of publication for research (see the examples on p. 209, and consult the Appendix for more information). This is a striking distinction from the MLA system. Social science research that was conducted fifty years ago may not be as useful as research conducted two years ago, so it's important to cite the date of the source in the text of the argument. Imagine how different the results would be for a study of the effects of violence in video games on youth twenty years ago versus a study conducted last year. Findings from twenty years ago probably have very little bearing on the contemporary social context and would not reflect the same video game content as today's games. As a result, the APA system requires the date of research publication as part of the in-text citation. The date enables readers to quickly evaluate the currency, and therefore the appropriateness, of the research being referenced. Learn more about the *Publication Manual of the American Psychological Association* and the APA itself at its website: www.apa.org.

The Council of Science Editors (CSE)

As the name suggests, the CSE documentation system is most prevalent among disciplines of the natural sciences, although many of the applied fields in the sciences, like engineering and medicine, rely on their own documentation systems. As in the other systems described here, CSE requires writers to document all materials derived from sources. Unlike MLA or APA, however, CSE allows multiple methods for in-text citations, corresponding to alternative forms of the reference page that appears at the end of research reports. For more detailed information on CSE documentation, consult the latest edition of *Scientific Style and Format: The CSE Manual for Authors, Editors, and Publishers.* You can learn more about the Council of Science Editors at its website: www.councilscienceeditors.org.

Writing an Annotated Bibliography

WRITING PROJECT

The annotated bibliography is a common genre in several academic disciplines because it provides a way to compile and take notes on — that is, annotate — resources that are potentially useful in a research project. **Annotated bibliographies** are essentially lists of citations, formatted in a consistent documentation style, that include concise summaries of source material. Some annotated bibliographies include additional commentary about the sources — perhaps evaluations of their usefulness for the research project or comments about how the sources complement one another within the bibliography (possibly by providing multiple perspectives). Annotated bibliographies are usually organized alphabetically, but longer bibliographies can be organized topically or in sections with subheadings. Each source entry gives the citation first and then a paragraph or two of summary, as in this example using MLA style:

> Carter, Michael. "Ways of Knowing, Doing, and Writing in the Disciplines." *College Composition and Communication*, vol. 58, no. 3, 2007, pp. 385–418.
>
> In this article, Carter outlines a process for helping faculty across different academic disciplines to understand the conventions of writing in their disciplines by encouraging them to think of disciplines as "ways of doing." He provides examples from his own interactions with faculty members in several disciplines, and he draws on data collected from these interactions to describe four "metagenres" that reflect ways of doing that are shared across multiple disciplines: problem-solving, empirical inquiry, research from sources, and performance. Finally, he concludes that the metagenres revealed by examining shared ways of doing can help to identify "metadisciplines."

For this assignment, you should write an annotated bibliography that seeks to find sources that will help you respond to a specific research question. Your purpose in writing the annotated bibliography is threefold: (1) to organize and keep track of the sources you've found on your own topic, (2) to better understand the relationships among different sources that address your topic, and (3) to demonstrate knowledge of the existing research about it.

To meet this purpose, choose sources that will help answer your research question, and think about a specific audience who might be interested in the research you're presenting. Your annotated bibliography should include the following elements.

- An introduction that clearly states your research question and describes the scope of your annotated bibliography.

- As many as eight to twelve sources (depending on the scope of the sources and the number of perspectives you want to represent), organized alphabetically. If you choose a different organization (e.g., topical), explain how you have organized your annotated bibliography in the introduction.

- An annotation for each source that includes:
  - A summary of the source that gives a concise description of the main findings, focused on what is most important for responding to your research question
  - Relevant information about the authors or sponsors of the source to indicate credibility, bias, perspective, and the like
  - An indication of what this source brings to your annotated bibliography that is unique and/or how it connects to the other sources
  - A citation (see the Appendix) in a consistent documentation style

Developing a Supported Argument on a Controversial Issue

For this writing assignment, you will apply your knowledge from Chapter 4 about developing an argument and from this chapter on finding and documenting appropriate sources. The sources you find will be evidence for the argument you develop. We ask you to make a claim about a controversial issue that is of importance to you and support that claim with evidence to persuade a particular audience of your position. As you write, you might follow the steps below to develop your argument.

- Begin by identifying an issue that you care about and likely have some experience with. We all write best about things that matter to us. For many students, choosing an issue that is specific to their experience or local context makes a narrower, more manageable topic to write about. For example, examining recycling options for students on your college campus would be more manageable than tackling the issue of global waste and recycling.

- Once you have identified an issue, start reading about it to discover what people are saying and what positions they are taking. Use the suggestions in this chapter to find scholarly sources about your issue so that you can "listen in on" the conversations already taking place about your issue. You might find that you want to narrow your topic further based on what you find.

- As you read, begin tracking the sources you find. These sources can serve as evidence later for multiple perspectives on the issue; they will be useful both in supporting your claim and in understanding counterarguments.

- Identify a clear claim you would like to support, an audience you would like to persuade, and a purpose for writing to that audience. Whom should you talk to about your issue, and what can they do about it?

As you work to develop your argument, consider the various elements of an argument you read about in Chapter 4.

- Identify a clear central claim, and determine if it should have a simple or complex thesis statement.

- Develop clear reasons for that claim, drawn from your knowledge of the issue and the sources you have found.

- Choose evidence from your sources to support each reason that will be persuasive to your audience, and consider the potential appeals of ethos, logos, and pathos.

- Identify any assumptions that need to be explained to or supported for your audience.

- Develop responses to any counterarguments you should include in your argument.

Insider Example
Student Argument on a Controversial Issue

The following sample student argument, produced in a first-year writing class, illustrates many of the principles discussed in Chapters 4 and 5. As you read, identify the thesis, reasons, and sources used as support for the argument. Notice also that the student writer, Jack Gomperts, followed CSE style conventions throughout his paper, in response to his instructor's direction to choose a documentation style appropriate to the subject of his argument.

JACK GOMPERTS

Evaluating Hydration Levels in High School Athletes

Jack Gomperts

Professor Melton
English 101
Project 4

Evaluating Hydration Levels in High School Athletes

Every day, high school athletes across the country put themselves at risk of heat-related injury, and even death, by failing to hydrate properly. Many athletes arrive at practice dehydrated, and abandon proper hydration throughout activity. This habit not only puts athletes at an increased risk of injury, but also decreases their performance (Gibson-Moore 2014). Numerous researchers have explored exactly when and how much fluid an athlete needs to maintain proper hydration. Some experimenters focus on which fluids, such as water, sports drinks, milk, juice, or various other drink options, produce the best hydration. The most important factor in making sure athletes maintain hydration, however, is not telling them how to obtain hydration, but rather testing their hydration status. Often, athletes forget or ignore hydration when coaches simply tell them to stay well hydrated. If athletes know that they will undergo testing for hydration every day, they will be more likely to take action to achieve the proper hydration status. Scientists possess dozens of methods for testing hydration in athletes, and urine specific gravity and body mass measurements are the most practical for everyday use. Urine specific gravity requires only one drop of urine from an athlete, and body mass measurements require athletes to step on a scale. In addition, athletes must sign a contract with their school before participating in any athletic event associated with the school. Schools use these contracts to ensure that they are not liable for any injury experienced by an athlete. However, most schools do not include any information about hydration in their contracts, thus exposing athletes to severe risk. Altogether, schools should alter their athletic contracts to include hydration testing for athletes with urine specific gravity and body mass measurements.

Argument begins by establishing a problem that exists

Establishes the need for further exploration and action with regard to hydration in athletes

Does this author identify or imply a particular audience for this argument? If so, who do you believe that audience might be?

Establishes a two-part central claim or position of the argument: schools should alter contracts to include hydration testing and they should use urine specific gravity and body mass measurements as the means to test hydration.

Every year, 10,000 high school athletes in the United States suffer from dehydration (Center for Disease Control and Prevention 2010). This staggering number only includes injuries that health professionals have diagnosed and does not account for the numerous athletes who suffer from dehydration without realizing it. Personally, I have never witnessed an athlete who was diagnosed with a heat-related illness, but I have seen several athletes suffer injuries that trace back to dehydration. I played on several sports teams throughout my high school career and witnessed a common theme; coaches often tell athletes to stay hydrated, but fail to explain the importance of hydration. At many football games, several of my teammates suffered from cramps caused by dehydration. During my senior year of high school, an athlete collapsed at three of my cross-country meets because of over-heating.

The athletes who neglected proper hydration at my school did not do so without consequences. Many of them experienced concussions; at least ten to twelve athletes from various sports at my school received concussions every year. According to Dr. Meehan, "Every time you get [a concussion], there's some effect on the brain that doesn't go away, concussions have a cumulative effect" (Costa 2015). Concussions negatively impact student-athletes for their entire lives, whereas most sports-related injuries do not have detrimental long-term effects. Scientists believe a strong correlation exists between hydration statuses and concussion risks. They have begun to study cerebrospinal fluid, which surrounds the brain and reduces the impact of heavy blows. With less fluid, athletes have a smaller cushion for their brain; scientists believe even a two percent decrease in hydration severely decreases the amount of cerebrospinal fluid (DripDrop 2016).

Consider the kinds of evidence the writer relies on this paragraph, including evidence from personal experience. Are they effective? What function does this paragraph serve in the overall structure of the student's argument?

How does this paragraph support part of the writer's central position about testing athletes' levels of hydration? What reason is supported here?

In addition to concussions, dehydration can also lead to a variety of heat-related illnesses, such as heat cramps, heat exhaustion, heat stroke, or even death. Heat cramps cause involuntary muscle contractions and can be treated by stretching and rehydration. Heat exhaustion causes redness of skin, profuse sweating, nausea, and vomiting, and is treated as a medical emergency by immediate rehydration and applying ice to the core. Heat stroke is the complete inability to thermo-regulate and causes clammy skin, cease of sweating, dizziness, nausea, and possible unconsciousness. In order to treat a person experiencing these symptoms, medical professionals immediately cool them in an ice bath or transport them to a trauma center (Gallucci 2014). Despite the consequences, many athletes and coaches overlook the problem of dehydration. According to the National Center for Catastrophic Sports Injury Research (2009), 40 high school football players have died from heat stroke since 1995. In addition, they report that dozens of athletes are hospitalized every year for heat-related illnesses, which directly correlates to hydration status. When as many as two thirds of young athletes arrive at practice dehydrated (Southwest Athletic Trainers' Association 2013), it is evident that high school athletic policies must be improved.

Once schools recognize the problem of dehydration, there are many possible solutions. Of the various methods, a combination of urine specific gravity and body mass measurements would be the most convenient and effective for daily use. Since urine specific gravity is easy to use and accurate, schools should utilize its capabilities. This system analyzes a drop of urine on the stage of a refractometer to evaluate the level of hydration in the athlete. If the device shows a value between 1.001 and 1.012, the athlete is likely over-hydrated. A value between 1.013 and 1.029 shows

This paragraph functions to support the writer's reasoning for his central position. What is the reason he presents to support his central claim or thesis?

How effectively does the writer incorporate evidence from statistics?

Provides reasoning to support this particular method of hydration testing proper hydration, and values above 1.030 show dehydration (Armstrong 2005). The device needed to take these measurements can cost anywhere from $60 to $400 (Lopez 2006)—a small price for teams to pay to ensure the safety of their athletes. According to Armstrong (2005), urine specific gravity is the best method to test hydration in an everyday setting because of its reliability, accuracy, and ease of use. Scientists possess several additional methods for testing hydration. These methods, however, are not practical for athletes on a daily basis, although they produce a higher level of accuracy than urine specific gravity. For instance, urine specific gravity loses accuracy as athletes' muscle mass increases. Hamouti et al. (2010) found that urine specific gravity devices falsely classify athletes with high muscle mass as dehydrated far more often than athletes with low muscle mass.

Due to the slightly inaccurate measurements produced by urine specific gravity, coaches should use body mass measurements in addition to urine specific gravity to test hydration. Body mass measurements are even more efficient and less expensive to record than urine specific gravity measurements. In order for coaches to use body mass measurements to determine hydration, they must simply weigh their athletes before and after every practice. If the athletes' mass decreases by more than two percent, they are dehydrated (Armstrong 2005). In addition, if their body mass decreases by more than two percent from the beginning of practice one day to the beginning of practice the next day, they are likely dehydrated. Body mass measurements provide a good estimate of hydration status. Recognizing that the body mass of high school athletes constantly changes due to growth, eating habits, and several other factors, coaches should use body mass measurements in addition to urine specific gravity. They should use urine specific gravity once

Writer provides further reasoning to support the methods of testing hydration levels in athletes

Writer ties together issues related to measuring hydration levels in order to support his contention that certain steps are necessary on the athletes at the beginning of the season, and two to three times randomly throughout the season. This system will provide the coaches with more accurate results than body mass measurements, while not requiring athletes to place a drop of urine on a device every day. This process will ensure the safety of athletes on a daily basis and drastically decrease their risk for illness or death.

Despite the many benefits of hydration testing, some people might disagree with this proposal. Some might argue that regulating hydration status invades the privacy of an athlete and assumes unnecessary control of an athlete's life. I propose that students should decide how much fluid they need, how often they need it, and which drinks best produce hydration. Lopez (2006), Maughan (2010), and Johannsen (2015) all argue for different amounts and types of fluid for proper hydration. These decisions should be left to the athlete since each athlete differs in how much fluid they need for hydration. The schools should only take responsibility for making sure that their athletes are well hydrated. Schools and athletic organizations have put dozens of rules in place to ensure the safety of athletes, like the types of hits allowed in football. If schools have the authority to make rules that protect football players, schools have the power to implement rules and regulations that concern hydration. If implementing hydration regulations can save just one life, schools should do so as quickly as possible. A life is worth more than the few hundred dollars spent on urine specific gravity devices and portable scales. A life is worth more than the slight hassle of taking a few minutes before and after practice to measure athletes' body mass. These rules, however, could have potentially saved the 40 lives that have been lost since 1995 because of heat-related illnesses (National Center for Catastrophic Sports Injury Research 2009). Hydration

> The writer acknowledges a potential counterargument. How does he use sources and evidence to refute the counterargument?

testing might have prevented several thousand athletes from experiencing heat-related illness every year, or saved dozens of athletes from hospitalization. The slight intrusion on athletes' privacy is well worth saving dozens of lives.

In addition to the intrusion on athletes, some people might argue that coaches already carry immense responsibility, and adding these tests would place a heavier burden on the coaches. However, the coaches' job is to teach the athletes how to improve their play and to keep them safe from injury. The hydration requirements I propose align directly with a coach's responsibility. Although it could be considered a burden to require coaches to measure athletes' hydration status, this burden takes no more than 20 minutes a day to complete. Additionally, these regulations exist in accordance with the coach's job, which is to protect his or her athletes, and enhance the athletes' performance however possible. These tests will help coaches do their job more fully and provide better care for their athletes.

Altogether, hydration should be tested in athletes with a combination of urine specific gravity and body mass measurements because these tests will ensure that athletes are practicing and performing under safe conditions. Dehydration poses a problem in high schools all across America because many teens do not understand the importance of proper hydration. Therefore, they arrive at practice dehydrated, which leads to thousands of injuries a year. I propose that to solve this problem, schools should include a policy in their athletic contract regarding hydration. This policy should require athletes to be subject to three to four urine specific gravity tests throughout the season and two daily body mass measurements. Even though people might argue that these tests intrude on athletes' privacy and place a burden on coaches, the tests are capable of saving

The author identifies another possible counterargument. What evidence is provided to refute the counterargument? Is that evidence convincing to you? Why or why not?

Can you identify other potential counterarguments that might undermine the writer's position here?

Do any of the writer's statements, presented in the conclusion to the argument, surprise you as a reader? Why or why not?

dozens of lives. I believe that this insignificant burden is well worth the sacrifice. I further propose that each athlete should be held responsible for determining how he or she can best achieve hydration. While researchers continue to find the best ways for athletes to maintain hydration, schools must take responsibility by implementing regulations to reduce the dangers associated with dehydration in athletics.

Are you convinced by this argument? Do you agree with the writer's position? Why or why not?

References

Armstrong LE. 2005. Hydration assessment techniques
[Internet]. Nutr Res. [accessed 2016 Dec 9]; 63(6):S40-S54.
Available from: https://www.ncbi.nlm.nih.gov/pubmed
/16028571

Center for Disease Control and Prevention. 2010. Heat illness
among high school athletes—United States, 2005-2009
[Internet]. Morb Mortal Wkly Rep. [accessed 2016 Dec 9];
59(32):1009-1053. Available from: https://www.cdc.gov
/mmwr/preview/mmwrhtml/mm5932a1.htm

Coe S, Williams R. 2011. Hydration and health [Internet].
Nutr Bull. [accessed 2016 Dec 9]; 36(2):259-266. Available
from: http://onlinelibrary.wiley.com/doi/10.1111/j.1467-3010
.2011.01899.x/abstract

Costa S. 2015. Just how dangerous are sports
concussions, anyway?: Concussions cause the brain
to dangerously move back and forth inside the skull
[Internet]. Huffington Post. [accessed 2016 Dec 9].
Available from: http://www.huffingtonpost.com/entry
/the-truth-about-concussions_us_564a0043e4b045bf3deff7fc

DripDrop Hydration. 2016. Does dehydration increase
an athlete's risk for concussion? [Internet]. [accessed
2016 Dec 9]. Available from: http://dripdrop.com
/dehydration-increase-athletes-risk-concussion/

Gallucci J. 2014. Soccer injury prevention and treatment:
A guide to optimal performance for players, parents
and coaches. New York (NY): Demos Medical Publishing.
p. 157-159.

Gibson-Moore H. 2014. Hydration and health [Internet].
Nutr Bull. [accessed 2016 Dec 9]; 39(1):4-8. Available
from: http://onlinelibrary.wiley.com/doi/10.1111/nbu
.12039/full

Notice the mix of sources the writer relies upon, both popular and academic, as well as any primary and secondary forms of research.

Notice the kinds of sources the author uses as support. If he were to conduct additional research for support, what kind of additional sources would you recommend he look to in order to strengthen his argument?

Hamouti N, Del Coso J, Avila A, Mora-Rodriquez R. 2010. Effects of athletes' muscle mass on urinary markers of hydration status [Internet]. Euro J Appl Physiol. [accessed 2016 Dec 9]; 109(2):213-219. Available from: https://www.ncbi.nlm.nih.gov/pubmed/20058021

Johannsen NM, Earnest CP. 2015. Fluid balance and hydration for human performance. In: Greenwood M, Cooke MB, Ziegenfuss T, Kalman DS, Antonio J, editors. Nutritional supplements in sports and exercise. Cham, Switzerland: Springer International Publishing. p. 105-119.

Lopez RM, Casa DJ. 2006. Hydration for athletes: What coaches can do to keep their athletes healthy and performing their best [Internet]. Coaches' Quarterly. [accessed 2016 Dec 9]. Available from: https://www.wiaawi.org/Portals/0/PDF/Sports/Wrestling/hydration4athletes.pdf

Maughan RJ, Shirreffs SM. 2010. Dehydration and rehydration in competitive sport [Internet]. Scand J Med Sci. [accessed 2016 Dec 9]; 20(3):40-47. Available from: http://onlinelibrary.wiley.com/doi/10.1111/j.1600-0838.2010.01207.x/abstract

National Center for Catastrophic Sports Injury Research (US) [NCCSIR]. 2009. Annual survey of football injury research: 1931-2008 [Internet]. [accessed 2016 Dec 9]. p. 2-29. Available from: http://nccsir.unc.edu/files/2014/05/FootballAnnual.pdf

Southwest Athletic Trainers' Association. 2013. Statistics on youth sports safety [Internet]. [accessed 2016 Dec 9]. Available from: http://www.swata.org/statistics/

Discussion Questions

1. Whom do you think Jack Gomperts is targeting as his audience in this assignment? Why do you think that is his audience?

2. What is Jack's thesis, and what does he provide as the reasons and evidence for his claim?

3. What assumptions connect his thesis to his reasons? Additionally, what assumptions would his audience have to accept in order to find his evidence persuasive? Really dig into this question, because this area is often where arguments fall apart.

4. What counterarguments does Jack address in his argument? Why do you think he addresses these particular counterarguments? Can you think of others that he might have addressed?

5. What kinds of sources does Jack rely on in his argument? How does he integrate them into his argument, and why do you think he has made those choices?

6. What would make this argument more persuasive and effective?

tip sheet

Academic Research

- **Research typically begins with a research question, which establishes the purpose and scope of a project.** As you develop research questions, keep in mind the following evaluative criteria: personal investment, debatable subject, researchable issue, feasibility, and contribution.

- **A researcher who has established a clear focus for her research, or who has generated a claim, must decide on the kinds of sources needed to support the research focus:** primary, secondary, or both.

- **While both scholarly and popular sources may be appropriate sources of evidence in differing contexts, be sure to understand what distinguishes these types of sources** so that you can choose evidence types purposefully.

- **Primary sources are the results of data that researchers might collect on their own.** These results could include data from surveys, interviews, or questionnaires. **Secondary sources include research collected by and/or commented on by others.** These might include information taken from newspaper articles, magazines, scholarly journal articles, and scholarly books, to name a few.

- **Keep in mind that as you conduct research, you will likely have to refine your search terms.** This process involves carefully selecting or narrowing the terms you use to locate information via search engines or databases.

- **Be aware of the challenges of conducting basic searches for sources via Internet search engines** like Google. While Google Scholar may be a better means of searching for sources in the academic context, researchers often rely on more specialized research databases.

- **Peer-reviewed academic journals are an excellent source of information for academic arguments.** The publication process for journal articles is typically much faster than for books, so using journal articles allows you access to the most current research.

- **Be aware of the strategies you can use to integrate the ideas of others into your own writing:** summarizing, paraphrasing, and/or quoting.

- **When you integrate the words or ideas of others, take care to ensure that you are documenting their words and ideas carefully to avoid instances of plagiarism,** and make sure you understand what constitutes plagiarism at your institution and/or in your individual classes. Follow appropriate rules for documenting your sources and constructing a bibliography. In academic contexts, this often means using MLA, APA, or CSE documentation systems.

PART TWO

Inside Academic Writing

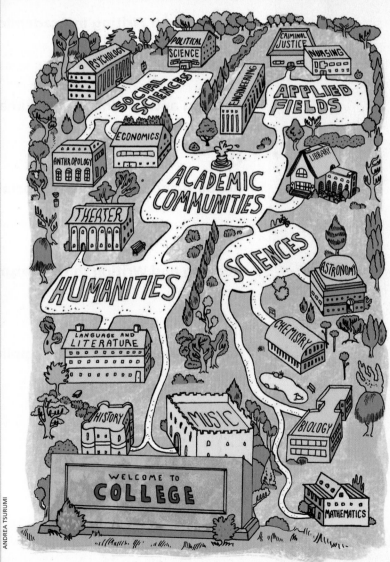

ANDREA TSURUMI

Reading and Writing in Academic Disciplines

The four chapters that follow this one introduce four broad disciplinary areas in higher education: humanities, social sciences, natural sciences, and applied fields. While some differences distinguish each of these areas, certain similarities show shared values that provide ways to analyze and understand the conventions of writing and research in those areas.

To help you navigate these chapters, we have organized Chapters 7 through 9 around the same key concerns:

- **Research in the Discipline** Every academic discipline has established conventions of research. One thing that unites them is the importance of **observation**. Whether you're a humanities scholar observing texts, or a social scientist observing human behavior, or a scientist observing the natural world, careful methods of observation are central to developing research questions and writing projects in each disciplinary area. Similarly, all disciplines rely on the concepts of **primary research** and **secondary research**. (If you gather data of your own, you're doing primary research. If you gather data by studying the research of others, you're doing secondary research. See pages 60–62 for more on different types of research.) Academic writers in a variety of disciplines engage in both primary and secondary research and find that they inform each other. For example, a social scientist studying human behavior might conduct secondary research first to learn what others have done and to develop her research questions. Then she might conduct primary research to test a hypothesis and report results. Similarly, a humanities scholar

ANDREA TSURUMI

Writing should be different in various situations

KAREN KEATON JACKSON, WRITING STUDIES

"I think students should consider that writing has to be and should be different in various situations. Students need to go through a kind of meta-process of thinking about their own writing, one that allows them to see that the skills they learn in first-year writing can transfer. When students go into their history class or psychology class, for instance, the expectations may be different, but they'll see how they can transfer what they've learned in first-year writing to that situation."

LaunchPad

Learn more about rhetorical situations.

studying historical documents might conduct secondary research to develop a review of literature that will lead to a guiding research question. That research question could then lead him to conduct primary research that includes analyzing a historical document to develop a thesis about his interpretation of that document.

- **Conventions of Writing in the Discipline** Each academic discipline has expectations about academic writing in its field. The chapters that follow this one all include sections that describe and help you analyze the **conventions** of writing in the disciplines, using the principles of rhetoric (the strategies of communication and persuasion) introduced in Part One and in this chapter.

- **Genres in the Discipline** Each chapter also provides examples of **genres**, or common types of writing, that often cross disciplines. These *Insider Examples* of writing, not only by professionals in the disciplines but also by students entering the discipline and composing in particular genres, are annotated to reveal key features that prompt your own analysis of them.

Chapter 10 then explores the kinds of genres produced in a number of applied fields, including health fields, education, business, and law.

Additionally, the chapters share other common features to help you broaden your understanding of each disciplinary area: *Insider's View* excerpts of scholars discussing disciplinary writing; *Inside Work* activities that prompt you to reflect on what you've learned; *Writing Projects* that help you develop your own academic compositions; and *Tip Sheets* that summarize key information.

Throughout these chapters, we ask you to analyze and practice writing in various academic disciplines. Keep in mind, though, that we *do not* expect you to master the writing of these communities by taking just one class or by reading one book. Instead, we introduce you to the concepts associated with **disciplinary discourse**, or the writing and speaking that is specific to different disciplines. Using these concepts, you can analyze future writing situations and make choices appropriate to the rhetorical contexts. It's worth noting that such rhetorical awareness may help you enter other **discourse communities**, or groups that share common values and similar communication practices, outside of your college classes as well, both socially and professionally.

Disciplinary conventions and styles are not just patterns to follow; rather, they represent shared values. In other words, there's a reason why academic texts are communicated in the way that they are: scholars in the same discipline might have similar ways of thinking about an issue, and they follow common ways of researching and investigating that represent their shared values and perspectives. The information we offer you on different academic disciplinary conventions in this book is not necessarily something to memorize, but rather something to analyze through the frame of *rhetorical context*. Ultimately, we want you to be able to look at an academic genre and determine:

1. What is the rhetorical context?
2. What conventions are present in the genre?

As you write for different courses throughout your college career, this ability will help you determine and follow the expectations of writing for the different academic contexts you encounter. It will also help you read the assignments in your other classes because you'll understand some of the reasons that texts are written in the way that they are.

Analyzing Genres and Identifying Conventions of Academic Writing

As you know, different writing situations call for different types of writing. Different types of writing—from short items such as tweets, bumper stickers, and recipes to longer and more complex compositions such as Ph.D. dissertations, annual reports, and novels—are called genres. We mentioned genres in Part One, but we want to dive a little deeper here to talk about the kinds of genres you'll encounter in academic contexts and how to analyze them. Scholars write in many different genres depending on their disciplinary areas, the kinds of work they do, and the situation in which they're writing. You have probably written in several different academic genres in your education already. You might have written a literary analysis in an English class, a lab report in a science class, a bibliography for a research paper, and maybe a personal narrative. Each of these genres has a distinct purpose and set of expectations that you must be familiar with in order to communicate effectively with your intended audience. In this text, you'll find information about writing in many of these genres—such as literary/artistic interpretations, rhetorical analyses, annotated bibliographies, reviews of literature, lab reports, and memos—with the ultimate goal of learning to analyze the rhetorical context so that you can determine the expected conventions of a genre in any writing situation.

Genres are not always bound by discipline, however. Some genres recur across disciplines because writers' purposes can be quite similar even in different fields. You'll find that the conventions of some genres are similar from one

"I think the three skills that students need to write in college settings are all tied into the rhetorical situation. If they can think about audience, purpose, and form, I think that will at least get them ready to start asking the kinds of questions they need of their professors to determine, how am I going to shape this for this particular audience, this particular discipline, this particular professor?"

LaunchPad

Learn more about analyzing genres.

disciplinary area to another. As you read Chapters 7 through 10 on humanities, the social sciences, the natural sciences, and applied fields, pay attention to which genres are repeated and how the conventions of those genres shift or remain constant from one disciplinary context to another.

You'll notice that similar writing situations within, and even sometimes across, disciplines call for a similar genre. In other words, academics might approach a piece of writing in the same (or a similar) way even though they come from different academic disciplines.

For example, you'll notice that scholars in all disciplines write reviews of literature for their research. Likewise, when reporting on the results of a research study, many academics follow the **IMRaD (Introduction, Methods, Results, and Discussion) format**, or a variation of it, to record and publish the results of their research, regardless of their discipline. There might be some subtle differences from one discipline or one situation to another, but common elements are evident. Literature reviews and IMRaD reports are two examples of common genres of academic writing.

As we begin to talk about specific disciplinary contexts, keep in mind these strategies to analyze the conventions of academic writing. When you read and write academic texts, you'll want to:

- understand the overall rhetorical context of the piece of writing: the author, the audience, the topic, and the purpose for writing
- identify and understand the disciplinary area—humanities, social sciences, natural sciences, applied fields—and make connections to what you know about that discipline
- identify the conventions of writing for that genre, including which elements of structure, language, and reference (explained below) govern the writing situation
- analyze the persuasive strategies used, if the author is developing an argument. (What claims are presented? How are they supported by reasons and evidence? What assumptions are in play?)

These analytical strategies will help you to approach any academic writing situation confidently and effectively.

Insider's View
Scientists must write all sorts of things
MIKE BROTHERTON, ASTRONOMY

"Aspiring scientists often don't appreciate the importance of communication skills. Science doesn't count until it's communicated to the rest of the scientific community, and eventually the public. Moreover, scientists must write all sorts of things to have a successful career, from journal articles to grant applications to press releases.

"Probably the most important thing to do well when writing as a scientist is simply to get everything right. Science is a methodology for developing reliable information about the world we live in, and getting things wrong is the surest way for scientists to lose their reputation; and for a scientist, reputation is the coin of the realm. While nearly everyone scientifically inclined finds getting things right to be an obvious and principal goal, it is also critically important to identify the audience of any particular piece of writing and address that audience in an effective way. The writing examples included in this text are all targeted for a different readership, and that represents a primary difference between them.

"Scientists write and are asked to write for all sorts of audiences. This isn't an easy task, but success in that adaptation can be the difference between a great career and failure, so it's important to treat it seriously. There isn't magic to this, and while brilliance can be challenging to achieve, competence can certainly be learned. It just takes some practice and thought."

Adapting to Different Rhetorical Contexts: An Academic Writer at Work

Even though some genres are more common in specific disciplines than others, many scholars write in more than one genre on a regular basis. Scholars write for different rhetorical contexts all the time, and they adapt their writing to the audience, topic, and purpose of the occasion. We'd like to take an in-depth look at one scholar's writing to show you an example of how he shifts the conventions of his writing for different contexts—often academic, but sometimes more general. We've chosen to look at a scholar in a scientific field that is rarely discussed in English classes: astronomy. Mike Brotherton is an astronomer at the University of Wyoming, and we'll look at two types of writing that he does on a regular basis. Brotherton writes scholarly articles in his field to report on his research to an audience of other academics—his peers. He also sometimes writes press releases about his research, and these are intended to help journalists report news to the general public. Each piece of writing represents a different genre that follows unique conventions for that rhetorical context, but together they show us the varying ways that Brotherton shares his work in the field of astronomy. Both of these rhetorical contexts call for an awareness of different genre conventions.

Reflecting on a Discipline

> In his Insider's View, "Scientists must write all sorts of things," Mike Brotherton makes several generalizations about science, scientists, and scientific writing. Which of these comments, if any, surprised you, and which ones didn't? Explain why. ▶

Using Rhetorical Context to Analyze Academic Writing

In Chapter 3, we introduced the concept of rhetorical context for analyzing different kinds of writing. Now we want to turn your attention toward the range of academic texts you might encounter in college and beyond to understand their unique rhetorical contexts. First we'll take a look at a piece of writing that Mike Brotherton composed for an audience of journalists who might be interested in research he conducted. Brotherton wrote a press release to communicate the results of his research in a genre familiar to journalists. As you read the press release, which we've annotated, keep in mind the elements of rhetorical context that are useful in analyzing all kinds of writing:

- *author* (who is the writer, and what does he or she bring to the text?)
- *audience* (for whom is the text intended?)
- *topic* (what issue is the text addressing?)
- *purpose* (why did the author write the text?)

Specifically, consider the following questions:

- How might Brotherton's position as the *author* of the press release influence the way he wrote it? What might have been different if someone else had written the press release after talking to him about his research?
- Who is the *audience* for this piece? What choices do you think Brotherton made that were specific to his audience for the press release?
- How does the *topic* of the press release affect the choices Brotherton made? Would you have made different choices to approach the topic for a general audience? What would they be?
- What is the *purpose* for writing the press release? How might that influence Brotherton's choices as a writer? Do you think he has met that purpose? Why or why not?

Excerpt from **Hubble Space Telescope Spies Galaxy/Black Hole Evolution in Action**

MIKE BROTHERTON

JUNE 2ND, 2008 — A set of 29 Hubble Space Telescope (HST) images of an exotic type of active galaxy known as a "post-starburst quasar" show that interactions and mergers drive both galaxy evolution and the growth of super-massive black holes at their centers. Mike Brotherton, Associate Professor at the University of Wyoming, is presenting his team's findings today at the American Astronomical Society meeting in St. Louis, Missouri. Other team members include Sabrina Cales, Rajib Ganguly, and Zhaohui Shang of the University of Wyoming, Gabriella Canalizo of the University of California at Riverside, Aleks Diamond-Stanic of the University of Arizona, and Dan Vanden Berk of the Penn State University. The result is of special interest because the images provide support for a leading theory of the evolution of massive galaxies, but also show that the situation is more complicated than previously thought.

Over the last decade, astronomers have discovered that essentially every galaxy harbors a super-massive black hole at its center, ranging from 10,000 times the mass of the sun to upwards of 1,000,000,000 times solar, and that there exists a close relationship between the mass of the black hole and properties of its host. When the black holes are fueled and grow, the galaxy becomes active, with the most luminous manifestation being a quasar, which can outshine the galaxy and make it difficult to observe.

In order to explain the relationships between galaxies and their central black holes, theorists have proposed detailed models in which both grow together as the result of galaxy mergers. This hierarchical picture suggests that large galaxies are built up over time through the assembly of smaller galaxies with corresponding bursts of star formation, and that this process also fuels the growth of the black holes, which eventually ignite to shine as quasars. Supernova explosions and their dusty debris shroud the infant starburst until the activated quasar blows out the obscuration.

Brotherton and his team turned the sharp-eyed Hubble Space Telescope and its Advanced Camera for Surveys to observe a subset of these post-starburst quasars that had the strongest and most luminous stellar content. Looking at these systems 3.5 billion light-years away, Hubble, operating without the distortions of an atmosphere, can resolve sub-kiloparsec scales necessary to see nuclear structure and host galaxy morphology.

"The images started coming in, and we were blown away," said Brotherton. "We see not only merger remnants as in the prototype of the class, but also

---

Sidebar annotations:

Identifies the topic of the research study and its relevant findings

Identifies members of the research team, who are all authors of the study upon which the press release is based

Fulfills the purpose of a press release by stating the importance of the research project. Appears in the first paragraph to make it prominent for the audience

Provides relevant background information about the topic for the audience

Provides a brief overview of the study's methods

post-starburst quasars with interacting companion galaxies, double nuclei, star-bursting rings, and all sorts of messy structures."

Astronomers have determined that our own Milky Way galaxy and the great spiral galaxy of Andromeda will collide three billion years from now. This event will create massive bursts of star formation and most likely fuel nuclear activity a few hundred million years later. Hubble has imaged post-starburst quasars three and a half billion light-years away, corresponding to three and a half billion years ago, and three and a half billion years from now our own galaxy is probably going to be one of these systems.

This work is supported by grants from NASA, through the Space Telescope Science Institute and the Long-Term Space Astrophysics program, and the National Science Foundation.

Acknowledges funding support for the research project, giving credit to funding agencies that might also be audiences for the journalists' news articles

Insider's View
The audience for a press release is very general
MIKE BROTHERTON, ASTRONOMY

"It isn't always the case that scientists write their own press releases. Often, there are writers on staff at various institutions who specialize in writing press releases and who work with scientists. I've written press releases solo (e.g., the contribution included here) and in collaboration with staff journalists at the University of Texas, Lawrence Livermore National Laboratory, and the University of Wyoming. Press releases should be able to be run as news stories themselves and contain enough content to be adapted or cut to length. The audience for a press release is very general, and you can't assume that they have any background in your field. You have to tell them why your result is important, clearly and briefly, and little else.

"While I don't think my effort here is bad, it is far from perfect and suffers one flaw. Reporters picking up press releases want to know what single result they should focus upon. They want to keep things simple. I tried to include several points in the release, rather than focusing on a single result. Some reporters became distracted about the notion that the Milky Way and Andromeda would someday merge and might become a post-starburst galaxy, which was not a result of my research project. Even though it gave the work some relevance, in hindsight I should have omitted it to keep the focus on the results of my research."

INSIDE WORK   **Reflecting on Rhetorical Context**

In his Insider's View, "The audience for a press release is very general," Mike Brotherton explains some of the specifics of writing a press release and what he sees as the strengths and weaknesses of his own press release. Review the press release with Brotherton's comments in mind, and explain whether you agree with his assessment of it. What advice might you give him for revising the press release? ▶

Using Structure, Language, and Reference to Analyze Genre Conventions

Earlier, we introduced two questions that are central to analyzing an academic text:

1. What is the rhetorical context?
2. What conventions are present in the text?

Understanding the rhetorical context is the first step toward understanding how a particular genre works. Knowing the audience and purpose for writing helps us to identify the situations in which different genres occur. In order to understand fully how a genre works, you must also understand the conventions that are present in the text and whether they follow the expectations for conventions in that genre.

To understand the conventions that are present in the text, though, we need an additional framework for analysis. The categories of **structure**, **language**, and **reference (SLR)*** offer more specific help in analyzing the conventions of genres at a deeper level. Although discourse conventions vary from discipline to discipline, once you understand how to analyze writing through these categories, you can determine what conventions and choices are appropriate for nearly any writing situation.

- **Structure, or Format and Organization**   Written texts are often organized according to specific disciplinary conventions. For example, scholars in the social sciences and natural sciences usually organize experimental study reports with an introduction first, followed by a description of their research methods, then their data/results, then the analysis of that data, and finally a discussion and conclusion (IMRaD format, discussed in more detail in Chapters 8 and 9 on the social sciences and natural sciences). By contrast, scholars in the humanities tend to write and value essays that are driven by a clear thesis (or main claim: what you are trying to prove) near the beginning of the essay that indicates the direction the argument will take. Scholars in the humanities also don't tend, as much, to use headings to divide a text.

- **Language, or Style and Word Choice**   The language used in academic writing follows disciplinary conventions. Consider the use of qualifiers (words such as *might*, *could*, *likely*), which are often used in the natural and social sciences to indicate the interpretive power of the data collected and to help persuade an audience to accept the results because they are not

---

*The SLR concept originated in the following essay: Patricia Linton, Robert Madigan, and Susan Johnson. "Introducing Students to Disciplinary Genres: The Role of the General Composition Course." *Language and Learning Across the Disciplines*, vol. 1, no. 2, 1994, pp. 63-78.

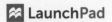

Get astronomer Mike Brotherton's take on qualifying and hedging.

generalizing inappropriately (*The positive correlation between the variables* <u>*likely*</u> *indicates a strong relationship between the motivation of a student and his or her achievement of learning objectives*). When qualifiers are used in the humanities, however, they often demonstrate uncertainty and weaken an argument (*Hamlet's soliloquies in acts 2 and 4* <u>*might*</u> *provide an interesting comparison because they frame the turning point of the play in act 3*).

- **Reference, or Citation and Documentation**   The conventions of how scholars refer to one another's work can also shift by discipline. You might already know, for example, that many scholars in the humanities use the documentation style of the Modern Language Association (MLA), while those in the social sciences generally use the style guide published by the American Psychological Association (APA). More citation styles are listed and discussed in the Appendix. Conventions for how often scholars quote, paraphrase, and summarize one another's work can also vary.

In the next example of Mike Brotherton's work, we'll look at the abstract and introduction to a scholarly journal article that he wrote with several co-authors. If we start with an understanding of the rhetorical context—that Brotherton and his co-authors are writing with the *purpose* of sharing research results and the *audience* of fellow astronomers—then we can move to understanding the conventions that are present in this type of writing. Considering the *structure*, *language*, and *reference conventions* used in the piece provides insight into the way such writing is structured within the sciences—and specifically in the field of astronomy.

As you read the excerpt from Brotherton's co-authored article, notice the structure, language, and reference conventions. The article contains a lot of specific scientific language, and for the purpose of your analysis right now it's not important to understand the concepts as much as it is to recognize some of the elements that make this writing unique from other writing you may have encountered in English classes in the past. Consider the following questions:

- Even though the entire article is not included, what conclusions can you draw about its **structure**? What comes first in the article, and how is it organized in the beginning?

- How would you describe the **language** that Brotherton and his co-authors choose to use in the article? What does it tell you about the audience for the article?

- What **reference conventions** does the article follow? Does the documentation style used for the parenthetical references look familiar? How often are other scholars cited, and what is the context for citing their work? What purpose do those references serve in the article?

Excerpt from **A Spectacular Poststarburst Quasar**

M. S. BROTHERTON, WIL VAN BREUGEL, S. A. STANFORD, R. J. SMITH, B. J. BOYLE, LANCE
MILLER, T. SHANKS, S. M. CROOM, AND ALEXEI V. FILIPPENKO

ABSTRACT

We report the discovery of a spectacular "poststarburst quasar" UN J10252–0040 ($B = 19$; $z = 0.634$). The optical spectrum is a chimera, displaying the broad Mg II λ2800 emission line and strong blue continuum characteristic of quasars, but is dominated in the red by a large Balmer jump and prominent high-order Balmer absorption lines indicative of a substantial young stellar population at similar redshift. Stellar synthesis population models show that the stellar component is consistent with a 400 Myr old instantaneous starburst with a mass of $\leq 10^{11} M_\odot$. A deep, K_s-band image taken in $\sim 0''.5$ seeing shows a point source surrounded by asymmetric extended fuzz. Approximately 70% of the light is unresolved, the majority of which is expected to be emitted by the starburst. While starbursts and galaxy interactions have been previously associated with quasars, no quasar ever before has been seen with such an extremely luminous young stellar population.

The language is highly specific and technical.

1. INTRODUCTION

Headings indicate a particular kind of structure.

Is there a connection between starbursts and quasar activity? There is circumstantial evidence to suggest so. The quasar 3C 48 is surrounded by nebulosity that shows the high-order Balmer absorption lines characteristic of A-type stars (Boroson & Oke 1984; Stockton & Ridgeway 1991). PG 1700+518 shows a nearby starburst ring (Hines et al. 1999) with the spectrum of a 10^8 yr old starburst (Stockton, Canalizo, & Close 1998). Near-IR and CO mapping reveals a massive ($\sim 10^{10} M_\odot$) circumnuclear starburst ring in I Zw 1 (Schinnerer, Eckart, & Tacconi 1998). The binary quasar member FIRST J164311.3+315618B shows a starburst host galaxy spectrum (Brotherton et al. 1999).

In addition to these individual objects, *samples* of active galactic nuclei (AGNs) show evidence of starbursts. Images of quasars taken with the *Hubble Space Telescope* show "chains of emission nebulae" and "near-nuclear emission knots" (e.g., Bahcall et al. 1997). Seyfert 2 and radio galaxies have significant populations of ~ 100 Myr old stars (e.g., Schmitt, Storchi-Bergmann, & Cid Fernandes 1999). Half of the ultraluminous infrared galaxies (ULIRGs) contain simultaneously an AGN and recent (10–100 Myr) starburst activity in a 1–2 kpc circumnuclear ring (Genzel et al. 1998).

The advent of *IRAS* provided evidence for an evolutionary link between starbursts and AGNs. The ULIRGs ($L_{IR} > 10^{12} L_\odot$) are strongly interacting merger systems with copious molecular gas [$(0.5–2) \times 10^{10}$ $M_\odot$] and dust heated by both starburst and AGN power sources. The ULIRG space density is sufficient to form the quasar parent population. These facts led Sanders et al. (1988) to hypothesize that ULIRGs represent the initial dust-enshrouded stage of a quasar. Supporting this hypothesis is the similarity in the evolution of the quasar luminosity density and the star formation rate (e.g., Boyle & Terlevich 1998; Percival & Miller 1999). Another clue is that supermassive black holes appear ubiquitously in local massive galaxies, which may be out-of-fuel quasars (e.g., Magorrian et al. 1998). AGN activity may therefore reflect a fundamental stage of galaxy evolution.

> Introduction references multiple prior studies by other scholars.

We report here the discovery of a poststarburst quasar. The extreme properties of this system may help shed light on the elusive AGN-starburst connection. We adopt $H_0 = 75$ km s^{-1} Mpc^{-1} and $q_0 = 0$.

INSIDE WORK   Reflecting on an Academic Article

In his Insider's View "Accuracy trumps strong writing," Mike Brotherton provides some guidelines for analyzing the conventions of his scientific article through the lenses of structure, language, and reference. Write down a few points he makes about each lens that will be helpful when you approach reading a scientific article on your own.

Insider's View
Accuracy trumps strong writing
MIKE BROTHERTON, ASTRONOMY

"The audience for a scientific journal should be experts in your field but also beginning graduate students. Articles should be specific, succinct, and correct. For better or worse, in scientific articles it is necessary to use a lot of qualifications, adverbs, and modifying phrases, to say exactly what you mean even though the result is not as strong or effective.

Accuracy trumps strong writing here, although there is plenty of room for good writing. Every piece of writing, fiction or non-fiction, should tell an interesting story. The format for a scientific article is rather standard.

"There is also an abstract that gives a summary of all the parts of the paper. In many instances, the entire paper is not read but skimmed, so being able to find things quickly and easily makes the paper more useful. Audiences for scientific papers are often measured only in the dozens, if that. While popular papers can be read and used by thousands, most papers have a small audience and contribute to advancement in some niche or other, which may or may not turn out to be important.

"Some people cite heavily, and some people don't cite as heavily. And, again, you need to keep in mind your audience and what's appropriate. In writing a telescope proposal, for instance, which is not quite the same as a scientific article but has the same conventions, some reviewers want you to cite a lot of things just to prove that you know the field. This is especially true for beginning students writing proposals."

- Reread the excerpt from "A Spectacular Poststarburst Quasar" (see pp. 129–30) and reflect on any new things you notice.

- Read the excerpt again, this time with an eye to rhetorical context (author, audience, topic, and purpose for writing). Try to generalize about the usefulness of the two approaches to your reading.

- Annotate a paper you've written for another class, noting the rhetorical context and the genre conventions as we have in our annotations on the press release and the scholarly article. What practices about your own writing do these approaches suggest? ❯

Writing a Genre Analysis of an Academic Article

WRITING PROJECT

For this project, you will analyze a full-length article in a discipline of your choice, published in an academic journal. Your instructor may assign an article or may ask you to seek his or her approval for the article you choose to use for this project.

Using the following guiding questions, describe the basic genre features of the article you've chosen to study:

1. What is the rhetorical context? Consider the author, audience, topic, and purpose of the article.

2. What conventions are present the text? Consider the structure, language, and reference conventions of the article.

Once you have described the genre features of the article, consider the choices the writer or writers made when they wrote the article. Why did they write the article in the way that they did? How do these genre features work together?

The introduction to your paper should name the article you will analyze, describe the primary methods you will use to analyze it, and explain the goal of your analysis—to analyze an academic article. The body of your paper might be organized around the two guiding questions, or you might focus on one or two of the genre features that are of specific interest in your article. Of course, you can subdivide the features you are analyzing to address specific elements of the larger categories. For example, if you were analyzing conventions of language, you could address the use of qualifiers, the use of first person, and so on, providing examples from the article and commenting on their usefulness for the writer. In your conclusion, reflect on what you've found. Are there other issues still to be addressed? What other rhetorical strategies could be explored to analyze the work further? How effective are the strategies the author used, given the intended audience?

Writing a Comparative Genre Analysis

WRITING PROJECT

The goal of this writing project is to allow you to consider further the shifts in rhetorical situation and genre expectations for writing across two disciplinary areas.

To begin, you'll need to locate two articles on the same topic in academic journals representing different disciplines. For example, you might find two articles discussing the issue of increasing taxes on the wealthy to deal with the U.S. national debt. You might find one article written by an economist that addresses the impact of the national debt and projects the feasibility of different solutions, and another article written by a humanist discussing how the media has portrayed the issue.

Once you have identified your two articles, use the following guiding questions to describe the basic genre features of the articles you've chosen to study:

1. What are the rhetorical contexts? Consider the authors, audiences, topic, and purposes of the articles.

2. What conventions are present in the texts? Consider the structure, language, and reference conventions of the articles.

Once you have described the genre features of the articles, consider the choices the writer or writers made when they wrote the article. Why did they write the article in the way that they did? How do these genre features work together?

You might also consider other elements of the articles: what kinds of questions the authors ask and what kinds of evidence they draw upon, for example. Formulate a thesis that assesses the degree to which the genre features in each category compare or contrast. Organize your analysis in a way that helps your reader follow the main points you want to make about your comparison. Throughout your paper, develop your comparisons and contrasts by illustrating your findings with examples from the texts. For example, if you find that one article (perhaps from the humanities) uses the active voice almost exclusively, then provide some examples. If the other article relies heavily on the passive voice, then provide examples of this use. End each section with a consideration of the implications of your findings: What does it say about the sciences that claims are often hedged by qualifiers? Do not avoid discussing findings that might contradict your assumptions about writing in these two academic domains. Instead, study them closely and try to rationalize the authors' rhetorical decision-making.

Comparing Scholarly and Popular Articles

Choose a scholarly article and an article written for a more general audience on a common topic. You might reread the discussion of the differences between scholarly and popular articles in Chapter 5 as you're looking for articles to choose. Then use these guiding questions to analyze the two texts as distinct, but perhaps related, genres:

1. What are the rhetorical contexts? Consider the authors, audiences, topic, and purposes of the articles.

2. What conventions are present in the texts? Consider the structure, language, and reference conventions of the articles.

In your comparison of the rhetorical contexts and the decisions the authors have made about conventions, consider the questions below:

1. How do the rhetorical contexts for writing compare?

2. Which genre conventions are similar, and which ones are different?

3. Why do you think the authors made the choices that they did in writing?

Translating Scholarly Writing for Different Rhetorical Contexts

At times, writing for an academic context, like Mike Brotherton's work, must be repurposed for presentation in another, more general context. Sometimes the writer does the translating, and sometimes other writers may help communicate the importance of a piece of scholarly writing to another audience.

Insider Example
Student Translation of a Scholarly Article

Jonathan Nastasi, a first-year writing student, translated a scholarly article about the possible habitability of another planet from the journal *Astronomy & Astrophysics* into a press release for a less specialized audience. He condensed the information into a two-page press release for a potential audience interested in publishing these research results in news venues. Also, he followed his writing instructor's advice to apply MLA style even though the article he summarized is scientific.

Release Date: 18 September 2014

Contact: W. von Bloh

bloh@pik-potsdam.de

Potsdam Institute for Climate Impact Research

Life May Be Possible on Other Planets

New data shows that a new planet found outside of our solar system may be habitable for life.

RALEIGH (SEPTEMBER 18, 2014)—A study from the Potsdam Institute for Climate Impact Research shows that a planet in another solar system is in the perfect position to harbor life. Additionally, the quantity of possibly habitable planets in our galaxy is much greater than expected.

Gliese 581g is one of up to six planets found to be orbiting the low-mass star Gliese 581, hence its name. Gliese 581g and its other planetary siblings are so-called "Super Earths," rocky

An artist's rendition of Gliese 581g orbiting its star.

planets from one to ten times the size of our Earth. This entire system is about twenty light-years away from our Sun. W. Von Bloh, M. Cuntz, S. Franck, and C. Bounama from the Potsdam Institute for Climate Impact Research chose to research Gliese 581g because of its size and distance from its star, which make it a perfect candidate to support life.

A planet must be a precise distance away from a star in order to sustain life. This distance is referred to as the habitable zone. According to Von Bloh et al., the habitable zones "are defined as regions around the central star where the physical conditions are favourable for liquid water to exist at the planet's surface for a period of time sufficient for biological evolution to occur." This "Goldilocks" zone can be affected by a number of variables, including the temperature of the star and the composition of the planet.

The actual distance of Gliese 581g from its star is known; the goal of this study was to find out if the planet is capable of supporting life at that distance. The researchers began by finding the habitable zone of the star Gliese 581 — specifically, the zone that allowed for photosynthesis. Photosynthesis is the production of oxygen from organic life forms and is indicative of life. In order for the planet to harbor this kind of life, a habitable zone that allows for a specific concentration of CO_2 in the atmosphere as well as liquid water would have to be found.

The scientists used mathematical models based on Earth's known attributes and adjusted different variables to find out which scenarios yielded the best results. Some of these variables include surface temperature, mass of the planet, and geological activity. The scientists also considered settings where the surface of the planet was all-land, all-water, or a mix of both.

Considering all of these scenarios, Von Bloh et al. determined that the habitable zone for Gliese 581g is between 0.125 and 0.155 astronomical units, where an astronomical unit is the distance between the Earth and the Sun. Other studies conclude that the *actual* orbital distance of Gliese 581g is 0.146 astronomical units. Because Gliese 581g is right in the middle of its determined habitable zone, the error and uncertainty in the variables that remain to be determined are negligible.

However, the ratio of land to ocean on the planet's surface is key in determining the "life span" of the habitable zone. The habitable zone can shift over time due to geological phenomena caused by a planet having more land than ocean. According to Von Bloh et al., a planet with a land-to-ocean ratio similar to ours would remain in the habitable zone for about seven billion years, shorter than Gliese 581g's estimated age. In other words, if Gliese 581g has an Earth-like composition, it cannot sustain life. But if the ratio is low (more ocean than land), the planet will remain in its habitable zone for a greater period of time, thus allowing for a greater chance of life to develop.

The researchers conclude that Gliese 581g is a strong candidate for life so long as it is a "water world." According to the authors, water worlds are defined as "planets of non-vanishing continental area mostly covered by oceans."

The discovery of Gliese 581g being a strong candidate for sustaining life is especially important considering the vast quantity of planets just like it. According to NASA's *Kepler Discoveries* Web page, the Kepler telescope alone has found over 4,234 planet candidates in just five years. With the collaboration of other research, 120 planets have been deemed "habitable," according to *The Habitable Exoplanets Catalog*.

"Our results are another step toward identifying the possibility of life beyond the Solar System, especially concerning Super-Earth planets, which appear to be more abundant than previously surmised," say the authors. More and more scientists are agreeing with the idea that extraterrestrial life is probable, given the abundance of Earth-like planets found in our galaxy already. If this is true, humanity will be one step closer to finding its place in the universe.

"[W]e have to await future missions to identify the pertinent geodynamical features of Gl[iese] 581g . . . to gain insight into whether or not Gl[iese] 581g harbors life," write the researchers. The science community agrees: continued focus in researching the cosmos is necessary to confirm if we have neighbors.

The full journal article can be found at http://www.aanda.org.prox.lib.ncsu .edu/articles/aa/full_html/2011/04/aa16534-11/aa16534-11.html.

Astronomy & Astrophysics, published by EDP Sciences since 1963, covers important developments in the research of theoretical, observational, and instrumental astronomy and astrophysics. For more information, visit http://www.aanda.org/.

Works Cited

"About Astronomy & Astrophysics." *Astronomy & Astrophysics*, www
.aanda.org/about-aa.

Annual Review of Astronomy and Astrophysics. Annual Reviews, 2014, www
.annualreviews.org/journal/astro.

Cook, Lynette. "Planets of the Gliese 581 System." *NASA Features*, NASA,
29 Sept. 2010, www.nasa.gov/topics/universe/features/Gliese_581.html.

The Habitable Exoplanets Catalog. Planetary Habitability Laboratory, 2 Sept.
2014, phl.upr.edu/projects/habitable-exoplanets-catalog.

Kepler Discoveries. NASA, 24 July 2014, kepler.nasa.gov/Mission/discoveries/.

Kepler Launch. NASA, 2 Apr. 2014, www.nasa.gov/mission_pages/kepler/
launch/.

Von Bloh, W., et al. "Habitability of the Goldilocks Planet Gliese 581g:
Results from Geodynamic Models." *Astronomy & Astrophysics*, vol. 528,
no. A133, 2011. *Summon*, doi:10.1051/0004-6361/201116534.

Discussion Questions

1. Who was Jonathan Nastasi's audience as he wrote his press release? What cues in the writing tell you whom Jonathan views as his audience?

2. How well did he tailor his description of the research to that audience?

3. What is the purpose behind Jonathan's communication of the research findings?

4. What other genre might work for translating this research to a public audience? What would Jonathan need to do differently in that rhetorical situation?

WRITING PROJECT

Translating a Scholarly Article for a Public Audience

The goal of this project is to translate a scholarly article for a public audience. To do so, you will first analyze the scholarly article rhetorically and then shift the genre through which the information in your article is reported. You will produce two documents in response to this assignment:

- the translation of your scholarly article
- a written analysis of the choices you made as you wrote your translation

IDENTIFY YOUR NEW AUDIENCE, PURPOSE, AND GENRE

To get started, you'll need to identify a new audience and purpose for the information in your selected article. The goal here is to shift the audience from an academic one to a public one and to consider whether the purpose for reporting the information also shifts. You may, for instance, choose to report the findings of the article in a magazine targeted toward a general audience of people who are interested in science, or you may choose to write a newspaper article that announces the research findings. You might also choose to write a script for a news show that reports research findings to a general television audience. Notice that once the rhetorical situation shifts, a new genre with unique conventions is often called for. The genre you produce will be contingent on the audience you're targeting and the purpose for writing: magazine article, newspaper article, news show script.

ANALYZE THE EXPECTATIONS OF YOUR GENRE

Closely analyze an example or two of the kind of genre you're attempting to create, and consider how those genre examples fulfill a particular purpose and the expectations of the target audience. Your project will be assessed according to its ability to reproduce those genre expectations, so you will need to explain, in detail, the choices you had to make in the construction of your piece. Be sure that you're able to explain those choices. In addition to thinking about the audience and purpose, consider the structure, language, and reference conventions of the genre.

CONSTRUCT THE GENRE

At this point, you're ready to begin constructing or translating the article into the new genre. The genre you're producing could take any number of forms. As such, the form, structure, and development of your ideas are contingent on the genre of public reporting you're attempting to construct. If you're constructing a magazine article, for example, then the article you produce should really look like one that would appear in a magazine. Try to mirror how the genre would appear in a real situation.

WRITE THE ANALYSIS

Once your translation is complete, compose a reflective analysis. As part of your analysis, consider the choices you made as you constructed your translation. Offer a rationale for each of your decisions that connects your translation to your larger rhetorical context and the conventions of the genre. For example, if you had to translate the title of the scholarly article for a public audience, explain why your new title is the most appropriate one for your public audience.

- **You should not expect to master the writing of every academic discipline by reading one book,** even this one.

- **It's important to become familiar with key concepts of disciplinary writing in academic discourse communities:** *research* expectations; *conventions* (expectations) of writing; *genres* (types) of writing.

- **Genres are not always bound by discipline, although their conventions may vary somewhat from discipline to discipline.** For example, you can expect to write literature reviews in many different courses across the curriculum.

- **Analyzing academic writing is a multistep process.**
  1. Understand the rhetorical context (author, audience, topic, purpose for writing).
  2. Identify the disciplinary area and what you know about it.
  3. Identify the conventions of writing for that genre, including *structure*, *language*, and *reference* expectations.
  4. Analyze the persuasive strategies if the writer is developing an argument.

- **Remember SLR.** The acronym for *structure*, *language*, and *reference* offers categories that can help you determine genre conventions and choices appropriate for most writing situations. These categories are particularly useful in academic writing situations.
  - *Structure* concerns how texts are organized. *Example:* IMRaD—signifying Introduction, Methods, Results, and Discussion—is a common format in both the social and natural sciences.
  - *Language* encompasses conventions of style or word choice. *Example:* Active voice is typically favored in the humanities, and passive voice is more characteristic of writing in the social and natural sciences.
  - *Reference* concerns the ways writers engage source material, including their use of conventions of citation and documentation. *Example:* Many humanities scholars use MLA style; many social science scholars use APA style.

- **Academic research is important beyond the academy.** Therefore, academic writing that conveys such research often must be repurposed—translated—for different venues and audiences.

Reading and Writing in the Humanities

Introduction to the Humanities

An interest in exploring the meaning, or interpretation, of something and how it reflects on the human experience is one of the defining characteristics of the **humanities** that sets it apart from the social sciences, the natural sciences, and applied fields. Look at the tree at the bottom of this page, and see if you recognize any fields within the humanities with which you're already familiar.

Scholars in the humanities are interested in, and closely observe, human thought, creativity, and experience. The American Council of Learned Societies explains that humanistic scholars "help us appreciate and understand what distinguishes us as human beings as well as what unites us." Scholars in the humanities ask questions such as these:

- What can we learn about human experience from examining the ways we think and express ourselves?
- How do we make sense of the world through various forms of expression?
- How do we interpret what we experience, or make meaning for ourselves and for others?

Professor John McCurdy teaches history at Eastern Michigan University. McCurdy's research focuses on the history of early America, and he teaches courses on the colonial era and the American Revolution. In his Insider's View comments, he offers thoughts on what humanists do and value, as well as the kind of research questions they ask. These comments come from an interview with him about his writing and about research in the humanities in general.

ANDREA TSURUMI

139

TEXTS AND MEANING

To understand the human condition and respond to these questions, humanists often turn to artifacts of human culture that they observe and interpret. These might be films, historical documents, comic strips, paintings, poems, religious artifacts, video games, essays, photographs, and songs. They might even include graffiti on the side of a building, a social media status update, or a YouTube video.

In addition to tangible artifacts, humanist writers might turn their attention to events, experiences, rituals, or other elements of human culture to develop meaning. When Ernest Hemingway wrote *Death in the Afternoon* about the traditions of bullfighting in Spain, he carefully observed and interpreted the meaning of a cultural ritual. And when historians interpret Hemingway's text through the lens of historical context, or when literary scholars compare the book to Hemingway's fiction of a later period, they are extending that understanding of human culture. Through such examination and interpretation of specific objects of study, scholars in the humanities can create artistic texts and develop theories that explain human expression and experience.

In this chapter, we'll often refer to artifacts and events that humanistic scholars study as **texts**. The ability to construct meaning from a text is an essential skill within the scholarship of the humanities. In high school English classes, students are often asked to interpret novels, poetry, or plays. You've likely written such analyses in the past, so you've developed a set of observational and interpretive skills that we'd like to build upon in this chapter. The same skills, such as the observational skills that lead you to find evidence in a literary text to develop and support an interpretation, can also help you analyze other kinds of texts.

Thinking about Texts

Write your responses to the following questions.

- What experiences do you already have with interpretation of texts in the humanities? Have you had to write a formal interpretation of a text before? If so, what questions did you ask?

- Imagine a text with which you are familiar. It might be a novel, a song, a painting, a sculpture, a play, a building, or a historical document. Brainstorm a list of *why* questions that you could ask about that text. ▶

OBSERVATION AND INTERPRETATION

You probably engage every day in observation of the kinds of things studied in the humanities, but you might not be doing it in the systematic way that humanistic scholars do. When you listen to music, how do you make meaning? Perhaps you listen to the words, the chord progressions, or repeated phrases. Or maybe you look to specific matters of context such as who wrote the song, what other music the artist has performed, and when it was recorded. You might consider how it is similar to or different from other songs. In order to understand the song's meaning, you might even think about social and cultural events surrounding the period when the song was recorded. These kinds of observational and interpretive acts are the very things humanists do when they research and write; they just use careful methods of observing, documenting, and interpreting that are generally more systematic than what most of us do when listening to music for enjoyment. Humanists also develop theories of interpretation or build on the theories of others in order to help still other scholars determine how to observe and interpret texts and find meaningful connections among them. In this chapter, you will learn about some of those methods of observation and interpretation, and you will also have the opportunity to practice some of the kinds of writing and research typically seen in the humanities.

Observing and Asking Questions

For this activity, pick a place to sit and observe, and bring something to write with. You might choose to do the activity in your dorm room or apartment, your workplace, a classroom, outside, in a restaurant or coffee shop, or at a gym, to name a few possibilities. For ten minutes, freewrite about all the things you see around you that could be "texts" that a humanist might interpret. Then think about the kinds of questions that a humanist might ask about those texts. Try to avoid writing about the actual activities people are engaging in; human behavior is more within the realm of the social sciences, not the humanities. Instead, think creatively about the kinds of artifacts that a humanist might analyze to understand and interpret human experience.

For example, if you observe and write in a coffee shop, you might consider the following artifacts, or texts.

- **The Sign or Logo Used for the Store**   Is there a logo? What does it include? How is it designed, and why? Is there a slogan? Whom might it relate to? What does it say about the store?

- **The Clothing of the People Working behind the Counter**   Do they have a dress code? Are they wearing uniforms? If so, what do the colors, materials, and/or style of the uniforms represent? What do they potentially tell you about the values of the business?

- **The Furniture**   Is it comfortable? New? Old? How is it arranged? What might the coffee shop be communicating to customers through that arrangement?

- **The Music Playing in the Background**   Is there music? What is playing? How loud is the music? What mood does it convey? Does it match the arrangement of the rest of the space? What emotions might the music evoke from customers?

- **The Materials Used to Serve Coffee**   Are the cups and napkins recycled? Does the store use glass or ceramic cups that can be washed and reused? Are there slogans or logos on the materials? If so, what do they say? What does the store communicate to customers through the materials used?

- **The Menu**   What kinds of items does the coffee shop serve? What language is used to describe menu items? How are the items written on the menu? Where is it displayed? Is food served? If so, what types of food are available, and what does that communicate to customers?

See how many different texts you can identify and how many questions you can generate. You might do this activity separately in the same place with a partner and then compare notes. What texts did you and your partner find in common? Which ones did you each identify that were unique? Why do you think you noticed the things you did? What was the most interesting text you identified? ▶

LaunchPad

Hear more about the different kinds of texts scholars draw on in their research.

Research in the Humanities

The collection of information, or data, is an integral part of the research process for scholars in all academic disciplines. The data that researchers collect form the foundation of evidence they use to answer a question. In the humanities, data are generally gathered from texts. Whether you're reading a novel, analyzing a sculpture, or speculating on the significance of a cultural ritual, your object of analysis is a text and the primary source of data you collect to use as evidence typically originates from that text.

Academic fields within the humanities have at their heart the creation and interpretation of texts. A history scholar may pore through photographs of Civil War soldiers for evidence to support a claim. An actor in a theater class might scour a script in order to develop an interpretation of a character he will perform onstage. And those who are primarily the creators of texts—visual artists, novelists, poets, playwrights, screenwriters, musicians—read widely in the field in order to master elements of style and contribute to their art in original and innovative ways. In the humanities, it's all about the text. Humanists are either creators or interpreters of texts, and often they are both.

To understand the research and writing in a specific disciplinary area, it is important to know not only what the objects of study are but also what methods scholars in that area use to analyze and study the objects of their attention. In the humanities, just as in other disciplines, scholars begin with observation. They closely observe the texts that interest them, looking for patterns, meaning, and connections that will help generate and support an interpretation. Humanists use their observations to pose questions about the human condition, to gather evidence to help answer those questions, and to generate theories about the human experience that can extend beyond one text or set of texts.

INSIDE WORK **Observing and Interpreting Images**

Consider each of the following images—graffiti (A), a painting (B), and a movie poster (C)—as texts that have something to say about human experience. Write your ideas in response to the following questions.

- What does the image mean?
- How do you make meaning from the image? What do you analyze to make meaning?
- What does the image make you think about?
- What emotion does the artist want you to feel? What aspect of the text do you base this on?
- Why do you think someone created this image? ❱

A. Graffiti as Text

B. Painting as Text

C. Movie Poster as Text

THE ROLE OF THEORY IN THE HUMANITIES

When scholars in the humanities analyze and interpret a text, they often draw on a specific theory of interpretation to help them make meaning. Theories in the humanities offer a particular perspective through which to understand human experience. Sometimes those perspectives are based on ideas about *how* we make meaning from a text; such theories include Formalism (sometimes called New Criticism, though it is far from new), Reader Response, and Deconstruction. Other theories, such as Feminist Theory and Queer Theory, are based more on ideas about how identity informs meaning-making. Still other theories, such as New Historicism, Postcolonialism, and Marxism, are centrally concerned with how historical, social, cultural, and other contexts inform meaning.

These are only a few of the many prominent theories of humanistic interpretation, barely scratching the surface of the theory-building work that has taken place in the humanities. Our goal is not for you to learn specific names of theories at this point, though. Rather, we want you to understand that when scholars in the humanities draw on a theory in the interpretation of a text, the theory gives them a *lens* through which to view the text and a set of questions they might ask about it. For example, they might ask:

- When was the text written, and what major social forces might have influenced the text at the time? (New Historicism)
- What characters exhibit the most power in their relationships to their partners? (Feminism)
- What kinds of tensions does the artifact create for the viewer through its use of shading and lighting? (New Criticism)

Different theories lead to different sets of questions and varying interpretations of the same text.

CLOSE READING IN THE HUMANITIES

To develop clear claims about the texts they're interpreting, scholars in the humanities must closely observe their texts and learn about them. Close observation might involve the kinds of reading strategies we discussed in Chapter 3, especially if the text is alphabetic (i.e., letter based), such as a book, a story, or a poem. One method that humanities scholars use is **close reading**, or careful observation of a text. It's possible to do a close reading of a story, of course, but you can also do a close reading of non-alphabetic texts such as films, buildings, paintings, events, or songs.

Most college students are highly skilled at reading for content knowledge, or for information, because that's what they're most often asked to do as students. This is what a professor generally expects when assigning a reading from a textbook. As you read such texts, you're primarily trying to figure out what the text is saying rather than thinking about how it functions, why the author makes certain stylistic choices, or how others might interpret the text. As we mentioned in Chapter 3, you might also read to be entertained, to learn, or to communicate.

Close observation or *reading* in the humanities, however, requires our focus to shift from reading for information to reading to understand how a text functions and how we can make meaning of it. Because texts are the primary sources of data used in humanistic research, it's important for those who work in the humanities to examine how a text conveys meaning to its audience. This kind of work—observing a text critically to analyze what it means and how it conveys meaning—is what we call close reading.

Insider Example
Professional Close Reading

In the following example of a close reading of a text, Dale Jacobs discusses how he constructs meaning from comics. He argues that comics are more complicated to interpret than texts composed only of words (e.g., a novel or short story) because graphic novel readers must also interpret visual, gestural, and spatial language at work in the panels. In doing so, Jacobs offers his own observation. Furthermore, he concludes his interpretation by calling on instructors to challenge students to think critically about how they construct meaning from texts. As you read his article, you might reflect on this question: When reading a text, how do you make meaning?

More Than Words: Comics as a Means of Teaching Multiple Literacies

DALE JACOBS

Over the last several years, comics have been an ever more visible and well-regarded part of mainstream culture. Comics are now reviewed in major newspapers and featured on the shelves of independent and chain bookstores. Major publishing houses such as Pantheon publish work in the comics medium, including books such as Marjane Satrapi's *Persepolis* and David B.'s *Epileptic*. Educational publishers such as Scholastic are also getting in on the act; in January 2005, Scholastic launched its own graphic novels imprint, Graphix, with the publication of Jeff Smith's highly acclaimed Bone series. At the NCTE [National Council of Teachers of English] Annual Convention, graphic novels and comics are displayed in ever greater numbers. School and public libraries are building graphic novels collections to try to get adolescents into the library. Comics have, indeed, emerged from the margins into the mainstream.

With all this activity and discussion surrounding comics, it is timely to consider how we as literacy teachers might think about the practice of using comics in our classrooms and how this practice fits into ongoing debates about comics and literacy. In examining these links between theory and practice, I wish to move beyond seeing the reading of comics as a debased or simplified word-based literacy. Instead, I want to advance two ideas: (1) reading comics involves a complex, multimodal literacy; and (2) by using comics in our classrooms, we can help students develop as critical and engaged readers of multimodal texts.

THE HISTORY OF ATTITUDES TOWARD COMICS AND LITERACY

Prior to their current renaissance, comics were often viewed, at best, as popular entertainment and, at worst, as a dangerous influence on youth. Such attitudes were certainly prevalent in the early 1950s when comics were at their most popular, with critics such as Fredric Wertham voicing the most strenuous arguments against comics in his 1954 book *Seduction of the Innocent* (for an extended discussion of this debate, see Dorrell, Curtis, and Rampal). Wertham baldly asserts that "[c]omic books are death on reading" (121). He goes on, "Reading troubles in children are on the increase. An important cause of this increase is the comic book. A very large proportion of children who cannot read well habitually read comic books. They are not really readers, but gaze mostly at the pictures, picking up a word here and there. Among the worst readers is a very high percentage of comic-book addicts who spend very much time 'reading' comic books. They are book-worms without books" (122). According to this thinking, children who read comic books are not really reading; they are simply looking at the pictures as a way to avoid engaging in the complex processes of learning to read. The problem, according to Wertham, is that in reading comics children focus far too much on the image to make meaning and avoid engaging with the written word, a semiotic system that Wertham clearly sees as both more complex and more important. Though he sees the visuality of comics as dangerous, Wertham shares the notion with current proponents of comics that the visual is more easily ingested and interpreted than the written. Whether the visual acts as a hindrance or a help to the acquisition of word-based literacy, the key idea remains that the visual is subservient to the written.

When I was growing up in the 1970s, I never saw comics in school or in the public library unless they were being read surreptitiously behind the cover of a novel or other officially sanctioned book. Over the last decade, however, there has been a movement to claim a value for comics in the literacy education of children. Comics have made their way into schools mainly as a scaffold for later learning that is perceived to be more difficult, in terms of both the literate practices and content involved. For example, *Comics in Education*, the online version of Gene Yang's final project for his master's degree at California State

University, Hayward, embodies thinking that is typical of many educators who advocate the use of comics in the classroom. Yang, a teacher and cartoonist, claims that the educational strength of comics is that they are motivating, visual, permanent, intermediary, and popular. In emphasizing the motivational, visual permanency (in the way it slows down the flow of information), intermediacy, and the popular, such approaches inadvertently and ironically align themselves with Wertham's ideas about the relationship between word and image, even while bringing comics into the mainstream of education. Comics in this formulation are seen simply as a stepping stone to the acquisition of other, higher skills. As a teaching tool, then, comics are seen primarily as a way to motivate through their popularity and to help slow-learning students, especially in the acquisition of reading skills (see Haugaard; Koenke). While I agree with these attempts to argue for the value of comics in education, such an approach has limited value.

Libraries have also been important in the reconsideration of the place of comics as appropriate texts for children in their literacy learning and acquisition. Recently, many librarians have been arguing for the introduction of comics into library collections, usually in the form of graphic novels, as a way to get children into the library and interested in reading. The main thrust of this argument is that the presence of graphic novels will make the library seem cool and interesting, especially among the so-called reluctant readers, mainly adolescent boys, who seem to show little interest in reading or in libraries (see Crawford; Simmons). Graphic novels can compete with video games, television, and movies, giving the library the advantage it needs to get this specifically targeted demographic through the door. Many public libraries and librarians have seen the power of comics and graphic novels as a tool for drawing young people into the library, getting them first to read those comics and then building on that scaffold to turn them into lifelong readers. Again, while I agree with the inclusion of comics and graphic novels in library collections, such an approach places severe limitations on the possibilities of our uses of the medium as literacy educators.

To think through these ideas, let's assume that this strategy has some of its desired effects in drawing reluctant readers into the library and coaxing them to read. What can we then say about the effects of this approach and its conception of comics and their relation to developing literate practices? On the one hand, the use of graphic novels is seen as one strategy in teaching and encouraging literacy and literate practices; on the other hand, graphic novels are still regarded as a way station on the road to "higher" forms of literacy and to more challenging and, by implication, worthwhile texts. I'm not trying to suggest that reading comics or graphic novels exists apart from the world of word-based texts as a whole or the complex matrix of literacy acquisition. Rather, I'm simply pointing out that in the development of children's and adolescents' literacies, reading comics has almost always been seen as a debased form of word-based literacy, albeit an important intermediate step to more advanced forms of textual literacy, rather than as a complex form of multimodal literacy.

COMICS AS MULTIMODAL LITERACY: THE THEORY

If we think about comics as multimodal texts that involve multiple kinds of meaning making, we do not give up the benefits of word-based literacy instruction but strengthen it through the inclusion of visual and other literacies. This complex view of literacy is touched on but never fully fleshed out in two excellent recent articles on comics and education: Rocco Versaci's "How Comic Books Can Change the Way Our Students See Literature: One Teacher's Perspective" and Bonny Norton's "The Motivating Power of Comic Books: Insights from Archie Comic Readers." By situating our thinking about comics, literacy, and education within a framework that views literacy as occurring in multiple modes, we can use comics to greater effectiveness in our teaching at all levels by helping us to arm students with the critical-literacy skills they need to negotiate diverse systems of meaning making.

I'm going to offer an example of how comics engage multiple literacies by looking at Ted Naifeh's *Polly and the Pirates*, but first let me give a brief outline of these multiple systems of meaning making. As texts, comics provide a complex environment for the negotiation of meaning, beginning with the layout of the page itself. The comics page is separated into multiple panels, divided from each other by gutters, physical or conceptual spaces through which connections are made and meanings are negotiated; readers must fill in the blanks within these gutters and make connections between panels. Images of people, objects, animals, and settings, word balloons, lettering, sound effects, and gutters all come together to form page layouts that work to create meaning in distinctive ways and in multiple realms of meaning making. In these multiple realms of meaning making, comics engage in what the New London Group of literacy scholars calls *multimodality*, a way of thinking that seeks to push literacy educators, broadly defined and at all levels of teaching, to think about literacy in ways that move beyond a focus on strictly word-based literacy. In the introduction to the New London Group's collection, *Multiliteracies: Literacy Learning and the Design of Social Futures*, Bill Cope and Mary Kalantzis write that their approach "relates to the increasing multiplicity and integration of significant modes of meaning-making, where the textual is also related to the visual, the audio, the spatial, the behavioural, and so on.... Meaning is made in ways that are increasingly multimodal—in which written-linguistic modes of meaning are part and parcel of visual, audio, and spatial patterns of meaning" (5). By embracing the idea of multimodal literacy in relation to comics, then, we can help students engage critically with ways of making meaning that exist all around them, since multimodal texts include much of the content on the Internet, interactive multimedia, newspapers, television, film, instructional textbooks, and many other texts in our contemporary society.

Such a multimodal approach to reading and writing asserts that in engaging with texts, we interact with up to six design elements, including linguistic, audio, visual, gestural, and spatial modes, as well as multimodal design, "of a different order to the others as it represents the patterns of interconnections among the other modes" (New London Group 25). In the first two pages from *Polly and the Pirates*, all of these design elements are present, including a textual and visual representation of the audio element. Despite the existence of these multiple modes of meaning making, however, the focus in thinking about the relationship between comics and education is almost always on the linguistic element, represented here by the words in the words balloons (or, in the conventions of comics, the dialogue from each of the characters) and the narrative text boxes in the first three panels (which we later find out are also spoken dialogue by a narrator present in the story).

As discussed earlier, comics are seen as a simplified version of word-based texts, with the words supplemented and made easier to understand by the pictures. If we take a multimodal approach to texts such as comics, however, the picture of meaning making becomes much more complex. In word-based texts, our interaction with words forms an environment for meaning making that is extremely complex. In comics and other multimodal texts, there are five other elements added to the mix. Thought about in this way, comics are not just simpler versions of word-based texts but can be viewed as the complex textual environments that they are.

COMICS AS MULTIMODAL LITERACY: *POLLY AND THE PIRATES* IN THE CLASSROOM

In comics, there are elements present besides words, but these elements are just as important in making meaning from the text. In fact, it is impossible to make full sense of the words on the page in isolation from the audio, visual, gestural, and spatial. For example, the first page of *Polly and the Pirates* (the first issue of a six-issue miniseries) opens with three panels of words from what the reader takes to be the story's narrative voice. Why? Partially it is because of *what* the words say—how they introduce a character and begin to set up the story—but also it is because of the text boxes that enclose the words. That is, most people understand from their experiences of reading comics at some point in their history that words in text boxes almost always contain the story's narrative voice and denote a different kind of voice than do words in dialogue balloons. What's more, these text boxes deviate in shape and design from the even rectangles usually seen in comics; instead, they are depicted more like scrolls, a visual element that calls to mind both the time period and genre associated with pirates. Not only does this visual element help to place the reader temporally and generically, but it, along with lettering and punctuation, also aids in indicating tone, voice inflection, cadence,

ONI PRESS INC.

Within the comic panels:

HER NAME WAS MEG MALLOY.

THEY CALLED HER THE PIRATE QUEEN.

THEY SAY THERE WAS NO VESSEL SHE COULDN'T OUTMATCH, NO TREASURE SHE COULDN'T PLUNDER.

AND WHILE THE NAVAL AUTHORITIES CURSED HER NAME...

SHE WAS THE TOAST OF ST. HELVETIA SOCIETY.

A History of the Pirate Queen

by Filbert R. Simon

AND, OF COURSE, IT WAS EVERY YOUNG GENTLEMAN'S DREAM TO MARRY HER.

and emotional tenor by giving visual representation to the text's audio element. We are better able to "hear" the narrator's voice because we can see what words are emphasized by the bold lettering, and we associate particular kinds of voices with the narrative voice of a pirate's tale, especially emphasized here by the shape of the text boxes. Both the visual and the audio thus influence the way we read the words in a comic, as can be seen in these three opening panels.

It seems to me, however, that the key lies in going beyond the way we make meaning from the words alone and considering the other visual elements, as well as the gestural and spatial. If I were teaching this text, I would engage students in a discussion about how they understand what is going on in the story and how they make meaning from it. Depending on the level of the class, I would stress different elements at varying levels of complexity. Here I will offer an example of how I make meaning from these pages and of some of the elements I might discuss with students.

In talking about the visual, I would consider such things as the use of line and white space, shading, perspective, distance, depth of field, and composition. The gestural refers to facial expression and body posture, while the spatial refers to the meanings of environmental and architectural space, which, in the case of comics, can be conceived as the layout of panels on the page and the relation between these panels through use of gutter space. The opening panel depicts a ship, mainly in silhouette, sailing on the ocean; we are not given details, but instead see the looming presence of a ship that we are led to believe is a pirate ship by the words in the text boxes. The ship is in the center of an unbordered panel and is the only element in focus, though its details are obscured. The unbordered panel indicates openness, literally and metaphorically, and this opening shot thus acts much in the same way as an establishing shot in a film, orienting us both in terms of place and in terms of genre. The second panel pulls in closer to reveal a silhouetted figure standing on the deck of the ship. She is framed between the sails, and the panel's composition draws our eyes toward her as the central figure in the frame. She is clearly at home, one arm thrust forward while the other points back with sword in hand, her legs anchoring herself securely as she gazes across the ocean. The third panel pulls in even farther to a close-up of her face, the top half in shadow and the bottom half showing a slight smile. She is framed by her sword on the left and the riggings of the ship on the right, perfectly in her element, yet obscured from our view. Here and in the previous panel, gestural and visual design indicate who is the center of the story and the way in which she confidently belongs in this setting. At the same time, the spatial layout of the page and the progression of the panels from establishing shot to close-up and from unbordered panels to bordered and internally framed panels help us to establish the relationship of the woman to the ship and to the story; as we move from one panel to the next, we must make connections between the panels that are implied by the gutter. Linguistic, visual, audio, gestural, and spatial elements combine in these first three panels to set up expectations in the reader for the type of story and its narrative approach. Taken together, these elements form a multimodal system of meaning making.

What happens in the fourth panel serves to undercut these expectations as we find out that the narrative voice actually belongs to one of the characters in the story, as evidenced by the shift from text box to dialogue balloon even though the voice is clearly the same as in the first three panels of the page. Spatially, we are presented with a larger panel that is visually dominated by the presence of a book called *A History of the Pirate Queen*. This book presumably details the story to which we had been introduced in the first three panels. The character holding the book is presenting it to someone and, because of the panel's composition, is also effectively presenting it to us, the readers. The gesture becomes one of offering this story up to us, a story that simultaneously becomes a romance as well as a pirate story as evidenced by the words the character says and the way she says them (with the bold emphasis on *dream* and *marry*). At this point, we do not know who this character is or to whom she is speaking, and the answers to these questions will be deferred until we turn to the second page.

On the first panel of page 2, we see three girls, each taking up about a third of the panel, with them and the background in focused detail. Both the words and facial expression of the first girl indicate her stance toward the story, while the words and facial expression of the second girl indicate her indignation at the attitude of the first girl (whom we learn is named Sarah). The third girl is looking to the right, away from the other two, and has a blank expression on her face. The next panel depicts the second and third girls, pulling in to a tighter close-up that balances one girl on either side of the panel and obscures the background so that we will focus on their faces and dialogue. The unbordered panel again indicates openness and momentary detachment from their surroundings. Polly is at a loss for words and is not paying attention to the other girl, as indicated by the ellipses and truncated dialogue balloons, as well as her eyes that are pointing to the right, away from the other girl. Spatially, the transition to panel 3 once more encloses them in the world that we now see is a classroom in an overhead shot that places the students in relation to the teacher. The teacher's words restore order to the class and, on a narrative level, name the third of the three girls and the narrative voice of the opening page. The story of the pirates that began on page 1 is now contained within the world of school, and we are left to wonder how the tensions between these two stories/worlds will play out in the remaining pages. As you can see, much more than words alone is used to make meaning in these first two pages of *Polly and the Pirates*.

CONCLUSION

My process of making meaning from these pages of *Polly and the Pirates* is one of many meanings within the matrix of possibilities inherent in the text. As a reader, I am actively engaging with the "grammars," including discourse and genre conventions, within this multimodal text as I seek to create/negotiate meaning; such a theory of meaning making with multimodal texts acknowledges the social and semiotic structures that surround us and within which we exist, while at the same time it recognizes individual agency and experience in the creation of meaning. Knowledge of linguistic, audio, visual, gestural, and spatial conventions within comics affects the ways in which we read and the meanings we assign to texts, just as knowledge of conventions within word-based literacy affects the ways in which those texts are read. For example, the conventions discussed above in terms of the grammar of comics would have been available to Naifeh as he created *Polly and the Pirates*, just as they are also available to me and to all other readers of his text. These conventions form the underlying structure of the process of making meaning, while familiarity with these conventions, practice in reading comics, interest, prior experience, and attention given to that reading all come into play in the exercise of agency on the part of the reader (and writer). Structure and agency interact so that we are influenced by design conventions and grammars as we read but are not determined by them; though we are subject to the same set of grammars, my reading of the text is not necessarily the same as that of someone else.

Reading and writing multimodal texts, then, is an active process, both for creators and for readers who by necessity engage in the active production of meaning and who use all resources available to them based on their familiarity with the comics medium and its inherent grammars, their histories, life experiences, and interests. In turn, every act of creating meaning from a multimodal text, happening as it does at the intersection of structure and agency, contributes to the ongoing process of becoming a multimodally literate person. By teaching students to become conscious and critical of the ways in which they make meaning from multimodal texts such as comics, we can also teach students to become more literate with a wide range of multimodal texts. By complicating our view of comics so that we do not see them as simply an intermediary step to more complex word-based literacy, we can more effectively help students become active creators, rather than passive consumers, of meaning in their interactions with a wide variety of multimodal texts. In doing so, we harness the real power of comics in the classroom and prepare students for better negotiating their worlds of meaning.

WORKS CITED

B., David. *Epileptic.* New York: Pantheon, 2005.

Cope, Bill, and Mary Kalantzis. "Introduction: Multiliteracies: The Beginnings of an Idea." *Multiliteracies: Literacy Learning and the Design of Social Futures.* Ed. Bill Cope and Mary Kalantzis. New York: Routledge, 2000. 3–8.

Crawford, Philip. "A Novel Approach: Using Graphic Novels to Attract Reluctant Readers." *Library Media Connection* 22.5 (Feb. 2004): 26–28.

Dorrell, Larry D., Dan B. Curtis, and Kuldip R. Rampal. "Book-Worms without Books? Students Reading Comic Books in the School House." *Journal of Popular Culture* 29 (Fall 1995): 223–34.

Haugaard, Kay. "Comic Books: Conduits to Culture?" *The Reading Teacher* 27.1 (Oct. 1973): 54–55.

Koenke, Karl. "The Careful Use of Comic Books." *The Reading Teacher* 34.5 (Feb. 1981): 592–95.

McCloud, Scott. *Understanding Comics: The Invisible Art.* New York: Harper, 1993.

Naifeh, Ted. *Polly and the Pirates* 1 (Sept. 2005): 1–2.

New London Group, The. "A Pedagogy of Multiliteracies: Designing Social Futures." *Multiliteracies: Literacy Learning and the Design of Social Futures.* Ed. Bill Cope and Mary Kalantzis. New York: Routledge, 2000. 9–37.

Norton, Bonny. "The Motivating Power of Comic Books: Insights from Archie Comic Readers." *The Reading Teacher* 57.2 (Oct. 2003): 140–47.

Satrapi, Marjane. *Persepolis.* New York: Pantheon, 2003.

Simmons, Tabitha. "Comic Books in My Library?" *PNLA Quarterly* 67.3 (Spring 2003): 12, 20.

Versaci, Rocco. "How Comic Books Can Change the Way Our Students See Literature: One Teacher's Perspective." *English Journal* 91.2 (Mar. 2001): 61–67.

Wertham, Fredric. *Seduction of the Innocent.* New York: Rinehart, 1954.

Yang, Gene. *Comics in Education.* 2003. 29 Aug. 2006 <http://www.humblecomics.com/comicsedu/index.html>.

Discussion Questions

1. In your own words, describe how Jacobs constructs meaning from the comics panels analyzed in this article.

2. What do you think he means by the phrase *multimodal text*?

3. Study one of the comics panels for a minute, and consider how you make meaning from it. Freewrite for five minutes about your own process for making sense of what the comic means.

4. Freewrite for five minutes discussing something you were asked to interpret in the past: perhaps a painting, a novel, a poem, or something else. How did you make meaning of what you were observing and interpreting?

STRATEGIES FOR CLOSE READING AND OBSERVATION

For most of us, when we observe a printed text closely, we highlight, underline, and take notes in the margins. If we're analyzing a visual or aural text, we might take notes on our thoughts, observations, and questions. We might keep a separate notebook or computer file in which we expand on our notes or clarify meaning. As with any skill, the more you practice these steps, the better you'll become at interpretation. We encourage you to take detailed notes, underline passages if applicable, and actively engage with a text when conducting your observation.

We recommend two specific data-collection steps for humanistic inquiry. First, we suggest that you take notes in the margins for a printed text or on a separate sheet of paper as you read, view, or listen to a text to be interpreted. These notes will draw your attention to passages that may serve as direct evidence to support points you'll make later. Additionally, you can elaborate in more detail when something meaningful in the text draws your attention. Jotting down page numbers, audio/video file time markers, and paragraph numbers is often a helpful step for cataloging your notes. The key is to commit fully to engaging with a text by systematically recording your observations.

Second, we recommend developing a **content/form-response grid** to organize the essential stages of your interpretation. The "content" is what happens in the text, and the "form" is how the text's creator structures the piece. In the case of a painting, you might comment on the materials used, the artist's technique, the color palette and imagery choice, or the historical context of the piece. In the case of a religious or political text, you might examine style, language, and literary devices used. The "response" is your interpretation of what the elements you've identified might mean.

Now read the opening paragraphs from "The Story of an Hour," a very brief short story by Kate Chopin published in 1894 that is now recognized as a classic work of American literature. The excerpt includes a student's notes in the margins followed by a content/form-response grid. Notice the frequency of notes the student takes in the margins and the kinds of questions she asks at this early stage. She offers a fairly equal balance of questions and claims. Pay attention to how she follows the two steps of humanistic inquiry mentioned above:

1. Examine the text and take careful notes. Try keeping marginal notes (if appropriate) and/or a separate notebook or sheets of paper to expand on your notes.

2. Complete a content/form-response grid based on the notes you collect.

Excerpt from **The Story of an Hour**

KATE CHOPIN

Knowing that Mrs. Mallard was afflicted with a heart trouble, great care was taken to break to her as gently as possible the news of her husband's death. It was her sister Josephine who told her, in broken sentences; veiled hints that revealed in half concealing. Her husband's friend Richards was there, too, near her. It was he who had been in the newspaper office when intelligence of the railroad disaster was received, with Brently Mallard's name leading the list of "killed." He had only taken the time to assure himself of its truth by a second telegram, and had hastened to forestall any less careful, less tender friend in bearing the sad message.

> *Heart trouble? I wonder what kind of trouble.*
>
> *The news of her husband's death is delivered by her sister.*

She did not hear the story as many women have heard the same, with a paralyzed inability to accept its significance. She wept at once, with sudden, wild abandonment, in her sister's arms. When the storm of grief had spent itself she went away to her room alone. She would have no one follow her.

> *Why would she act differently from other women hearing the same kind of news?*
>
> *Interesting comparison. The storm-like quality of her grief.*

There stood, facing the open window, a comfortable, roomy armchair. Into this she sank, pressed down by a physical exhaustion that haunted her body and seemed to reach into her soul.

> *Why is she "exhausted"? Interesting word choice.*

She could see in the open square before her house the tops of trees that were all aquiver with the new spring life. The delicious breath of rain was in the air. In the street below a peddler was crying his wares. The notes of a distant song which some one was singing reached her faintly, and countless sparrows were twittering in the eaves.

> *There are lots of images of life here. This really contrasts with the dark news of the story's opening.*

This student's annotations can be placed into a content/form-response grid that helps her keep track of the ideas she had as she read and observed closely, both for information (*what*) and for ways the text shaped her experience of it (*how*). Notice that the student uses the Content/Form section to summarize the comments from her annotations, and then she reflects on her annotations in the Response section:

Content/Form Notes *(what and how)*	Response (What effect does it have on me?)
Heart trouble? I wonder what kind of trouble.	*There's a mystery here. What's wrong with Mrs. Mallard's heart?*
The news of her husband's death is delivered by her sister.	*Interesting that a female relative is chosen to deliver the news. A man would be too rough?*
Why would she act differently from other women hearing the same kind of news?	*I wonder what is special about Mrs. Mallard that causes her reaction to be different. Is she putting on a show? Story says her reaction was "sudden" and "wild."*
Why is she "exhausted"? Interesting word choice.	*Maybe this has to do with her heart condition or with how physically draining her mourning is.*
There are lots of images of life here. This really contrasts with the dark news of the story's opening.	*This is a sudden change in feeling. Everything is so calm and pleasant now. What happened?*

The purpose of this activity is to construct meaning from the text based on the student's close observation of it. This is an interpretation. We can already see that major complexities in the story are beginning to emerge in the student's response notes—such as the importance of the story's setting and the change that occurs in Mrs. Mallard.

Because content/form-response grids like the one above allow you to visualize both your ideas and how you arrived at those ideas, we recommend using this activity any time you have to observe a text closely in order to interpret its meaning. For a non-alphabetic text, start with the content/form-response grid and use it to log your initial notes as you observe; then reflect later. In the end, such an activity provides a log of details that can help explain how you arrived at a particular conclusion or argument about the text.

INSIDE WORK **Annotating a Text**

Use this activity as an opportunity to practice close reading. Read the whole text of Kate Chopin's "The Story of an Hour" on pages 157–59, and then annotate the text as you read, paying particular attention to the following elements.

- **Content:** what is being said (the facts, the events, and who the characters are)

- **Form:** how it is being said (the style, language, literary techniques, and narrative perspective)

A follow-up activity at the conclusion of the story asks you to draw a content/form-response grid like the example above. It's important to take extensive marginal notes (perhaps one or two comments per paragraph) and highlight and underline passages as you read the story. These notes will help shape your content/form-response grid and will strengthen your interpretation. We encourage you to expand on your notes on a separate sheet of paper while you read the story. ❱

The Story of an Hour

KATE CHOPIN

Knowing that Mrs. Mallard was afflicted with a heart trouble, great care was taken to break to her as gently as possible the news of her husband's death.

It was her sister Josephine who told her, in broken sentences; veiled hints that revealed in half concealing. Her husband's friend Richards was there, too, near her. It was he who had been in the newspaper office when intelligence of the railroad disaster was received, with Brently Mallard's name leading the list of "killed." He had only taken the time to assure himself of its truth by a second telegram, and had hastened to forestall any less careful, less tender friend in bearing the sad message.

She did not hear the story as many women have heard the same, with a paralyzed inability to accept its significance. She wept at once, with sudden, wild abandonment, in her sister's arms. When the storm of grief had spent itself she went away to her room alone. She would have no one follow her.

There stood, facing the open window, a comfortable, roomy armchair. Into this she sank, pressed down by a physical exhaustion that haunted her body and seemed to reach into her soul.

She could see in the open square before her house the tops of trees that were all aquiver with the new spring life. The delicious breath of rain was in the air. In the street below a peddler was crying his wares. The notes of a distant song which some one was singing reached her faintly, and countless sparrows were twittering in the eaves.

There were patches of blue sky showing here and there through the clouds that had met and piled one above the other in the west facing her window.

She sat with her head thrown back upon the cushion of the chair, quite motionless, except when a sob came up into her throat and shook her, as a child who has cried itself to sleep continues to sob in its dreams.

She was young, with a fair, calm face, whose lines bespoke repression and even a certain strength. But now there was a dull stare in her eyes, whose gaze was fixed away off yonder on one of those patches of blue sky. It was not a glance of reflection, but rather indicated a suspension of intelligent thought.

There was something coming to her and she was waiting for it, fearfully. What was it? She did not know; it was too subtle and elusive to name. But she felt it, creeping out of the sky, reaching toward her through the sounds, the scents, the color that filled the air.

Now her bosom rose and fell tumultuously. She was beginning to recognize this thing that was approaching to possess her, and she was striving to beat it back with her will—as powerless as her two white slender hands would have been.

When she abandoned herself a little whispered word escaped her slightly parted lips. She said it over and over under her breath: "free, free, free!" The vacant stare and the look of terror that had followed it went from her eyes. They stayed keen and bright. Her pulses beat fast, and the coursing blood warmed and relaxed every inch of her body.

She did not stop to ask if it were or were not a monstrous joy that held her. A clear and exalted perception enabled her to dismiss the suggestion as trivial.

She knew that she would weep again when she saw the kind, tender hands folded in death; the face that had never looked save with love upon her, fixed and gray and dead. But she saw beyond that bitter moment a long procession of years to come that would belong to her absolutely. And she opened and spread her arms out to them in welcome.

There would be no one to live for during those coming years; she would live for herself. There would be no powerful will bending hers in that blind persistence with which men and women believe they have a right to impose a private will upon a fellow-creature. A kind intention or a cruel intention made the act seem no less a crime as she looked upon it in that brief moment of illumination.

And yet she had loved him—sometimes. Often she had not. What did it matter! What could love, the unsolved mystery, count for in face of this possession of self-assertion which she suddenly recognized as the strongest impulse of her being!

"Free! Body and soul free!" she kept whispering.

Josephine was kneeling before the closed door with her lips to the keyhole, imploring for admission. "Louise, open the door! I beg, open the door—you will make yourself ill. What are you doing, Louise? For heaven's sake open the door."

"Go away. I am not making myself ill." No; she was drinking in a very elixir of life through that open window.

Her fancy was running riot along those days ahead of her. Spring days, and summer days, and all sorts of days that would be her own. She breathed a quick prayer that life might be long. It was only yesterday she had thought with a shudder that life might be long.

She arose at length and opened the door to her sister's importunities. There was a feverish triumph in her eyes, and she carried herself unwittingly like a goddess of Victory. She clasped her sister's waist, and together they descended the stairs. Richards stood waiting for them at the bottom.

Some one was opening the front door with a latchkey. It was Brently Mallard who entered, a little travel-stained, composedly carrying his grip-sack and umbrella. He had been far from the scene of accident, and did not even know there had been one. He stood amazed at Josephine's piercing cry; at Richards' quick motion to screen him from the view of his wife.

But Richards was too late.

When the doctors came they said she had died of heart disease—of joy that kills.

INSIDE WORK **Preparing a Content/Form-Response Grid**

Based on your annotations and notes, construct a content/form-response grid modeled after the example on page 156. Be sure to include your responses to the items you identify in the Content/Form column. Remember that in this case "content" relates to what happens in the story, and "form," in the context of a literary text, relates to how the writer makes the story function through style, narrative perspective, and literary techniques.

Once you've completed your close reading, you might pair up with a classmate or two and share your content/form-response grids. When doing so, consider the following questions as part of your discussion.

- What facts or events did you note about the story?

- What did you notice about the ways Chopin shapes your experience of the story? What style or literary techniques did you note?

- What patterns do you see in the notes you've taken in the Form column? What repeated comments did you make, or what elements strike you in a similar way? How would you explain the meaning of those patterns? ▶

LaunchPad

Learn more about incorporating sources into your writing.

RESPONDING TO THE INTERPRETATIONS OF OTHERS

Before, during, and after observing a text, humanistic scholars also draw on the work of other scholars to build and support their interpretations. If you were interpreting Chopin's story, for example, you might review the notes you made in your content/form-response grid, search for interesting patterns, and then see if other scholars have noticed the same things. You might look for an element of the story that doesn't make sense to you and see if another scholar has

COURTESY OF SHELLEY GARRIGAN

"I learned [about the conventions of writing in my discipline] by trial and error. In graduate school, the papers that we wrote were expected to be publishable according to the academic standards of literary analysis, and yet I can recall no specific guidelines, rubrics, or feedback from professors geared toward teaching me to shape my writerly approach to the material. In fact, I remember that the feedback on a final paper that I received back from one professor in particular contained little more than a congratulations for so actively 'seeking my voice.' This effort was evidently enough to earn me an A– on the project, and yet I had no idea specifically what he meant. Nor was I sure that I should feel happy about being on the right track or bothered that I wasn't quite there yet.

"Peer-mentoring probably played the most significant role in the development of my professional writerly voice during graduate school. With a small group of fellow students, we regularly made informal arrangements with one another to read each other's papers. The praise and constructive criticism that we offered one another was a fundamental factor in my own development as a writer."

already offered an interpretation. If you agree with the interpretation, you might cite it as support for your own argument. If you disagree, you might look for evidence in the story to show why you disagree and then offer your own interpretation.

As in other disciplines, scholars in the humanities draw on the work of others to make sure they're contributing something new to the ongoing conversation about the artifact, event, or phenomenon they're studying. They also read the work of others to determine if they agree or disagree with an interpretation. Because of the importance of specific language and detail in the humanities, scholars in the humanities often quote one another's exact words, and they also quote directly from their primary sources. We'll discuss some of the reasons for these conventions, and others, in the next section.

Conventions of Writing in the Humanities

Some writing conventions are shared across different fields in the humanities. Because the kinds of texts humanistic scholars examine can vary so much, though, there are also sometimes distinctions in writing conventions among its various fields. One of the challenges of learning the conventions of a disciplinary discourse community is figuring out the specific expectations for communicating with a specific academic audience. In this section, we turn our attention from *research in the humanities* to examine and interpret artifacts themselves, to *strategies of rhetorical analysis* that help us examine how scholars in the humanities write about those artifacts.

Many scholars learn about disciplinary writing conventions through imitation and examination of articles in their fields. Recall that in Chapter 6 we introduced a three-part method for analyzing texts by examining the conventions of structure, language, and reference. Applying this analytical framework to professional writing in the various humanities fields can help you further understand conventions appropriate for any given subfield. An awareness of the conventions for writing in any academic context may facilitate your success in writing in those contexts.

Shelley Garrigan teaches Spanish language and literature at North Carolina State University. As Garrigan describes in her Insider's View, scholars learn conventions of writing in their field through a variety of means, including learning from peers.

STRUCTURAL CONVENTIONS

From your experience in high school, you might already be familiar with common structural features of writing in the humanities. Arguments in the humanities are generally "thesis-driven"; that is, they make an interpretive claim about a text and then support that claim with specific evidence from the text and sometimes with material from other sources that support their interpretation. By contrast, arguments in the social sciences and the natural sciences are usually driven by a hypothesis that must be tested in order to come to a conclusion, which encourages a different structure (see Chapters 8 and 9). First we'll talk about how humanistic scholars develop research questions and thesis statements. Then we'll turn our attention to a common structure that many students learn in secondary school to support their thesis statements with evidence, which is loosely based on the structure of the thesis-driven argument, and we'll compare it with published scholarship in the humanities.

DEVELOPING RESEARCH QUESTIONS AND THESIS STATEMENTS

An important part of the interpretation process is using observations to pose questions about a text. From these close observations, humanists develop *research questions* that they answer through their research. A research question in the humanities is the primary question a scholar asks about a text or set of texts. It is the first step in interpretation because questions grow out of our observations and the patterns or threads that we notice. A *thesis statement* is an answer to a research question and is most persuasive when supported by logical evidence. Thesis statements are discussed in more detail in

Insider's View
The research is going to support your own ideas
KAREN KEATON JACKSON, WRITING STUDIES

"When we talk about what the paper should look like, I let them know that the research part of your paper is not the longest part. I always say the longest part of your paper is this brainchild, your program that you're coming up with. And I say that purposely because I don't want the research running your paper. This is your paper, your voice. The research is going to support your own ideas.

"I think this sends the message that there's more to it than this; you can be more creative and not just rely on the research."

LaunchPad
Get expert advice on incorporating research.

Chapter 4 as the central claim of an argument. It's important to note that developing a research question works best when it is generated prior to writing a thesis statement. Novice writers can sometimes overlook this crucial step in the writing process and attempt to make a thesis statement without formulating a well-realized research question first.

As John McCurdy mentions earlier in this chapter, some of the most important questions for humanists begin by asking, "Why?" Why does George befriend Lenny in *Of Mice and Men*? Why did Pablo Picasso begin experimenting with cubism in his paintings in the early 1900s? Why did President Lincoln frequently use religious imagery and language in public discourse? To answer such questions, humanistic scholars must collect evidence to support their claims, and in the humanities, evidence often originates from texts.

Many students confess to struggling with the process of writing a good thesis statement. A key to overcoming this hurdle is to realize that a good thesis statement comes first from asking thoughtful questions about a text and searching for answers to those questions through observation.

A SUNDAY ON LA GRANDE JATTE, 1884-86 (OIL ON CANVAS)/SEURAT, GEORGES PIERRE (1859-91)/ART INSTITUTE OF CHICAGO/THE ART INSTITUTE OF CHICAGO, IL, USA/BRIDGEMAN IMAGES

Examples of Research Questions and Corresponding Thesis Statements

Research Question:	Why does F. Scott Fitzgerald use the adjective *great* to describe Gatsby in *The Great Gatsby*?
Thesis Statement:	The adjective *great* is used both ironically and derisively throughout F. Scott Fitzgerald's novel *The Great Gatsby*, as evidenced by the use of Nick Carraway as the narrator and the carnival-like depictions of Gatsby's home and parties.
Research Question:	Why did Georges-Pierre Seurat experiment with pointillism in the mid-1800s?
Thesis Statement:	Georges-Pierre Seurat drew upon the scientific research of Ogden Rood and other color theorists to create paintings with minute brushstrokes in a style now called pointillism, which Seurat believed unified optically to make colors more vivid than in traditional painting styles of the time.

Once you have carefully observed a text, gathered thorough notes, and developed a content/form-response grid as discussed earlier in the chapter, you're in a great position to begin brainstorming and drafting research questions. We encourage open-ended questions (*who, what, when, where, why,* and *how*) as opposed to closed questions (questions that can be answered with a *yes* or *no*) as a pivotal step before drafting a thesis statement. Scholars in the humanities often start by asking questions that begin with *why*, but you might also consider questions of *what* and *how*.

INSIDE WORK   Developing *Why, What,* and *How* Questions

> The process of asking questions after conducting a close reading of a text is part of interpretation, and it can help you generate effective research questions to guide the development of a thesis. In this activity, we walk you through developing research questions from your notes on "The Story of an Hour." You could easily follow these steps after observing another kind of text as well.
>
> 1. Review your notes on "The Story of an Hour," and develop three questions about the story's content and form using *Why* as a starter word.
>
> 2. Next, develop three questions using *What* as your starter word. Try to focus your questions on different aspects of the story's characters, language, style, literary techniques, or narrative perspective.
>
> 3. Then use *How* as a starter word to develop three more questions. Again, write your questions with a different aspect of the story as the central focus for each. That is, don't just repeat the same questions from your *What* or *Why* list, inserting *How* instead. Think of different questions that can help address the story's meaning.
>
> Try sharing your questions with a fellow student, and discuss which ones might lead to promising thesis statements to ground an extended interpretation. Effective research questions have the following characteristics:
>
> • They can be answered with specific evidence from the text and from your notes: an effective research question can be answered with evidence and not just feelings or opinions.
>
> • They can be answered in more than one way (i.e., they might require you to make a claim as opposed to being questions of fact): an effective research question is debatable. ▶

DEVELOPING EFFECTIVE THESIS STATEMENTS

The thesis statement, or the central claim, asserts *what* the author intends to prove, and it may also provide insight into *how* it will be proven. Providing both of these elements in a thesis allows writers to establish a blueprint for the structure of their entire argument—what we describe as a complex thesis statement in Chapter 4. Based on the thesis alone, a reader can determine the central claim and see how the writer intends to go about supporting it.

In the following example, Sarah Ray provides a thesis for her interpretation of Chopin's "The Story of an Hour." Notice that she includes clues as to how she will prove her claim in the thesis statement itself:

Blueprint for how Sarah will prove her claim

Sarah's interpretation of the story, provided as a clear claim

> Through Mrs. Mallard's emotional development and the concomitant juxta-position of the vitality of nature to the repressive indoors, Chopin exposes the role of marriage in the oppression of one's true self and desires.

Although it's not uncommon for thesis statements in humanistic scholarship to remain implied, as opposed to being stated explicitly, most interpretations explicitly assert a claim close to the beginning of the argument, often in the introductory paragraph (or, in a longer piece, paragraphs). Thesis statements may appear as single-sentence statements or may span multiple sentences.

Notice, for example, how Zenia Kish, a professor of American studies, states her claim at the end of the introductory section to her article "'My FEMA People': Hip-Hop as Disaster Recovery in the Katrina Diaspora." In the full text of the article, Kish builds up to this statement through several paragraphs of explanation, which all contribute to her thesis statement, shown here:

Blueprint for how Kish will prove her claim

Reasons provided for Kish's claim

Clear statement of Kish's claim

> I will examine how both national and local New Orleans artists identify with and rebel against the forces of marginalization that produced different senses of being a refugee, and also how they exploit marginality and the hustle as strategies to return home, however different or new that home may be. Providing listeners with an affective mapping of the social, economic, and discursive contradictions that produced the Katrina diaspora as refugees, post-Katrina hip-hop is a critical site for interrogating the ongoing tragedy of African American bodies that don't matter. (p. 673)

INSIDE WORK **Drafting Thesis Statements**

Review the questions and responses you drafted in the "Developing *Why, What,* and *How* Questions" Inside Work activity. Some scholars use "I" in thesis statements, like the example from Zenia Kish, while others avoid using "I." Make sure you pay attention to requirements for the particular type of writing you're doing in your discipline. (Don't hesitate to ask your professor if "I" state-ments are acceptable.) You can always edit the thesis statement later to take out "I" if needed, but sometimes it helps when figuring out what you want to say to include yourself in the statement. So, for now, consider structuring your responses to any three of your questions as separate thesis statements, using an "I" statement in the following form.

By examining _____ (a, b, c, etc.—the evidence you have found), I argue that _____ (your claim).

Example Thesis Statement: **By examining Mrs. Mallard's emotional development and the juxtaposition of the vitality of nature to the repressive indoors in the story, I argue that Chopin exposes the role of marriage in the story to show the oppression of a person's true self and desires.**

Now test the appropriateness of your claim by asking the following questions about it.

- **Is the thesis debatable?**   Claims in the humanities are propositions, not statements of fact. For example, the assertion that "The Story of an Hour" deals with a wife's response to the news of her husband's death is a fact. It is not, therefore, debatable and will not be a very useful thesis. If, however, we assert that the wife's response to her husband's death demonstrates some characteristic of her relationship with her husband and with the institution of marriage, then we're proposing a debatable claim. This is a proposition we can try to prove, instead of a fact that is already obviously true.

- **Is the thesis significant?**   Claims about texts should offer substantial insight into the meaning of the artifacts. They should account for as much of the artifacts as possible and avoid reducing their complexity. Have you paid attention to all of the evidence you collected, and have you looked at it in context? Are you considering all of the possible elements of the text that might contribute to your interpretation?

- **Does the thesis contribute to an ongoing scholarly conversation?**   Effective thesis statements contribute to an ongoing conversation without repeating what others have already said about the text. How does the claim extend, contradict, or affirm other interpretations of the text?

Once you've analyzed Chopin's story and constructed two separate thesis statements, consider sharing them with a classmate, identifying strengths and weaknesses in both. How is your claim both argumentative and significant? How many direct quotes from the story would help support your points? Which of the two thesis statements offers a more significant insight into the story's meaning? ❱

FIVE-PARAGRAPH ESSAYS AND OTHER THESIS-DRIVEN TEMPLATES

Many students learn to write academic arguments following a template taught in primary and secondary school as the **five-paragraph essay**. This template places a thesis, or claim, at the front of the argument (often at the end of an introductory paragraph), devotes the body of the essay to supporting the thesis, and then offers a final paragraph of conclusion that connects all the parts of the argument by summarizing the main points and reminding readers of the argument's overall significance.

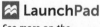

LaunchPad

See more on the transition into college writing.

While the premise behind this structure is based on some conventions of the humanities, following the template too closely could get you into trouble. Not every thesis has three points to prove, for example, giving you three body paragraphs in which to present evidence. And sometimes an introduction needs to be longer than one paragraph—as in the case of Zenia Kish's article "'My FEMA People': Hip-Hop as Disaster Recovery in the Katrina Diaspora," discussed below. The elements of the template that tend to be consistent in scholarship in the humanities, though, are these:

- Thesis statements generally appear toward the beginning of the argument in an introduction that explains the scope and importance of the topic.

- The body of the argument presents evidence gathered from the text to support the thesis.

- The conclusion connects the parts of the argument together to reinforce the thesis, summarizing the argument's important elements and reminding readers of its overall significance.

A template such as this one can provide a useful place to start as you organize your argument, but be careful not to allow a template to restrict your argument by oversimplifying your understanding of how humanistic scholars structure their writing.

OTHER STRUCTURAL CONVENTIONS IN THE HUMANITIES

There are other conventional structural features of writing in the humanities that you should consider when you begin a project in the discipline.

Title

Scholars in the humanities value the artistic and creative use of language, and titles of their work often reflect that value. In contrast to articles in the social sciences and the natural sciences, which often have descriptive titles that directly state the topic of study, articles in the humanities tend to have titles that play with language in creative ways, sometimes using quotations from the text in interesting ways. Humanistic scholars are also notorious for their love of subtitles. Here are a few examples:

- *Burlesque West: Showgirls, Sex, and Sin in Postwar Vancouver*
- "'The Fault of Being Purely French': The Practice and Theory of Landscape Painting in Post-Revolutionary France"
- "Reforming Bodies: Self-Governance, Anxiety, and Cape Colonial Architecture in South Africa, 1665–1860"
- "Resident Franchise: Theorizing the Science Fiction Genre, Conglomerations, and the Future of Synergy"

Paragraphs and Transitions

In arguments in the humanities, paragraphs tend to link back to the thesis by developing a reason and providing evidence. The paragraphs are often connected through **transitional words or phrases** (e.g., *similarly, in addition, in contrast, for example*) that guide readers by signaling shifts between and among the parts of an argument. These words and phrases help the reader understand the order in which the reasons are presented and how one paragraph connects to the preceding one.

LANGUAGE CONVENTIONS IN THE HUMANITIES

Writing in the humanities generally follows several conventions of language use that might sound familiar because they're often taught in English classes. Keep in mind, though, that even though these conventions are common in the humanities, they aren't necessarily conventional in other disciplinary areas.

Descriptive and Rhetorical Language

Writers in the humanities often use language that is creative or playful, not only when producing artistic texts but sometimes also when writing interpretations of texts. For example, you might notice that writing in the humanities uses figurative language and rhetorical devices (similes, metaphors, and alliteration, for example) more often than in other disciplines. Because writers in the humanities are studying texts so closely, they often pay similarly close attention to the text they're creating, and they take great care to choose precise, and sometimes artistic, language. In many cases, the language not only conveys information; it also engages in rhetorical activity of its own.

Active Voice

Writing in the humanities tends to privilege the use of the active voice rather than the passive voice. Sentences written in the **active voice** clearly state the subject of the sentence, the agent, as the person or thing doing the action. By contrast, the **passive voice** inverts the structure of the sentence, obscuring or eliminating mention of the agent. Let's look at three simple examples.

> **Active Voice:** The girl chased the dog.
>
> **Passive Voice (agent obscured):** The dog was chased by the girl.
>
> **Passive Voice (agent not mentioned):** The dog was chased.

In the first example, the girl is the subject of the sentence and the person (the agent) doing the action—chasing. In the second sentence, the girl is still there, but her presence is less prominent because the dog takes the subject's position at the beginning of the sentence. In the final sentence, the girl is not mentioned at all.

Now let's look at an example from a student paper in the humanities to understand why active voice is usually preferred. In her interpretation of "The Story of an Hour" (printed in full on pp. 174–80), Sarah Ray writes this sentence in the introduction, using active voice:

Active Voice: Kate Chopin presents a completely different view of marriage in "The Story of an Hour," published in 1894.

If Sarah were to write the sentence in the passive voice, eliminating the agent, it would look like this:

Passive Voice: A completely different view of marriage is presented in "The Story of an Hour," published in 1894.

In this case, the active voice is preferred because it gives credit to the author, Kate Chopin, who created the story and the character. Scholars in the humanities value giving credit to the person doing the action, conducting the study, or creating a text. Active voice also provides the clearest, most transparent meaning—another aspect of writing that is valued in the humanities.

Hedging

In the humanities, writers sometimes hedge the claims that they make when interpreting a text, even though they are generally quite fervent about defending their arguments once established. In fact, the sentence that you just read contains not one but three **hedges**, or qualifiers. Take a look:

In the humanities, writers tend to hedge the claims that they make when interpreting a text.

Each highlighted phrase limits the scope of the claim in a way that is important to improve accuracy and to allow for other possibilities. In contrast, consider the next claim:

Writers hedge the claims that they make.

If we had stated our claim that way, not only would it not be true, but you would immediately begin to think of exceptions. Even if we had limited the claim to writers in the humanities, you still might find exceptions to it. As the original sentence is written, we've allowed for other possibilities while still identifying a predominant trend in humanities writing.

Humanistic scholars hedge their claims for several reasons. The disciplines of the humanities don't tend to claim objectivity or neutrality in their research (for more detail, see Chapters 8 and 9), so they allow for other interpretations of and perspectives on texts. As an example, take a look at the first sentence of Dale Jacobs's Conclusion from his article printed earlier in the chapter:

My process of making meaning from these pages of *Polly and the Pirates* is one of many meanings within the matrix of possibilities inherent in the text. (par. 16)

In this example, Jacobs not only hedges the interpretation he has offered, but he explicitly states that there are many possible meanings in the text he has just analyzed.

REFERENCE CONVENTIONS IN THE HUMANITIES

Scholars in the humanities frequently cite the work of others in their scholarship, especially when supporting an interpretation of a text. They often quote the language from their primary sources exactly instead of summarizing or paraphrasing, because the exact words or details included in the primary source might be important to the argument.

Engagement with Other Scholars

When humanistic scholars cite the work of other scholars, they show how their research contributes to ongoing conversations about a subject—whether they're agreeing with a previous interpretation, extending someone else's interpretation, or offering an alternative one. These citations can strengthen their own argument and provide direct support by showing that another scholar had a similar idea or by demonstrating how another scholar's ideas are incorrect, imprecise, or not fully developed.

As we mentioned in Chapter 5, you can integrate the work of others into your writing by paraphrasing, summarizing, or quoting directly. Scholars in the humanities use all these options, but they quote directly more often than scholars in other disciplines because the exact language or details from their primary sources are often important to their argument.

Take a look at this example from Zenia Kish's article "'My FEMA People': Hip-Hop as Disaster Recovery in the Katrina Diaspora," which originally appeared in the academic journal *American Quarterly.* She situates her argument about the message of hip-hop music after Hurricane Katrina within the work of another scholar, Hazel Carby, who had written about the cultural meaning of the blues. Although Carby was writing about a genre that preceded hip-hop, Kish makes a connection between Carby's interpretation of the blues and her own interpretation of the message of hip-hop at a particular point in history:

> Where the early blues served to "sp[ea]k the desires which were released in the dramatic shift in social relations that occurred in a historical moment of crisis and dislocation," as Hazel Carby observes (36), I would argue that the post-Katrina moment is the first time that mainstream American hip-hop has taken up the thematic of contemporary black migration as a mass phenomenon in any significant way. (p. 674)

Establishing Focus/Stance

Most scholars in the humanities include references to the work of others early in their writing to establish what the focus and stance of their own research will be. Because abstracts appear in humanities scholarship less frequently than in social sciences and natural sciences research, the introduction to an article in the humanities provides a snapshot of how the researcher is positioning himself or herself in the ongoing conversation about an object of study.

As you read scholarship in the humanities, notice how frequently the text references or cites secondary sources in the opening paragraphs. Look at this example from the second page of Dale Jacobs's article on teaching literacy through the use of comics, on page 145 of this chapter. Jacobs situates his work historically among work published about comics in the 1950s, and he also references the research of other scholars who had already written about that history in more detail:

> Prior to their current renaissance, comics were often viewed, at best, as popular entertainment and, at worst, as a dangerous influence on youth. Such attitudes were certainly prevalent in the early 1950s when comics were at their most popular, with critics such as Fredric Wertham voicing the most strenuous arguments against comics in his 1954 book *Seduction of the Innocent* (for an extended discussion of this debate, see Dorrell, Curtis, and Rampal). (par. 3)

In these two sentences, Jacobs positions his work within that of other scholars, showing how it's connected to and distinct from it. Also, by citing the work of Dorrell, Curtis, and Rampal, Jacobs doesn't have to write a lengthy history about a period that's tangentially related to his argument but not central to it.

DOCUMENTATION

A few documentation styles are prevalent in the humanities, and those styles tend to highlight elements of a source that are important in humanistic study. Many scholars in the humanities, especially in literature and languages, follow the documentation style of the Modern Language Association (MLA). Scholars in history and some other disciplines of the humanities follow the *Chicago Manual of Style* (CMS). When using CMS, scholars can choose between two systems of citations: the notes and bibliography system or the author-date system. In the humanities, researchers generally use the notes and bibliography system.

The values of the humanities are most prevalent in the in-text citations of both MLA and CMS. In MLA, in-text citations appear in parenthetical references that include the author's last name and a page number, with no comma in between (Miller-Cochran et al. 139). The page number is included regardless of whether the cited passage was paraphrased, summarized, or quoted—unlike in other common styles like APA, where page numbers are usually given only for direct quotations. One reason for including the page number in the MLA in-text citation is that humanistic scholars highly value the original phrasing of an argument or passage and might want to look at the original source. The page number makes searching easy for the reader, facilitating the possibility of examining the original context of a quotation or the original language of something that was paraphrased or summarized.

CMS style also supports looking for the information in the original source by giving the citation information in a footnote on the same page as the referenced material. Additionally, CMS allows authors to include descriptive details in a footnote that provides more information about where a citation came from in a source.

INSIDE WORK Analyzing Scholarly Writing in the Humanities

Answer the following questions about a scholarly article in the humanities. You might choose to focus on an article from Part 3 of this book or find another article on a topic that interests you more.

A. Structural Elements

- **Title** Does the title of the interpretation seek to entertain, to challenge, or to impress the reader somehow? Does the title reveal anything about the writer and his or her relationship to the intended audience?

- **Thesis** Can you identify a clear statement of thesis? Where is it located? Does the thesis preview the stages of the claim that will be discussed throughout the paper? In other words, does the thesis explicitly or implicitly provide a "blueprint" for guiding the reader through the rest of the paper? If so, what is it?

- **Paragraphs and Transitions** Look closely at four successive body paragraphs in the paper. Explain how each paragraph relates to the paper's guiding thesis. How does the writer transition between each of the paragraphs such that his or her ideas in each one stay linked together?

B. Language Elements

- **Descriptive and Rhetorical Language** Is the language of the text meant only to convey information, or does it engage in rhetorical activity? In other words, do similes, metaphors, or other rhetorical devices demonstrate attempts to be creative with language? If so, what are they?

- **Voice** Is the voice of the text primarily active or passive?

- **Conviction and Hedging** Is the writer convinced that his or her interpretation is correct? If so, in what way(s) does specific language convey that conviction? Alternatively, if the writer doesn't seem convinced of the certainty of his or her argument, is there evidence of hedging? That is, does the writer qualify statements with words and phrases such as *tend, suggest, may, it is probable that*, or *it is reasonable to conclude that*? What is the significance of hedging?

C. Reference Elements

- **Engagement with Other Scholars** Choose two or three examples from the article showing the author's use of another scholar's words or ideas, if appropriate. Explain how the writer uses the words and ideas of another to support his or her own argument. Keep in mind that a writer may use another's words or ideas as direct support by showing that another scholar has the same or similar ideas, or by demonstrating how another scholar's ideas are incorrect, imprecise, or not fully developed. Also, does the writer use block quotations? Does he or she fully integrate others' words and ideas in his or her own sentences? Further, notice the writer's attitude toward other scholars: Does he or she treat other scholars' ideas fully and respectfully? Is there praise for others' ideas? Or are their ideas quickly dismissed? Is there any evidence of hostility in the writer's treatment of other voices?

- **Establishing Focus/Stance**   How frequently does the text reference or cite secondary source materials in the opening paragraphs? What function do such citations or references serve in the article's overall organization?

- **Documentation**   Look closely at examples of internal documentation as well as the writer's Works Cited or References page. What form of documentation applies? Why might the chosen documentation system be appropriate for writing about texts in the humanities? ▶

Insider's View
Academics often write for other academics

SHELLEY GARRIGAN, SPANISH LANGUAGE AND LITERATURE

COURTESY OF SHELLEY GARRIGAN

"I write academic articles and am currently editing a book-length manuscript. The articles that I have are peer-reviewed and published in academic journals, in which the readership is largely limited to other specialists in my field or in fields that touch upon what I study. Although the book has the possibility of inviting a wider range of readers, it is contracted with an academic press, and so the reading public that it may attract will most likely also be associated with or limited to academia."

Genres of Writing in the Humanities

The disciplines included under the umbrella of the humanities vary widely, but several genres occur frequently across disciplines. In her Insider's View response to interview questions, Shelley Garrigan, an associate professor of Spanish at North Carolina State University, describes the kind of academic writing that she does most frequently.

Similar to scholars in the social sciences and the natural sciences, scholars in the humanities often present their research at conferences and publish their work in journal articles and books. In some fields of the humanities, books are highly valued, and scholars here tend to work individually more frequently than scholars in the social sciences and the natural sciences. Also, many scholars in the humanities engage in creative work and might present it at an art installation, reading, or exhibit.

TEXTUAL INTERPRETATION

One of the primary genres that humanities researchers write is an interpretation of a text or set of texts. The research methods and activities outlined in this chapter provide support for interpretations of texts in a variety of fields in the humanities. A **textual interpretation** makes a clear claim about the object of study and then supports that claim with evidence from the text, and often with evidence drawn from the interpretations of other scholars.

Interpreting a Text

WRITING PROJECT

In this Writing Project, you'll complete a close reading and offer an interpretation of a text for an audience of your peers. Begin by selecting a text that you find particularly interesting. You may choose from a host of categories, including the ones listed here.

paintings	advertisements
photographs	short stories
sculptures	poems
buildings	music videos or recordings

As a model for reading closely, follow the procedures outlined earlier in this chapter for creating a content/form-response grid. As you read, view, listen to, and/or study the text and make notes, consider the ways you are interacting with the text by creating a content/form-response grid: *What* are you learning, and *how* is the text itself shaping your experience of it?

Once your close reading is complete, formulate a thesis (or a claim) about the text. You'll need to provide evidence to support your thesis from the text itself. You might also include evidence from secondary sources as support. (See Chapter 4 for more information on developing a clear thesis and Chapter 5 for gathering secondary sources.) Remember that depending on the scope of your thesis, your interpretation may or may not require you to do additional research beyond your close reading of the text. As you compose your interpretation, also keep in mind the conventions of structure, language, and reference that typically appear in scholarship in the humanities. Integrate them into your interpretation as appropriate.

Insider Example
Student Interpretation of a Text

In the following essay, "Till Death Do Us Part: An Analysis of Kate Chopin's 'The Story of an Hour,'" Sarah Ray offers an interpretation of Chopin's story that relies on close observation of the text for support. Read her essay below, and pay particular attention to her thesis statement and to her use of evidence. Note how her thesis responds to the question, "How does Mrs. Mallard's marriage function in the story?" Sarah didn't use outside scholars to support her interpretation, so you could also consider how secondary sources might have provided additional support for her claim.

Sarah Ray

ENG 101

10 April 201-

Till Death Do Us Part: An Analysis of Kate Chopin's

"The Story of an Hour"

The nineteenth century saw the publication of some of
the most renowned romances in literary history, including the
novels of Jane Austen and the Brontë sisters, Charlotte, Emily,
and Anne. While their stories certainly have lasting appeal,
they also inspired an unrealistic and sometimes unattainable
ideal of joyful love and marriage. In this romanticized vision,
a couple is merely two halves of a whole; one without the
other compromises the happiness of both. The couple's lives,
and even destinies, are so intertwined that neither individual
worries about what personal desires and goals are being
forsaken by commitment to the other. By the end of the
century, in her "The Story of an Hour" (1894), Kate Chopin
presents a completely different view of marriage. Through
the perspective of a female protagonist, Louise Mallard, who
believes her husband has just died, the author explores the
more challenging aspects of marriage in a time when divorce
was rare and disapproved of. Through Mrs. Mallard's emotional
development and the concomitant juxtaposition of the vitality
of nature to the repressive indoors, Chopin explores marriage
as the oppression of one's true self and desires.

"The Story of an Hour" begins its critique of marriage
by ending one, when the news of Brently Mallard's death
is gently conveyed to his wife, Louise. Chopin then follows
Mrs. Mallard's different emotional stages in response to her
husband's death. When the news is initially broken to
Louise, "[s]he did not hear the story as many women have
heard the same, with a paralyzed inability to accept its

FORM: Ray uses a common line from marriage vows to indirectly indicate that she focuses on the role of marriage in her interpretation.

CONTENT: Ray clearly states her thesis and provides a preview about how she will develop and support her claim.

CONTENT: In this paragraph, Ray develops the first part of her thesis, the stages of Mrs. Mallard's emotional development.

---

significance" (Chopin par. 3). She instead weeps suddenly and briefly, a "storm of grief" that passes as quickly as it had come (par. 3). This wild, emotional outburst and quick acceptance says a great deal about Louise's feelings toward her marriage. "[S]he had loved [her husband]—sometimes" (par. 15), but a reader may infer that Louise's quick acceptance implies that she has considered an early death for her spouse before. That she even envisions such a dark prospect reveals her unhappiness with the marriage. She begins to see, and even desire, a future without her husband. This desire is expressed when Louise is easily able to see past her husband's death to "a long procession of years to come that would belong to her absolutely" (par. 13). Furthermore, it is unclear whether her "storm of grief" is genuine or faked for the benefit of the family members surrounding her. The "sudden, wild abandonment" (par. 3) with which she weeps almost seems like Louise is trying to mask that she does not react to the news as a loving wife would. Moreover, the display of grief passes quickly; Chopin devotes only a single sentence to the action. Her tears are quickly succeeded by consideration of the prospects of a future on her own.

Chopin uses the setting to create a symbolic context for Louise's emotional outburst in response to the news of her husband's death. Louise is informed of Brently's death in the downstairs level of her home: "It was her sister Josephine who told her, in broken sentences; veiled hints that revealed in half concealing" (par. 2). No mention is made of windows, and the only portal that connects to the outside world is the door that admits the bearers of bad news. By excluding a link to nature, Chopin creates an almost claustrophobic environment to symbolize the oppression Louise feels from her marriage. It is no mistake that this setting plays host to Mrs. Mallard's initial

FORM: Ray primarily uses active voice to clarify who is doing the action in her sentences.

emotional breakdown. Her desires have been suppressed throughout her relationship, and symbolically, she is being suffocated by the confines of her house. Therefore, in this toxic atmosphere, Louise is only able to feel and show the emotions that are expected of her, not those that she truly experiences. Her earlier expression of "grief" underscores this disconnect, overcompensating for emotions that should come naturally to a wife who has just lost her husband, but that must be forced in Mrs. Mallard's case.

Chopin continues Mrs. Mallard's emotional journey only after she is alone and able to process her genuine feelings. After her brief display of grief has run its course, she migrates to her upstairs bedroom and sits in front of a window looking upon the beauty of nature. It is then and only then that Louise gives in not only to her emotions about the day's exploits, but also to those feelings she could only experience after the oppression of her husband died with him — dark desires barely explored outside the boundaries of her own mind, if at all. They were at first foreign to her, but as soon as Louise began to "recognize this thing that was approaching to possess her . . . she [strove] to beat it back with her will" (par. 10). Even then, after the source of her repression is gone, she fights to stifle her desires and physical reactions. The habit is so engrained that Louise is unable to release her emotions for fear of the unknown, of that which has been repressed for so long. However, "her bosom rose and fell tumultuously . . . When she abandoned herself a little whispered word escaped her slightly parted lips. She said it over and over under her breath: 'free, free, free!' . . . Her pulses beat fast, and the coursing blood warmed and relaxed every inch of her body" (pars. 10, 11). When she's allowed to experience them, Louise's feelings and desires provide a glimpse into a possible joyous future without

FORM: Ray uses transitions between paragraphs that indicate her organization and connect different ideas.

her husband, a future where "[t]here would be no powerful will bending hers in that blind persistence with which men and women believe they have a right to impose" (par. 14). Her marriage is over, and Louise appears finally to be able to liberate her true identity and look upon the future with not dread but anticipation.

The author's setting for this scene is crucial in the development of not only the plot but also her critique of marriage. Chopin sought to encapsulate the freedom Louise began to feel in her room with this scene's depiction of nature. For example, Chopin describes the view from Louise's bedroom window with language that expresses its vitality: "She could see in the open square before her house the tops of trees that were all aquiver with the new spring life" (par. 5). She goes on to say, "The delicious breath of rain was in the air. In the street below a peddler was crying his wares . . . and countless sparrows were twittering in the eaves" (par. 5). The very adjectives and phrases used to describe the outdoors seem to speak of bustling activity and life. This is in stark contrast to the complete lack of vivacity in the description of downstairs.

The language used in the portrayal of these contrasting settings is not the only way Chopin strives to emphasize the difference between the two. She also uses the effect these scenes have on Mrs. Mallard to convey their meaning and depth. On the one hand, the wild, perhaps faked, emotional outburst that takes place in the stifling lower level of the house leaves Louise in a state of "physical exhaustion that haunted her body and seemed to reach into her soul" (par. 4). On the other hand, Louise "[drank] in a very elixir of life through that open window" (par. 18) of her bedroom through which nature bloomed. Because the author strove to symbolize Mrs. Mallard's marriage with the oppressive downstairs

FORM: When making assumptions about the author's intentions, Ray sometimes uses hedging words—in this case, "seem to."

and her impending life without her husband with the open, healing depiction of nature, Chopin suggests that spouses are sometimes better off without each other because marriage can take a physical toll on a person's well-being while the freedom of living for no one but one's self breathes life into even the most burdened wife. After all, "[w]hat could love, the unsolved mystery, count for in face of this possession of self-assertion" (par. 15) felt by Mrs. Mallard in the wake of her emancipation from oppression?

Chopin goes on to emphasize the healing capabilities and joy of living only for one's self by showing the consequences of brutally taking it all away, in one quick turn of a latchkey. With thoughts of her freedom of days to come, "she carried herself unwittingly like a goddess of Victory. She clasped her sister's waist, and together they descended the stairs" (par. 20). Already Chopin is preparing the reader for Mrs. Mallard's looming fate. Not only is she no longer alone in her room with the proverbial elixir of life pouring in from the window, but also she is once again sinking into the oppression of the downstairs, an area that embodies all marital duties as well as the suffocation of Louise's true self and desires. When Brently Mallard enters the house slightly confused but unharmed, the loss of her newly found freedom is too much for Louise's weak heart to bear. Chopin ends the story with a hint of irony: "When the doctors came they said she had died of heart disease—of joy that kills" (par. 23). It may be easier for society to accept that Mrs. Mallard died of joy at seeing her husband alive, but in all actuality, it was the violent death of her future prospects and the hope she had allowed to blossom that sent Louise to the grave. Here lies Chopin's ultimate critique of marriage: when there was no other viable escape, only death could provide freedom from an oppressive marriage. By killing

Louise, Chopin solidifies this ultimatum and also suggests that even death is kinder when the only other option is the slow and continuous addition of the crushing weight of marital oppression.

In "The Story of an Hour," Kate Chopin challenges the typical, romanticized view of love and marriage in the era in which she lived. She chooses to reveal some of the sacrifices one must make in order to bind oneself to another in matrimony. Chopin develops these critiques of marriage through Louise Mallard's emotional responses to her husband's supposed death, whether it is a quick, if not faked, outburst of grief, her body's highly sexualized awakening to the freedoms to come, or the utter despair at finding that he still survives. These are not typical emotions for a "grieving" wife, and Chopin uses this stark contrast as well as the concomitant juxtaposition of nature to the indoors to further emphasize her critique. Louise Mallard may have died in the quest to gain independence from the oppression of her true self and desires, but now she is at least "[f]ree! Body and soul free!" (par. 16).

CONTENT: Ray provides a broad summary of her argument in the concluding paragraph.

CONTENT: In her last sentence, Ray reveals a portion of the significance of the story to an understanding of marital oppression.

Work Cited

Chopin, Kate. "The Story of an Hour." 1894. Ann Woodlief's
Web Study Texts, www.vcu.edu/engweb/webtexts/hour.

Discussion Questions

1. Describe how Sarah Ray's thesis is both debatable and significant.

2. How does the author use evidence from the text to support her interpretation?

3. How has she organized her interpretation?

4. How could it help Sarah's interpretation if she looked at the work of other scholars who have studied Chopin's story?

ARTISTIC TEXTS

Many scholars in the humanities are creators of artistic texts. It has been said about artistic texts that when you create them, they're the arts, and when you study them, they're the humanities. This formulation oversimplifies somewhat, but it's helpful as shorthand for thinking about the relationship between arts and humanities. Artistic texts can occur in many different forms and media. Some of the more common artistic texts that students create include the following:

paintings	songs	stories
sculptures	pottery	video games
poems	models	short films

The process that you follow to create an artistic text will vary according to the type of text you create. In a writing class, an instructor might ask you to create an artistic text and then reflect on the process of creating it. Additionally, he or she might ask you to interpret your own text or that of another student.

Creating an Artistic Text

In this three-part project, you'll create a text, reflect on the process of creating it, and then develop a preliminary interpretation of the text. Your assessment will be based primarily on your reflection on and close reading of your text. We encourage you to try something new; indeed, you might discover a talent you didn't realize you had, or you might understand something new about the creative process by trying an art form you haven't experimented with before.

PART 1
Choose an art form that you'd like to experiment with for this activity. You might try something that you've done before, or you might want to experiment with something new. Some possibilities are listed below.

- sketching or painting a figure or a landscape
- composing a poem or a song
- using a pottery wheel or sculpting with clay
- writing a short story
- creating an advertisement or Public Service Announcement for an issue important to you
- designing a video game
- directing a (very) short film

PART 2
After completing the creative portion of this project, respond to the following prompts for reflection about the process of creating the text. First reflect on the process of creating your text and what you learned from it.

- What was the most challenging part of the project for you?
- What was the most enjoyable part of the project?
- What did you discover about yourself as you participated in this activity?
- Did you find yourself trying to imitate other examples you've seen, heard, or experienced, or were you trying to develop something very different?
- What inspired you as you were working?

PART 3
Once you've reflected on the process of creating your text, examine the text closely and take notes regarding the elements of it that you see as important to its meaning. Once you've developed notes, do the following.

1. Complete a content/form-response grid to highlight the notes you see as most important for constructing meaning from the text. Be sure to articulate responses about why you see each note as important and relevant toward interpreting meaning.

2. Brainstorm a list of *how*, *what*, and *why* questions regarding various aspects of the text related to its meaning(s).

3. Select one or two questions that seem most promising to try and answer. You should be able to draw direct evidence from the text (and your notes) that supports your answer.

4. Select and rewrite the best question that has evidence, and then write a thesis statement.

You should construct the remainder of your interpretation of the text based on the thesis statement. Try to develop an interpretation that's organized with clear reasons and evidence (see Chapter 4). Use examples actually taken from your text as evidence.

---

tip sheet

Reading and Writing in the Humanities

- **In the humanities, scholars seek to understand and interpret human experience.** To do so, they often create, analyze, and interpret texts.

- **Scholars in the humanities often conduct close readings of texts** to interpret and make meaning from them, and they might draw on a particular theoretical perspective to ask questions about those texts.

- **Keeping a content/form-response grid can help you track important elements of a text** and your response to them as you do a close reading.

- **Writing in the humanities often draws on the interpretations of others,** either as support or to position an interpretation within prior scholarship.

- **Arguments in the humanities generally begin with a thesis statement** that asserts what the author intends to prove, and it may also provide insight into how the author will prove it. Each section of the argument should provide support for the thesis.

Reading and Writing in the Social Sciences

Introduction to the Social Sciences

Social scientists study human behavior and interaction along with the systems and social structures we create to organize our world. Professionals in the fields of the **social sciences** help us understand why we do what we do as well as how processes (political, economic, personal, etc.) contribute to our lives. As the image at the bottom of this page shows, the social sciences encompass a broad area of academic inquiry that comprises numerous fields of study. These include sociology, psychology, anthropology, communication studies, and political science, among others.

Maybe you've observed a friend or family member spiral into addictive or self-destructive behavior and struggled to understand how it happened. Maybe you've spent time wondering how cliques were formed and maintained among students in your high school, or how friends are typically chosen. Perhaps larger social issues like war, poverty, or famine concern you the most. If you've ever stopped to consider any of these kinds of issues, then you've already begun to explore the world of the social sciences.

Social scientist Kevin Rathunde, who teaches at the University of Utah, shares his perspective on the work and writing of social scientists in Insider's View features in this chapter. Excerpts from Rathunde's paper entitled "Middle School Students' Motivation and Quality of Experience: A Comparison of Montessori and Traditional School Environments,"

ANDREA TSURUMI

183

Social scientists care about the conditions that allow people to connect

KEVIN RATHUNDE, SOCIAL SCIENCES

COURTESY OF KEVIN RATHUNDE

"There are many branches of social science. In general, as the name 'social science' implies, the main focus of scientific action and dialogue is on people and social processes. My training was in an interdisciplinary program on human development at the University of Chicago. As a result, my perspective on social science tends to reach across disciplinary boundaries. I also work in an interdisciplinary department at the University of Utah. The professional conversations I have with colleagues—both within and outside of my department—are wide-ranging. If there is a common denominator to them, it might be the well-being of individuals, families, and society. Social scientists care about the conditions that allow people to connect with others, participate in the lives of their communities, and reach their full potential."

which he wrote and published with his colleague Mihaly Csikszentmihalyi in the *American Journal of Education*, also appear throughout this chapter. Rathunde and Csikszentmihalyi's study investigated the types of educational settings that contribute to the best outcomes for students. Specifically, they compared traditional public school environments with those of Montessori schools to assess how students learn, interact, and perceive the quality of their experiences in these differing environments.

As a social scientist, you might study issues like therapy options for autism, the effects of substance abuse on families, peer pressure, the dynamics of dating, social networking websites, stress, or the communication practices of men and women. You might study family counseling techniques or the effects of divorce on teens. Or perhaps you might wonder (as Rathunde and Csikszentmihalyi do) about the effects of differing educational environments on student satisfaction and success.

Whatever the case may be, if you're interested in studying human behavior and understanding why we do what we do, you'll want to consider further how social scientists conduct research and how they present their results in writing. As in all the academic domains, progress in the social sciences rests upon researchers' primary skills at making observations of the world around them.

INSIDE WORK Observing Behavior

For this activity, pick a place to sit and observe people. You can choose a place that you enjoy going to regularly, but make sure you can observe and take notes without being interrupted or distracted. For example, you might observe people in your school's library or another space on campus. Try to avoid places where you could feel compelled to engage in conversation with people you know.

For ten minutes, freewrite about the people around you and what they're doing. Look for the kinds of interactions and engagements that characterize their behavior. Then draft some questions that you think a social scientist observing the same people might ask about them. For example, if you wrote about behaviors you observed in a college classroom or lecture hall, you might consider questions like the ones listed here.

- How are students arranged around the room? What does the seating arrangement look like? What effect does the room's arrangement have on classroom interaction, if any?

- What are students doing? Are they taking notes? Writing? Sleeping? Typing? Texting? Listening? Doing something else?

- Are students doing different things in different parts of the room, or are the activities similar throughout the room? Why?

- What is the instructor doing in the classroom? Where is he or she positioned? How are students responding?

- Are students using technology? If so, what kinds of technology? What are they using the technology to do?

- If people are interacting with one another in the classroom, what are they talking about? How are they interacting? How are they positioned when they interact? Are numerous people contributing to the conversation? Is someone leading the conversation? If so, how?

See how many different behaviors, people, and interactions you can observe and how many questions you can generate. You might do this activity in the same place with a partner and then compare notes. What did you or your partner find in common? What did you each observe that was unique? Why do you think you noticed the things you did? What was the most interesting thing you observed? ◗

Research in the Social Sciences

As we've indicated, the social sciences comprise a diverse group of academic fields that aim to understand human behavior and systems. But it may be difficult to see the commonalities among these disciplines that make it possible to refer to them as social sciences. One of the ways we can link these disciplines and the values they share, beyond their basic concern for why and how people do things, is by considering how social scientists conduct and report their research.

THE ROLE OF THEORY

Unlike in the natural sciences, where research often takes place in a laboratory setting under controlled conditions, research in the social sciences is necessarily "messier." The reason is fairly simple: human beings and the systems they organize cannot generally be studied in laboratory conditions, where variables are controlled. For this reason, social scientists do not generally establish fixed laws or argue for absolute truths, as natural scientists sometimes do. For instance, while natural scientists are able to argue, with certainty, that a water molecule contains two atoms of hydrogen and one of oxygen, social scientists cannot claim to know the absolute fixed nature of a person's psychology (why a person does what she does in any particular instance, for example) or that of a social system or problem (why homelessness persists, for instance).

Much social science research is therefore based on **theories of human behavior and human systems**, which are propositions that scholars use to explain specific phenomena. Theories can be evaluated on the basis of their ability to explain why or how or when a phenomenon occurs, and they generally result from research that has been replicated time and again to confirm their accuracy, appropriateness, and usefulness. Still, it's important to understand that theories are not laws; they are not absolute, fixed, or perfect explanations. Instead, social science theories are always being refined as research on particular social phenomena develops. The Rathunde and Csikszentmihalyi study we highlight in the Insider's View boxes, for instance, makes use of goal theory and optimal experience theory as part of the research design to evaluate the type of middle school environment that best contributes to students' education.

Insider Example
Exploring Social Science Theory

Read the following excerpt from Kalervo Oberg's "Cultural Shock: Adjustment to New Cultural Environments," and then reflect on his theory by answering the questions that follow the selection. Oberg (1901–1973) was a pioneer in economic anthropology and applied anthropology, and his foundational work in this study has been cited hundreds of times by sociologists and anthropologists who are interested in the phenomenon. Oberg himself coined the term *culture shock*.

Excerpt from Cultural Shock: Adjustment to New Cultural Environments

KALERVO OBERG

Culture shock is precipitated by the anxiety that results from losing all our familiar signs and symbols of social intercourse. These signs or cues include the thousand and one ways in which we orient ourselves to the situations of daily life: when to shake hands and what to say when we meet people, when and how to give tips, how to give orders to servants, how to make purchases, when to accept and when to refuse invitations, when to take statements seriously and when not. Now these cues—which may be words, gestures, facial expressions, customs, or norms—are acquired by all of us in the course of growing up and are as much a part of our culture as the language we speak or the beliefs we accept. All of us depend for our peace of mind and our efficiency on hundreds of these cues, most of which we do not carry on the level of conscious awareness.

Now when an individual enters a strange culture, all or most of these familiar cues are removed. He or she is like a fish out of water. No matter how broad-minded or full of good will you may be, a series of props have been knocked from under you, followed by a feeling of frustration and anxiety. People react to the frustration in much the same way. First they *reject* the environment which causes the discomfort: "the ways of the host country are bad because they make us feel bad." When Americans or other foreigners in a strange land get together to grouse about the host country and its people—you can be sure they are suffering from culture shock. Another phase of culture shock is *regression*. The home environment suddenly assumes a tremendous importance. To an American everything American becomes irrationally glorified. All the difficulties and problems are forgotten and only the good things back home are remembered. It usually takes a trip home to bring one back to reality.

SYMPTOMS OF CULTURE SHOCK

Some of the symptoms of culture shock are: excessive washing of the hands; excessive concern over drinking water, food, dishes, and bedding; fear of physical contact with attendants or servants; the absent-minded, far-away stare (sometimes called "the tropical stare"); a feeling of helplessness and a desire for dependence on long-term residents of one's own nationality; fits of anger over delays and other minor frustrations; delay and outright refusal to learn the language of the host country; excessive fear of being cheated, robbed, or injured; great concern over minor pains and irruptions of the skin; and finally, that terrible longing to be back home, to be able to have a good cup of coffee and a piece of apple pie, to walk into that corner drugstore, to visit one's relatives, and, in general, to talk to people who really make sense.

Individuals differ greatly in the degree in which culture shock affects them. Although not common, there are individuals who cannot live in foreign countries. Those who have seen people go through culture shock and on to a satisfactory adjustment can discern steps in the process. During the first few weeks most individuals are fascinated by the new. They stay in hotels and associate with nationals who speak their language and are polite and gracious to foreigners.

This honeymoon stage may last from a few days or weeks to six months depending on circumstances. If one is a very important person he or she will be shown the show places, will be pampered and petted, and in a press interview will speak glowingly about progress, good will, and international amity, and if he returns home he may well write a book about his pleasant if superficial experience abroad.

But this Cook's tour type of mentality does not normally last if the foreign visitor remains abroad and has seriously to cope with real conditions of life. It is then that the second stage begins, characterized by a hostile and aggressive attitude towards the host country. This hostility evidently grows out of the genuine difficulty which the visitor experiences in the process of adjustment. There is maid trouble, school trouble, language trouble, house trouble, transportation trouble, shopping trouble, and the fact that people in the host country are largely indifferent to all these troubles. They help but they just don't understand your great concern over these difficulties. Therefore, they must be insensible and unsympathetic to you and your worries. The result, "I just don't like them." You become aggressive, you band together with your fellow countrymen and criticize the host country, its ways, and its people. But this criticism is not an objective appraisal but a derogatory one. Instead of trying to account for conditions as they are through an honest analysis of the actual conditions and the historical circumstances which have created them, you talk as if the difficulties you experienced are more or less created by the people of the host country for your special discomfort. You take refuge in the colony of your countrymen and its cocktail circuit, which often becomes the fountain-head of emotionally charged labels known as stereotypes. This is a peculiar kind of invidious shorthand which caricatures the host country and its people in a negative manner. The "dollar-grasping American" and the "indolent Latin American" are samples of mild forms of stereotypes. The use of stereotypes may salve the ego of someone with a severe case of culture shock but it certainly does not lead to any genuine understanding of the host country and its people. This second stage of culture shock is in a sense a crisis in the disease. If you overcome it, you stay; if not, you leave before you reach the stage of a nervous breakdown.

If the visitor succeeds in getting some knowledge of the language and begins to get around by himself, he is beginning to open the way into the new cultural environment. The visitor still has difficulties but he takes a "this is my cross and I have to bear it" attitude. Usually in this stage the visitor takes a superior attitude to people of the host country. His sense of humor begins to exert itself. Instead of criticizing he jokes about the people and even cracks jokes about his or her own difficulties. He or she is now on the way to recovery. And there is also the poor devil who is worse off than yourself whom you can help, which in turn gives you confidence in your ability to speak and get around.

In the fourth stage your adjustment is about as complete as it can be. The visitor now accepts the customs of the country as just another way of living. You operate within the new milieu without a feeling of anxiety although there are moments of strain. Only with a complete grasp of all the cues of social intercourse will this strain disappear. For a long time the individual will understand what the national is saying but he is not always sure what the national means. With a complete adjustment you not only accept the foods, drinks, habits, and customs, but actually begin to enjoy them. When you go on home leave you may even take things back with you and if you leave for good you generally miss the country and the people to whom you have become accustomed.

Discussion Questions

1. In your own words, define what you think Kalervo Oberg means by *culture shock*.

2. What are the four stages of culture shock, according to Oberg?

3. Oberg's essay was written more than half a century ago. In what ways does it seem dated? In what ways does it strike you as still valid or relevant?

INSIDE WORK Tracing a Theory's Development

As we indicated, theories in the social sciences exist to be developed and refined over time, based on our developing understandings of a social phenomenon as a result of continued research. Conduct a search (using the web or your academic database access) to determine if you can make a rough estimate as to how often Oberg's theory of culture shock has been cited in published research. You might even make a timeline, or another visual representation, of what you find. As you look at the research, identify any evidence or indicators that the theory has been updated or altered since its first appearance. In what ways has the theory been refined? ❭

RESEARCH QUESTIONS AND HYPOTHESES

As we've noted throughout this book, research questions are typically formulated on the basis of observations. In the social sciences, such observations focus on human behavior, human systems, and/or the interactions between the two. Observations of a social phenomenon can give rise to questions about how a phenomenon operates or what effects it has on people or, as Rathunde suggests, how it could be changed to improve individuals' well-being. For example, in their social science study, "'Under the Radar': Educators and Cyberbullying in Schools," W. Cassidy, K. Brown, and M.

Jackson (2012) offer the following as guiding research questions for their investigation:

> Our study of educators focused on three research questions: Do they [educators] consider cyberbullying a problem at their school and how familiar are they with the extent and impact among their students? What policies and practices are in place to prevent or counter cyberbullying? What solutions do they have for encouraging a kinder online world? (p. 522)

Research that is designed to inform a theory of human behavior or to provide data that contributes to a fuller understanding of some social or political structure (i.e., to answer a social science research question) also often begins with the presentation of a *hypothesis*. As we saw in Chapter 4, a hypothesis is a testable proposition that provides an answer or predicts an outcome in response to the research question(s) at hand. It's important to note that not all social science reports include a statement of hypothesis. Some social science research establishes its focus by presenting the questions that guide researchers' inquiry into a particular phenomenon instead of establishing a hypothesis. C. Kerns and K. Ko (2009) present the following hypothesis, or predicted outcome, for their social science study, "Exploring Happiness and Performance at Work." The researchers make a prediction concerning what they believed their research would show before presenting their findings later in their research report:

> The intent of this analysis was to review how happiness and performance related to each other in this workplace. It is the authors' belief that for performance to be sustained in an organization, individuals and groups within that organization need to experience a threshold level of happiness. It is difficult for unhappy individuals and work groups to continue performing at high levels without appropriate leadership intervention. (p. 5)

Hypotheses differ from *thesis statements*, which are more commonly associated with arguments in the humanities. While thesis statements offer researchers' final conclusions on a topic or issue, hypothesis statements offer a predicted outcome. The proposition expressed in a hypothesis may be either accepted or rejected based on the results of the research. For example, an educational researcher might hypothesize that teachers' use of open-ended questioning increases students' level of participation in class. However, the researcher wouldn't be able to confirm or reject such a hypothesis until the end of his or her research report.

INSIDE WORK **Developing Hypotheses**

1. For five minutes, brainstorm *social science* topics or issues that have affected your life. One approach is to consider issues that are causing you stress in your life right now. Examples might include peer pressure, academic performance, substance abuse, dating, or a relative's cancer treatment.

2. Once you have a list of topics, focus on two or three that you believe have had the greatest impact on you personally. Next, generate a list of possible

research questions concerning the topics that, if answered, would offer you a greater understanding of them. Examples: *What triggers most people to try their first drink of alcohol? What types of therapies are most effective for working with children on the autism spectrum? What kinds of technology actually aid in student learning?*

3. When you've reached the stage of proposing a possible answer to one or more of your questions, then you're ready to state a hypothesis. Try proposing a *hypothesis*, or testable proposition, as an answer to one of the research questions you've posed. For example, if your research question is "What triggers most people to try their first drink of alcohol?" then your hypothesis might be "Peer pressure generally causes most people to try their first drink of alcohol, especially for those who try their first drink before reaching the legal drinking age." ▶

METHODS

Research in the diverse fields of the social sciences is, as you probably suspect, quite varied, and social scientists collect data to answer their research questions or test their hypotheses in several different ways. Their choice of methods is directly influenced by the kinds of questions they ask in any particular instance, as well as by their own disciplinary backgrounds. In his Insider's View on page 192, Kevin Rathunde highlights the connection between the kinds of research questions a social scientist asks and the particular methods the researcher uses to answer those questions.

We can group most of the research you're likely to encounter in the fields of the social sciences into three possible types: quantitative, qualitative, and mixed methods. Researchers make choices about which types of methods they'll employ in any given situation based on the nature of their line of inquiry. A particular research question may very well dictate the methods used to answer that question. If you wanted to determine the number of homeless veterans in a specific city, for instance, then collecting numerical, or quantitative, data would likely suffice to answer that question. However, if you wanted to know what factors affect the rates of homelessness among veterans in your community, then you would need to do more than tally the number of homeless veterans. You'd need to collect a different type of data to help construct an answer — perhaps responses to surveys or interview questions.

Quantitative Methods

Quantitative studies include those that rely on collecting numerical data and performing statistical analyses to reveal findings in research. Basic statistical data, like those provided by *means* (averages), *modes* (most often occurring value), and *medians* (middle values), are fundamental to quantitative social science research. More sophisticated statistical procedures commonly used in

Insider's View
A good question is usually worth looking at from multiple perspectives
KEVIN RATHUNDE, SOCIAL SCIENCES

COURTESY OF KEVIN RATHUNDE

"I have strong interests in how people experience their lives and what helps them stay interested, engaged, and on a path of lifelong learning and development. I tend to ask questions about the quality of life and experience. How are students experiencing their time in class? When are they most engaged? How does being interested affect the learning process? How can parents and teachers create conditions in homes and families that facilitate interest?

"The fields of developmental psychology and educational psychology are especially important to my work. The questions I ask, therefore, are framed the way a developmental or educational psychologist might ask them. Social scientists from other disciplines would probably look at the same topic (i.e., human engagement and interest) in a different way. My daughter is studying anthropology in graduate school. She would probably approach this topic from a cultural perspective. Where I might design a study using questionnaires that are administered in family or school contexts, she might focus on interviews and cultural frameworks that shed light on the meaning and organization of educational institutions. Although my research is primarily quantitative and uses statistical analysis to interpret the results, I have also used a variety of qualitative techniques (i.e., interviews and observations) over the years. A good question is usually worth looking at from multiple perspectives."

professional quantitative studies include correlations, chi-square tests, analysis of variance (ANOVA), and multivariate analysis of variance (MANOVA), as well as regression model testing, just to name a few. Not all statistical procedures are appropriate in all situations, however, so researchers must carefully select procedures based on the nature of their data and the kinds of findings they seek. Researchers who engage in advanced statistical procedures as part of their methods are typically highly skilled in such procedures. At the very least, these researchers consult or work in cooperation with statisticians to design their studies and/or to analyze their data.

You may find, in fact, that a team of researchers collaborating on a social science project often includes individuals who are also experienced statisticians. Obviously, we don't expect you to be familiar with the details of statistical procedures, but it's important that you be able to notice when researchers rely on statistical methods to test their hypotheses and to inform their results.

Also, you should take note of how researchers incorporate discussion of such methods into their writing. In the following example, we've highlighted a few elements in the reporting that you'll want to notice when reading social science studies that make use of statistical procedures:

- **Procedures**   What statistical procedures are used?
- **Variables**   What variables are examined in the procedures?
- **Results**   What do the statistical procedures reveal?

- **Participants** From whom are the data collected, and how are those individuals chosen?

In their study, Rathunde and Csikszentmihalyi report on the statistical procedures they used to examine different types of schools:

> The first analysis compared the main motivation and quality-of-experience variables across school type (Montessori vs. traditional) and grade level (sixth vs. eighth) using a two-way MANCOVA with parental education, gender, and ethnic background as covariates. Significant differences were found for school context (Wilks's lambda = .84, $F(5, 275) = 10.84$, $p < .001$), indicating that students in the two school contexts reported differences in motivation and quality of experience. After adjusting for the covariates, the multivariate eta squared indicated that 17 percent of the variance of the dependent variables was associated with the school context factor. The omnibus test for grade level was not significant (Wilks's lambda = .99, $F(5, 275) = .68$, $p = .64$) indicating that students in sixth and eighth grade reported similar motivation and quality of experience. Finally, the omnibus test for the interaction of school context x grade level was not significant (Wilks's lambda = .97, $F(5, 275) = 2.02$, $p = .08$). None of the multivariate tests for the covariates—parental education, gender, and ethnic background—reached the .05 level. (p. 357)

Variables examined, participants or populations involved in the study, and statistical procedure employed— MANCOVA, or a multivariate analysis of covariance—are identified.

Results of the statistical procedure are identified.

Qualitative Methods

Qualitative studies generally rely on language, observation, and reporting of individual human experiences to reveal findings in research. Research reports often communicate these methods through the form of a study's results, which rely on in-depth narrative reporting. Methods for collecting data in qualitative studies include interviews, document analysis, surveys, and observations.

We can see examples of these methods put into practice in Barbara Allen's "Environmental Justice, Local Knowledge, and After-Disaster Planning in New Orleans" (2007), published in the academic social science journal *Technology and Society*. In this example, we've highlighted a few elements in the reporting that you'll want to notice when reading qualitative research methods:

- **Method** What method of data collection is used?
- **Data** What data is gathered from that method?
- **Results** What are the results? What explanation do the researchers provide for the data, or what meaning do they find in the data?
- **Participants** From whom is the data collected, and how are these individuals chosen?

> Six months after the hurricane I contacted public health officials and researchers, many of whom were reluctant to talk. One who did talk asked that I did not use her name, but she made some interesting observations. According to my informant, health officials were in a difficult position. Half a year after the devastation, only 25% of the city's residents had returned; a year after the

Participants

Data-collection method: interview

Data, followed by explanation or meaning of data — storm, that number rose to about 40%. Negative publicity regarding public health issues would deter such repatriation, particularly families with children who had not returned in any large numbers to the city. The informant also told me to pursue the state public health websites where the most prominent worries were still smoking and obesity, not Hurricane Katrina. While the

Data — information on various public health websites did eventually reflect concerns about mold, mildew, and other contamination, it was never presented as the health threat that independent environmental scientists, such as Wilma Subra, thought it was. (pp. 154–55)

. . .

Participant — About five months after Hurricane Katrina, I received an e-mail from a high school student living in a rural parish west of New Orleans along the Mississippi River (an area EJ advocates have renamed Cancer Alley). After Hurricane Katrina, an old landfill near her house was opened to receive waste and began emitting noxious odors. She took samples of the "black ooze" from the site and contacted the Louisiana Department of Environmental Quality, only to be told that the landfill was accepting only construction waste, and the smell she described was probably decaying gypsum board. I suspect her story

Explanation or meaning of data — will be repeated many times across south Louisiana as these marginal waste sites receive the debris from homes and businesses ruined by the hurricane. The full environmental impact of Hurricane Katrina's waste and its hastily designated removal sites will not be known for many years. (p. 155)

Mixed Methods

Studies that make use of both qualitative and quantitative data-collection techniques are generally referred to as **mixed-methodology studies**. Rathunde and Csikszentmihalyi's study used mixed methods: the authors report findings from both qualitative and quantitative data. In this excerpt, they share results from qualitative data they collected as they sought to distinguish among the types of educational settings selected for participation in their study:

> After verifying that the demographic profile of the two sets of schools was similar, the next step was to determine if the schools differed with respect to the five selection criteria outlined above. We used a variety of qualitative sources to verify contextual differences, including observations by the research staff; teacher and parent interviews; school newsletters, information packets, mission statements, and parent teacher handbooks; summaries from board of education and school council meetings; and a review of class schedules and textbook choices discussed in strategic plans. These sources also provided information about the level of middle grade reform that may or may not have been implemented by the schools and whether the label "traditional" was appropriate. (p. 64)

However, Rathunde and Csikszentmihalyi's central hypothesis, "that students in Montessori middle schools would report more positive perceptions of their school environment and their teachers, more often perceive their classmates as friends, and spend more time in collaborative and/or individual work rather than didactic educational formats such as listening to a lecture" (p. 68), was tested by using quantitative methods:

> The main analyses used two-way multivariate analysis of covariance (MANCOVA) with school type (Montessori vs. traditional) and grade level (sixth vs. eighth) as the two factors. Gender, ethnicity, and parental education were covariates in all of the analyses. Overall multivariate F tests (Wilks's lambda) were performed first on related sets of dependent variables. If an overall F test was significant, we performed univariate ANOVAs as follow-up tests to the MANCOVAs. If necessary, post hoc analyses were done using Bonferroni corrections to control for Type I errors. Only students with at least 15 ESM signals were included in the multivariate analyses, and follow-up ANOVAs used students who had valid scores on all of the dependent variables. (p. 68)

Addressing Bias

Because social scientists study people and organizations, their research is considered more valuable when conducted within a framework that minimizes the influence of personal or researcher bias on the study's outcome(s). When possible, social scientists strive for **objectivity** (in quantitative research) or **neutrality** (in qualitative research) in their research. This means that researchers undertake all possible measures to reduce the influence of biases on their research. Bias is sometimes inevitable, however, so social science research places a high value on honesty and transparency in the reporting of data. Each of the methods outlined above requires social scientists to engage in rigorous procedures and checks (e.g., ensuring appropriate sample sizes and/or using multiple forms of qualitative data) to ensure that the influence of any biases is as limited as possible.

LaunchPad

A political scientist weighs in on avoiding bias.

INSIDE WORK **Considering Research Methods**

In the previous activity, we asked you to consider possible hypotheses, or testable propositions, to the research questions you posed. Now choose one of your hypothesis statements, and consider the types of methods that might be appropriate for testing the hypothesis. Think about the kinds of data you'll generate from the different methods.

- Would quantitative, qualitative, or mixed research methods be the most appropriate for testing your hypothesis? Why?

- What specific methods would you use—statistical procedures, surveys, observations, interviews? Why?

- Who would you want to have participate in your research? From whom would you need to collect your data in order to answer your research question? ❭

THE IRB PROCESS AND USE OF HUMAN SUBJECTS

All research, whether student or faculty initiated and directed, must treat its subjects, or participants, with the greatest of care and consider the ethical implications of all its procedures. Although institutions establish their own systems and procedures for verifying the ethical treatment of subjects, most of these include an **institutional review board (IRB)**, or a committee of individuals whose job is to review research proposals in light of ethical concerns for subjects and applicable laws. Such proposals typically include specific forms of documentation that identify a study's purpose; rigorously detail the research procedures to be followed; evaluate potential risks and rewards of a study, especially for study participants; and ensure (whenever possible) that participants are fully informed about a study and the implications of their participation in it.

We encourage you to learn more about the IRB process at your own institution and, when appropriate, to consider your own research in light of the IRB policies and procedures established for your institution. Many schools maintain informational, educational, and interactive websites. You'll notice similarities in the mission statements of institutional review boards from a number of colleges and universities:

Duke University: To ensure the protection of human research subjects by conducting scientific and ethical review of research studies while providing leadership and education for the research community.

The George Washington University: To support [the] research community in the conduct of innovative and ethical research by providing guidance, education, and oversight for the protection of human subjects.

Maricopa County Community College District: [T]o review all proposed research involving human subjects to ensure that subjects are treated ethically and that their rights and welfare are adequately protected.

Conventions of Writing in the Social Sciences

In light of the variety of research methods used by social scientists, it's not surprising that there are also a number of ways social scientists report their research findings. In this section, we highlight general conventional expectations of *structure*, *language*, and *reference* that social scientists follow to communicate their research to one another. Understanding these conventions, we believe, can help foster your understanding of this academic domain more broadly.

Aya Matsuda is a linguist and social science researcher at Arizona State University, where she studies the use of English as an international language, the integration of a "World Englishes" perspective into U.S. education, and the ways bilingual writers negotiate identity. In her Insider's View, Matsuda explains that she learned the conventions of writing as a social scientist, and more particularly as a linguist, "mostly through writing, getting feedback, and revising."

As Matsuda also suggests, reading can be an important part of understanding the writing of a discipline. Furthermore, reading academic writing with a particular focus on the rhetorical elements used is a powerful way to acquire insight into the academic discipline itself, as well as a way to learn the literacy practices that professional writers commonly follow in whatever academic domain you happen to be studying.

STRUCTURAL CONVENTIONS AND IMRaD FORMAT

Structural conventions within the fields of the social sciences can vary quite dramatically, but the structure of a social science report should follow logically from the type of study conducted or the methodological framework (quantitative, qualitative, or mixed-methods) it employs. The more quantitative a study is, the more likely its reporting will reflect the conventions for scientific research, using IMRaD format. Qualitative studies, though, sometimes appear in other organizational forms that reflect the particular qualitative methods used in the study. But just as numerous fields within the social sciences rely on quantitative research methods, so too do many social scientists report their results according to the conventional form for scientific inquiry: *IMRaD (Introduction, Methods, Results, and Discussion) format.*

Introduction

The introduction of a social science report establishes the context for a study, providing appropriate background on the issue or topic under scrutiny. The introduction is also where you're likely to find evidence of researchers' review of previous scholarship on a topic. As part of these reviews, researchers typically report what's already known about a phenomenon or what's relevant in the current scholarship for their own research. They may also situate their research goals within some gap in the scholarship—that is, they

Insider's View
Reading the kind of writing I needed to do helped me learn about the conventions
AYA MATSUDA, LINGUISTICS

COURTESY OF AYA MATSUDA

"In undergraduate and graduate courses, I had writing assignments that are similar to the kind of writing I do now. For those, I wrote (often using the published materials as a model) and got feedback from the professors. Sometimes I had a chance to revise according to those comments. Other times I didn't, but used the comments when I had to do a similar writing assignment in later courses. As I became more advanced in my academic career (starting in graduate school), I started submitting my papers for publication. I would draft my manuscript and then share it with my professors or fellow students (when I was in graduate school) or with my colleagues (now) to get their feedback. I also got comments from reviewers and editors. The process of writing, getting feedback, and revising helped me not only learn about but also learn to follow and negotiate the conventions.

"Reading the kind of writing I needed to do (e.g., journal articles) helped me learn about the conventions, but that alone did not help me learn to follow them. I needed to write and use what I learned in order to feel I had actually added it to my writing repertoire."

explain how their research contributes to the growing body of scholarship on the phenomenon under investigation. If a theoretical perspective drives a study, as often occurs in more qualitative studies, then the introduction may also contain an explanation of the central tenets or the parameters of the researchers' theoretical lens. Regardless, an introduction in the social sciences generally builds to a statement of specific purpose for the study. This may take the form of a hypothesis or thesis, or it may appear explicitly as a general statement of the researchers' purpose, perhaps including a presentation of research questions. The introduction to Rathunde and Csikszentmihalyi's study provides an example:

Provides an introduction to the topic at hand: the problem of motivation for adolescents in middle school. The problem is situated in the scholarship of others.

> The difficulties that many young adolescents encounter in middle school have been well documented (Carnegie Council on Adolescent Development 1989, 1995; Eccles et al. 1993; U.S. Department of Education 1991). During this precarious transition from the elementary school years, young adolescents may begin to doubt the value of their academic work and their abilities to succeed (Simmons and Blyth 1987; Wigfield et al. 1991). A central concern of many studies is motivation (Anderman and Maehr 1994); a disturbingly consistent finding associated with middle school is a drop in students' intrinsic motivation to learn (Anderman et al. 1999; Gottfried 1985; Harter et al. 1992).

Reviews relevant scholarship: the researchers review previous studies that have bearing on their own aims—addressing the decline in motivation among students.

> Such downward trends in motivation are not inevitable. Over the past decade, several researchers have concluded that the typical learning environment in middle school is often mismatched with adolescents' developmental needs (Eccles et al. 1993). Several large-scale research programs have focused on the qualities of classrooms and school cultures that may enhance student achievement and motivation (Ames 1992; Lipsitz et al. 1997; Maehr and Midgley 1991). School environments that provide a more appropriate developmental fit (e.g., more relevant tasks, student-directed learning, less of an emphasis on grades and competition, more collaboration, etc.) have been shown to enhance students' intrinsic, task motivation (Anderman et al. 1999).

Identifies researchers' particular areas of interest

> The present study explores the issues of developmental fit and young adolescents' quality of experience and motivation by comparing five Montessori middle schools to six "traditional" public middle schools. Although the Montessori educational philosophy is primarily associated with early childhood education, a number of schools have extended its core principles to early adolescent education. These principles are in general agreement with the reform proposals associated with various motivation theories (Anderman et al. 1999; Maehr and Midgley 1991), developmental fit theories (Eccles et al. 1993), as well as insights from various recommendations for middle school reform (e.g., the Carnegie Foundation's "Turning Points" recommendations; see Lipsitz et al. 1997). In addition, the Montessori philosophy is consistent with the theoretical and practical implications of optimal experience (flow) theory (Csikszentmihalyi and Rathunde 1998). The present study places a special emphasis on students' quality of experience in middle school. More specifically, it uses the Experience Sampling Method (ESM) (Csikszentmihalyi and Larson 1987) to compare the school experiences of Montessori middle school students with a comparable sample of public school students in traditional classrooms. (pp. 341–42)

Although the introductory elements of Rathunde and Csikszentmihalyi's study actually continue for a number of pages, these opening paragraphs reveal common rhetorical moves in social science research reporting: establishing a topic of interest, reviewing the scholarship on that topic, and connecting the current study to the ongoing scholarly conversation on the topic.

Methods

Social science researchers are very particular about the precise reporting of their methods of research. No matter what the type of study (quantitative, qualitative, or mixed-methods), researchers are very careful not only to identify the methods used in their research but also to explain why they chose certain ones, in light of the goals of their study. Because researchers want to reduce the influence of researcher bias and to provide enough context so others might replicate or confirm their findings, social scientists make sure that their reports thoroughly explain the kinds of data they have collected and the precise procedures they used to collect that data (interviews, document analysis, surveys, etc.). Also, there is often much discussion of the ways the data were interpreted or analyzed (using case studies, narrative analysis, statistical procedures, etc.).

An excerpt from W. Cassidy, K. Brown, and M. Jackson's study on educators and cyberbullying provides an example of the level of detail at which scholars typically report their methods:

> Each participant chose a pseudonym and was asked a series of 16 in-depth, semi-structured, open-ended questions (Lancy, 2001) and three closed-category questions in a private setting, allowing their views to be voiced in confidence (Cook-Sather, 2002). Each 45- to 60-minute audiotaped interview was conducted by one of the authors, while maintaining a neutral, nonjudgmental stance in regards to the responses (Merriam, 1988).
>
> Once the interviews were transcribed, each participant was given the opportunity to review the transcript and make changes. The transcripts were then reviewed and re-reviewed in a backward and forward motion (Glaser & Strauss, 1967; McMillan & Schumacher, 1997) separately by two of the three researchers to determine commonalities and differences among responses as well as any salient themes that surfaced due to the frequency or the strength of the response (Miles & Huberman, 1994). Each researcher's analysis was then compared with the other's to jointly determine emergent themes and perceptions.
>
> The dominant themes were then reviewed in relation to the existing literature on educators' perceptions and responses to cyberbullying. The approach taken was "bottom-up," to inductively uncover themes and contribute to theory, rather than apply existing theory as a predetermined frame for analysis (Miles & Huberman, 1994). (p. 523)

Provides highly specific details about data-collection methods, and emphasizes researchers' neutral stance

Provides detailed explanation of procedures used to support the reliability of the study's findings

Connects the research to the development of theory

You'll notice that the researchers do not simply indicate that the data were collected via interviews. Rather, they go to some lengths to describe the kinds of interviews they conducted and how they were conducted, as well as how those interviews were analyzed. This level of detail supports the writers' ethos, and it further highlights their commitment to reducing bias in their research. Similar studies might also report the interview questions at the end of the report in an appendix. Seeing the actual questions helps readers interpret the results on their own and also provides enough detail for readers to replicate the study or test the hypothesis with a different population, should they desire to do so. Readers of the study need to understand as precisely as possible the methods for data collection and analysis.

Results

There can be much variety in the ways social science reports present the results, or findings, of a study. You may encounter a section identified by the title "Results," especially if the study follows IMRaD format, but you may not find that heading at all. Instead, researchers often present their results by using headings and subheadings that reflect their actual findings. As examples, we provide here excerpts from two studies: (1) Rathunde and Csikszentmihalyi's 2005 study on middle school student motivation, and (2) Cassidy, Brown, and Jackson's 2012 study on educators and cyberbullying.

In the Results section of their report, Rathunde and Csikszentmihalyi provide findings from their study under the subheading "Motivation and Quality-of-Experience Differences: Nonacademic Activities at School." Those results read in part:

> Follow-up ANCOVAs were done on each of the five ESM variables. Table 3 summarizes the means, standard errors, and significance levels for each of the variables.

Table 3

Univariate F-Tests for Quality of Experience in Nonacademic Activities at School by School Context

| | School Context | | | |
| | Montessori (N = 131) | Traditional (N = 150) | | |
ESM Measure			**F-test**	**p**
Flow (%)	11.0 (1.7)	17.3 (1.6)	7.19	.008
Affect	.32 (.05)	.14 (.05)	6.87	.009
Potency	.22 (.05)	.16 (.05)	1.90	NS
Motivation	−.03 (.05)	−.12 (.05)	1.70	NS
Salience	−.38 (.04)	−.19 (.04)	11.14	.001

Means are z-scores (i.e., zero is average experience for the entire week) and are adjusted for the covariates gender, parental education, and ethnicity. Standard errors appear in parentheses. Flow percent indicates the amount of time students indicated above-average challenge and skill while doing nonacademic activities.

Consistent with the relaxed nature of the activities, students in both school contexts reported higher levels of affect, potency, and intrinsic motivation in nonacademic activities, as well as lower levels of salience and flow (see table 2). In contrast to the findings for academic work, students in both groups reported similar levels of intrinsic motivation and potency. In addition, students in the traditional group reported significantly more flow in nonacademic activities, although the overall percentage of flow was low. Similar to the findings for academic activities, the Montessori students reported better overall affect, and despite the fact that levels of salience were below average for both student groups, the traditional students reported that their activities were more important. (pp. 360–61)

Result

Result

Result

Result

You'll notice that in this section, the researchers remain focused on reporting their findings. They do not, at this point, go into great detail about what those findings mean or what the implications are.

Cassidy, Brown, and Jackson also report their findings in a Results section, and they subdivide their findings into a number of areas of inquiry (identified in the subheadings) examined as part of their larger study. Only the results are presented at this point in the article; they are not yet interpreted:

RESULTS

Familiarity with technology

Despite the district's emphasis on technology, the educators (except for two younger teachers and one vice-principal) indicated that they were not very familiar with chat rooms and blogs, were moderately familiar with YouTube and Facebook and were most familiar with the older forms of communication—email and cellular phones.

Results

Cyberbullying policies

We asked respondents about specific cyberbullying policies in place at their school and their perceived effectiveness. Despite the district's priorities around technology, neither the school district nor either school had a specific cyberbullying policy; instead educators were supposed to follow the district's bullying policy. When VP17-A was asked if the district's bullying handbook effectively addressed the problem of cyberbullying, he replied: "It effectively addresses the people that are identified as bullying others [but] it doesn't address the educational side of it . . . about what is proper use of the Internet as a tool."

P14-B wanted to see a new policy put in place that was flexible enough to deal with the different situations as they arose. VP19-B thought that a cyberbullying policy should be separate from a face-to-face bullying policy since the impact on students is different. He also felt that there should be a concerted district policy regarding "risk assessment in which you have a team that's trained at determining the level of threat and it should be taken very seriously whether it's a phone threat, a verbal threat, or a cyber threat." Participants indicated that they had not considered the idea of a separate cyberbullying policy before the interview, with several commenting that they now saw it as important. (pp. 524, 526–27)

Result

Result

Visual Representations of Data The Results section of a report may also provide data sets in the form of tables and/or figures. Figures may appear as photos, images, charts, or graphs. When you find visual representations of data in texts, it's important that you pause to consider these elements carefully. Researchers typically use *tables* when they want to make data sets, or raw data, available for comparisons. These tables, such as the one Rathunde and Csikszentmihalyi include in their study of middle school students' motivation, present variables in columns and rows, as seen above.

Table 1

Comparison of Montessori and Traditional Middle School Samples on Various Background Variables

Background Variable	School Context	
	Montessori	Traditional
Ethnicity (%):		
European American	72.6	74.9
Asian American	10.2	7.8
Latino	1.9	3.4
African American	12.7	12.6
Other	2.6	1.2
Parental education	5.5	5.4
Home resources	29.6	29.5
School-related:		
Parental discussion	2.41	2.49
Parental involvement	2.11	2.10
Parental monitoring	1.69	1.66
Number of siblings	1.8	2.0
Mother employment (%)	71.6	74.1
Father employment (%)	83.7	88.1
Intact (two-parent) family (%)	81.0	84.0
Grade point average	1.97	1.93

Note. None of the differences reported in the table were statistically significant.

In this instance, the "background variable[s]" used to describe the student populations are listed in the column, and the rows compare values from two "school context[s]," Montessori and traditional schools. The table's title reveals its overall purpose: to compare "Montessori and Traditional Middle School Samples on Various Background Variables." Rathunde and Csikszentmihalyi describe the contents of their table this way:

> Table 1 summarizes this comparison. The ethnic diversity of the samples was almost identical. Both shared similar advantages in terms of high parental

education (baccalaureate degree or higher), high rates of two-parent families, high family resources, and other indicators of strong parental involvement in their children's education. Although only one-third of the Montessori students received grades, *t*-tests indicated that both samples were comprised of good students (i.e., they received about half As and half Bs). (p. 356)

Researchers use *figures* when they want to highlight the results of research or the derived relationships between data sets or variables. *Graphs*, a type of figure, contain two axes—the horizontal x-axis and the vertical y-axis. The relationship between variables on these axes is indicated by the cells of overlap between the two axes in the body of the figure. Conventionally, the *x-axis* identifies an independent variable, or a variable that can be controlled; by contrast, the *y-axis* identifies the dependent variable, which is dependent on the variable identified in the x-axis. Here's a figure from Rathunde and Csikszentmihalyi's study:

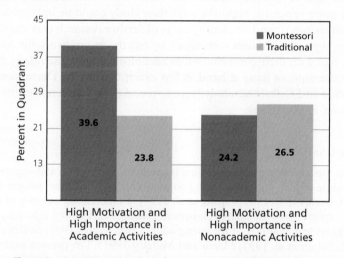

Figure 2. Percentage of undivided interest in academic and nonacademic activities

As with tables, the titles of figures reveal their overall purpose. In this case, the researchers demonstrate the "[p]ercentage of undivided interest in academic and nonacademic activities." Reading the figure, in this instance, comes down to identifying the percentage of "undivided interest" that students in Montessori and traditional middle schools (revealed in different colors, as the legend indicates) expressed in the quadrants "High Motivation and High Importance in Academic Activities" and "High Motivation and High Importance in Nonacademic Activities." Colored cells in the body of the graph reveal the percentages. Rathunde and Csikszentmihalyi note about this figure: "[O]n the key variable undivided interest, students in the traditional group reported a slightly higher percent of high-motivation and high-importance activities; this noteworthy change from academic activities is illustrated in figure 2" (p. 361).

Whenever you see charts or figures in social science reports, you should take time to do the following:

- study the titles carefully
- look for legends, which provide keys to understanding elements in the chart or figure
- identify the factors or variables represented, and understand how those factors or variables are related, as well as how they are measured
- look closely for possible patterns

Discussion

The Discussion of a social science report explains the significance of the findings in light of the study's aims. This is also where researchers reflect on the study more generally, highlight ways their study could be improved (often called "limitations"), and/or identify areas of further research that the study has brought to light. Researchers sometimes lay out the groundwork for continued research, based on their contribution, as part of the ongoing scholarly conversation on the topic or issue at hand. A few excerpts from the Discussion section of Rathunde and Csikszentmihalyi's study reveal their adherence to these conventional expectations:

DISCUSSION

Reveals why their study is important to the ongoing conversation on this topic

Given the well-documented decline in students' motivation and engagement in middle school, and the ongoing emphasis on middle school reform (Cross 1990; Eccles et al. 1993; Lipsitz et al. 1997), an increasing number of studies have explored how to change classroom practices and school cultures in ways that provide a healthier fit for young adolescents (Ames 1992; Eccles et al. 1993; Felner et al. 1997; Maehr and Midgley 1991). The present study adds to this area of research by comparing the motivation and quality of experience of students from five Montessori middle schools and six traditional middle schools. (p. 362)

. . .

Discusses important findings

Results from the study showed that while engaged in academic work at school, Montessori students reported higher affect, potency (i.e., feeling alert and energetic), intrinsic motivation (i.e., enjoyment, interest), and flow experience than students from traditional middle schools. (p. 363)

. . .

Identifies limitations in the study and an area for possible future research

The present study did not look at whether such experiential differences translated into positive achievement and behavioral outcomes for the students. This is an important topic for future research. (p. 363)

Following are some additional structural conventions to consider when you are reading or writing in the fields of the social sciences.

OTHER STRUCTURAL CONVENTIONS

Conclusion

On occasion, researchers separate out coverage of the implications of their findings (as part of a Discussion section) from other elements in the Discussion. When this occurs, these researchers typically construct a separate Conclusion section in which they address conventional content coverage of their study's limitations, as well as their findings' implications for future research.

Titles

Research reports in the social sciences, as in the natural sciences, tend to have rather straightforward titles that are concise and that contain key words highlighting important components of the study. Titles in the social sciences tend not to be creative or rhetorical, although there is a greater tendency toward creativity in titles in qualitative studies, which are more typically language driven than numerically driven. The title of Barbara Allen's study reported in the academic journal *Technology in Society*, for instance, identifies the central issues her study examined as well as the study location: "Environmental Justice, Local Knowledge, and After-Disaster Planning in New Orleans." Similarly, the title of Rathunde and Csikszentmihalyi's article is concise in its identification of the study's purpose: "Middle School Students' Motivation and Quality of Experience: A Comparison of Montessori and Traditional School Environments."

Abstracts

Another structural feature of reports in the social sciences is the abstract. **Abstracts** typically follow the title of the report and the identification of the researchers. They provide a brief overview of the study, explaining the topic or issue under study, the specific purpose of the study and its methods, and offering a concise statement of the results. These elements are usually summarized in a few sentences. Abstracts can be useful to other researchers who want to determine if a study might prove helpful for their own work or if the methods might inform their own research purposes. Abstracts thus serve to promote collaboration among researchers. Though abstracts appear at the beginning of research reports, they're typically written after both the study and the research report are otherwise completed. Abstracts reduce the most important parts of a study into a compact space.

The following example from Rathunde and Csikszentmihalyi illustrates a number of the conventions of abstracts:

> This study compared the motivation and quality of experience of demographically matched students from Montessori and traditional middle school programs. Approximately 290 students responded to the Experience Sampling Method (ESM) and filled out questionnaires. Multivariate analyses showed

The study's purpose is identified.

Methods are briefly outlined.

that the Montessori students reported greater affect, potency (i.e., feeling energetic), intrinsic motivation, flow experience, and undivided interest (i.e., the combination of high intrinsic motivation and high salience or importance) while engaged in academic activities at school. The traditional middle school students reported higher salience while doing academic work; however, such responses were often accompanied by low intrinsic motivation. When engaged in informal, nonacademic activities, the students in both school contexts reported similar experiences. These results are discussed in terms of current thought on motivation in education and middle school reform.

Results are provided.

Implications of the research findings are noted.

Acknowledgments

Acknowledgment sections sometimes appear at the end of social science reports. Usually very brief, they offer a quick word of thanks to organizations and/or individuals who have helped to fund a study, collect data, review the study, or provide another form of assistance during the production of the study. This section can be particularly telling if you're interested in the source of a researcher's funding. Barbara Allen's "Environmental Justice, Local Knowledge, and After-Disaster Planning in New Orleans" contains the following Acknowledgments section:

> ### ACKNOWLEDGMENTS
>
> I would like to thank Carl Mitcham, Robert Frodeman, and all the participants of the Cities and Rivers II conference in New Orleans, March 21–25, 2006. The ideas and discussions at this event enabled me to think in a more interdisciplinary manner about the disaster....
>
> In addition, I would like to thank the American Academy in Rome for giving me the time to think and write about this important topic. Conversations with my colleagues at the academy were invaluable in helping me to think in new ways about historic preservation and rebuilding. (p. 159)

References

The documentation system most often used in the social sciences is the style regulated by the American Psychological Association, which is referred to as **APA format**. (For more details about APA style conventions, see p. 100 of Chapter 5 and the Appendix.) Studies in the social sciences end with a References page that follows APA guidelines — or the formatting style used in the study, if not APA.

Appendices

Social science research reports sometimes end with one or more appendices. Items here are often referenced within the body of the report itself, as appropriate. These items may include additional data sets, calculations, interview questions, diagrams, and images. The materials typically offer context or support for discussions that occur in the body of a research report.

INSIDE WORK   **Observing Structural Features**

> Although we've discussed a number of structural expectations for reports in the social sciences, we need to stress again that these expectations are conventional. As such, you'll likely encounter numerous studies in the social sciences that rely on only a few of these structural features or that alter the conventional expectations in light of the researchers' particular aims. For this activity, we'd like you to do the following.
>
> - Select a social science topic.
> - Locate two articles published in peer-reviewed academic journals that address some aspect of your selected topic.
> - Compare and contrast the two articles in terms of their structural features. Note both (1) instances when the articles follow the conventional expectations for social science reporting as explained in this chapter, and (2) instances when the articles alter or diverge from these expectations. Speculate as to the authors' reasoning for following the conventional expectations or diverging from them. ▶

LANGUAGE CONVENTIONS

As with structural conventions, the way social scientists use language can vary widely with respect to differing audiences and/or genres. Nevertheless, we can explore several language-level conventional expectations for writing in the social sciences. In the following sections, we consider the use of both active and passive voice, as well as the use of hedging (or hedge words) to limit the scope and applicability of assertions.

Active and Passive Voice

Many students have had the experience of receiving a graded paper back from an English teacher in high school and discovering that a sentence or two was marked for awkward or inappropriate use of the passive voice. This problem occurs fairly often as students acclimate their writing to differing disciplinary communities. As we discussed in Chapter 7, the passive voice usually appears with less frequency in the fields of the humanities, but writers in the social sciences and natural sciences use it more frequently, and with good purpose. (For a fuller discussion and examples of the differences between active and passive voice constructions, see pp. 167–68 in Chapter 7.)

You may wonder why anyone would want to add words unnecessarily or remove altogether the actor/agent from a sentence. The passive voice is often preferable in writing in the social sciences and natural sciences because, although it may seem wordy or unclear to some readers in some instances, skillful use of the passive voice can actually foster a sense that researchers are acting objectively or with neutrality. This does not mean that natural or social scientists are averse to the active voice. However, in particular instances, the passive voice can go a long way toward supporting an ethos of objectivity, and its use appears most commonly in the Methods sections of social science reports. Consider these two sentences that might appear in the Methods section of a hypothetical social science report:

Active Voice: We asked participants to identify the factors that most influenced their decision.

Passive Voice: Participants were asked to identify the factors that most influenced their decision.

With the agent, *we*, removed, the sentence in passive voice deemphasizes the researchers conducting the study. In this way, the researchers maintain more of a sense of objectivity or neutrality in their report.

Hedging

Another language feature common to writing in the social sciences is hedging. Hedging typically occurs when researchers want to make a claim or propose an explanation but also want to be extremely careful not to overstep the scope of their findings based on their actual data set. Consider the following sentences:

Participants seemed to be anxious about sharing their feelings on the topic.
Participants were anxious about sharing their feelings on the topic.

When you compare the two, you'll notice that the first sentence "hedges" against making a broad or sweeping claim about the participants. The use of *seemed to be* is a hedge against overstepping, or saying something that may or may not be absolutely true in every case. Other words or phrases that are often used to hedge include the following, just to name a handful:

probably	perhaps
some	possibly
sometimes	might
likely	it appears that
apparently	partially

Considering that social scientists make claims about human behavior, and that participants in a study may or may not agree with the conclusions, it's perhaps not surprising that writers in these fields often make use of hedging.

INSIDE WORK   Observing Language Features

Use the two articles you located for the previous Inside Work exercise, in which you compared and contrasted their structural conventions.

- This time, study the language of the articles for instances of the two language conventions we've discussed in this section. Try to determine in what sections of the reports passive voice and hedging occur most frequently.

- Offer a rationale for your findings. If you find more instances of the use of passive voice in the Methods sections than in the Results sections, for instance, attempt to explain why that would be the case. Or, if you find more instances of verbal hedging in the Results sections than in the Methods sections, what do you think explains those findings? ❱

REFERENCE CONVENTIONS

The style guide for writing followed in most (but not all) social science fields is the *Publication Manual of the American Psychological Association* (APA). Many referencing conventions of the social sciences are governed by the APA, and some are worth examining in more detail.

In-Text Documentation

One of the distinguishing features of the APA method for documenting sources that are paraphrased, summarized, or cited as part of a report is the inclusion of a source's year of publication as part of the parenthetical notation in or at the end of a sentence in which a source is used. We can compare this to the MLA documentation system described in Chapter 6 through the following examples:

MLA: The study reports that "in some participants, writing block appears to be tied to exhaustion" (Jacobs 23).

APA: The study reports that "in some participants, writing block appears to be tied to exhaustion" (Jacobs, 2009, p. 23).

Although these examples by no means illustrate all the differences between MLA and APA styles of documentation, they do highlight the elevated importance that social science fields place on the year of a source's publication. Why? Imagine that you're reading a sociological study conducted in 2010 that examines the use of tobacco products among teenagers. The study references the finding of a similar study from 1990. By seeing the date of the referenced study in the in-text citation, readers can quickly consider the usefulness of the 1990 study for the one being reported on. Social scientists value recency, or the most current data possible, and their documentation requirements reflect this preference.

Summary and Paraphrase

Another reference distinction among the academic domains concerns how writers reference others' ideas. You've probably had experience writing papers for teachers who required you to cite sources as support for your ideas. You may have done this by copying the language directly from a source. If so, then you noted that these words belonged to another person by putting quotation marks around them and by adding a parenthetical comment identifying the source of the cited language. These practices hold true for writers in the social sciences as well.

However, as you become more familiar with the reference practices of researchers in these fields, you'll discover that social scientists quote researchers in other fields far less frequently than scholars in the humanities do. Why is this so? For humanist scholars, language is of the utmost importance, and how someone conveys an idea can seem almost inseparable from the idea being conveyed. Additionally, for humanists, language is often the "unit of measure"—that is, *how* someone says something (like a novelist or a poet) is actually *what* is being studied. Typically, this is not the case for social science researchers (with the exception of fields such as linguistics and communication, although they primarily address how study participants say something and not how prior research reported its findings). Instead, social scientists tend to be much more interested in other researchers' methodology and findings than they are in the language through which those methods or finding are conveyed. As a result, social scientists are more likely to summarize or paraphrase source materials than to quote them directly.

INSIDE WORK **Observing Reference Features**

In this section, we've suggested that two areas of conventional reference features in social science writing are (1) the elevated position of year of publication in the internal documentation of source material, and (2) the preference among social scientists for summarizing and paraphrasing sources.

- Use the same two studies that you examined for the last two Inside Work activities.
- Based on the principle that social scientists are concerned with the recency of research in their areas, examine the References page (the ending bibliography) for each study. How does the form of entries on the References page reflect the social science concern with the recency of sources?
- Look more closely at the introductions of the two articles, and note the number of times in each article another source is referenced. Count the number of times these sources are paraphrased, summarized, or quoted directly. Based on your findings, what can you conclude about the ways social scientists reference source material? ❥

Genres of Writing in the Social Sciences

Scholars in the social sciences share the results of their research in various ways. As Aya Matsuda reveals in her Insider's View, social scientists write in a variety of forms for differing venues. They might, for instance, present their work at a conference or publish their research results in a journal or a book.

In this section, we offer descriptions of, and steps for producing, two of the most common types of writing, or genres, required of students in introductory-level courses in the social sciences. These are the literature review and the theory-response paper. As genres, literature reviews and responses to social science theories sometimes appear as parts of other, longer works. Sometimes, though, they stand alone as complete works.

THE LITERATURE REVIEW

The literature review (also referred to as a review of scholarship) is one of the most common genres you will encounter in academic writing. Though this chapter is dedicated to writing in the social sciences, and the literature review genre occurs quite frequently in the social sciences, you can find evidence of reviews of scholarship in virtually every academic field—including the humanities, the natural sciences, and applied fields. The skills required for this genre are thus important to the kinds of inquiry that occur across all the academic disciplines.

At its core, the **literature review** is an analysis of published resources related to a specific topic. The purposes of a literature review may vary: students and researchers may conduct a review of scholarship simply to establish what research has already been conducted on a topic, or the review may make a case for how new research can fill in gaps or advance knowledge about a topic. In the former situation, the resulting literature review may appear as a freestanding piece of writing; in the latter, a briefer review of scholarship may be embedded at the start (usually in the introduction) of a research study.

In fact, most published scholarly articles include a review of literature in the first few pages. Besides serving as a means to identify a gap in the scholarship or a place for new scholarship, a literature review helps to establish

Insider's View
There are many kinds of writing that applied linguists do
AYA MATSUDA, LINGUISTICS

COURTESY OF AYA MATSUDA

"My writing is mostly in the form of research papers that are published as articles in scholarly journals or chapters in scholarly books. I also review other applied linguists' manuscripts and write evaluation reports on them, usually to help journal editors decide whether or not to publish manuscripts in their journals. I also write book reviews that are published in scholarly journals. But because of the 'real-life' nature of the kinds of questions my field addresses, there are many other kinds of writing that applied linguists do. Textbooks, articles in newspapers and general magazines, policies, consultation reports, and public education materials (e.g., brochures) are some examples of other types of writing that my colleagues do. Grant writing is also an important kind of writing that researchers in my field do."

researchers' credibility by demonstrating their awareness of what has been discovered about a particular topic or issue. It further respectfully acknowledges the hard work of others within the community of scholarship. Equally important, the literature review illustrates how previous studies interrelate. A good literature review may examine how prior research is similar and different, or it may suggest how a group of researchers' work developed over several years and how scholars have advanced the work of others.

Insider Example
An Embedded Literature Review

Read the first two paragraphs of "Happiness in Everyday Life: The Uses of Experience Sampling," a social science study reported by Mihaly Csikszentmihalyi and Jeremy Hunter, as an example of a review of scholarship that is embedded within a larger study report. As you read, consider the purposes of a literature review to which it responds, including:

- reviewing what is known on a topic or issue
- identifying a gap in scholarship
- establishing the researchers' ethos

Excerpt from Happiness in Everyday Life: The Uses of Experience Sampling

MIHALY CSIKSZENTMIHALYI AND JEREMY HUNTER

MIHALY CSIKSZENTMIHALYI

PHOTO BY WILLIAM VASTA

INTRODUCTION

Current understanding of human happiness points at five major effects on this emotion. These are, moving from those most impervious to change to those that are most under personal control: genetic determinants, macro-social conditions, chance events, proximal environment, and personality. It is not unlikely that, as behavioral geneticists insist, a "set level" coded in our chromosomes accounts for perhaps as much as half of the variance in self-reported happiness (Lykken & Tellegen, 1996; Tellegen et al., 1988). These effects are probably mediated by temperamental traits like extraversion, which are partly genetically determined and which are in turn linked to happiness (Myers, 1993). Cross-national comparisons suggest that macro-social conditions such as extreme poverty, war, and social injustice are all obstacles to happiness (Inglehart &

> This section of the study's introduction establishes what is known about the topic at hand. It reviews the scholarship of others.

Klingemann, 2000; Veenhoven, 1995). Chance events like personal tragedies, illness, or sudden strokes of good fortune may drastically affect the level of happiness, but apparently these effects do not last long (Brickman et al., 1978; Diener, 2000). One might include under the heading of the proximal environment the social class, community, family, and economic situation—in other words, those factors in the immediate surroundings that may have an impact on a person's well-being. And finally, habits and coping behaviors developed by the individual will have an important effect. Hope, optimism, and the ability to experience flow can be learned and thus moderate one's level of happiness (Csikszentmihalyi, 1997; Seligman, 2002).

In this paper, we present a method that allows investigators to study the impact of momentary changes in the environment on people's happiness levels, as well as its more lasting, trait-like correlates. Research on happiness generally considers this emotion to be a personal trait. The overall happiness level of individuals is measured by a survey or questionnaire, and then "happy" people—those who score higher on a one-time response scale—are contrasted with less happy ones. Whatever distinguishes the two groups is then assumed to be a condition affecting happiness. This perspective is a logical outcome of the methods used, namely, one-time measures. If a person's happiness level is measured only once, it is by definition impossible to detect intra-individual variations. Yet, we know quite well that emotional states, including happiness, are quite volatile and responsive to environmental conditions.

> How does this review of previous scholarship affect your view of the writers? What does it say about them?

> Reveals the researchers' purpose in the context of the review of scholarship. Identifies a space, or gap, in the scholarship for investigation.

WRITING A LITERATURE REVIEW

The scope of a freestanding literature review can vary greatly, depending on the knowledge and level of interest of the investigator conducting the review. For instance, you may have very little knowledge about autism, so your review of the scholarship might be aimed at learning about various aspects of the condition and issues related to it. If this is the case, your research would cast a pretty wide net. However, let's say you're quite familiar with certain critical aspects of issues related to autism and are interested in one aspect in particular—for example, the best therapies for addressing autism in young children. If this is the case, then you could conduct a review of scholarship with a more focused purpose, narrowing your net to only the studies that address your specific interest. Regardless of the scope of your research interest, though, literature reviews should begin with a clear sense of your topic. One way to narrow the focus of your topic is by proposing one or more research questions about it. (See Chapter 5 for more support for crafting such research questions.)

Once you've clearly established your topic, the next step is to conduct your research. The research you discover and choose to read, which may be quite substantial for a literature review, is chosen according to the scope of your research interest. (For help in narrowing a search based on key terms in your research question, see Chapter 5.) Here are some tips to conducting research:

- As you search for and review possible sources, pay particular attention to the *abstracts* of studies, as they may help you quickly decide if a study is right for your purposes.

- Unless your review of scholarship targets the tracing of a particular thread of research across a range of years, you should probably focus on the most current research available.

- After you've examined and gathered a range of source materials, determine the best way to keep track of the ideas you discover. Many students find this is a good time to produce an annotated bibliography as a first step in creating a literature review. (See Chapter 5, pp. 101–2 for more help on constructing annotated bibliographies.)

Another useful strategy for organizing your sources is a **source synthesis chart**. We recommend this as a way to visualize the areas of overlap in your research, whether for a broad focus (*What are researchers studying with regard to autism?*) or a more narrow one (*What are the best therapies for addressing autism in young children?*). Here's an abbreviated example of a source synthesis chart for a broad review of scholarship on autism:

	Topics We Expect to Emerge in Scholarship			
Authors of Study	*Issues of Diagnosis*	*Treatments*	*Debate over Causes*	*Wider Familial Effects*
Solomon et al. (2012)	pp. 252–55 Notes: emphasizes problems families face with diagnosis	pp. 257–60 Notes: examines and proposes strategies for family therapists	p. 253 Notes: acknowledges a series of possible contributing factors	
Vanderborght et al. (2012)		pp. 359–67 (results) Notes: examines use of robot for storytelling		
Grindle et al. (2012)		pp. 208–313 (results) Notes: school-based behavioral intervention program (ABA)		p. 229 Notes: home-based therapy programs
Lilley (2011)	pp. 135–37 Notes: explores the roles of mothers in diagnosis processes	pp. 143–51 Notes: explores rationales and lived experiences of ABA and non-ABA supporters		

In this case, the studies that we read are named in the column under "Authors of Study." The topics or issues that we anticipated would emerge from our review of the sources are shown in the top row. Based on our reading of a limited number of studies, four at this point, we can already discern a couple of areas of overlap in the scholarship: the diagnosis of autism in children, and intervention programs for children with autism. We can tell which researchers talked about what issues at any given time because we've noted the areas (by page number, along with some detail) where they addressed these issues. The empty cells in the synthesis chart reveal that our review of the sources, thus far at least, suggests there is less concern for those topics. We should note, however, that our review of sources is far from exhaustive. If you're able to create a visual representation of your research such as this one, then you're well on your way to creating a successful literature review. Keep in mind that the more detailed you can make your synthesis chart, the easier your process may be moving forward.

The last step before writing is perhaps the most challenging. You must synthesize the sources. **Synthesizing sources** is the process of identifying and describing the relationships between and among researchers' ideas or approaches: What trends emerge? Does the Grindle et al. study say something similar to the Lilley study about behavioral interventions? Something different? Do they share methods? Do they approach the issue of behavioral interventions similarly or differently? Defining the relationships between the studies and making these relationships explicit is critically important to your success. As you read the sources, you'll likely engage in an internal process of comparing and contrasting the researchers' ideas. You might even recognize similarities and differences in the researchers' approaches to the topic. Many of these ideas will probably be reflected in your synthesis chart, and you might consider color-coding (or highlighting in different colors) various cells to indicate types of relationships among the researchers you note.

A quick review of the abstract to "The Experience of Infertility: A Review of Recent Literature," a freestanding literature review published in the academic journal *Sociology of Health and Illness*, demonstrates the areas of synthesis that emerged from the professionals' examination of recent research on infertility:

> About 10 years ago Greil published a review and critique of the literature on the socio-psychological impact of infertility. He found at the time that most scholars treated infertility as a medical condition with psychological consequences rather than as a socially constructed reality. This article examines research published since the last review. More studies now place infertility within larger social contexts and social scientific frameworks, although clinical emphases persist. Methodological problems remain, but important improvements are also evident. We identify two vigorous research traditions in the social scientific study of infertility. One tradition uses primarily quantitative techniques to study clinic patients in order to improve service delivery and to

Four synthesis points: (1) more recent studies approach the topic of infertility differently; (2) there remains a focus on examining infertility from a clinical viewpoint; (3) there are still questions about research methods, but there have also been "important improvements" in methods; (4) two trends emerged from these scholars' review of the current research.

Presents conclusions reached as a result of the literature review project

assess the need for psychological counseling. The other tradition uses primarily qualitative research to capture the experiences of infertile people in a sociocultural context. We conclude that more attention is now being paid to the ways in which the experience of infertility is shaped by social context. We call for continued progress in the development of a distinctly sociological approach to infertility and for the continued integration of the two research traditions identified here.

Another example, this one a brief excerpt from the introduction to Csikszentmihalyi and Hunter's "Happiness in Everyday Life: The Uses of Experience Sampling," demonstrates the kind of synthesis that typically appears in reviews of scholarship when they're embedded as part of a larger study:

The writers indicate that there is agreement between researchers: both Inglehart & Klingemann (2000) and Veenhoven (1995) have confirmed the finding in "cross-national comparisons."

> Cross-national comparisons suggest that macro-social conditions such as extreme poverty, war, and social injustice are all obstacles to happiness (Inglehart & Klingemann, 2000; Veenhoven, 1995). Chance events like personal tragedies, illness, or sudden strokes of good fortune may drastically affect the level of happiness, but apparently these effects do not last long (Brickman et al., 1978; Diener, 2000).

Again, the writers indicate there is agreement between researchers: both Brickman et al. (1978) and Diener (2000) have confirmed this finding.

WRITING PROJECT

Writing a Literature Review

Your goal in this writing project, a freestanding literature review, is to provide an overview of the research that has been conducted on a topic of interest to you.

THE INTRODUCTION

The opening of your literature review should introduce the topic you're exploring and assess the state of the available scholarship on it: What are the current areas of interest? What are the issues or elements related to a particular topic being discussed? Is there general agreement? Are there other clear trends in the scholarship? Are there areas of convergence and divergence?

THE BODY

Paragraphs within the body of your literature review should be organized according to the issues or synthesized areas you're exploring. For example, based on the synthesis chart shown earlier, we might suggest that one of the body sections of a broadly focused review of scholarship on autism concern issues of diagnosis. We might further reveal, in our topic sentence to that section of the literature review, that we've synthesized the available research in this area and that it seems uniformly to suggest that although many factors have been studied, no credible studies establish a direct link between any contributing factor and the occurrence of autism in children. The rest of that section of our paper would explore the factors that have been examined in the research to support the claim in our topic sentence.

Keep in mind that the body paragraphs should be organized according to a claim about the topic or ideas being explored. They should not be organized merely as successive summaries of the sources. Such an organization does not promote effective synthesis.

THE CONCLUSION

Your conclusion should reiterate your overall assessment of the scholarship. Notify your readers of any gaps you've determined in the scholarship, and consider suggesting areas where future scholarship can make more contributions.

TECHNICAL CONSIDERATIONS

Keep in mind the conventions of writing in the social sciences that you've learned about throughout this chapter. Use APA documentation procedures for in-text documentation of summarized, paraphrased, and cited materials, as well as for the References page at the end of your literature review.

Insider Example
Student Literature Review

William O'Brien, a first-year writing student who had a particular interest in understanding the effects of sleep deprivation, composed the following literature review. As you read, notice how William's text indicates evidence of synthesis both between and among the sources he used to build his project. Notice also that he follows APA style conventions in his review.

Effects of Sleep Deprivation: A Literature Review

William O'Brien

North Carolina State University

Effects of Sleep Deprivation: A Literature Review

Introduction

Everybody knows the feeling of having to struggle through a long day after a night of poor sleep, or sometimes even none at all. You may feel groggy, cloudy, clumsy, or unable to think of simple things. Sometimes you may even feel completely fine but then get angry or frustrated at things that normally would not affect you. No matter how you deal with it on that particular day, the reality is that even slight sleep deprivation can have extremely negative effects on mental ability. These effects are amplified when poor sleep continues for a long period of time. In a society with an ever-increasing number of distractions, it is becoming harder for many people to get the recommended amount of sleep. Sleep issues plague the majority of the U.S. population in one way or another. The Centers for Disease Control recognizes insufficient sleep as a public health epidemic.

A lot of research is being conducted relating to sleep and sleep deprivation, and for good reason. Most researchers seem to agree that short-term sleep deprivation has purely negative effects on mental functioning in general. However, the particular types of effects caused by poor sleep are still being debated, as are the long-term implications of sleep deprivation. The questions for researchers, then, are under what circumstances do these negative effects begin to show, to what extent do they show, and most significant, what exactly are these negative effects?

Short-Term Effects of Sleep Deprivation

In order to examine the direct and immediate effects of sleep deprivation, numerous researchers rely on experimentation, to control for other variables, for results. Research by Minkel et al. (2012) identified a gap in the

The writer establishes the general topic, sleep deprivation, in the opening paragraph.

SYNTHESIS POINT: scholars agree on the negative effects of short-term sleep deprivation.

SYNTHESIS POINT: questions remain about the effects of long-term sleep deprivation.

Focuses on scholarship that uses experimental studies to examine the effects of short-term sleep deprivation.

research relating to how sleep deprivation affects the stress response (p. 1015). In order to test how inadequate sleep affects the stress response, the researchers divided healthy adults into two groups. Participants in the first group acted as the control and were allowed a 9-hour sleeping opportunity during the night. The second group was not allowed to sleep at all during that night. The next day, the participants completed stressful mental tasks (primarily math) and were asked to report their stress levels and mood via visual scales (Minkel et al., 2012, pp. 1016-1017). The researchers hypothesized that insufficient sleep would increase the stress response to each stressor as compared to the rested group, and that sleep loss would increase the stress response in proportion to the severity of the stressor (p. 1016). Their findings, however, showed that while the negative response to stressors was more profound for the sleep-deprived group, the differences in stress response between groups were not significant for the high-stressor condition. Still, the research clearly showed that sleep-deprived people have "significantly greater subjective stress, anger, and anxiety" in response to low-level stressors (p. 1019).

Links the two studies reviewed according to their similar focus on short-term effects of sleep deprivation

Research by Jugovac and Cavallero (2012) also focused on the immediate effects of sleep deprivation on attention. This study's purpose was to research the effects of sleep deprivation on attention through three attentional networks: phasic alerting, covert orienting, and executive control (Jugovac & Cavallero, 2012, p. 115). The study tested 30 young adults using the Attention Network Test (ANT), the Stanford Sleepiness Scale (SSS), and the Global Vigor-Affect Scale (GVA) before and after a 24-hour sleep deprivation period (p. 116). (All participants were subjected to sleep deprivation, because the tests before the sleep deprivation served as the control.) The findings built upon the idea that sleep deprivation decreases vigilance and that it impairs the "executive control" attentional network, while appearing to leave the other components (alerting and orienting) relatively unchanged (pp. 121-122). These findings help explain how one night of missed sleep negatively affects a person's attention, by distinguishing the effects on each of the three particular attentional networks.

Research by Giesbrecht, Smeets, Leppink, Jelicic, and Merckelbach (2013) focused on the effects that short-term sleep deprivation has on dissociation. This research is interesting and different from the other research in that it connects sleep deprivation to mental illness rather than just temporarily reduced mental functioning. The researchers used 25 healthy undergraduate students and kept all participants awake throughout one night. Four different scales were used to record their feelings and dissociative reactions while being subjected to two different cognitive tasks (Giesbrecht et al., 2013, pp. 150-152). The cognitive tasks completed before the night of sleep deprivation were used to compare the results of the cognitive tasks completed after the night of sleep deprivation. Although the study was small and the implications are still somewhat unclear, the study showed a clear link between sleep deprivation and dissociative symptoms (pp. 156-158).

> The writer links this study to the continuing discussion of short-term effects of sleep deprivation but also notes a difference.

It is clear that sleep deprivation negatively affects people in many different ways. These researchers each considered a different type of specific effect, and together they form a wide knowledge base supporting the idea that even a very short-term (24-hour) loss of sleep for a healthy adult may have multiple negative impacts on mental and emotional well-being. These effects include increased anxiety, anger,

> This paragraph provides a summative synthesis, or an overview of the findings among the sources reviewed.

and stress in response to small stressors (Minkel et al., 2012), inhibited attention—the executive control attentional network more specifically (Jugovac & Cavallero, 2012)—and increased dissociative symptoms (Giesbrecht et al., 2013).

Long-Term Effects of Sleep Deprivation

Although the research on short-term effects of sleep deprivation reveals numerous negative consequences, there may be other, less obvious, implications that studies on short-term effect cannot illuminate. In order to better understand these other implications, we must examine research relating to the possible long-term effects of limited sleep. Unfortunately, long-term sleep deprivation experiments do not seem to have been done and are probably not possible (due to ethical reasons and safety reasons, among other factors). A study by Duggan, Reynolds, Kern, and Friedman (2014) pointed out the general lack of previous research into the long-term effects of sleep deprivation, but it examined whether there was a link between average sleep duration during childhood and life-long mortality risk (p. 1195). The researchers analyzed data from 1,145 participants in the Terman Life Cycle Study from the early 1900s, which measured bedtime and wake time along with year of death. The amount of sleep was adjusted by age in order to find the deviations from average sleep time for each age group. The data were also separated by sex (Duggan et al., 2014, pp. 1196-1197). The results showed that, for males, sleeping either more or less than the regular amount of time for each age group correlated with an increased life-long mortality risk (p. 1199). Strangely, this connection was not present for females. For males, however, this is a very important finding. Since we can surmise that the childhood sleep patterns are independent of and unrelated to any underlying health issues that ultimately cause the deaths later

The writer shifts to an examination of the long-term effects of sleep deprivation and acknowledges a shift in the methods for these studies.

on in life, it is more reasonable to assume causation rather than simply correlation. Thus, the pattern that emerged may demonstrate that too little, or too much, sleep during childhood can cause physiological issues, leading to death earlier in life, which also reaffirms the idea that sleep is extremely important for maintaining good health.

    While this study examined the relationship between sleep duration and death, a study by Kelly and El-Sheikh (2014) examined the relationship between sleep and a slightly less serious, but still very important, subject: the adjustment and development of children in school over a period of time. The study followed 176 third grade children (this number dropped to 113 by the end of the study) as they progressed through school for five years, recording sleep patterns and characteristics of adjustment (Kelly & El-Sheikh, 2014, pp. 1137-1139). Sleep was recorded both subjectively through self-reporting and objectively though "actigraphy" in order to assess a large variety of sleep parameters (p. 1137). The study results indicated that reduced sleep time and poorer-quality sleep are risk factors for problems adjusting over time to new situations. The results also indicate that the opposite effect is true, but to a lesser extent (p. 1146).

    From this research, we gain the understanding that sleep deprivation and poor sleep quality are related to problems adjusting over time. This effect is likely due to the generally accepted idea that sleep deprivation negatively affects cognitive performance and emotional regulation, as described in the Kelly and El-Sheikh article (2014, pp. 1144-1145). If cognitive performance and emotional regulation are negatively affected by a lack of sleep, then it makes sense that the sleep-deprived child would struggle to adjust over time as compared to a well-rested child. This hypothesis has

> Establishes one of the study's central findings related to long-term effects of sleep deprivation

important implications. It once again affirms the idea that receiving the appropriate amount of quality sleep is very important for developing children. This basic idea does not go against the research by Duggan et al. (2014) in any way; rather, it complements it. The main difference between each study is that the research by Duggan et al. shows that too much sleep can also be related to a greater risk of death earlier in life. Together, both articles provide evidence that deviation from the appropriate amount of sleep causes very negative long-term effects, including, but certainly not limited to, worse adjustment over time (Kelly & El-Sheikh, 2014) and increased mortality rates (Duggan et al., 2014).

Provides a summative synthesis that examines relationships between the sources and considers implications of findings

Conclusion

This research provides great insight into the short-term and long-term effects of sleep deprivation. Duggan et al. (2014) showed increased mortality rates among people who slept too much as well as too little. This result could use some additional research. Through the analysis of each article, we see just how damaging sleep deprivation can be, even after a short period of time, and thus it is important to seriously consider preventative measures. While sleep issues can manifest themselves in many different ways, especially in legitimate sleep disorders such as insomnia, just the simple act of not allowing oneself to get enough sleep every night can have significant negative effects. Building on this, there seems to be a general lack of discussion on *why* people (who do not have sleep disorders) do not get enough time to sleep. One possible reason is the ever-increasing number of distractions, especially in the form of electronics, that may lead to overstimulation. Another answer may be that high demands placed on students and adults through school and work, respectively, do not give them time to sleep enough.

Conclusion acknowledges what appears as a gap in the scholarship reviewed

The most probable, yet most generalized, answer, however, is that people simply do not appropriately manage their time in order to get enough sleep. People seem to prioritize everything else ahead of sleeping, thus causing the damaging effects of sleep deprivation to emerge. Regardless, this research is valuable for anyone who wants to live a healthy lifestyle and function at full mental capacity. Sleep deprivation seems to have solely negative consequences; thus, it is in every person's best interests to get a full night of quality sleep as often as possible.

References

Duggan, K., Reynolds, C., Kern, M., & Friedman, H. (2014). Childhood sleep duration and lifelong mortality risk. *Health Psychology*, *33*(10), 1195-1203. https://doi.org /10.1037/hea0000078

Giesbrecht, T., Smeets, T., Leppink, J., Jelicic, M., & Merckelbach, H. (2013). Acute dissociation after one night of sleep loss. *Psychology of Consciousness: Theory, Research, and Practice*, *1*(S), 150-159. https://doi.org /10.1037/2326-5523.1.S.150

Jugovac, D., & Cavallero, C. (2012). Twenty-four hours of total sleep deprivation selectively impairs attentional networks. *Experimental Psychology*, *59*(3), 115-123. https://doi.org/10.1027/1618-3169/a000133

Kelly, R., & El-Sheikh, M. (2014). Reciprocal relations between children's sleep and their adjustment over time. *Developmental Psychology*, *50*(4), 1137-1147. https://doi .org/10.1037/a0034501

Minkel, J., Banks, S., Htaik, O., Moreta, M., Jones, C., McGlinchey, E., Simpson, N., & Dinges, D. (2012). Sleep deprivation and stressors: Evidence for elevated negative affect in response to mild stressors when sleep deprived. *Emotion*, *12*(5), 1015-1020. https://doi.org/10.1037 /a0026871

THEORY RESPONSE ESSAY

Faculty in the fields of the social sciences often ask students to apply a social science theory to their own experiences. Psychology, sociology, and communication professors may ask students to use a psychological, sociological, or communication theory as a lens through which to explain their own or others' behaviors. Assignments like these involve writing a **theory response essay**. These assignments are popular for a number of reasons: (1) they allow students to engage with the fundamental elements of social sciences (theories); (2) they allow students to attend to the basic processes of data collection that are common in the social sciences; and (3) they are often quite engaging for faculty to read and are among the most interesting for students to write.

Whether you're using elements of Freud's dream theories to help understand your own dreams or you're using an interpersonal communication theory to understand why people so easily engage with you, the theory you're working with provides the frame for your analysis of some event or action. The theory is the core of any theory response.

Precisely because the theory is the core of such a writing project, it's crucial that in the beginning stage of such a project, you work with a theory that is actually applicable to the event, action, or phenomenon you want to understand better. You also want to choose a theory that genuinely interests you. Luckily, theories of human behavior and human system interactions abound. If you aren't assigned a theory for the project, then consider the places where you might go about locating a workable theory. Textbooks in the social sciences frequently make reference to theories, and numerous academic websites maintain lists and explanations of social science theories. Here are a few categories of theories that students often find interesting:

birth order theories	friendship theories
parenting style theories	stage theories of grieving
addiction theories	

If you're unable to locate a workable theory that's "ready-made" for application to some experience(s), then consider building a theory based on your reading of a social science study. Though this certainly makes completing the assignment challenging, it is not without rewards.

Personal Experience

Regardless of whether you're working with a particular theory or constructing a theory of behavior based on one or more studies, consider making a list of the "moments" or events in your life that the theory might help you understand further. Your next step might be to write out detailed descriptions of those events as you see or remember them. Capture as much detail as you can, especially if you're writing from memory. Then apply the theory (all of its component parts) to your event or moment to see what it can illuminate for you: Where does it really help you understand something? Where does it fail to help? How might the theory need to change to account for your experiences?

Others' Experiences

Some instructors might ask you to collect and analyze the experiences of others. If you're assigned to do this, then you'll need to consider a data-collection method very carefully and ask your instructor if there are specific procedures at your institution that you should follow when collecting data from other people. We recommend, for now, that you think about the methods most commonly associated with qualitative research: observations, interviews, and open-ended surveys. These rich data-producing methods are most likely to provide the level of detail about others' experiences needed to evaluate the elements of your theory. Trying to understand others' experiences in light of the theory you're working with means considering the same analytical questions that you applied to your own experiences: Where does the theory really help you understand something? Where does it fail to help? How might the theory need to change to account for the experiences of those in your study?

WRITING PROJECT

Writing a Theory Response

The goal of this writing project is to apply a theoretical framework from an area of the social sciences to your own experiences, to the experiences of others, or to both. The first step is to choose a theoretical framework that has some relevance to you, providing ample opportunity to reflect on and write about your own experiences in relation to the theory.

THE INTRODUCTION

The introduction to your study should introduce readers to the theory and explain all of its essential elements. You should also be clear about whether you're applying the theory to your own experiences, to the experiences of others, or to both. In light of the work you did applying the theory, formulate a thesis that assesses the value of the theory for helping to understand the "moments," events, or phenomena you studied.

THE BODY

The body can be organized in a number of ways. If your theory has clear stages or elements, then you can explain each one and apply it to relevant parts of your experiences or those of others. If the theory operates in such a way that it's difficult to break into parts or stages or elements, then consider whether or not it's better to have subheadings that identify either (1) the themes that emerged from your application, or (2) your research subjects (by pseudonym). In this case, your body sections would be more like case studies. Ultimately, the organization strategy you choose will depend on the nature of the theory you're applying and the kinds of events you apply it to. The body of your project should establish connections among the theory's component elements.

THE CONCLUSION

The conclusion of your study should assert your overall assessment of the theory's usefulness. Reiterate how the theory was useful and how it wasn't. Make recommendations for how it might need to be changed in order to account for the experiences you examined in light of the theory.

TECHNICAL CONSIDERATIONS

Keep in mind the conventions of writing in the social sciences that you've learned about throughout this chapter. Use APA documentation procedures for in-text documentation of summarized, paraphrased, and cited materials, as well as for the References page at the end of your study.

Insider Example
Student Theory Response Paper

Matt Kapadia, a first-year writing student, was interested in understanding the ways people rationalize their own successes and failures. In the following paper, he analyzes and evaluates a theory about the social science phenomenon of attribution (as described at changingminds.org) through the lenses of both his own and others' experiences. As you read Matt's paper, pay close attention to the moments when he offers evaluation of the theory. Ask yourself if his evaluation in each instance makes sense to you, based on the evidence he provides. Notice also that he follows APA style conventions in his paper.

1

Evaluation of the Attribution Theory

Matt Kapadia

Department of English, North Carolina State University

Comp II: Writing in the Disciplines

Dr. Caroline Ruiz

October 29, 2016

Evaluation of the Attribution Theory

In an attempt to get a better sense of control, human beings are constantly attributing cause to the events that happen around them (Straker, 2008). Of all the things people attribute causes to, behavior is among the most common. The attribution theory aims to explain how people attribute the causes of their own behaviors compared to the behaviors of those around them. Behaviors can be attributed to both internal and external causes. Internal causes are things that people can control or are part of their personality, whereas external causes are purely circumstantial and people have no control over the resulting events (Straker, 2008). The attribution theory uses these internal and external causes to explain its two major components: the self-serving bias and the fundamental attribution error. The self-serving bias evaluates how we attribute our own behaviors, whereas the fundamental attribution error evaluates how we attribute the behaviors of those around us (Straker, 2008). This paper evaluates how applicable the attribution theory and its components are, using examples from personal experience as well as data collected from others. Based on the findings of this evaluation, I believe the attribution theory holds true on nearly all accounts; however, the category of the self-serving bias might need revision in the specific area dealing with professionals in any field of study or in the case of professional athletes.

Attribution Theory: An Explanation

The foundation of the attribution theory is based in the nature of the causes people attribute behaviors to, whether it be internal or external. A person has no control over an external cause (Straker, 2008). An example would be a student failing a math test because the instructor used the

> The writer establishes a thesis that includes an evaluation of the theory's usefulness in various contexts.

> In this paragraph and the next two, the writer reviews and exemplifies the component parts of the theory. That is, the writer offers an explanation of the theory, with examples to illustrate points, as appropriate.

wrong answer key. In this case, the student had no control over the grade he received, and it did not matter how much he had studied. A bad grade was inevitable. A person can also attribute behavioral causes to internal causes. Internal causes are in complete control of the person distributing the behavior and are typically attributed to part of the individual's personality (Straker, 2008). An example would be a student getting a poor grade on his math test because he is generally lazy and does not study. In this case, the student had complete control of his grade and chose not to study, which resulted in the poor grade. These two causes build up to the two major categories within the attribution theory.

The first major category of the attribution theory is that of self-serving bias. This category explores how people attribute causes to their own behaviors. It essentially states that people are more likely to give themselves the benefit of the doubt. People tend to attribute their poor behaviors to external causes and their good behaviors to internal causes (Straker, 2008). An example would be a student saying he received a poor grade on a test because his instructor does not like him. In this case, the student is attributing his poor behavior, making a poor grade on the test, to the external cause of his instructor not liking him. However, following the logic of the theory, if the student had made a good grade on the test, then he would attribute that behavior to an internal cause such as his own good study habits.

The second category of the attribution theory, the fundamental attribution error, states the opposite of the self-serving bias. The fundamental attribution error talks about how people attribute cause to the behaviors of those around them. It states that people are more likely to attribute others' poor behaviors to internal causes and their good behaviors to external causes (Straker, 2008). An example would be a student saying his friend got a better grade on the math test than him because the instructor likes his friend more. The student jumps to the conclusion that his friend's good grade was due to the external cause of the instructor liking the friend more. Moreover, if his friend had done poorly on the test, the student would most likely attribute the poor grade to an internal factor, such as his friend not studying for tests.

Personal Experiences

A situation from my personal experiences that exemplifies the ideas of the attribution theory is my high school golfing career. For my first two years of high school, I performed relatively poorly on the golf course. My team consistently placed last in tournaments, and I ranked nowhere near the top golfers from neighboring high schools. I blamed my performance on factors such as the wind and flat-out bad luck. At the same time, I attributed my teammates' poor performances to factors such as not practicing hard enough to compete in tournament play. In doing this, I became no better a golfer because I was denying that the true cause of my poor scores was the fact that I was making bad swings and not putting in the hours of work needed to perform at a higher level. I finally recognized this during my junior year of high school. I started to realize that blaming everything but myself was getting me nowhere and that the only way to improve was to take responsibility for my own play. I started practicing in areas where my game needed improvement and putting in hours at the driving range to improve my swing memory. In doing this, I became a much better player; by the time my senior season came around, I was ranked one of the top golfers in my conference and one of the best amateur players in the state of North Carolina. However, my team still did not perform

> The writer details a particular personal experience that he'll later analyze through the lens of the theory.

well due to my teammates' performance, which I continued to attribute to their poor practice habits.

This experience reflects the attribution theory in several ways. I displayed self-serving bias in my early years of high school golf. I attributed all of my poor performances to external causes, such as the wind, that I could not control. At the same time, I was displaying the fundamental attribution error in attributing my teammates' poor performances to internal causes such as not practicing hard enough. Throughout my high school golf career, I displayed the ideas of the attribution theory's category of the fundamental attribution error. However, during my junior and senior seasons my attributions moved away from the attribution theory's category of the self-serving bias. I began to attribute my poor performance to internal causes instead of the external causes I had previously blamed for my mishaps.

I believe that this is generally true for any athlete or professional seeking improvement in his or her prospective field. If a person continues to follow the ideas discussed in the category of the self-serving bias, he is not likely to improve at what he is trying to do. If Tiger Woods had constantly attributed his bad play to external causes and not taken responsibility for his actions as internal causes, he would have never become the best golfer in the world. Without attributing his poor behaviors to internal causes, he would have never gained the motivation to put in the hours of work necessary to make him the best. This observation can be applied to any other professional field, not only athletics. Personal improvement is only likely to take place when a person begins to attribute his or her poor behaviors to internal causes. I believe athletes and professionals represent problem areas for the theory of self-serving bias. However, the ideas of the fundamental attribution error generally hold true.

In this section, the writer analyzes his experiences through the lens of the theory.

Experiences of Others

To evaluate the attribution theory, I conducted an experiment to test both the fundamental attribution error and the self-serving bias. The test subjects were three friends in the same class at North Carolina State University: MEA101, Introduction to Geology. The students were asked to write down if their grades were good or bad on the first test of the semester ("good" meant they received an 80 or higher on the test, and "bad" meant they received below an 80). After the three students had done this for themselves, they were asked to attribute the grades of the others to a cause. This activity provided a clear sample of data that could test the validity of the self-serving bias and the fundamental attribution error. The reason I chose a group of friends versus a group of random strangers was that when people know each other they are more likely to attribute behavioral causes truthfully, without worrying about hurting anyone's feelings.

For the purposes of this experiment, the test subjects will be addressed as Students X, Y, and Z to keep their names confidential. The results of the experiment were as follows. The first student, Student X, received a "bad" grade on the test and attributed this to the instructor not adequately explaining the information in class and not telling the students everything the test would ultimately cover. However, Students Y and Z seemed to conclude that the reason Student X got a "bad" grade was because he did not study enough and is generally lazy when it comes to college test taking. Student Y received a "good" grade on the test and attributed this to studying hard the night before and to the fact that the test was relatively easy if one studied the notes. Students X and Z seemed to conclude that Student Y is a naturally smart student who usually receives good grades on tests regardless of how

The writer provides some insight into his methods for collecting data on the experiences of others.

In this section, the writer provides the results of his data collection.

7

much he or she studies. Finally, Student Z received a "bad" grade on the test and attributed this to the instructor not covering the material on the test well enough for students to do well, a similar response to Student X. However, Students X and Y attributed Student Z's poor grade to bad study habits and not taking the class seriously.

These results tend to prove the ideas of both of the attribution theory's categories. Student X attributed his poor grade to the external cause of the instructor not covering the material well enough, demonstrating the self-serving bias. Students Y and Z attributed Student X's poor grade to the internal cause of Student X not studying hard enough and being a generally lazy college student, exemplifying the ideas of the fundamental attribution error. Student Y attributed her good grade to the internal cause of good study habits, also exemplifying the self-serving bias. However, Students X and Z felt that the reason for Student Y's success was the external cause of being a naturally good student who does well with or without studying, reflecting the ideas of the fundamental attribution error. Student Z's results also hold true to the theory. Student Z attributed his poor grade to the external cause of the instructor not covering the material adequately, a belief shared by Student X. Also holding true to the fundamental attribution error, both Students X and Y attributed Student Z's failure to the internal cause of poor study habits. Based on the findings of this experiment, I can say that both the fundamental attribution error and the self-serving bias hold true on all accounts.

Conclusion

Overall, I believe the attribution theory's categories of the self-serving bias and the fundamental attribution error are very applicable to everyday life. Based on the data gathered

In this section, the writer discusses the implications of his findings for his overall evaluation of the theory.

The writer concludes his response paper by reviewing his overall evaluation of the theory in light of his own and others' experiences he analyzed.

236 8 • READING AND WRITING IN THE SOCIAL SCIENCES

through personal experiences and the experiences of others through the experiment described in this analysis, I believe the theory holds true in the vast majority of situations where people attribute causes to behaviors and/or actions. The only area needing revisions is the self-serving bias when applied to the specific situations of professionals in a field of study or in the case of professional athletes. In both situations, improvement must occur in order to become a professional, and the only way this is likely to happen is by accepting internal fault for poor behaviors. By accepting internal fault, a person gains the motivation to put in the hours of work necessary to learn and improve at what he or she is trying to do. Without this improvement and learning, the ability to reach the professional level is slim to none. This displays the exact opposite of the attribution ideas that are described in the self-serving bias. With the exception of this small niche of situations that falsify the self-serving bias, the validity of the attribution theory is confirmed on all accounts.

9

Reference

Straker, D. (2008). *Attribution theory*. Changingminds.org.
http://changingminds.org/explanations/theories
/attribution_theory.htm

- **Observation plays a critical role in the social sciences.** The academic fields of the social sciences, including sociology, psychology, anthropology, communication studies, and political science, among others, make observations about human behavior and interactions, as well as the systems and social structures we create to organize the world around us.

- **Social science research rests on theories of human behavior and human systems,** propositions that are used to explain specific phenomena. Social science research contributes to the continual process of refining these theories.

- **Researchers in the social sciences typically establish a hypothesis,** or a testable proposition that provides an answer or predicts an outcome in response to the research question(s) at hand, at the beginning of a research project.

- **Social science researchers must make choices about the types of methods they use** in any research situation, based on the nature of their line of inquiry and the kind of research question(s) they seek to answer. They may use a quantitative, qualitative, or mixed-methods research design to collect data for analysis.

- **Social scientists must guard against bias in their research.** They rely on rigorous procedures and checks (e.g., ensuring appropriate sample sizes and/or using multiple forms of qualitative data) to ensure that the influence of any biases is as limited as possible.

- **IMRaD format—Introduction, Methods, Results, and Discussion—is a common structure used for the organization of research reports in the social sciences.** Although research reports in the social sciences may appear in any number of forms, much of the scholarship published in these fields appears in the IMRaD format.

- **The passive voice and hedging are uses of *language* that characterize,** for good reason, social scientific writing.

- **APA style is the most common documentation style used for *reference*** in the fields of the social sciences.

- **The genres of the literature review and the theory response paper are often produced in the fields of the social sciences.**

CHAPTER

9

Reading and Writing in the Natural Sciences

Introduction to the Natural Sciences

E ach of us has likely observed something peculiar in the natural world and asked, "Why does it do that?" or "Why does that happen?" Perhaps you've observed twinkling stars in the night sky and wanted to know why such distant light seems to move and pulse. Or perhaps you've wondered why, as you drive, trees closer to your car appear to rush by much faster than trees in the distance. Maybe you can recall the first time you looked at a living cell under a microscope in a biology course and wondered about the world revealed on the slide.

For most scientists, observation of natural phenomena is the first step in the process of conducting research. Something in the natural world captures their attention and compels them to pose questions. Some moments of scientific observation are iconic—such as Newton's observation of an apple falling from a tree as inspiration for his theory of gravity.

We interviewed Sian Proctor, a geologist at South Mountain Community College in Phoenix, Arizona, where she teaches classes in physical, environmental, and historical geology. Proctor has participated in several unique research team experiences, including the Hawaii Space Exploration Analog and Simulation (HI-SEAS) Mars habitat, the NASA Spaceflight and Life Sciences Training Program (she was a finalist for the 2009 NASA Astronaut Program), and the PolarTREC (Teachers and Researchers Exploring and Collaborating) program in Barrow, Alaska. Her work has taken her out

ANDREA TSURUMI

240

of the college/university setting many times. In her Insider's View, she describes the varied places in which scientists conduct observations and collect data as part of their work to understand the natural world.

Proctor's description of her field explains that those who work in the **natural sciences** study observable phenomena in the natural world and search for answers to the questions that spark their interests about these phenomena. The disciplines of the natural sciences include a wide array of fields of academic research, including those in agricultural and life sciences, as well as physical sciences. As Proctor's own life experiences suggest, the search for understanding of natural phenomena can take scientists to many different places, and there is much variety in the ways they engage in research. One aspect that holds this diverse group of disciplines together, though, is a set of common values and procedures used in conducting research. You're probably already familiar with or at least have heard about the **scientific method**, a protocol for conducting research in the sciences that includes the following elements, or steps:

1. Observe.
2. Ask a research question.
3. Formulate a hypothesis.
4. Test the hypothesis.
5. Explain the results.

Insider's View
Geologists work out in the field, in labs, in educational institutions, and in the corporate world
SIAN PROCTOR, GEOLOGY

COURTESY OF SIAN PROCTOR

"Geology is an extremely diverse discipline encompassing specialties such as planetary geology, geochemistry, volcanology, paleontology, and more. The goal of a general geologist is to develop understanding of Earth processes such as the formation of mineral or energy resources, the evolution of landscapes, or the cause of natural disasters. Geologists work out in the field, in labs, in educational institutions, and in the corporate world. They collect data, analyze samples, generate maps, and write reports. Geology instructors teach students how to conceptualize all the information and processes mentioned above. It is our job to get students to think like a geologist (if you are teaching majors) or gain an appreciation for the Earth and Earth processes (if you are teaching non-majors)."

In this chapter, we describe a process of writing activities involved in scientific research. We present a four-step **scientific writing process** that maps onto the elements of the scientific method. The process begins with careful observation of natural phenomena and leads to the development of research questions. This step is followed by an investigation that culminates in the reporting or publication of the research:

1. Observe and describe.
2. Speculate.
3. Experiment.
4. Report.

The following table illustrates how the elements of the scientific method map onto a scientific writing process:

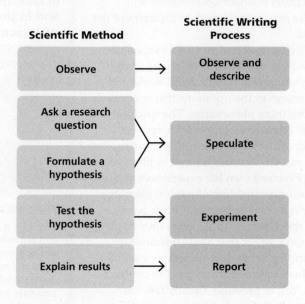

Scientific Method	Scientific Writing Process
Observe	Observe and describe
Ask a research question	Speculate
Formulate a hypothesis	Speculate
Test the hypothesis	Experiment
Explain results	Report

Before we delve too deeply into the research and writing practices of students and scholars of the sciences and how they connect, though, let's consider some of the areas of inquiry that make up the natural sciences.

Astronomy, biology, chemistry, earth science, physics, and mathematics are some of the core disciplinary areas within the natural sciences. Each area of inquiry includes numerous areas of specialty, or fields. For example, quantum physics, acoustics, and thermodynamics are three fields of physics. Conservation biology and marine science are fields of biology. Ecology (the study of organisms and their relationships to their environments) also operates under the umbrella of biology.

Interdisciplinary research is quite common in the natural sciences. An **interdisciplinary field** is an area of study in which different disciplinary perspectives or methods are combined into one. In such instances, methods for data collection often associated with one field may be used within another field of study. Consider biochemistry and biophysics, two interdisciplinary fields. In biochemistry, methods often associated with chemistry research are useful in answering questions about living organisms and biological systems. A biochemist may study aspects of a living organism such as blood alkalinity and its impact on liver function. Likewise, researchers in biophysics may use methods typical of physicists to answer research questions about biological systems. Biophysicists, for instance, might use the methodology of physics to unlock the mysteries of human DNA.

Research in the Natural Sciences

No matter the specific fields in which scientists work, they all collect, analyze, and explain data. Scientists tend to embrace a shared set of values, and as a result they typically share similar desires about how best to conduct research. The importance of any scientific study and its power to explain a natural phenomenon, then, are largely based on how well a researcher or research team designs and carries out a study in light of the shared values and desires of the community's members.

Completing the steps of a research project in a logical order and reporting the results accurately are keys to mastering research and writing in the natural sciences. You must observe and describe an object of study before you can speculate as to what it is or why it does what it does. Once you've described and speculated about a particular phenomenon, and posed a research question and a hypothesis about it, then you're positioned well to construct an experiment (if appropriate) and collect data to test whether your hypothesis holds true. When you report the results of your research, you must describe these steps and the data collected accurately and clearly. These research and writing steps build on one another, and we explore each step in more detail moving forward.

We interviewed biomedical scientist Paige Geiger, who teaches in the Department of Molecular and Integrative Physiology at the University of Kansas Medical Center, where she conducts experimental research in a laboratory on the effects of exercise and age on muscle metabolism and insulin resistance in Type II diabetes. In her Insider's View, she describes the kind of work that natural scientists do in her field and the importance of conducting careful, thorough data collection in the sciences.

Natural scientists collect evidence through systematic observation and experimentation, and they value methods that are quantifiable and replicable. In some instances, the natural sciences are described as "hard" sciences and the social sciences as "soft." This distinction stems from the tendency for natural scientists to value quantitative methods over qualitative methods, whereas social scientists often engage in both forms of data collection and sometimes combine quantitative and qualitative methods in a single study. (See Chapter 8,

Insider's View
We value innovation, ideas, accurate interpretation of data, and scientific integrity

PAIGE GEIGER, MOLECULAR AND INTEGRATIVE PHYSIOLOGY

COURTESY OF PAIGE GEIGER

"A biomedical scientist performs basic research on questions that have relevance to human health and disease, biological processes and systems. We design scientific studies to answer a particular research question and then report our results in the form of a manuscript for publication. Good science is only as good as the research study design itself. We value innovation, ideas, accurate interpretation of data, and scientific integrity. There is an honor system to science that the results are accurate and true as reported. Manuscripts are peer-reviewed, and there is inherent trust and belief in this system."

pp. 191–95, for more discussion of quantitative and qualitative methods.) Natural scientists value experiments and data collection processes that can be repeated to achieve the same or similar results, often for the purposes of generalizing their findings. Social scientists acknowledge the fluidity and variability of social systems and therefore also highly value qualitative data, which helps them to understand more contextual experiences.

INSIDE WORK **Considering a Natural Science Topic**

Generate a list of natural science topics or issues that interest you. Include any you may have read about or heard about recently, perhaps in a magazine or blog or from a television news report. Then select one for further consideration. Try to focus on a topic in which you're genuinely interested or for which you have some concern. If you're currently taking a natural science course or studying in one of the fields of the natural sciences, you might consider a topic that has emerged from your classroom or laboratory experiences. Answer the following questions.

- What is the topic?

- What do you think scientists are currently interested in discovering about this topic? What would you like to know about the topic?

- Could the topic be addressed by researchers in more than one field of the sciences? Is the topic multidisciplinary in nature? What fields of the natural sciences are currently exploring or could potentially explore the topic?

- How do or could scientists observe and collect data on some aspect of the topic?

- In a broader sense, how does the topic connect with you personally? ❥

OBSERVATION AND DESCRIPTION IN THE NATURAL SCIENCES

Observing in the natural world is an important first step in scientific inquiry. Indeed, the first step of the scientific method is observation, as we show in the table on page 242. Beyond simple observation, though, researchers in the natural sciences conduct **systematic observations** of their objects of study. A systematic approach to observation requires a researcher to follow a regular, logical schedule of observation and to conduct focused and *neutral* observations of the object of study. In other words, the researcher tries to minimize or eliminate any bias about the subject matter and simply records everything he or she experiences, using the five senses. These observations, when written up to share with others as part of a research report, form the basis of description of the object of study. In order to move from observation to description, researchers must keep careful notes about their systematic observations. We discuss one method of tracking those observations, an observation logbook, on pages 258–70.

Thinking about Systematic Observation in the Sciences

Read student Kedric Lemon's account of his observations (on pp. 260–70) of various batteries, which he completed between October 11 and October 19, 2017, as part of his observation logbook. Then answer the following questions.

- What do you know about who the author is, based on the language used in this description? Provide at least two specific examples of how the language suggests something about the author's background, knowledge, or frame of reference.

- What can you determine about the observation schedule that the author—the researcher—followed to write this description?

- What kinds of details must the researcher have noted when observing to write this description?

- Did you find any language that seems to reveal bias on the part of the researcher? If so, make a note of this language.

- Based on your answers to the previous questions, what kind of plan for systematic observation would you recommend for the topic you chose in the previous Inside Work activity? ▶

MOVING FROM DESCRIPTION TO SPECULATION

The distinction between description and speculation is a subtle but important one to understand as it relates to scientific inquiry. As we've seen, descriptive writing in the sciences is based on observations. Of course, descriptive writing in the sciences isn't only applicable to a physical space or a stored energy device. A researcher could use similar observational methods to describe, say, the movements of an ant crawling along a sidewalk or tidal erosion along a section of a beach. **Descriptive writing**, then, is the action outcome associated with the first step of the scientific method—observation.

Speculative writing, in contrast, seeks to explain *how* or *why* something behaves the way that it does, and it is most commonly associated with asking a research question and formulating a hypothesis—the second and third steps of the scientific method. In order to speculate about how or why something exists or behaves as it does, a researcher must first observe and describe. Developing a thorough observational strategy and completing a descriptive writing process will help you to lay a solid foundation for speculating about your object of study so that you can later develop a clear research question and formulate a credible hypothesis worthy of testing through experimentation.

To understand the difference between description and speculation, compare the following two zoo memos written by middle school students.* Which one is the better example of descriptive writing? Which one engages more fully in speculative writing?

*From Carolyn W. Keys. "Revitalizing Instruction in Scientific Genres: Connecting Knowledge Production with Writing to Learn in Science." *Science Education*, vol. 83, no. 2 (1999), pp. 115–30.

Middle School Students' Science Memo #1 (12-year-old girls)

On Monday, July 17, DC and I observed the Muntjac. We learned that this animal comes from Asia. And that they eat the bottom part of the grass because it is fresher. We also learned that Muntjacs are very secretive animals. We also observed the difference between a male and female. The male has a [sic] earring in his left ear and he has horns. To urinate they stand on three legs. They like to disappear into the bushes. Their habbitat [sic] is bushy land.

Another behavior that we observed was the adult Muntjac often moved toward the fence and sniffed. We believe he was sniffing for food. He also rolled back his ears and stuck out his neck. We think he is always alert to protect his family from danger. On one occasion, the male Muntjac came toward the fence. KT [another student] held her shirt toward him. He ran away quickly.

In conclusion, we can say that the Muntjac constantly hunts for food, but is always alert to protect itself and its family.

Middle School Students' Science Memo #2 (13-year-old boys)

Today we went to the Atlanta zoo, where we looked at different animals such as zebras, giraffes, gorilas [sic], monkeys, and orangatangs [sic]. From my observations of the giraffe I found out that they are rather slow and are always eating. They do many strange things, such as wagging their tails, wiggling their ears, and poking out their tounges [sic]. They are very large and I read that they weigh more than a rhinoserous [sic], which is close to 2 or 2½ tons, and their necks extend out 7 ft. long. Their tails are 3 ft. long and are sometimes used for swating [sic] flies. At times the giraffes will stand completely motionless.

Discussion Questions

1. What similarities and differences do you notice between the two samples?
2. Which sample engages in speculative writing more fully, and which one adheres to mostly descriptive writing?

The process of articulating an explanation for an observed phenomenon and speculating about its meaning is an integral part of scientific discovery. By collecting data on your own and then interpreting it, you're engaging in the production of knowledge even before you begin testing a proposed hypothesis. In this respect, scientific discovery is similar to writing in the humanities and the social sciences. Scientists interpret data gained through observation, modeling, or experimentation much in the same way that humanists interpret data collected through observation of texts. The ability to *observe systematically* and *make meaning* is the common thread that runs through all academic research.

Descriptive writing seeks to define an object of study, and it functions like a photograph. Speculative writing engages by asking *how* or *why* something behaves the way that it does, and in this sense it triggers a kind of knowledge production that is essential to scientific discovery. Following a writing process that moves a researcher from describing a phenomenon to considering *how* or *why* something does what it does is a great strategy for supporting scientific inquiry.

To this end, we encourage you to collect original data as modeled in the writing projects presented at the end of this chapter—the observation logbook (p. 258), the research proposal (p. 271), and the lab report (p. 279). Your view on the natural world is your own, and the data you collect and how you interpret that data are yours to decide. The arguments you form based on your data and your interpretation of that data can impact your world in small or very large ways.

INSIDE WORK **Practicing Description and Speculation**

For this activity, you should go outdoors and locate any type of animal (a squirrel, bird, butterfly, frog, etc.) as an object of study. Decide beforehand the amount of time you'll spend observing your subject (five minutes may be enough), and write down in a notebook as many observable facts as possible about your subject and its behavior. Consider elements of size, color, weight, distance traveled, and interaction with other animals or physical objects. If you're able to make a video or take a picture (e.g., with a cell phone camera), please do so.

After you've collected your notes and/or video, return to your classroom and write two paragraphs about your subject. Label the first paragraph "Description" and the second paragraph "Speculation," and use the following writing prompt.

Writing Prompt: The director of your local wildlife management agency needs a written report detailing the behaviors that you observed while watching your animal. Be sure to use your notes or video for accuracy. In the first paragraph, write a *description* of the subject and its behavior. Limit your description to observable facts; resist explaining why the subject appears the way it does or behaves the way it does. In the second paragraph, *speculate* about why the animal appears or behaves the way it does. Limit your speculation to the subject's behavior (or appearance) based on the observable data you wrote in your description. Finally, consider writing questions at the end of the second paragraph that might be answered in future research but that cannot be answered on the basis of your observations alone. ❯

Once you've conducted observations and collected data, you can move on to formalize your speculation by writing research questions and formulating a hypothesis, consistent with the second and third steps of the scientific method. Writing research questions and hypotheses in the natural sciences is a similar process to those activities in the social sciences (see Chapter 8). Devoting time to several days of focused observation, collecting data, and writing and reflecting on your object of study should trigger questions about what you're observing.

As you write research questions, you might consider the difference between open-ended and closed-ended research questions. A **closed-ended question** can be answered by *yes* or *no*. By contrast, an **open-ended question** provokes a fuller response. Here are two examples:

Closed-Ended Question: Is acid rain killing off the Fraser fir population near Mount Mitchell in North Carolina?

Open-Ended Question: What factors contribute to killing off the Fraser fir population near Mount Mitchell in North Carolina?

Scientists use both open-ended and closed-ended questions. Open-ended questions usually begin with *What*, *How*, or *Why*. Closed-ended questions can be appropriate in certain instances, but they can also be quite polarizing. They often begin with *Is* or *Does*. Consider the following two questions:

Closed-Ended Question: Is global warming real?

Open-Ended Question: What factors contribute to global warming?

Rhetorically, the closed-ended question divides responses into *yes* or *no* answers, whereas the open-ended question provokes a more thoughtful response. Neither form of question is better per se, but the forms do function differently. If you're engaging in a controversial subject, a closed-ended research question might serve your purpose. If you're looking for a more complete answer to a complex issue, an open-ended question might serve you better.

Once you've established a focused research question, informed by or derived on the basis of your observation and speculation about a natural science phenomenon, then you're ready to formulate a hypothesis. This will be a testable proposition that provides an answer or that predicts an outcome in response to the research question(s) at hand.

INSIDE WORK   **Developing Research Questions and a Hypothesis**

Review the observation notes and the descriptions and explanations you produced in the Inside Work activity on page 247. What potential research questions emerged? For example, in an observation logbook about house finches and nesting practices written by one of the authors of this textbook, a question that remained unanswered was why two eggs from the initial brood of five were removed from the nest. Potential research questions for a study might include the one shown here.

> **Research Question:** Do female house finches remove eggs from their own nests?

From such a question, we can formulate a hypothesis.

> **Hypothesis:** Our hypothesis is that female house finches do remove eggs from their own nests. Furthermore, our observational data supports other scholars' claims that female house finches cannibalize their brood on occasion.

Now you try it. Write down at least two research questions that emerged from your observations, and then attempt to answer each question in the form of a hypothesis. Finally, discuss your hypotheses with a classmate or small group, and make the case for which one most warrants further study. Freewrite for five minutes about the evidence you have or additional evidence you could collect that would support your chosen hypothesis. ▶

DESIGNING A RESEARCH STUDY IN THE NATURAL SCIENCES

As we've noted, research in the natural sciences most often relies on quantitative data to answer research questions. While there are many ways to collect and analyze quantitative data, most professional scientists rely on complex statistical procedures to test hypotheses and generate results.

We interviewed Michelle LaRue, a research fellow at the Polar Geospatial Center, a research group based at the University of Minnesota. Her doctorate is in conservation biology, and her research has focused mainly on large-mammal habitat selection and movement—in particular, the phenomenon of potential recolonization of cougars in the American Midwest. In her Insider's View excerpt, LaRue describes the kinds of questions she asks as a scientist and the kinds of data collection and analysis she typically undertakes as part of her efforts to answer her research questions.

In the previous two sections, we discussed how to conduct systematic observation that leads to description of a phenomenon, and then we explored processes for speculating about what you observed in order to construct a research question and a hypothesis. One way to test a hypothesis is to engage in a systematic observation of the target of your research phenomenon. Imagine that you're interested in discovering factors that affect the migration patterns of bluefin tuna, and you've hypothesized that water temperature has some effect on those patterns. You could then conduct a focused observation to test your hypothesis. You might, for instance, observe bluefin tuna in their migration patterns and measure water temperatures along the routes.

COURTESY OF MICHELLE LaRUE

"I am interested in asking questions that address how populations of animals behave across broad spatial and temporal scales (i.e., large regions such as the Midwest or the Ross Sea, Antarctica,

over decades), and which methods are most suitable to answer them. Do suitable habitat or dispersal corridors exist for cougars in midwestern North America? Can we use distance sampling to estimate densities of white-tail deer? How many Weddell seals are there in the Ross Sea? Does glacial retreat impact emigration rates of Adélie penguins?

"I typically form study questions from personal observations or communication with my colleagues. Because my questions come from the perspective of a spatial ecologist, I gather data from myriad sources: field work (e.g., aerial surveys), remote sensing and GIS [Geographic Information Systems] data (land cover, locations of animal occurrence, satellite imagery), population dynamics data (fecundities and survival rates), and climate data (air temperature, wind speed). Compiling data from various disciplines helps me understand the landscape more broadly than focusing on just one aspect. Analysis of these types of data includes GIS and statistical procedures."

LaunchPad

Hear more about the prewriting process from a professional mathematician.

Another way to test a hypothesis, of course, is to design an experiment. Experiments come in all shapes and sizes, and one way to learn about the experimental methods common to your discipline is by reading the Methods sections of peer-reviewed scholarly articles in your field. Every discipline has slightly different approaches to experimental design. Some disciplines, such as astronomy, rely almost exclusively on non-experimental systematic observation, while others rely on highly controlled experiments. Chemistry is a good example of the latter.

One of the most common forms of experimental design is the **comparative experiment**, in which a researcher tests two or more types of objects and assesses the results. For example, an engineering student may want to test different types of skateboard ball bearings. She may design an experiment that compares a skateboard's distance rolled when using steel versus ceramic bearings. She could measure distances rolled, speed, or the time it takes to cover a preset distance when the skateboard has steel bearings and when it has ceramic bearings.

In some disciplines of the natural sciences, it's common practice to test different objects against a control group. A **control group** is used in a comparative experimental design to act as a baseline with which to compare other objects. For example, a student researcher might compare how subjects score on a memorization test after having consumed (a) no coffee, (b) two cups of decaf coffee, or (c) two cups of caffeinated coffee. In this example, the group of subjects consuming no coffee would function as a control group.

Regardless of a study's design, it is important to realize that academic institutions have very clear policies regarding experimental designs that involve human subjects, whether that research is being conducted by individuals in the humanities, the social sciences, or the natural sciences. Both professional and student researchers are required to submit proposals through an institutional review board, or IRB. In the United States, *institutional review boards* operate under federal law to ensure that any experiment involving humans is ethical. This is often something entirely new to undergraduate students, and it should be taken seriously. No matter how harmless a test involving human subjects may seem, you should determine if you must submit your research plans through an IRB. This can often be done online. Depending on the nature and scope of your research, though, the processes of outlining the parameters of your research for review may be quite labor-intensive and time-consuming. You should familiarize yourself with the protocol for your particular academic institution. An online search for "institutional review board" and the name of your school should get you started. (For more on the role of institutional review boards, see Chapter 8.)

INSIDE WORK   **Freewriting about an Experiment**

Start this activity by writing, in one sentence, what your initial research goal was when you began an observation about a phenomenon that interested you. You might draw on your writing from earlier Inside Work activities to start.

Example: **My goal was to study a bird's nest I discovered on my front porch.**

For many students beginning their inquiry in the sciences, learning about a topic may be the extent of their initial objective. For more advanced students, however, starting an observation from a strong knowledge base may sharpen the objective. The example below draws on prior knowledge of the object of study.

Example: **My goal was to determine whether a female house finch eats her own eggs.**

Once you've written down what your initial objective was, then freewrite for five minutes about what you now know. What are the most important things you learned about your object of study?

Most important, what hypothesis can you make about your object of study?

Hypothesis: **My observational data suggest that female house finches often remove eggs from their nest and may occasionally cannibalize their brood.**

After developing a hypothesis, the next step in the scientific method is to test the hypothesis. Keep in mind that data in the sciences to support a hypothesis come from either a systematic observation or an experiment.

Freewrite for five minutes about how you could collect data that would test your hypothesis. As you write, consider feasible methods that you could follow soon, as well as methods that might extend beyond the current semester but that you could develop into a larger project for later use in your undergraduate studies. Consider whether an experiment or a systematic observation would be more useful. Most important, use your imagination and have fun. ▶

After observing and describing, speculating and hypothesizing, and conducting an experimental study or systematic observation, scientists move toward publishing the results of their research. This is the final step of the scientific method and the final stage of the scientific writing process that we introduced at the beginning of the chapter: scientists explain their results by reporting their data and discussing its implications. There are multiple forms through which scientists report their findings, and these often depend on the target audience. For instance, a scientist presenting his research results at an academic conference for the consideration of his peers might report results in the form of a poster presentation. Research results can also be presented in the form of an academic journal article. A scientist who wants to present her results to a more general audience, though, might issue a press release. In the next two sections of this chapter, we discuss conventions for reporting results in the natural sciences and provide examples of common genres that researchers in the natural sciences produce as a means of reporting their results.

Conventions of Writing in the Natural Sciences

Although the different fields of study that make up the natural sciences have characteristics that distinguish them from one another, a set of core values and conventions connects these areas of inquiry. The values shared among members of the scientific community have an impact on the communication practices and writing conventions of professionals in natural science fields:

- objectivity
- replicability

- recency
- cooperation and collaboration

In this section, we examine each of these commonly held values in more detail. And we suggest that these values are directly linked to many of the conventions that scientists follow when they write, or to the ways scientists communicate with one another more generally.

Insider's View
I also learned the KISS principle during my undergraduate career
MICHELLE LaRUE, CONSERVATION BIOLOGY

COURTESY OF MICHELLE LaRUE

"I learned the conventions of science writing through literature review, imitation, and a lot of practice: this often included pages and pages of feedback from advisors and colleagues. Further, reading wildlife and modeling articles helped me focus on the tone, writing style, and format expected for each journal. After that, it was all about practicing my writing skills.

"I also learned the KISS principle during my undergraduate career: Keep It Simple, Stupid. This mantra reminds me to revise my writing so it's clear, concise, and informative. It is my opinion that science writing can be inherently difficult to understand, so it's important to keep the message clear and straightforward.

"I find that as I progress and hone my writing and research skills, sitting down to write gets easier, and I have been able to move up in the caliber of journal in which I publish papers. Writing is a skill that is never perfected; striving for the next best journal keeps me focused on improvement."

OBJECTIVITY

In her Insider's View, Michelle LaRue notes the importance of maintaining clarity in the presentation of ideas in science writing. Of course, clarity is a general expectation for all writing, but the desire for clarity in science writing can also be linked to the community's shared value of objectivity. As we noted earlier, *objectivity* (or neutrality) in observation and experimentation is essential to the research that scientists do. Most researchers in the natural sciences believe that bias undermines the reliability of research results. When scientists report their results, therefore, they often use rhetorical strategies that bolster the appearance of objectivity in their work. (Note that our marginal annotations below indicate which parts of the SLR model apply—structure, language, and reference; see Chapter 6.)

Rhetorical Features That Convey Objectivity

- **Titles** Scientists tend to give their reports very clear titles. Rarely will you find a "creative" or rhetorical title in science writing. Instead, scientists prefer non-rhetorical, descriptive titles, or titles that say exactly what the reports are about.

Titles may be considered a language and/or a structural feature of a text.

The IMRaD format is a common structure used in scientific writing.

- **IMRaD**   Researchers in the sciences generally expect research reports to appear in the IMRaD format (for more detail, see Chapters 6 and 8):

  Introduction

  Methods

  Results

  Discussion

  Notice how the structure of IMRaD parallels the ordered processes of the scientific writing process (observe and describe, speculate, experiment, and report). This reporting structure underscores the importance of objectivity because it reflects the prescribed steps of the scientific method, which is itself a research process that scientists follow to reduce or eliminate bias.

Jargon is a language feature.

- **Jargon**   Scientists often communicate in highly complex systems of words and symbols that hold specific meaning for other members of the scientific community. These words and symbols enable scientists to communicate their ideas as clearly as possible. For example, a scientific researcher might refer to a rose as *Rosa spinosissima*. By using the Latin name, she communicates that the specific type of rose being referenced is actually the one commonly referred to as the Scotch rose. The use of jargon, in this instance, is actually clarifying for the intended audience. Using jargon is a means of communicating with precision, and precision in language is fundamental to objective expression.

Numbers and other symbol systems function in much the same way as words, so they may be understood as a language feature.

- **Numbers**   Scientific reports are often filled with charts and figures, and these are often filled with numbers. Scientists prefer to communicate in numbers because unlike words, which can inadvertently convey the wrong meaning, numbers are more fixed in terms of their ability to communicate specific meaning. Consider the difference between describing a tree as "tall" and giving a tree's height in feet and inches. This represents the difference between communicating somewhat qualitatively and entirely quantitatively. The preference for communicating in numbers, or quantitatively, enables members of the scientific community to reduce, as much as possible, the use of words. As writers use fewer words and more numbers in scientific reports, the reports appear to be more objective.

INSIDE WORK   **Looking for Conventions of Objectivity**

Although we've discussed a number of writing expectations related to objectivity in the sciences, we need to stress again that these expectations are conventional. As such, you'll likely encounter numerous studies in the sciences that rely on only a few of these features or that alter the conventional expectations in light of a study's particular aims.

- Choose a scientific topic of interest to you, and locate a research article on some aspect of that topic in a peer-reviewed academic journal article.

- Once you've found an appropriate article, look at the features of the article that reflect the writers' desire for objectivity in science reporting. Note evidence of the following in particular:
  - straightforward, descriptive titles
  - IMRaD
  - jargon
  - numbers

- Take notes on instances where the article follows conventional expectations for science reporting as explained in this chapter, as well as instances where the article alters or diverges from these expectations. Speculate as to the authors' reasoning for their decisions to follow the conventional expectations or to diverge from them. ❯

REPLICABILITY

Like objectivity, the **replicability** of research methods and findings is important to the production and continuation of scientific inquiry. Imagine that a scientific report reveals the discovery that eating an orange every day could help prevent the onset of Alzheimer's disease. This sounds great, right? But how would the larger scientific community go about verifying such a finding? Multiple studies would likely be undertaken in an attempt to replicate the original study's finding. If the finding couldn't be replicated by carefully following the research procedures outlined in the original study, then that discovery wouldn't contribute much, if anything at all, to ongoing research on Alzheimer's disease precisely because the finding's veracity couldn't be confirmed.

Several conventional aspects of writing in the natural sciences help ensure the replicability of a study's findings and underscore replicability as an important value shared by members of the scientific community:

- **Detail**   One of the conventional expectations for scientific writing involves the level of detail and specificity, particularly in certain areas of research reporting (e.g., Methods sections). Scientists report their research methods in meticulous detail to ensure that others can replicate their results. This is how scientific knowledge builds. Verification through repeated testing and retesting of results establishes the relative value of particular research findings. It's not surprising, then, that the Methods sections of scientific research reports are typically highly detailed and specific.

  > Detail may be considered a language or a structural feature.

- **Hypotheses**   Hypothesis statements predict the outcome of a research study, but the very nature of a prediction leaves open the possibility of

  > Hypotheses are a structural feature.

other outcomes. By opening this "space" of possibility, scientists acknowledge that other researchers could potentially find results that differ from their own. In this way, scientists confirm the importance of replicability to their inquiry process.

Precision is a language feature of scientific writing.

- **Precision**   Scientific communication must be precise. Just as researchers must choose words and numbers with attention to accuracy and exactness, so too must they present their findings and other elements of scientific communication with absolute precision. As you engage with scientific discourse, you should be able to develop a sense of the precise nature of scientific description and explanation.

LaunchPad

Learn about putting your research in context.

RECENCY

Scientific research is an ongoing process wherein individual studies or research projects contribute bits of information that help fill in a larger picture or research question. As research builds, earlier studies and projects become the bases for additional questioning and research. As in other fields, like the social sciences, it's important that scientific researchers remain current on the developments in research in their respective fields of study. To ensure that their work demonstrates **recency**—that is, it is current and draws on knowledge of other recent work—researchers in the sciences may follow numerous conventions in their writing, including those listed here:

The purposeful selection of resources is a reference feature.

- **Reference Selection**   Scientific writers typically reference work that has been published recently on their topic. One way to observe the importance of recency is to examine the dates of studies and other materials referenced in a recent scientific publication. If you do this, then you'll likely discover that many studies referenced are relatively recent. By emphasizing recent research in their reports, scientists convey the importance of remaining on top of the current state of research in their areas of expertise. Knowledge production in the natural sciences is highly methodical and builds slowly over time. It's not surprising, then, that the recency of research is important to members of this community.

Scientific documentation systems of reference are often APA or CSE, but they are frequently also specific to the journal in which an article is published.

- **Documentation**   The importance of recency is also evident in the methods of documentation most often employed in the fields of the natural sciences, like APA (American Psychological Association), CSE (Council of Science Editors), and others. Unlike MLA, for instance, where only page numbers appear next to authors' names in parenthetical citations—as in (Jacobs 1109)—the APA system requires a date next to authors' names, both for in-text references to research and, often, in parenthetical remarks when this is not provided in text—as in (Jacobs, 2012, pp. 198–199). The fact that the APA method generally requires a date highlights scientists' concern for the recency of the research they reference and on which they build their own research.

Start with the same article that you used in the previous Inside Work activity to search for writing conventions that demonstrate objectivity. If you don't already have an article selected, search for an academic article published in a peer-reviewed journal on a scientific topic of interest to you.

- Look for at least one example of the researchers' use of the following conventions that might demonstrate how much they value replicability and recency. Note evidence of the following:

  - details
  - precision
  - timely reference selection
  - choice of documentation style

- Take notes on instances where the article follows conventional expectations for science reporting as explained in this chapter and instances where the article alters or diverges from these expectations. Speculate as to the authors' reasoning for their decisions to follow the conventional expectations or to diverge from them. ◗

COOPERATION AND COLLABORATION

Unlike the clichéd image of the solitary scientist spending hours alone in a laboratory, most scientists would probably tell you that research in their fields takes place in a highly cooperative and collaborative manner. In fact, large networks of researchers in any particular area often comprise smaller networks of scholars who are similarly focused on certain aspects of a larger research question. These networks may work together to refine their research goals in light of the work of others in the network, and researchers are constantly sharing—through publication of reports, team researching, and scholarly conferences—the results of their work. Several common elements in scientific writing demonstrate this value:

- **Presentation of Researchers' Names** As you examine published research reports, you'll find that very often they provide a list, prominently, of the names of individuals who contributed to the research and to the reporting of that research. This information usually appears at the top of reports just after the title, and it may also identify the researchers' institutional and/or organizational affiliations. Names typically appear in an order that identifies principal researchers first. Naming all the members of a research team acknowledges the highly cooperative nature of the researching processes that many scientists undertake.

> The presentation of researchers' names is a structural feature.

- **Treatment of Other Researchers** Another feature you might notice is the way science professionals treat one another's work. In the humanities,

> How researchers in the natural sciences treat one another is a feature of reference.

where ideas are a reflection of the individuals who present them, researchers and writers often direct commentary toward individuals for their ideas when there's cause for disagreement or dissatisfaction with other researchers' ideas. Conventionally, however, science researchers treat others in their field more indirectly when objections to their research or findings come up. Instead of linking research problems to individuals, scientists generally direct their dissatisfaction with others' work at problems in the research process or design. This approach highlights the importance of cooperation and collaboration as shared values of members of the scientific community.

Genres of Writing in the Natural Sciences

Once again we interviewed Paige Geiger, whom you met earlier in this chapter. She teaches in the Department of Molecular and Integrative Physiology at the University of Kansas Medical Center. In the following Insider's View, she describes two important genres of writing in her discipline.

In this section, we provide descriptions of, and steps for producing, three of the most common genres that writers in the natural sciences produce: an observation logbook, a research proposal, and a lab report. The observation logbook provides a location for carefully recording systematic observations at the beginning of a research process. The research proposal forms the basis for the important grant proposals that Geiger describes, and it might draw on information gathered during initial observations. It also incorporates other elements such as a careful review of the literature on a subject. Lab reports are the final results of research, and they reflect the form in which a scientist might ultimately publish a scholarly journal article.

AN OBSERVATION LOGBOOK

Systematic and carefully recorded observations can lay a solid foundation for further exploration of a subject. These observations might take place as an initial step in the scientific writing process, or they might be part of the data collection that occurs when testing a hypothesis.

The tools that we discuss over the next few pages parallel the kind of systematic observation that's needed to undertake scientific inquiry. One way to focus and record your observations of a phenomenon is to keep an **observation logbook**, which functions as both a data collection tool and a reflective strategy that becomes useful later in research writing and reporting stages. The observation logbook is a foundational part of the research process that precedes the construction of a formal lab report.

Sometimes observation logbooks include speculation in addition to description, but the two types of writing should be clearly separated from each other to ensure that the more objective observations are not confused with any speculation. Speculation, you'll remember, occurs at the stage of formulating research questions and a hypothesis.

Two different forms serve very different purposes

PAIGE GEIGER, MOLECULAR AND INTEGRATIVE PHYSIOLOGY

COURTESY OF PAIGE GEIGER

"There are two kinds of writing in my discipline—writing manuscripts for publication and writing grant applications. The two different forms serve very different purposes. We must write grant applications to obtain funding to perform our research. The applications are usually for three to five years of funding and are very broad in scope. These applications describe what you plan to do and the results you expect to see. This requires a comprehensive assessment of the literature, an explanation of what is known and what is unknown regarding the specific research question. You must describe how you will design the studies, how you will collect and analyze data, and how you will handle problems or unexpected results. This kind of writing is considered an art form. It is something that you improve upon throughout your career.

"Writing manuscripts for publication is quite different. A manuscript deals with a very specific research question, and you report the direct results of your investigation. There is some background information to place the study in a greater context, but the focus is on the data and the interpretation of the data from this one study. This form of writing is very direct, and overinterpretation of the data is frowned upon. In addition to these two forms of writing, scientists also write review articles and textbook chapters on their area of expertise."

Keeping an Observation Logbook

For this project, you'll need to decide on a particular object of study and collect at least five days of observations about it. We encourage you to develop a multi-modal data collection process that includes digital photos and videorecorded evidence. For each daily entry, begin with description before moving into speculation. A natural outgrowth of descriptive writing should include brainstormed research questions that could be answered with further experiments, research, or observation.

For each day, you should do the following.

1. Collect and include photographic evidence.

2. Write a description of your object of study.

3. Generate questions for future research.

At the conclusion of five days, answer the following questions.

1. What did I learn about my object of study?

2. What claims can I now make regarding my object of study?

3. What evidence could I use from my observational logbook to support those claims?

Finally, write a one- to two-page paper that includes two sections.

1. Description
2. Speculation

For the **Description** section, write a description of your object of study. Refrain from explaining or speculating about behavior in this section; simply write the observations that are most important to give a clear picture of what you studied and how you studied it. Make use of time measurements and physical measurements such as weight, size, and distance. For the **Speculation** section, assert suggestions as to why certain behaviors emerged in your object of study. You might begin by deciding which behaviors most surprised you or seem most interesting to you.

You might also use the Speculation section as a place to begin thinking about future questions that could be explored as a follow-up to your observations.

Insider Example
Student Observation Logbook

In the following observation logbook, written using APA style conventions, student Kedric Lemon catalogs his observations concerning the efficiency of several types of batteries over a five-day period. His observations form the basis for his experimental study, which appears later on pages 280–90. You'll notice that he carefully separates his observations and description from any speculation about why he observed what he did.

Comparing the Efficiency of Various Batteries Being Used over Time

Kedric Lemon

North Carolina State University

Professor Matthew Chu

November 4, 2017

Comparing the Efficiency of Various Batteries Being Used over Time

Logbook

Introduction

The purpose of this study is to see if some batteries can hold their charge for longer periods of time than others. Also, this observational study will determine if there is an overwhelming difference between generic brand and the top name-brand batteries, or if people are really just paying

for the name. I will perform this study by first recording all of the batteries' initial voltages, and then each day I will allow each of the batteries to go on for an hour and a half and then again check the voltage. It is important that I test the voltage immediately after the batteries come out of the flashlight. Otherwise, results could vary. Before putting in the second set of batteries, I will allow the flashlight to cool down for an hour because after being in use for an hour and a half they are likely hot, and I am unsure if this can affect how fast the other batteries will be consumed. I will look first at how much charge was lost over the duration that they were used in the flashlight. Then I will compare them to one another to determine which one has lost the most over a day, and second, which of the batteries still holds the highest

voltage. I hypothesize that the Duracell battery will decrease at the slowest rate and that it will have the highest initial voltage.

Friday, October 11, 2013

Today was the first day that I observed results from my batteries. I believe that the first thing is to state the initial voltages of all three types of batteries. (Also, it is important to note that these are the averages of the batteries, as the flashlight demands two AA batteries.)

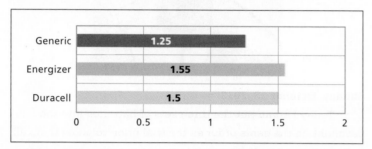

So from these initial observations the Energizer battery has the highest initial voltage.

After allowing all of the batteries to run for an hour and a half, I again took the voltages of the batteries and found this:

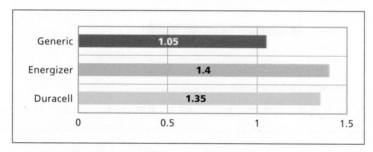

Energizer and Duracell both appear to be decreasing at approximately the same rates thus far in the observation, whereas the generic brand has already dropped much faster than the other two types of batteries. From this observation I have raised the question: What is the composition of the

Begins a report on systematic observation of the phenomenon

Observations leading to questions

Duracell and Energizer batteries that allows them to hold a better initial charge than the generic brand of batteries?

Sunday, October 13, 2013

Today I again put the three sets of batteries into the flashlight, in the same order as the trial prior, to allow them all to have close to the same time between usages, again to try and avoid any variables. Today my data showed similar results after allowing all of the batteries to run in the flashlight for an hour and a half:

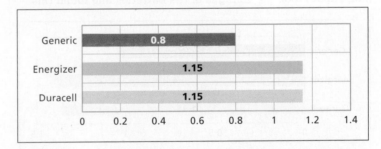

After this day of observing the results I found that the generic brand of batteries did not decrease as significantly as it did after the first trial. This day the generic brand lost close to the same voltage as the other two types of batteries. Another interesting observation I found was that Energizer and Duracell had the same voltages.

Provides evidence of the researcher's attempt to remain systematic in his observations

Tuesday, October 15, 2013

On this day of observation I again put the batteries into the flashlights for the trial time. The data I found for this day was as follows:

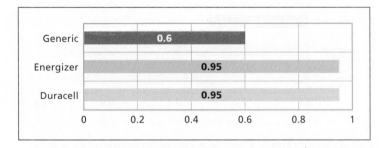

On this day I found that again the generic brand decreased by an amount similar to the other two batteries. Also I found that the generic brand's intensity has begun to decrease. However, both the other two batteries still give off a strong light intensity. This observation raises the question: At what voltage does the light intensity begin to waver? Another question is: Will the other two batteries begin to have lower light intensity at approximately the same voltage as the generic, or will they continue to have a stronger light intensity for longer? The figures below show the change of light intensity of the generic brand of batteries from the beginning until this day's observation.

Student's observations continue to raise questions

Figure 1. Before

Figure 2. After

Thursday, October 17, 2013

Today is my fourth day of observation. The readings for the voltages for this day were:

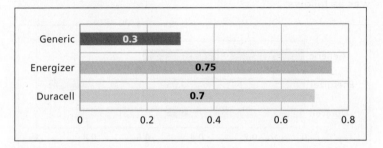

The generic brand is losing even more intensity when it is in the flashlight. It is obvious that it is getting near the end of its battery charge. Today was also the biggest decrease in charge for the generic brand of batteries. This is interesting because it is actually producing less light than before, so why does it lose more voltage toward the end of its life? Also, another thing I observed for this day was that again the Energizer brand holds more voltages than the Duracell, like before. There is still no change in light intensity for the two name brands.

Saturday, October 19, 2013

Today is my final day of observation. This is the data I collected for this day:

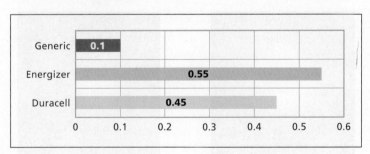

Today the generic battery hardly produced any light out of the flashlight by the end of the time period, although it still didn't drop to 0 voltage, so there are clearly still some electrons flowing in the current throughout the battery. Also, I observed that the Duracell battery has clearly dropped well below the Energizer now. The Duracell has shown a slight decrease in the light intensity compared to when the observational study first started. So what is the composition of the Energizer battery that makes it outlast the Duracell battery?

Narrative

Description

Five days of observations were conducted over an eight-day period. It did not matter what day of the week I took these observations nor the conditions of the environment around my object of study at the time of the observations. The only thing that I made sure that was constant environmentally for all of the batteries in the study was the temperature because more heat results in higher kinetic energy, which causes electrons to move faster. I had to decide on the types of batteries that I wanted to study for the observational study. The batteries I decided on were: Duracell, Energizer, and a generic brand from Wal-Mart. Before I took my first observation I tested each of the batteries that were to be used with the voltmeter to know the initial charge of the battery. Doing this gave me an idea from the beginning of which battery is typically the most powerful and also how much the batteries would be losing in comparison to their initial charge.

Each of these battery types was tested for the same amount of time for each day that they were observed. Since the flashlight took two batteries to run properly I was planning on taking the average of the two batteries, but I found them to be very similar in all of the trials. I believe that this occurrence

The narrative description provides a summary of the student's systematic observation.

is a result of the entire circuit acting at the same time, causing equal electron transfer between the two batteries to occur, thus causing them to have equal voltages.

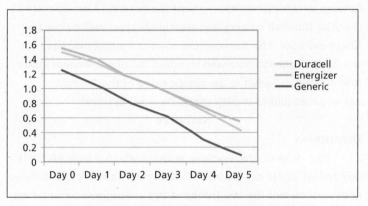

Final Graph from Five Days of Observations

The graph above shows the change in voltage over the five-day period that I took the observations. As you can see, Duracell and Energizer are very similar to one another, with Energizer performing slightly higher than the Duracell brand. The generic has a lower initial voltage than the other two batteries and continues to decrease at a faster rate than the other two batteries. Another thing you can see from this graph is how quickly the generic brand lost its voltage toward the end of its life, whereas the other two batteries seemed to continue to decrease at approximately the same rate throughout.

Speculation

My initial hypothesis that the Duracell battery would decrease at the slowest rate was not supported by this data. I have done a little bit of research on the composition of the cathodes of the Duracell and Energizer batteries. I found that

Evaluates initial hypothesis (speculation) in light of the data the Duracell battery uses a copper tip on the cathode, whereas the Energizer uses a combination of lithium with the copper tip to allow longer battery life. This would explain why the Energizer battery decreases at a slightly lower rate than the Duracell battery does. Also, the generic brand of batteries uses a carbon and copper tip. This would explain why it decreases at a higher rate than the other two name-brand batteries. Also, the cathodes and anodes of the generic batteries may not be as professionally manufactured as the other two types of batteries. All of these reasons could explain why there is a higher voltage density in the Energizer battery than in the other two batteries.

Also, my initial hypothesis that the Duracell battery would have the highest initial voltage was incorrect. From the research that I have gathered, the only explanation for the higher initial voltage in the Energizer battery would be the presence of the alkaline metals that the manufacturer puts into its batteries, whereas the Duracell manufacturer does no such thing. However, there is little information on the Internet about the generic brand of batteries that I used for the experiment, but I was able to find that the reason it has such a lower initial voltage than the other two types of batteries is because it is not packed as well. It takes special equipment to make all the electrons store properly, and the equipment used is not as powerful as the ones that Duracell and Energizer use for their batteries. These ideas all make up my understanding of why there is such a major difference in the rates at which the batteries lose their charge.

For further research into this topic I would recommend using a larger sample, because I used only two batteries for each type of battery. Also, I would recommend looking into the new rechargeable batteries, as that is what a lot of people

> Further speculates about factors that contributed to rejection of the hypothesis

> Provides suggestions for future research on the subject

are turning to more recently. Another thing that I would try is leaving the batteries on longer because from some of the research that I have done, Duracell does better than Energizer over continuous usage. This means that maybe there is something in the Energizer batteries that causes them to speed up reactions over long periods of use that will cause them to decrease faster over this period. A study like that would be very interesting to compare to my own.

Another interesting topic to follow up on would be the cost of each of the batteries and which battery would be the most cost-effective for users. A lot of people today are buying the generic brand of batteries because they think that this is saving them money. Yes, the generic brand is sold at a lower price, but it is also being used up faster than the other two types of batteries.

RESEARCH PROPOSAL

The research proposal is one of the most common genres of academic writing in the natural sciences. Professional scholars use the **research proposal** to plan out complex studies, to formulate their thoughts, and to submit their research designs to institutional review boards or to grant-funding agencies. The ability to secure grant funding (i.e., to write an effective research proposal and connect it to a realistic, clear budget) is a highly sought-after skill in a job candidate for many academic, government, and private industry positions. In many cases, an effective proposal results from practice with and knowledge of the conventions expected for the genre. No doubt, much of the work of science could not get done without the research proposal, because it is such an important vehicle for securing the funding and materials necessary to conduct research.

Most research proposals include the following sections:

- Title page
- Introduction (and literature review)
- Methods
- References

The *title page* should include (1) the title of your proposal, (2) your name and the names of any co-authors/researchers, and (3) the name of your academic institution. Your instructor may require additional information such as a running header, date, or author's note. Be sure to ask your instructor what documentation and formatting style to use and what information is required in any specific writing context.

The *introduction* of a research proposal explains the topic and purpose of the proposed research. Be sure to include your research question and/or your proposed hypothesis. Additionally, your introduction should contextualize your research by reviewing scholarly articles related to your topic and showing how your proposed research fills a gap in what is already known about the topic. Specifically, the introduction should explain how other researchers have approached your topic (or a closely related one) in the past, with attention to the major overlapping findings in that research. An effective introduction incorporates a literature review that demonstrates your knowledge of other scholars' research. As such, it builds your credibility to conduct your proposed research. (See Chapter 8, pp. 211–26, for more information about writing a literature review.)

The *Methods section* of a research proposal explains exactly what you will do to test your hypothesis (or answer your research question) and how you will do it. It differs from the Methods section of a lab report in several ways: (1) it should be written in future tense, and (2) it should include more detail about your plans. Further, the Methods section should address how long your study will take and should specify how you will collect data (in a step-by-step descriptive manner).

The *references list* for a research proposal is essentially the same as the references list for a lab report or any other academic project. You'll need to include the full citation information for any work you used in your literature review or in planning or researching your topic.

<table>
<tr><td>WRITING PROJECT</td><td>

Developing a Research Proposal

Drawing on a topic of interest to you, develop a research proposal that outlines a specific research question and/or hypothesis, and describe how you would go about answering the question or testing the hypothesis. Keep in mind that successful research proposals include the elements listed below.

- Title page
- Introduction (and literature review)
- Methods
- References

You might try drawing on the observations you collected while completing an observation logbook to develop your research question and/or hypothesis.

</td></tr>
</table>

Insider Example
Research Proposal

In the following example of a professional research proposal by Gary Ritchison, a biologist at Eastern Kentucky University, note how the Introduction section begins with a brief introduction to the topic (par. 1) and then proceeds to review the relevant literature on the topic (pars. 1 and 2). As you read, consider how a potential funding entity would likely view both the content and the form in which that content is presented. Also note that the references list is titled "Literature Cited." Minor variations like this are common from discipline to discipline and in various contexts. Here, Ritchison has followed CSE style conventions in his proposal.

9 • READING AND WRITING IN THE NATURAL SCIENCES

Hunting Behavior, Territory Quality, and Individual
Quality of American Kestrels (*Falco sparverius*)

Gary Ritchison

Department of Biological Sciences
Eastern Kentucky University

Introduction

American Kestrels (*Falco sparverius*) are widely distributed throughout North America. In Kentucky, these falcons are permanent residents and are most abundant in rural farmland, where they hunt over fields and pastures (Palmer-Ball 1996). Although primarily sit-and-wait predators, hunting from elevated perches and scanning the surrounding areas for prey, kestrels also hunt while hovering (Balgooyen 1976). Kellner (1985) reported that nearly 20% of all attacks observed in central Kentucky were made while kestrels were hovering. Habitats used by hunting kestrels in central Kentucky include mowed and unmowed fields, cropland, pastures, and plowed fields (Kellner 1985).

Several investigators have suggested that male and female American Kestrels may exhibit differences in habitat use during the non-breeding period, with males typically found in areas with greater numbers of trees, such as wooded pastures, and females in open fields and pastures (Stinson et al. 1981; Bohall-Wood and Collopy 1986). However, Smallwood (1988) suggested that, when available, male and female kestrels in south-central Florida established winter territories in the same type of habitat. Differential habitat use occurred only because migratory female kestrels usually arrived on wintering areas before males and, therefore, were more likely to establish territories in the better-quality, more open habitats before males arrived (Smallwood 1988).

In central Kentucky, many American Kestrels are residents. As a result, male and female kestrels would likely have equal opportunity to establish winter territories in the higher-quality, open habitats. If so, habitat segregation should be less apparent in central Kentucky than in areas further south, where wintering populations of kestrels are largely migratory. In addition, territory quality should be correlated

Establishes the topic and provides background information on American Kestrels

Reveals evidence of a review of previous scholarship

Establishes a local context for research

with individual quality because higher-quality resident kestrels should be able to defend higher-quality territories.

The objectives of my proposed study of American Kestrels will be to examine possible relationships among and between hunting behavior, territory quality, and individual quality in male and female American Kestrels. The results of this study will provide important information about habitat and perch selection by American Kestrels in central Kentucky in addition to the possible role of individual quality on hunting behavior and habitat use.

Reveals research purposes and identifies significance of the proposed research

Methods

Field work will take place from 15 October 2000 through 15 May 2001 at the Blue Grass Army Depot, Madison Co., Kentucky. During the study period, I will search for American Kestrels throughout accessible portions of the depot. Searches will be conducted on foot as well by automobile.

An attempt will be made to capture all kestrels observed using bal-chatri traps baited with mice. Once captured, kestrels will be banded with a numbered aluminum band plus a unique combination of colored plastic bands to permit individual identification. For each captured individual, I will take standard morphological measurements (wing chord, tarsus length, tail length, and mass). In addition, 8 to 10 feathers will be plucked from the head, breast, back, and wing, respectively. Plumage in these areas is either reddish or bluish, and the quality of such colors is known to be correlated with individual quality (Hill 1991, 1992; Keyser 1998). Variation in the color and intensity of plumage will be determined using a reflectance spectrometer (Ocean Optics S2000 fiber optic spectrometer, Dunedin, FL), and these values will be used as a measure of individual quality. To confirm that plumage color and intensity are dependent on condition, we will use

This section provides a highly detailed description of proposed research procedures, or methods.

tail feather growth rates as a measure of nutritional condition during molt. At the time of capture, the outermost tail feathers will be removed and the mean width of daily growth bars, which is correlated with nutritional condition (Hill and Montgomerie 1994), will be determined.

Each focal American Kestrel (N = at least 14; 7 males and 7 females) will be observed at least once a week. Observations will be made at various times during the day, with observation periods typically 1 to 3 hours in duration. During focal bird observations, individuals will be monitored using binoculars and spotting scopes. Information will be recorded on a portable tape recorder for later transcription. During each observation, I will record all attacks and whether attacks were initiated from a perch or while hovering. For perches, I will note the time a kestrel lands on a perch and the time until the kestrel either initiates an attack or leaves for another perch (giving up time). If an attack is made, I will note attack distances (the distance from a perch to the point where a prey item was attacked) and outcome (successful or not). If successful, an attempt will be made to identify the prey (to the lowest taxonomic category possible).

The activity budgets of kestrels will also be determined by observing the frequency and duration of kestrel behaviors during randomly selected 20-min observation periods (i.e., a randomly selected period during the 1- to 3-hour observation period). During these 20-minute periods, the frequency of occurrence of each of the following behaviors will be recorded: capturing prey, preening, engaging in nonpreening comfort movements (including scratching, stretching wing or tail, shaking body plumage, cleaning foot with bill, and yawning), vocalizing, and flying. The context in which flight occurs, including pounces on prey, and the duration of flights and of preening bouts will also be recorded.

Territories will be delineated by noting the locations of focal kestrels, and the vegetation in each kestrel's winter territory will be characterized following the methods of Smallwood (1987). Possible relationships among hunting behavior (mode of attack, perch time, attack distance and outcome [successful or unsuccessful], and type of prey attacked), territory vegetation, time budgets, sex, and individual quality will be examined. All analyses will be conducted using the Statistical Analysis System (SAS Institute 1989).

Literature Cited

Balgooyen TG. 1976. Behavior and ecology of the American Kestrel in the Sierra Nevada of California. Univ Calif Publ Zool 103:1-83.

Bohall-Wood P, Collopy MW. 1986. Abundance and habitat selection of two American Kestrel subspecies in north-central Florida. Auk 103:557-563.

Craighead JJ, Craighead FC Jr. 1956. Hawks, owls, and wildlife. Harrisburg (PA): Stackpole.

Hill GE. 1991. Plumage coloration is a sexually selected indicator of male quality. Nature 350:337-339.

Hill GE. 1992. Proximate basis of variation in carotenoid pigmentation in male House Finches. Auk 109:1-12.

Hill GE, Montgomerie R. 1994. Plumage colour signals nutritional condition in the House Finch. Proc R Soc Lond B Biol Sci 258:47-52.

Kellner CJ. 1985. A comparative analysis of the foraging behavior of male and female American Kestrels in central Kentucky [master's thesis]. [Richmond (KY)]: Eastern Kentucky University.

Keyser AJ. 1998. Is structural color a reliable signal of quality in Blue Grosbeaks? [master's thesis]. [Auburn (AL)]: Auburn University.

Mengel RM. 1965. The birds of Kentucky. Lawrence (KS): Allen Press. (American Ornithologists' Union monograph; 3).

Palmer-Ball B. 1996. The Kentucky breeding bird atlas. Lexington (KY): Univ. Press of Kentucky.

SAS Institute. 1989. SAS user's guide: statistics. Cary (NC): SAS Institute.

Smallwood JA. 1987. Sexual segregation by habitat in American Kestrels wintering in southcentral Florida: vegetative structure and responses of differential prey availability. Condor 89:842-849.

Smallwood JA. 1988. The relationship of vegetative cover to daily rhythms of prey consumption by American Kestrels wintering in southcentral Florida. J Raptor Res 22:77-80.

Stinson CH, Crawford DL, Lauthner J. 1981. Sex differences in winter habitat of American Kestrels in Georgia. J. Field Ornithol 52:29-35.

LAB REPORT

Lab reports are the formal reporting mechanism for research in the sciences. When a scientist publishes an article that reports the results of a research study, it is generally in the form of a lab report. Lab reports include information reported in IMRaD format, and the sections of the lab report are often listed exactly in that order:

- Introduction
- Methods
- Results
- Discussion

Be sure to read through the section on pages 197–204 of Chapter 8 that describes the different kinds of information typically presented in each of these sections.

If a group of researchers writes a research proposal before writing a lab report, they've already completed the first two sections of the lab report and only need to revise the report to reflect what they actually accomplished in the study (instead of what they planned to do). The Results and Discussion sections report new information about the data they gathered and what they offer as explanations and interpretations of what those results might mean. The Discussion section might also include suggestions for future research, demonstrating how research in the sciences is always building upon prior research.

Composing a Lab Report

The final writing project for this chapter is a lab report. You might report results from either experimentation or systematic observation. Your research could take place in an actual laboratory setting, or it could just as easily take place in the wider environment around you. Regardless, be sure to check with your instructor about whether your lab report should be based on formal observation or experimentation.

Since lab reports use IMRaD organizational format, your report should include the following sections:

- Introduction
- Methods
- Results
- Discussion

As you report your results and discuss their significance, you might include elements of visual design to help communicate the results to your audience. These might include tables or figures. Also, you might include an abstract, and you'll need to include a reference list that cites all sources used in your report. (See Chapter 8 for more information on writing tables and figures, and more information on abstracts.)

Insider Example
Student Lab Report

In the following sample lab report, Kedric Lemon revisits the question of which battery type is most effective. He draws on the information gathered in his observation logbook (pp. 260–70) to design a research study that allows him to conduct further investigation to answer his research question.

Which Type of Battery Is the Most Effective When Energy Is Drawn Rapidly?

The researcher provides a descriptive, non-rhetorical title.

Kedric Lemon

North Carolina State University

Professor Matthew Chu

November 4, 2017

Which Type of Battery Is the Most Effective
When Energy Is Drawn Rapidly?

Introduction

The report follows the conventional IMRaD format.

The researcher establishes a focus for his research by positing a research question.

Today batteries are used in many of the products that we use every day, from the TV remote to the car we drive to work. AA batteries are one of the most widely used battery types, but which of these AA batteries is the most effective? Almeida, Xará, Delgado, and Costa (2006) tested five different types of batteries in a study similar to mine. They allowed each of the batteries to run the product for an hour. The product they were powering alternated from open to closed circuit, so the batteries went from not giving off energy to giving off energy very quickly. The researchers then measured the pulse of the battery to determine the charge. The pulse test is a very effective way of reading the battery because it is closed circuit, meaning it doesn't run the battery to find the voltage, and it is highly accurate. They found that the Energizer battery had the largest amount of pulses after the experiment. The energizer had on average 20 more pulses than the Duracell battery, giving the Energizer battery approximately a half hour longer in battery life when being used rapidly. Booth (1999) also performed his experiment using the pulse test. However, this experiment involved allowing the batteries to constantly give off energy for two hours, and then Booth measured the pulse. So his experiment is more comparable to my observational study because it was constantly drawing energy from the battery. In this experiment he found that the Duracell battery was the most effective. The Duracell battery had over 40 more pulses per minute than the Energizer battery, which means that the battery could last for an hour longer than the Energizer battery would.

Reviews previous research, and connects that research to the current research project

However, in today's market, rechargeable batteries are becoming increasing popular. Zucker (2005) compared 16 different types of rechargeable batteries. Most of these batteries were Nickel Metal Hydride, but a couple of them were the more traditional rechargeable AA battery, the Nickel Cadmium. In his study Zucker was testing how these batteries faired on their second charge after being discharged as closely as they could; rechargeable batteries are not allowed to go to 0 volts because then they cannot be recharged. In the end Zucker found that all but four of the batteries came back up to at least 70% of their initial charge, two of which did not even recharge at all. He found that, not surprisingly, the two most effective rechargeable batteries were Duracell and Energizer, which both came back to 86% of the first charge. However, the Energizer rechargeable battery had the higher initial charge, so Zucker concluded that the Energizer battery was the most effective rechargeable battery. Yu, Lai, Yan, and Wu (1999) looked at the capacity of three different Nickel Metal Hydride (NiMH) rechargeable batteries. They first took three different types of NiMH batteries and found the electrical capacity through a voltmeter. After, they measured the volume of each of the batteries to discover where it fell in the AA battery range of 600 to 660 mAh/cm3. They used this to test the efficiency of the NiMH batteries, as there are slightly different chemical compositions inside the batteries. In the end they concluded that the NiMH battery from the Duracell brand was the most efficient.

Li, Daniel, and Wood (2011) looked at the improvements being made to lithium ion AA batteries. The lithium ion AA batteries are extremely powerful, but in recent years they have become increasingly more popular for studying by many researchers. Li et al. tested the voltage of the lithium ion AA rechargeable battery and found that the starting voltage was

Prominence of dates points to the researcher's concern for the recency of source materials

Continues review of previous scholarship on this topic

on average 3.2 volts. That is more than the average onetime-use AA battery. They further found that what makes modern lithium ion batteries so much more powerful is the cathodes. Research into cathode materials has significantly increased the rate of reactions for lithium ion batteries.

Establishes specific research questions on the basis of previous observations

The objective of this study is to determine which brand of batteries is the most efficient and to compare a generic rechargeable battery to these regular AA batteries. My original research question for my logbook was Which brand of AA batteries is the most effective over extended usage? However, for my final study I wanted to look at how batteries reacted when they were being used very quickly, so I formed two research questions for this study: Which type of battery is the most effective for rapid uses? How do regular AA batteries compare to a generic AA rechargeable battery? My hypothesis for this experiment is that the Energizer battery will be the most effective battery when energy is being taken from the battery rapidly.

Hypothesis

Method

Observation Logbook

Reports on research previously conducted

In my observation logbook I looked at how different types of batteries compared when they were being tested through a flashlight. The batteries I observed were Duracell, Energizer, and a generic brand. I allowed the flashlight to run for an hour with the set of batteries inside. I did this step for all three types of batteries that I observed in that study. After the hour was up I tested the voltage with a voltmeter. I continued to do this for five consecutive days. For each of the tests I made sure that the temperature was the same for each of the batteries while they were being tested. I also allowed the flashlight to remain off for an hour to let it cool down. These steps were taken to avoid any unknown variables.

For my follow-up study, I decided to look at how batteries compare when they are being used in quick bursts, meaning that they quickly change from using no energy to using a lot of energy rapidly. In order to test the battery this way I had to change the flashlight to a strobe light so that it quickly turns on and off automatically. I also decided to add a rechargeable battery to my tests since this is an increasingly popular item today. I found my data by attaching the batteries to a voltmeter immediately after they were taken out of the strobe light. Each of the set of batteries was in the strobe light for 20 minutes.

Variables that I made sure remained constant for this experiment were the temperature of the room as well as the temperature of the strobe light. For this reason I allowed the strobe light a 30-minute cooldown before I put the next set of batteries into it.

> Provides a detailed account of research procedures

Limitations

One of the limitations that I faced in this study was an inability to get the thermocouple that I wanted to measure the temperature of the battery. Also I had a small sample size, so if I had taken more samples, then my results would have been more valid. I could improve on these by getting a thermocouple that would measure the temperature. This would allow me to compare the expected voltage of the battery through the

> The researcher uses technical language, or jargon.

thermocouple and the voltmeter. After the battery got out of the strobe light I would hook it up to the thermocouple and then measure the voltage by looking at the voltmeter. I could tell what the voltage of the battery is through the thermocouple using a graph that one of my secondary sources provided. Another limitation that I faced in this experiment was that I lacked better equipment that could have made my results more accurate—like a pulse reader or a better voltmeter, as I was using a fairly inexpensive one.

Results

My results from my logbook provided me with primarily quantitative data. For each of the types of batteries I found these results.

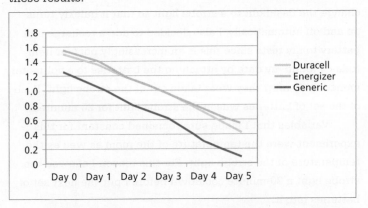

For the Energizer battery I found that it started off with the largest initial charge of 1.55 volts. On average the Energizer battery lost .16 volts for every hour. The Duracell battery had an initial charge of 1.5 volts and lost an average of .18 volts per hour. Last, the generic brand of battery had an initial voltage of 1.25 volts and lost on average .23 volts every hour.

In this experiment I found that the Energizer battery again had the highest starting charge and highest ending charge. The Duracell AA battery was close behind the

The researcher notes limitations he encountered with the methods.

Outlines the major findings of the study. A number of results are also presented visually, in the form of graphs and figures.

The researcher frequently presents results in tables and charts.

Energizer. The generic brand of batteries came next, followed by the rechargeable battery.

This experiment showed similar results to what I had found in my logbook. The Duracell and Energizer batteries were both very similar, while the generic brand lagged behind.

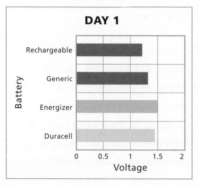

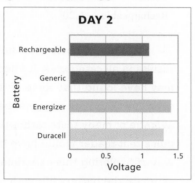

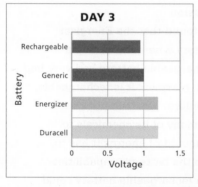

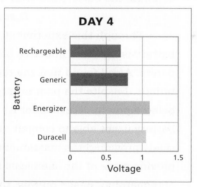

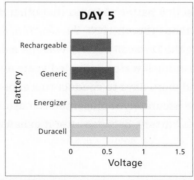

Battery	Initial voltage (volts)	Final voltage (volts)	Average volts lost (volts/20 min)
Energizer	1.60	1.10	0.10
Duracell	1.55	0.95	0.12
Generic	1.40	0.60	0.16
Rechargeable	1.20	0.55	0.13

The table shows that the Energizer battery had the best results in all categories. If I had taken more samples, then I may have found that some of the batteries performed better or worse than they did here, because I could have taken the average of many tests rather than looking at only one. Using a pulse test reader would have been an even more informative way of exploring this experiment because that instrument can estimate the battery life with high precision.

Discussion

Through this experiment I found that the Energizer battery is the most effective battery when used in rapid bursts. Also I found that the rechargeable battery had very bad ratings. Despite the poor ratings, however, it is rechargeable, being a potential reason for its failure. The rechargeable battery is not able to commit as many of its chemicals to solely providing the maximum amount of energy; it has to provide some of the chemicals to the battery's capabilities of recharging. Based on this, the rechargeable battery could be the most effective battery. I found that other studies with similar methods (Booth 1999; Yu, Lai, Yan, & Wu 1999) determined that the Duracell battery was the most effective. However, these studies were conducted years ago.

If I had had more days to conduct this experiment, I could have more accurately represented the usefulness of the rechargeable battery, because after it exhausted its first

Provides an overview of the implications of major findings in light of previous scholarship charge it came back completely recharged for the next day. Another limitation that I faced in this experiment was that I overestimated how fast the battery voltages would decrease in the strobe light, so I was unable to see how the batteries acted near the end of their charge. An area of study for further research would be to compare different types of rechargeable batteries. For instance, I already know that the lithium ion AA rechargeable batteries carry more volts than regular AA batteries, and they are rechargeable.

If I had had more time to perform this experiment or had allowed the batteries to be in the strobe light for a longer time, I think that I would have found that the rechargeable battery would be ahead of the generic battery in terms of the average voltage lost. Also I think that the gap would have been larger between the Duracell battery and the Energizer battery because looking at my results from the observation logbook shows that the Energizer battery does a lot better than the Duracell battery toward the end of its life. This being said, I think that the Duracell battery does not handle the rapid uses as well as the extended uses.

Discusses limitations of the study overall

These results show that the Energizer battery is the most effective battery for rapid use and, from my observation logbook, the most effective for extended use. The rechargeable battery used in this experiment is hard to compare to these regular AA batteries because I wasn't able to exploit its sole advantage, recharging. However, this was just a generic brand of rechargeable batteries, so it would be interesting to see how the Duracell and Energizer rechargeable batteries compare to their regular batteries.

References

Almeida, M. F., Xará, S. M., Delgado, J., & Costa, C. A. (2006). Characterization of spent AA household alkaline batteries. *Waste Management, 26*(5), 466-476. https://doi.org/10.1016/j.wasman.2005.04.005

Booth, S. A. (1999). High-drain alkaline AA-batteries. *Popular Electronics, 16*(1), 5.

Li, J., Daniel, C., & Wood, D. (2011). Materials processing for lithium-ion batteries. *Journal of Power Sources, 196*(5), 2452-2460. https://doi.org/10.1016/j.jpowsour.2010.11.001

Yu, C. Z., Lai, W. H., Yan, G. J., & Wu, J. Y. (1999). Study of preparation technology for high performance AA size Ni–MH batteries. *Journal of Alloys and Compounds, 293*(1-2), 784-787. https://doi.org/10.1016/S0925-8388(99)00463-6

Zucker, P. (2005). AA batteries tested: Rechargeable batteries. *Australian PC User, 17*(6), 51.

Provides a list of sources used in the construction of the lab report.

Reading and Writing in the Natural Sciences

- **Systematic observation plays a critical role in the natural sciences.** The disciplines of the natural sciences rely on methods of observation to generate and answer research questions about how and why natural phenomena act as they do.

- **Many natural scientists work in interdisciplinary fields of study.** These fields, such as biochemistry and biophysics, combine subject matter and methods from more than one field to address research questions.

- **Scientists typically conduct research according to the steps of the scientific method:** observe, ask a research question, formulate a hypothesis, test the hypothesis through experimentation, and explain results.

- **The scientific writing process follows logically from the steps of the scientific method:** observe and describe, speculate, experiment, and report.

- **To test their hypotheses, or their proposed answers to research questions, natural scientists may use multiple methods.** Two common methods are systematic observation and experimentation.

- **Scientific research proposals are typically vetted by institutional review boards (IRB).** Committees that review research proposals are charged with the task of examining all elements of a scientific study to ensure that it treats subjects equitably and ethically.

- **Conventional rhetorical features of the scientific community reflect the shared values of the community's members.** Some of these values are objectivity, replicability, recency, and cooperation and collaboration.

- **Members of the scientific community frequently produce a number of genres.** These include the observation logbook, the research proposal, and the lab report.

10

Reading and Writing in the Applied Fields

Introduction to the Applied Fields

In this chapter, we explore some of the applied fields that students often encounter or choose to study as part of their college experience. In some cases, one or more of these applied fields may correspond to your intended major or to your selected area of focus for your career. Throughout the chapter, we also examine some of the common genres through which professionals in these fields communicate to various audiences.

WHAT ARE APPLIED FIELDS?

Applied fields are areas of academic study that focus on the production of practical knowledge and that share a core mission of preparing students for specific careers. Often, such preparation includes hands-on training. Examples of applied fields that prepare students for particular careers include nursing, business, law, education, and engineering, just to name a few. A list of some additional applied fields appears below.

Some Applied Fields

Sports psychology	Counseling
Business	Statistics
Law	Engineering
Education	Speech pathology
Nursing	Public administration
Applied physics	Architecture
Applied linguistics	Broadcast journalism
Social work	

ANDREA TSURUMI

As you might expect, research that occurs in the applied fields is quite varied. These variations among the fields are often reflected in the kinds of questions each field asks and attempts to answer, the forms of evidence it relies on, the data-collection methods it employs, and the ways it reports findings from research to differing audiences. Nevertheless, research in the applied fields typically attempts to solve problems. An automotive engineering team, for example, might start with a problem like consumers' reluctance to buy an all-electric vehicle. To address the issue, the engineering team would first attempt to define the scope of the problem. Why does the problem exist? What are the factors contributing to consumers' reluctance to buy an all-electric vehicle? Once the problem has been identified and clearly defined, the team of researchers can then begin to explore possible solutions.

Examples of large-scale problems that require practical applications of research include issues such as racial inequality in the American criminal justice system, the lack of clean drinking water in some nonindustrialized nations, obesity and heart disease, and ways to provide outstanding public education to children with behavioral problems. These are all real-world problems scholars and practitioners in the applied fields are working to solve this very moment.

INSIDE WORK **Defining and Solving Problems**

> Describe a time when you conducted research to solve a problem. Start by defining the problem and explaining why you needed to solve it. When did you first identify the problem? What caused you to seek solutions to it? How did you research and understand the problem? What methods did you use to solve it? Finally, make a list of applied field professionals (e.g., engineer, lawyer, nutritionist) who might have some interest in helping to solve the kind of problem you identified. What do you think each of these fields could contribute to an understanding of or solution to the problem? ❱

Professionals in applied fields often work in collaboration with one another, or in teams, to complete research and other projects, and professors who teach in these areas frequently assign tasks that require interaction and cooperation among a group of students to create a product or to solve a problem. In the field of business management, for example, teams of professionals often must work together to market a new product. Solid communication and interpersonal skills are necessary for a team to manage a budget, design a marketing or advertising campaign, and engage with a client successfully all at the same time. As such, the ability to work cooperatively—to demonstrate effective interpersonal and team communication skills—is highly valued among professionals in the applied fields. You shouldn't be surprised, then, if you're one day applying for a job in an applied field and an interviewer asks you to share a little about your previous experiences working in teams to successfully complete a project. As you learn more about the applied fields examined in this chapter, take care to note those writing tasks completed by teams, or those moments when cooperation among professionals working in a particular field are highlighted by the content of the genres we explore.

Our purpose in this chapter is to offer a basic introduction to a few of the many applied fields of study and to explore some of the kinds of writing that typically occur in these fields. Because the applied fields vary so much, and since it would be impossible to generalize conventional expectations for communication across these diverse fields, we've chosen to focus on specific fields as examples. The rest of the chapter, then, explores specific applied fields and provides examples of the kinds of writing routinely produced by professionals in these fields. Our aim here is to highlight a rhetorical approach to these fields that would be helpful for any student attempting to acclimate to one or more of these communities.

INSIDE WORK **Considering Additional Applied Fields**

Visit your college or university's website, and locate a listing of the majors or concentrations offered in any academic department. In light of the definition of an *applied field* proposed above, consider whether any of the majors or concentrations identified for that particular discipline could be described as applied fields. Additionally, spend some time considering your own major or potential area of concentration: Are you studying an applied field? Are there areas of study within your major or concentration that could be considered applied fields? If so, what are they, and why would you consider them applied fields? ▶

Rhetoric and the Applied Fields

Because applied fields are centrally focused on preparing professionals who will work in those fields, students are often asked to engage audiences associated with the work they'll do in those fields after graduation. Imagine that you've just graduated from college with a degree in business management and have secured a job as a marketing director for a business. What kinds of writing do you expect to encounter in this new position? What audiences do you expect to be writing for? You may well be asked to prepare business analyses or market reports. You may be asked to involve yourself in new product management or even the advertising campaign for a product. All these activities, which call for different kinds of writing, will require you to manage information and to shape your communication of that information into texts that are designed specifically for other professionals in your field—such as boards of directors, financial officers, or advertising executives. As a student in the applied field of business management, you therefore need to become familiar with the audiences, genres, conventions, and other expectations for writing specific to your career path that extend beyond academic audiences. Being mindful of the rhetorical situation in which you must communicate with other professionals is essential to your potential success as a writer in an applied field.

As with more traditional academic writing, we recommend that you analyze carefully any writing situation you encounter in an applied field. You might begin by responding to the following questions:

LaunchPad

Criminal justice instructor Michelle Richter discusses the role of audience.

1. **Who is my audience?** Unlike the audience for a lab report for a chemistry class or the audience for an interpretation of a poem in a literature class, your audience for writing in an applied field is just as likely to be non-academic as academic. Certainly, the writing most students will do in their actual careers will be aimed at other professionals in their field, not researchers or professors in a university. In addition to understanding exactly who your audience is, you'll want to be sure to consider the specific needs of your target audience.

2. **In light of my purpose and my audience's needs, is there an appropriate genre I should rely on to communicate my information?** As in the more traditional academic disciplines, there are many genres through which professionals in applied fields communicate. Based on an analysis of your rhetorical situation, and keeping your purpose for writing in mind, you'll want to consider whether the information you have to share should be reported in a specific genre: Should you write a memorandum, a marketing proposal, or an executive summary, for instance? Answering this question can help you determine if there is an appropriate form, or genre, through which to communicate your information.

3. **Are there additional conventional expectations I should consider for the kind of writing task I need to complete?** Beyond simply identifying an appropriate genre, answering this question can help you determine how to shape the information you need to communicate to your target audience. If the writing task requires a particular genre, then you're likely to rely on features that conventionally appear as part of that genre. Of course, there are many good reasons to communicate information in other ways. In these situations, we recommend that you carefully consider the appropriateness of the structural, language, and reference features you employ.

Genres in Selected Applied Fields

In the sections that follow, we offer brief introductions to some applied fields of study and provide examples of genres that students and professionals working in these fields often produce. We explore expectations for these genres by highlighting conventional structure, language, and reference features that writers in these fields frequently employ.

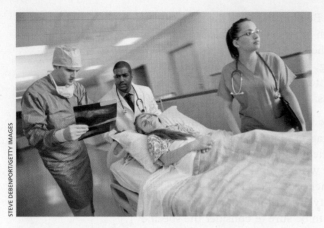

HEALTH FIELDS

One of the fastest-growing segments of the U.S. economy is related to health services. As the population of the country ages, and as science and medicine come together to lengthen average life spans, it's not surprising that health professionals of all sorts, including those with various levels of training and expertise in providing emotional, mental, and physical health services, are in high demand.

Allied Health Professions

Along with this increased demand and the continued development of the medical arts as a result of scientific discoveries and technological advances, it's also not surprising that the allied health fields are constantly expanding and evolving to meet the needs of patients. The Association of Schools of Allied Health Professionals defines "allied health" as "those health professions that are distinct from medicine and nursing." Allied health professionals typically work in a highly cooperative manner with other professionals, including medical doctors and nurses, to provide various forms of direct and indirect care to patients. In fact, allied health professionals regularly have a role to play in the prevention, diagnosis, treatment, and recovery from illness for most patients. A small sampling of the many diverse allied health fields includes:

- Medical Assistant
- Nutritionist
- Occupational Therapist
- Phlebotomist
- Physical Therapist
- Physician Assistant
- Radiographer
- Respiratory Therapist
- Speech Pathologist

Nursing

Most of us have had experiences with nurses, who, along with physicians and other health professionals, serve on the front lines of preventing and treating illness in our society. In addition to their hands-on engagement with individuals in clinical and community settings, nurses spend a good deal of their time writing—whether documenting their observations about patients in medical charts, preparing orders for medical procedures, designing care plans, or communicating with patients. A student of nursing might encounter any number of additional forms of writing tasks, including nursing care plans for individuals, reviews of literature, and community or public health assessment papers, just to name a few. Each of these forms of communication requires that nurses be especially attuned to the needs of various audiences. A nurse communicating with a patient, for example, might have to translate medical jargon so that the individual can fully understand his or her treatment. Alternatively, a nurse who is producing a care plan for a patient would likely need to craft the document such that other nurses and medical professionals could follow methodically the assessments and recommendations for care. Some nurses, especially those who undertake advanced study or who prepare others to become nurses, often design, implement, or participate in research studies.

We interviewed Janna Dieckmann, a registered nurse and clinical associate professor in the School of Nursing at the University of North Carolina at Chapel Hill. In her Insider's View, she offers valuable insights into the writing and researching practices of the nursing community.

As Dieckmann notes, many nurses, especially those working to prepare other nurses, may also participate in various kinds of scholarly research endeavors. In the section that follows, we provide an excerpted look at a 2005 research study published in the nursing journal *Newborn and Infant Nursing Reviews*, along with an example of discharge instructions. The former is a genre of writing common across health professions, and the latter is a genre of writing that nurses who work in a clinical setting often produce for patients.

Insider's View

Nurses and nursing consider many different areas of research and interest

JANNA DIECKMANN, NURSING

COURTESY OF JANNA DIECKMANN

"Research in nursing is varied, including quantitative research into health and illness patterns, as well as intervention to maximize health and reduce illness. Qualitative research varies widely, including research in the history of nursing, which is my focus. There is a wide variety of types of writing demanded in a nursing program. It is so varied that many connections are possible. Cross-discipline collaborations among faculty of various professional schools are valued at many academic institutions today. One of my colleagues conducted research on rats. Another looked at sleep patterns in older adults as a basis for understanding dementia onset. One public health nursing colleague conducts research on out-of-work women, and another examines cross-cultural competence. These interests speak to our reasons for becoming nurses—our seeking out of real life, of direct experience, of being right there with people, and of understanding others and their worlds."

Scholarly Research Report Some professionals in health fields are both practitioners and scholars. As practitioners, they assess and care for patients in cooperation with other medical professionals. As scholars, they may, as Dieckmann indicates, conduct research on a host of issues, including the history and best practices of nursing, the best therapy for healing repetitive stress injuries, or the benefits of food tracking apps in maintaining a balanced diet. In addition to producing scholarship that advances the health fields, these professionals typically work in colleges or universities with programs that prepare individuals for careers in nursing or the allied health fields. Such professionals, then, may assume multiple roles as researchers and educators, and as practitioners.

Insider Example
Professional Research Report

As you read the following research report, pay particular attention to the structure, language, and reference parallels between the form of the report and those you've encountered already in the fields of the natural sciences and the social sciences. Keep in mind that the text presented here is made up of a series of excerpts from a much lengthier and more substantial research report.

Rural African-American Mothers Parenting Prematurely Born Infants: An Ecological Systems Perspective

MARGARET SHANDOR MILES, PhD, FAAN; DIANE HOLDITCH-DAVIS, PhD, FAAN; SUZANNE THOYRE, PhD; LINDA BEEBER, PhD

The abstract provides an overview of the report, including a description of the study's purpose, its methods, and its central findings.

— **ABSTRACT**

This qualitative descriptive study describes the concerns and issues of rural African-American mothers with prematurely born infants. Mothers were part of a larger nurse-parent support intervention. The 18 mothers lived in rural areas in the Southeast, and their infants were younger than 35 weeks gestational age at birth and at high risk for developmental problems because they either weighed less than 1500 grams at birth or required mechanical ventilation. Field notes written by the intervention nurses providing support to the mothers after discharge from the hospital were analyzed using methods of content analysis. Concerns of the mothers related to the infant's health and development, the maternal role in parenting the infant, personal aspects of their lives, and relationship issues particularly with the fathers. Findings support the importance of an ecological systems perspective when designing research and caring for rural African-American mothers with prematurely born children.

REVIEW OF THE LITERATURE

The review of the literature begins with a synthesis point: mothers experience a period of transitioning. Both McHaffie and May confirm this conclusion.

Although mothers are excited about taking the preterm infant home, a number of studies have noted that they are also anxious during this important transition. McHaffie[1] found mothers insecure and lacking in confidence at first, followed by a period of accommodation as they learned about the infant's behavioral cues and needs. During this period, mothers became overwhelmed with responsibilities, and fatigue resulted. As the infants settled into their new surroundings and the mothers felt the rewards of caregiving, they became confident in their maternal role. May[2] also found that mothers went through a process of learning about the added responsibilities of caregiving, and this resulted in strains on their time and energy. Mothers were vigilant about looking for changes in the infant's status and for signs of progress through improved physical health and development. During this process, they looked for signs that their child was normal and sought support from others. . . .

METHOD

This study used a qualitative descriptive design[3] to identify the concerns and issues of the mothers based on field notes written by the intervention nurses providing support to the mothers after discharge from the hospital.[4] The Nursing Support Intervention was an 18-month in-person and telephone intervention provided by master's-prepared nurses starting around the time of discharge of the infant and ending when the infants were around 18 months old corrected for prematurity. The nurses helped the mothers to process the mothering experience and resolve emotional distress that is caused by prematurity, identify and reduce parenting and other life stresses, develop relationships with their infants, and identify and use acceptable resources to meet needs of the infant and the mother. . . .

Qualitative research methods are explained.

RESULTS

The concerns and issues raised by the mothers with the intervention nurses fell into four major categories: infant health and development, parenting, personal concerns, and relationship issues (Table 1). _____

Results of the study, or categories of concerns identified among mothers, are presented in the form of a summary table. The researchers explore these results in more detail in a number of additional paragraphs.

Table 1.
Maternal concerns of rural African-American mothers in parenting prematurely born infants

Infant health and development	Establishing feeding and managing gastrointestinal tract distress
	Managing medical technologies
	Preventing and managing infections
	Establishing sleep patterning
	Learning developmental expectations
Parenting	Learning the infant's needs
	Establishing daily patterns
	Balancing roles
Personal concerns	Coping with financial problems
	Managing stressful jobs while securing appropriate childcare
	Losing and trying to regain educational opportunities toward a better life
	Working toward securing a home of one's own
	Managing depressive symptoms
Relationship issues	Working through relationship with infant's father

The study's
Discussion section
connects findings to
potential changes
in support that
could improve
outcomes for
mothers and their
children.

— DISCUSSION

Findings from this study provide insight into the needs of mothers of prematurely born infants after discharge from the hospital. In the early months after discharge, support is needed related to caring for the infant. As their infants grow, mothers may need help in identifying and getting resources for developmental problems. Agencies that provide services to mothers need to consider the complex lives of the mothers, especially those who are single and living in poverty. Of utmost importance is helping the mothers to manage issues related to finding a job, managing work, and care of their infant. Finding acceptable day care is a particularly important need. Furthermore, community programs are needed to help the mothers achieve their dreams of furthering their education and finding acceptable homes for themselves and their children.

REFERENCES

1. McHaffie HE. Mothers of very low birthweight babies: how do they adjust? *J Adv Nurs.* 1990;15:6–11.

2. May KM. Searching for normalcy: mothers' caregiving for low birthweight infants. *Pediatr Nurs.* 1997;23:17–20.

3. Sandelowski M. Whatever happened to qualitative description? *Res Nurs Health.* 2000;23:334–340.

4. Holditch-Davis D. A nursing support intervention for mothers of preterm infants. Grant funded by the National Institute of Nursing Research (NR05263). 2001.

Discharge Instructions If you've ever been hospitalized, then you probably remember the experience quite vividly. It's likely that you interacted with a nurse, who perhaps assessed your health upon arrival. You were also likely cared for by a nurse, or a particular group of nurses, during your stay. Nurses also often play an integral role in a patient's discharge from a hospital. Typically, before a patient is released from a hospital, a nurse explains to the patient (and perhaps a family member or two, or another intended primary caregiver) and provides in written form a set of instructions for aftercare. This constitutes the **discharge instructions**.

This document, or series of documents, includes instructions for how to care for oneself at home. The instructions may focus on managing diet and medications, as well as caring for other needs, such as post-operative bandaging procedures. They may also include exercise or diet management plans recommended for long-term recovery and health maintenance. These plans may include seeing an allied health professional such as a physical or occupational therapist. Often presented in a series of bulleted items or statements, these lists are usually highly generic; that is, the same instructions frequently apply for patients with the same or similar health conditions. For this reason, discharge instruction forms may include spaces for nurses or other health-care professionals to write in more specific information relating to a patient's individual circumstances. As well, discharge instructions frequently include information about a patient's follow-up care with his or her doctor or primary caregiver. This could take the form of a future appointment time or directions to call for a follow-up appointment or to consult with another physician. An additional conventional element of discharge instructions is a list of signs of a medical emergency and directions concerning when and how to seek medical attention immediately, should certain signs or symptoms appear in the patient. Finally, discharge instructions are typically signed and dated by a physician or nurse, and they are sometimes signed by the patient as well.

   Many patients are in unclear states of mind or are extremely vulnerable at the time of release from a hospital, so nurses who provide and explain discharge instructions to patients are highly skilled at assessing patients' understanding of these instructions.

Insider Example
Discharge Instructions

The following text is an example of a typical set of discharge instructions. As you read the document, consider areas in the instructions that you think a nurse would be more likely to stress to a patient in a discharge meeting: What would a nurse cover quickly? What would he or she want to communicate most clearly to a patient?

Provides identifying information about the patient, as well as name and contact information of healthcare provider

Much of the information provided in discharge instructions is generic, so nurses can provide "personalized notes" here.

Provides a brief overview of the patient's medical issue treated by the healthcare provider

Provides specific instructions for the patient to follow upon release from the medical facility

Note that each of these directions begins with a verb, stressing the importance of taking the action indicated.

Note that specific directions are listed in a series of bulleted sections. Bulleted lists make the information easier to read and follow.

FIRST HOSPITAL
Where Care Comes First

Patient's Name: John Q. Patient
Healthcare Provider's Name: First Hospital
Department: Cardiology
Phone: 617-555-1212
Date: Thursday, May 8, 2014
Notes: **Nurses can write personalized notes to the patient here.**

Discharge Instructions for Heart Attack

A heart attack occurs when blood flow to the heart muscle is interrupted. This deprives the heart muscle of oxygen, causing tissue damage or tissue death. Common treatments include lifestyle changes, oxygen, medicines, and surgery.

Steps to Take

Home Care

- Rest until your doctor says it is okay to return to work or other activities.
- Take all medicines as prescribed by your doctor. Beta-blockers, ACE inhibitors, and antiplatelet therapy are often recommended.
- Attend a cardiac rehabilitation program if recommended by your doctor.

Diet

Eat a heart-healthy diet:

- Limit your intake of fat, cholesterol, and sodium. Foods such as ice cream, cheese, baked goods, and red meat are not the best choices.
- Increase your intake of whole grains, fish, fruits, vegetables, and nuts.
- Discuss supplements with your doctor.

Your doctor may refer you to a dietician to advise you on meal planning.

Physical Activity

The American Heart Association recommends at least 30 minutes of exercise daily, or at least 3–4 times per week, for patients who have had a heart attack. Your doctor will let you know when you are ready to begin regular exercise.

- Ask your doctor when you will be able to return to work.
- Ask your doctor when you may resume sexual activity.
- Do not drive unless your doctor has given you permission to do so.

Medications

The following medicines may be prescribed to prevent you from having another heart attack:

- Aspirin, which has been shown to decrease the risk of heart attacks
  ○ Certain painkillers, such as ibuprofen, when taken together with aspirin, may put you at high risk for gastrointestinal bleeding and also reduce the effectiveness of aspirin.
- Clopidogrel or prasugrel
  ○ Avoid omeprazole or esomeprazole if you take clopidogrel. They may make clopidogrel not work. Ask your doctor for other drug choices.
- ACE inhibitors
- Nitroglycerin
- Beta-blockers or calcium channel blockers

- Cholesterol-lowering medicines
- Blood pressure medicines
- Pain medicines
- Anti-anxiety or antidepressant medicines

If you are taking medicines, follow these general guidelines:

- Take your medicine as directed. Do not change the amount or the schedule.
- Do not stop taking them without talking to your doctor.
- Do not share them.
- Ask what the results and side effects are. Report them to your doctor.
- Some drugs can be dangerous when mixed. Talk to a doctor or pharmacist if you are taking more than one drug. This includes over-the-counter medicine and herbal or dietary supplements.
- Plan ahead for refills so you do not run out.

Lifestyle Changes and Prevention

Together, you and your doctor will plan proper lifestyle changes that will aid in your recovery. Some things to keep in mind to recover and prevent another heart attack include:

- If you smoke, talk to your doctor about ways to help you quit. There are many options to choose from, like using nicotine replacement products, taking prescription medicines to ease cravings and withdrawal symptoms, participating in smoking cessation classes, or doing an online self-help program.
- Have your cholesterol checked regularly.
- Get regular medical check-ups.
- Control your blood pressure.
- Eat a healthful diet, one that is low in saturated fat and rich in whole grains, fruits, and vegetables.
- Have a regular, low-impact exercise program.
- Maintain a healthy weight.
- Manage stress through activities such as yoga, meditation, and counseling.
- If you have diabetes, maintain good control of your condition.

Follow-Up

Since your recovery needs to be monitored, be sure to keep all appointments and have exams done regularly as directed by your doctor. In addition, some people have feelings of depression or anxiety after a heart attack. To get the help you need, be sure to discuss these feelings with your doctor.

Schedule a follow-up appointment as directed by your doctor.

Call for Medical Help Right Away If Any of the Following Occurs

Call for medical help right away if you have symptoms of another heart attack, including:

- Chest pain, which may feel like a crushing weight on your chest
- A sense of fullness, squeezing, or pressure in the chest
- Anxiety, especially feeling a sense of doom or panic without apparent reason
- Rapid, irregular heartbeat
- Pain, tingling, or numbness in the left shoulder and arm, the neck or jaw, or the right arm
- Sweating
- Nausea or vomiting
- Indigestion or heartburn
- Lightheadedness, weakness, or fainting
- Shortness of breath
- Abdominal pain

If you think you have an emergency, call for medical help right away.

Directions are provided in as few words as possible.

Provides directions for how to "follow up" with medical provider(s)

Identifies emergency indicators

In Table 1 on page 299, the authors of the qualitative research report "Rural African-American Mothers Parenting Prematurely Born Infants: An Ecological Systems Perspective" identify a number of "concerns and issues" among rural mothers with premature infants. Choose one of these "concerns and issues," and develop a discharge plan for a mother and child in response. Using "Discharge Instructions for Heart Attack" as a model for your own set of discharge instructions, complete the following.

- Provide a brief introduction in which you offer a quick overview of the concern or issue.

- Provide supporting instructions for patients in three central areas: Steps to Take, Follow-Up, and Emergency Response. Note that many, or all, of the directives or recommendations that make up your instructions may be non-medical treatments, interventions, or therapies. You may consult additional sources for support, as needed.

- Authorize the discharge orders by signing and dating your document.

Once you've completed the discharge instructions, spend some time reflecting on the challenges you faced in the process of devising your instructions: What were the least and most challenging parts of writing the instructions? ❱

EDUCATION

When your teachers tell you that writing is important, they're probably conveying a belief based on their own experiences. Professional educators do a lot of writing. As students, you're aware of many contexts in which teachers write on a daily basis. They have project assignment sheets to design, papers to comment on and grade, websites to design, and e-mails to answer, just to name a few. However, educators also spend a great deal of time planning classes

and designing lesson plans. Though students rarely see these written products, they are essential, if challenging and time-consuming, endeavors for teachers. We provide examples and discussion of two forms of writing frequently produced by professionals in the various fields of education: the lesson plan and the Individualized Education Program (IEP).

Lesson Plan

When designing a **lesson plan**, teachers must consider many factors, including their goals and objectives for student learning, the materials needed to execute a lesson, the activities students will participate in as part of a lesson, and the methods they'll use to assess student learning. Among other considerations, teachers must also make sure their lesson plans help them meet prescribed curricular mandates.

Insider Example
Student Lesson Plan

The following lesson plan for a tenth-grade English class was designed by Myra Moses, who at the time of writing the plan was a doctoral candidate in education. In this plan, Moses begins by identifying the state-mandated curricular standards the lesson addresses. She then identifies the broader goals of her lesson plan before establishing the more specific objectives, or exactly what students will do to reach the broader learning goals. As you read, notice that all the plan's statements of objectives begin with a verb, as they identify actions students will take to demonstrate their learning. The plan ends by explaining the classroom activities the teacher will use to facilitate learning and by identifying the methods the instructor will use to assess student learning. These structural moves are conventional for the genre of a lesson plan.

Educational Standard → Goals → Objectives → Materials → Classroom Activities → Assessment

Lesson Plan

Overview and Purpose

This lesson is part of a unit on Homer's *Odyssey*. Prior to this lesson students will have had a lesson on Greek cultural and social values during the time of Homer, and they will have read the *Odyssey*. In the lesson, students will analyze passages from the *Odyssey* to examine the author's and characters' points of view. Students will participate in whole class discussion, work in small groups, and work individually to identify and evaluate point of view.

Education Standards Addressed

This lesson addresses the following objectives from the NC Standard Course of Study for Language Arts: English II:

1.02 Respond reflectively (through small group discussion, class discussion, journal entry, essay, letter, dialogue) to written and visual texts by:

- relating personal knowledge to textual information or class discussion.
- showing an awareness of one's own culture as well as the cultures of others.
- exhibiting an awareness of culture in which text is set or in which text was written.

> Identifies the state-mandated curricular elements, or the educational objectives, the lesson addresses. Notice that these are quite broad in scope.

1.03 Demonstrate the ability to read, listen to, and view a variety of increasingly complex print and non-print expressive texts appropriate to grade level and course literary focus, by:

- identifying and analyzing text components (such as organizational structures, story elements, organizational features) and evaluating their impact on the text.
- providing textual evidence to support understanding of and reader's response to text.
- making inferences, predicting, and drawing conclusions based on text.
- identifying and analyzing personal, social, historical, or cultural influences, contexts, or biases.

5.01 Read and analyze selected works of world literature by:

- understanding the importance of cultural and historical impact on literary texts.

Goals

1. To teach students how to identify and evaluate an author's point of view and purpose by examining the characters' point of view.
2. To teach students to critically examine alternate points of view.

Objectives

Students will:

1. Identify point of view in a story by examining the text and evaluating how the main character views his/her world at different points in the story.
2. Demonstrate that they understand point of view by using examples and evidence from the text to support what they state is the character's point of view.
3. Apply their knowledge and understanding of point of view by taking a passage from the text and rewriting it from a supporting character's point of view.
4. Evaluate the rationality of a character's point of view by measuring it against additional information gathered from the text, or their own life experience.

Materials, Resources

- Copies of *The Odyssey*
- DVD with video clips from television and/or movies
- Flip chart paper
- Markers
- Directions and rubric for individual assignment

Identifies materials needed for the lesson

Activities

Session 1

Outlines classroom procedures for the two-day lesson plan

1. Review information from previous lesson about popular cultural and social views held during Homer's time (e.g., Greek law of hospitality). This would be a combination of a quiz and whole class discussion.
2. Teacher-led class discussion defining and examining point of view by viewing clips from popular television shows and movies.
3. Teacher-led discussion of 1 example from *The Odyssey*. E.g., examine Odysseus's point of view when he violates Greek law of hospitality during his encounter with the Cyclops, Polyphemus. Examine this encounter through the lens of what Homer might be saying about the value Greeks placed on hospitality.
4. In small groups the students will choose 3 places in the epic and evaluate Odysseus's point of view. Students will then determine what Odysseus's point of view might reflect about Homer's point of view and purpose for that part of the epic.
5. Groups will begin to create a visual using flip chart paper and markers to represent their interpretations of Odysseus's point of view to reflect about Homer's point of view and purpose.

Session 2

1. Groups will complete visual.
2. Groups will present their work to the rest of the class.
3. The class will discuss possible alternate interpretations of Homer's point of view and purpose.
4. Class will review aspects of point of view based on information teacher provided at the beginning of the class.
5. Beginning during class and finishing for homework, students will individually take one passage from the epic that was not discussed by their groups and do the following:
   - write a brief description of a main character's point of view

- write a response to prompts that guide students in evaluating the rationality of the main character's point of view based on information gathered from the text, or the students' own life experience
- rewrite the passage from a supporting character's point of view

Identifies how the teacher will assess students' mastery of the concepts and material covered in the lesson

Assessment

- Evaluate students' understanding of Greek cultural/social values from Homer's time through the quiz.
- Evaluate group's understanding of point of view by examining the visual product—this artifact will not be graded, but oral feedback will be provided that should help the students in completing the independent assignment.
- Evaluate the written, individual assignment.

Individualized Education Program (IEP)

Professional educators are often required to design education plans that address the specific needs of individual students who, according to federal definitions, are identified with a disability. These are examples of an **individualized education program (IEP)**. IEP development most often results from cooperation among educational professionals (teachers, school administrators, guidance counselors, etc.) and parents as they plan a student's educational course in light of his or her individual disability and needs. IEPs, like general lesson plans, are guided by the identification of goals and objectives for individual students, taking into account the student's disability or disabilities.

Insider Example
Student IEP

The sample IEP that follows indicates both an academic goal and a functional goal for the student. The academic goal relates to the student's desired academic achievement, while the functional goal specifies a desired behavioral outcome. These goals are followed by statements of objectives that represent steps the student will take to achieve the specified goals. Both sections end with descriptions of how the student's progress toward the desired goals will be measured or assessed.

Student Description for IEP

Joey Smith is a 16-year-old 11th grader. He has a learning disability in reading, and he also has attention deficit hyperactivity disorder.

Joey generally works well with others and has a good sense of humor. He likes to be helpful and is good at encouraging others. He tries hard when assigned tasks, but gets extremely frustrated and gives up quickly when he has difficulty completing a task as easily or quickly as he thinks he should. He responds well to being asked to try again if someone can work with him individually to get him started on the task again. Sometimes he acts up in class, usually in a joking manner. This tends to result in him frequently being off-task, as well as affecting the students around him. He displays the classic characteristics of a student with attention deficit hyperactivity disorder, including losing focus easily, needing to move around frequently, exhibiting difficulty paying attention to details, and continually blurting out inappropriate comments, or talking at inappropriate times.

Check Purpose: ☐ Initial
☒ Annual Review
☐ Reevaluation
☐ Addendum
☐ Transition Part C to B

INDIVIDUALIZED EDUCATION PROGRAM (IEP)

Duration of Special Education and Related Services: From: 06/05/2008 To: 06/04/2009

Student: <u>Joey Smith</u>   DOB: 08/21/1992

School: <u>ABC High School</u>   Grade: <u>10</u>

Primary Area of Eligibility* Learning Disability
Secondary Area(s) of Eligibility (if applicable): Other Health Impairment
(*Reported on Child Count)

Student Profile

Student's overall strengths:
Joey works hard to complete assignments and accomplish his goals. He interacts well with others, including his peers. He is very helpful and often encourages his peers when they are trying to accomplish their own goals. Joey has a good sense of humor and is good at entertaining others.

Summarize assessment information (e.g., from early intervention providers, child outcome measures, curriculum based measures, state and district assessments results, etc.), and review of progress on current IEP/IFSP goals:
Overall, Joey is making significant progress on his IEP goals. He continues to do well with improving his reading skills. He still struggles with implementing strategies consistently to help him remain focused and committed to completing his tasks; however, he continues to make progress.

Parent's concerns, if any, for enhancing the student's education:
Parent had no concerns at this time.

Parent's/Student's vision for student's future:
Joey will learn to motivate himself to complete tasks and learn to rely less on external motivation from others. He will complete high school and then attend community college.

INDIVIDUALIZED EDUCATION PROGRAM (IEP)

**Duration of Special Education and Related Services: From: 06/05/2008
To: 06/04/2009**

Student: Joey Smith   **DOB: 08/21/1992**

School: ABC High School   **Grade: 10**

Consideration of Transitions

> If a transition (e.g., new school, family circumstances, etc.) is anticipated during the life of this IEP/IFSP, what information is known about the student that will assist in facilitating a smooth process? ☒ N/A
>
> The student is age 14 or older or will be during the duration of the IEP.
> ☒ Yes ☐ No

Consideration of Special Factors (Note: If you check yes, you must address in the IEP.)

> Does the student have behavior(s) that impede his/her learning or that of others? ☒ Yes ☐ No
>
> Does the student have Limited English Proficiency? ☐ Yes ☒ No
>
> If the student is blind or partially sighted, will the instruction in or use of Braille be needed? ☐ Yes ☐ No ☒ N/A
>
> Does the student have any special communication needs? ☐ Yes ☒ No
>
> Is the student deaf or hard of hearing? ☐ Yes ☒ No
> ☐ The child's language and communication needs.
> ☐ Opportunities for direct communications with peers and professional personnel in the child's language and communication mode.
> ☐ Academic level.
> ☐ Full range of needs, including opportunities for direct instruction in the child's language, and
> ☐ Communication mode.
> (Communication Plan Worksheet available at www.ncpublicschools.org/ec/policy/forms.)
>
> Does the student require specially designed physical education?
> ☐ Yes ☒ No

Present Level(s) of Academic and Functional Performance
Include specific descriptions of what the student can and cannot do in relationship to this area. Include current academic and functional performance, behaviors, social/emotional development, other relevant information, and how the student's disability affects his/her involvement and progress in the general curriculum.

> Joey consistently reads at grade level. He can answer comprehension questions accurately if given additional time. He does well on tests and assignments that require reading if given additional time and if allowed to be in a separate setting with minimized distractions during longer tests.

INDIVIDUALIZED EDUCATION PROGRAM (IEP)

Duration of Special Education and Related Services: From: 06/05/2008 To: 06/04/2009

Student: Joey Smith   DOB: 08/21/1992

School: ABC High School   **Grade:** 10

Annual Goal

☒ Academic Goal   ☐ Functional Goal

> Joey will continue to learn and demonstrate functional reading skill at grade level.

The academic goal for the student is identified here.

Does the student require assistive technology devices and/or services?
☐ Yes   ☒ No

If yes, describe needs:

(Address after determination of related services.) Is this goal integrated with related service(s)?   ☐ Yes*   ☒ No
*If yes, list the related service area(s) of integration:

Competency Goal

Required for areas (if any) where student participates in state assessments using modified achievement standards.
Select Subject Area: ☐ Language Arts   ☐ Mathematics   ☐ Science
List Competency Goal from the NC Standard Course of Study:
(Standard must match the student's assigned grade.)

Note: Selected Grade Standard Competency Goals listed are those identified for specially designed instruction. In addition to those listed, the student has access to grade-level content standards through general education requirements.

Benchmarks or Short-Term Objectives (if applicable)
(Required for students participating in state alternate assessments aligned to alternate achievement standards)

> 1) Joey will recognize and use vocabulary appropriate for grade level with 90% accuracy.
> 2) Joey will recognize the author's point of view and purpose with 85% accuracy.
> 3) Joey will apply decoding strategies to comprehend grade-level text with 85% accuracy.

The IEP identifies specific objectives the student will achieve toward reaching the academic goal.

Describe how progress toward the annual goal will be measured

> Progress toward this annual goal will be measured by work samples and tests or quizzes.

The IEP identifies ways the student's progress will be measured.

INDIVIDUALIZED EDUCATION PROGRAM (IEP)

**Duration of Special Education and Related Services: From: 06/05/2008
To: 06/04/2009**

Student: Joey Smith   **DOB:** 08/21/1992

School: ABC High School   **Grade:** 10

Present Level(s) of Academic and Functional Performance
Include specific descriptions of what the student can and cannot do in relationship to this area. Include current academic and functional performance, behaviors, social/emotional development, other relevant information, and how the student's disability affects his/her involvement and progress in the general curriculum.

> Joey does well getting back on task with assistance and when he implements attention-focusing strategies. He needs to improve working on his ability to self-monitor and keep himself on task.

Annual Goal
☐ Academic Goal   ☒ Functional Goal

> Joey will continue learning to identify situations where he is more likely to lose focus. He will learn to identify and apply appropriate attention-focusing strategies in a variety of situations.

Does the student require assistive technology devices and/or services?
☐ Yes   ☒ No

If yes, describe needs:

(Address after determination of related services.) Is this goal integrated with related service(s)?   ☐ Yes*   ☒ No
*If yes, list the related service area(s) of integration:

Competency Goal

Required for areas (if any) where student participates in state assessments using modified achievement standards.
Select Subject Area: ☐ Language Arts   ☐ Mathematics   ☐ Science
List Competency Goal from the NC Standard Course of Study:
(Standard must match the student's assigned grade.)

Note: Selected Grade Standard Competency Goals listed are those identified for specially designed instruction. In addition to those listed, the student has access to grade-level content standards through general education requirements.

The functional goal for the student is identified here.

INDIVIDUALIZED EDUCATION PROGRAM (IEP)

**Duration of Special Education and Related Services: From: 06/05/2008
To: 06/04/2009**

Student: Joey Smith   DOB: 08/21/1992

School: ABC High School   Grade: 10

Benchmarks or Short-Term Objectives (if applicable)
(Required for students participating in state alternate assessments aligned
to alternate achievement standards)

> 1) Joey will be able to articulate how he feels when he becomes frustrated when
>   work gets difficult on 4 trials over a 2-week period as evaluated by structured
>   observations every 6 weeks.
> 2) By January, Joey will independently request a break from work when he needs it
>   to prevent class disruptions and allow himself to refocus.

Describe how progress toward the annual goal will be measured

> Progress will be monitored through documented teacher observation, student self-
> monitoring checklist, and anecdotal logs.

The IEP identifies specific objectives the student will achieve toward reaching the functional goal.

The IEP identifies ways that the student's progress will be measured.

For this exercise, imagine that you've just taken a job teaching in your major area of study. Identify a specific concept or skill you can see yourself teaching to a group of students. Consider the background and previous knowledge of your target audience. Then, with the concept or skill in mind, design a single-day lesson plan that addresses each of the following elements of a typical lesson plan.

- **Goal(s)** State the specific goal(s) for the skill you want to teach.

- **Objectives** Identify what students will do to better understand the concept or learn the target skill.

- **Materials** Identify the materials needed to carry out the lesson plan successfully.

- **Classroom Activities** Outline the procedures, in chronological order, for the day's lesson.

- **Assessment** Explain how you will assess your students' mastery of the concept or skill. ❱

BUSINESS

Communication in businesses takes many forms, and professionals writing in business settings may spend substantial amounts of time drafting e-mails and memos, or writing letters and proposals. In some instances, businesses may hire individuals solely for their expertise in business communication practices. Such individuals are highly skilled in the analysis and practice of business communication, and their education and training are often aimed at these purposes. Still, if your experiences lead you to employment in a business setting, you're likely to face the task of communicating in one or more of the genres frequently used in those settings. It's no surprise, then, that schools of business, which prepare students to work in companies and corporations, often require their students to take classes that foster an understanding of the vehicles of communication common to the business setting. In the following section, we provide some introductory context and annotated examples of a couple of the more common forms of communication you're likely to encounter in a business setting: the memorandum and the business plan.

Memorandum

The **memorandum**, or memo, is a specialized form of communication used within businesses to make announcements and to share information among colleagues and employees. Although memos serve a range of purposes, like sharing information, providing directives, or even arguing a particular position, they are not generally used to communicate with outside parties, like other companies or clients. While they may range in length from a couple of

paragraphs to multiple pages, they're typically highly structured according to conventional expectations. In fact, you'd be hard-pressed to find an example of a professional memo that didn't follow the conventional format for identifying the writer, the audience, the central subject matter, and the date of production in the header. Also, information in memos typically appears in a block format, and the content is often developed from a clear, centralized purpose that is revealed early on in the memo itself.

Insider Example
Student Memorandum

The following is an example of a memo produced by a student in a professional writing class. His purpose for writing was to share his assessment of the advantages and drawbacks of a particular company he's interested in working for in the future. As you read, notice how the information in the opening paragraphs forecasts the memo's content and how the memo summarizes its contents in the concluding passages. We've highlighted a number of the other conventional expectations for the memo that you'll want to notice.

MEMO

To: Jamie Larsen
           Professor, North Carolina State University

From: James Blackwell
           Biological Engineering, North Carolina State University

Date: September 2, 2014

Subject: Investigative Report on Hazen and Sawyer

I plan on one day using my knowledge gained in biological engineering to help alleviate the growing environmental problems that our society faces. Hazen and Sawyer is a well-known environmental engineering firm. However, I need to research the firm's background in order to decide if it would be a suitable place for me to work. Consequently, I decided to research the following areas of Hazen and Sawyer engineering firm:

- Current and Past Projects
- Opportunities for Employment and Advancement
- Work Environment

The purpose of this report is to present you with my findings on Hazen and Sawyer, so that you may assist me in writing an application letter that proves my skills and knowledge are worthy of an employment opportunity.

Current and Past Projects

Founded in 1951, Hazen and Sawyer has had a long history of providing clean drinking water and minimizing the effects of water pollution. The company has undertaken many projects in the United States as well as internationally. One of its first projects was improving the infrastructure of Monrovia, Liberia, in 1952. I am interested in using my knowledge of environmental problems to promote sustainability. Designing sustainable solutions for its clients is one of the firm's main goals. Hazen and Sawyer is currently engaged in a project to provide water infrastructure to over one million people in Jordan. Supplying clean drinking water is a problem that is continuously growing, and I hope to work on a similar project someday.

Opportunities for Employment and Advancement

Hazen and Sawyer has over forty offices worldwide, with regional offices in Raleigh, NC, Cincinnati, OH, Dallas, TX, Hollywood, FL, Los Angeles, CA, and its headquarters in New York City. The company currently has over thirty job openings at offices across the United States. I would like to live in the Raleigh area following graduation, so having a regional office here in Raleigh greatly helps my chances of finding a local job with the company. Hazen and Sawyer also has offices in Greensboro and Charlotte, which also helps my chances of finding a job in North Carolina. I am interested in finding a job dealing with stream restoration, and the Raleigh office currently has an opening for a Stream Restoration Designer. The position requires experience with AutoCAD and GIS, and I have used both of these programs in my Biological Engineering courses.

In addition to numerous job openings, Hazen and Sawyer also offers opportunities for professional development within the company. The Pathway Program for Professional Development is designed to keep employees up-to-date on topics in their fields and also stay educated to meet license requirements in different states. Even if I found a job at the Raleigh office, I would most likely have to travel out of state to work on projects, so this program could be very beneficial. I am seeking to work with a company that promotes continuous professional growth, so this program makes me very interested in Hazen and Sawyer.

Work Environment

Hazen and Sawyer supports innovation and creativity, and at the same time tries to limit bureaucracy. I am seeking a company that will allow me to be creative and assist with projects while not being in charge initially. As I gain experience and learn on the job, I hope to move into positions with greater responsibility. The firm offers a mentoring program that places newly hired engineers with someone more experienced. This program would help me adapt to the company and provide guidance as I gain professional experience. I hope to eventually receive my Professional Engineering license, so working under a professional engineer with years of experience would be a great opportunity for me. Hazen and Sawyer supports positive relationships among its employees, by engaging them in social outings such as sporting events, parties, picnics, and other activities.

References

Hazen and Sawyer—Environmental Engineers and Scientists. Web. 2 Sept. 2014. <http://www.hazenandsawyer.com/home/>.

The writer uses conventional formatting in the To, From, Date, and Subject lines.

Paragraphs are blocked and single-spaced.

Reasons for the student's interest in this company are bulleted and become the developed sections in the remainder of the memo. Important information is often bulleted in memos.

The memo announces its purpose clearly, forecasting the content to follow.

Headers are used to break up the content in memos. In this instance, the student uses headers that correspond to the areas of interest in the company he is exploring for potential employment.

The writer relies on formal language, evidenced here by avoiding contractions.

Double spacing between paragraphs

Notice the organizational pattern employed in the body paragraphs. The writer begins by describing the potential employer and then relates that information to his particular needs, desires, or circumstances.

References are usually indicated in an attachment.

Many people dream of being their own bosses. One avenue for achieving this dream is to create a successful business, or to own and operate a service or company. Anyone undertaking such a task in the economy today will need a solid business background that includes knowledge of the many forms of written communication required to start and continue the operation of a successful business. Two very important genres for these purposes are the business plan and the business proposal. If you're a business owner looking to raise capital, or if you've got a good idea or product that you want to sell to potential investors, then you're going to need a solid **business plan**, a document that clearly and efficiently describes your business and its essential operations, analyzes your market competition, and assesses the expected expenses and potential for profit. Let's say that you've got a great idea for a new lawn care service, but you need capital to purchase the necessary equipment and to advertise your services to potential customers. To obtain that capital, you're likely going to need a business plan that others can read when deciding whether to invest in your business.

By contrast, the **business proposal** is a form of communication through which a company proposes a relationship of some sort with another entity— often another company. Companies frequently receive unsolicited business proposals. A photocopying company, for instance, may design a proposal to begin a relationship that involves installing and maintaining all the photocopiers owned by a particular city or municipality. At other times, companies request business proposals. Imagine that you're the president of a landscaping service, for example, and you've decided to outsource all work that involves tree removal. To determine whom you want to hire for those jobs, you call for proposals from those companies or individuals to determine whose services best match your needs. In the world of business, effective communication means making money.

Insider Example
Student Business Plan

The following business plan was produced by a student in a writing class that addressed the communication needs of his major. As you read, notice how the student shapes the plan to satisfy the needs of the target audience, a bank, as a potential source of funding.

The cover page for the plan highlights the name of the proposed company, along with the author of the plan.

The Electricity Monitor Company

This document is a request for a start-up business loan for a company that will design, manufacture, and sell an electricity-monitoring product that will answer customers' demands for a solution to high power bills.

The author identifies a specific audience for the plan—in this case a potential source of funding. More than a generic plan, then, this document is crafted specifically for the purpose of seeking start-up capital.

To: Ms. Jane Harmon Bausch, President

First National Bank

10 Money Street

Raleigh, North Carolina 27695

Prepared By:

Identifies the writer/company submitting the plan for consideration, along with appropriate contact information

Daniel Chase Mills

The Electricity Monitor Company

100 Satellite Lane

City, North Carolina 20000

Email: dcmills@ncsu.edu

Phone: (919) 555-2233

November 21, 2014

In the executive summary, the writer provides a general overview of the plan: identifies a problem, briefly describes the company's unique product and market, and highlights potential customers. The section ends by noting the dollar amount requested from the bank.

Executive Summary

The Electricity Monitor Company

Prepared by Daniel Chase Mills, November 21, 2014

This document is a start-up business proposal for the Electricity Monitor Company and a request for an investment from First National Bank of Raleigh, North Carolina. The Company will design, manufacture, and sell the Electricity Monitor. Families with a traditional circuit-breaker box often struggle with high power bills, due to their inability to monitor their electricity usage. The Electricity Monitor is a device that will answer this pain point. This device is an adapter that attaches to any existing breaker box with installation simple enough for consumers to perform on their own. The device monitors current electricity usage and determines ways to reduce energy consumption. The device is superior to alternatives in the market in that it is cheaper, easier to install, and more effectively solves the problem of not knowing how much electricity is being used. The overall purpose of the Electricity Monitor Company is to develop a high-quality

In what way is an executive summary like an abstract?

product that can generate excitement in the electricity monitor market and turn a profit for its business owners and investors. The total loan request from First National Bank is three hundred and fifty-four thousand dollars ($354,000.00).

Table of Contents

List of Tables and Figures

Introduction to the Electricity Monitor Company

A. Purpose

The purpose of this document is to request funding from First National Bank for a start-up business called the Electricity Monitor Company. This

> Notice the ordering of elements of the plan. How would you describe the order of these elements?

> Briefly identifies the general purpose of the document and offers a preview of the document's contents

document will contain an overview of the problem that the company will address in the market, how the Electricity Monitor will solve this problem, and a plan for this business.

Explains a problem that consumers face

B. Problem: High Power Bills

In twenty-first century America, and in most first world countries, electricity is a necessity. In the home, electricity is used for a variety of devices. Due to the vast number of devices that use electricity, and no good way of knowing how much power they are consuming on a daily basis, families with a traditional circuit-breaker box often struggle with using too much electricity. The problem is high power bills.

Provides a brief market analysis, and identifies a gap in the market

C. Current Alternatives to High Power Bills

There are three currently available solutions to measuring home energy usage in an attempt to lower power bills: Plug-in Meters, Energy Meter Monitors, and Home Energy Monitors. Plug-in Meters are devices that plug in to individual outlets to measure energy usage of a single device. An Energy Meter Monitor attaches to an electricity meter, measures total energy consumption of a home, and estimates what the power bill will be for the month. Neither device is effective in determining energy usage of the entire home across multiple devices. The Home Energy Monitors contain multiple channels to measure energy usage across multiple devices in the home, but these devices are extremely expensive and require detailed installation that increases the cost of the products. Three Home Energy Monitoring Devices are the TED 5000, eGuage, and EnviR, with respective prices of $239, $494, and $129. I have determined that the current solutions in this market are too expensive and do not adequately provide families with an affordable way to monitor their electricity usage. I have developed a better solution to this pain point.

How is this section of the report similar to or different from a review of scholarship?

Stresses reasons that support the business's potential for success

D. The Electricity Monitor

The Electricity Monitor is a device that can solve the pain point of high power bills by measuring the electricity usage of each device in the home. This device can easily attach to any existing breaker box. Installation of the device can be performed by any customer with the instructions provided with the device. At a price of $75, this device will be much cheaper than current solutions to monitoring power usage. A price comparison is shown in Figure 1 below. By measuring electricity usage of each device in the home, the Electricity Monitor will be able to accurately estimate the power bill for the month (within 1% error) and update daily with changes to electricity usage trends in the home. All data will be transmitted to a monitoring display. This device is also superior to the competition in that it makes suggestions as to how to decrease energy consumption and provides information on which devices in the home are using the most energy. Using the data from the Electricity Monitor, families will finally have the tool they need to save money on their power bill.

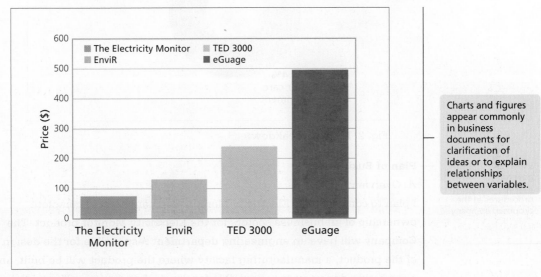

Fig. 1. Price comparison

Charts and figures appear commonly in business documents for clarification of ideas or to explain relationships between variables.

E. Market for This Product

Industry market research from the IBIS World database shows small household appliance manufacturing to have $3.1 billion in annual revenue with $77.9 million in annual profit. This number alone shows the vastness of this market. In addition, IBIS World estimates 38.4% of this market to account for small household devices similar to the Electricity Monitor. Figure 2 below from IBIS World shows the market breakdown. The main demographic for this product will be families of three or more who are unhappy with their current power bill. The United States Census Bureau estimated there to be 4.4 million households with families of three or more people, accounting for 39% of all households in 2011. IBIS World describes the technology change in this market to be "Medium." This leads me to believe that a new product in this market could really shake the market and attract interest from consumers. Assuming that the current trend for revenue

Performs a more detailed market analysis

and profit in the small household appliance industry performs as predicted, the market for the Electricity Monitor will be large.

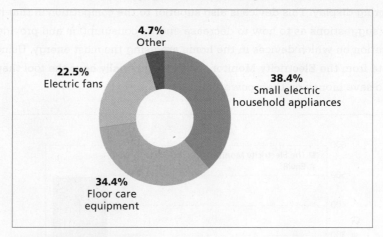

4.7% Other

22.5% Electric fans

38.4% Small electric household appliances

34.4% Floor care equipment

Fig. 2. Market breakdown

Plan of Business

A. Overview

I plan to construct the Electricity Monitor Company to hold complete ownership of all business sectors for the Electricity Monitor product. The Company will have an engineering department responsible for the design of the product, a manufacturing facility where the product will be built, and a marketing department responsible for the marketing and selling of the product. The overall cost for the start-up is analyzed below. This breakdown of cost can also be found in the Attachments section of this document.

B. Cost Analysis

Table 1
Design Expense

Design Expense	Description	Total Cost
Building	Rented office space	$ 5,000.00
Software	CAD modeling and FEA software license	$ 4,000.00
Total		**$ 9,000.00**

Table 1 is an analysis of the cost for designing the product. The requested loan will need to cover the first month of rent for an office and also a license for software that will be used to design the product. The labor is not included in the cost here because I will be designing the product myself.

Explains governance and operating procedures of the proposed company

Offers a detailed analysis of costs associated with the business start-up

Table 2
Manufacturing Expense

Manufacturing Expense (First 500 Products)	Description	Total Cost
Building	Small manufacturing facility	$ 100,000.00
Manufacturing equipment	Laser cutting machine, etc.	$ 200,000.00
Tools	Screwdrivers, socket wrenches, Allen wrenches, etc.	$ 5,000.00
Materials	First 500 monitors (avg cost $20/ monitor)	$ 10,000.00
Labor	$25/hr with five employees @ 40 hours a week	$ 20,000.00
Total		$ 335,000.00

Table 2 is an analysis of the cost for manufacturing the product. The building and manufacturing equipment are one-time costs for the initial start-up. The materials and labor will be ongoing costs, but the loan request is only enough to cover the first 500 products manufactured. Five hundred products have been estimated as enough to cover the first month of sales and will allow my company to be self-sufficient after selling the first 500 products.

Table 3
Marketing Expense

Marketing Expense	Description	Total Cost
Commercial	Television ad	$ 5,000.00
Web search	Google AdWords	$ 5,000.00
Total		$ 10,000.00

Table 3 is an analysis of the total marketing expense. I will additionally market this product to retail stores that could also sell this product, but cost for labor of this marketing is not included here because I will do it myself.

Table 4
Total Cost Analysis

Business Sector	Total Cost
Design	$ 9,000.00
Manufacturing	$ 335,000.00
Marketing	$ 10,000.00
Total	$ 354,000.00

Table 4 is a summary of the total cost analysis for this product. The highlighted cell in Table 4 represents the total start-up cost for the Electricity Monitor Company. This is also the total requested loan amount from First National Bank.

C. Summary

The total cost for this start-up was analyzed in Tables 1 through 4 above. The cost of materials was estimated from current market cost of materials and is subject to change with the market. However, my request for the bottom-line loan amount for this start-up is three hundred and fifty-four thousand dollars ($354,000.00), and this request will not change with cost of materials. A sound business plan has been constructed that will allow the Electricity Monitor Company to become self-sufficient after one month. In order for this business plan to work, the product must be successful in attracting customers quickly as projected by the market research.

The conclusion reiterates the proposed product's unique characteristics and potential for success in hopes of securing the capital investment.

Conclusion

The overall purpose of the Electricity Monitor start-up business is to develop a high-quality product that can generate excitement in the electricity monitor market and turn a profit for its business owners and investors. This product will benefit not only its investors, but also its consumers in that it will solve their pain point of not being able to affordably measure their current energy consumption. In comparison to other products in the market that attempt to solve the problem of high power bills, the Electricity Monitor is superior in price, ease of installation, and overall ability to solve the problem. There is nothing quite like this product currently in the market, and this is why it will be successful. The market research has proven that there is a large potential market and that current technology change is not very high. I am excited about starting the Electricity Monitor Company, the potential of this product, and the benefits for all parties involved. Please grant the requested loan amount of three hundred and fifty-four thousand dollars ($354,000.00) and help me make unnecessarily high power bills a thing of the past.

Documents sources consulted in the preparation of the business document

Bibliography

Entrepreneur. "TV Ads." Web. <http://www.entrepreneur.com/article/83108>.

IBIS World. "Vacuum, Fan, & Small Household Appliance Manufacturing in the US." Web. <http://clients1.ibisworld.com.prox.lib.ncsu.edu/reports /us/industry/ataglance.aspx?indid=786>.

Kreider, Rose M. "America's Families and Living Arrangements: 2012."
    United States Census Bureau. Web. <https://www.census.gov/prod
    /2013pubs/p20-570.pdf>.
Thornton Oliver Keller Commercial Real Estate. "Rental Rate Calculations."
    Web. <http://tokcommercial.com/MarketInformation/LearningCenter
    /RentalRateCalculations.aspx>.

Attachments

A. Cost Breakdown

Design Expense	Description	Total Cost
Building	Rented office space	$ 5,000.00
Software	CAD modeling and FEA software license	$ 4,000.00
Total		**$ 9,000.00**

Manufacturing Expense (First 500 Products)	Description	Total Cost
Building	Small manufacturing facility	$ 100,000.00
Manufacturing equipment	Laser cutting machine, etc.	$ 200,000.00
Tools	Screwdrivers, socket wrenches, Allen wrenches, etc.	$ 5,000.00
Materials	First 500 monitors (avg cost $20/monitor)	$ 10,000.00
Labor	$25/hr with five employees @ 40 hours a week	$ 20,000.00
Total		**$ 335,000.00**

Marketing Expense	Description	Total Cost
Commercial	Television ad	$ 5,000.00
Web search	Google AdWords	$ 5,000.00
Total		**$ 10,000.00**

Business Sector	Total Cost	
Design	$ 9,000.00	
Manufacturing	$ 335,000.00	
Marketing	$ 10,000.00	
Total	**$ 354,000.00**	

Compiles the costs associated with the business start-up. See the reference to the attachment on page 322.

INSIDE WORK CFO for a Day

For this exercise, imagine that you're the chief financial officer for a company, Music Studio Emporium. Your company has twenty employees, and you've been charged with the task of notifying ten of them that they'll be receiving a 2 percent annual pay increase, effective immediately, based on their sales records. Unfortunately, you must also notify your other ten employees that they will not be receiving raises. Draft a brief memo to each group of employees—one for those receiving raises and one for those who aren't—in which you explain the company's decisions regarding your employees' compensation. Feel free to provide additional reasoning for those decisions, as you see fit.

Refer to the memo on page 316 as a model of the structural features you'll want to employ in constructing your memo. Once you're done, consider how the nature of the news you had to convey to each audience influenced the way you delivered that news. What did you do the same for each of your audiences? What did you do differently in constructing the two memos? ▶

CRIMINAL JUSTICE AND LAW

Millions of people are employed in the areas of law and criminal justice in the United States. When we encounter the terms "law" and "criminal justice," the image of a lawyer, or attorney, often comes to mind first. No doubt, attorneys make vital contributions to almost every aspect of our lives; their work helps us to understand, to enforce, and even to change our policies, procedures, and laws, whether they are civil or criminal in nature. Though attorneys make a significant contribution to our system of governance, they actually represent only a fraction of the vast number of professionals who work in the U.S. criminal justice system.

Criminal Justice

If you've ever watched a crime show on television, then you've likely been exposed to some of the many areas of training and expertise that make up the U.S. criminal justice system. Professionals who work in the fields of criminal justice are responsible for enforcing our laws and ensuring the safety of our communities. They are also responsible for such jobs as investigating crime scenes, staffing our jails and prisons, and providing essential services to victims of crimes and to those charged with or convicted of a crime. Careers in the fields of criminal justice range from forensic technician to parole officer to corrections counselor. While each of these career paths requires a different level of training and expertise, and many colleges and universities offer specific plans of study that culminate in certification or licensure in these diverse areas, they are unified by a commitment to the just treatment of all individuals under the law.

As criminologist Michelle Richter notes in her "Insider's View," there are various reasons that might compel an individual to choose a career in criminal justice, and there are various constituencies to whom differing careers in the fields of criminal justice must deliver support and services. Here's a small sampling of the many career paths available to those interested in the field of criminal justice:

- Bailiff
- Correctional Officer
- Corrections Counselor
- Court Reporter
- Emergency Management Director
- Fire Inspector
- Forensic Science Technician
- Legal Secretary
- Paralegal
- Police Detective
- Sheriff and Deputy Sheriff

Law

Most of us probably have clichéd understandings of the law at work. Many of these likely originated from television shows and movies. In these scenarios, there's almost always lots of drama as the lawyers battle in court, parse witnesses' words, and attempt to sway a judge or jury to their side of a case.

In real life, the practice of law may not always be quite as dramatic or enthralling as it appears on the screen. In fact, many lawyers rarely, or maybe never, appear in court. A criminal defense attorney may regularly appear before a judge or jury in a courtroom setting, but a corporate lawyer may spend the majority of her time drafting and analyzing business contracts. This difference is directly related to the field of law an individual specializes in, be it criminal law, family law, tax law, or environmental law, just to name a few.

Regardless of an attorney's chosen specialization, though, the study of law remains fundamentally concerned with debates over the interpretation of language. This is because the various rules that govern our lives—statutes, ordinances, regulations, and laws, for example—are all constructed in language. As you surely recognize, language can be quite slippery, and rules can often be interpreted in many different ways. We need only briefly to consider current

debates over free speech issues or the "right to bear arms" or marriage equality to understand how complicated the business of interpreting laws can become. In the United States, the U.S. Supreme Court holds the authority to provide the final interpretation on the meaning of disputed laws. However, there are lots of legal interpretations and arguments that lower courts must make on a daily basis, and only a tiny portion of cases are ever heard by the U.S. Supreme Court.

As in the other applied fields, there are many common forms of communication in the various fields of law, as lawyers must regularly communicate with different kinds of stakeholders, including clients, other lawyers, judges, and law enforcement officials. For this reason, individuals working in the legal professions are generally expert at composing e-mail messages, memos, letters to clients, and legal briefs, among other genres. The following examples provide a glimpse into two types of writing through which lawyers frequently communicate.

Legal Brief   One of the first forms of writing students of law are likely to encounter in their academic study is the **legal brief**. Briefs can serve any number of functions, but their primary purpose is to outline the critical components of a legal argument to a specified audience. They may be descriptive or argumentative. A typical assignment for a student in law school might include writing a legal brief that describes a particular court's decision and explains how the court reached that decision. Cases that appear before the U.S. Supreme Court are usually accompanied by numerous legal briefs that are written and filed with the Court by parties who are interested in the outcomes of those cases. Many of these briefs are argumentative. Students of law, then, must be familiar with the basic structural components, or the structural conventions, of the legal brief. And law schools regularly instruct their students to produce legal briefs using the generalized form known as **IRAC**—an acronym for **Introduction, Rule, Application, and Conclusion**—as a means to describe past court decisions and/or to present written arguments to a court:

- **Introduction: Identify the Legal Issue(s) in the Case**   Legal cases can be very complicated. It is a lawyer's task to explore the facts of a case, along with its legal history, to determine which facts are actually relevant and which are irrelevant as they pertain to a legal question or dispute.

- **Rule: Identify and Explain the Relevant Law(s) to the Case** Often, many different statutes, regulations, laws, or other court precedents are applicable and need exploration as part of a legal dispute. A lawyer must identify the applicable rules of law and explain their relevance to the legal question or dispute at hand.

- **Application: Apply the Relevant Rules to the Facts of the Case** The facts of the case are explored through the lens of relevant rules. Arguments are presented in these sections of a brief.

- **Conclusion: Argue for a Particular Decision or Outcome** Based on the application of relevant rules to the facts of the case, a lawyer makes a recommendation that the judge or court should reach a particular conclusion.

Insider Example
Professional Legal Brief

The following excerpts are from a 55-page legal brief that was filed with the U.S. Supreme Court on behalf of the University of Texas at Austin, et al., which was sued by an applicant after being denied admission to the university. In arguing their case, attorneys writing on behalf of the respondents, or the university, defended its decision to deny admission to the complainant, or the petitioner, Abigail Fisher. As you read the excerpted sections below, try to identify parts of the brief that correspond to the elements of the IRAC structure for presenting legal arguments: Introduction, Rule, Application, and Conclusion.

No. 11-345

𝕴𝖓 𝖙𝖍𝖊
𝕾𝖚𝖕𝖗𝖊𝖒𝖊 𝕮𝖔𝖚𝖗𝖙 𝖔𝖋 𝖙𝖍𝖊 𝖀𝖓𝖎𝖙𝖊𝖉 𝕾𝖙𝖆𝖙𝖊𝖘

ABIGAIL NOEL FISHER,
Petitioner,

v.

UNIVERSITY OF TEXAS AT AUSTIN, ET AL.,
Respondents.

ON WRIT OF CERTIORARI TO THE
UNITED STATES COURT OF APPEALS
FOR THE FIFTH CIRCUIT

BRIEF FOR RESPONDENTS

PATRICIA C. OHLENDORF
*Vice President for
Legal Affairs*

GREGORY G. GARRE
Counsel of Record
MAUREEN E. MAHONEY

THE UNIVERSITY OF
TEXAS AT AUSTIN
Flawn Academic Center
2304 Whitis Avenue
Stop G4800
Austin, TX 78712

DOUGLAS LAYCOCK
UNIVERSITY OF VIRGINIA
SCHOOL OF LAW
580 Massie Road
Charlottesville, VA 22903

J. SCOTT BALLENGER
LORI ALVINO MCGILL
KATYA S. GEORGIEVA
LATHAM & WATKINS LLP
555 11th Street, NW
Suite 1000
Washington, DC 20004
(202) 637-2207
gregory.garre@lw.com

JAMES C. HO
GIBSON, DUNN &
CRUTCHER LLP
2100 McKinney Avenue
Suite 1110
Dallas, TX 75201-6912

Counsel for Respondents

INTRODUCTION

Identifies the critical issue at stake, and lays out the respondents' position

After considering largely the same objections raised by petitioner and her amici here, this Court strongly embraced Justice Powell's controlling opinion in *Regents of the University of California v. Bakke*, 438 U.S. 265 (1978), and refused to prohibit the consideration of race as a factor in admissions at the Nation's universities and graduate schools. *Grutter v. Bollinger*, 539 U.S. 306 (2003); *see id.* at 387 (Kennedy, J., dissenting). And although the Court has made clear that any consideration of race in this context must be limited, it has been understood for decades that "a university admissions program may take account of race as one, non-predominant factor in a system designed to consider each applicant as an individual, provided the program can meet the test of strict scrutiny by the judiciary." *Id.* at 387 (Kennedy, J., dissenting) (citing *Bakke*, 438 U.S. at 289-91, 315-18 (Powell, J.)); *see id.* at 322-23. The University of Texas at Austin (UT)'s highly individualized consideration of race for applicants not admitted under the State's top 10% law satisfies that demand, and meets strict scrutiny under any conception of that test not designed simply to bar the consideration of race altogether.

Reviews relevant precedents, or earlier conclusions reached by the Court

That conclusion follows *a fortiori* from existing precedent. UT's admissions plan was modeled on the type of plan upheld in *Grutter* and commended by Justice Powell in *Bakke*. Moreover, UT's plan lacks the features criticized in *Grutter* by Justice Kennedy—who agreed with the majority that *Bakke* is the "correct rule." *Id.* at 387 (dissenting). Justice Kennedy concluded that Michigan Law School's admissions plan used race "to achieve numerical goals indistinguishable from quotas." *Id.* at 389. Here, it is undisputed that UT has not set any "target" or "goal" for minority admissions. JA 131a. Justice Kennedy stressed that Michigan's "admissions officers consulted . . . daily reports which indicated the composition of the incoming class along racial lines." *Grutter*, 539 U.S. at 391 (dissenting). Here, it is undeniable that no such monitoring occurs. JA 398a. And Justice Kennedy believed that race was "a predominant factor" under Michigan's plan. *Grutter*, 539 U.S. at 393 (dissenting). Here, petitioner argues (at 20) that UT's consideration of race is too "minimal" to be constitutional. That paradoxical contention not only overlooks the indisputably meaningful impact that UT's plan has on diversity, *infra* at 36-38, it turns on its head Justice Powell's conception of the appropriately nuanced and modest consideration of race in this special context.

Because petitioner cannot dispute that UT's consideration of race is both highly individualized and modest, she is forced to take positions directly at odds with the record and existing precedent. Her headline claim that UT is engaged in "racial balancing" (Pet. Br. 6-7, 19, 27-28, 45-46) is refuted by her own concession that UT has *not* set any "target" for minority admissions. JA 131a. Her argument that the State's top 10% law bars UT from considering race in its holistic review of applicants not eligible under that law is foreclosed by *Grutter*'s holding that percentage plans are not a complete, workable alternative to the individualized consideration of race in full-file review. 539 U.S. at 340. And her argument that, in 2004, UT had already achieved all the diversity that the Constitution allowed is based on "a limited notion of diversity" (*Parents Involved in Cmty. Schs. v. Seattle Sch. Dist. No. 1*, 551 U.S. 701, 723 (2007)) rejected by this Court—one that crudely lumps together distinct racial groups and ignores the importance of diversity among individuals *within* racial groups.

Presents the complainant's central claims, and offers response

In the end, petitioner really is just asking this Court to move the goal posts on higher education in America—and overrule its precedent going back 35 years to *Bakke*. Pet. Br. 53-57. *Stare decisis* alone counsels decisively against doing so. Petitioner has provided no persuasive justification for the Court to reexamine, much less overrule, its precedent, just nine years after this Court decided *Grutter* and eliminated any doubt about the controlling force of Justice Powell's opinion in *Bakke*. And overruling *Grutter* and *Bakke* (or effectively gutting them by adopting petitioner's conception of strict scrutiny) would jeopardize the Nation's paramount interest in educating its future leaders in an environment that best prepares them for the society and workforce they will encounter. Moreover, the question that petitioner herself asked this Court to decide is the constitutionality of UT's policy under *existing* precedent, including *Grutter*. *See* Pet. i; Pet. Br. i. Because the court of appeals correctly answered that question, the judgment below should be affirmed.

Identifies stakes for the outcome of the decision, and reasserts the respondents' position

STATEMENT OF THE CASE

. . .

E. Petitioner's Application for Admission

Petitioner, a Texas resident, applied for admission to UT's Fall 2008 freshman class in Business Administration or Liberal Arts, with a combined SAT score of 1180 out of 1600 and a cumulative 3.59 GPA. JA 40a-41a. Because petitioner was not in the top 10% of her high school class, her application was considered pursuant to the holistic review process described above. JA 40a. Petitioner scored an AI of 3.1, JA 415a, and received a PAI score of less than 6 (the actual score is contained in a sealed brief, ECF No. 52). The summary judgment record is uncontradicted that—due to the stiff competition in 2008 and petitioner's relatively low AI score—petitioner would not have been admitted to the Fall 2008 freshman class even if she had received "a 'perfect' PAI score of 6." JA 416a.

Petitioner also was denied admission to the summer program, which offered provisional admission to some applicants who were denied admission to the fall class, subject to completing certain academic requirements over the summer. JA 413a-14a. (UT discontinued this program in 2009.) Although one African-American and four Hispanic applicants with lower combined AI/PAI scores than petitioner's were offered admission to the summer program, so were 42 Caucasian applicants with combined AI/PAI scores identical to or lower than petitioner's. In addition, 168 African-American and Hispanic applicants in this pool who had combined AI/PAI scores identical to or *higher* than petitioner's were *denied* admission to the summer program.[1]

---

[1] These figures are drawn from UT's admissions data and are provided in response to petitioner's unsupported assertion (at 2) that her "academic credentials exceeded those of many admitted minority applicants." Petitioner presented a subset of this data (admitted minority students) to the district court as Plaintiffs' Exhibits 26 and 27 at the preliminary injunction hearing (the court later returned the exhibits). See W.D. Tex. Record Transmittal Letter (July 27, 2012), ECF No. 136. UT summarized additional data in a sealed letter brief after the hearing. ECF No. 52; JA 20a (discussing data and explaining that petitioner had not requested data regarding the applicants "who were *not* admitted to UT"). In denying a preliminary injunction, the district court stated (without citation) that 64 minority applicants with lower AI scores than petitioner were *admitted* to Liberal Arts. *Fisher v. Texas*, 556 F. Supp. 2d 603, 607 & n.2 (W.D. Tex. 2008). That statement is not binding at the merits stage. *University of Texas v. Camenisch*, 451 U.S. 390, 395 (1981). Although the district court did not specify whether it was referring to admissions to the fall class or the summer program, that figure can only encompass admits to the summer program. As explained in the unrebutted summary judgment record, with her AI score, petitioner could not "have gained admission through the fall review process," even with a "perfect" PAI score. JA 415a-16a. Petitioner has submitted no contrary evidence (and UT is aware of none). That leaves the now-defunct summer program. The district court's statement that minority applicants with lower AI scores than petitioner were admitted does not establish that race was a factor in petitioner's

UT did offer petitioner admission to the Coordinated Admissions Program, which allows Texas residents to gain admission to UT for their sophomore year by completing 30 credits at a participating UT System campus and maintaining a 3.2 GPA. JA 414a. Petitioner declined that offer and enrolled at Louisiana State University, from which she graduated in May.

F. Procedural History

Petitioner and another applicant—"no longer involved in this case," Pet. Br. ii—filed suit in the Western District of Texas against UT and various University officials under 42 U.S.C. § 1983, alleging, *inter alia*, that UT's 2008 full-file admissions procedures violate the Equal Protection Clause. JA 38a. They sued only on their own behalf (not on behalf of any class of applicants) and sought a declaratory judgment and injunctive relief barring UT's consideration of race and requiring UT to reconsider their own applications in a race-blind process. JA 39a. They also sought a "refund of [their] application fees and all associated expenses incurred . . . in connection with applying to UT." *Id.*; *see* App. 3a-4a.

The district court denied petitioner's request for a preliminary injunction. The parties filed cross-motions for summary judgment and supporting statements of fact (JA 103a-51a, 363a-403a). Applying strict scrutiny (App. 139a), the court granted judgment to UT, holding that UT has a compelling interest in attaining a diverse student body and the educational benefits flowing from such diversity, and that UT's individualized and holistic review process is narrowly tailored to further that interest. App. 168-69a.

The Fifth Circuit affirmed. Like the district court, the court of appeals found that "it would be difficult for UT to construct an admissions policy that more closely resembles the policy approved by the Supreme Court in *Grutter*." App. 5a. And the court likewise took it as "a given" that UT's policy "is subject to strict scrutiny with its requirement of narrow tailoring." App. 35a. While acknowledging that *Bakke* and *Grutter* call for some deference to a university's "educational judgment," the court emphasized that "the scrutiny triggered by

> Provides a brief history of the case in the courts, explaining decisions by lower courts

---

denial from the summer program, because (as noted above) many more minority applicants (168) with identical or *higher* AI/PAI scores were *denied* admission to the summer program. It is thus hard to see how petitioner could establish any cognizable injury for her § 1983 damages claim—the only claim still alive in this case—or, for that matter, standing to maintain that claim. *See Texas v. Lesage*, 528 U.S. 18, 19, 21 (1999) (per curiam); *Lujan v. Defenders of Wildlife*, 504 U.S. 555, 562 (1992). (Petitioner's claims for injunctive relief dropped out of the case at least once she graduated from a different university in May 2012, making this issue pertinent now.) And that is just one apparent vehicle—if not jurisdictional—defect with this case. *See* Br. in Opp. 6-22; *see also* Adam D. Chandler, *How (Not) to Bring an Affirmative-Action Challenge*, 122 Yale L. J. Online (forthcoming Sept. 2012), *available at* http://ssrn.com/abstract_id=2122956 (discussing vehicle defects stemming from, among other things, the unusual manner in which this case was framed).

racial classification 'is no less strict for taking into account' the special circumstances of higher education." App. 34a, 36a. Applying strict scrutiny, the court upheld UT's admissions policy. App. 71a.

Judge Garza concurred. He recognized that the court's opinion was "faithful" to *Grutter*, but argued that *Grutter* was wrongly decided. App. 72a-73a.

SUMMARY OF ARGUMENT

Presents a summary of arguments in defense of the respondents' position in light of the facts of the case

UT's individualized consideration of race in holistic admissions did not subject petitioner to unequal treatment in violation of the Fourteenth Amendment.

I. Racial classifications are subject to strict scrutiny, including in the higher education context. But ever since Justice Powell's opinion in *Bakke*, this Court has recognized that universities have a compelling interest in promoting student body diversity, and that a university may consider the race of applicants in an individualized and modest manner—such that race is just one of many characteristics that form the mosaic presented by an applicant's file.

UT's holistic admissions policy exemplifies the type of plan this Court has allowed: race is only one modest factor among many others weighed; it is considered only in an individualized and contextual way that "examine[s] the student in 'their totality,'" JA 129a; and admissions officers do not know an applicant's race when they decide which "cells" to admit in UT's process. At the same time, UT's policy *lacks* the features that Justice Kennedy found disqualifying in *Grutter*: it is undisputed that UT has not established any race-based target; race is not assigned any automatic value; and the racial or ethnic composition of admits is not monitored during the admissions cycle.

II. Petitioner's arguments that she was nevertheless subjected to unequal treatment in violation of the Fourteenth Amendment are refuted by both the record and existing precedent.

. . .

III. The Court should decline petitioner's far-reaching request to reopen and overrule *Bakke* and *Grutter*. That request is outside the scope of the question presented, which asks the Court to review UT's policy under *existing* precedent, including *Grutter*. In any event, petitioner has failed to identify any special justification for taking the extraordinary step of overruling *Grutter*, just nine years after this Court decided *Grutter* and unequivocally answered any doubt about the validity of Justice Powell's opinion in *Bakke*. Abruptly reversing course here would upset legitimate expectations in the rule of law—not to mention the profoundly important societal interests in ensuring that the future leaders of America are trained in a campus environment in which they are exposed to the full educational benefits of diversity.

. . .

CONCLUSION

The judgment of the court of appeals should be affirmed.

Respectfully submitted,

PATRICIA C. OHLENDORF
Vice President for
Legal Affairs
THE UNIVERSITY OF
TEXAS AT AUSTIN
Flawn Academic Center
2304 Whitis Avenue
Stop G4800
Austin, TX 78712

DOUGLAS LAYCOCK
UNIVERSITY OF VIRGINIA
SCHOOL OF LAW
580 Massie Road
Charlottesville, VA 22903

GREGORY G. GARRE
Counsel of Record
MAUREEN E. MAHONEY
J. SCOTT BALLENGER
LORI ALVINO McGILL
KATYA S. GEORGIEVA
LATHAM & WATKINS LLP
555 11th Street, NW
Suite 1000
Washington, DC 20004
(202) 637-2207
gregory.garre@lw.com

JAMES C. HO
GIBSON, DUNN &
  CRUTCHER LLP
2100 McKinney Avenue
Suite 1110
Dallas, TX 75201-6912

AUGUST 2012

Counsel for Respondents

> Concludes by asserting the decision that respondents believe the Court should reach

E-Mail Correspondence As you might expect, technological advances can have a profound impact on the communication practices of professionals. There may always be a place for hard copies of documents, but e-mail communication has no doubt replaced many of the letters that used to pass between parties via the U.S. Postal Service. Like most professionals these days, those employed in the legal fields often spend a lot of time communicating with stakeholders via e-mail. These professionals carefully assess each rhetorical situation for which an e-mail communication is necessary, both (1) to make sure the ideas they share with stakeholders (the explanations of legal procedures, or legal options, or applicable precedents, etc.) are accurate, and (2) to make sure they communicate those ideas in an appropriate fashion (with the appropriate tone, clarity, precision, etc.).

Insider Example
E-Mail Correspondence from Attorney

The following example is an e-mail sent from a practicing lawyer to a client. In this instance, the lawyer offers legal advice concerning a possible donation from a party to a foundation. As you read the lawyer's description of the documents attached to his e-mail correspondence with the client, pay attention to the ways the attorney demonstrates an acute awareness of his audience, both in terms of the actual legal advice he provides and in terms of the structure and language of his message.

Establishes the level of familiarity and tone

Provides transactional advice, explaining what procedure needs to occur between the two parties involved: a donor and a receiving foundation

Provides additional advice to protect the interests of the parties in the event that either party decides to back out of the transaction

Explains more specific details included in the attached legal documents to protect the interests of the Foundation

Communicates a willingness to continue the relationship with the client

Provides standard identification and contact information for communication between and among professionals

---

Dear _____

As promised, here are two documents related to the proposed gift of the ABC property to the XYZ Foundation (the "Foundation"). The first document summarizes the recommended due diligence steps (including the creation of a limited liability company) that should take place prior to the acceptance of the property, accompanied by estimated costs associated with each such step. The second document contains a draft "pre-acceptance" agreement that the Foundation could use to recover its documented costs in the event that either the donor or the Foundation backs out of a gift agreement following the due diligence process.

You will note that we have limited the Foundation's ability to recover costs in the event that the Foundation is the party that "pulls the plug." In such a scenario, the Foundation could recover costs only if it reasonably determines that either (i) the property would create a risk of material exposure to environmentally related liabilities or (ii) the remediation of environmental issues would impose material costs on the Foundation. We realize that even in light of this limiting language, the agreement represents a fairly aggressive approach with the donor, and we will be glad to work with you if you wish to take a softer stance.

Please don't hesitate to call me with any questions, concerns, or critiques. As always, we appreciate the opportunity to serve you in furthering the Foundation's good work.

Best regards,

Joe

Joseph E. Miller, Jr.
Partner
joe.miller@FaegreBD.com
Direct: +1 317 237 1415
FaegreBD.com Download vCard
FAEGRE BAKER DANIELS LLP
300 N. Meridian Street
Suite 2700
Indianapolis, IN 46204, USA

Lawyer for a Day

Imagine that you're an attorney, and you've just been hired as a consultant by the Board of Governors of a local college that's in the process of designing new guidelines for student admissions. As part of that process, the Board has asked you to review legal briefs presented on behalf of various stakeholders in *Fisher v. University of Texas at Austin,* et al. Additionally, the Board wants you to provide a summary of UT–Austin's response to the charge that its admissions procedures violated the petitioner's rights under the Fourteenth Amendment to the U.S. Constitution.

Read again the section of the legal brief filed with the U.S. Supreme Court entitled "Summary of Argument" (on p. 334), and then draft an e-mail to your client (the Board of Governors) in which you offer an overview of UT–Austin's response to its possible violation of a prospective student's constitutional rights. As part of your summary, offer your client an assessment of the likely effectiveness of UT–Austin's argument. Be clear and precise in your presentation of UT–Austin's argument in defense of its position. Keep your audience and your relationship to that audience in mind as you compose your e-mail. ❱

Discovering Genres of Writing in an Applied Field

WRITING PROJECT

In this chapter, you've read about some of the conventions of writing in the applied fields of health, education, business, criminal justice, and law. You might be interested in a field that's not represented in this chapter, though. For this assignment, you will conduct research to discover more about the kinds of writing that are common within a particular applied field—ideally, one you're interested in. You might conduct either primary or secondary research to respond to this assignment. However, you should focus on collecting examples of the kinds of writing done in the field. Consider following the steps below to complete this assignment.

1. Collect examples of the kinds of writing done in the field.

2. Describe the different genres and how they relate to the work of that applied field.

3. Look for comparisons and contrasts across those genres. Do any commonalities point to conventions shared across genres? Are there differences that are important to notice? What do the patterns across the genres tell you about the work and values of that applied field?

Variation: Imagine that your audience is a group of incoming students interested in the same field of study you've researched for this project. Your task is to write a guide for those students about the conventions of writing expected in this applied field. Depending on what you have found, you may need to identify what conventions are appropriate for specific genres of writing.

- **The applied fields focus on the practical application of knowledge and career preparation.** Many applied fields also focus on problem-solving as part of the practical application of knowledge.

- **When beginning a writing task in applied fields, carefully analyze the rhetorical situation.** Consider your purpose and your audience carefully, and assess the appropriateness of responding in a particular genre.

- **Much of the writing in applied fields follows conventional expectations for structure, language, and reference appropriate to the fields.** Regardless of your writing task, you should be aware of these conventional expectations.

- **Students and professionals in applied fields often communicate information through field-specific genres.** Nurses, for example, often construct discharge directions, just as students and professionals in the fields of law often compose legal briefs.

PART THREE

Entering Academic Conversations

Readings and Case Studies

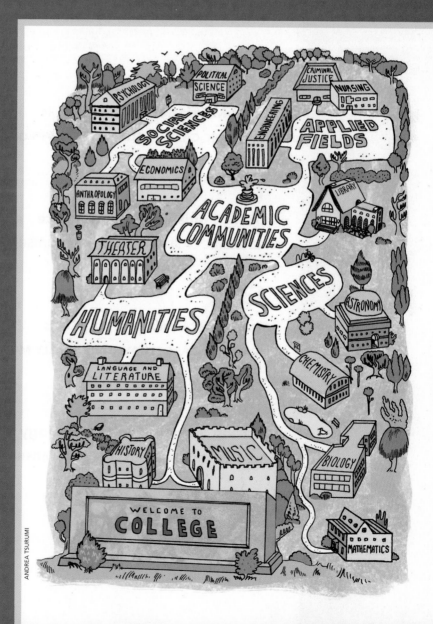

ANDREA TSURUMI

Love, Marriage, and Family

The readings in this chapter provide a glimpse into various aspects of love, marriage, and family. Bringing together a wide variety of sources, the chapter presents multiple views on these topics, ranging from insights drawn from large survey data to interviews about individual experiences.

The chapter begins with a reading that explores the cultural influences that have shaped the current state of marriage in the United States. The text that follows examines the relationships between parents and children, focusing on the relatively recent phenomenon of "helicopter parents," or parents who are overly involved in their children's lives. Other readings in the chapter focus on two types of families that have historically been excluded from, or have faced significant challenges with attaining, social acceptance and legal legitimacy: same-sex families and multi-racial families. In addition to reviewing general trends in the way others perceive these types of families, these final readings focus on the experiences of being marginalized or excluded and on the ways in which families cope with those experiences.

As you read selections from the chapter, we hope you will consider the relationships between your own experiences and those presented in the popular and academic readings offered. We encourage you to consider critically the issues they raise and to pose your own questions about those issues. These might include the following:

- What constitutes a marriage, a family?
- How have definitions of "family" changed over time?
- How are individuals included and excluded from social legitimacy as a family? How are those lines drawn in our society?
- How do individuals negotiate their own family identities in times of trial or change?
- How do your own family experiences align with those described in the readings?

The academic case study for this chapter focuses on love. It comprises readings that explore the topic from a range of scholarly perspectives:

- **Humanities**   How have dominant notions of love and marriage been challenged historically?
- **Social Sciences**   Who falls in love first, men or women?
- **Natural Sciences**   How does our body chemistry change when we experience love?
- **Applied Fields**   How do men and women market themselves online in the quest for love?

How American Family Life Is Different

ANDREW CHERLIN

Andrew Cherlin is a professor of sociology at Johns Hopkins University, specializing in families and public policy. He publishes regularly in both scholarly and popular venues on topics such as marriage and divorce, children's well-being, intergenerational relations, family policy, and welfare policy. The following excerpt is from *The Marriage-Go-Round: The State of Marriage and the Family Today* (2009), a popular text informed by scholarship that places American families within an international context to demonstrate how they differ from families in other wealthy countries. In this excerpt, Cherlin argues that it is America's contradictory emphasis on marriage and individualism that differentiates it from other countries.

THE CONTRADICTIONS OF AMERICAN CULTURE

There are many similarities, of course, between the United States and other Western nations. All have industrialized in similar ways, and all are making the transition from factory work to office work. All are being affected by the globalizing economy. Moreover, all of the Western nations are democracies, and they share a common cultural heritage. The United States has even more in common with Great Britain than with the rest of Europe, including a language, a legal system, and a colonial past. All of these similarities reflect important characteristics of Western societies, but they won't help us to explain distinctive American family patterns. To do that, we have to look for differences, not similarities, between the United States and other countries.

One difference lies in the realm of culture: the contradictory emphases on marriage and individualism

found only in the United States. People tend to think of a nation's culture as consistent and unified — a set of values and expectations that fit together to create a coherent whole. We learn this culture in childhood, it is commonly thought, from parents, teachers, and the media, and each of us applies it the same way as adults. But this understanding is simplistic. Culture often contains multiple, inconsistent ways of viewing the same reality, and individuals choose, sometimes without even realizing it, which view to adopt. We have more culture in our heads than we use, in other words, and not all of it coheres. To use an earlier metaphor, culture is a vast tool kit, and people reach into this kit to select the tools they need to organize their lives. In the kit are sets of tools I will call cultural models — frameworks for interpreting common situations we encounter. Cultural models are habits of thought, taken-for-granted ways of interpreting the world that we draw upon in everyday life. But sometimes there is more than one cultural model—more than one set of tools—that we can apply to a given situation. That is the case with intimate partnerships, where Americans can draw upon both a cultural model of marriage and a cultural model of individualism.

In a similar vein, Karla B. Hackstaff wrote a book about the "contesting ideologies" of a marriage culture and a divorce culture in contemporary American society. The marriage culture, she maintained, has three bases. First, marriage is a given: you have to marry, it's something everyone does, it's the only proper way to live your adult life. Second, marriage is forever. Third, divorce is a last resort. I think that fifty or sixty years ago marriage was indeed a given in American culture. But I don't think it's a given anymore. You can choose not to marry and still live a socially acceptable life. Nevertheless, marriage continues to be the most desired and most prestigious way to have a family.

Consequently, I would amend Hackstaff's definition to say that marriage is no longer a given but is still the preferred way to live one's personal life. I agree with her that people still think of marriage as lasting forever and of divorce as a last resort. Everyone, of course, is aware that these days marriages often end in separation or divorce. Yet most people still think that marriage *should* last forever and that divorce should be avoided. For instance, Americans were asked in a national survey whether they agreed or disagreed with this statement: "Marriage is a lifetime relationship that should never be ended except under extreme circumstances." Seventy-six percent agreed, 13 percent said they neither agreed nor disagreed, and only 11 percent said they disagreed. Moreover, when people marry, almost all of them intend for their own marriage to last forever. When a journalist interviewed sixty people whose marriages had ended within five years, she found that every one of them expected at first that their marriages would last forever. Nor are these expectations limited to the middle class. Low-income, unmarried mothers in the Philadelphia area told two sociologists that they would marry only if they were sure the relationship would last forever. A twenty-year-old Puerto Rican mother said, "If I get married, I wanna be with this person for the rest of my life. I don't wanna just get

married and then our relationship goes wrong, and then I have to go and get a *divorce!*"

This tendency to draw a line between other people's 5 families (lots of marriages fail these days) and your own (my marriage will last forever) can be seen in other opinions about family life. For instance, in another national survey, people were asked, "In general, do you think that because of such things as divorce, more working mothers, or single parents, etc., family ties in the U.S. are breaking down—or don't you think so?" Seventy-six percent responded that they thought family ties were breaking down. Yet their responses were very different to the follow-up question "What about your own family? Are family ties breaking down, or not?" Eighty-two percent said that their own family ties were *not* breaking down. Some may call it denial, but people think their own family is in good shape even though they think the family in general is in decline. Similarly, they are optimistic that their own marriage will last forever—at least when they start it—although they know that many other marriages will not.

Americans also believe that spouses should be sexually faithful to each other. In fact, over the past few decades, people have become *more* disapproving of extramarital sex. The number of Americans who answered "always wrong" to the question "What is your opinion about a married person having sexual relations with someone other than the marriage partner—is it always wrong, almost always wrong, wrong only sometimes, or not wrong at all?" increased from 70 percent in 1973 to 82 percent in 2004. This trend is all the more notable since, during the same period, people have become much more tolerant of sex before marriage, with close to a majority now saying that premarital sex is not wrong at all.

Overall, then, I would suggest that the American cultural model of marriage contains the following elements today:

- Marriage is the best way to live one's family life.
- A marriage should be a permanent, loving relationship.
- A marriage should be a sexually exclusive partnership.
- Divorce should be a last resort.

There may be other elements, but these are the ones that matter for the argument I am making. Despite the decline in the percentage of people who ever marry, the rise of cohabitation, and the increase in divorce, Americans still have this set of tools in their kit.

The cultural model of marriage is stronger in the United States than in most other Western countries. In 2006, the U.S. Congress debated the wisdom of a federal constitutional amendment stating, in part, "Marriage in the United States shall consist only of the union of a man and a woman." In his weekly radio address two days before the senatorial debate, President George W. Bush, a supporter of the amendment, told the nation, "Marriage cannot be cut off from its cultural, religious, and natural roots without weakening this good influence on society." No political observers expected this amendment to be approved by Congress, because a two-thirds majority is required, and indeed it was defeated. But a simple majority of senators and representatives voted for it.

In another sign of support for heterosexual marriage, Congress, in early 2006, enacted a law providing $150 million per year for research and demonstration projects that promote "healthy marriage and responsible fatherhood." These funds can be used for activities such as relationship skills training for young couples who want to marry or married couples who want to avoid divorce, public advertising campaigns on the value of marriage, and education programs in high school that promote marriage. The advertisements that I saw on the sides of buses in Baltimore saying "Marriage works" were privately funded, but they were a prototype of what the healthy marriage funds may support.

These government interventions on behalf of marriage have no counterpart in other Western nations, because nowhere else is the meaning and function of marriage such a contested issue. No other government provides funds for promoting marriage. Just north of the border in 2004, Paul Martin, the prime minister of Canada, announced plans to introduce legislation that would legalize same-sex marriage. He told reporters he expected the measure to pass because

"I've always thought Canada is the most postmodern country," an assertion one cannot imagine an American president making. By 2005 Canada and a few other Western countries (Belgium, the Netherlands, Spain) allowed same-sex marriage. Many European countries, including Britain and France, had enacted national, civil union–like statuses for same-sex partners. A British legal scholar, John Eekelaar, wrote, "The Civil Partnership Act of 2004 has cleverly created an institution for England and Wales for same-sex partners that is equivalent to marriage with hardly a murmur of protest." Such a measure in the United States would cause a cacophony of protest. Only in the United States is marriage so central a value that conservatives and liberals battle fiercely over its definition and over providing government support.

How Americans' beliefs about marriage compare to other nations can also be seen in the World Values Surveys, conducted in more than sixty countries, including all members of the European Union, Canada, and the United States, between 1999 and 2002. Adults in each country were asked whether they agreed or disagreed with the statement "Marriage is an outdated institution." Fewer Americans agreed (10 percent)—that is, fewer endorsed the idea that marriage is outdated—than in any other Western country, including Italy (17 percent), Sweden (20 percent), Canada (22 percent), Great Britain (26 percent), or France (36 percent). Americans are more likely to think that marriage is still appropriate for the times.

There's not much written about the strength of the cultural model of marriage because many observers mistakenly think that marriage is fading away. But the literature on the cultural model of individualism today is vast. The rise of individualism, historians and social commentators have argued, has been one of the master trends in the development of Western society over the past few centuries. And most would agree that an individualistic outlook on family and personal life has become more important since the mid-twentieth century. Robert Bellah and his colleagues, in an influential book on individualism and commitment in American life, distinguished between two types of individualism. They called the older form "utilitarian individualism." Think of the utilitarian individualist as the self-reliant, independent entrepreneur pursuing material success, such as a high position in a corporation or a senior partnership in a law firm. The great German social theorist Max Weber, in a classic book, suggested that there is a link between a similar concept, which he called "the Protestant ethic," and the economic development of the West. He noted that Calvinists (including the group that became known as the Puritans in England and America) believed that some individuals had been predestined by God for earthly success. This doctrine encouraged people to work hard so that they could prove to others (and themselves) that they were among the elect. Weber used the writings of Benjamin Franklin, a prototype of the utilitarian individualist, to illustrate this spirit of industriousness. "Early to bed and early to rise," Franklin advised in one of his famous aphorisms, "makes a man healthy, wealthy, and wise."

The newer form of individualism, which Bellah and his colleagues called "expressive individualism," germinated in the late nineteenth and early twentieth centuries and flowered in the second half of the twentieth. It is a view of life that emphasizes the development of one's sense of self, the pursuit of emotional satisfaction, and the expression of one's feelings. Until the past half century, individuals moved through a series of roles (student, spouse, parent, housewife or breadwinner) in a way that seemed more or less natural. Choices were constrained. In mill towns, two or three generations of kin might work at the same factory. Getting married was the only acceptable way to have children, except perhaps among the poor. Young people often chose their spouses from among a pool of acquaintances in their neighborhood, church, or school. But now you can't get a job in the factory where your father and grandfather worked because overseas competition has forced it to close, so you must choose another career. You get little help from relatives in finding a partner, so you sign on to an Internet dating service and review hundreds of personal profiles. As other lifestyles become more

acceptable, you must choose whether to get married and whether to have children. You develop your own sense of self by continually examining your situation, reflecting on it, and deciding whether to alter your behavior as a result. People pay attention to their experiences and make changes in their lives if they are not satisfied. They want to continue to grow and change throughout adulthood.

This kind of expressive individualism has flourished as prosperity has given more Americans the time and money to develop their senses of self—to cultivate their own emotional gardens, as it were. It suggests a view of intimate partnerships as continually changing as the partners' inner selves develop. It encourages people to view the success of their partnerships in individualistic terms. And it suggests that commitments to spouses and partners are personal choices that can be, and perhaps should be, ended if they become unsatisfying.

The World Values Surveys asked about expressive 15 individualism using a cluster of questions that contrast "survival versus self-expression" values. The answers to these questions suggest that the level of expressive individualism among Americans is high but not out of line for a wealthy Western nation: a little below that in Sweden and the Netherlands, comparable to the levels in Norway and West Germany, and greater than in Britain, Canada, or France. One question in this cluster asked people to place themselves on a scale of 1 to 10, where 1 means that they think the actions they take have no real effect on what happens to them (which indicates survival values) and 10 means they think they have completely free choice and control over their lives (self-expression values). More Americans placed themselves at the free choice end than did people in any other Western country, but some of the other countries were close: 82 percent of Americans chose 7, 8, 9, or 10, compared to 77 percent of Canadians, 74 percent of Swedes, and 73 percent of Germans.

The cultural model of individualism, then, holds that self-development and personal satisfaction are the key rewards of an intimate partnership. Your partnership must provide you with the opportunity to develop your sense of who you are and to express that sense through your relations with your partner. If it does not, then you should end it.

Cohabiting relationships, especially those without children, come closest to this kind of partnership. They are held together solely by the voluntary commitments of the partners, and should either party become dissatisfied with the relationship, it is expected that she or he will end it. The rise of cohabitation reflects the growing influence of the cultural model of individualism on personal and family life. Living together provides a way of obtaining the emotional rewards of a partnership while minimizing the commitment to it.

Even among married couples, we have seen the rise of what Barbara Whitehead calls "expressive divorce." Beginning in the 1960s people began to judge the success of their marriages not by their material standard of living or how well they raised children but rather by whether they felt their personal needs and desires were being fulfilled. They turned inward and examined whether their marriages restricted their personal development. They were more likely to turn to psychotherapists for help in seeking out the causes of their unhappiness with their marriages. And if they perceived that their marriages were personally unfulfilling, they considered leaving. According to this logic, if a person finds that he or she has changed since marriage in a direction different from the one his or her spouse has taken, then that person is justified in leaving the marriage in order to express this newer, fuller sense of self. It's too bad, the feeling goes, especially if the couple is raising children, but to stay in a marriage that constrains the partners' sense of who they are would be worse.

Concerning family life, then, the cultural model of individualism in the United States today emphasizes these elements:

- One's primary obligation is to oneself rather than to one's partner and children.
- Individuals must make choices over the life course about the kinds of intimate lives they wish to lead.
- A variety of living arrangements are acceptable.

- People who are personally dissatisfied with marriages and other intimate partnerships are justified in ending them.

As a twenty-first-century individual, you must choose your style of personal life. You are allowed to—in fact, you are almost required to—continually monitor your sense of self and to look inward to see how well your inner life fits with your married (or cohabiting) life. If the fit deteriorates, you are almost required to leave. For according to the cultural model of individualism, a relationship that no longer fits your needs is inauthentic and hollow. It limits the personal rewards that you, and perhaps your partner, can achieve. In this event, a breakup is unfortunate, but you will, and must, move on.

In practice, few Americans use just the cultural 20 tools of the marriage model or just the tools of the individualism model. Rather, most Americans draw upon both. As a result, our actual marriages and cohabiting relationships typically combine them. People may rely on both sets of tools at the same time, or they may move from one to the other over time as their assessment of their personal lives changes. Moreover, they may not realize that they are combining two inconsistent models.

For instance, let's return to the national survey in which people were asked whether they thought marriage was a lifetime relationship that shouldn't be ended except under extreme circumstances. You'll recall that 76 percent agreed. The great majority, then, answered in a way consistent with the cultural model of marriage. Just a few pages farther along in the questionnaire they were asked whether they agreed or disagreed with this statement: "When a marriage is troubled and unhappy, it is generally better for the children if the couple stays together." It, too, reflects the marriage model, because the troubled and unhappy individual, by staying in the marriage, subordinates his or her personal satisfaction to the greater goal of raising the children well. It would seem logical, therefore, that most of the people who agreed that marriage is for life would also agree that it's better if the couple stays together.

But they don't. Only 25 percent of the people who said marriage is for life also said that the couple should stay together. Forty percent disagreed and 35 percent said they neither agreed nor disagreed. How can it be that a few minutes after they all agreed that marriage is for life, only one-fourth agreed that unhappy people should stay in marriages for the sake of the children? These respondents, like many Americans, are drawing from two different cultural models simultaneously. When people think about the way marriage should be, they tend to say that it should be for life. But when people think about individual satisfaction, they tend to give others wide latitude to leave unhappy living arrangements. Cue them in one direction, and you get one picture; cue them in another, and you get a different picture. Both pictures, contradictory as they may be, are part of the way that Americans live their family lives. Together they spin the American merry-go-round of intimate partnerships.

Reading Questions

1. How does Cherlin define *cultural model*? What metaphor does he adopt to help his readers understand cultural models?

2. How does Cherlin amend Hackstaff's definition of *marriage culture*? What evidence does he use to support his amendment?

3. What is the difference between "utilitarian individualism" and "expressive individualism"?

4. In what ways are the cultural models of marriage and individualism contradictory?

Rhetoric Questions

5. Cherlin relies heavily on survey data to support his claims about marriage and individualism. What other types of evidence could be used to support, refute, or amend his claims?

6. How would you describe Cherlin's style of presenting ideas from other academics? How does this style affect the overall tone of the piece?

Response and Research Questions

7. Cherlin writes that the United States stands out from other nations in that the meaning and function of marriage are constantly contested here. Other than discussions surrounding government intervention in marriage, what national debates might signify disagreement about the meaning and function of marriage?

8. According to Cherlin, survey data reveal that most people believe marriage in general is breaking down in the United States, yet they also believe that their own marriage is in good shape. What might explain this contradiction?

9. Cherlin proposes Benjamin Franklin as a model of "utilitarian individualism." What prominent figure could serve as a model for "expressive individualism"? Explain your choice.

The Myth of the Helicopter Parent

SUSAN KRAUSS WHITBOURNE

Susan Krauss Whitbourne is a professor emerita of psychological and brain sciences at the University of Massachusetts–Amherst. She publishes regularly in both scholarly and popular outlets on topics of adult development and aging. Whitbourne is the author of several books, including *The Search for Fulfillment* (2010). Additionally, she writes a popular blog for *Psychology Today* entitled "Fulfillment at Any Age" and contributes to the *Huffington Post*. In the article below, written for *Psychology Today*, Whitbourne explores the effects of "helicopter parenting" on both children and parents. Specifically, she asks, "Will indulgent parents hurt their children—and themselves? Or will helicoptering young adult children benefit all concerned?" Drawing on scholarship from the discipline of psychology, Whitbourne tailors her answers for a non-technical audience.

So-called "helicopter parents" are roundly criticized by everyone from teachers to media experts for smothering [their children] with too much loving. If you want to "land your kids in therapy," according to psychotherapist Lori Gottlieb writing in *Atlantic* magazine, then by all means give them everything under the sun. If you want them to become productive members of society with reasonably normal lives, then keep the hugs and kisses to a minimum and even deny them things once in a while. "Well-meaning parents can ruin their children," so the claim goes.

These observations led University of Texas psychologist Karen Fingerman and her colleagues (2012) to put the claims to the empirical test. They believed that today's children, especially when they're young adults, need more support than ever from their parents—ranging from advice to financial help. Today's young adults don't necessarily expect support from parents. Given the stretching out of adolescence, and particularly "emerging adulthood" (ages 18–29; Arnett, 2000), such expectations, if not hope, are not out of the question. Parents today may worry that they're providing more help than they "should" based on the social norms of their own youth. Therefore, they may fear violating social norms for parental support. On the other hand, research based on the Longitudinal Study of Generations (Byers, Levy, Allore, Bruce, & Kasl, 2008) suggests that parents of young adults report fewer depressive symptoms when they are heavily involved with their kids. Providing tangible and emotional support helps people feel that they are part of the lives of their children by making them feel they "matter."

So which will it be? Will indulgent parents hurt their children—and themselves? Or will helicoptering young adult children benefit all concerned? Fingerman and team had at their disposal a sample of 399 parents (reporting on 886 children) and 592 children (reporting on 1,158 parents) living in the greater Philadelphia area who completed a computer-assisted telephone interview. They were asked questions from the Intergenerational Support Index, a measure in which parents and children indicate the extent to which parents provide support ranging from advice and listening to financial and practical help. Both parents and children rated the intensity of support parents provided: "too little" to "more than you would like" with the middle point being "about right." This was the measure of intense support. Children answered questions about their own adjustment and life satisfaction, and parents rated their life satisfaction as well.

The children ranged in age from 19 to 41 years old, with a mean of 24. They lived from 0 to 5,000 miles away from their parents, with an average distance of 172 miles. [Moreover,] 30% of them actually lived with their parents, 24% had children of their own, and 35% were full-time students.

A substantial number of children (about one-fifth) 5 reported that their parents in fact provided them with intense support, but more felt this came from their mothers (27%) than from their fathers (15%). These numbers corresponded closely to what parents said about the support they felt they provided. In fact, parents and children were remarkably consistent in reporting the areas of their relationship in which parents provided intense support. Parents provided the most support in the emotional areas that included listening, emotional help, and advice; and less in the areas of practical, financial, and socializing. However, parents did not provide support equally to all of their children. About 30% of parents provided support to only one child (for those who had more than one child). Those children most likely to receive support tended to be younger, to live with their parents, or to have children of their own, and mothers were more likely than fathers to provide intense support.

How did these helicoptered children fare? According to the findings presented by Fingerman and her group, the children whose parents provided them with intense support experienced better outcomes. Helicoptered children actually had higher life satisfaction and more clearly defined goals. However, helicoptering parents had many self-doubts as indicated by their lower life satisfaction.

Helicopter parenting, at least for grown children, seems to have its benefits. Parents who are involved and supportive across a wide range of areas produce young adult children who have a clearer sense of self and are more satisfied with their lives. However, parents who felt that their children need too much support were themselves lower in life satisfaction.

Parental support to grown children isn't a one-size-fits-all affair. The adult children who seemed to benefit the most from the involvement of their parents in their lives tended to be younger, lived with their parents, and had children of their own. It is possible that the reason they found this support so helpful was that they were in a life stage when the continued help of their parents could ease their adjustment into adulthood. Parents and children characterized by these intense support bonds may be feeling some pangs of guilty pleasure. They enjoy their relationship, and the children seem to do well as a result. However, because they hear so much in the media about the dangers of over-involved parents, they feel that there's something wrong with them for being in this type of relationship.

You might be thinking, and you'd be right, that as a correlational study, we can't conclude that intense parenting causes better outcomes in grown children. Perhaps parents provide more intense support for children who they see as "worthy" of investment. Furthermore, parents who are dissatisfied with their lives may also rate their children as less successful or needier. It's also possible that parents and children who have better relationships feel more satisfied with their lives in general and may even be mentally healthier.

Nevertheless, the findings lead to a new understanding of parent-child support in the years of emerging adulthood. For parents, having your 20-something (or even 30-something) kids depend on you for everything from advice to a little financial help now and then doesn't mean you've failed. For grown children, you don't have to break yourself off entirely from your parents in order to be considered successful or mature.

Another piece of good news from this study is that there are many ways for parents and children to stay connected. Even if you don't live with or near your family, email, Facebook, and other social media can allow you to provide support at many levels. To be a successful helicopter parent, just listening can help your kids navigate the sometimes rocky years of early adulthood. And kids, it's not a bad idea to listen to your parents. It may be good for your mental health!

REFERENCES

Arnett, J. J. (2000). Emerging adulthood: A theory of development from the late teens through the twenties. *American Psychologist, 55,* 469–480. doi:10.1037/0003-066X.55.5.469

Byers, A. L., Levy, B. R., Allore, H. G., Bruce, M. L., & Kasl, S. V. (2008). When parents matter to their adult children: Filial reliance associated with parents' depressive symptoms. *Journals of Gerontology: Series B: Psychological Science and Social Sciences, 63,* P33–P40.

Fingerman, K. L., Cheng, Y. P., Wesselmann, E. D., Zarit, S., Furstenberg, F., & Birditt, K. S. (2012). Helicopter parents and landing pad kids: Intense parental support of grown children. *Journal of Marriage and Family, 74,* 880–896.

Reading Questions

1. How does Whitbourne define *helicopter parents*? What debate concerning helicopter parents is Whitbourne addressing?

2. What research methods were used to collect data in the Fingerman et al. study? What specific demographics did the study draw from?

3. What conclusions about helicopter parents (and their children) does Whitbourne draw from the Intergenerational Support Index?

Rhetoric Questions

4. Whitbourne writes that "as a correlational study, we can't conclude that intense parenting causes better outcomes in grown children" (par. 9). How does Whitbourne hedge her claims throughout the article and anticipate her audience's questions?

5. Throughout the article, Whitbourne both summarizes and analyzes data. How does she transition between summary and analysis? How might you use one or more of these techniques in your own writing?

6. Analyze the structure of Whitbourne's article. Specifically, note what each paragraph in the article is meant to accomplish. Then compare Whitbourne's article to a similar one in *Psychology Today*. Identify any structural patterns you're able to see.

Response and Research Questions

7. What connections can you make between your own life experiences (as a child and/or as a parent) and the ideas Whitbourne explores in her work?

8. Locate the original Fingerman et al. study using your library's journal database. What techniques does Whitbourne use to make sense of academic scholarship for a non-technical audience?

Changing Counts, Counting Change: Toward a More Inclusive Definition of Family

BRIAN POWELL, CATHERINE BOLZENDAHL, CLAUDIA GEIST, AND LALA CARR STEELMAN

As a team of researchers and writers, Brian Powell, Catherine Bolzendahl, Claudia Geist, and Lala Carr Steelman utilize their collective experience and training in the field of sociology to explore various definitions of family that circulate in American culture. This excerpt from *Counted Out: Same-Sex Relations and Americans' Definitions of Family* (2010) draws on survey data collected from more than 1,500 people in 2003 and 2006, years before the 2015 Supreme Court decision that legalized same-sex marriage in the United States. These surveys asked respondents to explain their views about marriage, adoption, cohabitation, and many other issues related to family. In the passage below, the authors explore attitudes toward same-sex marriage as a way to understand Americans' perception of family more generally.

Family counts. Few would dispute this statement. Family is assigned a great many responsibilities and in turn is afforded a great number of benefits. It has a profound influence on our lives. But "family" counts too. How "family" is defined determines which living arrangements are expected to perform these responsibilities, which are granted these benefits, and upon which social legitimacy is conferred. Definitions of family—and especially whether same-sex couples should be seen as family—currently lie at the heart of passionate scholarly and public controversy and debate. Whether same-sex couples are counted in or out of this definition, we argue, is a crucial touchstone for understanding family more generally and accordingly is intertwined with views regarding a host of family issues—among them, the relative influence of parenting versus genetic inheritance, gender and parenting, and marital naming practices. Yet we have known little about the boundaries that Americans erect between family and nonfamily—that is, which living arrangements they include as family and which ones they do not. The unique and comprehensive approach taken in this book, however, narrows this gap by explicitly canvassing Americans' views on the definition of family.

In this closing chapter, we revisit the key patterns and themes that emerged from our interviews and discuss what these patterns may indicate about family in American society now and into the future. Despite their disagreements regarding whether same-sex couples should be seen as family and accorded, by extension, marital and other familial rights, "pro-family" and gay rights activists do agree about the centrality of the question of same-sex couples for our understanding of family. The conservative commentator Maggie Gallagher, for example, observes that "gay marriage is not some sideline issue, it *is* the marriage debate" (Gallagher 2003). Since the very first interviews we conducted in 2003, there have been remarkable changes surrounding the debate about same-sex couples and their actual legal status. These changes have not followed a predictably linear path. Rather, they have swung back and forth so much that they have triggered everything from unbridled optimism

to devastating despair among both advocates of the extension of family rights to same-sex couples and critics apprehensive about the possible loss of "traditional" families. We have seen gains—or losses, in the view of certain "pro-family" groups—in the rapidly shifting legal and political landscape where the rights of same-sex couples have been advanced. Among these gains are court-initiated legalization of same-sex marriage in Massachusetts, Connecticut, Iowa, and, for a short period of time, California; legislatively approved same-sex marriage in Vermont, New Hampshire, Washington, D.C., and, temporarily, Maine; a publicly supported vote (Referendum 71) in Washington State in favor of expansion of domestic partnership rights and protections for same-sex couples, as well as for senior heterosexual couples;[1] and, at the time of the writing of this chapter, attempts by political leaders to at least tread softly toward extension of some familial rights to same-sex couples (for example, President Barack Obama's executive order granting hospital visitation rights to same-sex couples) or sometimes to more boldly follow the lead of the states.

At the same time, we have experienced losses—or gains according to traditional "pro-family" groups. Some sharply divided courts, including those with fairly liberal traditions (such as New York's), declined to overturn the long-standing prohibition against same-sex marriage in their states. Often these courts justify their ruling by deferring to the legislature and the will of the people. More than twenty states—representing a cross-section of this nation and wide divergence in political views and geographical locations—have put forth ballot initiatives to outlaw same-sex marriage. Some political commentators contend that this flurry of initiatives played a nontrivial role in the 2004 presidential election and increased support for Republican candidates in state elections: in fact, some pundits maintain that the ballot initiatives in swing states (such as Ohio) were a cynical ploy to secure George W. Bush's reelection. All but one effort passed—many of them decisively. And in Arizona, the one exception, the success was short-lived: voters opposed Proposition 107 ("protection of marriage") in 2006, but in 2008 they cast ballots in favor of Proposition 102, which amended the state constitution to define marriage as a union between one man and one woman. Even in California, one of the most socially liberal states—indeed, a state that several of our respondents labeled as overly liberal or far removed from the American mainstream—voters jettisoned the previously discussed breakthrough court decision when they narrowly voted in favor of Proposition 8, which revised the state constitution to restrict marital status to heterosexual couples.[2] These setbacks often extend beyond the debate regarding marriage. In Arkansas, legislation mainly designed to bar same-sex couples from adopting children or offering a home to foster children also passed.[3]

It is tricky to make predictions about the future of same-sex families, especially given the sheer fluidity of the situation and the intensified public reaction to the debate and to issues regarding sexuality more broadly. Even traditional forms of American entertainment are engaging this issue—from television personalities who advocate for or against same-sex marriage, to contestants in beauty pageants who are asked their views on same-sex marriage, to bloggers who gossip over whether a reality show contestant is gay. Currently, and somewhat surprisingly, some pundits and spokespersons for political parties and advocacy groups act as if the debate is over and proponents of same-sex marriage have prevailed with the American public, or shortly will do so (Waldman 2009). Neither the numbers from our data nor actual votes on initiatives are anywhere near the sufficient magnitude to support the idea that the public is ready to embrace same-sex couples with open arms.[4] To be sure, there still are many Americans who are—in their own words—"appalled," "disgusted," and "repelled" by the very idea of same-sex families and the extension of rights to these groups. Nevertheless, we remain confident that the resistance to same-sex partnerships will dissipate in the not-too-distant future.

Social scientists typically are more comfortable 5 making claims about the past and present, while shying away from forecasting the future. Yet, if we tie together the various pieces of evidence that stand out in the previous chapters, we can make some admittedly cautious but empirically based predictions. We began by identifying and deciphering three distinguishable categories of Americans who vary in the lines that they draw between family and nonfamily: inclusionists, moderates, and exclusionists. These categories have provided a recurring baseline throughout the book that, in turn, is connected to other views about the family. At one end of the spectrum, exclusionists are restrictive in whom they welcome into the realm of family, while at the other end inclusionists are more receptive to living arrangements that exclusionists routinely reject. Moderates may be the most interesting group—or at least most important in terms of the future of American attitudes and beliefs. Moderates are at the very least open to new ways of defining family, but remain more guarded than inclusionists when it comes to granting family status to same-sex couples.

CHANGING COUNTS AND RECOUNTS

It is telling that even in a short period of time—just three years—we experienced a notable decrease in the percentage of exclusionists and a corresponding increase in the percentage of inclusionists. By 2006 a very clear majority (over three-fifths) of Americans had come to include same-sex couples with children and/or childless same-sex couples under the rubric of "family." This change is all the more impressive given that during that three-year period—from 2003 to 2006—anti-gay-marriage and, more broadly, anti-same-sex-relationships rhetoric reached perhaps its most heated level and arguably was also at its most effective. Although one might question whether this change is merely a blip in one particular data set, the corresponding open-ended comments provided by respondents convinced us that these changes are quite real. Moreover, these patterns are corroborated by a recently added and, in our opinion, most welcome question regarding same-sex marriage provided in the National Opinion Research Center's General Social Survey. Interviewees in the General Social Survey were asked their view regarding same-sex marriage in 2004, 2006, and 2008.[5] Between 2004 and 2006, the percentage of Americans who agreed that "homosexuals should have the right to marry" rose from 29.8 percent to 35.3 percent. Our own survey did not go beyond 2006, but the 2008 General Social Survey suggests that support for same-sex marriage increased further, up to 39.3 percent. Admittedly, these figures fall below any threshold that signals an irreversible tipping point, and therefore they challenge the idea promoted by some pundits that the debate is over. But these figures do indicate that the patterns we report throughout the book are not idiosyncratic to our data. These figures also signify that there is good reason to be confident that views of family and family rights will continue to expand, perhaps with increasing speed.

Had we not listened to the comments that Americans gave to explain the boundaries that they make between family and nonfamily, we might not be as optimistic. The quantitative data give us a picture of the boundaries, but the qualitative data animate the struggles that Americans face in defining family — struggles that should compel them to reevaluate their definitions of family. We do not see much struggle, however, among inclusionists. They believe that love and commitment make a family and bind it together. They embrace a broad definition of family that not only privileges love and commitment but also recognizes the various instrumental and expressive purposes of family and further defers to others' self-definitions of their own living situation. Inclusionists are unambiguous in their views and seem to be impervious to the arguments proffered by those who endorse narrower definitions of family. In fact, we are hard-pressed to envision a scenario in which a large segment of the inclusionist group would reverse itself and rein in its broad-ranging definition of family.

Most exclusionists also do not struggle with their definition of family. Or more precisely, they typically do not wrestle over the question of same-sex couples, although they do face challenges in their views regarding cohabiting heterosexual couples, especially those with children. Regarding same-sex couples, however, exclusionists do not show much potential for change in their views. Exclusionists insist upon heterosexuality, censure homosexuality (sometimes with palpable hostility), rely on interpretations of biblical text that putatively condemn same-sex unions, and emphasize the importance of biological parents — or "blood" relations. These frames may be so powerful that they counteract any attempts to broaden the definition of family, therefore rendering exclusionists unlikely candidates for change.

Still, we see some opportunities for movement even among some exclusionists. Although most exclusionists believe that the structure of families — notably, the presence of marriage — trumps the functions that families provide, some do not. This latter group may be receptive to entreaties to expand the definition of family to those living arrangements in which the needs and functions of family are met by its members regardless of legal documents or sexual orientation. Ironically, the focus on structure — more specifically, the legally endorsed familial structure — may ultimately be an effective strategy to relax exclusionists' resistance to same-sex couples. From our interviews, it is apparent that several exclusionists saw legal marriage as the key ingredient of family status and, in fact, as the only requirement to warrant that status. If legal definitions carry weight with exclusionists who respect legal tradition above all else, then legalization of same-sex marriage in various states may be sufficient to push some exclusionists toward a more moderate, if not inclusionist, stance. Thus, while our overall assumption is that definitions of family precipitate changes in views regarding the extension of legal rights to nontraditional living arrangements, for this group a change in the law might simultaneously shape both their views about same-sex marriage and the line of demarcation they draw between family and nonfamily. Legal changes in the status of same-sex couples, then, may move some exclusionists incrementally toward acceptance of same-sex couples as family.

We see much greater potential for movement among moderates, who — more so than either inclusionists or exclusionists — appear to genuinely struggle as they try to reconcile their traditionalism with their openness to change. This group, however, does not waver on the issue of children: if there is a child in the household, 10 moderates deem the living arrangement to be a family. Given the pivotal role that moderates as a bloc may play in the future of same-sex marriage (and in the extension of other rights to nontraditional family forms), campaigns that emphasize the positive effect that marital rights have on children of same-sex couples may be a winning formula. Moreover, with sophisticated and ever-changing reproductive technologies and increased opportunities for adoption, the number and visibility of same-sex couples residing with their children certainly may increase. From a political standpoint, framing the equality of same-sex couples in terms of "the best interests of the child" may prove to be a successful gateway that, when opened, fosters greater acceptance of same-sex households, along with equal rights and protections.

Still, moderates are hesitant to define childless same-sex couples — and childless heterosexual cohabiting couples — as family. But even here we foresee this reluctance eventually being transformed into steadier or even unwavering support. Surely, we see little evidence that moderates will become more restrictive in their definitions of family. In fact, the arguments that appear most persuasive to exclusionists — for example, pronouncements regarding the immorality of homosexual relations and reliance on biblical text (or particular interpretations of biblical text) — carry little weight among moderates. In contrast, arguments that appeal to inclusionists ultimately may also convert moderates. Given that so many moderates stipulate that the presence of children signals commitment among same-sex and heterosexual partners, the increasing visibility of other signals of commitment may also become a persuasive wellspring of change.

Among these signals is the length of time spent living together — as demonstrated by the sizable number of moderates who agree that a childless same-sex couple who have lived together for ten years constitute a family. Another signal, however, is detected from the functions that partners perform as a unit. Moderates are fully aware that families comprise members who are interdependent in accomplishing shared goals.

The more moderates are aware of or actually witness people in loving nontraditional living arrangements carrying out the various emotional and instrumental functions of family, the more receptive they should become to a more expansive definition of family. And this awareness is indeed likely to expand, given the growing number of media representations of loving same-sex families and the greater openness of same-sex couples themselves in schools, work settings, and communities. As moderates reexamine their views regarding same-sex families, social scientists might need to take a fresh look at their own views regarding functional approaches to family.[6] Although functionalism was once the mainstay of much sociological thought, recently it has been summarily dismissed by many social scientists as mere rationalization of the status quo and therefore an unremitting source of conservatism. But our interviews suggest an alternative interpretation: when the functions of families were brought up in our interviews, this topic tended, perhaps counterintuitively, to liberalize individual viewpoints.

Moderates' cognizance of their ambivalence and the inconsistencies in their responses makes us even more convinced of future changes in the boundaries that Americans make between family and nonfamily. In our interviews, moderates often realized that their emphasis on love and commitment, as well as on meeting familial needs, was at odds with their initial exclusion of childless same-sex and cohabiting heterosexual couples from the definition of family. Upon acknowledging their contradictory responses, some asked to change their responses — almost always in the direction of more inclusion. Others did not make this request but clearly felt uneasy with the dissonance in their responses. Some even volunteered that their views might switch or at least soften in the near future. The response of a fifty-year-old moderate woman from Georgia personifies the kind of ambivalence that might give way to a more inclusive view:

> I don't . . . I don't know if . . . I don't know, between my religious upbringing and my traditional upbringing, I don't know. I'm still working on this one for myself, and I still don't have one answer. . . . We're not adamant

against it [same-sex couples], but like I said, I mean, process is changing. If you call me next year, I might change my mind.

She continued by describing her upbringing and the ongoing process by which she was evaluating her own views:

> Well, you know, it's just traditional southern upbringing, where it's not like we knew homosexuals. But you know, it's just, I don't know, it's just . . . it's hard to explain. With my age group we're still learning to consider other—I can't think of the word. I can't think of the word: goodness, it's like once I hit fifty, I forget things! I was brought up one way, but I am slowly changing and considering other options. But I'm not totally, you know, I haven't totally changed some of the things. So, I'm, that's why some of my answers have been like flip-flopping, 'cause I'm not adamant about some of the things. So like I said, this is one of the areas that I am still thinking about. . . . It might be that under the right circumstances I could be convinced that it would be okay.

This respondent might have been apologetic about her lack of clarity or consistency, but her comments spoke volumes about what we believe is an inevitable pull toward greater acceptance of same-sex living arrangements. She exemplifies the many moderates who are poised to ultimately embrace a broader definition of family. A climate of acceptance is encouraging for those who advocate the extension of familial rights to same-sex couples—and to cohabiting heterosexual ones—but conversely, it is alarming to opponents and may further gird their resistance. Some commentators on this subject suggest that defenders of "traditional marriage" realize that there remains only a small window of time in which they can proactively prevent the extension of familial rights to nontraditional living arrangements. This realization could well be the precipitating factor behind the flurry of anti-gay-marriage initiatives that were advanced in the past few years. To the dismay of inclusionists, these initiatives have been enormously successful. But even among some exclusionists, we hear resigned recognition that these successes are likely to be short-lived: "In the end I believe all will prevail for the gay community. I will never agree with it. But that will be something I will have to live and die with."

CHANGING DIVISIONS

This sense of resignation may be due in large measure 15 to exclusionists' appreciation of the vast generational cleavages in definitions of family. Exclusionists realize that youths are no longer living in, as one person puts it, "the *Leave It to Beaver* world anymore." Older respondents were especially attuned to generational differences; in fact, they mentioned these differences more frequently than did younger Americans. The patterns are clear: the younger generation is strikingly more expansive in their definition of family than are their elders, especially those age sixty-five or older. Over 75 percent of adults under the age of thirty view some types of same-sex couples as family, while over 60 percent of adults sixty-five years of age or older refuse to acknowledge any living arrangement involving gay men or lesbians as family.

Some commentators speculate that youths will outgrow their more liberal views about family. We are less convinced. Instead, generations matter. For example, the members of the baby boom generation espouse more liberal views regarding family than would ordinarily be expected, breaking the otherwise smooth linear relationship between age and conservative views on family. This departure in the pattern highlights the powerful influence that a historical climate of tolerance has on individuals as they approach adulthood. Our younger respondents came of age—or are coming of age—at a time when gay issues have been more widely discussed and certainly gays have been less stigmatized. Some mass media have been at the cutting edge in presenting nontraditional families—showing, for example, single-parent and step-parent households at times when out-of-wedlock childbearing and divorce were not generally accepted. The same is true today for media images of gays and lesbians. Contemporary media and other conduits of information are more open about same-sex relations and overall are less heterosexist than they were even just a decade ago. Ironically, even the most virulently negative characterizations of gays and lesbians in public discourse may have the unintended consequence of making a taboo topic less taboo. While one can rightfully critique some images of gays and lesbians in the media (Gamson 1998; Walters 2001), the increased visibility of gays and lesbians in the public domain may be pivotal to the receptiveness of younger adults to a broader definition of family. If trends continue on the same path that they appear to favor, then the replacement of older cohorts by younger ones should invariably reshape the boundaries between family and nonfamily.

Educational differences should create a similar demographic pull toward inclusivity. As also confirmed in past scholarship about social attitudes, Americans with higher levels of education typically are more cosmopolitan in their views. Compared to their peers with lower levels of education, they report greater receptivity to including same-sex couples in their definitions of family. Such increased liberalism is not unexpected. College exposes youths to new ideas and experiences that challenge the often more insular viewpoints they might have had upon entering college. Moreover, college students may know and have contact with gay peers, a pattern that might soften once staunchly held exclusionist positions.[7]

Contact with gay men and lesbians is not limited, however, to the college-educated. Having a gay friend or relative in one's network or even just knowing someone who is gay is related quite strongly to the acceptance of same-sex living arrangements as family. The notable increase between 2003 and 2006 in the percentage of Americans who reported having a gay friend or relative suggests two things. First, gay and lesbian Americans are becoming more open about their sexuality to their friends, relatives, and acquaintances—even during or perhaps because of the heightened negative rhetoric about same-sex couples that took place between 2003 and 2006. Second, heterosexual Americans increasingly acknowledge the presence of gays and lesbians in their personal and professional social networks. These changes parallel the greater visibility of gay and lesbian public figures and, importantly, show no sign of abating. Additionally, current forms of communication (such as blogs, Twitter, and email) all encourage dialogue and openness about sexuality rather than denial of it. In the business world, many companies already offer same-sex benefits and programs, thus perhaps making employees feel more comfortable informing their colleagues about their sexual preference. Taken together, these trends insinuate more openness by the gay community, increasing recognition of gays and lesbians by others, and, in turn, greater receptivity to a broader conceptualization of family.

Earlier in this book, we identified other sociodemographic factors that also are implicated in Americans' definition of family. Regarding gender, women cast a wider net than do men when making decisions about who counts as family. This pattern also foretells a shift toward greater acceptance of various living arrangements as family. Women remain the primary caretakers of children and thus may hold greater sway over what their children come to believe. In a country where divorce and single-parenthood rates remain high, the effects of mothers' views may be especially pronounced. Consequently, children may learn from the example set by their mothers to be more open-minded about other types of families. Women also are as likely as men to vote, if not more so (Carroll and Fox 2006). Thus, as a voting bloc, women may have great sway over future elections and ballot initiative outcomes. Of course, not all women are inclusionists and not all men are exclusionists, but the average pattern is suggestive. Should the majority of women favor a more expansive vision of family, then politicians' hesitation to endorse the same may correspondingly lessen.

This is not to say that men are impervious to change. [20] On the contrary, increased education and contact with gay friends and relatives are at least as liberalizing for men as they are for women. Younger generations of men, not unlike the women of their age cohorts, also are more receptive to inclusionist definitions of family than are their older counterparts. Young men often are portrayed as unrelentingly homophobic, presumably because homosexuality challenges hegemonic* ideas of masculinity. But the patterns found in our data challenge the idea that young men constitute the group most resistant to inclusionist visions of family. The patterns also suggest room for future change among

*hegemonic: the dominant social or political perspective.

men, especially if we listen to how men talk about family. The different frames that men and women use to define family may be useful in campaigns that target male voters. For example, appeals to the responsibilities that are met in the family may provide a winning strategy for gay rights advocates in gaining support among men.

Spatial boundaries also figure into the boundaries that individuals draw between family and nonfamily. Urban-rural and regional schisms in Americans' definitions of family suggest that change will be uneven—with fairly rapid steps taken toward inclusivity in certain areas and nontrivial pushback in others. These differences to some degree explain why, for example, some Americans living in urban areas in the Northeast are so perplexed by strong hostility to same-sex marriage—and more broadly to the idea that a same-sex couple constitutes a family—when they consider it a non-issue, while other Americans living in rural areas of the South are baffled by and even fearful of the acknowledgment of the rights of same-sex couples that is perhaps inexorably under way.

What we already know about attitudes toward interracial couples also may be instructive here. The reader may recall that [in a previous chapter] we not only showed that age (cohort) and education affect Americans' current definitions of family (that is, whether they are exclusionist) but also noted that these factors closely parallel the age and educational differences in Americans' views regarding interracial marriage several decades ago. The very same survey—the General Social Survey—confirms a huge gap between urban and rural dwellers in 1972, the first year of the survey. In that year, over half (57.4 percent) of rural Americans favored "laws against marriages between (Negroes/Blacks/African Americans) and whites," while over three-fourths (78.9 percent) of respondents living in large cities were opposed to such discriminatory mandates. Although the rural-urban gap never entirely disappeared, over time rural Americans' views drifted closer to those of urban Americans (in other words, became more tolerant). By the mid-1990s, more than three-fourths of rural Americans also expressed opposition to miscegenation laws (76.2 percent in 1994). The very same changes transpired among southerners, although stubborn pockets of resistance in some southern states lingered. These patterns are not atypical: scholars have confirmed that social attitudes—especially innovative and liberal ones—typically spread in the United States from urban to rural areas and from nonsouthern to southern states (Fischer 1978; Firebaugh and Davis 1988). Urban-rural and regional gaps may not entirely disappear, but rural and southern views are more likely to move in the direction of urban and nonsouthern views than the other way around.

Currently, one might characterize the social and political climate regarding familial definitions as one in which pockets of acceptance are scattered. That is, in a small number of states, individuals are more receptive to a broadened definition of family that includes same-sex couples and ultimately promotes the extension of rights and benefits to these couples. The number of such states is small, but if the regional and urban-rural changes in attitudes toward interracial marriage are any indication, the number will continue to grow. Although such growth is likely to encounter additional resistance, this opposition will diminish to the point where only pockets of resistance remain—as we have witnessed with respect to attitudes toward interracial marriage.

Most sociodemographic trends seem to propel us in the direction of a more inclusive definition of family. One influence, however, may stand in the way. Religious ideology and identity—measured in several ways, but most notably by interpretations of the Bible as literal—are powerfully entwined with some Americans' definitions of family. Homosexuality and same-sex relationships are often couched by exclusionists in terms of violating biblical doctrine—as flouting "God's law," "the biblical standard," and "*the rules.*" For Americans who resolutely hold on to these positions, it is difficult to envision much movement toward greater inclusivity. The use of these religious frames is so powerful that the greater adherence of some Americans to religious orthodoxy—at least compared to the rest of the Western world—may be a major stumbling block that stands in the way of acceptance of nontraditional groups as families.

Should the number of Americans who subscribe to religiously orthodox or fundamentalist views increase in the future, then we might expect a slowing down or even a reversal in the trend toward a more inclusive definition of family. Whether religious conservatism and fundamentalism in the United States will increase, however, has been widely debated. Some scholars contend that fundamentalism has reached its peak in popularity and is now noticeably on the decline. Instead, they forecast, Americans will become more and more secularized, as indicated by the rise in the number of Americans who indicate that they are agnostic, atheist, or unaffiliated with any particular religion. Others do not deny that religion remains important in the everyday lives of Americans, but they believe that the absolutism associated with fundamentalism is being supplanted by a more expansive religious worldview—an expansiveness that is manifested, for example, in greater concern over global warming and poverty in the developing countries (Bolzendahl and Brooks 2005). The possibility that this greater liberalism will extend to views regarding same-sex relationships is certainly not out of the question. After all, religious messages can and do shift dramatically over time—as witnessed, for example, in the civil rights movement. Many messages in religious texts encourage tolerance above and beyond other values. Relying on these messages, some denominations explicitly welcome gays and lesbians, such as the United Church of Christ and the Episcopal Church (in the United States). Casting religion as an insurmountable and unalterable bulwark holding back the extension of familial definitions and of civil liberties to include gay citizens therefore may itself be too rigid a view.

CHANGING ACCOUNTS

The invocation of "God's will" takes a surprising twist when used to explain the etiology of sexual preference. Ordinarily, we might expect religious reasoning—or, at least, the insertion of "God's will" into causal explanations—to behave in conservative ways. Yet Americans who believe that "God's will" is the principal factor determining sexual preference are surprisingly liberal in their definitions of family. Also unexpected is the age profile of the Americans who are most likely to subscribe to this account: younger adults. These two perhaps jarring patterns do not necessarily imply that religious views per se now automatically convert into liberalism or are on the rise. But they do suggest that some Americans see sexuality as determined not by the individual or the environment, but instead by forces that exist well beyond our understanding. In other words, it is possible to use the concept of "God's will" in a way that reinforces the immutability of sexuality and challenges claims that sexual preference can be changed. Importantly, as comments by the interviewees clarify, this frame may simultaneously appeal to those who are religious and supportive of same-sex families and to those who do not necessarily see themselves as religious (atheists, agnostics, and spiritualists). Just as appeals to "God's will" have been successfully employed in various progressive social causes, the use of this apparent religious frame may be called upon to justify equality for same-sex couples.

Religion and science typically are not thought of as natural allies. Instead, they often are pitted against each other and as such are portrayed as promoting incompatible accounts of human behavior. But here we see a clear exception. Ostensibly religious ("God's will") and scientific (genetic inheritance) explanations of sexual preference share a great deal in common. Paralleling "God's will" explanations, genetic accounts are robustly coupled with a more inclusive definition of family. When Americans attribute sexual preference to genetics—or to "God's will"—they in essence reject the idea that homosexuality is a "lifestyle" choice and therefore is reversible or, in the parlance of gay reparative therapy, "curable." Instead, adherents of genetic accounts—like those who endorse "God's will" explanations—view sexual preference not as a choice, but rather as an intrinsic and immutable trait of individuals.

This view is becoming increasingly popular—as indicated by the growing number of Americans between 2003 and 2006 who selected genetic or "God's will" explanations in the closed-ended questions and correspondingly the declining number who placed responsibility on parenting and parenting practices. Open-ended remarks, especially regarding the extension of marital and other rights to same-sex couples, further demonstrate the resonance of explanations that underscore the genetic or fixed nature of sexual preference. In 2003, the notion that the origins of sexual preference are beyond the realm of individual control rarely appeared in Americans' comments. By 2006, however, Americans had begun to employ this line of reasoning as a compelling factor behind their support of, among other things, gay marriage. Clearly, Americans are hearing and sharing the message promoted by many—but certainly not all—gay rights activists that individuals should not be disparately treated because of a trait that is beyond their control. Should increasing reliance on genetic and "God's will" accounts follow the growth that was witnessed between 2003 and 2006, then support for a more inclusive vision of family should correspondingly accelerate.

These patterns may simultaneously hearten and unsettle social scientists. They certainly should be encouraging to social scientists who advocate expanding familial definitions because they suggest a likely and perhaps unavoidable movement toward inclusivity. But these same patterns also may be disquieting to those social scientists who express serious reservations about the use of genetic accounts of human or social behavior—reservations predicated to a large extent on the historical usage of genetic differences to rationalize racial and gender discrimination. Despite a recent upswing in scholarly ventures that explore the joint influence of social and biological or genetic factors on human behavior, a very large contingency of social scientists remains intransigently opposed to such endeavors, dismissing them as a contemporary rationalization for inequality and unequal treatment.[8] Yet equating genetic frames with a reactionary position is a dangerous oversimplification. As we can see from the responses that Americans give, genetic explanations need not be inherently conservative. Instead, they can be a source of liberalism in some cases. Just as Americans are reevaluating their

beliefs about family, many social scientists will need to reconsider their assumptions regarding "nature" and "nurture"—especially in the case of sexual preference, where "nature" currently yields the more liberal response while "nurture" produces the more conservative one.

UNCHANGING BARRIERS

The most exclusionist definitions of family come from Americans who believe that parents and parenting practices are primarily accountable for sexual preference. This group sees few limits to parenting—even, or especially, when it comes to sexuality, which they believe can and should be controlled. In listening to Americans' comments regarding the optimal living situation for girls and boys in single-parent households, we come to appreciate how intertwined Americans' views on sexual preference and gender really can be. Americans who believe that boys are better off living with their fathers and girls are better off living with their mothers also are more likely to believe that sexual preference is due to parents and, more importantly, are more likely to take a strongly exclusionist stance when defining the boundaries between family and nonfamily. They do not believe in same-sex couples, but they do believe in the importance of a same-sex parent: fathers for boys and mothers for girls. The same-sex parent is seen as the frontline role model who instills in boys appropriate and desirable masculine traits and behaviors and in girls requisite feminine traits and behaviors. The marked sex differentiation endorsed by Americans may be surprising given the assertions made by many social commentators that gender divisions have loosened greatly. Yet remarks by Americans who highlight the merits of same-sex role models—especially the importance of a male figure in a boy's life as a means to counteract the feminizing influence of women—echo similar arguments made over a century ago. These arguments suggest a sustained fear, disdain, or loathing of feminine qualities in boys—which appears to be coupled with a continuing fear, disdain, or loathing of homosexuality.

But the ongoing durability of gender stereotypes and the power of gender expectations also are seen in the comments by Americans who presume that both boys and girls would be better off living with their mother. This group of Americans is skeptical about fathers' ability to parent and instead perhaps overstates the unique qualifications that women possess in this arena. Clearly, they hold distinct gendered stereotypes regarding parents. Nevertheless, their focus on nurturance and their less rigid differentiation between boys and girls may be critical factors in their greater willingness to include same-sex couples with children as family and may be influential in moving them to even greater inclusivity in the future. That inclusivity may eventually approach that of the group of Americans who believe that a parent's gender and a child's gender are less consequential than the actual quality of the parent-child relationship. Tellingly, members of this group constitute a much smaller percentage than the other two—further evidence of the tenacity of gendered expectations and the wide-ranging effects of these expectations, most notably on definitions of family.

The resiliency of certain gendered assumptions amid a sea of other social changes is clearly on display when Americans discuss their views about marital name change. Nearly three-fourths of Americans agree that it is better for a woman to change her name at marriage, while one-half concur that women should be legally required to change their name at marriage, and almost one-half believe that it is unacceptable for a man to take the name of his wife. These responses not only tell us about Americans' views regarding name practices but also reveal a great deal about their understanding of gender in family life, their openness to a variety of gendered identities, and their receptiveness to a broader definition of family. Despite a clear correspondence between liberal views regarding marital name change and expansive definitions of family, it appears that the rate of change in the latter is much more rapid than in the former. This disparity, we believe, is due mostly to the intensified public attention to the issue of same-sex relations (even in such a short period as 2003 through 2006),

in contrast to the virtual absence of public dialogue over marital name change. This pattern also suggests that, ironically, despite the current inextricable link between views regarding gender and sexuality, changes in Americans' views regarding the definition of family may liberalize so swiftly that they may well be decoupled from at least some views regarding gender in the future.

CHANGING BOUNDARIES

Throughout this book, we have found persuasive evidence that Americans are moving toward a more encompassing definition of family that includes same-sex households. In other words, the boundary between family and nonfamily is being redrawn. For most proponents of equality for same-sex families, this is good news. Still, moving the boundary does not eliminate it. The boundary is simply repositioned. Placing same-sex couples within the category of family does not deny that other living arrangements will continue to be counted out—such as friends living together, nonromantic relationships, and non-exclusive partnerships. Although many of the Americans we interviewed challenged some heteronormative conceptions of "the family," there were limits. For example, over 90 percent—including most inclusionists—categorically dismissed housemates as nonfamily. Would this response have shifted had we focused on the functions of this living arrangement rather than on its form? It is possible, especially for some inclusionists who in their open-ended comments suggested that families can come in a variety of packages that perform familial functions. Still, an unintentional consequence of efforts to include same-sex couples as family—and correspondingly, to recognize same-sex marriage—might be further marginalization of other living arrangements, or "chosen families," that do not enjoy legal recognition and the rights and benefits attendant with such a status.

Two legal scholars, Martha Fineman and Nancy Polikoff, both make arguments along these lines. Fineman (1995, 2004) proposes a more narrow model—or legal definition—of family that expressly privileges relationships between a dependent and his or her caretaker.[9] She also believes that the intimate nature of horizontal relationships between adults should be left out of the question of family and that state-sanctioned marriage should be replaced by private contracts between adult partners. Mirroring Fineman's line of reasoning, Polikoff (2008) critiques the use of marriage as a means of conveying legal and social status. She grants the advantages that legal marital status would provide to same-sex couples, but also is troubled that same-sex marriage would create and strengthen boundaries between the married and nonmarried (see also Ettelbrick 2001; Walters 2001; Warner 1999). According to Polikoff, compelling couples to marry in order to obtain benefits and legal status necessarily results in the exclusion of a number of familial (biological or not) forms that need and deserve protection and benefits under the law, such as adult children taking care of parents, couples who choose not to marry, and cohabiting friends who share a long-standing (though nonsexual) economic and emotional interdependence. Polikoff proposes that marriage be converted to a merely cultural or religious ceremony and that family laws be based on the choices that people make in forming their own family. We bring up Fineman's and Polikoff's positions not because they represent the modal viewpoint currently held among scholars, gay rights activists, or gay men and lesbians (for a detailed description of the various debates within the gay community regarding same-sex marriage, see Hull 2006). But their comments remind us that when efforts to define same-sex couples as family—and relatedly, to legalize same-sex marriage—are successful, the battleground regarding the definition of family will shift, just as it shifted after other barriers to family or marital status were broken.

COUNTING CHANGE

The United States includes a rich diversity of families 35 whether or not they are officially recognized as such. In fact, "the family," although still invoked far too often in public and scholarly venues, is an increasingly untenable and obsolete concept. Many nontraditional or hitherto transgressive living arrangements—single-parent households, voluntarily childless couples, divorced homes—no longer carry strongly negative connotations or elicit highly judgmental reactions, as in the past. The idea of the legal recognition of interracial marriage, for example, at one time was unthinkable in most parts of the United States. Decades after the Supreme Court ordered the removal of antimiscegenation laws, interracial relations are tolerated, accepted, or even embraced by most Americans.[10]

Despite resistance in some communities to acknowledging a similarity between interracial and same-sex couples, the parallels between the two as highlighted throughout this book are impossible to ignore. The very same sociodemographic cleavages that distinguished supporters and vehement opponents of interracial marriage have reemerged to differentiate between advocates of an inclusive definition of family and critics who take a more exclusionist stance. The discomfort with same-sex couples and, more broadly, contact with gays and lesbians that Americans express closely resembles the discomfort with interracial couples and contact with other races. Arguments to resist the inclusion of same-sex couples as family echo the arguments that were advanced against interracial couples: for example, that these couples are abhorrent, unnatural, and against the law of God. By the same token, the reasons currently offered on behalf of an inclusive vision of family are strikingly similar to the reasons given to support interracial marriage: for example, that love and commitment define the family regardless of its members, that one cannot choose one's sexual preference just as one cannot choose one's race, and that whom one falls in love with cannot be controlled.

But today the fact that interracial relations were legally prohibited not so long ago seems unfathomable, beyond the pale of possibility. Given the cumulative and compelling evidence presented in this book, we envisage a day in the near future when same-sex families also will gain acceptance by a large plurality of the public, the denial of similar rights to same-sex couples will be nothing more than an antiquated memory, and same-sex couples will no longer be counted out.

NOTES

1. Referendum 71 offers expanded domestic partner rights to heterosexual couples when at least one of the partners is sixty-two years old or older.

2. At the time of the writing of this chapter, the constitutionality of Proposition 8 has been challenged before the California Supreme Court.

3. Although a state judge overturned the law, some "pro-family" groups have indicated that they likely will appeal this judicial decision.

4. Even in New York, surely among the most consistently liberal states, Governor David Paterson's attempts to bring forth a vote in the New York Senate to legalize same-sex marriage initially were met with a tepid reaction—and in some cases vehement opposition—by New York legislators from both the Democratic and Republican Parties who were leery of reactions from constituents. Although advocates of same-sex marriage were able to bring a marriage equality bill to a full vote, they did not succeed in getting the bill passed.

5. This question also was asked in 1988.

6. For discussions of how an emphasis on familial functions need not bolster conservative visions of family and instead can undercut them, see Fineman (1995, 2004).

7. The liberalizing effect of education has not gone unnoticed by college students. In our undergraduate classes, we routinely ask students to complete the same set of closed-ended questions and to write their open-ended personal definitions of family. Their responses confirm not only a strikingly large percentage who see same-sex couples as family but also an appreciation of the powerful role played in their inclusive conceptualization of family by college and, in particular, their contact with a diverse group of students.

8. Similarly, some gay activists worry that, taken to the extreme, the position that sexuality is fixed and beyond an individual's control could justify disparate treatment of bisexuals, transsexuals, those who change sexual identities later in life, and others who choose not to identify as either "gay" or "straight."

9. Fineman's preferred typology of family is shared by very few Americans who were interviewed in the Constructing the Family Survey. Only 3 percent indicated that only households in which there is a parent-child relationship count as a family. Fineman's definitions of family may be more attractive in other countries, however. After hearing the results of the Constructing the Family Survey, David Reimer, Cornelia Hausen, Irena Kogan, and Markus Gangl from the University of Mannheim and Mannheim Centre for European Social Research led a data collection effort in 2005 in which more than nine hundred Germans who lived in or near Mannheim, an urban area with a strong manufacturing base, were presented with ten living arrangements (the same as those asked in the Constructing the Family Survey, with the exception of housemates) and asked to indicate which living arrangements they believed count as family. Among this German sample, the most common pattern was to define family solely on the basis of the presence of children. Whereas marriage by itself is a decisive factor among Americans, Germans grant more weight to living arrangements that include children—so much weight, in fact, that married couples without children are less likely than same-sex couples with children to be deemed a family. That said, Germans also are less likely than Americans to privilege single-parent households, perhaps because there is a fairly low proportion of single-parent households and because Germany's public policies and institutional practices especially encourage a two-parent—and in particular, a breadwinner-homemaker—arrangement.

10. This is not to deny the continued disavowal of interracial relationships among a certain segment of the population. Media representations of interracial couples still provoke strongly visceral reactions by some. The cover story in a recent edition of the *St. Louis Post-Dispatch* (Moore 2009), for example, featured an interracial couple kissing, prompting thousands of comments, mostly complaints:

> Haven't read the story but don't like to see blacks and whites kissing.

> . . . The reality here is that the silent majority does not accept interracial behavior and views it as unnatural. Most responsible parents do not allow cross-relationships such as these and for valid reasons.

The parallel with same-sex couples was explicitly brought up by several readers:

> Next year it will be two people of the same sex. Not that there's anything wrong with that. . . .

> It should be two men kissing because those are the morals that the media wants the public to adopt and if you're offended, the liberals tell you it's because only their morals matter and what you want doesn't matter because they're in control and you're a mentally unstable hater.

REFERENCES

Bolzendahl, Catherine I., and Clem Brooks. 2005. "Polarization, Secularization, or Differences as Usual? The Denominational Cleavage in U.S. Social Attitudes since the 1970s." *Sociological Quarterly* 46(1): 47–78.

Carroll, Susan J., and Richard Logan Fox, eds. 2006. *Gender and Elections: Shaping the Future of American Politics*. New York: Cambridge University Press.

Ettelbrick, Paula L. 2001. "Domestic Partnership, Civil Unions, or Marriage: One Size Does Not Fit All." *Albany Law Review* 64(3): 905–14.

Fineman, Martha Albertson. 1995. *The Neutered Mother, the Sexual Family, and Other Twentieth-Century Tragedies.* New York: Routledge.

Fineman, Martha Albertson. 2004. *The Autonomy Myth: A Theory of Dependency.* New York: New Press.

Firebaugh, Glenn, and Kenneth E. Davis. 1988. "Trends in Antiblack Prejudice, 1972–1984: Region and Cohort Effects." *American Journal of Sociology* 94(2): 251–72.

Fischer, Claude S. 1978. "Urban-to-Non-Urban Diffusion of Opinions in Contemporary America." *American Journal of Sociology* 94(2): 251–72.

Gallagher, Maggie. 2003. "The Stakes." *National Review Online* (July 14). Available at: http://article.nationalreview.com/269352/the-stakes/maggie-gallagher (accessed May 18, 2010).

Gamson, Joshua. 1998. *Freaks Talk Back: Tabloid Talk Shows and Sexual Nonconformity.* Chicago: University of Chicago Press.

Hull, Kathleen E. 2006. *Same-Sex Marriage: The Cultural Politics of Love and Law.* Cambridge: Cambridge University Press.

Polikoff, Nancy D. 2008. *Beyond (Straight and Gay) Marriage: Valuing All Families under the Law.* Boston: Beacon Press.

Waldman, Paul. 2009. "We've Already Won the Battle over Gay Marriage." *The American Prospect* (April 14). Available at: http://www.prospect.org/cs/articles?article-weve_already_won_the_battle_over_gay_marriage (accessed May 3, 2010).

Walters, Susana Dunata. 2001. *All the Rage: The Story of Gay Visibility in America.* Chicago: University of Chicago Press.

Warner, Michael. 1999. *The Trouble with Normal: Sex, Politics, and the Ethics of Queer Life.* New York: Free Press.

Reading Questions

1. How do the authors define *inclusionists*, *moderates*, and *exclusionists*?

2. The authors draw a parallel between changing attitudes about same-sex marriage and attitudes about interracial marriage. What patterns do the authors identify? What does this history of interracial marriage suggest about same-sex marriage?

Rhetoric Questions

3. Identify moments of forecasting and previewing in the structure of the text. Where are these paragraphs located within the essay, and why?

4. Choose two passages in which the authors rely heavily on survey data to support their claims. How do they integrate data within these passages? What phrases or key words do they use?

Response and Research Questions

5. Writing about their methodology, the authors note that "quantitative data give us a picture of the boundaries, but the qualitative data animate the struggles that Americans face in defining family" (par. 7). Choose and explain an instance from the text when the authors demonstrate the ideas expressed in this statement.

6. The authors write that their data suggest an "alternative interpretation" (12) to those typically proposed in the field of sociology. Think about a topic that you're writing about or might choose to write about in the future. Explain how you might determine if there is room for change, refinement, and/or redefinition of what others have written on the topic.

In Strangers' Glances at Family, Tensions Linger

SUSAN SAULNY

As a journalist and former national correspondent for the *New York Times*, Susan Saulny has written about a wide array of topics for popular audiences. From politics to gun control to race, Saulny crafts compelling news stories that are both informative and persuasive for readers. In the article below, published in the *New York Times* in October 2011, Saulny describes the experiences of two generations of a multiracial family, the Greenwoods and the Dragans. At times heartbreaking, this article relays anecdotes to convey each family's struggles as they are met with confusion by the outside world and the ways they make sense of these experiences.

Toms River, N.J. — *"How come she's so white and you're so dark?"*

The question tore through Heather Greenwood as she was about to check out at a store here one afternoon this summer. Her brown hands were pushing the shopping cart that held her babbling toddler, Noelle, all platinum curls, fair skin, and ice-blue eyes.

The woman behind Mrs. Greenwood, who was white, asked once she realized, by the way they were talking, that they were mother and child. "It's just not possible," she charged indignantly. "You're so . . . dark!"

It was not the first time someone had demanded an explanation from Mrs. Greenwood about her biological daughter, but it was among the more aggressive. Shaken almost to tears, she wanted to flee, to shield her little one from this kind of talk. But after quickly paying the cashier, she managed a reply. "How come?" she said. "Because that's the way God made us."

The Greenwood family tree, emblematic of a growing number of American bloodlines, has roots on many continents. Its mix of races—by marriage, adoption, and other close relationships—can be challenging to track, sometimes confusing even for the family itself.

For starters: Mrs. Greenwood, 37, is the daughter 5 of a black father and a white mother. She was adopted into a white family as a child. Mrs. Greenwood married a white man with whom she has two daughters. Her son from a previous relationship is half Costa Rican. She also has a half brother who is white, and siblings in her adoptive family who are biracial, among a host of other close relatives—one from as far away as South Korea.

The population of mixed-race Americans like Mrs. Greenwood and her children is growing quickly, driven largely by immigration and intermarriage. One in seven new marriages is between spouses of different races or ethnicities, for example. And among American children, the multiracial population has increased almost 50 percent, to 4.2 million, since 2000.

But the experiences of mixed-race Americans can be vastly different. Many mixed-race youths say they feel wider acceptance than past generations, particularly on college campuses and in pop culture. Extensive interviews and days spent with the Greenwoods show that, when they are alone, the family strives to be colorblind. But what they face outside their home is another story. People seem to notice nothing but race. Strangers gawk. Make rude and racist comments. Tell offensive jokes. Ask impolite questions.

The Greenwoods' experiences offer a telling glimpse into contemporary race relations, according to sociologists and members of other mixed-race families.

It is a life of small but relentless reminders that old tensions about race remain, said Mrs. Greenwood, a homemaker with training in social work.

"People confront you, and it's not once in a while, it's 10 all the time," she said. "Each time is like a little paper cut, and you might think, 'Well, that's not a big deal.' But imagine a lifetime of that. It hurts."

Jenifer L. Bratter, an associate sociology professor at Rice University who has studied multiracialism, said that as long as race continued to affect where people live, how much money they make, and how they are treated, then multiracial families would be met with double-takes. "Unless we solve those issues of inequality in other areas, interracial families are going to be questioned about why they'd cross that line," she said.

According to Census data, interracial couples have a slightly higher divorce rate than same-race couples — perhaps, sociologists say, because of the heightened stress in their lives as they buck enduring norms. And children in mixed families face the challenge of navigating questions about their identities.

"If we could just go about whatever we're doing and not be asked anything about our family's colors," Mrs. Greenwood said, "that would be a dream."

A FAMILY'S STORY

The colors that strangers find so intriguing when they see the Greenwood family are the result of two generations of intermixing.

Their story begins with Mrs. Greenwood's 15 adoptive parents, Dolores and Edward Dragan, of Slovak and Polish descent, veterans of Woodstock and the March on Washington, who always knew they wanted to adopt. They were drawn to children who were hardest to place in permanent homes. In the early 1970s, those children were mixed race.

Mrs. Dragan, a retired art teacher, remembers telling her adoption agency that she and her husband, then a principal, would take "any child, any color," at a time when most people like themselves were looking for healthy white infants.

They adopted two mixed-race children within two years. The family seemed complete until Mr. Dragan came home from school one day and joked to his wife, "I'm in love with another woman." It was the sprightly 6-year-old Heather, a student. She had been living with foster parents and was up for adoption.

"Holy cow, she just brought the energy into our home," Mrs. Dragan recalled of their early days together in Flemington, N.J.

As the children grew, the Dragans tried to infuse their world with African-American culture. There were family trips to museums in Washington, as well as beauty salons in Philadelphia, where Mrs. Dragan learned black hairstyling skills.

However, the children were not particularly 20 interested, and do not remember race being a big part of their identities when they were younger. "We were happy to be whoever we thought we were at that time," Mrs. Greenwood said.

But as she moved into adulthood, she began to identify herself as a black woman of mixed heritage. She also felt more of a connection with whites and Latinos, and had a son, Silas Aguilar, now 18, with a Costa Rican boyfriend. She later married Aaron Greenwood, a computer network engineer who is a descendant of Quakers. A few years ago, they bought a split-level ranch house in Toms River and started a bigger family.

STINGING INSULTS

The shoulder shrugs about being mixed race within the family are in stark contrast to insults outside the home — too many for the Dragans and the Greenwoods to recount.

But some still sting more than others. On one occasion, a boy on the school bus called young Heather a nigger, and she had no idea what the word meant, so Mrs. Dragan, now 69, got the question over homework one night: "Mom, what's a nigger?"

Once, on a beach chair at a resort in Florida years ago, a white woman sunning herself next to Mrs. Dragan bemoaned the fact that black children were running around the pool. "Isn't it awful?" Mrs. Dragan recalled the woman confiding to her.

Within minutes, Mrs. Dragan, ever feisty despite 25 her reserved appearance, had her brood by her side. "I'd like to introduce you to my children," she told the woman. Awkward silence ensued.

"You know what? She deserved it," Mrs. Dragan recalled during an interview at her home in

Lambertville, N.J. "I figured, why miss an opportunity to embarrass someone if they needed it?"

Sometimes, the racism directed toward the Dragans seemed similar to what a single-race minority family might experience.

When the children were still young, a real estate agent in Flemington warned prospective buyers in her neighborhood about the Dragan household, saying that "there are black people living there, and I feel it's my duty to let you know." The people bought the house anyway, and later told the Dragans about the incident, once they had become friends.

"We weren't blind to the reality of racism," Mr. Dragan explained, "yet when you get into a situation where it's your family, it really takes on a different dimension."

Mrs. Dragan said her life came to revolve 30 around shielding the children: "I was always on my A-game. My antennas were always up. I was aware all the time."

Fast-forward 30 years, and Mrs. Dragan sees her daughter, Mrs. Greenwood, going through similar episodes with her own children — all because mother and child are not the same color.

"She gets the same stares I got when I was a young mother in the supermarket, with three African-American kids hanging off the cart," said Mrs. Dragan, whose wisps of blond hair frame a fair-skinned face.

"You sort of put it out of your mind once your children are grown and you think, I just want to relax, that part's over for now," she continued. "But I've gotten a little more agitated lately."

She does not like what she is hearing from her daughter these days. A typical story: On the boardwalk at the shore over the summer, Noelle scampered toward the carousel, her parents in tow. Even at 21 months, Noelle is a regular customer, so the ride operator, Risa Ierra, felt free to have a little fun.

"You know this little one isn't really theirs, right?" 35 Ms. Ierra joked to the other people in line. "Must have been switched at the hospital."

Since Mr. and Mrs. Greenwood are friendly with her, they said later that they were not offended. But the exchange was typical of remarks Mrs. Greenwood hears often, even from people who seem well-meaning.

"Oh my God! Are they yours? Or are you their nanny?" she said she was often asked. (By contrast, her mother, Mrs. Dragan, was often asked if she was hosting inner-city children as part of a charitable effort.)

"That's the most common thing I get," Mrs. Greenwood said of the nanny question. "But I don't want to go there. I don't want to justify me being their mother to strangers."

HUMOR AND STRENGTH

The family has always used humor to cope, but sometimes that is not enough.

When the Dragan children were young, for 40 instance, the family stopped at a restaurant near Disney World and people seemed to drop their forks when they walked in. "Yes, it's true!" one of the Dragan children yelled. "These folks aren't from around here!"

At least the family laughed, if no one else did.

Of the constant confrontations, Mrs. Dragan said, "I don't always feel successful. I feel like I could have thrown my hands up a number of times, with the kids and other people."

Often, she found the energy to fight. "Other times," she said, "I locked myself in the house."

The Dragans concede that at times they felt a strain on their relationship. "There is a lot of stress when people are looking at you and scrutinizing and judging," Mr. Dragan said. "You might not hear it but you feel it. We felt it. That is stressful for a marriage. You do have to help and reinforce each other. Humor has really gotten us through a lot of heartache."

Mrs. Greenwood uses the same strategy. She likes 45 T-shirts with messages. She has one that she wears on St. Patrick's Day: "This is what Irish looks like," it says, a reference to her biological mother's lineage. She is thinking about having one made that says, "Yes, I'm the mom."

Mrs. Greenwood is not ready to have a conversation about race with Sophia, now 7. But Sophia is starting to notice the stares, the jokes, the questions. Mrs. Greenwood feels as though the world is forcing race into her home, which has been a respite from race ever since she was a little girl herself.

"I actually don't know what to tell Sophia and Noelle when they start asking me, 'Am I black?'" she said.

"If they look in the mirror or to society, they're not going to be black," she said, worried about what sort of internal conflicts this might cause.

"I'm afraid she's going to start questioning who she is, and she shouldn't have to," Mrs. Greenwood added.

Mr. Greenwood has already tried something. "I've 50 told Sophia that she is a perfect mix of her mommy and daddy," he said, "but we're going to have to talk more."

Silas, Mrs. Greenwood's half-Latino son from a previous relationship, started to ask race questions around age 7.

"I went up to my mom and said, 'What am I?'" Silas recalled. "And, 'What are you? Are we the same thing?' I was just shooting questions. It was like a brain mash. I looked at my family and thought, 'What is going on here?' I was just lost. But after a really long explanation, I eventually understood."

He paused, adding later, "I think my little sisters will be fine."

Race is not something Silas says he spends a lot of time worrying about. He learned long ago about the family tree, and that he is part black, that his grandmother is Slovakian, his cousin is Asian, and so on—and hardly any of that matters to him.

"Barriers are breaking down," he said. 55

For the moment, the matter seems simple enough for Sophia, too. She responds confidently when asked what race she is. "Tan!" says the second-grade student. "Can't you tell by just looking?"

Reading Questions

1. Drawing on sociological work on multiracialism, what social issues does Saulny suggest our society needs to address?

2. According to Saulny, what are some contributing factors to the rise in the number of multi-racial families in America?

3. How does the Dragan family cope with negative responses to their racial identity?

Rhetoric Questions

4. At the end of the article, Saulny focuses primarily on Silas and Sophia's understandings of race. How do the children's understandings of race differ from that of their parents? What is the rhetorical effect of ending the article in this way?

5. Identify three instances in the text that rely on an emotional response from the reader. How does the text elicit this response in each instance?

Response and Research Questions

6. Despite the thirty-year differences between Mrs. Dragan and her daughter, Heather Greenwood, Saulny reports that they received much the same reactions to their interracial family. Does this surprise you? Why or why not?

7. In paragraph 7, Saulny writes, "People seem to notice nothing but race." What is your reaction to such an assertion? Does this notion fit in the context of your own experiences?

8. Think of a time when your own racial identity was made apparent to you. How did your response compare to the Dragan family's?

The Strategies of Forbidden Love: Family across Racial Boundaries in Nineteenth-Century North Carolina

WARREN E. MILTEER JR.

Warren E. Milteer Jr. is currently an assistant professor of history at the University of South Carolina. In this article, which appeared in the Spring 2014 edition of the *Journal of Social History*, Milteer explores "forbidden love" and makes the case that "free women of mixed ancestry and white men developed relationships that mimicked legally sanctioned marriages" in nineteenth-century North Carolina. His argument, which relies heavily on primary document analysis, explores the wider implications for these seemingly impossible historical constructs.

> Learn more about the use of descriptive titles in the humanities on page 166.

> Although abstracts are more common in the social and natural sciences, they do sometimes occur in the humanities. Learn more about abstracts on pages 205–6.

ABSTRACT

This article contends that although local beliefs and legal edicts attempted to discourage sexual and familial relationships between women of color and white men in North Carolina, free women of mixed ancestry and white men developed relationships that mimicked legally sanctioned marriages. These unions often produced children who maintained frequent interaction with both parents. In nineteenth-century Hertford County, North Carolina, free women of mixed ancestry and their white partners developed creative strategies to deal with the legal limitations inherent in their situation. Women and men in these relationships found ways to secure property rights for women and children and developed methods to prevent legal scrutiny of their living arrangements.

By the early to mid-nineteenth century, Hertford County, located in the tobacco- and cotton-growing intercoastal plain of North Carolina, had developed a reputation throughout the eastern seaboard as a place where free women of mixed ancestry lived outside of marriage with white men.[1] In 1853, William D. Valentine, a prominent organizer in the Hertford County Whig Party, wrote in reference to the practice: "So common has it long been that I apprehend it is tolerated by married men in this locality. They too indulge. The whites are more blamable than the low degraded colored."[2] Calvin Scott Brown heard similar tales of sexual encounters across racial boundaries as he traveled toward Hertford County to begin his work as an administrator of a new school for people of color during the 1880s: "I remember on my way here for the first time from Franklin, Virginia, a man on the boat asked me where I was going . . . I told him I was going to Winton." The man responded that the inhabitants of Hertford County "were the most degraded people upon the face of the earth." He said that mulatto women "lived with white men and that white men came from as far as Baltimore to have the mulatto girls."[3]

Historical records, including accounts from children produced from relationships between free women of mixed ancestry and white men, support these rumors of sexual exploitation in nineteenth-century Hertford County. Mollie Cherry Hall Catus remembered that her white father, Albert Vann,

Learn more about the use of primary source evidence on pages 82–83.

> would come in at bed-time and even before his wife died he would come and stay with my mother [Sallie Ann Hall] all night and get up and go to his house the next morning. His children despised us and I despised them and all their folks, and I despised him. . . . He had plenty of property but didn't give mother one thing.[4]

Many non-white women, both enslaved and free, lived under similar conditions as Sallie Ann Hall, and many of their children had the same attitudes about their white fathers' actions. However, the historical record demonstrates that not all free women of mixed ancestry served their white partners as concubines. In several instances, relationships between free women of mixed ancestry and white men took the form of long-term dedicated partnerships.[5]

This study focuses on long-term monogamous relationships between free women of mixed ancestry and white men who probably would have married if legal and social circumstances had been different. North Carolina law banned marriage between whites and non-whites for most of the nineteenth century, yet many free women of mixed ancestry and white men still built lifetime partnerships. Legal restrictions alone could not dissuade these men and women from sharing their lives together. Although historical sources reveal relatively few relationships of this type in contrast with the often-cited situations of concubinage, scholars must acknowledge that some whites and non-whites in the nineteenth century, just as people today, desired to share their lives together regardless of the lack of legal recognition and social approval. Because the law did not permit these unions, evidence of their existence is at best hidden and sometimes does not appear at all in surviving documents. These unions' lack of legal recognition coupled with destruction of the majority of Hertford County's pre–Civil War court records preclude an exact count of how many of these relationships existed at any particular time. Yet the surviving evidence still allows scholars to understand how free women of mixed ancestry and white men navigated through a society that refused to publicly approve their relationships.[6]

Milteer identifies the subject of his study, "long-term monogamous relationships between free women of mixed ancestry and white men," but acknowledges a lack of available primary evidence to help us understand those relationships.

Milteer establishes the focus of his argument as exploring how these couples "navigated through a society that refused to publicly approve their relationships."

Learn more about thesis statements in the humanities on pages 161–65.

This article contends that although local beliefs and legal edicts discouraged sexual and familial relationships between women of color and white men, some free women of mixed ancestry actively developed relationships with white men that often resembled legally sanctioned marriages. These illegal unions often produced children who maintained frequent interaction with both parents. Free women of mixed ancestry and their white partners developed creative strategies to deal with the legal limitations inherent in any unrecognized union. Even as state lawmakers banned and illegitimated their relationships, women and men in these relationships found ways to secure property rights for women. They developed creative strategies to pass on wealth to their children, who by law were illegitimate and therefore not entitled to their fathers' estates. These couples even found ways to obscure the illegality of their living arrangements in an era when an unmarried couple living in the same house constituted fornication and adultery, which courts treated as a single crime in North Carolina.

Although contemporary observers suggested that Hertford County had an unusual propensity for unions between non-white women and white men, a closer examination of family histories and surviving documents from other areas would likely reveal that couples across the United States sought solutions for similar domestic issues. Through much of the nineteenth century, the majority of states prohibited marriages between whites and non-whites.[7] Free non-white women and white men in these parts of the nation undoubtedly used many of the same strategies employed by couples in Hertford County to overcome legal obstacles and social stigmas. They along with couples composed of white women and non-white men, both without the legal protections of marriage, would have needed to seek out special arrangements to protect and pass down family assets, provide care to children, and shield themselves from public scrutiny and legal prosecution.

Since 1715, North Carolina law had either discouraged or banned marriage between whites and non-whites. The first law to address marriage fined any white man or woman who intermarried with "any Negro, Mulatto or Indyan Man or Woman" fifty pounds. The General Assembly updated this law in 1741 by levying the same fine on any white man or woman who married "an Indian, negro, mustee, or mulatto man or woman, or any person of mixed blood to the third generation, bond or free."[8] Neither of these laws actually prohibited intermarriage between whites and non-whites but simply discouraged marriages by imposing heavy fines. Both laws also fined clergy and other officials who married whites to non-whites. These laws appear to have discouraged the issuances of legal marriage bonds to mixed couples in Hertford County and many other parts of the state. Nevertheless, in 1830 the General Assembly passed an act banning "any free negro or free person of color" from marrying "a white person."[9] In 1875, a state convention added a similar intermarriage ban to the North Carolina Constitution.[10]

For the past generation, historians have endeavored to understand relationships between non-white women and white men in the United States through the laws governing marriage in the colonial and national periods. Historians have reviewed court cases at the municipal, state, and federal levels in order to understand how different localities treated people living in unlawful mixed unions. Past scholars have focused on the exploitative nature of many of these relationships, in which white men extracted sexual favors from women of color, most of whom had no form of recourse in a society that ignored the sexual indiscretions of offending white men. However, more than a generation of new scholarship has clearly demonstrated that white planters, politicians, and plebeians* also took part in liaisons with women of color that were more mutually beneficial and often long-term.[11]

Yet only the most recent scholarship has begun to uncover the intricacies of daily life for women of color, white men, and their families. Scholars have shown that familial relationships between whites and non-whites existed despite legal prohibitions, but much work still needs to be completed in order to understand how women of color and white men managed family life in communities that refused to give legal recognition to their unions. Even less is understood about the unique position of free women of color involved in illicit unions with white men. Slave status placed limitations on women that caused relationships between enslaved women and white men to be inherently skewed in the favor of white men, whether those white men intended to treat those women as long-term partners or brief subjects of their sexual aggression. However, freedom offered women of color a greater variety of possible relationships with white men, which scholars have yet to fully explore. Free women of color had choices far beyond those available to enslaved women. These women, like white women, had the option to marry free men of their own race, engage in contracts, and own and sell property. When they chose to engage in relationships with white men, free women of color had greater freedom than enslaved women to determine and shape their familial relations and could reap greater benefits from those interactions. Most importantly, these couples helped to develop the rationale for such relationships and the guidelines for how free women of color and white men carried out their relationships in public and private spaces.

The free women of mixed ancestry who chose to develop life-long relationships 10 with white men in nineteenth-century Hertford County came from a variety of family backgrounds, but most were not wealthy. Louisiana Weaver's father, Charles Weaver, was a poor and sickly man of color who struggled to provide for his family and often depended on the labor of his wife, Delilah, and their children in order to make ends meet. Celia Garnes, the daughter of Daniel and Betsey Garnes, grew up in a household in which her parents had trouble supporting their children and were almost forced by the courts to bind out** several of their sons. Sallie Yeates Bizzell was the daughter of Velia Bizzell, a free-born woman of mixed ancestry, who toiled in local fisheries as a fish cleaner, making only half what her male counterparts made for the same day's work. Whoever Sallie's father was, he did not provide for the family. Mary Jane and Susan Chavis also grew up under tough circumstances. Both girls were the daughters

Milteer reviews the work of other scholars on this topic and identifies a gap in the scholarship to which his study responds. Learn more about establishing a scholarly focus in the context of others' work on pages 197–99.

*plebeians: members of lower social classes.

**bind out: to apprentice, or place someone in service to another.

of Emmaline Chavis, a free woman of color; however, they had different fathers. Mary Jane was the daughter of Samuel Powell, a white man, who left her mother alone with six children after he was shot and killed in a brawl. Susan was reportedly the daughter of Nathaniel Turner, a free man of color, who was between marriages at the time of Susan's birth. Strong tensions appear to have existed between Susan's parents, as Turner brought larceny charges against Emmaline Chavis for stealing bacon from his storehouse. These women who chose to build relationships with white men sought better adult lives than those they experienced as children and did not find legal husbands who could help them reach that goal.[12]

Milteer identifies a number of factors that likely influenced "women's companion choices," including financial stability, as well as their social and political positioning.

Financial mobility likely played a significant role in the choices of free women of mixed ancestry. In an era in which women in general had limited opportunities for work and faced significant wage discrimination, free women of mixed ancestry had to consider the financial security and social standing of potential mates. For a poor woman looking to move up financially, a relationship with a well-established white man who was willing to build a long-term relation was a promising opportunity. A white man could not directly pass on the benefits of whiteness to a woman of color and her children as he could for a white woman and her children. White enforcement of racial boundaries limited free people of color's access to certain exclusively white networks, therefore limiting a white man's ability to extend his social connections. However, a white man could convey property obtained through connections to these networks and, as long as he lived, he could pass on some of the intangible benefits of being part of middle- and upper-class white social circles.

The second-class social and political position of non-white men in North Carolina's social hierarchy may have influenced women's companion choices. During much of the nineteenth century, the law and social customs granted white men privileges, which men of color, especially slaves, could not enjoy. White superiority, in effect, was not simply an ideology, but in many instances a social reality. Free women of mixed ancestry may have taken this reality into consideration and used it to rationalize their mate selections. Calvin Scott Brown recalled, "When I first came here [to Hertford County] I often heard mulatto women say that they would rather be a white man's concubine than a nigger's wife."[13] Brown's statement suggests that at least some women of mixed ancestry in Hertford County viewed certain non-whites as the inferiors of white men. Historians have found non-white women in other societies including much of Latin America and the Caribbean who used similar logic to support their choices to embrace illicit arrangements with white men over legally sanctioned marriages to non-whites.[14] As in other slave or former slave societies, Hertford County residents drew significant distinctions between different groups of non-white people. Free people of color were politically and legally distinct from enslaved people, who had no civil rights in American slave societies. After emancipation, people continued to draw meaningful distinctions between the old free people of color and newly emancipated slaves and their descendants. In Hertford County, social divisions between "mulattoes," which included almost all of the old free population of color, and "blacks" reinforced these lines of distinction. Women of mixed ancestry in Hertford County may have taken these distinctions into consideration when choosing marriage partners. A woman's choice of a partner had long-term implications for both her and any children that she might have. Associations with a man of lower social status would have ultimately diminished the social standing of a woman of higher social position.

Basic feelings of love, admiration, and affection versus purely economic and social motivations may have driven relationships between free women of mixed ancestry and white men. Examples exist from all time periods and areas of the world where people with different social statuses, ancestral origins, economic positions, and belief systems have crossed socially constructed boundaries in order to build loving relationships. At least some free women of mixed ancestry and white men likely moved beyond the social constructions that attempted to order their world to fulfill their desires for love and acceptance from another human being whom they found attractive and desirable. The racial categories used to divide people with different ancestries, appearances, and community positions could not always overcome natural attraction. Laws against marriage between whites and non-whites attempted to curb the influences of attraction and affection and make unions across racial boundaries socially unacceptable. The people who engineered marriage laws attempted to impose their beliefs about appropriate behavior through granting or denying the privilege of marriage. However, their attempts could not convince every couple to deny their own feelings in order to conform to the societal norm.

Although love and attraction likely played an important part in the development of relationships between free women of mixed ancestry and white men, the social and economic realities still carried considerable weight in the rationale of relationships. Social and economic status of the participants in these relationships could determine the feasibility of living in a socially unacceptable manner. Free women of mixed ancestry who chose white mates usually selected men of high standing in the community. Christian Wiggins partnered with Noah Cotton, a planter and descendant of a long-established Hertford County family. Louisiana Weaver established a family with James Kiff, the county tax collector and a businessman. Sallie Yeates Bizzell developed a long-term relationship with Richard Henry Shield, a well-respected doctor. Mary Jane Chavis's partner was James Norfleet Holloman, a successful merchant and active participant in local Democratic Party politics.[15] Most free women of mixed ancestry who had white partners chose men of wealth and prestige. Free women of mixed ancestry made their mate selections just as carefully as women who contracted in legal marriage with the hope of securing economic stability.

For non-white women, associations with men of high social position were imperative to social mobility as well as immunity from legal prosecution for fornication and adultery. Hertford County's courts never brought white men of high status into court for committing fornication and adultery with women of color. The elite white power structure that controlled the local judiciary was generally unwilling to shame publicly members of its own group by placing well-to-do white male fornicators on trial. Social respectability resulting from birth into well-established families, economic success, or connections to important white-only social networks protected these men from legal prosecution. Only the relationships of white men who lacked these attributes faced prosecution.

Learn more about transitions in the humanities on page 167.

Learn more about documentation of sources in the humanities on pages 170–72.

15

The backgrounds of two white men prosecuted for fornication and adultery with women of color during the March 1854 term of Hertford County Court illustrate this class-based legal double standard. The court charged two couples, William Futrell and Frusa Reid and Wiley Ezell and Celia Garnes, with fornication and adultery. William Futrell appears to have come from a poor farming family. The 1850 Census lists the Futrell family as owners of real estate worth only $48. Wiley Ezell owned a modest amount of real property, but the circumstances of his birth as the son of an unwed mother likely stained his reputation in the community. At their trials, both couples pled not guilty, and in the end the jury found only Futrell and Reid guilty of fornication and adultery. The jury acquitted Ezell and Garnes of all charges, although their cohabitation and children should have served as enough evidence to find the couple in the wrong. The Hertford County court records do not explain how Ezell and Garnes won their case; however, the list of jurors contains a possible clue. Starkey Sharpe Harrell, one of the jurors in the Ezell and Garnes case, carried on a relationship with Emma Butler, a free woman of color, and may have sympathized with Ezell. Records from a later period suggest that Harrell and Ezell maintained a close relationship, and Ezell named Harrell the executor of his estate. Ezell came from a lower-class background, but at the time of trial may have begun to surround himself with people of wealth and good reputation. Cases like the *State v. Futrell and Reid* and the *State v. Ezell and Garnes* were a rarity in Hertford County, appearing on the court docket usually no more than once every five or ten years. The second of these cases shows that of those white men and women of color brought into court, only a few actually ended with a guilty verdict and punishment for the couples.[16]

Even though relations between free women of mixed ancestry and white men usually went unprosecuted, couples took precautions to limit the public visibility of their unlawful arrangements. In the antebellum period, some free women of mixed ancestry openly lived with their white partners, but most white men, attempting to maintain a façade to protect their respectability, kept two separate houses. One house, usually the main family quarters, served as the primary residence of the woman and her children. Another house, sometimes larger and sometimes smaller, was the permanent residence of the white father. This was the arrangement that Sallie Yeates Bizzell and Richard Henry Shield set up for their family. In the 1850s, Shield purchased a piece of property to maintain as his own residence. Then Bizzell purchased a small five-acre tract beside Shield, which served as her regular residence.[17] Jesse Rob Weaver remembered that his mother, Louisiana Weaver, and father, James Kiff, set up a similar situation for their family in the 1870s and 1880s. Weaver stated, "My father provided a good large farm. One part was [my mother's] through his efforts. . . . He had one farm and house joining our field and he with our help worked both farms."[18]

When mothers and fathers maintained separate residences, children and both parents still often came together in one or the other of these physical spaces for family time. Jesse Rob Weaver recalled going back and forth between his mother's and father's houses as a youngster. A Hertford County teacher recollected that one of the daughters of Mary Jane Chavis and James Norfleet Holloman, who grew up at the turn of the century, told this teacher that "her father used to come see her mother every day and every

Notice the use of hedging, or qualifying language, in this paragraph. Learn more about hedging on page 168.

night. He would sit around the fire with the whole family and talk just like any other father."[19] Although many free women of mixed ancestry and white men attempted to create an illusion of physical separation, their families experienced a life more similar to those headed by two parents than those headed by only a single parent. These families' façades were formalities, not realistic attempts to hide illicit relationships. As shown in the example of the teacher, people in the neighborhood knew the reality of their neighbors' situations.

Inside these households, free women of mixed ancestry and their white partners negotiated the operations of daily life for their families. Women engaged in long-term relationships with white partners could maintain significant power in family decision making. They ruled the domestic realm of their households and worked side by side with their white partners to make decisions about other family matters such as finances. Clarence Chavis, son of Mary Jane Chavis and James Norfleet Holloman, remembered that his father was "very attentive" to his mother and stated, "What was produced on the farm he and she agreed mutually as to how best to dispose of it. He always consulted her about how was best to spend the money."[20] Jesse Rob Weaver recalled that his mother "handled" the money that his father brought home.[21] Cooperation between women and men in these mixed-status relationships was imperative to their survival. Neither the woman nor man was bound by law to maintain their partnership. Unlike the relationships of married couples, the state had not sanctioned their relationship, so the law could not require court or legislative approval if the woman and man chose to dissolve their union. Of course the woman was less likely than the man to walk away from a relationship that provided financial security, but unlike some enslaved women, a free woman of color did have a choice. A long-term relationship with a white man was not her only option.

Like most legally recognized couples, free women of mixed ancestry and white men living in long-term relationships produced children, who often became the focus of these couples' energies and affections. Although the law did not acknowledge the relationship between white fathers and their mixed children, fathers in long-term partnerships with those children's mothers typically played an important role in their children's support and development. An acquaintance of the Chavis family recalled that one of James Norfleet Holloman's daughters

> said that her father was a merchant and would often go to Baltimore and Norfolk and buy things and would never come home without bringing all of them something, from dolls to suits of clothes. She said she felt proud that he was her father. She said that although in public they called him Mr. H[olloman], at home they called him daddy, and he was as sweet and loving to them as any father. . . . I have known this family all my life and know most of these things were true.

Holloman's daughter Bessie added that her father would allow his children to borrow his horses and buggies. Clarence Chavis remembered that his father "paid the children's school bills."[22]

Wiley Ezell recognized his children by Celia Garnes in a similar manner by providing for their needs. Even when they were adults, Ezell helped his children financially. Ezell ran an account with the merchants Knight and Barham on behalf of his son

Joseph Garnes. Purchases on the account included essential items such as shoes and clothing. Ezell also aided his son Albert Garnes and son-in-law Henry T. Lassiter, husband of his daughter Delia Ann, by purchasing corn on their behalves through his own credit account.[23]

James Kiff supported his children as many of his contemporaries in the same situation did. His son Jesse Rob Weaver recalled that Kiff

> would come to our house every morning and every night. He would eat there sometimes. He would tell us what to do each day. . . . He arranged for us to have gifts and things as any father would do. I stayed with him mostly till he died. I would stay at nights and sleep with him.

Milteer identifies a number of strategies that white men and non-white women used to "create the kind of family experience for themselves and their children that their married neighbors had."

Kiff also provided his children with many other essential needs, including sending them to school and helping them to maintain their mother's farm.[24] Although the law denied recognition to families like the Kiff-Weaver family, they still found ways to carve out spaces where members could live like the legally recognized families around them. White fathers' contributions to their non-white families reveal their desires to create the kind of family experience for themselves and their children that their married neighbors had. By failing to grant white men and non-white women the right to marry, the law placed a handicap on attempts to create a legitimate household. However, the dedication of white fathers who bypassed legally and socially imposed obstacles in order to care for their loved ones elucidates the complicated nature of respectability in nineteenth-century Southern society. Social norms and North Carolina law required fathers to take care of their children if both parties were free. However, those same social norms and laws created obstacles for white fathers to provide for non-white children.

Deep ties to extended family across the color line further highlight the determination of couples to enjoy an unbounded family life. Wiley Ezell went beyond simply helping his children. In 1851, he extended a loan to his partner's brother, Noah Garnes, for $18.68, which Ezell never collected.[25] James Kiff's sister, Penny Hedgepath, played an important role in the lives of his children. Jesse Rob Weaver retained very fond memories of his aunt, whom he helped to take care of after the death of his father. He remembered, "I thought she could cook the best food I ever ate. She was good to all of us and would give us some of anything she had to eat."[26] These examples demonstrate that racial divisions and lack of legal recognition sometimes failed to overcome the social significance given to common ancestry and extended kinship. Lawmakers sought to define the family as a racially uniform unit by prohibiting marriage across the color line, but people on the ground, at least occasionally, rejected this notion.[27]

Women of mixed ancestry, when they spent many years in close unions with white men, worked with their partners to set up some form of financial security for themselves and their children. White men used a number of legally enforceable options in order to provide for their families at the time of their deaths. Wills, promissory notes, and property transfers before death were all methods to provide financial security to partners and children with no legally recognized familial relationship. During the nineteenth century, several white men left wills in the hands of trusted friends who promised to take care of children and partners. Before his death in 1815, Noah Cotton dictated a will leaving all his property to his nine children and partner, Christian Wiggins, whom some people in the community recognized as "Christian Cotton." John Vann, the executor of the will, made a conscious effort to obtain shelter, food, and education for Noah's and Christian's children. Using funds from Noah's estate sale and receipts from the rental of his plantation and two slaves, Vann paid the monthly bills for the children's upkeep.[28]

Many years later, Richard W. Knight followed the example of men like Noah Cotton and used a will to protect the future interests of his family. Sometime in the late nineteenth century, Knight had begun a long-term relationship with Susan Chavis, which produced three daughters. Desiring to pass on his wealth to them, Knight wrote his will in 1908 leaving all of his property, "real, personal, and mixed," to Susan Chavis. He requested that at Susan's death, all of his property be divided among the couple's three daughters, Mary S. Roberts, Mattie J. Chavis, and Hattie F. Graves. Knight appointed James Norfleet Holloman, the partner of Mary Jane Chavis, Susan's half-sister, as the executor of his estate. In 1913, two witnesses supported the authenticity of the will at the probate court after Knight's death. There is no evidence to suggest that Susan and her children did not ultimately receive the property left to them.

Wiley Ezell attempted to create a similar situation for his partner Celia Garnes and their children. In his will, Ezell left his home place to his children with the prerequisite that they care for their mother for the rest of her life. Ezell made Starkey Sharpe Harrell, the juror from the 1854 fornication and adultery case, his executor.[29] Unlike the cases of Noah Cotton and Richard Knight, however, several people challenged Ezell's last wishes. Soon after Ezell's death in 1879, Harrell sent notice to the court renouncing his right as executor of the Ezell estate. The court then replaced Harrell with John F. Newsome. Newsome moved quickly after his appointment and began the process of settling Ezell's numerous debts, including several notes on behalf of Celia Garnes and her sons, Joseph, Daniel, and Albert. While Newsome was in the process of settling the estate, Ezell's niece, C. Elizabeth Futrell, and her husband Amos filed a suit against Celia Garnes and her four children claiming that the will devising all of Ezell's property to the Garneses was not Ezell's true last will and testament. Benjamin B. Winborne, the lawyer for the Futrells, argued that Elizabeth, as the sole daughter of Ezell's only sister, was her uncle's only heir at law. The probate judge ruled in favor of the Futrells, but Newsome refused to surrender the assets of the estate to them. Failing to gain Newsome's cooperation, the Futrells sued Newsome as the administrator of the estate and in 1882 won a judgment in their favor.

Wills were imperfect means to transfer property to loved ones. When legitimate heirs challenged the rights of children and partners with no legally recognized connection to a man, the law could be swayed against the wishes of the progenitor. Celia Garnes and her children never collected all that Ezell intended for them to have from his estate. However, the Garneses successfully procured some of Ezell's assets through other means. Daniel, Albert, and Celia Garnes collected debts from the estate for various sorts of work. Whether the Garneses actually performed this work or Ezell simply gave them notes to collect against his estate for fear that someone might challenge his will is not clear. The Garneses also took possession of much of Ezell's personal property,

> Milteer explores instances where white men used wills, promissory notes, and property transfers through deed changes to "protect the future interests" of their families.

including the contents of his house by purchasing them at his estate sale. Celia Garnes and her children failed to gain all that Ezell intended to leave to them, but under the circumstances, the outcome could have been much worse.[30]

Some white men relied solely on promissory notes to convey wealth to their partners and progeny. Before their deaths, men would issue these notes to their partners and children. Upon their deaths, the women and children could use the notes to make claims against the estates of the white progenitors. This was the arrangement made between Sallie Yeates Bizzell and Richard Henry Shield. In 1867, Shield gave Bizzell a promissory note for $1,500 with interest. In the note, he specifically stated that he, his heirs, and executors guaranteed this debt to Bizzell. After Shield's death in 1870, Sallie collected the value of the note from the executor of his estate.[31] Surviving sources do not explain Shield's reasoning for leaving Bizzell a promissory note versus leaving a will with instructions. Shield probably understood that while wills could be contested, promissory notes were collectible no matter who was the bearer.

Although promissory notes were a safer method for white men to pass on wealth to their partners and children, legal heirs still challenged the exchange of notes. James Kiff left his children "notes or mortgages amounting to $18,000," as his son Jesse Rob Weaver remembered. Just days before his death in 1882, Kiff gave the notes to his son Samuel Weaver. James may have suspected that his brother, William Kiff, would try to block his wishes. Indeed, William qualified as administrator of his brother's estate and then attempted to claim all of his brother's property, including the notes. William sued James's children for the notes, taking the case all the way to the North Carolina Supreme Court. Jesse Rob explained that his uncle "tried to get everything from us but he failed. My father had things so fixed that he couldn't get it."[32] After each of William Kiff's appeals, the courts sided with the defendants and secured the Weavers' rights to their father's property.[33]

Promissory notes were the most effective means of passing property posthumously on to illegitimate children whose inheritance rights could be challenged by legal heirs, such as siblings or nieces and nephews. The Kiff and Weaver case demonstrates that many participants in mixed relationships were well aware of the dissatisfaction of close family members in regards to their relationships. They knew that if they set up the executions of their estates carefully, the legal system was bound to back their actions. Into the 1880s, at least some courts were unwilling to challenge the exchange of notes, even when people of color were involved. A ruling against the Weaver children would have represented a ruling for chicanery. In the Weaver case, the courts were unwilling to create a precedent with such disastrous potential.

While promissory notes were more reliable than wills, making real estate property transfers through deeds during the man's lifetime was the most secure way to transfer property to his family. Unlike with wills and promissory notes, men could personally prevent challenges to their wishes by guaranteeing that the register of deeds recorded the deeds in the county records. In 1870, James Kiff made his first land transfer to his partner, Louisiana Weaver. The deed states that Kiff sold Weaver several tracts of land for $498.33. Two subsequent deeds also state that Weaver paid Kiff for real estate. The facts that Kiff and Weaver were engaged in an intimate relationship and that single women in nineteenth-century Hertford County had little ability to accrue large sums of money suggest that an actual exchange of money between Kiff and Weaver was very unlikely. But Kiff knew that a deed of sale was much stronger than a deed of gift, the method often chosen to exchange property through relatives. He likely chose a deed of sale because creditors and other parties could challenge deeds of gift.[34]

Other partners and fathers used deeds of sale to transfer land to their families. Soon after the birth of his last child, James Norfleet Holloman deeded his partner, Mary Jane Chavis, a tract of land adjoining his other properties. The deed of sale states that Mary Jane Chavis paid Holloman $200. Almost twenty years later, Holloman transferred the cemetery lot where the family had recently buried Mary Jane Chavis to his son, Clarence Chavis. The deed for this land transfer implied that Clarence Chavis paid his father for the small cemetery plot. Richard W. Knight used similar tactics to grant land to his daughter, Mattie J. Chavis. In 1906, shortly before his death, Knight transferred a lot in the town of Union to his daughter under the supposition that Mattie J. Chavis paid him $130 for the property.[35] None of these men used the more contestable deeds of gift to transfer property to their families. As long-time buyers and sellers of land, they were cognizant of the possible implications of one type of land transfer over another. In the cases of Kiff, Holloman, and Knight, the historical record clearly demonstrates that all of these men knew one another and operated within some of the same social circles. Similarities in the methods used by white men to convey real estate to their non-white families suggest that these men may have shared strategies for the secure transfer of property.

Free women of mixed ancestry and their white partners worked with ingenuity to create environments for their families to thrive despite living in a state that denied their partnerships and children legal recognition. The material circumstances of the women of mixed ancestry involved in long-term partnerships with white men improved drastically over their lives. All of the women in this article grew up poor, but by the time of their deaths most owned their own homes and sometimes additional properties. At her death in 1914, Louisiana Weaver was one of the wealthiest women of color in her locality. Weaver owned several tracts of land and in her will bequeathed $100 in gold to each of her five sons. The children of these women enjoyed much more comfortable lives than their mothers experienced in their early years. Most of the children of these couples married, established families, owned property, and generally enjoyed financial success. Some of the children and grandchildren of these couples intermarried and others married the children of other successful families.[36] Although the law discouraged or prevented women of mixed ancestry from marrying their white partners, these women clearly demonstrated that inconsistencies in the law could be exploited to their benefit and that of their children.

These conclusions should not imply that free women of mixed ancestry built long-term partnerships with white men only for financial gain. While the historical record has a difficult time revealing love between human beings, the examples cited in this paper reveal that at least in some situations, relationships between free women of mixed ancestry and white men were bound together by mutual respect. Furthermore, some neighbors and friends recognized the bonds between free women of mixed ancestry,

Milteer is careful to explain that the role of "love" is difficult to assess from the available historical records.

white men, and their children, and went to great lengths to respect those bonds even when the law granted those bonds no such respect.

Peggy Pascoe's work has shown that communities continued to debate the extent to 35 which these laws should be enforced against white men even as lawmakers and judges attempted to strengthen white supremacy through tougher enforcement of laws banning relationships between whites and non-whites. Scholars have demonstrated that stronger enforcement of marriage restrictions and the proliferation of extralegal activities to punish and discourage sex between whites and non-whites came about during and after the Civil War. However, Pascoe noted that lawmakers and judges sought to target with increased persecution a particular type of relationship, those between white women and non-white men. She argues that not until the 1890s did the desire to uphold white supremacy make officials, judges, and juries more likely to subject white men "to the full range of the disabilities of miscegenation law." Even past this period up to the *Loving v. Virginia* decision, which found state miscegenation laws unconstitutional, the rights of white men continued to threaten the full enforcement of marriage and cohabitation restrictions.[37] The examples in this article show that even into the first decade of the twentieth century, the white power structure in Hertford County, at least in some cases, decided to uphold the rights of white men to choose their partners over widespread demands to prosecute white-non-white relationships.

The relationships discussed in this article reveal the limitations of race as a method to stratify society. Many people in the nineteenth century argued that the separation of races was a product of nature or even divine provenance. However, long-term partnerships between free women of mixed ancestry and white men demonstrate that such arguments were more political in nature than grounded in biological science or biblical scripture. The relationships in this study suggest that had such faulty argumentation not dominated nineteenth-century law and society, many mixed couples would have sought legal recognition. Their determination to build strong families, secure property rights, and uphold a public image of respectability supports the supposition that given the choice, they would have selected marriage. Free women of mixed ancestry and their white partners did not want to live on the edge of society; they simply hoped—and strived—to define their own relationships and build their own families.

ENDNOTES

I completed the research for this article with support from the Center for the Study of the American South and North Caroliniana Society. I would like to thank Kathleen DuVal, Susannah Loumiet, and the two anonymous reviewers for the *Journal of Social History* for their thoughtful comments and suggestions. Participants at the Thinking Gender Conference at UCLA and Virginia Tech's Bertoti Conference also provided valuable feedback on earlier versions of this article. I would also like to acknowledge the staffs of the State Archives of North Carolina, the Moorland-Spingarn Center, and

Milteer summarizes the major findings of his study and indicates their overall significance. Learn more about **conclusions** in the humanities on pages 161–63.

See the Appendix to learn more about the use of documentation systems in the academic disciplines.

the Southern Historical Collection for helping me procure primary source materials. Finally, I would like to express my gratitude to the descendants of the families discussed in this article for their friendship and support. Address correspondence via email: wemilteer@hotmail.com.

1. "Women of mixed ancestry" in this context refers to women with various combinations of European, Native American, and African ancestry. Throughout the nineteenth century, Hertford County residents drew important distinctions between slaves and their descendants, who locals generally categorized as black, and free people of color, most who usually fell under the mulatto category. In nineteenth-century North Carolina, the term *mulatto* was not used exclusively to refer to people of African descent. People descended from native peoples and Europeans also fell under the mulatto category. "Women of mixed ancestry" reinforces this ambiguity. See William D. Valentine Diary, Volume 12, 164–65, Southern Historical Collection (hereafter SHC); *State v. William Chavers* (Dec. 1857), Supreme Court Cases, State Archives of North Carolina (hereafter SANC).

2. William D. Valentine Diary, Volume 13, 85, SHC.

3. E. Franklin Frazier Papers Box 131–92, Folder 7; Manuscript Division, Moorland-Spingarn Research Center, Howard University (hereafter EFFP Box 131–92, Folder 7, MDMSRCHU).

4. EFFP Box 131–92, Folder 7, MDMSRCHU.

5. For further discussion of the contrast between concubinage and long-term relationships between free women of color and white men, see Kenneth Aslakson, "The 'Quadroon-Plaçage' Myth of Antebellum New Orleans: Anglo-American (Mis)interpretations of a French-Caribbean Phenomenon," *Journal of Social History* 3 (2012): 709–34.

6. *Guide to Research Materials in the North Carolina State Archives: County Records* (Raleigh, 2002), 177. For further discussion of marriage as a public institution, see Nancy Cott, *Public Vows: A History of Marriage and the Nation* (Cambridge, 2000).

7. Peggy Pascoe, *What Comes Naturally: Miscegenation Law and the Making of Race in America* (New York, 2009), 42–43.

8. Walter Clark, ed., *The State Records of North Carolina*, vol. 23 (Goldsboro, 1904), 65, 160. For further discussion of the impacts of these laws in colonial North Carolina, see Kirsten Fischer, *Suspect Relations: Sex, Race, and Resistance in Colonial North Carolina* (Ithaca, 2002).

9. *Acts Passed By the General Assembly of the State of North Carolina at the Session of 1830–1831* (Raleigh, 1831), 9–10.

10. *Amendments to the Constitution of North Carolina, Proposed by the Constitutional Convention of 1875 and the Constitution As It Will Read As Proposed to Be Amended* (Raleigh, 1875), 65.

11. For general studies of mixed marriages in the United States, see Gary B. Nash, *Forbidden Love: The Secret History of Mixed-Race America* (New York, 1999); Peter Wallenstein, *Tell the Court I Love My Wife: Race, Marriage, and Law—An American History* (New York, 2002). For further discussion of relations between enslaved women and white men see Deborah Gray White, *Ar'n't I a Woman: Female Slaves in the Plantation South* (New York, 1985); Kent Anderson Leslie, *Woman of Color, Daughter of Privilege: Amanda America Dickson 1849–1893* (Athens, 1995); Jean Fagan Yellin, *Harriet Jacobs: A Life* (New York, 2004); Annette Gordon-Reed, *The Hemingses of Monticello: An American Family* (New York, 2008). For further discussion of relations between free women of color and white men, see Adele Logan Alexander, *Ambiguous Lives: Free Women of Color in Rural Georgia, 1789–1879* (Fayetteville, 1991); Victoria E. Bynum, *Unruly Women: The Politics of Social and Sexual Control in the Old South* (Chapel Hill, 1992); Joan Martin, "Plaçage and the Louisiana

Gens de Couleur Libre: How Race and Sex Defined the Lifestyles of Free Women of Color" in *Creole: The History and Legacy of Louisiana's Free People of Color*, ed. Sybil Kein (Baton Rouge, 2000); Joshua D. Rothman, *Notorious in the Neighborhood: Sex and Families across the Color Line in Virginia, 1787–1861* (Chapel Hill, 2003); Amrita Chakrabarti Myers, *Forging Freedom: Black Women and the Pursuit of Liberty in Antebellum Charleston* (Chapel Hill, 2011).

12. Richard R. Weaver Pension File, National Archives and Records Administration; Hertford County County Court Minutes, Volume 1, May 1832, SANC; Letter J. A. Anderson to Chesson and Armstead, John B. Chesson Papers, Box 1, Chesson Papers Miscellaneous, SANC; William D. Valentine Diary, Volume 13, 188, SHC; State v. Emmy Chavers, Hertford County Civil and Criminal Action Papers, Box 1, Civil and Criminal Cases 1864, SANC; Death Certificate of Susan Chavis, SANC.

13. EFFP Box 131–92, Folder 7, MDMSRCHU. The context of Calvin Scott Brown's statement appears to suggest that the term "nigger" may have referred specifically to people recognized in the community as "black" and would not have included "mulattoes" or people recognized as being of mixed ancestry.

14. Mavis Christine Campbell, *The Dynamics of Change in a Slave Society: A Sociopolitical History of the Free Coloreds of Jamaica, 1800–1865* (London, 1976), 51; David Brion Davis, *Inhuman Bondage: The Rise and Fall of Slavery in the New World* (New York, 2006), 180.

15. Benjamin B. Winborne, *The Colonial and State Political History of Hertford County* (Raleigh, 1906), 235, 333.

16. Hertford County County Court Minutes, Volume 3, March 1854, SANC; 1850 United States Federal Census, Hertford County, North Carolina, Northern District, 291a, 309a; EFFP Box 131–92, Folder 7, MDMSRCHU. The 1850 Census lists two men named William Futrell living in the same Hertford County household. Which of these men was involved in the case with Frusa Reid is unclear.

17. Hertford County Record of Deeds, Volume A, 653, SANC.

18. EFFP Box 131–92, Folder 7, MDMSRCHU. The 1870 Census confirms the proximity between Louisiana Weaver's house and James Kiff's place as described by Jesse Rob Weaver. See 1870 United States Federal Census, Hertford County, North Carolina, Winton Township, 54.

19. EFFP Box 131–92, Folder 7, MDMSRCHU.

20. EFFP Box 131–92, Folder 7, MDMSRCHU.

21. EFFP Box 131–92, Folder 7, MDMSRCHU.

22. EFFP Box 131–92, Folder 7, MDMSRCHU.

23. Hertford County Estates Records, Box 13, Ezell, Wiley, SANC.

24. EFFP Box 131–92, Folder 7, MDMSRCHU.

25. Hertford County Estates Records, Box 13, Ezell, Wiley, SANC.

26. EFFP Box 131–92, Folder 7, MDMSRCHU.

27. For further discussion of the way lawmakers attempted to define family through marriage laws, see Cott, *Public Vows*, 24–55.

28. Will of Noah Cotton 1815, John Vann Papers, Box 4, SANC; Estate of Noah Cotton, John Vann Papers, Box 3, SANC.

29. Hertford County Record of Wills, Volume C, 222, SANC.

30. Hertford County Estates Records, Box 13, Ezell, Wiley, SANC.

31. Hertford County Estates Records, Box 40, Shields, Richard H., SANC.

32. EFFP Box 131–92, Folder 7, MDMSRCHU.

33. North Carolina Supreme Court ruled that Samuel Weaver was entitled to his father's notes after the settlement of all of James Kiff's debts. See *William Kiff Admr. v. Samuel Weaver et al.* 94 NC 274 (Feb 1886), Supreme Court Cases, SANC.

34. Hertford County Record of Deeds, Volume B, 50–51, SANC; Hertford County Record of Deeds, Volume F, 548–49, SANC; Hertford County Record of Deeds, Volume H, 196–97, SANC.

35. Hertford County Record of Deeds, Volume V, 172–73, SANC; Hertford County Record of Deeds, Volume 50, 172, SANC; Hertford County Record of Deeds, Volume 32, 88, SANC.

36. Hertford County Record of Wills, Volume D, 324–26, SANC. Examples of intermarriages between families include the marriage of Louisiana Weaver's and James Kiff's son to Sallie Yeates Bizzell's and R. H. Shield's daughter and the marriage between Mary Jane Chavis's and J. N. Holloman's son, to Sallie Yeates Bizzell's and R. H. Shield's granddaughter. See Hertford County Marriage Register and Hertford County Marriage Licenses in the State Archives of North Carolina for further examples.

37. Pascoe, *What Comes Naturally*, 10–11. For further discussion of changes in the regulation of relationships between whites and non-whites after the Civil War, see Martha Hodes, *White Women, Black Men: Illicit Sex in the Nineteenth-Century South* (New Haven, 1997).

Reading Questions

1. Milteer acknowledges a number of difficulties that attend the kind of historical research presented in the article. What are they?

2. According to Milteer, what is a likely financial justification for mixed free women choosing to develop long-term relationships with white men? What evidence does he provide for this?

3. What, according to Milteer, seems to be the role of love in mate selection for the mixed free women he discusses in the article?

4. Why were certain white men unlikely to face legal or social scrutiny for developing relationships with mixed free women?

5. Why were promissory notes "a safer method for white men to pass on wealth to their partners and children" (par. 29)? What, according to Milteer, was the most secure way to transfer property to partners and children?

Rhetoric Questions

6. What is the primary form of evidence that Milteer uses to support his conclusions?

7. The article's introduction includes testimony from a number of individuals. What is the effect of the use of personal testimony on you as a reader?

8. Milteer spends a great deal of time interpreting historical documents and records as part of his argument. Did you find any of his interpretations particularly strong? Weak? Explain why.

Response and Research Questions

9. Milteer writes, "Lawmakers sought to define the family as a racially uniform unit by prohibiting marriage across the color line, but people on the ground, at least occasionally, rejected this notion" (23). Do you see evidence of individuals rejecting lawmakers' definitions of marriage or family in society today? Explain.

10. What does Milteer mean when he writes, "The relationships discussed in this article reveal the limitations of race as a method to stratify society" (36)? In what ways does Milteer's article reveal these limitations?

ACADEMIC CASE STUDY • PERSPECTIVES ON LOVE   SOCIAL SCIENCES

Women and Men in Love: Who Really Feels It and Says It First?

MARISSA A. HARRISON AND JENNIFER C. SHORTALL

Marissa A. Harrison is currently an associate professor of psychology, behavioral sciences, and education at Pennsylvania State University. She has published multiple articles on topics concerning human behavior, including sexuality. "Women and Men in Love: Who Really Feels It and Says It First?" was written with co-author Jennifer C. Shortall, a graduate student at Duquesne University at the time of the article's 2011 publication in the *Journal of Social Psychology*. The article explores attitudes toward love and romance among men and women, concluding that "women may not be the greater 'fools for love' that society assumes."

ABSTRACT

A widely held belief exists that women are more romantic and tend to fall in love faster than men. Responses from 172 college students indicated that although both men and women believe that women will fall in love and say "I love you" first in a relationship, men reported falling in love earlier and expressing it earlier than women reported. Analyses also showed no sex differences in attitudinal responses to items about love and romance. These results indicate that women may not be the greater "fools for love" that society assumes and are consistent with the notion that a pragmatic and cautious view of love has adaptive significance for women.

Love has been called "the deepest and most meaningful of sentiments" (Rubin, 1970), although what constitutes "love" can have a myriad of meanings, ranging from concepts involving an initial state of attraction, to falling in love, to being/staying in love (Aron et al., 2008). Yet even though it is difficult to define *falling in love*, and the consideration of such may not ever rise entirely

above subjectivity (Hendrick & Hendrick, 1986; Sternberg & Weis, 2006), researchers have commented that almost everyone can relate to being or falling in love (Esch & Stefano, 2005; Stefano & Esch, 2007).

How love is expressed and experienced may differ between women and men. With respect to the expression of love, surprisingly little research has focused on the locution "I love you," even though these three small words appear to be a critical delineation in relationships (Owen, 1987), as such expressions of affection are thought to be decisive moments for the advancement of romantic relationships (Baxter & Braithewaite, 2008). Researchers have indicated that cross-culturally, females tend to use the locution "I love you" more than males (Wilkins & Gareis, 2006). This is not surprising, since evidence suggests that women and men differ in their expression of emotions and in their descriptions of related cognitions (Barbara, 2008). Women tend to be more expressive in relationships, and women are *expected* by others to be more expressive (Rubin, 1970; Hess, Adams, & Kleck, 2007), particularly in instances of romantic love (Durik et al., 2006). Interestingly, women appear to enjoy a neurological advantage in terms of processing multisensory, emotional experiences (Collignon et al., 2010); this is likely one reason why women are faster at perceiving others' emotions (Hampson, van Anders, & Mullin, 2006) and have more confidence than do men when expressing affection, liking, and love to the opposite sex (Blier & Blier-Wilson, 1989). In contrast, due to their "inexpressiveness and restrictive emotionality" (Blier & Blier-Wilson, 1989, p. 287) men may experience intimacy, parenting, and relationship problems (Dosser, 1982; Balswick, 1988).

Despite men's purported emotional restriction, however, a few older studies have shown that men report saying "I love you" first in a relationship (Owen, 1987; Brantley, Knox, & Zusman, 2002). Owen (1987) posited that this transpires because men are socialized to take the initiative in relationships, and that this verbal declaration may prompt women to reciprocate this iteration and commit prematurely to a relationship. Brantley, Knox, and Zusman (2002) interpreted this through an evolutionary lens, positing that men use this locution first in a relationship as an inroad to sexual access. In support of Brantley and colleagues' theory, Tucker, Marvin, and Vivian (1991) noted that women listed their partners' expressions of "I love you" in their top 10 romantic acts, but men did not. If men possess knowledge that women find "I love you" to be romantic, men may communicate what their partners want to hear so as to advance a relationship sexually and/or emotionally. This makes sense evolutionarily, as women in our ancestral environment, who have few gametes compared to men, would have benefitted from pair-bond assurance more than would males (Symons, 1979) and saying "I love you" appears to communicate a commitment. Moreover, men place a greater premium on sex than women do (Buss, 2004, 2006), and this is theorized to be the case because of the reproductive advantage that sex with multiple women confers to men, who have a virtually unlimited supply of sperm. Thus, any strategy serving as the means to a

sexual end would be beneficial to men, including declarations of love. With this in mind, then, one might wonder if the public's perception of women as the more romantic sex (Hatfield & Walster, 1978; Hyde & DeLamater, 2009) might simply be due to the fact that men report being and are perceived as more sexual than are women, and are therefore viewed as less romantic.

It should be noted, however, that men may have 5 a different sexual attitude toward long-term, committed partners than they do toward short-term, sex-only partners. Evidence shows that men and women report similar preferences for a long-term partner who is kind, intelligent, and understanding, and one who loves them in return (Buss, 2007).

In terms of romance, a widely held stereotype in our society contends that women are more romantic than are men, although older data from college students show men to have a greater number of romantic attitudes than women do (Knox & Sporakowski, 1968). Further, researchers have reported that men fall in love earlier than do women (Kanin, Davidson, & Schreck, 1970; Rubin, Peplau, & Hill, 2004). Even adolescent boys seem to fall in love earlier than do adolescent girls (Montgomery & Sorrell, 1998), and these individuals are at an age when passionate love is thought to be more intense (Hatfield & Sprecher, 1986). Although at what age we fall in love for the first time has been the topic of scientific scrutiny (e.g., Montgomery & Sorrell, 1998; Reagan, Durvasula, Howell, Ureno, & Rea, 2004), the exact *time frame* of falling in love (e.g., hours, days, weeks, months into a relationship) is difficult to study empirically because of the retrospective nature of the question. Perhaps this is why this not been extensively explored in previous studies.

Much of the seminal research of "love" was conducted more than a generation ago (e.g., 1960s, 1970s). The present study used a contemporary sample of college students in an attempt to determine if there has been a social change in this phenomenon. Our study attempts to replicate, integrate, and extend upon previous work on which sex falls in love first, when they fall in love, and who says "I love you" first. This study also sought to examine if women's perceptions of love and romance are really that different from men's perceptions by asking questions about these phenomena, thus attempting to dispel the popular notion that women are hopeless romantics and support the notion that women are careful, comparison shoppers in terms of relationships.

METHOD

All procedures were approved by the local Institutional Review Board. A 28-item Internet-based instrument was created to assess similarities and differences between men's and women's attitudes, expectations, and experiences with respect to love and relationships. As researchers have reported that first- and second-year college students have an expected high incidence of falling in love (Aron, Paris, & Aron, 1995), the choice of a college sample was appropriate for the purposes of this study. We attempted to obtain a diverse sample by recruiting participants from the subject pool of a mid-sized university and by recruiting volunteer respondents from a large community college in a major metropolitan city in the northeastern United States. Of the 188 participants who responded to the questionnaire, 10 did not indicate their sex and were excluded from analysis. Although of interest, the sample of homosexual and bisexual respondents was not large enough for analysis, and therefore the data from seven individuals (6 men and 1 woman) who reported preferring to date and have sex with men and women equally, mostly the same sex, or only the same sex were excluded from the analysis to control for error variance. The resulting sample of 171 heterosexual individuals consisted of 72 men and 99 women with a mean age of 20.28 (SD = 5.25). Ethnicities reported were: 77.1% White, 13.0% Asian, 5.3% Black, 3.5% Hispanic, and 1.1% Other.

RESULTS

Analyses revealed that 61 men (84.72%) and 88 (90.90%) women reported they had been involved in a committed, romantic relationship at some point in their lives, with no sex difference, $X^2(1, N = 171) = 1.54, p > .214$, N.S. Additionally, 27 men (38.02%) and 56 women (56.57%) reported that they were *currently* involved in a committed, romantic relationship and this sex difference was significant, $X^2(1, N = 170) = 5.69, p < .017$. Of people who were currently in relationships, most men (91.30%) and women (98.21%) reported being "in love" with their partner, with no sex difference in frequency, $X^2(1, N = 76) = 2.13, p > .144$.

As this study was interested in relationship dynamics, only responses from those with previous relationship experience were included in subsequent analyses. Participants were asked, "In your most recent romantic relationship, how long did it take you to realize you were in love?" Answer choices were: 1 = "*I am not in love*," 2 = "*Immediately*," 3 = "*A few days*," 4 = "*A few weeks*," 5 = "*A few months*," 6 = "*A year*," and 7 = "*More than a year*." Men (M = 4.47, SD = 1.23) reported falling in love more quickly than women (M = 5.01, SD = .99) reported falling in love, $t(127) = 2.74, p < .007, d = .48$. In addition, in response to the question, "In your most recent committed, romantic relationship, who said 'I love you' FIRST?" only 12.10% reported that neither partner did. Among those for whom this was expressed, there was a relationship to sex, with 64% of men compared to 18.51% of women reporting they said "I love you" to their partners first, $X^2(1, N = 131) = 27.80, p < .000$.

Participants were also asked, "Who falls in love first in a relationship, a man or a woman?" Interestingly, 87.78% of participants believed that a woman falls in love first in a relationship, $X^2(1, N = 131) = 74.82, p < .000$, and this response was unrelated to sex, $X^2(1, N = 131) = .939, p > .332$. Participants were further asked, "Do you think a man or a woman is more likely to say 'I love you' first in a relationship?" Results showed that 75.20% of participants believed that a woman is more likely to express this sentiment first, $X^2(1, N = 125) = 31.75, p < .000$, and there was no relationship to sex, $X^2(1, N = 125) = 2.04, p > .153$.

Participants were asked, "About how far into a relationship would you be able to tell you were in love?" and "About how far into a relationship would you be able to tell your partner was in love?" Answer choices were presented on a Likert-type scale: 1 = "*Immediately*"; 2 = "*A few days*"; 3 = "*A few weeks*"; 4 = "*A few months*"; 5 = "*A year*"; and 6 = "*More than a year.*" Women anticipated knowing they were in love with a partner ($M = 4.00$, $SD = .67$) later than men anticipated knowing they were in love ($M = 3.62$, $SD = 1.14$), $t(148) = 2.54$, $p < .012$, $d = .41$, and women anticipated being able to tell their partner was in love with them later ($M = 4.09$, $SD = .80$) than men anticipated being able to tell ($M = 3.70$, $SD = .99$), $t(147) = 2.63$, $p < .009$, $d = .43$. However, both sexes reported anticipating they would know they were in love with a partner the same time they knew their partners were in love with them [women: $t(87) = 1.82$, $p = .072$; men: $t(60) = .820$, $p = .416$]. Participants were also asked, "How far into a committed, romantic relationship would you want to have sex with a partner?" The same scale reported above was used for responses. Women reported a desire to wait longer to have sex ($M = 3.83$, $SD = 1.14$) than men reported ($M = 3.42$, $SD = 1.18$), $t(147) = 2.15$, $p < .034$, $d = .35$ Additional analyses showed that men's responses indicated that they anticipated wanting to have sex at the same time they would know they were in love, $t(59) = 1.01$, $p < .318$, and that their partners were in love, $t(59) = 1.61$, $p < .112$. Women's responses indicated they also anticipated wanting to have sex at the same time they would know they were in love, $t(87) = 1.39$, $p < .167$, and their responses indicated they would want to have sex before knowing their partners were in love, $t(86) = 2.19$, $p < .031$, but a Bonferroni correction to alpha for multiple comparisons renders this result non-significant.

Participants were then presented with a series of statements about love, dating, romance, sex, and physical attraction, and were asked to report on a scale the degree to which they agreed with each statement, with again, 1 = "*Totally disagree*"; 2 = "*Slightly disagree*"; 3 = "*Neither agree nor disagree*"; 4 = "*Slightly agree*"; and 5 = "*Totally agree.*" When employing a Bonferroni correction to alpha for multiple comparisons, there were no sex differences in responses to any questions about love and romance. Results are presented in Table 1.

DISCUSSION

In our contemporary college sample, nearly 9 out of 10 people who have had relationship experience expressed that it is likely a woman who will fall in love first in a relationship. Further, 7 out of 10 people believed that a woman will say "I love you" first. However, our data showed that men reported falling in love sooner and that three times as many men as women said "I love you" first to their partners. These results show no change from those in older studies (e.g., Dion & Dion, 1973) in that men report falling in love and saying it first. This suggests that women tend to be more pragmatic about love than society tends to believe, i.e., not rushing fool-heartedly into a relationship. The emergence of the locution "I love you" in relationship vocabulary is important, as emotional narration can offer a window into the speaker's affective state (Barbara, 2008). It can be argued that men's falling in love and exclaiming this love first may be explained as a byproduct of men equating love with sexual desire, as evidence suggests that men are more interested in sex than are women (see Buss, 2006). However, researchers have proposed that passionate love and sexual desire are distinctly different mechanisms (see Reis & Aron, 2008), and our data showed that men and women showed equivocal agreement that they become increasingly physically attracted to someone with whom they are in love, indicating an understanding of the difference. Again, evidence does suggest that people in North American culture (from which our sample was obtained) can relate to what it means to fall in love (Aron et al., 2008).

Our results indicated that when asked to speculate, women reported anticipating they would know they were in love with a partner in about a few months and that they would also know the feeling was mutual within a few months. This was significantly later than the timeline indicated by men, who reported anticipating knowing they were in love and knowing their partner's mutual feelings in about a few weeks to a few months. These findings are novel and provide support that women do not rush into a romance before men do. Additionally, neither sex indicated an expected temporal difference between realizing one's own and one's partner's feelings. This further indicates that women are not hopeless

Table 1

Men's and Women's Responses to Items about Love and Romance

Item	Men (*n* = 72) *M (SD)*	Women (*n* = 100) *M (SD)*	*t(df)*	*p*
Romantic love is a biological trick to get you to reproduce.	2.53 (1.32)	2.04 (1.07)	2.69 (170)	.008
You really need to get to know someone's personality before you can be in love with them.	4.32 (.80)	4.57 (.66)	2.20 (169)	.029
Love at first sight exists.	3.08 (1.20)	3.08 (1.20)	.015 (167)	.988
Love is a waste of time.	1.85 (1.10)	1.39 (.82)	3.10 (169)	.029
My being in love is important to me.	3.76 (1.04)	3.89 (1.14)	.758 (169)	.450
Physical attraction fades over time.	2.90 (1.20)	2.61 (1.08)	1.67 (170)	.096
Being in love fades over time.	2.46 (1.17)	2.32 (1.10)	.791 (170)	.430
I am a fool for love.	2.86 (1.25)	3.20 (1.28)	1.74 (169)	.084
I become more and more in love with the person I am attracted to.	3.88 (.96)	3.98 (.91)	.73 (170)	.467
I become more and more physically attracted to the person I love.	4.08 (1.12)	4.31 (.84)	1.47 (167)	.143

Notes. No differences were significant after employing a Bonferroni correction to alpha for multiple comparisons. Answers were given on a 5-point Likert-type scale where 1 = "*Totally disagree*"; 2 = "*Slightly disagree*"; 3 = "*Neither agree nor disagree*"; 4 = "*Slightly agree*"; and 5 = "*Totally agree.*"

romantics engulfed in unrequited or unsure love any more or less than are men.

Most men and women in our study reported being involved in a committed relationship before, and almost all who were in romantic relationships at the time of participation reported being in love with their partners. As in previous research, men's reports of when they fell in love with their partners indicated that they did so sooner than women's reports indicated they did. However, unlike previous studies, our data highlighted a timeline, whereby men reported falling in love with their most recent, committed partner in about a few weeks to a few months, and women reported falling in love in about a few months. These findings corroborate our data, as mentioned above, that show men are more likely than women to say "I love you" first to their partners.

Not surprisingly, women in our study reported a preference to engage in first sex later in a new relationship (a few months into it) than men's reported preference (a few weeks to a few months into it), but both sexes reported a desire to have sex at the same time they were certain of their own and their partner's feelings. This suggests that women, relative to men, are making more careful assessments of their partners before committing sexually and emotionally to a relationship.

Interestingly, other than the above, our data indicated no significant differences between the sexes, revealing that women's general viewpoints (including cynical beliefs, e.g., "Love is a waste of time") about love, dating, and romance are not different than those of men. These data reveal a trend for women which apparently goes against the popular belief that women are more romantic and idealistic about love than are men. There were no sex differences in agreement to statements such as "Love at first sight exists," "My being in love is important to me," "Physical attraction fades over time," "Being in love fades over time," and "I am a fool for love." These data show that women are *not* greater fools for love than are men as is the common societal stereotype, and are not, as Heiss (2005) reported, "handicapped in the competition" (p. 575). In fact, these data arguably show that both sexes are equally as pragmatic and as foolish about love.

It is curious why the belief that women are fools for love persists, as the notion that women should logically and realistically view love and commitment follows evolutionary theory that women need to be discriminative in their mate choices due to their relatively limited reproductive capabilities (Symons, 1979). That is, it is reproductively advantageous for a woman to be tentative and not simply jump into a sexual or romantic relationship until she is sure of her partner's intent to commit, as this would have assured resources and protection in the ancestral environment which was likely not very female-friendly.

Still, alternative explanations may exist for such 20 beliefs and therefore our findings. Who says what to whom and at what time in a relationship may simply be learned from others as appropriate or inappropriate. Personal perceptions and cognitions of sex roles likely lead men and women to behave in love relationships as they feel they are expected to behave. For example, it may be part of a man's gender schema (Bem, 1981) to be the one to facilitate the solidification of a relationship by stating "I love you" first. Likewise, it may be enmeshed in a woman's gender schema to wait for the man in a relationship to make such a move first. Societal expectations may dictate and place pressure upon men and women to act accordingly as well, likely beginning very early in life, and messages on how men and women "typically" behave as their respective genders are presented though the family, school, friends, and media (for discussion, see Macionis, 2004, p. 250). As beliefs can be culturally transmitted, however, they can create selection pressures for behavioral adaptations (Confer

et al., 2010). With respect to interpreting the findings of the present study through an evolutionary framework, perhaps it is men who expressed love to their partners first that left more descendants than men who did not, and likewise, perhaps it is women who waited for men to make the first move left more descendants. It seems plausible that both evolutionary and cultural theory can come into play when interpreting the results presented herein.

There are admitted limitations to the present study. First, participants' responses, as is the case with any self-report research, may reflect inaccuracies due to social desirability, difficulties with estimates, and problems with retrospective judgments (Hyde & DeLamater, 2009). Future studies might involve longitudinal assessments of individuals who have recently become romantically involved, recording progression of love experiences and expressions. For example, a diary study would allow fairly accurate determination of the time frame and expression of love feelings. In addition, the love and romance experiences of college men and women from the northeastern United States may not represent the psychology of men and women in all cultures. As such, additional research may wish to replicate these findings in other countries.

In conclusion, our data show that women tend to be more cautious about love and the expression thereof than what is commonly believed. Perhaps women are perceived as less rational about love compared to men because women have a greater capacity for processing emotional experiences (Collignon et al., 2010) and have a more emotionally expressive nature than do men (Rubin, 1970; Hess, Adams, & Kleck, 2007; Barbara, 2008). If this is the case, then the stereotype of women as hopeless romantics compared to men will likely persist even in the face of scientific evidence to the contrary.

REFERENCES

Aron, A., Fisher, H., Strong, G., Acevedo, B., Riela, S., & Tsapelas, I. (2008). Falling in love. In S. Sprecher, A. Wenzel, & J. Harvey (Eds.), *Handbook of relationship initiation* (pp. 315–336). New York, NY: Psychology Press.

Aron, A., Paris, M., & Aron, E. (1995). Falling in love: Pro-spective studies of self-concept change. *Journal of Personality and Social Psychology, 69,* 1102–1112.

Balswick, J. (1988). *The inexpressive male.* Lexington, MA: Lexington Books.

Barbara, G. (2008). Gender differences in verbal expression of love schema. *Sex Roles, 58,* 814–821.

Baxter, L., & Braithewaite, D. (2008). *Engaging theories in interpersonal communication: Multiple perspectives.* Thousand Oaks, CA: Sage.

Bem, S. (1981). Gender schema theory: A cognitive account of sex typing. *Psychological Review, 88,* 354–364.

Blier, M., & Blier-Wilson, L. (1989). Gender differences in self-rated emotional expressiveness. *Sex Roles, 21,* 287–295.

Brantley, A., Knox, D., & Zusman, M. (2002). When and why gender differences in saying "I love you" among college students. *College Student Journal, 36,* 614–615.

Buss, D. (2004). *The evolution of desire.* New York, NY: Basic Books.

Buss, D. (2006). The evolution of love. In R. Sternberg & K. Weis (Eds.), *The new psychology of love* (pp. 65–86). New Haven, CT: Yale University Press.

Buss, D. (2007). The evolution of human mating. *Acta Psychologia Sinica, 39,* 502–512.

Collignon, O., Girard, S., Gosselin, F., Saint-Amour, D., Lepore, F., & Lassonde, M. (2010). Women process multisensory emotion expressions more efficiently than men. *Neuropsychologia, 48,* 220–214.

Confer, J., Easton, J., Fleischman, D., Goetz, C., Lewis, D., Perilloux, C., & Buss, D. (2010). Evolutionary psychology: Controversies, questions, prospects, and limitations. *American Psychologist, 65,* 110–126. doi: 10.1037/a0018413

Dion, K., & Dion, K. (1973). Correlates of romantic love. *Journal of Consulting and Clinical Psychology, 41*(1), 51–56.

Dosser, D. (1982). Male expressiveness behavioral intervention. In K. Solomon & M. Levy (Eds.), *Men in transition: Theory and therapy.* New York, NY: Plenum.

Durik, A., Hyde, J., Marks, A., Roy, A., Anaya, D., & Schultz, G. (2006). Ethnicity and gender stereotypes of emotion. *Sex Roles, 54,* 429–445.

Esch, T., & Stefano, G. (2005). The neurobiology of falling in love. *Neuroendocrinology Letters, 26,* 175–192.

Hampson, E., van Anders, S., & Mullin, L. (2006). A female advantage in the recognition of emotional facial expressions: Test of an evolutionary hypothesis. *Evolution and Human Behavior, 27,* 401–416.

Hatfield, E., & Sprecher, S. (1986). Measuring passionate love in intimate relationships. *Journal of Adolescence, 9,* 383–410.

Hatfield, E., & Walster, W. (1978). *A new look at love.* Lanham, MD: University Press of America.

Heiss, J. (2005). Gender and romantic love roles. *Sociological Quarterly, 32,* 575–591.

Hendrick, C., & Hendrick, S. (1986). A theory and method of love. *Journal of Personality and Social Psychology, 50,* 392–402.

Hess, U., Adams, R., & Kleck, R. (2007). When two do the same it might not mean the same: The perception of emotional expressions shown by men and women. In U. Hess & P. Phillipot (Eds.), *Group dynamics and emotional expression: Studies in emotion and social interaction, 2nd series* (pp. 33–50). New York, NY: Cambridge University Press.

Hyde, J., & DeLamater, J. (2009). *Understanding human sexuality* (10th ed.). New York, NY: McGraw-Hill.

Kanin, E., Davidson, K., & Schreck, S. (1970). A research note on male-female differentials in the experience of heterosexual love. *Journal of Sex Research, 6,* 64–72.

Knox, D., & Sporakowski, M. (1968). Attitudes of college students toward love. *Journal of Marriage and the Family, 30,* 638–642.

Macionis, J. (2004). *Society: The basics* (7th ed.). Upper Saddle River, NJ: Pearson Education.

Montgomery, M., & Sorrell, G. (1998). Love and dating experience in early and middle adolescence: Grade and gender comparisons. *Journal of Adolescence, 21,* 677–689.

Owen, W. (1987). The verbal expression of love by women and men as a critical communication event in personal relationships. *Women's Studies in Communication, 10*(1), 15–24.

Reagan, P. C., Durvasula, R., Howell, L., Ureno, O., & Rea, M. (2004). Gender, ethnicity, and the developmental timing of first sexual and romantic experiences. *Social Behavior and Personality, 32,* 667–676.

Reis, H., & Aron, A. (2008). Love: What is it, why does it matter, and how does it operate? *Perspectives on Psychological Science, 3*(1), 80–86.

Rubin, Z. (1970). Measurement of romantic love. *Journal of Personality and Social Psychology, 16,* 265–273.

Rubin, Z., Peplau, L., & Hill, C. (2004). Loving and leaving: Sex differences in romantic attachments. *Sex Roles, 7,* 821–835.

Stefano, G., & Esch, T. (2007). Love and stress. *Activitas Nervosa Superior, 49*(3–4), 112–113.

Sternberg, R., & Weis, K. (2006). *The new psychology of love.* New Haven, CT: Yale University Press.

Symons, D. (1979). *The evolution of human sexuality.* New York, NY: Oxford University Press.

Tucker, R., Marvin, M., & Vivian, B. (1991). What constitutes a romantic act? An empirical study. *Psychological Reports, 69,* 651–654.

Wilkins, R., & Gareis, E. (2006). Emotional expression and the locution "I love you": A cross-cultural study. *International Journal of Intercultural Relations, 30,* 51–75.

Reading Questions

1. The researchers note that "a few older studies have shown that men report saying 'I love you' first in a relationship" (par. 4). Based on the authors' review of scholarship, what are two possible reasons for this?

2. The researchers outline at least three main areas of inquiry for their study. What are these areas?

3. The researchers report excluding data from analysis from a number of their respondents. Why were these particular individuals excluded from the study?

4. Based on the researchers' findings, who reported falling in love more quickly, men or women? Who tended to believe that women would fall in love first in a relationship?

5. What evidence does the research provide to support the idea that "women do not rush into a romance before men do" (15)?

Rhetoric Questions

6. What does the table "Men's and Women's Responses to Items about Love and Romance" add to the study's effectiveness?

7. Read the study's concluding paragraph again. How would you assess the researchers' tone and attitude in this moment? What is the effect of that tone on you as a reader?

Response and Research Questions

8. The researchers note the limitations associated with using self-reported data in their research. Do you see any additional limitations in their study?

9. As they suggest, the researchers' work assumes that people tend to believe that women are more romantic and less cautious about falling in love. Do you agree or disagree with this notion? Why?

10. Do you find the study's results at all surprising? Why or why not? What might your answer reveal about some of your own beliefs and attitudes?

ACADEMIC CASE STUDY • PERSPECTIVES ON LOVE   NATURAL SCIENCES

Hormonal Changes When Falling in Love

DONATELLA MARAZZITI AND DOMENICO CANALE

Donatella Marazziti is a professor of psychiatry and the director of the laboratory of psychopharmacology at the University of Pisa, Italy. She has researched and published widely on the subjects of love and biochemistry, and she is author of the best-seller *The Nature of Love* (2002), among other scholarly texts. In this study, co-written with Domenico Canale, the researchers examine hormone changes in individuals who have recently fallen in love. They conclude that the hormone changes identified are "reversible, state-dependent, and probably related to some physical and/or psychological features typically associated with falling in love." The study was published in the journal *Psychoneuroendocrinology* in 2004.

SUMMARY

To fall in love is the first step in pair formation in humans and is a complex process which only recently has become the object of neuroscientific investigation. The little information available in this field prompted us to measure the levels of some pituitary, adrenal, and gonadal hormones in a group of 24 subjects of both sexes who had recently (within the previous six months) fallen in love, and to compare them with those of 24 subjects who were single or were part of a long-lasting relationship. The following hormones were evaluated by means of standard techniques: FSH, LH, estradiol, progesterone, dehydroepiandrosterone sulphate (DHEAS), cortisol, testosterone, and androstenedione.

The results showed that estradiol, progesterone, DHEAS, and androstenedione levels did not differ between the groups and were within the normal ranges. Cortisol levels were significantly higher amongst those subjects who had recently fallen in love, as compared with those who had not. FSH and testosterone levels were lower in men in love, while women of the same group presented higher testosterone levels. All hormonal differences were eliminated when the subjects were retested from 12 to 24 months later. The increased cortisol and low FSH levels are suggestive of the "stressful" and arousing conditions associated with the initiation of a social contact. The changes of testosterone concentrations, which varied in opposite directions in the two sexes, may reflect changes in behavioral and/or temperamental traits which have yet to be clarified. In conclusion, the findings of the present study would indicate that to fall in love provokes transient hormonal changes, some of which seem to be specific to each sex.

1. INTRODUCTION

The formation of pair bonding is relevant in several animal species, and particularly in mammals since, in some cases, it ensures not only that a new couple is formed which can thus generate offspring, but also that a safe and stable environment is set up wherein the newborn can receive sufficient care to enable them to mature and become capable of surviving alone (Bowlby, 1969; Kleiman, 1977; Carter et al., 1997a, 1997b).

The process of pair bonding in humans begins with the subjective experience of falling in love, which sometimes leads to the establishment of long-lasting relationships: for this reason, its function exceeds that of reproduction alone and, given its relevance to the survival of the species, it would not be surprising if it were regulated by precise and long-standing neural mechanisms (Uvnäs-Moberg, 1997, 1998; Carter, 1998). Indirect evidence of the biological process involved in falling in love is provided by cross-cultural studies which suggest that it is present in virtually all societies and is, perhaps, genetically determined (Jankoviak and Fischer, 1992). Furthermore, common features of this process can be identified in studies from all over the world and include: perception of an altered mental state, intrusive thoughts and images of the other, sets of behavioral patterns aimed at eliciting a reciprocal response, and a definite course and predictable outcome (Leckman and Mayes, 1999).

One of the first biological hypotheses with regard 5 to falling in love associates this state to increased levels of phenylethylamine, on the basis of the similarities between the chemical structure of this neurotransmitter and that of amphetamines which provoke mood changes resembling those typical of the initial stage of a romance; however, no empirical data have been gathered to support this theory (Liebowitz, 1983). The strong suggestion is that different mechanisms may be involved (Panksepp, 1982; Jankoviak, 1986; Hazan and Shaver, 1987; Fisher, 1992; Porges, 1998; Insel and Young, 1997), and it has been recently demonstrated that the intrusive thoughts of the early, romantic phase of falling in love are underlaid by a decreased functionality of the serotonin transporter (Marazziti et al., 1999).

The complexity of the process would seem, therefore, to be understood better when we consider falling in love as a basic emotion, such as anxiety or fear, due to the activation of the amygdala and related circuits and neurotransmitters (Bartels and Zeki, 2000; LeDoux, 2000). Consistent with this hypothesis is the observation that stress and threatening situations may facilitate the onset of new social bonds and intimate ties (Bowlby, 1973; Reite, 1985; Kraemer, 1992; Panksepp et al., 1994). The review of animal data is beyond the scope of this paper; however, it should perhaps be noted also that stress and corticosterone have been demonstrated to promote pair bonding formation in different species (DeVries et al., 1995, 1996; Hennessy, 1997; Levine et al., 1997; Mendoza and Mason, 1997). Furthermore, these elements induce the synthesis and release of neuropeptides, such as oxytocin, which are involved in the subsequent processes, including sexual and maternal behaviors and, more in general, positive social contacts, which reduce anxiety (McCarthy et al., 1992; Numan, 1994; Carter, 1998). The literature relevant to humans in this regard is meager, albeit in agreement with animal findings, and suggests that the activation of the hypothalamic-pituitary-adrenal (HPA) axis due to stressful experiences or, more in general, to arousal, may trigger the development of different kinds of social attachment, possibly also that which begins with falling in love (Milgram, 1986; Chiodera et al., 1991; Simpson and Rhole, 1994).

Given the paucity of data in this field and the unexplored questions regarding the possible role of gonadal hormones, our study aimed at evaluating the levels of some pituitary, adrenal, and gonadal hormones in a homogenous group of subjects of both sexes who were in the early, romantic phase of a loving relationship, and to compare them with those of subjects who were single or were already in a long-lasting relationship.

2. SUBJECTS AND METHODS

2.1. Subjects

Twenty-four subjects (12 male and 12 female, mean age ± SD: 27 ± 4 years) who declared that they had recently fallen in love were recruited from amongst residents (17) and medical students (7), by means of advertisement. They were selected according to the criteria already applied in a previous study (Marazziti et al., 1999), in particular: the relationship was required to have begun within the previous 6 months (mean ± SD: 3 ± 1 months) and at least four hours a day spent in thinking about the partner (mean ± SD: 9 ± 3 hours), as recorded by a specifically designed questionnaire.

Twenty-four subjects (12 female and 12 male, mean age ± SD: 29 ± 3), belonging to the same environment and with similar educational levels, with either a long-lasting (mean ± SD: 67 ± 28 months) or no relationship, served as the control group.

No subject had a family or personal history of [10] any major psychiatric disorder or even subthreshold symptoms, or had ever taken psychotropic drugs, except for three who occasionally took benzodiazepines because of difficulties in sleeping at night, as assessed by a detailed psychiatric interview conducted by one of the authors (DM). In addition, all subjects had undergone the following rating scales: the Hamilton Rating Scale for Depression (Hamilton, 1960), the Hamilton Rating Scale for Anxiety (Hamilton, 1959), and the Yale-Brown Obsessive-Compulsive Rating Scale (Goodman et al., 1986), with the results that all total scores fell within the normal range.

All subjects, except for four singles (three women and one man), were indulging in normal and regular sexual activity, as assessed by self-report questionnaires and, during the psychiatric interview, no differences were noted between the romantic lovers and the control subjects.

The women had regular menstrual cycles and were not taking contraceptive pills. Their blood samples were drawn in the early follicular phase (between the third and the fifth day of the menses); the men had no history of genital disease or hypogonadism. All subjects were free of physical illness, were neither heavy cigarette smokers nor belonged to high-risk HIV individuals, and all underwent a general and detailed check-up, carried out by one of the authors (DC).

All gave their informed written consent to their inclusion in the study.

2.2. Hormonal measurements

Venous blood (10 ml) was collected between 8 and 9 a.m. from fasting subjects and centrifuged at low-speed centrifugation (200 × g, for 20 min, at 22°C) to obtain serum which was stored at −20°C until the assays, which were performed within a few days.

The following hormones were evaluated by means of standard techniques in duplicate for each point, by biologists who were blind to each subject's conditions: FSH, LH, estradiol, progesterone (chemiluminescent immuno-assay, CMIA, Architect, Abbott, Abbott Park, USA), dehydroepiandrosterone sulphate (DHEAS) (Spectria, Orion Diagnostic, Essoo, Finland), cortisol (CMIA, DPC, Immulite, Los Angeles, USA), testosterone, and androstenedione (RIA, Testo-CTK, Diasorin Biomedica, Saluggia, Italy).

2.3. Statistics

The differences in hormone levels between subjects of the two sexes who recently had or had not fallen in love were measured by means of the Student t-test (unpaired, two-tailed). The possible effects of the length of the relationship or of the time devoted to thinking about the partner on the hormonal levels were assessed according to Pearson's analysis. All analyses were carried out using the SSPS version 4.0, by means of personal computer programs (StatView V) (Nie et al., 1998).

3. RESULTS

Table 1 shows that cortisol levels (ng/ml) were significantly higher in the subjects who had recently fallen in love, as compared with control subjects (239 ± 39 vs 168 ± 31, $p < 0.001$), with no difference between women and men.

The levels of LH, estradiol, progesterone, DHEAS, and androstenedione did not differ between the groups and were within normal ranges according to the sex and the follicular phase of the women.

On the other hand, testosterone levels (ng/ml) in men who had recently fallen in love were significantly lower than in singles or individuals with a long-lasting relationship (4.1 ± 1.0 vs 6.8 ± 2.1, $p > 0.003$); the results in women were the opposite, that is, higher levels in the women from the first group, as compared with those from the second (1.2 ± 0.4 vs 0.6 ± 0.2, $p < 0.001$).

FSH levels were significantly lower in men who had fallen in love than in those from the control group ($p < 0.0001$).

When the cortisol, testosterone, and FSH levels were re-tested in 16 out of the total of 24 subjects in love, from 12 to 28 months later, no differences from control subject levels were detected. Hormonal measurements were also repeated in 15 out of the total of 24 control subjects after the same time interval, but no significant differences from those of the first assessment were noted (data not shown).

The length of the relationship and the time spent in thinking about the partner did not affect hormonal levels.

Singles or subjects with a long-lasting relationship did not differ in any of the parameters evaluated.

4. DISCUSSION

The main bias of this study is probably represented by the criteria used for selecting the subjects who had fallen in love since, despite our best efforts, no definite indication was available. Since the altered mental state associated with falling in love seems to have a precise time course, with an average duration of between 18 months and 3 years (Tennov, 1979; Marazziti et al., 1999), we chose the length of the relationship as one criterion which, furthermore, can easily be recorded. The other main criterion adopted was the time spent in thinking about the partner which, according to various authors, represents a core feature of this phase (Tesser and Paulhus, 1976; Tennov, 1979; Shea and Adams, 1984). One might perhaps infer that the subjects who are in love suffer from a moderate form of OCD, or have an obsessive-compulsive personality, a positive family history of OCD or even obsessive-compulsive subthreshold symptoms; however, we excluded all these possibilities by means of the psychiatric interview and specific questionnaires. It might also be judged questionable that our hormonal evaluation was performed on a single sample; however, this could represent a bias for LH measurement only, for which a pulsatile pattern is well recognized.

However, in spite of this limitation, our study led to some intriguing and innovative findings, in particular that healthy subjects of both sexes who had recently fallen in love did show some hormonal changes.

The first finding was that the cortisol levels were higher in subjects in love, as compared with those

Table 1

Hormonal Levels in Subjects in the Early Stage of Falling in Love and in Control Subjects

	Subjects in love		Control subjects	
	M	**F**	**M**	**F**
FSH	3.2 ± 1.1^	8.1 ± 4.2	9.3 ± 3.8	9.1 ± 3.1
LH	6.9 ± 2.3	12.3 ± 3.4	7.1 ± 2.8	10 ± 4.3
Estradiol	< 50	170 ± 23	< 50	145 ± 32
Progesterone	< 0.2	0.57 ± 0.3	< 0.2	0.55 ± 0.3
Testosterone	4.1 ± 1.0*	1.2 ± 0.4**	6.8 ± 2.1	0.6 ± 0.2
DHEAS	2736 ± 1122	2232 ± 986	2450 ± 1000	2315 ± 980
Cortisol	224 ± 21°	243 ± 41°°	165 ± 21	172 ± 44
Androstenedione	2.0 ± 1.0	2.1 ± 0.7	2.1 ± 0.7	1.9 ± 0.7

M, male; F, female.
^Significant: $p < 0.0001$; *Significant: $p < 0.003$; **Significant: $p < 0.001$; °Significant: $p < 0.001$;
°°Significant: $p < 0.0001$.

from the control group. This condition of "hyper-cortisolemia" is probably a non-specific indicator of some changes which occur during the early phase of a relationship, reflecting the stressful conditions or arousal associated with the initiation of a social contact which helps to overcome neophobia.* Such conditions appear to be fundamental, as a moderate level of stress has been demonstrated to promote attachment and social contacts in both animals and humans (DeVries et al., 1995, 1996; Hennessy, 1997; Levine et al., 1997; Mendoza and Mason, 1997). In addition, different data indicate an association between HPA activation following stressful experiences and the development of social attachment which, in turn, promotes physiological states which reduce anxiety and related negative sensations (Hinde, 1974; Milgram, 1986; Simpson and Rhole, 1994; Legros, 2001). We observed no difference in cortisol levels between women and men, but this is perhaps not surprising, given indications that they represent rather an unspecific reaction to different triggers.

*neophobia: fear of new things.

On the other hand, while LH, estradiol, progesterone, DHEAS, and androstenedione levels did not differ between men and women, the testosterone concentrations showed some sex-related peculiarities: in both men and women who were at the early stage of a relationship, they were lower and higher, respectively, than those in men and women from the control group. Although none reached pathological levels, all subjects presented this finding, as if falling in love tended temporarily to eliminate some differences between the sexes, or to soften some male features in men and, in parallel, to increase them in women. It is tempting to link the changes in testosterone levels to changes in behaviors, sexual attitudes, or, perhaps, aggressive traits which move in different directions in the two sexes (Zitzmann and Nieschlag, 2001); however, apart from some anecdotal evidence, we have no data substantiating this which would justify further research. Similarly, we have no explanation for the decreased level of FSH in male subjects who were in love, apart from the suggestions that it may represent another marker of hypothalamic involvement in the process of falling in love.

It is noteworthy that when we measured the cortisol, testosterone, and FSH levels for a second time,

12–18 months later, in those 16 (out of the total of 24) subjects who had maintained the same relationship but were no longer in the same mental state to which they had referred during the first assessment and now reported feeling calmer and no longer "obsessed" with the partner, the hormone levels were no different from those of the control group. This finding would suggest that the hormonal changes which we observed are reversible, state-dependent, and probably related to some physical and/or psychological features typically associated with falling in love.

In conclusion, our study would suggest that falling in love represents a "physiological" and transient condition which is characterized (or underlaid) by peculiar hormonal patterns, one of which, involving testosterone, seems to show a sex-related specificity.

Studies are now in progress to establish whether 30 the noted hormonal changes may be related to the modifications of specific behaviors, such as aggression or sexual or attachment attitudes.

ACKNOWLEDGMENTS

We thank Prof. Lucia Grasso and the technical staff of the hormone laboratory of the "Dipartimento di Endocrinologia" of the University of Pisa for performing the hormone assay. We express our gratitude to Prof. Aldo Pinchera and Prof. Enio Martino of the same department for the fruitful discussion during the preparation of the manuscript, and to Dr. Elena Di Nasso from the "Dipartimento di Psichiatria, Neurobiologia, Farmacologia e Biotecnologie," who was helpful in selecting the subjects included in the study.

REFERENCES

Bartels, A., Zeki, S., 2000. The neural basis of romantic love. Neuroreport 11, 3829–3838.

Bowlby, J., 1969. Attachment and Loss. Attachment. vol. 1. Basic Books, New York.

Bowlby, J., 1973. Attachment and Loss. Separation: anxiety and anger. vol. 2. Basic Books, New York.

Carter, C.S., 1998. Neuroendocrine perspectives on social attachment and love. Psychoneuroendocrinol 23, 779–818.

Carter, C.S., DeVries, A.C., Taymans, S.E., 1997a. Peptides, steroids and pair bonding. Ann NY Acad Sci 807, 260–268.

Carter, C.S., Lederhendler, I.I., Kilpatrick, B. (eds.), 1997b. The integrative neurobiology of affiliation. Ann NY Acad Sci 807.

Chiodera, P., Salvarani, C., Bacchi-Modena, A., Spallanzani, R., Cigarini, C., Alboni, A., Gardini, E., Coiro, V., 1991. Relationship between plasma profiles of oxytocin and adrenocorticotropic hormone during suckling or breast stimulation in women. Horm & Res 35, 119–123.

DeVries, A.C., DeVries, M.B., Taymans, S.E., Carter, S.C., 1995. The modulation of pair bonding by corticosteroids in female prairie voles. Proc Natl Acad Sci USA 92, 7744–7748.

DeVries, A.C., DeVries, M.B., Taymans, S.E., Carter, S.C., 1996. The effects of stress on social preferences are sexually dimorphic in prairie voles. Proc Natl Acad Sci USA 93, 11980–11990.

Fisher, H., 1992. Anatomy of Love. Fawcett Columbine, New York.

Goodman, W.K., Price, L.H., Rasmussen, S.A., 1986. The Yale Brown Obsessive-Compulsive Scale I: Development, use and reliability. Arch Gen Psychiatry 46, 1006–1011.

Hamilton, M., 1959. The assessment of anxiety state by rating. Br J Med Psychol 32, 50–55.

Hamilton, M., 1960. A rating scale for depression. J Neurol Neurosurg Psychiatry 23, 56–62.

Hazan, C., Shaver, P., 1987. Romantic love conceptualized as an attachment process. J Personal Soc Psychol 52, 511–524.

Hennessy, M.B., 1997. Hypothalamic-pituitary-adrenal responses to brief social separation. Neur Biobehav Rev 21, 11–29.

Hinde, R.A., 1974. Biological Bases of Human Social Behavior. McGraw-Hill, New York.

Insel, T.R., Young, L.J., 1997. The neurobiology of attachment. Nature Rev 2, 129–136.

Jankoviak, W.R., 1986. A psychobiological theory of love. Psychol Rev 93, 119–130.

Jankoviak, W.R., Fischer, E.F., 1992. A cross-cultural perspective on romantic love. Ethol 31, 149–155.

Kleiman, D., 1977. Monogamy in mammals. Quart Rev Biol 52, 39–69.

Kraemer, G.W., 1992. A psychobiological theory of attachment. Behav Brain Sci 15, 493–520.

Leckman, J.F., Mayes, L.C., 1999. Preoccupations and behaviors associated with romantic and parental love. Perspectives on the origin of obsessive-compulsive disorder. Child & Adol Psychiatry Clin North Am 1, 635–665.

LeDoux, J.E., 2000. Emotion circuits in the brain. Ann Rev Neurosci 2, 155–184.

Legros, J.J., 2001. Inhibitory effects of oxytocin on corticotrope function in humans: are vasopressin and oxytocin ying-yang neurohormones? Psychoneuroendocrinol 26, 649–655.

Levine, S., Lyons, D.M., Schatzberg, A.F., 1997. Psychobiological consequences of social relationships. Ann NY Acad Sci 807, 210–218.

Liebowitz, M.R., 1983. The Chemistry of Love. Little, Brown and Company, Boston.

Marazziti, D., Akiskal, H.S., Rossi, A., Cassano, G.B., 1999. Alteration of the platelet serotonin transporter in romantic love. Psychol Med 29, 741–745.

McCarthy, M.M., Kow, L.M., Pfaff, D.W., 1992. Speculations concerning the physiological significance of central oxytocin in maternal behavior. Ann NY Acad Sci 652, 70–82.

Mendoza, S.P., Mason, W.A., 1997. Attachment relationships in New World primates. Ann NY Acad Sci 807, 203–209.

Milgram, N.A., 1986. Stress and Coping in Time of War: Generalizations from the Israeli Experiences. Brunner Mazel, New York.

Nie, N.H., Hull, C.H., Steinbrenner, K., Bent, D.H., 1998. Statistical Package for the Social Science (SPSS), 4th ed. McGraw-Hill, New York.

Numan, M., 1994. Maternal behavior. In: Knobil, E., Neill, I. (eds.), The Physiology of Reproduction. Raven Press, New York, pp. 221–302.

Panksepp, J., 1982. Toward a psychobiological theory of emotions. Behav Brain Res 5, 407–467.

Panksepp, J., Nelson, E., Silvy, S., 1994. Brain opioids and mother-infant social motivation. Acta Pediatr Suppl 397, 40–46.

Porges, S.W., 1998. Love and emotions. Psychoneuroendocrinol 23, 837–861.

Reite, M., 1985. The Psychobiology of Attachment and Separation. Academic Press, New York.

Shea, J.A., Adams, G.R., 1984. Correlates of romantic attachment: a path analysis study. J Youth Adol 13, 27–31.

Simpson, J.A., Rhole, W.A., 1994. Stress and secure base relationships in adulthood. Adv Pers Relat 5, 181–204.

Tennov, D., 1979. Love and Limerence. The Experience of Being in Love. Stein and Day, New York.

Tesser, A., Paulhus, D.L., 1976. Toward a causal model of love. J Pers & Soc Psychol 34, 1095–1103.

Uvnäs-Moberg, K., 1997. Physiological and endocrine effects of social contact. Ann NY Acad Sci 807, 146–163.

Uvnäs-Moberg, K., 1998. Oxytocin may mediate the benefit of positive social interaction and emotions. Psychoneuroendocrinol 23, 819–835.

Zitzmann, M., Nieschlag, E., 2001. Testosterone levels in healthy men and the relation to behavioural and physical characteristics: facts and constructs. Eur J Endocrinol 144, 183–197.

Reading Questions

1. The study's introduction explicitly establishes the researchers' goals for their study. What are those goals?

2. Based on what criteria do the researchers select study participants for their experimental group—those who had recently fallen in love?

3. Following analysis of blood samples, what statistical procedure is used to compare differences in hormone levels between subjects who had or had not recently fallen in love?

4. What central limitation, or bias, are the researchers concerned with, based on the study's Discussion section?

Rhetoric Questions

5. How does the introduction establish the significance or importance of the researchers' work for their audience?

6. Closely analyze the structure of the study's Discussion section. Based on your analysis, what do you see as the section's organizational logic? In other words, what do you believe the researchers set out to achieve in this section of the study?

7. Identify areas in the study where the researchers first acknowledge and then offer response to the effects of possible limitations to their study's methods or findings. Do these areas strengthen or weaken their report? Explain your response.

8. How does the Acknowledgments section affect the researchers' ethos?

9. The researchers write that falling in love "tended temporarily to eliminate some differences between the sexes, or to soften some male features in men and, in parallel, to increase them in women" (par. 27). Consider a time when you've fallen in love or when you've witnessed what you thought was someone falling in love. Do your experiences support the researchers' conclusion in this instance?

10. Do you have any anecdotal evidence, based on personal experiences, that might support or challenge any of the researchers' central findings? If so, what are they? Explain your answers.

ACADEMIC CASE STUDY • PERSPECTIVES ON LOVE   APPLIED FIELDS

Looking for Love on Craigslist: An Examination of Gender Differences in Self-Marketing Online

CARA O. PETERS, JANE B. THOMAS, AND RICHARD MORRIS

Cara O. Peters is a professor of marketing at Winthrop University in South Carolina. The following study, conducted with her colleagues Jane B. Thomas and Richard Morris, also of Winthrop University, examines differences in the ways men and women represent, or market, themselves online in Craigslist advertisements for relationships. According to the authors, their study provides "unique insight into differences between males and females that can be used when creating marketing messages from a managerial perspective." The article appeared in the *Journal of Marketing Development and Competitiveness* in 2013.

The purpose of this research is to examine the self-marketing occurring among heterosexual men and women who are advertising for a prospective date on the social media site Craigslist. Qualitative and quantitative analysis of 1,200 posts was conducted. The findings offer unique insight into differences between males and females that can be used when creating marketing messages. The results illustrate that language is an imprecise form in how people read and understand the written and spoken word. It is important for marketers to understand the criteria that consumers are searching for and the language that they use in self-marketing.

INTRODUCTION

Those in the popular press have begun to assert that men and women use social media differently.

For example, some have argued that certain social media sites, like Pinterest, are only utilized by women (Conaway, 2013a). Others contend that women, when compared to men, are more likely to use Facebook and other social media to foster and reinforce social connections (Bond, 2009; Joinson, 2008). Furthermore, some researchers have found that women are more likely to have a public Facebook profile, put up more photos of family and friends, frequently update their own profile photos, and post more often about their ongoing activities (Bond, 2009; Strano, 2008). In contrast, recent research reports that women are less likely to report their detailed, personal information (such as phone numbers) on social media sites when compared to men (Conaway,

2013b). While these studies have begun to identify the different ways men and women use social media, they only present part of the picture. There is virtually no examination to date of how men and women present and "market" themselves differently via social media.

Given that studies show men and women use social media differently and the fact that academics have known for quite some time that the two genders communicate differently (cf. Lakoff & Bucholtz, 2004), it seems important for marketers to understand the differences in communication used by males and females in social media and how these language differences assist in the development of an online identity that is packaged and presented to others. Marketers could better communicate with potential target audiences if they had a stronger understanding of the language utilized by the different genders. Moreover, knowing more about gendered language also helps understand online consumer behavior, not only for social media sites (like Pinterest) but also for other websites that are selling goods and services (like eHarmony.com and Match.com).

In both the popular press and among academics, there is a small but growing literature around the idea of "self-marketing" (a.k.a., "personal branding") in which individual consumers carefully construct a personal identity, much like a brand image, that is presented to others (McCaffrey, 1983; Montoya & Vandehey, 2008; Peters, 1997; Shepherd, 2005). "Self-marketing" appears to happen in a variety of contexts, ranging from functional to social reasons, such as in search of employment, promotion, self-expression, social connections (i.e., familial relationships and friendships), and romantic relationships (i.e., dating) (Labrecque, Markos, & Milne, 2011). Furthermore, many assert that much of self-marketing takes place online via social media (Chase, 2011; Elmore, 2010; Greer, 2010; Hearn, 2008; Hyatt, 2010).

As explained in our literature review below, 5 e-dating is the ultimate form of "self-marketing," which presents a unique opportunity to explore differences in the language used by men and women in social media. Self-marketing via Craigslist.com

served as the focus of the current study because this website is one of the most well-known online communities that is public (i.e., no fee required). In the United States alone, more than 50 million people use Craigslist, and the site has 30 billion page views per month (http://www.craigslist.org/about/factsheet). Craigslist provides more than 100 topical forums that contain more than 200 million user postings at any given time. One of Craigslist's topical forums is "personal advertisements." These advertisements are a unique blend of content that mirrors traditional newspaper personal ads with online dating. However, unlike traditional newspaper ads and e-dating websites, personal ads on Craigslist require no fees, no contracts, no limits on text, and provide for more real-time communication between interested individuals. Within these personal ads on Craigslist, individuals are using self-marketing to communicate with prospective partners, who then decide to make connections based on information provided in the online post.

The purpose of this research is to examine the self-marketing occurring among heterosexual men and women who are advertising for a prospective date/partner on the popular social media site Craigslist. The central aim of this study is to review the content of these online ads and then explore how men and women communicate differently as they self-market online. This paper makes a unique contribution to the literature, as research in self-marketing via social media has yet to delve into gender differences. Little is known about how men and women market and present themselves differently via social media sites. Findings from this study also provide insights for understanding gendered language and developing marketing communication for online communities, social media, and other marketing activities. Following is the theoretical foundation, methodology, findings, and discussion.

LITERATURE REVIEW

Schau and Gilly (2003) argue that consumers consciously construct online identities, using a combination of words and pictures. Although they were studying web pages and not social media per se, these authors seem to have planted the early seeds of the online self-marketing literature that is currently growing into a field of study on its own. Although self-marketing has been around for quite some time in the popular press (McCaffrey, 1983; Peters, 1997), the literature has flourished among practitioners (cf. Chase, 2011; Elmore, 2010; Greer, 2010; Hyatt, 2010; Montoya & Vandehey, 2008) and is beginning to take hold among academics as well. From an academic perspective, Shepherd (2005) defines self-marketing as "those activities undertaken by individuals to make themselves known in the market place" (p. 590). Shepherd suggests that individuals are continually reinventing themselves in an effort to remain desirable to others. Lair, Sullivan, and Cheney (2005) similarly describe self-marketing as efforts by individuals to create and position the self as a package that is presented to others. Hearn (2008) also examined self-marketing, although from the perspective of consumer culture theory. She states that in marketing themselves online, people purposefully direct messages outward and this self-production is "narrated, marked by visual codes of mainstream culture industry, and subject to extraction value" (p. 197).

One of the few academic studies of self-marketing to date that actually includes data collection, as opposed to being conceptual in nature, is Labrecque, Markos, and Milne's (2011) examination of twelve individuals' online profiles. These researchers found that individuals purposefully craft and post material on social media to project a personal identity. Through interviews, Labrecque et al. found that most of the informants had a "branding strategy" and were "consciously aware" of what they were posting. The twelve individuals attempted to highlight their positive attributes that they believed were of value to the target audience (and were also ways to differentiate themselves from others). After interviewing the informants, the researchers then conducted "brand audits" of these online profiles, inviting HR professionals and undergraduate students to judge the content of these profiles. The results of these brand audits suggested that at times the audience did not fully comprehend the positioning of the informants and authenticity was often important in posting and interpreting the content of the profiles.

The literature on e-dating suggests that in their efforts to find prospective partners/dates, consumers are practicing self-marketing online. E-dating consists of a set of "activities such as subscribing to a dating website, posting a personal ad, and/or replying to dating messages online" (Close & Zinkhan, 2004, p. 153). The primary means for communicating with others in the e-dating process is via an online personal ad that lists the person's personal data, self-description, and states what they are looking for (Malchow-Moller, 2003). Because these online personal ads communicate what is "valuable" about the person in order to attract prospective partners, several researchers have argued that these online personal ads are self-marketing (Arvidsson, 2006; Coupland, 1996; Patterson & Hodgson, 2006).

Malchow-Moller (2003) found that when posting 10 e-dating personal ads, consumers experience tension as they balance highlighting their positive attributes against presenting their authentic or true selves. While the mediation in e-dating allows for greater control over the presentation of self and can create opportunities for misrepresentation, it also allows for consumers to be more open in the self-disclosure process (Malchow-Moller, 2003). Malchow-Moller (2003) actually found that consumers present themselves how they want to be perceived, as opposed to how they actually are, which could lead to the tension described by Ellison et al. (2006). Another factor that weighs into what consumers post about themselves in the e-dating process is that prospective daters use subtle cues in the posts to make judgments about the content of the post and whether he/she wants to reply to the e-dater (Malchow-Moller, 2003). For example, *Rosen*, Cheever, Cummings, and Felt (2008) found that the amount of emotionality and self-disclosure in the personal ad were key factors that affected a person's perception of a potential e-dating partner. Posts with more emotional language (like *excited* or *wonderful*) had a more positive effect on the reader, but the amount of self-disclosure needed to be more moderate because too much self-disclosure led to negative perceptions.

There is a small but growing literature on gender differences in e-dating personal ads, but these studies tend to focus more on traditional media, as there are only a few that examine gender differences in an online context. Butler-Smith, Cameron, and Collins (1998) examined personal ads from the Sunday newspaper and found that content typically fell along lines of gendered stereotypes. Men more often sought younger partners and offered financial security, when compared to women. Women specified that men must have financial security more frequently than men. These researchers did not find gender differences among a host of other variables, including relationship commitment (i.e., fling versus long term), declared age, divorced, and family status (i.e., children). In a follow-up study, Cameron and Collins (1999) analyzed personal ads from the newspaper and found that women's declaration of wealth and divorced status had a positive impact on the demand for male looks. In other words, when women reported being wealthy, they were more likely to be seeking an attractive male. In addition, Cameron and Collins (1999) found that older women were less likely to require attractiveness in a prospective partner.

Jagger (1998), like Butler-Smith et al. (1988), analyzed newspaper ads and found that the content mirrored gendered stereotypes. Men offered financial status and sought physical attractiveness in prospective partners, while women offered physical attractiveness and sought men with financial resources. However, what was unique to Jagger's study was that she also found that both men and women equally marketed their bodies as a primary selling point. In fact, both genders marketed their bodies more frequently than their other resources. Jagger suggests that this may be the case because lifestyle choices may be displacing financial resources as identity markers for men in today's society. However, despite these findings, more recent studies examining newspaper personal ads have continued to reinforce the assertion that content of personal ads follows typical gender stereotypes. For example, Tither (2000) found

that females were more likely to offer weight and seek financial security, while men were more likely to offer height, stipulate weight, and prefer to date someone younger.

There are a few studies that examine personal ads online. Specifically, Dawson and McIntosh (2006) analyzed Internet dating ads for attractiveness, income, physical attributes, and other positive personal characteristics (i.e., personality, lifestyle, interests). These researchers found that when men stated that they had wealth and were attractive, they were less likely to place emphasis on positive personal characteristics. For women, when they placed emphasis on their physical attractiveness, they too were less likely to emphasize other positive personal characteristics. These findings put a new twist on the previous literature on gender differences in personal advertisements. Simply put, Dawson and McIntosh's findings support the assertion that personal ad content is largely consistent with gender stereotypes (in that men seek physical attractiveness in women and women seek financial resources in men), but their findings also support previous research in that they suggest when these factors are not prominent in the personal advertiser, he/she will then emphasize other positive attributes such as lifestyle, personality, and interests. Interestingly, Gallant, Williams, Fisher, and Cox (2011) analyzed photos posted in e-dating sites and found that, while women emphasized reproductive fitness in their photos, the men's photos did not emphasize the ability to provide resources.

Bond (2009) appears to have provided one of the few studies to date that specifically examines gendered self-marketing on social media. While Bond does not explicitly examine e-dating per se, he surveyed 137 college students with respect to the amount and content of their self-disclosure on social media. Bond found that women, when compared to men, were more likely to include images and information related to friends, family, romantic partners, holidays, school, and alcohol. (The only variable where men disclosed more than women was sports.) The content of the posts was also analyzed for sexual expressiveness, but females were only marginally more sexually expressive when compared to men (i.e., the finding was not statistically significant). While Bond's study was important, it merely proves that there may be differences among men and women in self-marketing via social media. Studies have yet to uncover the specific gender differences that exist when women and men self-market via social media. Toward that end, the methodology is presented next.

METHODOLOGY

Craigslist.org was selected for data collection because it is one of the most popular self-advertising websites in the world. This online community is the 15th most viewed site on the Internet in the United States (http://www.craigslist.org/about/factsheet). Craigslist's platform does not require a set time a posting has to be up, which gives users the ability to post whenever they want, leave it up for an extended time, and take it down when needed. This site does not require consumers to use a template when creating an advertisement. This provides users more freedom of self-expression than traditional e-dating sites, which require fees and use of an existing template. Thus, Craigslist.com was chosen for the current study since self-expression was less restrictive.

The sampling process utilized methods employed by Kroft and Pope (2008) in their research on the matching efficiency for job and apartment postings on Craigslist and Thomas, Peters, and Tolson (2007) in their research on Myspace.com. To obtain the sample data from Craigslist.org, the United States was divided into six different regions (Northeast, Southeast, etc.) and the two cities with the largest number of posts were selected from each region. Table 1 presents a summary of the sampling process. It should be noted that the cities with the largest number of posts also had substantial population bases, allowing for greater diversity among those who posted. Data was selected from the Craigslist "personal advertisements" section. The personal advertisements section had eight sub-categories: strictly platonic, women seeking women, women seeking men, men seeking women, men seeking men, miscellaneous romance, casual encounters, and missed connections. Because this study focused on differences between heterosexual men and women, data were drawn from two of the eight sub-categories, women seeking men and men seeking women. For each selected city, the first fifty posts within these two sub-categories were extracted and saved as a Word document. This resulted in a total of 1,200 posts in the data set.

Table 1

Sampling Process

Region	Cities with largest number of posts	Categories selected*
Southeast	Jacksonville	Men seeking women
	Memphis	Women seeking men
Upper Midwest	Chicago	Men seeking women
	Milwaukee	Women seeking men
Northeast	New York City	Men seeking women
	Philadelphia	Women seeking men
Southwest	Los Angeles	Men seeking women
	Phoenix	Women seeking men
Lower Midwest	Houston	Men seeking women
	San Antonio	Women seeking men
Northwest	Portland	Men seeking women
	Seattle	Women seeking men

*The first fifty posts were selected from each of these categories.

A two-step process was used to examine the self-marketing occurring among men and women on Craigslist. This two-step approach provided a more holistic view of the data and clearer insights into how men and women differ in regards to gender and self-marketing. Categories from the data were first explored from a heterosexual cohort viewpoint (i.e., the two categories men seeking women and women seeking men were analyzed for common themes). This process was then followed by examination of the differences by gender (i.e., men seeking women and women seeking men were separated and compared).

For the first phase of the study, content analysis was selected as the method for analyzing the 1,200 posts because it provides a well-accepted, objective, systematic, and scientific process for analyzing communication (Kassarjian, 1977, pp. 8–9). Each of the two authors participating in the study (who are trained, qualitative researchers) printed hard copies of data. Utilizing the transcripts, the authors then followed an emergent coding process as described by Stemler (2001). To identify the categories for classification, the two authors independently reviewed the transcripts, noting the general categories of content as they read through the data. The authors then met and shared their independent classification schemes. After discussing the commonalities and differences in the classification schemes, the authors identified a set of common categories for purposes of classification. After independently returning to transcripts and coding each of the individual posts until all the data had been accounted (Stemler, 2001), the authors got back together and shared their independent coding of the data. Inter-rater reliability was computed using the number of agreements divided by the total number of observations (Hartman, 2006). The authors had 98.4% agreement and discrepancies were reviewed and resolved via debate and discussion. The frequency of occurrence for each category is reported in Table 2. In addition to tabulating the frequency of occurrence, each category of data was interpreted for its specific meaning. Finally, exemplary verbatim quotes were drawn from the data to be incorporated into the interpretation presented in the findings.

For the second phase of the study, the authors conducted a quantitative analysis comparing the frequency of occurrence by gender. The frequency and percentage of each category and subtopic of discussion was calculated for men and then women. This step was followed with a Chi-square test of the proportions to uncover statistically significant differences in the topics discussed by men and women. Table 3 presents the frequency and percentage of occurrence by gender. Because of the exploratory nature of the study, the authors utilized the 2-tailed p-value when interpreting the significance of the z-scores (i.e., $p \leq .05$ was used as the significance level).

FINDINGS

The categories that emerged from the data and the analysis of differences by gender are presented together in order to provide for a comprehensive understanding of the themes utilized in self-marketing and also allow for a parceling out of the differences that may exist between the self-marketing of men and women. Furthermore, this approach also provides a clearer understanding of how marketers and advertisers can use these findings when marketing to men and women. Four general categories emerged from the data: types of interaction, criteria for partner, self-disclosure, and tone (see Table 2). Within each of these general categories there was a subset of four to seven items that comprised the category. It should be noted that the total number of responses for these four categories was much greater than 1,200 (i.e., the total number of posts selected for the sample) because more than one category could have been represented in a given post. In other words, a consumer's post could contain information that fell into more than one category. In addition, Craigslist provides the consumer with a number when posting on the site and thus all data was treated anonymously and no identifying markers (such as name or email address) are reported below.

Types of Interaction

Data included in this category provide insight into what a person is seeking from the relationship. When reading the posts, it appeared that many of the participants specified the type of interaction that they were

Table 2
Content of the Ads

	Frequency	Percentage
1. Types of Interaction		
a. Kinky	53	0.0654085
b. Sex	71	0.088476
c. Dating (Friend to More)	282	0.3644395
d. LTR (Long-Term Relationship)	141	0.1848945
e. Friend/New to Area/Bored	117	0.149766
f. Other	114	0.1470145
Sub-total:	778	
2. Criteria for Partner		
a. Relationship Status	113	0.1402915
b. STD-Free/Drug-Free	83	0.106293
c. Demographics (Race, Religion, Employed)	193	0.2442595
d. Physical Characteristics (Age, Weight, Height)	374	0.509156
Sub-total:	763	
3. Self-Disclosure		
a. Physical Characteristics (Age, Weight, Height)	492	0.2754425
b. Personality (Shy, Outgoing)	279	0.1558555
c. Hobbies/Interests	332	0.185488
d. Sex Life (Desire)	40	0.0224245
e. Family Structure (Divorced, Kids, Pets)	205	0.11458
f. Demographics (Race, Religion, Professional, Employed)	328	0.1834985
g. Non-Smoking/Disease-Free/Non-Drinking/Drug-Free	112	0.06271
Sub-total:	1788	
4. Tone		
a. Sales Pitch	30	0.0652505
b. Wordy	72	0.156796
c. Honesty (Real/Not Real)	101	0.2196915
d. Picture for Picture	258	0.558262
Sub-total:	461	
Total:	3697	

Table 3

Gender Differences in Self-Marketing by Category

	Frequency (%)			2-tailed
	Women	Men	z-score	p-value
1. Types of Interaction				
a. Kinky	9 (0.025)	44 (0.106)	−4.486	0.000*
b. Sex	17 (0.047)	54 (0.130)	−4.025	0.000*
c. Dating (Friend to More)	143 (0.394)	139 (0.335)	1.708	0.087
d. LTR	87 (0.240)	54 (0.130)	3.957	0.000*
e. Friend/New to Area/Bored	51 (0.140)	66 (0.159)	−0.722	0.472
f. Other	56 (0.154)	58 (0.140)	0.571	0.569
2. Criteria for Partner				
a. Relationship Status	82 (0.169)	31 (0.112)	2.154	0.032*
b. STD-Free/Drug-Free	56 (0.115)	27 (0.097)	0.783	0.435
c. Demographics (Race, Religion, Employed)	134 (0.276)	59 (0.212)	1.959	0.050*
d. Physical Characteristics (Age, Weight, Height)	213 (0.439)	161 (0.579)	−3.722	0.000*
3. Self-Disclosure				
a. Physical Characteristics (Age, Weight, Height)	211 (0.234)	281 (0.316)	−3.882	0.000*
b. Personality (Shy, Outgoing)	165 (0.183)	114 (0.128)	3.202	0.001*
c. Hobbies/Interests	193 (0.214)	139 (0.157)	3.149	0.002*
d. Sex Life (Desire)	13 (0.014)	27 (0.030)	−2.282	0.023*
e. Family Structure (Divorced, Kids, Pets)	113 (0.126)	92 (0.104)	1.457	0.144
f. Demographics (Race, Religion, Professional, Employed)	158 (0.176)	170 (0.191)	−0.868	0.384
g. Non-Smoking/Disease-Free/ Non-Drinking/Drug-Free (vice versa)	47 (0.052)	65 (0.073)	−1.830	0.067
4. Tone				
a. Sales Pitch	14 (0.059)	31 (0.138)	−2.868	0.004*
b. Wordy	32 (0.135)	27 (0.121)	0.465	0.638
c. Honesty (Real/Not Real)	47 (0.198)	59 (0.263)	−1.660	0.097
d. Picture for Picture	144 (0.608)	161 (0.719)	−2.521	0.012*

*p ≤ .05 significance level

seeking. The types of interaction sought represented a range of sexual to non-sexual interactions, including kinky, sex, dating, long-term relationship (LTR), friend, and other (see Table 2). While a small number of the posts contained lewd comments, most of the content reflected posters who were seeking those types of interactions that would commonly occur in traditional, offline dating situations.

The most frequently mentioned type of interaction was dating (n = 282, 36%) and the least frequent type of interaction discussed was kinky (n = 53, 6%). Dating involved individuals stating that they were looking for someone to start out as friends, go out on a few dates (like to lunch or the theater), with the idea that the relationship could potentially turn into a romantic [one] if both parties agree. The second most frequently discussed type of interaction was long-term relationship (n = 141, 18%). In contrast to dating, which was based more on friendship with the potential (but no expectation of) a relationship, the long-term relationship posters clearly stated that they were looking for an exclusive, committed relationship for an extended period of time. For example, a woman in New York City wrote an advertisement that began with a description of her physical appearance and a clear statement that she is seeking a long-term relationship.

> I am a very attractive full-figured Black and Puerto Rican woman. I am very voluptuous with a great shape. I work out so I am getting my body tight. I have body and face shots as well. I have no children, crazy ex-boyfriends, or stalkers in my life. I am college educated with a great career. I love sports, including WWE wrestling (yes I know it is fake). I love going dancing because I am a good dancer. I like going to museums especially art museums. I like going away on vacations even though the restrictions for flying are a bit tedious. I like playing video games and just staying home to relax. I work very hard and sometimes I have to travel for business so if you can be understanding about my career, then we will have no problems. I will make every effort to make for a relationship. I have a good career, however no one special in my life. Race is not important. I am not looking for someone over forty-five. Please be employed, attractive, and looking to be in a relationship. I am not interested in men with children. I have no children so I am seeking someone with no children as well. I don't smoke so please be a non-smoker as well. I like to laugh and have a good time. If you are seeking someone who has no drama and wants to be in a committed relationship, then please respond back. Take care!

In contrast to dating or long-term relationship posts, the friend types of interactions (n = 117, 15%) consisted of someone who was bored or lonely (many of which were new to the area) and were looking for platonic relationships. This man from San Antonio, who is new to the area, creates a short post that clearly explains what he wants.

> I have a good job and am self sustaining. I just moved to the San Antonio area for my job and would love to get to know the area. I hear there is much to see, I only need someone to see it with. I would like you to have a job as well.

The least-discussed types of interaction were sexual (n = 71, 9%) and kinky (n = 53, 6%) interactions. These types of interactions sought consisted of one-night stands where the poster is asking someone to fulfill his/her sexual or physical fantasies, with little expectation of a friendship or long-term relationship coming from the interaction. Sexual posts merely stated that the person was looking for sex, while kinky posts stated that the person was looking for a more erotic type of physical interaction (like sexual fetishes). For example, the following post from a man in Chicago is written similar to a job description. In this post he describes the type of woman he is seeking for this "full time position."

> Am accepting applications and reviewing resumes for the full time position with extreme benefits for a sexy young lady to play the role of "Spoiled Sex Princess." As Hiring Manager, I require that you submit the following documentation: 1. Resume, 2. Photograph (Clothing is optional; extra bonus points for lingerie shots), 3. Work Experience, 4. Talents. The hiring manager (who just happens to be the person you will be reporting to) is an upper managerial type, advanced degreed with stylish wavy hair, hazel eyes, smart, intelligent, passionate, romantic with stylish clothes, stylish shoes, smart, sensual and very sexual. Duties include, but not limited to, serious role playing so a flair for the dramatic will be handy. "Boss after work with sexy Secretary." "Teacher keeping Naughty Girl After School for Discipline," and my personal favorite—"Catholic School Girl Gone Bad." Physically, must be able to withstand extended sessions of foreplay. Serious spoiling, pampering and pleasing available. Whatever your beautiful heart desires . . . within reason. Lingerie showings are on the itinerary as well as mutually pleasurable "oral activities." Physically must be able to withstand extended sessions of foreplay and be able to simulate a variety of different positions for the extreme sessions of

intercourse. For the intelligent, open minded, college educated and extremely sexual young woman only. Serious Inquiries from seriously sexually advanced women only.

With respect to differences in the types of interactions sought, the analysis did reveal some statistically significant differences by gender (see Table 3). Men (n = 54, 13%) were more likely to state that they were interested in sex when compared to women (n = 17, 4%). Moreover, men (n = 44, 11%) were more likely to be seeking kinky interactions than women (n = 9, 2%). However, women (n = 87, 24%) were more likely to be seeking a long-term relationship, when compared to men (n = 54, 13%). These findings suggest that men seem to seek out more one-time, sexual encounters while women may be seeking more long-term, committed relationships, which is consistent with previous research (Dawson & McIntosh, 2006; Gallant et al., 2011). From a marketing perspective, this finding suggests that men and women utilize somewhat traditional norms (i.e., men seek sex and women seek relationships) when specifying what they want from e-dating on Craigslist.

Criteria for a Partner

The criteria for a partner category was defined as the characteristics that are required for a potential date/partner to be considered suitable. Four criteria were identified in the data: physical characteristics, demographics, relationship status, and drug/sexually transmitted disease (STD; see Table 2). The most frequently discussed criteria for a prospective partner was preferred physical characteristics. More than half of the posts clearly articulated preferences for the physical characteristics of a partner, including age, weight, and height (n = 374, 51%). For example, a female from San Antonio not only describes her criteria for a partner, but also comments that she offers a complete package to a potential suitor.

> Yes, like most other women, I am looking for the whole package, but I feel that I can because I offer the whole package in return :) I want someone who is attractive, smart, funny, great personality, responsible/ mature, up for random fun and who is open to a more serious relationship if things worked out well between

the two of us. I must admit I'm not looking to be someone's hook-up or casual friend. Taller than 5'7", average body type or better, somewhere between 25 and 35, race is of no issue to me — I've dated across the board. Also, I don't have children and would prefer that you don't as well.

The second most frequently discussed topic related to criteria for a partner was related to demographics, such as race, religion, and professional status (*n* = 193, 24%, Table 2). The following post from a 35-year-old male musician in Houston, Texas, demonstrates how self-marketing is used when describing the criteria for a partner.

> I am looking for a 24 to 43, fit, non-smoker, not yet spoiled, able to have fun and be happy no matter what the event is, educated with employable skills. You should like: music (including hard rock), kids, cats, good conversation, motorcycles, going out for dinner and drinks, concerts.

Less frequently discussed criteria for a partner included preferred relationship status (n = 113, 14%) and drug/alcohol/STD-free status (n = 83, 11%). For some posters it was important that they state up front that they were looking for someone to date who was not already in an existing relationship or married. In addition, a minority of the posts also clearly articulated that a person who answers the ad must not have a sexually transmitted disease or any issues with alcohol and drugs.

With respect to statistically significant gender differences (see Table 3), women (n = 213, 44%) tended to specify preferred physical characteristics when compared to men (n = 161, 58%). This difference could be attributed to the absence of a face-to-face encounter, but the lack of interpersonal interaction exists for both genders. To the extent that gender is a contributing factor, the results are counter-intuitive when compared to previous research on personal ads. Past research on personal ads in newspapers suggests that men are more likely to specify preferred physical characteristics when compared to women (Jagger, 1998; Tither, 2000). The findings of the present study are different in the context of self-marketing on Craigslist.

In addition, when compared to men (n = 59, 21%), women were more likely to create personal advertisements that specified preferences on demographics (n = 134, 28%). In contrast to the findings on pre-ferred physical characteristics, the finding on demo-graphics is consistent with previous research on personal ads in newspapers. Research on personal ads in newspapers found women, who are seeking resources, are likely to prefer partners that are pro-fessional and employed in contrast to men (But-ler-Smith et al., 1998; Dawson & McIntosh, 2006; Gallant et al., 2011; Jagger, 1998).

Finally, the data also suggest that women (n = 82, 17%) were more likely to specify the pre-ferred relationship status of a prospective partner when compared to men (n = 31, 11%). This finding is consistent with the literature on e-dating as some studies have found that authenticity can be an issue in this context. Men, more often than women, misreport their relationship status (i.e., claim they are single when actually married) when participating in online dating activity (Close & Zinkhan, 2004).

Self-Disclosure

Self-disclosure is the essence of self-marketing. It is through the process of self-disclosure that partici-pants in the Craigslist personal ads revealed as much or as little as they wanted the other person to know about themselves. Furthermore, self-disclosure is required to establish trust and mutual understand-ing in interpersonal relationships (Derlega, 1979; Ellison et al., 2006). Seven key pieces of personal information were revealed in the data: physical char-acteristics, personality, hobbies/interests, desire for a sex life, family structure, demographics, and smoker/drug-free/disease-free (see Table 2). Consumers uti-lized these seven pieces of information to carefully construct an image of themselves for a prospective dater.

Individuals most frequently offered information about their physical characteristics (n = 492, 27%), hobbies/interests (n = 332, 19%), and demographics (n = 328, 18%). Personality (n = 279, 16%) charac-teristics and family structure (n = 205, 11%) were also disclosed frequently in the posts. And while discussed less frequently, non-smoking/drug-free/disease-free (n = 112, 6%) and desire for a sex life (n = 40, 2%)

were also present in the data. The following post from a woman in Chicago illustrates how she discloses her physical characteristics and hobbies/interests.

> More about me—Height/Weight proportionate, 5′3, 110 lbs., blue eyes, brown hair, I'm spiritual but not religious. I enjoy reading, watching movies, hanging out, dining out, drinking, live music, dance clubbing, com-muning with nature, going on impulsive adventures, and just walking the beach can be a work out.

It is interesting that while individuals were seek-ing partners that met specific criteria (see criteria for partner above), they were also not afraid to disclose their personal information. This finding was not nec-essarily surprising because, in some ways, e-dating allows individuals a forum for less inhibited self-expression when compared to face-to-face commu-nication (Malchow-Moller, 2003; Rosen et al., 2008).

At the same time, authenticity is important, and individuals often project their ideal (as opposed to actual selves) online (Close & Zinkhan, 2004; Malchow-Moller, 2003). Consumers, after all, are self-marketing in looking for a prospective date on Craigslist. Individuals seeking online for a date or part-ner understand the importance of these personal facts and use this information to help them form a complete image of the other person. Similar to how consumer brands are recognized by their trademark, self-market-ing provides cues such as physical characteristics and hobbies that are used to help others determine whether or not the person is a fit for them (Arvidsson, 2006; Hearn, 2008; Patterson & Hodgson, 2006). It could be that much of what consumers put in the posts was in response to what they see in preferred criteria for a partner. This may be why consumers self-disclosed on items like family structure, being drug/disease-free, and their desire for a sex life, as shown in the example below from a woman in Memphis.

> I am a single parent of one and am really frustrated right now because I don't have any friends who I can call on in my time of need. I have been single for 4 yrs. Men seem to play so many games and that has led me to Craigslist. I'm sexy, smart, independent, fun, have paperwork to prove I'm STD FREE and still that's not enough I guess. I am not trying to get over on anyone but I am really

frustrated right now due to some recent circumstances that may lead to some bad things that I need someone to help me avoid. We can talk about the specific things later. I have my own apt, car, and job but it's still a strain especially when you don't have anyone to have your back and vice versa. I really would like to just meet a knight in shining armor to take away some of my stress that may need a good girl to cook, clean, or be there for them as a companion and see where things go. I'm tired of stressing and would love to just be happy for a while to just enjoy someone but that's not the case. I am serious about life especially since I have a son to raise alone so please ONLY the mature and sincere apply.

The data analysis revealed gender differences in four of the seven items that comprised the self-disclosure category (see Table 3). Men were more likely to reveal information about their physical characteristics (n = 281, 32%), when compared to women (n = 211, 23%). This finding is somewhat counter-intuitive in light of previous research on newspaper personal ads. Previous research by Jagger (1998), Dawson & McIntosh (2006), and Gallant et al. (2011) suggests women would be more likely to advertise their physical characteristics. However, men (n = 27, 3%) were also more likely to self-disclose their preferences for a certain type of sex life than women (n = 13, 1%), which is somewhat consistent with sexual strategies theory (Dawson & McIntosh, 2006; Gallant et al., 2011). It is interesting that while women were less likely to disclose their physical characteristics and sex life preferences, they were more likely to describe their personality (n = 165, 18%) and hobbies/interests (n = 193, 21%) in their self-marketing, when compared to men (n = 114, 13%; and n = 139, 16%, respectively). Thus, gender differences do appear to exist in self-marketing related to utilizing personality and hobbies/interests in attempting to attract a prospective date.

Tone

The tone of the personal ad conveyed the overall feeling and approach that the individual was using for the self-marketing. The tone of the post is important because the language selected for use in the post becomes the subtle cues utilized by others in judging the content (Rosen et al., 2008). If the post is deemed too wordy or the individual is believed to be dishonest, her personal advertisement may be ignored. Four sub-categories were identified related to the tone: sales pitch, wordy, honesty, and picture for picture (see Table 2).

Picture for picture (n = 258, 56%) and honesty (i.e., "Keeping things real") (n = 101, 22%) were the most frequent tone utilized in the ads. These findings are supported by previous research that says authenticity can be important in e-dating (Close & Zinkhan, 2004). Because of the mediated nature of e-dating, there is a tendency for the consumer to not always be completely accurate in his/her post and may tend to project their ideal (as opposed to real) self (Malchow-Moller, 2003). The tone of the ads asking for honesty and asking to exchange current photos suggests that the posters want to be forthright and are looking for frank information in return. This post from a woman in Jacksonville illustrates the importance of honesty.

> Keep it real and no one gets hurt. Just be yourself unless you're one of "those kind of guys." A façade living out a charade. Then umm yea; buh-bye.

The other tones that appeared to emerge from the data were extreme wordiness (n = 72, 16%) and a sales pitch (n = 30, 7%). The wordiness could have been the fact that the poster did not plan out his/her advertisement and, instead, wrote the ad in a "stream of consciousness." Furthermore, wordiness could also have been due to the fact that he/she was nervous and unsure exactly what to post, so he/she put down everything that came to mind when typing up the ad. Although less frequent, there were also ads that had a tone that appeared to mirror a sales pitch for a consumer good. This man from Chicago utilized a sales tone.

> I am a masculine, yet boyish, sexy American white boy. 34, that's me in the body, blond hair, hazel eyes, and super smooth with a great body. Discreet, personable, sane, healthy, d/d free. Looking for an attractive woman, and most importantly, someone with a good attitude and an open mind. Contact me for more. Yes the ad is real!!!!!!! . . . Lastly—no hassles, no drama, no b/s, no attitudes, and no wasting of each other's time.

Utilizing a tone with a sales pitch when writing a [40] personal ad suggests that the consumer realizes that the post for a date is truly a form of self-marketing, where the poster is trying to attract a potential partner into the exchange, as suggested by previous research (Arvidsson, 2006; Patterson & Hodgson, 2006).

When examining gender differences by the type of tone, the data also suggested differences exist among men versus women. While there was no difference on the two genders with respect to preference for honesty and wordiness, men were more likely than women to request a picture for a picture (n = 31, 14% for men; n = 14, 6% for women) and to utilize the sales pitch (n = 171, 72% for men; n = 144, 61% for women) in their self-marketing. Men asking for a current photo is consistent with previous research. Close and Zinkhan (2004) found that authenticity can be an issue in e-dating. While men tend to misreport their relationship status (i.e., they say that they are single when really married), women tend to misrepresent their age and weight. If they share a photo, it can even be from many years ago (Close & Zinkhan, 2004). To the extent this is a common occurrence in the context of e-dating, men may be more likely to request an updated photo from women, as found in the data from the present study.

DISCUSSION

The findings from this study reinforce some of what is already known in the e-dating and personal ads literature. And yet, some of the findings are innovative, making a contribution to both of these literatures, as well as the literature on self-marketing. In fact, no study to date has examined gender differences in self-marketing. The present study not only extends the literature on e-dating and personal ads, but it also unpacks how men and women market themselves differently in the context of personal ads on Craigslist.

To begin, the results of this study support some of the existing findings in previous research on e-dating. Specifically, this study suggests that authenticity in the context of e-dating is an issue for both men and women. There was no difference in gender with respect to honesty (i.e., "keep it real"). However, in our sample, women were more likely to state a preferred relationship status for a prospective dater when compared to men. This is a significant finding related to authenticity because previous research has indicated men are more likely (than women) to misreport being involved in a relationship when participating in e-dating (Close & Zinkhan, 2004). Similarly, the present study found that men were more likely to articulate that they wanted to exchange photos with a prospective dater when compared to the women in the sample. This also reinforces existing findings by Close and Zinkhan (2004), who found women were more likely to share old photos and not disclose current age and weight when interacting with a prospective e-dater.

The results of this study also reinforce existing findings in the literature on personal ads. This study's findings show that much of the content of online personal ads in the context of Craigslist is based on traditional gender stereotypes, such as men want sex and women are seeking long-term relationships. Furthermore, the findings also show that women, when compared to men, are more likely to state preferred demographics (such as employment status) in their online personal ads. This finding also suggests that women are seeking men that can provide resources, as suggested by previous research.

And yet, this study's findings also make some [45] novel contributions to the literature on personal ads and e-dating. For example, the content of the Craigslist ads showed a range of types of relationships sought. Not all interactions sought were romantic in nature, nor were they all based on the idea of an extended relationship. Some relationships sought were more platonic in nature (i.e., new to the area and looking for a friend) and others were more one-time, discrete interactions (i.e., a one-night stand). In addition, criteria for a partner, such as relationship status and being disease/drug-free, are new to the literature on personal ads. It is possible that these things have always been important to dating via personal ads, but the free-form and unlimited space available on Craigslist could have brought these issues to the forefront of the advertising content.

This study also makes a contribution to the literature on self-marketing in that it begins to unpack gender differences that exist as consumers begin to market and brand themselves online. One interesting finding from this study was that men utilized a tone of a sales pitch more often than women. Why this is the case has yet to be determined. Do men view e-dating more as a form of self-marketing than women? Or are men more comfortable selling and marketing themselves than women? Clearly, this gender difference merits future research. Other gender differences that occurred in self-marketing included that men pitched more of their physical characteristics in the ads, while women pitched more of their personality characteristics and hobbies/interests. Again, this was a counter-intuitive finding in that sexual strategies theory suggests that women should want to sell their physical characteristics (in order to attract more prospective partners), while men should want to sell their ability to produce resources (i.e., their demographics). This was not the case in the data. Future research needs to unpack these gender differences to determine the extent to which consumers plan out what kind of content they build into a personal ad in order to maximize their chance at obtaining a potential date. Finally, the results of this study also showed that women were more likely than men to specify preferred physical characteristics of prospective partners. This finding also suggests that future studies are needed to understand why, given that men want to attract fertile females, women are more likely to specify what they want with respect to the physical attractiveness of a man.

The findings of this study also offer unique insight into differences between males and females that can be used when creating marketing messages from a managerial perspective. In advertising consumer products, crafting the right message and using the right person to deliver the message is crucial for the success of the campaign. The present study suggests that the same premises are true in self-marketing on Craigslist. Online dating is replete with obvious marketing tactics where the presentation of the self is consciously sales oriented. The types of interaction, criteria for partner, self-disclosure, and tone of the post suggest that online

self-marketing is carefully constructed and communicated. Thus, the findings of this study provide insight into how gendered identities are constructed, which is insightful for those creating marketing messages. For example, consumers often try a product because they like the package and/or remember a slogan or brand message. In much the same way, when online self-marketing is effective, an individual might connect with someone whose post matches his/her personal views. Thus, it is important when creating marketing messages to understand what types of messages would appeal to the target market. Should the message be about building a relationship with the consumer or about benefits offered by the product? What selection criteria are important to members of the target market? Is the criteria more fact based (i.e., like demographics) or is it related to emotions? Finally, how should the marketing message be constructed? Answers to these questions can assist marketers in crafting a message and improving positioning of brands. And answers to these types of questions should also be studied among consumers who are self-marketing online as well.

Another interesting implication of this study is that the Internet is an important space for finding and exhibiting one's self because it is free from the immediate bias often present in face-to-face communication (McKenna and Bargh, 2000). According to Arvidsson (2006), Internet dating sites are the perfect branding tool where communication and interaction are based on the brand image (i.e., self-marketing) that is created and accepted. Marketers are encountering an untapped resource with social media tools, like Craigslist. Information from online communities represents an important source of marketing information that can be acquired at minimal cost. Our findings illuminate opportunities for marketers to expand their understanding of how the genders self-market and what they are looking for in heterosexual relationships. Not only is this information useful for a host of online dating companies (like eHarmony.com), but it is also relevant for media companies (like VH1, Cosmopolitan, Playboy, Facebook) and consumer product companies, like fashion designers (i.e., Abercrombie & Fitch), beauty products (i.e., Calvin

Klein), and other product categories that are marketed via appeals to identity and sex.

Finally, the results of this study also illustrate that language is an imprecise form in how people read and understand the written and spoken word. It is important for marketers, especially advertisers, to understand the criteria that consumers are searching for and the language that they use to describe the criterion. In the case of self-marketing via Craigslist, words are used to motivate another person to get in touch with the poster in the hope that the first encounter (i.e., an e-mail hopefully followed by a face-to-face meeting) will lead to something more. The same scenario happens in advertising. The advertising message is carefully crafted to encourage the consumer to desire an experience with the product. The message is a strategic combination of words and sometimes pictures that provide a reason to believe. And yet, no matter how right the copywriter "gets" the words, it is the picture that may often seal the deal. In Craigslist, a thoughtfully crafted personal ad may attract someone's attention, but it might be a picture-for-a-picture exchange that generates the next level of interest.

REFERENCES

Arvidsson, A. (2006). "Quality singles": Internet dating and the work of fantasy. *New Media and Society, 8*(4), 671–690.

Bond, B. J. (2009). He posted, she posted: Gender differences in self-disclosure on social network sites. *Rocky Mountain Communication Review, 6*(2), 29–37.

Butler-Smith, P., Cameron, S., & Collins, A. (1998). Gender differences in mate search effort: An exploratory economic analysis of personal advertisements. *Applied Economics, 30*(10), 1277–1285.

Cameron, S., & Collins, A. (1999). Looks unimportant? A demand function for male attractiveness by female personal advertisers. *Applied Economics Letters, 6*(6), 381.

Chase, L. (2011). The power of personal branding. *American Salesman, 56*(6), 7.

Close, A., & Zinkhan, G. M. (2004). Romance and the Internet: The e-mergence of e-dating. *Advances in Consumer Research, 31*, 153–157.

Conaway, C. (2013a). Are men more risky with social media? May 1. Retrieved from http://goodmenproject.com/good-feed-blog/are-men-more-risky-with-social-media/

Conaway, C. (2013b). Pinterest is for girls, Gentlemint is for boys, February 26. Retrieved from http://cameronconaway.com/pinterest-is-for-girls-gentlemint-is-for-boys/

Coupland J. (1996). Dating advertisements: Discourses of the commodified self. *Discourse & Society, 7*(2), 187–207.

Dawson, B., & McIntosh, W. D. (2006). Sexual strategies theory and Internet personal advertisements. *Cyberpsychology & Behavior, 9*(5), 614–617.

Derlega, V. (1979). Appropriateness of self-disclosure. In Gordon J. Chelune (Ed.), *Self-disclosure: Origins, patterns, and implications of openness in interpersonal relationships* (pp. 151–176). San Francisco: Jossey-Bass.

Ellison, N., Heino, R., & Gibbs, J. (2006). Managing impressions online: Self-presentation processes in the online dating environment. *Journal of Computer-Mediated Communication, 11*(2), 415–441.

Elmore, L. (2010). Personal branding 2.0. *Women in Business, 62*(1), 12.

Gallant, S., Williams, L., Fisher, M., & Cox, A. (2011). Mating strategies and self-presentation in online personal advertisement photographs. *Journal of Social, Evolutionary, and Cultural Psychology, 5*(1), 106–121.

Greer, J. (2010). The art of self-marketing online. *U.S. News & World Report, 147*(5), 30.

Hartman, K. (2006). Television and movie representations of salespeople: Beyond Willy Loman. *Journal of Personal Selling & Sales Management, 26*(3), 283–292.

Hearn, A. (2008). "Meat, mask, burden": Probing the contours of the branded self. *Journal of Consumer Culture, 8*(2), 197–217.

Hyatt, J. (2010). Building your brand (and keeping your job). *Fortune, 162*(3), 70–76.

Jagger, E. (1998). Marketing the self, buying another: Dating in a postmodern, consumer society. *Sociology, 32*(4), 795–814.

Joinson, A. N. (2008). Looking at, looking up, or keeping up with people? Motives and uses of Facebook. *CHI 2008 Proceedings*, 1027–1036.

Kassarjian, H. H. (1977). Content analysis in consumer research. *Journal of Consumer Research, 4*(1), 8–18.

Kroft, K., & Pope, D. (2008). *Does online search crowd out traditional search and improve matching efficiency? Evidence from Craigslist.* Working paper.

Labrecque, L. I., Markos, E., & Milne, G. R. (2011). Online personal branding: Processes, challenges, and implications. *Journal of Interactive Marketing, 25*(1), 37–50.

Lair, D., Sullivan, K., & Cheney, G. (2005). Marketization and the recasting of the professional self: The rhetoric and ethics of personal branding. *Management Communications Quarterly, 18*(3), 307–343.

Lakoff, R. T., & Bucholtz, M. (2004). *Language and woman's place: Text and commentaries.* New York, NY: Oxford University Press.

Malchow-Moller, A. (2003). Internet dating. A focus group investigation of young Danes' and Frenchmen's attitudes towards the phenomenon. *Kontur, 7*, 11–20.

McCaffrey, M. (1983). *Personal marketing strategies: How to sell yourself, your ideas, & your services.* Englewood Cliffs, NJ: Prentice Hall.

McKenna, K. A., & Bargh, J. A. (2000). Plan 9 from cyberspace: The implication of the Internet for personality and social psychology. *Personality & Social Psychology Review* (Lawrence Erlbaum Associates), 4(1), 57–75.

Montoya, P., & Vandehey, T. (2008). *The brand called you: Create a personal brand that wins attention and grows your business.* New York, NY: McGraw-Hill.

Patterson, A., & Hodgson, J. (2006). A speeddating story: The lover's guide to marketing excellence. *Journal of Marketing Management, 22*(5/6), 455–471.

Peters, T. (1997). The brand called you. *Fast Company, 10,* 83–88.

Rosen, L. D., Cheever, N. A., Cummings, C., & Felt, J. (2008). The impact of emotionality and self-disclosure on online dating versus traditional dating. *Computers in Human Behavior, 24*(5), 2124–2157.

Schau, H., & Gilly, M. C. (2003). We are what we post? Self-presentation in personal web space. *Journal of Consumer Research, 30*(3), 385–404.

Shepherd, I. H. (2005). From cattle and Coke to Charlie: Meeting the challenge of self-marketing and personal branding. *Journal of Marketing Management, 21*(5/6), 589–606.

Stemler, S. (2001). An overview of content analysis. *Practical Assessment, Research, and Evaluation, 7*(17).

Strano, M. (2008). User descriptions and interpretations of self-presentation through Facebook profile images. *Cyberpsychology: Journal of Psychosocial Research on Cyberspace, 2*(2), Retrieved from http://www.cyberpsychology.eu/view.php?cisloclanku=2008110402&article=(search in Issues)

Thomas, J., Peters, C., & Tolson, H. (2007). An exploratory investigation of the virtual community MySpace.com: What are consumers saying about fashion? *Journal of Fashion Marketing & Management, 11*(4), 587–603.

Tither, J. M. (2000). Selling yourself and procuring another: Investigating gender differences in NZ dating advertisements. *New Zealand English Journal, 14,* 66–74.

Reading Questions

1. The authors of this study identify a gap in the scholarship as part of their introduction. According to the authors, what is that gap?

2. In your own words, explain how the researchers selected the cities they focused on for their collection of Craigslist postings.

3. According to Table 2, what was the most frequent criterion for a partner identified in the content of the ads?

4. Based on their examination of self-disclosure in the ads, the researchers suggest that "gender differences do appear to exist in self-marketing related to utilizing personality and hobbies/interests in attempting to attract a prospective date" (par. 36). What specific findings do the researchers use to support this conclusion?

Rhetoric Questions

5. Based on the article's (unlabeled) abstract, who are the researchers' intended audiences? What evidence does the abstract provide to support your conclusions?

6. In the Methodology section, the authors describe the two phases of their research "used to examine the self-marketing occurring among men and women on Craigslist" (17). Contrast the authors' descriptions of these two phases in terms of length and level of detail. What accounts for the differences in the two descriptions?

7. Describe the authors' strategy, or the organizational principle, for reporting their findings.

8. To whom are the final paragraphs of the study directed? How do you know this?

Response and Research Questions

9. What do you see as the potential advantages or drawbacks of attempting to find love by self-marketing online?

10. In the Discussion section, the authors note that "[o]ne interesting finding from this study was that men utilized a tone of a sales pitch more often than women." They then pose the following questions: "Do men view e-dating more as a form of self-marketing than women? Or are men more comfortable selling and marketing themselves than women?" (46). Based on your own life experiences, how would you answer the researchers' questions?

11. Imagine for a moment that you're on a quest to find love online. Construct a brief Craigslist ad in which you describe yourself and your ideal partner. Once you're done, reflect on the strategies you used to "market" yourself. What did you include or choose to leave out? What do you see as most effective about your self-marketing?

WRITING PROJECT

Contributing to a Scholarly Conversation

For this assignment, choose a family-related topic and compose an academic essay that contributes to the scholarly conversation surrounding that topic in a field or discipline of your choice. For example, in "Changing Counts, Counting Change," Brian Powell et al. position themselves within the scholarly conversation in the field of sociology regarding the functional view of families. Arguing that scholars need to take a "fresh look," the authors use their own survey data to provide an alternative interpretation. In other words, by understanding the scholarly conversations about the topic and conducting their own research, the authors were able to help others understand the topic in a new way.

Using the readings in this chapter as a model, you might choose a topic related to how "family" is defined within different cultures or how definitions of marriage have historically shifted over time. Additionally, you might investigate how gender roles and expectations are perceived by diverse groups of people. No matter what topic you choose, think about how particular disciplinary perspectives might ask questions about the topic and how those questions can inform your research.

One of your first steps will therefore be to explore others' ideas by conducting research into your topic. Using the research skills you developed in Chapter 4, remember to think about research not just as gathering supporting evidence for your own argument. Think about research also as tracing out a conversation among scholars:

- What are others saying about your topic?

- Is there room for change, refinements, or redefinition in what they are saying about your topic?

- How might you contribute to this conversation?

Depending on your instructor and the expectations of your disciplinary perspective, you may choose to conduct research by designing a study, collecting data, and analyzing your results. Follow appropriate disciplinary and genre expectations in structuring your argument, providing evidence for your claims, and citing your sources.

Writing a Comparative Analysis of Research Methodologies

WRITING PROJECT

In this chapter, the writers draw on a wide variety of research methodologies to explore their research questions. For example, Warren Milteer Jr. relies heavily on analysis of historical documents to explore racial boundaries in nineteenth-century North Carolina, whereas Brian Powell et al. rely on a mixed methodology that includes the use of survey data to understand shifting perspectives on same-sex marriage.

Drawing on the readings in the academic case study in this chapter, compose a descriptive analysis of the methods utilized in two differing academic disciplines. You might begin by identifying the following for each research report:

- **Research Question(s)** What phenomenon are the researchers studying, and what do they want to know about it?

- **Research Methods** What research methods are used to find answers to the research question(s)?

As you describe the researchers' methods, be sure to engage in analysis as well. In other words, consider why the researchers use the methods they do and how those methods compare to others. Conclude your descriptive analysis by highlighting any similarities or differences in the two disciplines' methods.

12

Crime, Punishment, and Justice

This chapter includes a number of popular and academic texts aimed at examining various aspects of crime, punishment, and justice in American society. The opening selections present perspectives from a number of popular sources. The first identifies some of the highly controversial implications for criminal prosecution and punishment that have resulted from recent advances in the fields of neuroscience and neuroimaging. The second selection presents a series of statistics about our criminal justice system as evidence of its bias in the treatment of people of color. The third article examines trends in America's high incarceration rates to demonstrate how they have reached the point at which a continued rise in incarceration rates may be more harmful than helpful. The last popular selection tells the story of a successful financial planner who spent four months incarcerated at Rikers Island, New York, one of the most notoriously violent prisons in America, after being convicted of a white-collar crime.

We hope these readings will foster your own further consideration of a few of the many complex issues related to the topics of crime, punishment, and justice in America:

- Is criminal behavior biologically driven? If so, then how do we punish individuals for criminal behavior?

- Is our criminal justice system color-blind? Does it treat people equitably, regardless of race?

- Are white-collar criminals punished appropriately?

- What factors contribute to America's extraordinarily high incarceration rates, and what can be done about them?

- What is life in jail or prison really like? Does punishment in America need to change? If so, in what ways?

Beyond the typical lines of inquiry directed at the topic of the death penalty in America (e.g., Does it act as a deterrent? Can it be fairly applied? Does it constitute "cruel or unusual" punishment?), the academic case study for this chapter explores capital punishment from a number of perspectives that reveal, collectively, a wide variety in the kinds of inquiry that characterize distinct disciplinary approaches:

- **Humanities** What meaning can be found by analyzing capital punishment as cultural performance in America, from Puritan New England to today?
- **Social Sciences** How do movies affect viewers' moods about and attitudes toward the death penalty?
- **Natural Sciences** Does the current execution drug cocktail work as it was intended? Is it constitutional?
- **Applied Fields** How might proponents of the death penalty respond to its critics?

Inside a Psychopath's Brain: The Sentencing Debate

BARBARA BRADLEY HAGERTY

Barbara Bradley Hagerty is a former National Public Radio (NPR) religion correspondent. She is also the author of the *New York Times* best-selling book *Fingerprints of God: The Search for the Science of Spirituality* (2009). In the following article, published on NPR's website in June 2010 as the second part of a three-part series entitled *Inside the Criminal Brain*, Hagerty reports on the implications of emerging technologies in neuroscience and neuroimaging for the prosecution of crimes and for the punishment of criminals.

Kent Kiehl has studied hundreds of psychopaths. Kiehl is one of the world's leading investigators of psychopathy and a professor at the University of New Mexico. He says he can often see it in their eyes: There's an intensity in their stare, as if they're trying to pick up signals on how to respond. But the eyes are not an element of psychopathy, just a clue.

Officially, Kiehl scores their pathology on the Hare Psychopathy Checklist, which measures traits such as the inability to feel empathy or remorse, pathological lying, or impulsivity.

"The scores range from zero to 40," Kiehl explains in his sunny office overlooking a golf course. "The average person in the community, a male, will score about 4 or 5. Your average inmate will score about 22. An individual with psychopathy is typically described as 30 or above. Brian scored 38.5 basically. He was in the 99th percentile."

"Brian" is Brian Dugan, a man who is serving two life sentences for rape and murder in Chicago. Last July, Dugan pleaded guilty to raping and murdering 10-year-old Jeanine Nicarico in 1983, and he was put on trial to determine whether he should be executed. Kiehl was hired by the defense to do a psychiatric evaluation.

In a videotaped interview with Kiehl, Dugan 5 describes how he only meant to rob the Nicaricos' home. But then he saw the little girl inside.

"She came to the door and . . . I clicked," Dugan says in a flat, emotionless voice. "I turned into Mr. Hyde from Dr. Jekyll."

On screen, Dugan is dressed in an orange jumpsuit. He seems calm, even normal—until he lifts his hands to take a sip of water and you see the handcuffs. Dugan is smart—his IQ is over 140—but he admits he has always had shallow emotions. He tells

Kiehl that in his quarter century in prison, he believes he's developed a sense of remorse.

"And I have empathy, too—but it's like it just stops," he says. "I mean, I start to feel, but something just blocks it. I don't know what it is."

Kiehl says he's heard all this before: All psychopaths claim they feel terrible about their crimes for the benefit of the parole board.

"But then you ask them, 'What do you mean, you 10 feel really bad?' And Brian will look at you and go, 'What do you mean, what does it mean?' They look at you like, 'Can you give me some help? A hint? Can I call a friend?' They have no way of really getting at that at all," Kiehl says.

Kiehl says the reason people like Dugan cannot access their emotions is that their physical brains are different. And he believes he has the brain scans to prove it.

BRAIN SCANNING IN A MOBILE MRI

On a crystal clear June morning at Albuquerque's Youth Diagnostic and Development Center, juveniles who have been convicted of violent offenses march by, craning their necks as a huge trailer drives through the gates. This is Kiehl's prize—a $2 million mobile MRI provided by the Mind Research Network at the University of New Mexico. Kiehl transports the mobile MRI to maximum-security prisons around the state, and over the past few years, he has scanned the brains of more than 1,100 inmates, about 20 percent of whom are psychopaths.

For ethical reasons, Kiehl could not allow me to watch an inmate's brain being scanned, so he asked his researchers to demonstrate.

After a few minutes of preparation, researcher Kevin Bache settles into the brain scanner, where he can look up and see a screen. On the screen flash three types of pictures. One kind depicts a moral violation: He sees several hooded Klansmen setting a cross on fire. Another type is emotional but morally ambiguous: a car that is on fire but you don't know why. Another type of photo is neutral: for example, students standing around a Bunsen burner.

The subjects rate whether the picture is a moral 15 violation on a scale of 1 to 5. Kiehl says most psychopaths do not differ from normal subjects in the way they rate the photos: Both psychopaths and the average person rank the KKK with a burning cross as a moral violation. But there's a key difference: Psychopaths' brains behave differently from that of a nonpsychopathic person. When a normal person sees a morally objectionable photo, his limbic system lights up. This is what Kiehl calls the "emotional circuit," involving the orbital cortex above the eyes and the amygdala deep in the brain. But Kiehl says when psychopaths like Dugan see the KKK picture, their emotional circuit does not engage in the same way.

"We have a lot of data that shows psychopaths do tend to process this information differently," Kiehl says. "And Brian looked like he was processing it like the other individuals we've studied with psychopathy."

Kiehl says the emotional circuit may be what stops a person from breaking into that house or killing that girl. But in psychopaths like Dugan, the brakes don't work. Kiehl says psychopaths are a little like people with very low IQs who are not fully responsible for their actions. The courts treat people with low IQs differently. For example, they can't get the death penalty.

"What if I told you that a psychopath has an emotional IQ that's like a 5-year-old?" Kiehl asks. "Well, if that was the case, we'd make the same argument for individuals with low emotional IQ—that maybe they're not as deserving of punishment, not as deserving of culpability, etc."

IMPLICATIONS OF THE DIAGNOSIS

And that's exactly what Dugan's lawyers argued at trial last November. Attorney Steven Greenberg said that Dugan was not criminally insane. He knew right from wrong. But he was incapable of making the right choices.

"Someone shouldn't be executed for a condition 20 that they were born with, because it's not their fault," Greenberg says. "The crime is their fault, and he wasn't saying it wasn't his fault, and he wasn't saying, give [me] a free pass. But he was saying, don't kill me because it's not my fault that I was born this way."

This argument troubles Steven Erickson, a forensic psychologist and legal scholar at Widener University School of Law. He notes that alcoholics have brain abnormalities. Do we give them a pass if they kill someone while driving drunk?

"What about folks who suffer from depression? They have brain abnormalities, too. Should they be entitled to [an] excuse under the law?" he asks. "I think the key idea here is the law is not interested in brain abnormalities. The law is interested in whether or not someone at the time that the criminal act occurred understood the difference between right and wrong."

At trial, Jonathan Brodie, a psychiatrist at NYU Medical School who was the prosecution's expert witness, went further. Even if Dugan's brain is abnormal, he testified, the brain does *not* dictate behavior.

"There may be many, many people who also have psychopathic tendencies and have similar scans, who don't do antisocial behavior, who don't rape and kill," Brodie says.

Moreover, Brodie told the jury, Dugan's brain 25 scan in 2009 says nothing about what his brain was like when he killed Jeanine Nicarico.

"I don't know with Brian Dugan what was going on in his brain" when he committed his crime, Brodie says. "And I certainly don't know what was going on from a brain scan that was taken 24 years later."

The jury seemed to zero in on the science, asking to reread all the testimony about the neuroscience during 10 hours of deliberation. But in the end, they sentenced Dugan to death. Dugan is appealing the sentence.

In the meantime, this case signals the beginning of a revolution in the courtroom, Kiehl says.

"Neuroscience and neuroimaging is going to change the whole philosophy about how we punish and how we decide who to incapacitate and how we decide how to deal with people," he says, echoing comments of a growing number of leading scholars across the country, including Princeton and Harvard.

Just like DNA, he believes brain scans will even- 30 tually be standard fare. And that, he and others say, could upend our notions of culpability, crime, and punishment.

Reading Questions

1. Why does Kiehl believe that psychopaths like Dugan, a self-confessed murderer and rapist, cannot access their emotions in the same way the average person can?

2. What do MRI results reveal about psychopaths' limbic systems that separate them from non-psychopathic individuals?

3. What appears to be the defense strategy of Dugan's attorneys at trial? What is their argument with regard to his guilt or innocence?

4. What are psychiatrist Jonathan Brodie's objections to the Dugan defense strategy?

5. Kiehl says that the Dugan case "signals the beginning of a revolution in the courtroom" (par. 28). How does this position make sense in light of the jury's verdict in the Dugan case?

Rhetoric Questions

6. This part of the NPR series *Inside the Criminal Brain* is presented in three sections. Consider the structural design of the text, and provide a brief explanation for the writer's decision to divide the text as she does.

7. Choose any one of the three sections in this article, and determine the average number of sentences per paragraph in the section. As well, calculate the average number of quotations per paragraph. Why do you suppose Hagerty makes such language and reference decisions?

8. If possible, read the other two parts of the series of reports included in *Inside the Criminal Brain.* Describe the relationship of Part Two, "Inside a Psychopath's Brain: The Sentencing Debate," to the other two parts. Why is it positioned as the second report in the series?

Response and Research Questions

9. According to forensic psychologist Steven Erickson, "the law is not interested in brain abnormalities" (22). Should it be? Why or why not?

10. Kiehl suggests that neuroscience and neuroimaging are going to change the way society thinks about how it punishes criminal behavior. Do you agree with this suggestion? What kinds of potential changes might we anticipate?

The Top 10 Most Startling Facts about People of Color and Criminal Justice in the United States: A Look at the Racial Disparities Inherent in Our Nation's Criminal-Justice System

SOPHIA KERBY

Sophia Kerby is a policy associate at New York University School of Law's Brennan Center for Justice and a former special assistant to the Center for American Progress's *Progress 2050* project, which provides support for the development of progressive ideas in response to the nation's increasingly diverse population. The following report was published online at the Center for American Progress's website in March 2012. Kerby's report presents a series of statistics as evidence to suggest that "eliminating the racial disparities inherent to our nation's criminal-justice policies and practices must be at the heart of a renewed, refocused, and reenergized movement for racial justice in America."

This month the United States celebrates the Selma-to-Montgomery marches of 1965 to commemorate our shared history of the civil rights movement and our nation's continued progress toward racial equality. Yet decades later a broken criminal-justice system has proven that we still have a long way to go in achieving racial equality.

Today people of color continue to be disproportionately incarcerated, policed, and sentenced to death at significantly higher rates than their white counterparts.

Further, racial disparities in the criminal-justice system threaten communities of color—disenfranchising thousands by limiting voting rights and denying equal access to employment, housing, public benefits, and education to millions more. In light of these disparities, it is imperative that criminal-justice reform evolves as the civil rights issue of the 21st century.

Below we outline the top 10 facts pertaining to the criminal-justice system's impact on communities of color.

1. *While people of color make up about 30 percent of the United States' population, they account for 60 percent of those imprisoned.* The prison population grew by 700 percent from 1970 to 2005, a rate that is outpacing crime and population rates. The incarceration rates disproportionately impact men of color: 1 in every 15 African American men and 1 in every 36 Hispanic men are incarcerated in comparison to 1 in every 106 white men.

2. *According to the Bureau of Justice Statistics, one in three black men can expect to go to prison in their lifetime.* Individuals of color have a disproportionate number of encounters with law enforcement, indicating that racial profiling continues to be a problem. A report by the Department of Justice found that blacks and Hispanics were approximately three times more likely to be searched during a traffic stop than white motorists. African Americans were twice as likely to be arrested and almost four times as likely to experience the use of force during encounters with the police.

3. *Students of color face harsher punishments in school than their white peers, leading to a higher number of youth of color incarcerated.* Black and Hispanic students represent more than 70 percent of those involved in school-related arrests or referrals to law enforcement. Currently, African Americans make up two-fifths and Hispanics one-fifth of confined youth today.

4. *According to recent data by the Department of Education, African American students are arrested far more often than their white classmates.* The data showed that 96,000 students were arrested and 242,000 referred to law enforcement by schools during the 2009–10 school year. Of those students, black and Hispanic students made up more than 70 percent of arrested or referred students. Harsh school punishments, from suspensions to arrests, have led to high numbers of youth of color coming into contact with the juvenile-justice system and at an earlier age.

5. *African American youth have higher rates of juvenile incarceration and are more likely to be sentenced to adult prison.* According to the Sentencing Project, even though African American juvenile youth are about 16 percent of the youth population, 37 percent of their cases are moved to criminal court and 58 percent of African American youth are sent to adult prisons.

6. *As the number of women incarcerated has increased by 800 percent over the last three decades, women of color have been disproportionately represented.* While the number of women incarcerated is relatively low, the racial and ethnic disparities are startling. African American women are three times more likely than white women to be incarcerated, while Hispanic women are 69 percent more likely than white women to be incarcerated.

7. *The war on drugs has been waged primarily in communities of color where people of color are more likely to receive higher offenses.* According to the Human Rights Watch, people of color are no more likely to use or sell illegal drugs than whites, but they have higher rates of arrests. African Americans comprise 14 percent of regular drug users but are 37 percent of those arrested for drug offenses. From 1980 to 2007 about one in three of the 25.4 million adults arrested for drugs was African American.

8. *Once convicted, black offenders receive longer sentences compared to white offenders.* The U.S. Sentencing Commission stated that in the federal system black offenders receive sentences that are 10 percent longer than white offenders for the same crimes. The Sentencing Project reports that African Americans are 21 percent more likely to receive mandatory-minimum sentences than white defendants and are 20 percent more likely to be sentenced to prison.

9. *Voter laws that prohibit people with felony convictions to vote disproportionately impact men of color.* An estimated 5.3 million Americans are denied the right to vote based on a past felony conviction. Felony disenfranchisement is exaggerated by racial disparities in the criminal-justice system, ultimately denying 13 percent of African American men the right to vote. Felony-disenfranchisement policies

have led to 11 states denying the right to vote to more than 10 percent of their African American population.

10. *Studies have shown that people of color face disparities in wage trajectory following release from prison.* Evidence shows that spending time in prison affects wage trajectories with a disproportionate impact on black men and women. The results show no evidence of racial divergence in wages prior to incarceration; however, following release from prison, wages grow at a 21 percent slower rate for black former inmates compared to white ex-convicts. A number of states have bans on people with certain convictions working in domestic health-service industries such as nursing, child care, and home health care—areas in which many poor women and women of color are disproportionately concentrated.

These racial disparities have deprived people of color of their most basic civil rights, making criminal-justice reform the civil rights issue of our time. Through mass imprisonment and the overrepresentation of individuals of color within the criminal justice and prison system, people of color have experienced an adverse impact on themselves and on their communities from barriers to reintegrating into society to engaging in the democratic process. Eliminating the racial disparities inherent to our nation's criminal-justice policies and practices must be at the heart of a renewed, refocused, and reenergized movement for racial justice in America.

There have been a number of initiatives on the state and federal level to address the racial disparities in youth incarceration. Last summer Secretary of Education Arne Duncan announced the Schools Discipline Initiative to bring increased awareness of effective policies and practices to ultimately dismantle the school-to-prison pipeline. States like California and Massachusetts are considering legislation to address the disproportionate suspensions among students of color. And in Clayton County, Georgia, collaborative local reforms have resulted in a 47 percent reduction in juvenile-court referrals and a 51 percent decrease in juvenile felony rates. These initiatives could serve as models of success for lessening the disparities in incarceration rates.

Reading Questions

1. According to Kerby, what are three negative effects on communities of color caused by the racial disparities in the treatment of people of color by the criminal justice system?

2. The article reports that people of color make up what percentage of the prison population in the United States?

3. What percentage of African American men have lost the right to vote as a result of a felony conviction, according to Kerby's reporting?

4. What evidence is there to suggest that women of color are treated differently from white women in the criminal justice system?

5. According to the U.S. Sentencing Commission, as reported in Kerby's article, how much longer are sentences imposed on African American offenders than sentences given to white offenders for the same crime?

Rhetoric Questions

6. Kerby presents the core content of her piece in a numbered list. Is this an effective strategy in light of her audience and goals?

7. Spend some time learning more about the Center for American Progress. With what political organizations or beliefs is it associated? Do these associations have any impact on your evaluation of the information presented in Kerby's report, or on the writer's ethos? Why or why not?

Response and Research Questions

8. Kerby provides evidence to suggest that the American criminal justice system is broken. Do you agree that it is broken? Why or why not?

9. Kerby's final paragraph mentions the "school-to-prison pipeline." What is this, and what role might it play in the unequal treatment of people of color by the criminal justice system?

10. Choose any one of the statistical findings, as reported by Kerby, presented in the piece. Locate a reputable source that either substantiates or challenges that finding.

The Many Causes of America's Decline in Crime: A New Report Finds That Locking Up More Offenders Isn't Making People Any Safer—and May Even Be Counterproductive

INIMAI CHETTIAR

Inimai Chettiar is director of the Justice Program at the New York University School of Law's Brennan Center for Justice. She previously worked at the New York University Law School's Institute for Policy Integrity as well as the American Civil Liberties Union. She is coeditor of the book *Solutions: American Leaders Speak Out on Criminal Justice* (2015). Chettiar's work on topics related to mass incarceration and criminal justice reform appears frequently in popular publications like the *New York Times, Washington Post, Bloomberg*, and the *Wall Street Journal*. In the article below, published in the *Atlantic* in February 2015, Chettiar presents research to suggest that increasing rates of incarceration do not necessarily make Americans safer.

The dramatic rise of incarceration and the precipitous fall in crime have shaped the landscape of American criminal justice over the last two decades. Both have been unprecedented. Many believe that the explosion in incarceration created the crime drop. In fact, the enormous growth in imprisonment only had a limited impact. And, for the past thirteen years, it has passed the point of diminishing returns, making no effective difference. We now know that we can reduce our prison populations and simultaneously reduce crime.

This has profound implications for criminal justice policy: We lock up millions of people in an effort to fight crime. But this is not working.

The link between rising incarceration and falling crime seems logical. Draconian penalties and a startling expansion in prison capacity were advertised as measures that would bring down crime. That's what happened, right?

Not so fast. There is wide agreement that we do not yet fully know what caused crime to drop. Theories abound, from an aging population to growing police forces to reducing lead in the air. A jumble of data and theories makes it hard to sort out this big, if happy, mystery. And it has been especially difficult to pin down the role of growing incarceration.

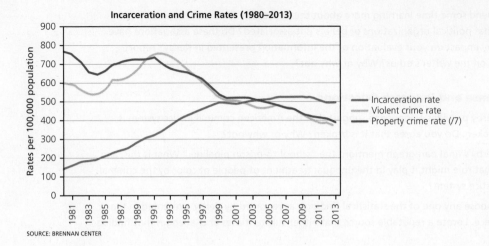

Incarceration and Crime Rates (1980–2013)

Y-axis: Rates per 100,000 population (0 to 900)

X-axis: 1981 to 2013

Legend:
- Incarceration rate
- Violent crime rate
- Property crime rate (/7)

SOURCE: BRENNAN CENTER

So incarceration skyrocketed and crime was 5 in free fall. But conflating simple correlation with causation in this case is a costly mistake. A report from the Brennan Center for Justice at NYU School of Law, called *What Caused the Crime Decline?*, finds that increasing incarceration is not the answer. As Nobel laureate economist Joseph Stiglitz writes in the foreword, "This prodigious rate of incarceration is not only inhumane, it is economic folly."

Our team of economic and criminal justice researchers spent the last twenty months testing fourteen popular theories for the crime decline. We delved deep into over thirty years of data collected from all fifty states and the fifty largest cities. The results are sharply etched: We do not know with precision what caused the crime decline, but the growth in incarceration played only a minor role, and now has a negligible impact.

The drop in crime stands as one of the more fascinating and remarkable social phenomena of our time. For decades, crime soared. Cities were viewed as unlivable. Politicians competed to run the most lurid campaign ads and sponsor the most punitive laws. Racially tinged "wedge issues" marked American politics from Richard Nixon's "law and order" campaign of 1968 to the "Willie Horton" ads

credited with helping George H. W. Bush win the 1988 election.

But over the past twenty-five years, the tide of crime and violence seemed to simply recede. Crime is about half of what it was at its peak in 1991. Violent crime plummeted 51 percent. Property crime fell 43 percent. Homicides are down 54 percent. In 1985, there were 1,384 murders in New York City. Last year there were 333. The country is an undeniably safer place. Growing urban populations are one positive consequence.

During that same period, we saw the birth of mass incarceration in the United States. Since 1990, incarceration nearly doubled, adding 1.1 million people behind bars. Today, our nation has 5 percent of the world's population and 25 percent of the world's prison population. The United States is the world's most prodigious incarcerator.

THE ROLE OF INCARCERATION

What do the numbers say? Did this explosion in 10 incarceration cause the crime decline?

It turns out that increased incarceration had a much more limited effect on crime than popularly thought. We find that this growth in incarceration was responsible for approximately 5 percent of the drop in crime in the 1990s. (This could vary from 0 to 10 percent.) Since then, however, increases in incarceration have had essentially *zero* effect on crime. The positive returns are gone. That means the colossal number of Americans cycling in and out of prisons and jails over the last thirteen years was not responsible for any meaningful fraction of the drop in crime.

The figure below shows our main result: increased incarceration's effectiveness since 1980. This is measured as the change in the crime rate expected to result from a 1 percent increase in imprisonment—what economists call an "elasticity." During the 1980s and 1990s, as incarceration climbed, its effectiveness waned. Its effectiveness currently dwells in the basement. Today, a 1 percent increase in incarceration would lead to a microscopic 0.02 percent decline in crime. This is statistically indistinguishable from having no effect at all.

Increased incarceration accounted for about 6 percent of the property crime decline in the 1990s, and 1 percent of that drop in the 2000s. The growth of incarceration had no observable effect on violent crime in the 1990s or 2000s. This last finding may initially seem surprising. But given that we are sending more and more low-level and non-violent offenders to prison (who may never have been prone

to violent crime), the finding makes sense. Sending a non-violent offender to prison will not necessarily have an effect on *violent* crime.

How Rising Incarceration's Effect on Crime Waned

There is no question that some level of incarceration had some positive impact on bringing down crime. There are many habitual offenders and people committing serious, violent crimes who may need to be kept out of society. Criminologists call this the "incapacitation" effect: Removing someone from society prevents them from committing crimes.

But after a certain point, that positive impact ceases. The new people filling prisons do so without bringing down crime much. In other words, *rising* incarceration rates produce less of an effect on crime reduction. This is what economists call "diminishing returns." It turns out that the criminal justice system offers a near perfect picture of this phenomenon.

As incarceration doubled from 1990 to today, it became less effective. At its relatively low levels twenty years ago, incarceration may indeed have had some effect on crime. The positive returns may not have yet diminished.

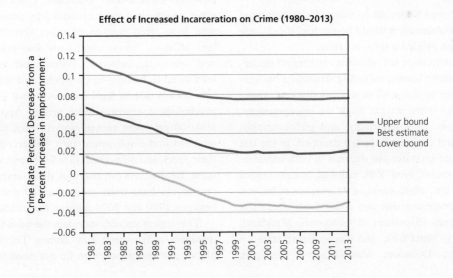

Effect of Increased Incarceration on Crime (1980–2013)

Incarceration rates have now risen so high that further increases in incarceration are ineffective. Due to the war on drugs and the influx of harsher sentencing laws in the 1980s and 1990s, an increasing proportion of the 1.1 million prisoners added since 1990 were imprisoned for low-level or non-violent crimes. Today, almost half of state prisoners are convicted of non-violent crimes. More than half of federal prisoners are serving time for drug offenses. The system is no longer prioritizing arresting, prosecuting, and incarcerating the most dangerous or habitual offenders. In this case, each additional prisoner will, on average, yield less in terms of crime reduction. We have incarcerated those we should not have. This is where the "more incarceration equals less crime" theory busts.

Even those who have argued for the effectiveness of incarceration acknowledge this possibility. University of Chicago economist and *Freakonomics* co-author Steven Levitt found in his 2004 study that incarceration was responsible for over a third of the 1990s drop in violent crime. He noted that, "Given the wide divergence in the frequency and severity of offending across criminals, sharply declining marginal benefits of incarceration are a possibility," which, if present, could have affected his findings.

Decrease in Incarceration and *Crime*

Can the United States safely reduce its incarcerated population? After all, it would be too bad if reducing incarceration yielded a spike in crime.

Fortunately, there is a real-time experiment underway. For many reasons, including straitened budgets and a desire to diminish prison populations, many states have started to cut back on imprisonment. What happened? Interestingly, and encouragingly, crime did not explode. In fact, it dropped. In the last decade, fourteen states saw declines in both incarceration and crime. New York reduced imprisonment by 26 percent, while seeing a 28 percent reduction in crime. Imprisonment and crime both decreased by more than 15 percent in California, Maryland, New Jersey, New York, and Texas. Eight states— Connecticut, Delaware, Massachusetts, Michigan,

Nevada, North Carolina, South Carolina, and Utah—lowered their imprisonment rates by 2 to 15 percent while seeing more than a 15 percent decrease in crime.

This is all very significant. Incarceration is not just any government policy. Mass incarceration comes at an incredible cost. "A year in prison can cost more than a year at Harvard," Stiglitz points out. Taxpayers spend $260 billion a year on criminal justice. And there will continue to be less and less to show for it, as more people are incarcerated.

There are significant human costs as well—to individuals, families, communities, and the country. Spending a dollar on prisons is not the same as spending it on public television or the military. Prisons result in an enormous waste of human capital. Instead of so many low-level offenders languishing behind bars, they could be earning wages and contributing to the economy. Incarceration is so concentrated in certain communities that it has disrupted the gender balance and marriage rates. The costs are intergenerational. There are 2.7 million minor children with a parent behind bars. More than one in nine black children have a parent incarcerated.

Research also shows that incarceration can actually *increase* future crime. Criminologists call this the "criminogenic effect" of prison. It is particularly powerful on low-level offenders. Once individuals enter prison, they are surrounded by other prisoners who have often committed more serious and violent offenses. Prison conditions also breed violent and antisocial behavior. Former prisoners often have trouble finding employment and reintegrating into society due to legal barriers, social stigma, and psychological scarring from prison. Approximately 600,000 prisoners reenter society each year. Those who can find employment earn 40 percent less than their peers, and 60 percent face long-term unemployment. Researchers estimate that the country's poverty rate would have been more than 20 percent lower between 1980 and 2004 without mass incarceration.

This lack of stability increases the odds that former prisoners will commit new crimes. The more people we put into prison who do not need to be there,

20

the more this criminogenic effect increases. That is another plausible explanation for why our massive levels of incarceration are resulting in less crime control.

Our findings do not exist in a vacuum. A body of empirical research is slowly coalescing around the ineffectiveness of increased incarceration. Last year, the Hamilton Project issued a report calling incarceration a "classic case of diminishing returns," based on findings from California and Italy. The National Research Council issued a hefty report last year, finding that crime was not the cause of mass incarceration. And, based on a summary of past research, the authors concluded that "the magnitude of the crime reduction [due to increased incarceration] remains highly uncertain and the evidence suggests it was unlikely to have been large."

We go a few steps further to fully reveal the complex relationship between crime and incarceration. By using thirteen years of more recent data, gathered in the modern era of heavily elevated incarceration, combined with an empirical model that accounts for diminishing returns and controls for other variables, we are able to quantify the sharply declining benefits of overusing prison.

Other Factors Reducing Crime

But if it was not incarceration, then what did cause the crime decline?

There is no shortage of candidates. Every year, it seems, a new study advances a novel explanation. Levitt attributes about half the crime drop to the legalization of abortion. Amherst economist Jessica Reyes attributes about half the violent crime drop to the unleading of gasoline after the Clean Air Act. Berkeley law professor Franklin Zimring credits the police as the central cause. All three theories likely played some role.

Instead of a single, dominant cause, our research points to a vast web of factors, often complex, often interacting, and some unexpected. Of the theories we examined, we found the following factors had some effect on bringing down crime: a growth in income (5 to 10 percent), changes in alcohol consumption (5 to 10 percent), the aging population (0 to 5 percent),

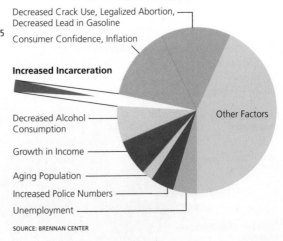

Popular Theories on the Crime Decline: Percent of Crime Decline (1990–1999)

Decreased Crack Use, Legalized Abortion, Decreased Lead in Gasoline

Consumer Confidence, Inflation

Increased Incarceration

Decreased Alcohol Consumption

Growth in Income

Aging Population

Increased Police Numbers

Unemployment

Other Factors

SOURCE: BRENNAN CENTER

and decreased unemployment (0 to 3 percent). Policing also played a role, with increased numbers of police in the 1990s reducing crime (0 to 10 percent) and the introduction of CompStat* having an even larger effect (5 to 15 percent).

But none is solely, or even largely, responsible for the crime drop. Unfortunately, we could not fully test a few theories, as the data did not exist at the detailed level we needed for our analysis. For those, we analyzed past research, finding that inflation and consumer confidence (individuals' belief about the strength of the economy) probably had some effect on crime. The legalization of abortion and unleading of gasoline may also have played some role.

In aggregate, the fourteen factors we identified can explain some of the drop in crime in the 1990s. But even adding all of them together fails to explain the majority of the decrease.

A Sensible Way Forward

No one factor brought down crime. Today, incarceration has become the default option in the fight

---

* *CompStat:* a crime-management system that identifies increases in crimes and assists in targeting resources to address those increases.

**Popular Theories on the Crime Decline:
Percent of Crime Decline (2000–2013)**

Increased Incarceration

Growth in Income

Decreased Alcohol
Consumption

Introduction of
CompStat

Consumer Confidence,
Inflation

Other Factors

SOURCE: BRENNAN CENTER

against crime. But more incarceration is not a silver bullet. It has, in fact, ceased to be effective in reducing crime—and the country is slowly awakening to that reality. Incarceration can be reduced while crime

continues to decline. The research shows this and many states are watching it unfold.

Where do we go from here? As President Obama said it in his State of the Union last month, "Surely we can agree that it's a good thing that for the first time in 40 years, crime and incarceration have come down together, and use that as a starting point for Democrats and Republicans, community leaders and law enforcement, to reform America's criminal justice system so that it protects and serves all of us." And indeed, reforming our criminal justice system is emerging as a bipartisan cause. Everyone from Jeb Bush to Hillary Clinton to the Koch Brothers to George Soros has made similar calls.

We should listen to them. There are bold, practical policy solutions starting to gain bipartisan support. Incarceration can be removed as a punishment for many non-violent, non-serious crimes. Violations of technical conditions of parole and probation should not lead to a return trip to prison. Sentence maximum and minimum lengths can be downscaled across the board. There is little reason to jail low-risk defendants who are simply waiting for their trials to begin. And, government funding streams can change to reward reducing incarceration.

Crime is expensive. We do well to fight it. But 35 increasing incarceration is definitely not the answer.

Reading Questions

1. According to Chettiar, what are three possible theories that some use to account for the declining rates of crime in America over the last two decades?

2. Why, according to Chettiar, is it "a costly mistake" to conflate "simple correlation with causation" (par. 5) when it comes to the relationship between rates of incarceration and crime?

3. What statistical evidence does Chettiar provide to support her contention that the United States "is the world's most prodigious incarcerator" (9)?

4. Explain the concept of "elasticity" and how it relates to Chettiar's argument about the current relationship between incarceration and crime rates.

5. What has happened to crime rates in states like New York, Texas, Massachusetts, and North Carolina, where imprisonment rates have been lowered in the last decade, according to Chettiar?

6. Identify three government policy decisions Chettiar recommends or supports at the end of her argument.

Rhetoric Questions

7. What purpose does the article's subtitle serve, and what is the likely effect of the subtitle on the reader?

8. What sentence (or group of sentences) best reveals Chettiar's central position, or her argument's unifying claim? Explain why you chose the sentence or sentences you did.

9. Chettiar references economic concepts, like "elasticity" and "diminishing returns," on a number of occasions. What is the effect of Chettiar couching her arguments in the language of economics on you as a reader?

10. Identify a paragraph in which Chettiar acknowledges a possible counterargument or an alternative view. Explain how she presents and handles that counterargument or alternative view.

11. In addition to exploring the effects of incarceration on crime rates, Chettiar also acknowledges, in a couple of paragraphs of her article, its effects on families and the economy. How useful do you find Chettiar's arguments concerning incarceration and its effects on families and the economy as support for her central position? Explain your response.

12. Chettiar's article includes four visual representations of data (charts and graphs). Look closely at each graph or chart and write four brief paragraphs in which you explain how each supports or contributes to a central part of Chettiar's argument.

Response and Research Questions

13. Chettiar's article was first published in the *Atlantic* in 2015. Research the *Atlantic* and offer a description of the magazine's likely intended audience. Why would Chettiar's piece likely be appealing to the magazine's readership?

14. Chettiar makes reference to "Willie Horton" ads that may have played a role in the election of George H. W. Bush as president of the United States in 1988. Research Willie Horton to learn more about the circumstances that thrust his crime into the 1988 election, and then locate a "Willie Horton" ad. Study the ad carefully and explain how the ad is designed to support the "law and order" candidate (Bush) for the presidential election.

15. Research and explain the general trends in crime statistics for your city, town, county, or state over the past two decades. Do the statistics you are able to locate match the national trends for crimes rates Chettiar reports in her article? If so, why do you think they are in close alignment? If not, why do you think the rates in your city, town, county, or state differ from national trends?

16. The final paragraph of Chettiar's argument is made up of three short sentences. Imagine that you've been tasked with writing a new conclusion for Chettiar's article that is made up of five sentences and maintains the short-sentence style. Write a new conclusion for Chettiar's article.

I Survived Prison: What Really Happens behind Bars

ABIGAIL PESTA (REPORTING)

Abigail Pesta is an award-winning investigative and features reporter who has published articles in a number of national and international venues, including the *Wall Street Journal*, the *New York Times*, the *Atlantic*, and *Newsweek*. In "I Survived Prison: What Really Happens behind Bars," which appeared in *Marie Claire* online in March 2009, Pesta relates the experience of a highly successful financial planner, Jennifer Wilkov, who was sentenced to four months in jail at Rikers Island, New York, following her conviction for a white-collar crime. Pesta reports the experience from Wilkov's point of view.

I'm rolling up to Rikers Island, a notoriously violent prison in New York City, on a bus with about a dozen other women. My wrist is handcuffed to a lifelong drug addict whose stomach is distended from fibroids, she tells me. One of the ladies clearly hasn't bathed for weeks, and the smell is unbearable.

Simply boarding this bus was a feat in itself. If you think it sounds challenging to round up a group of hyperactive third-graders for a field trip, you should've seen the guards trying to get a bunch of loud-mouthed, drugged-out, furious female convicts to shut up, stand in line, and get on the bus.

A plain, redbrick building looms before me. I'm about to become a prisoner in a massive penitentiary, and I feel an overwhelming sense of dread. I'm surrounded by people who have been here before, who know the system, who know how to work the guards. But I know nothing. I'm thinking, I have to get through this. I have to stay safe. Stay alive. I tell myself that maybe someone in this prison needs me; perhaps that's the reason life has thrown me this curveball. For a moment, I think I hear a distant voice calling for help.

As the bus pulls to a stop, I try for about the millionth time to wrap my head around how I got here.

Just a couple of years ago, I was working as a 5 Certified Financial Planner for American Express Financial Advisors and living with my cat, Figaro, in a leafy Brooklyn neighborhood. The trouble started when a relative recommended an investment opportunity in California—an operation that was buying foreclosed homes, fixing them up, then reselling them at a profit. He'd invested himself, and I followed suit.

At the same time, some of my clients started inquiring about real-estate opportunities, and I asked the compliance officer at American Express if I could mention this one. He said AmEx didn't deal with "hard property" real estate but that I could refer people independently if I filled out the proper securities forms. I did so, then told a few people about the investment, while advising them to do their own homework.

About a year later, in August 2005, I launched my own financial-planning business. Things went swimmingly for the first year, until investors—including members of my family and me—stopped getting any returns on that real-estate deal. So an attorney and I paid a visit to the owners of the California company. After our meeting, the attorney deemed the operation a scam and said I should report it to the authorities.

I did so immediately, in October 2006. A month later, several plainclothes officers confronted me on my street. "You're gonna let us in your apartment, or we're gonna beat the door down," one of them snarled. They confiscated my cell phone, computer, and files, while another set of police cleared out my office nearby. I was stunned, but I thought my stuff might help them nail the crooks.

Eight months later, when I was sitting in my office one morning in a favorite outfit—Ralph Lauren top, white pants, white heels—the police returned. I was arrested and accused of being part of a $1.6 million real-estate fraud, since I'd recommended the investment and had received standard referral fees. (Of course my family and I had lost a substantial amount of money in the con ourselves, but that didn't seem to matter.) After I answered a slew of questions from an assistant district attorney, my criminal-defense lawyer—who, by the way, was from the firm that had unsuccessfully defended Martha Stewart—advised me to agree to a deal with the DA. If I pleaded guilty, I'd get sentenced to six months in jail but could be out in four. "Four months is better than four years, which is what you could get if you go to trial and lose," my lawyer said. I hated the idea of making that deal, but since I was new to the legal field, I took his advice and signed the papers. That was January 2008.

For the next few months, while I awaited my sentencing, I moved my belongings into storage and stayed with friends, as I'd put my apartment on the market prior to the legal nightmare. I worked as a book consultant, since I'd written and published three finance books myself. I tried to do some research on Rikers, but Googling turned out to be a mistake. What popped up were reports of abuse, injustice, and rape, along with news of guards running an alleged prison fight club, in which inmates were forced to beat each other to a pulp. Nonetheless, any New York City dweller sentenced to less than a year on state charges gets sent there.

Terrified, I started preparing for hell. I sought advice from self-defense experts, and enlisted them to shout insults in my face so I could practice my response. I cut my hair and donated it to charity, because I'd been warned that prisoners could yank it, hard. I talked to my mom constantly. She believed I was innocent, as did my friends—at least, my true friends, who even wrote letters to the judge about me. A few people couldn't cope and dropped out of my life. Meanwhile, a tsunami of unflattering stories about me hit the media—the *New York Times*, *New York Daily News*, the Associated Press. The headlines were infuriating, and humiliating. I felt increasingly angry about pleading guilty.

10 In June 2008, I went to a criminal courthouse in downtown Manhattan to be formally sentenced. The courtroom looked like something straight out of *Law & Order*, with old-fashioned wood-paneled walls, wooden pews, and a sign above the judge's head that said "In God We Trust." I stood before the judge and asked her if I could withdraw my guilty plea. The answer: No.

That same day, I said good-bye to my family, my cell phone, my normal life. Then I was handcuffed and escorted to a dingy basement room called "the bridge," where I waited with a bunch of prostitutes and drug addicts for the bus to Rikers.

When I replay it all in my mind, it seems like a bad movie or a nightmare—not anything real. But the reality sets in as soon as I step off the bus at Rikers, where the indignities begin promptly. For starters, I'm told to strip naked and squat—the idea being that any contraband I might be hiding inside me will tumble out. Then the guards make me sit in a computerized chair called the B.O.S.S.; the chair seems to be doing an X-ray of my insides to detect anything I might have swallowed in order to conceal it. I tell myself not to take any of this personally, but it's hard not to let it mess with my mind. I feel like I'm in a foreign country where I don't know the language or the rules, and no one wants to help. Anything I say can be misinterpreted. I'm afraid to ask even the simplest questions. Guards and inmates are staring at me; they know I'm new here. I have to stay alert.

15 I undergo a series of medical tests (for tuberculosis, HIV) for the next six hours. Then I put on a dark-green jumpsuit and head to my new home: a minuscule, private cinder-block cell (about eight feet by three feet) that contains a metal cot with a block of foam on top and a sheet but no pillow. There's a white porcelain toilet and sink right out in the open; I'm handed a towel, a bar of scratchy white soap that's more like bleach, and half a roll of toilet paper. No hot water. A tiny window looks out onto a parking lot.

I sit on the cot, take a deep breath, and thank God I'm alive; I've made it this far. I think, *Whatever I'm supposed to do here, let me do it well.* I remind myself that I can survive by becoming invisible: I will not act superior, or fearful. I'll follow directions, and I won't ask any questions of anyone. By this time, it's 4 in the morning, and I've been up for more than 24 hours. Breakfast will be served in one hour. I lie awake, not sure if I'm allowed to sleep; I'm afraid of getting in trouble if I miss breakfast.

After a week marked by entire days of keeping mostly to myself, I move to a dorm with 50 other women. The beds are crowded onto an open floor surrounded by tan Sheetrock walls. Most of the women here have aligned themselves with people from the housing projects they come from, so there are Latin factions, African-American ones, and so forth. I keep my head down, and pray.

There are regular confrontations. One woman randomly decides she doesn't want me to use the phone and tries to pick fights with me in front of the guards when I call my mother. One day she says, unprovoked, "Did you call me an idiot?" I reply that I don't say that type of thing, and luckily, the situation doesn't escalate. I know I have to stand up for myself and not show fear.

One evening, I witness a fight just before dinner. We're all assembling in the dormitory, with the guards barking at us to "shut up and line up," as usual. Suddenly, one woman flies at another, punching her everywhere—in the face, the gut. I've never seen a fistfight in real life, with two people trying to kill each other. Another woman jumps in, and the trio turns into a tornado, careening around the room. The guards gradually isolate them, ordering everyone else out. I imagine that the women were sent to solitary confinement in a dreaded place known as "the bin."

The most threatening person is a brute of a 20 woman who leers at me menacingly one night in the communal showers. I know she wants to rape me; I've been warned of the signs. Rumor has it that another woman was recently raped by three female inmates in the high-security wing, which is a heavily patrolled area, so presumably the guards knew what was happening. In my case, a fellow inmate comes and stands defiantly by my side in the shower, and the bully backs off.

I lose 14 pounds in the first six weeks, due to stress and also to the fact that I've been an organic vegetarian for years. I have Crohn's disease, a serious digestive disorder, and my diet has helped me keep it under control. But there is hardly anything green or even remotely fresh served in jail. Meals mostly consist of slices of bread and turkey patties or fried chicken quarters, which the prisoners like to refer to as "seagull meat." I don't eat much, to the delight of my fellow inmates, who constantly ask for my leftovers. There's also a commissary, which is stocked with cookies, candy, and Kool-Aid packets that inmates can purchase once a week. Only a prison dietitian knows of my condition. Her advice? "You have to find a way to survive here."

Our days are extremely regimented; we're counted several times by guards changing shifts so they can make sure we're present, and alive. There's a law library and an outdoor area for exercise, such as jump rope. A TV blasts shows like *Jerry Springer* and *Maury Povich* in a common room. We're allowed to make the occasional cup of tea, but only if the entire dorm is clean, which is a regular source of friction. Religious services are popular, with prisoners frequently spouting, "Only God can judge." All of us have jobs; I make 39 cents an hour working in the prison garden, as part of a training program provided by the Horticultural Society of New York. Nighttime is a cacophony of raucous arguments among all the wound-up women who have been consuming sugar and starch all day, with the guards threatening to flip on the fluorescent lights if people don't pipe down.

As time creeps by, what keeps me sane is the continuing belief that I'm here for a reason, that I might be able to help someone. Gradually, I do. I manage to teach a woman from Trinidad to read, and I show others how to do yoga. I hold poetry readings with the woman who bunks next to me, an African-American Muslim who has been homeless at times. When I describe how I'd once heard someone calling for help, she says it was her.

On the final day of my ordeal, in October 2008, my mother and a dear friend escort me out into a bright, brisk fall afternoon. At this point, I've contracted a full-body yeast infection called candida, but I've never felt better—or freer—in my life. With my 40th birthday just around the corner, I feel oddly proud of myself. I'm tougher than I realized, and now I know I can win the respect of people from worlds very different from my own. I can keep a positive outlook in the worst of circumstances. Ironically, I have my experience at Rikers to thank for that knowledge. As one of the guards once said to me, "If you can survive this place, you can survive anything."

Reading Questions

1. What specific fears related to her impending stay at Rikers Island does Wilkov express on the bus ride to the prison?

2. What is the crime to which Wilkov pleads guilty? What is her punishment?

3. Wilkov mentions food a number of times throughout her story. How is food used as both a punishment and a reward in her prison experience?

4. Wilkov raises the issue of privacy frequently. In what ways is her privacy seemingly violated by the experience of prison?

5. To what belief does Wilkov credit her ability to maintain her sanity while in prison?

Rhetoric Questions

6. What purpose does Wilkov have in telling her story? What purpose do you think *Marie Claire* had in publishing it? What do you see as the story's intended effects on the magazine's readers?

7. How would you describe the tone of Pesta's work overall? How does her work establish that tone? What impact does the tone have on you as a reader?

8. In what ways does Pesta's piece follow conventional expectations for a news article?

Response and Research Questions

9. Regardless of her actual guilt or innocence, do you think the punishment Wilkov receives fits the white-collar crime for which she was convicted? Why or why not?

10. Wilkov reports that immediately following her sentencing, she was "handcuffed and escorted to a dingy basement room called 'the bridge,' where [she] waited with a bunch of prostitutes and drug addicts for the bus to Rikers" (par. 13). How would you describe Wilkov's attitude toward the other criminals?

11. Wilkov says, at the end of her experience in prison, that she felt "proud" of herself. Why does she feel proud? Do you think she has reason to be proud?

Lethal Theatre: Performance, Punishment, and the Death Penalty

DWIGHT CONQUERGOOD

Before his death in 2004, Dwight Conquergood was an associate professor and former chair of the Department of Performance Studies at Northwestern University. Conquergood's research, grounded in ethnographic and cultural studies, often focused on marginalized groups within societies, including refugees in Thailand and Gaza and the immigrant populations of Chicago. In the article below, Conquergood explores the implications of understanding capital punishment, from Puritan New England to modern America, as ritual and performance. The article was first published in *Theatre Journal* in 2002.

I'm not going to struggle physically against any restraints. I'm not going to shout, use profanity or make idle threats. Understand though that I'm not only upset, but I'm saddened by what is happening here tonight. . . .

If someone tried to dispose of everyone here for participating in this killing, I'd scream a resounding, "No." I'd tell them to give them all the gift that they would not give me, and that's to give them all a second chance. . . .

There are a lot of men like me on death row—good men—who fell to the same misguided emotions, but may not have recovered as I have. Give those men a chance to do what's right. Give them a chance to undo their wrongs. A lot of them want to fix the mess they started, but don't know how. . . .

No one wins tonight. No one gets closure.

—Napoleon Beazley[1]

There will be no lasting peace either in the heart of individuals or in social customs until death is outlawed.   —Albert Camus[2]

Like it or not, you are putting on a show.

—John Whitley[3]

Show, spectacle, theatre, these representational media are central to the rituals of state killing.

—Austin Sarat[4]

In 1975 Michel Foucault published *Discipline and Punish: The Birth of the Prison*, a landmark book that opened with two astonishing chapters, "The Body of the Condemned" and "The Spectacle of the Scaffold," harrowing accounts in gruesome detail of the performance of capital punishment in the premodern era.[5] These chapters served as points of departure for charting the historical shift from the dramatic infliction of corporal and capital punishment to modernity's more subtle and insidious infiltrations of power through mechanisms of discipline linked with knowledge. Punishment transformed, Foucault argued, from a theatre of violence and repression to a medical model of rehabilitation metonymically connected to other normalizing mechanisms and internalized techniques of coercion, compliance, and surveillance. According to Foucault, the performance of power in modern society has changed radically from spectacular capital punishments—that point at which the violence of the state is most nakedly displayed—to undercover capillary penetrations, insinuations, secretions, and circulations of power that is difficult to flesh out. He closed the book with the confident claim that "we are now far away from the country of tortures," the spectacle of the scaffold, because contemporary legal punishment "appears to be free of all excess and all violence."[6]

I reread *Discipline and Punish* in the summer of 2001, during the same time that I traveled twice in eight days to Terre Haute, Indiana, to march and stand in vigil outside the prison death chamber to protest the serial executions of Timothy McVeigh and Juan Raul

Garza, the first federal prisoners put to death since 1963. I found Foucault's opening chapters on executions more resonant and familiar than later chapters titled "The Gentle Way of Punishment." Emotionally drained from attending the June 11 and June 19 executions, I kept writing "not in June, 2001" in the margins of passages about how modern judicial punishment had advanced well beyond the deployment of raw, physical force. I drew an incredulous exclamation point across from this passage in the conclusion: "There is nothing in it now that recalls the former excess of sovereign power when it revenged its authority" on the body of the condemned.[7]

To be fair, Foucault wrote *Discipline and Punish* in 1975, at a time when the medical model of rehabilitation was in the ascendancy in penological thought and practice. The death penalty was rarely deployed, and France, along with the rest of Europe, was on the verge of abolishing capital punishment for good. Although it is amazing to think of it now, the United States was in step with and even ahead of the international community on the issue of the death penalty. In 1975, there were no executions in the US, not even in Texas. In 1972 the Supreme Court in *Furman v. Georgia* had declared capital punishment—"as then practiced," which proved to be a fatal loophole phrase—"cruel and unusual punishment" and therefore unconstitutional. Many assumed that the death penalty had been abolished for good, instead of temporarily suspended. After World War II and the shock of Holocaust atrocities, executions had declined steadily. In 1965, the same year that Britain abolished the death penalty, there were seven executions, compared to the peak decade of the depression-ravaged 1930s when there were 167 executions a year on average. Then in the next year, 1966, there were two, and the following year, 1967, only one. No executions were performed in the five years leading up to the Supreme Court's formal ruling against the death penalty in 1972, and in particular the Federal government had not executed anyone since 1963. From the vantage point of May, 2002 (the time of the final draft of this article), when we have already put 31 people to death in the first five months of this

year, it is astounding to think that from 1968 through 1976 there was not a single execution in America.[8]

How have we come so far from the social sensibility that Foucault indexed in *Discipline and Punish*? Since 1975 there has been a major shift of societal attitudes toward punishment. Current support for the death penalty hovers between 70 and 75 percent, having peaked at 80 percent in 1994, the year of the conservative Republican takeover of congress. As of April 1, 2002, there are 3,701 men and women—including 83 juvenile offenders—awaiting execution on death row compared to 334 in 1972 when the Supreme Court struck down the death penalty.[9] So deep is the revanchist enthusiasm for spectacles of the scaffold that when Senator Dianne Feinstein, the former mayor of San Francisco, ran for governor of California in 1990 she displayed images of the San Quentin gas chamber in her television campaign commercials. She came from behind to win the Democratic primary by 19 percent after campaigning on the slogan, "the only Democrat who supports the death penalty."[10]

Especially with the resurgent popularity of capital punishment, it is important to remember that the history of the death penalty in the United States has been one of challenge and contention.[11] Almost from the beginning, capital punishment has been a fraught and contested performance practice. The performance genealogy of executions periodically requires fresh blood to keep this macabre tradition alive. Contemporary defenders of capital punishment shore up its shaky premises, not by logic or rational argument, but by invoking scapegoats, poster boys for the death penalty: Timothy McVeigh, John Wayne Gacy, Jeffrey Dahmer, Richard Speck—and now Osama bin Laden and his henchmen. With each exemplary monster executed, capital punishment is legitimated and revitalized. Thus it is no surprise that George W. Bush, who has presided over 156 executions during his relatively short time in public life, issued executive orders very soon after September 11, 2001, to create military tribunals designed to expedite executions with an efficiency and speed that would exceed that of Texas.[12] Theatre and performance studies have an ethical as well as intellectual obligation to examine this resurgent theatre of death that anchors conservative politics in the United States. The very word "execute" means to accomplish, to carry out, and to perform, to do. "Execution" also means "a mode or style of performance."[13] The death penalty cannot be understood simply as a matter of public policy debate or an aspect of criminology, apart from what it is pre-eminently: performance.

PERFORMANCE RITUALS OF STATE KILLING

Executions are awesome rituals of human sacrifice through which the state dramatizes its absolute power and monopoly on violence. We know from the anthropological record that a key to the efficacy of rituals is their capacity to embrace paradox, to gloss contradictions, to mediate profound oppositions, tensions, ambivalences, anxieties. The ritual frame is elastic enough to encompass conflict and chaos, yet sufficiently sturdy to channel volatile forces and disruptive tensions into an aesthetic shape, a repeatable pattern. Rituals draw their drama, dynamism, and intensity from the crises they redress. A host of important anthropologists, notably Victor Turner, Mary Douglas, Clifford Geertz, Roy Rappaport, and others, have noted that ritual performance proliferates along social faultlines, pressure points, cracks in the system, the jagged edge of belief.[14] Rituals carry their weight and earn their cultural keep by restoring, replenishing, repairing, and remaking belief, transforming vague ideas, mixed feelings, and shaky commitments into dramatic clarity and alignment. As embodied performances, rituals incarnate and make visible abstract principles and inchoate concepts—such as "Justice." What is Justice? Justice is an abstraction, a spirit that commands tremendous faith, power, and huge investments both economic and emotional. Like religion and other powerful abstractions, Justice—to paraphrase Victor Turner—lives only in performance, "only in so far as its rituals are 'going concerns'"; Justice can be seen only when it is acted out.[15] All the interlocking rituals of criminal punishment—arrest, detention, interrogation, trial, conviction, incarceration, execution—are performed so that citizens can see "justice done":

"All of justice is a stage; it is the appearance—the ritual—that is the meaningful thing."[16]

Moreover, rituals are neither static nor discrete. They draw their meaning, structure, style, and affective resonance from the traditions they reenact. But they never simply repeat a given form, but, like all "restored behavior," they reverberate within the traditions they simultaneously reinvent and redeploy for historically situated needs and purposes.[17] The ritual replaying of traditional form always plays with, and plays off and against, the performance genealogy that it recites.[18] Rituals of execution in the United States are part of a dynamic performance genealogy that has undergone profound shifts in feeling, form, and dramaturgy. The seismic shift has been from the public, open-air, communal, hortatory rituals of redemption in colonial and revolutionary era America to the privatized, elite, class-stratified rituals of retribution and exclusion that were created in the early nineteenth century to accommodate an emergent middle-class ethos of restraint, propriety, gentility and new standards of bourgeois taste and refinement. Beginning in the 1830s, execution rituals moved from the public square where they drew diverse audiences numbering in the thousands to inside prison walls where, withdrawn from public view, they became private performances for a small, homosocial, invitation-only audience of elites. Historian Louis Masur summarizes the wider social significance of this change in the mise-en-scène of execution rituals:

> The creation of private executions [during the 1830s] . . . was an act charged with multiple meanings: it marked the triumph of a certain code of conduct and set of social attitudes among the middle and upper classes; it symbolized a broader trend toward privatization and class segmentation; it turned the execution of criminals into an elite event centered around class and gender exclusion.[19]

The withdrawal and relocation of executions from the public green to censored enclosures signaled a major shift in structures of feeling about criminals and capital punishment.

To understand better this profoundly meaningful change in dramaturgy, let us examine the execution rituals characteristic of early America. Public hangings in seventeenth- and eighteenth-century New England were mass spectacles that drew the largest audiences ever assembled for any occasion. Especially in Puritan New England, with no maypoles, carnivals, staged theatre, or even Christmas celebrations, a public hanging was an avidly attended "Tragical Spectacle."[20] For the 1686 execution of John Morgan, crowds began gathering in Boston a week before the hanging. According to John Dunston, a bookseller from London visiting Boston at the time, some "have come 50 miles to see it."[21] On the morning of March 11, more than 5,000 people jammed into Boston's Second Old North Church to see the condemned prisoner prominently seated in front of the pulpit to hear Cotton Mather preach his execution sermon, a key part of the dramaturgy of hanging day rituals. When the floor and walls of the church gallery began to crack and buckle under the tremendous weight and pressure of the crowd, Mather interrupted his sermon to move the audience to Samuel Willard's Third Old South Church, which had a larger gallery.[22] And the outdoor staging of the gallows accommodated multitudes who could not squeeze into the church or were inclined to skip the sermon. One scholar estimated that executions in colonial New England attracted as many as 12,000 spectators.[23] In terms of sheer audience size, executions were the most popular performance genre in seventeenth- and eighteenth-century America: "Well into the nineteenth century, execution crowds still outnumbered crowds gathered for any other purpose."[24]

Puritan executions were elaborately staged and exquisitely paced ritual dramas seething with suspense, tension, ambivalence, crisis, reversals, revelations, and breathtaking spectacle. The hanging day ritual included the public procession from the jail to the church, where the prisoner was displayed as a "sorrowful spectacle" and embodied "example," a focal point and prop for the minister's fiery execution sermon.[25] The celebrated ministers appointed to preside at these high profile events rose to their greatest oratorical heights, knowing that they were addressing the largest audiences of their careers, and given the magnitude of an execution, the sermons were often published and sold, thus circulating in print to an ever widening audience.[26]

After the sermon, there was the doleful parade to the gallows, which often took one or more hours. The prisoner typically was carried slowly through the crowd elevated on a cart, sometimes with a rope around his or her neck, and with the coffin conspicuously alongside. At the gallows, there were more speeches and audible prayers, and often hymns were sung communally to pitch the emotions of the audience. Then the sheriff read the death warrant aloud. All of the dramaturgy at the foot of the gallows was designed to anticipate, draw out, and heighten the spellbinding moment when the prisoner climbed the ladder and, precariously perched, delivered a speech to the rapt audience thronged below. This long-awaited speech from the prisoner—who, more often than not, was a young servant or slave, a person of little or no education and low social standing—could eclipse the rhetorical grandeur of the elite, Harvard-trained minister-orators. The "last Dying Words"[27] of the condemned gathered compelling presencing powers precisely because they were uttered from a space of death and disappearance that impressed on the audience the urgency of their vanishing: "I am upon the brink of Eternity."[28] Then the hood was lowered and the noose tightened around the neck. To clinch the climactic force of the condemned's dying speech, the hangman kicked the ladder out from under the prisoner's feet, and, as one historian put it, "then came a riot of motion."[29]

The suspense that excited and transfixed execution audiences was not about the temporal plot or unfolding physical action—the hanging day scenario was well known and predictably choreographed. All the suspense hovered over the fate of the prisoner's immortal soul. What riveted audience attention was whether or not the condemned had truly repented, and, even if so, would her or his faith hold fast under the tremendous distress and horror of "the present circumstances for Terrification"?[30] Executions, like every other temporal aspect of life in Puritan New

England, were inserted within a cosmic spiritual drama of sin and salvation. The real suspense was not about anything so mundane as whether the condemned would get a last-minute reprieve, but would the condemned confess convincingly, manifest true repentance, and be able to deliver an affecting dying speech that would serve as warning to sinners and inspiration to the sanctified? If that happened—no easy feat, by any measure—then the worst malefactor could hope for eternal life. Puritan audiences scrutinized the body and speech of the condemned for "Signals of Divine Grace," and when they recognized true penitence then they could interpretively reframe the hideous torture of a hanging into a catalyst for salvation: "This Serves only to draw the Curtain, that thou mayst behold a Tragick Scene, strangely changed into a Theater of Mercy."[31]

To appreciate better the complex theatricality of executions in early America, let us look more closely at one particular case. On July 31, 1701, Esther Rodgers, a twenty-one-year-old indentured servant convicted of infanticide, was hanged outside the town of Ipswich before a crowd estimated between four and five thousand.[32] She had confessed to fornication, "Carnal Pollution with the Negro" with whom she worked in the same household, and to killing the "bastard" newborn "begotten in Whoredom."[33] After arraignment and imprisonment for this heinous crime, she confessed to another, earlier murder: when she was seventeen she had fallen into "that foul Sin of Uncleanness, suffering my self to be defiled by a Negro Lad" and she had killed that mixed-race baby as well. In between the two pregnancies, she had lived in a tavern, "giving my self up to other wicked Company and ways of Evil."[34] A vast multitude of spectators assembled at the gallows, the largest audience "as was scarcely ever heard of or seen upon any occasion in any part of New England."[35] They had come "to behold the Tragical End" of this young but "very great Criminal."[36] In addition to the notoriety and sexual-racial sensationalism of her crimes, part of the draw could have been the circulating reports of her "marvelous change" from the pastors and pious townspeople who had visited and ministered to her during her eight months in prison awaiting execution.[37] As one of the ministers attested: "a poor Wretch, entering into Prison a Bloody Malefactor, her Conscience laden with Sins of a Scarlet Die . . . she came forth, Sprinkled, Cleansed, Comforted, a Candidate of Heaven."[38]

For all its "antitheatrical prejudice," Puritan life was saturated with a performance consciousness that delighted in transformations, metamorphoses, reversals, astonishing wonders, and the language of theatrical representation: "tragical spectacle," "tragick scene," "tragick end," "theater of mercy."[39] Everyday people and events could become spectacles, displays, signs, examples, monuments. Esther was depicted as "a Pillar of Salt Transformed into a Monument of Free Grace."[40] But Puritan ways of seeing increased the dramatic tension because any "monument of grace" was unstable and fallible, always in danger of falling, of debasing itself, of shape-shifting into "a Monument of Shame and Ignominy."[41] The drama of the fall and the relentless conflict with evil suffused the workaday world where everyday action, gesture, and speech suddenly could shimmer with spiritual significance to the discerning eye. The execution sermon provided a figural proscenium arch, the theological frame, through which a Puritan audience viewed a public hanging. Puritan ministers endeavored, at great discursive length, to turn the earthly scene of capital punishment into a stunning morality play, a vivid acting out of the allegory of divine wrath and judgment, and, if the ritual succeeded, "an Instance of Converting Grace and Mercy."[42] They uplifted the physical action of the state "Business of Death" onto a sacred plane of performative metaphors, images, and symbols.[43] Thus when describing the vast multitude of thousands gathered to watch Esther Rodgers hang, one minister commented, "Which could not but put all serious and thoughtful Spirits in mind of the Great and General Assembly that will appear at the Great Day to receive their final Sentence."[44]

Puritan theology underpinned robust "interpretive communities" of active spectators for whom, in a very deep sense, all the world was a stage, a place for seeing.[45] They inculcated "watchfulness"—of themselves and their neighbors—as part of the habitus of daily life.[46] According to their Calvinist outlook, everyone was innately depraved, and conversion, never final, was an arduous and incessant struggle. For several weeks prior to her execution, Esther Rodgers consistently enacted the role of an exemplary sinner, showing all the signs of repentance and conversion. Nonetheless, she emerged from prison on the morning of her execution as a *"Candidate* of Heaven," her salvation by no means yet assured.[47] She still had to face the greatest and most severe test and trial of her newfound faith. The sabbath before her hanging she had dictated a written message to be read aloud in church enlisting the support and prayers of the congregation, "that the Lord would Strengthen and Uphold her, and carry her through that hard and difficult Work when called thereunto, that she may not be dismayed at the Sight and Fear of Death."[48] These same congregants formed part of the vigilant and expectant circle of spectators around the gallows who scrutinized every move she made. Everyone wondered: what was the state of her mind, heart, and soul as she looked death in the face? Had she accomplished the laborious work of conversion sufficiently?

And if these questions were not already in many spectators' minds, they certainly would have been stirred up by the attending clergy who continuously questioned her conversion as they cross-examined her throughout the grim proceedings. Toward the end of his execution morning sermon, the Reverend Rogers challenged her:

> But what preparation hast thy Soul made to appear at Gods Tribunal before this Day be ended? . . . Hast thou desired and laboured for Holiness to Sanctify thee, as well as Righteousness to justify thee? What means hast thou used to get thy Soul purged as well as sin pardoned . . .? Hast thou waited and prayed with David, Psal[m] 51. *Wash me throughly from my sins, purge me with Hyssop* . . . or hast thou thought a few Tears sufficient for this?[49]

And as she walked the long "dolorous way" to the gallows, the accompanying ministers pressed her with frightening questions, "mixing with words of Consolation, something of Terrour":

> O Esther, How can your heart abide! Don't you here behold terrible displays of Justice: you are surrounded with Armed men. . . . The terrible place and Engines of Destruction, are but a little before us, where you must in a few Minutes Expire; and there lyes your Coffin that must receive your perishing Body: How can you bear the sight of all these things?[50]

And even after she had climbed the scaffold ladder, and delivered a deeply moving speech to the audience of thousands, and an even more emotionally pitched and passionate prayer, and after the sheriff had tied the blindfold over her face, just moments before he placed the noose over her head, another attending minister, Reverend Wise, stepped forward and took that moment to cross-examine her again: "Now is the great Crisis of Time. Does your Faith hold in God and Christ still? She answers, *God be thanked it does, God be thanked.*" Then, with the rope around her neck, and after her final, almost frantic, outcry—"O Lord Jesus, Now Lord Jesus, I am a coming. . . ." (152)—even at that most vulnerable, plaintive moment, as she waited for the drop, "Lifting up her Hands to Heaven," the unflappable Reverend Wise stepped forward again, and extended her only the conditional comfort of the subjunctive mood: "If your Hopes can lay hold upon the irresistible Grace and Mercy of God in Christ, and [if] you can cast your self into His Armes, you are Happy for Ever. And so we must bid you Fare-Well."[51]

The Ipswich pastors seized the occasion of Esther Rodgers's execution to dramatize and drive home the point that conversion was a moment-by-moment contingency: at any instant mortals could be "assaulted with Temptations to Unbelief or Fear."[52] Esther died a saint, but throughout the protracted drama of her execution-*cum*-salvation her state of grace was both affirmed and deferred, contrapuntally played out and kept in agonizing suspense right up until the end. The processual, equivocal, anxious, contested dynamics of conversion heightened the tension and turned a familiar execution scenario into a cliffhanger. The moral drama was heightened and made compelling by this deep interplay between knowing, and not knowing, for sure.

Further, Puritan sermons were filled with warnings against dissemblers, hypocrites, and charlatans who masqueraded piety: "Lyars: Such as are deceitful, and dissembling, who speak otherwise then they think; and do otherwise then they speak; such as accustom themselves to speak falsly" and those who are "partial and feigned in their repentance."[53] Esther Rodgers was a person who knew how to keep secrets, how to feign and hide: she had concealed not one, but two pregnancies, carried the babies to term, secretly delivered, and no one knew, not even the fathers. And she had successfully covered up the first murder. At least one supporter felt the need to preempt questions about the sincerity of her jailhouse conversion: "Neither shall any need to question the truth of the repentance of the person Condemned, and after Executed, from the shortness of the time of her Experiences: The Thief that Commenced Converted on the Cross . . . is a proof of the possibility hereof."[54]

The ambivalence of her spiritual condition, the gap between closure and uncertainty that the ministers pried open, also provided a space for multiple ways of seeing and other spectatorial positions unbounded by Puritan orthodoxy. Executions encouraged spectators to gaze intently at the body on display and granted extraordinary ritual license for the condemned, especially if they were women, to make spectacles out of their bodies.[55] Just as the sentence of death had to be "executed on her body," so also the signs of grace had to be manifested bodily.[56] Execution audiences closely monitored the prisoner's gesture, carriage, countenance, demeanor, deportment, vocal intonation, inflection, timber. An "admiring observer" noted Esther's "Composure of spirit, Cheerfulness of Countenance, pleasantness of Speech, and a sort of Complaisantness in Carriage towards the Ministers who were assistant to her."[57] But was there slippage in the frames through which she was viewed? And did even a pious allegorical reading pivot on a doubling of vision, an interplay of perspectives that saw her as both a wanton woman and an aspiring Christian? She had been, until very recently, a harlot. Everyone knew the sexual nature of her crime and her "scarlet" past. She had confessed that she was a creature wholly given over to "lust."[58] Reverend Rogers reminded her, and everyone else, in his morning execution sermon: "Thy ways have been all filthy, thy whole Walk, a walk after the Flesh; thy course a course of filthy Communication and Conversation."[59]

With that phrase still ringing in their ears, how did spectators view her "Walk" to the gallows? Her choice to forego the customary cart and to "walk on foot"?[60] How did they observe the moving body of this young, sexually active woman, surrounded by men, as it paraded by them? Was she a walking palimpsest, the imprint of her harlot past shadowing and alternating with her Christian image? Which image came into sharper and more sustained focus for whom, at what points in the procession? How did bystanders interpret her vivacious physicality, especially the remarkable moment when she responded to a minister's question by "turn[ing] about, and looking him in the face with a very smiling countenance"?[61] What did various spectators make of the moment when she stumbled upon first seeing the gallows, and then, after this "Reluctancy of the Flesh," her recovery when "she lift up her Feet, and Marched on with an Erected, and Radiant Countenance"?[62] How did different audience members construe "the very affecting Gestures" with which she took her leave of the ministers at the foot of the gallows?[63] How did they watch her as she paused, composed herself, "and so without stop or trembling went up the Ladder"? And what went through their minds during the physically delicate moment of "turning herself about" on the narrow ladder so that she could face the crowd? And how did they take in her spectacularly displayed body, especially when she arched it, "being bid [by the sheriff] to lean her Head back upon the Ladder, to receive the Halter"?[64]

We can be sure that profane ways of looking commingled with pious perspectives within this huge gathering. The sheer size of the crowd, numbering in the thousands, must have created a social effervescence. Executions in England during the same time period were rowdy, rambunctious, "carnivalesque" 20 affairs.[65] And the large number of young people in the audience—"great Numbers whereof were expected" and their large presence was "accordingly" noted—must have charged the event with libidinal energy.[66] Puritan sermons reverberated with warnings about "youthful lusts."[67] The massive ideological pressure of the execution sermons attests indirectly to the excitement and desire that the preachers struggled so forcefully to rein in and control. If we read these official documents against the grain of their orthodoxy, we can understand that all the appeals to "serious and thoughtful spirits" were pulling against other, more unruly and irreverent dispositions.[68] Moreover, sensuality was not banished from Puritan piety. Recent historical research disputes the stereotype of the dour, sexually repressed Puritans and argues that they exuberantly "conjoined earthly and spiritual passion" and that a striking aspect of their religious life was "the eroticisation of the spiritual."[69]

Execution audiences were encouraged to identify deeply with the condemned as fellow sinners. They did not shrink in moral revulsion from even the most despised and heinous criminals. The typical response was "there but for the grace of God, go I." At the 1674 execution of Benjamin Goad for sodomy, Samuel Danforth vehemently denounced his horrid and unnatural "lasciviousness" but then reminded the audience: "there are sins with the Spectators, as well as with the Sufferers. . . . If we ransack our own hearts . . . we shall finde such sins with us. . . . The holiest man hath as vile and filthy a Nature, as the Sodomites. . . ."[70] This way of seeing encouraged a deeply sympathetic, theatrical identification in which the spectators could imaginatively exchange places with the condemned, instead of holding themselves aloof in distanced judgment. The ideal spectator at executions became a deeply engaged, coperformative witness.

The Puritan structure of feeling that embraced wrongdoers as members of the same moral community in need of repentance was superseded in the nineteenth century by a gothic view of criminals as "moral aliens" and "moral monsters."[71] The dramaturgy of executions changed from large-scale public rituals of redemption and reincorporation to exclusive, privatized rituals of retribution and expulsion. This new, bourgeois structure of feeling about criminals is registered powerfully in an 1848 *American Whig Review* article, "On the Use of Chloroform in Hanging."[72] Criminals are now seen as "miserable wretches whom we simply wish to cast contemptuously out of existence."[73] Class lines are now sharply drawn and patrolled by social performances of civility and respectability, all based on bodily deportment: "the rude have one species, the refined another."[74] A "gentlemanly nation" should be "severe towards crime"; therefore the respectable classes "must overcome sympathy"[75] to criminals who are "aliens to the race":

> The reason should condemn them, the fancy recoil from them, and the pride scorn them. All that can spring from the deepest determination to wipe out such stains from humanity, or express the universal strong disgust which they inspire, should be brought to bear against them. Mankind are bound to affect towards them the manners of loathing and horror.[76]

Peck proposed chloroforming prisoners before hanging them, not out of any compassion for the condemned, but because some of the loathsome creatures had the bad manners to struggle and convulse while being executed, "thus tending to disturb the nervous peace, which is the support of refinement." A botched execution was "against good manners, and unbecoming in a civilized Christian people."[77] Coming midway between the 1701 execution of Esther Rodgers and the 2001 executions of Timothy McVeigh and Juan Raul Garza, Peck's pivotal document registers the profound shift in structure of feeling about the death penalty and prefigures the modern interest in new methods and technologies for sanitizing death. Although Peck's idea to anesthetize criminals before executing them was not adopted in his day, it resurfaced in 1977 when Oklahoma invented lethal injection as the preferred mode of capital punishment for the modern age. The lethal injection protocol includes a first dose of sodium pentothal, which puts the prisoner to sleep, followed by a muscle relaxant that paralyzes the lungs, and then potassium chloride that stops the heart.[78] Putting the prisoner to sleep before killing him or her is more about cosmetics than compassion; it keeps up the appearance of decency, protects the witnesses from messy scenes, and masks the violence of state killing with a humane medical procedure.

THE MAGICAL REALISM OF MODERN CAPITAL PUNISHMENT

The multibillion dollar business of incarceration with its ramified rituals of punishment provides the bodies—and they are disproportionately racialized and working-class bodies—that serve as the concrete referents for society's ideas about "justice," "law and order," and "public safety."[79] Executions anchor belief in the criminal justice system, dramatizing in an especially vivid way that "something is being done," that the system is in control, order has been restored. Foucault argued: "without the right to kill, would the judicial system be anything more than a public utility a bit less efficient than the post office? The right to kill is the last emblem of its supremacy."[80] Never has Foucault's insight been demonstrated more clearly than in the FBI bungling of the McVeigh evidence in the most high-profile capital trial in recent history; the FBI lost 4,400 documents, evidence that should have been turned over to the defense team. This was such a breach of due process that Attorney General John Ashcroft had to issue a one-month stay of execution.[81] If the judicial system can break down and bungle a case of this magnitude, under an international media spotlight, imagine what happens with everyday prosecutions. This crisis of confidence was redressed by speedy review, and within a few weeks the McVeigh execution bandwagon was back on track and a new death warrant signed for June 11. These events dramatically drive home Foucault's larger point that executions justify Justice, that they provide a satisfying sense of closure and cover for a shaky system that pretends to be infallible. Northwestern University's Center for Wrongful Convictions has documented more than one hundred cases of men and women who were sentenced to death and then exonerated. In Illinois, thirteen men in recent years have been freed from death row; that is one more than the state has executed since the United States reinstated capital punishment in 1976. One of these released men, Anthony Porter, came within 48 hours of being put to death; he had already ordered his last meal and been measured for his coffin.[82]

Contemporary execution rituals work their magic and derive their efficacy from the effusive power of the effigy. Here I draw together Joseph Roach's performance theory of the effigy in *Cities of the Dead* with Michael Taussig's rereading of the anthropological literature on effigies and magic in *Mimesis and Alterity*.[83] Effigies are crudely fashioned surrogates that bear little resemblance to the person for whom they stand in. They produce magical power from parts, pieces, effluvia, operating on principles of contiguity and synecdoche—the piece, the part that stands for the whole—more than likeness or resemblance. Effigies are rough fabrications made from distorted parts of a person, often excrements such as saliva, blood, hair, fingernail parings, semen, fingerprints, footprints, which are then performatively deployed to put the real person in harm's way. An effigy is the fusion of image and body, symbol and source, the figurative and the physical. Because a jury will never vote to kill a human being, the fundamental task of the prosecutor is to turn the accused into an effigy composed of his or her worst parts and bad deeds. Before they are strip-searched and strapped down to the execution gurney, the condemned must first be stripped of all human complexity and reduced to human waste, the worst of the worst. These waste parts are then crafted onto prefabricated figures: stereotypes of the violent criminal, coldblooded killer, animal, beast, brute, predator, fiend, monster. Thus a young, attractive, completely rehabilitated, devoutly spiritual Karla Faye Tucker was transformed into an effigy, a scarecrow, and methodically put to death as "the Pick-Axe Killer." These effigies take on manifest powers and become not just surrogates for the accused, but stand-ins for crime and all antisocial forces of evil that threaten law and order. When the Federal government strapped Juan Garza onto a gurney on June 19, 2001, and stuck a needle into the calf of his right leg, it was not killing a loving father of young children who was much, much more than the single worst thing that he had ever done. They were sticking pins into an effigy: "Drug Kingpin," the headlines blared on execution day. And they did this in the name of Justice and for the sake of Order to ward off omnipresent social dangers and the specter of crime.

Race figures prominently in the construction 25 of these effigies. Glaring racial disparities at every level of the death penalty system are shocking and egregious. Of the 760 people put to death since capital punishment was reinstated in 1977, 44 percent have been minorities, when minorities are only 29 percent of the population. And this disproportion is even more skewed if we focus on blacks: 35 percent of the people executed were black, when blacks are only 12 percent of the population (Table 1). And 43 percent of the prisoners currently on death row are black (Table 2). The racial profile of people put to death becomes even more stark when we look at juvenile offenders. First, I need to point out that the United States is one of a small number of countries in the world that still has a juvenile death penalty. Not only is the US out of step with other western democracies that long since have stopped putting their citizens to death—abolition of the death penalty is a condition of membership in the European Union—but also only five countries that still retain capital punishment to execute minors: Iran, Nigeria, Pakistan, Saudi Arabia, and the United States. And no nation in the world has reported executions of minors since 1997, except the United States: we have executed seven juvenile offenders since 1998, three in 2000, one in May, 2002 (Napoleon Beazley, the young African American man, whose last words I quoted in the epigraph for this essay). Not even China, the world leader in number of executions per year, still executes juvenile offenders. Of the thirty-eight states with death penalty statutes, twenty-three authorize the execution of children; eighteen states allow the execution of children as young as sixteen (Table 3). Texas has executed eleven of the nineteen juvenile offenders who have been put

to death since 1985, and 64 percent of that group were minorities (Table 4). And twenty-six of the eighty-three juvenile offenders currently awaiting execution are on Texas's death row: 85 percent of them are minorities (Table 5).[84]

Table 1

Race of 760 Defendants Executed, 1977–2002

(US pop.)			
White	430	56%	(71%)
Minority	330	44%	(29%)
Black	265	35%	(12%)
Latino	50	7%	(12%)
Other	15	2%	(5%)

U.S. Census 2000
Execution count up to February 19, 2002

Table 2

Race of Death Row Inmates

Minority	54%
Black	43%
Latino	9%
Other	2%
White	46%

January 1, 2002

Table 3

Juvenile Death Penalty

23 of the 38 Death Penalty States Permit the Execution of Minors

Minimum Age	
16	(18 states)
17	(5 states)
18	(15 states)

Table 4

19 Juvenile Offenders Executed Since 1985

Texas Executed 11	
7 Minority	64%
6 Black	
1 Latino	
4 White	36%

May, 2002

Table 5

83 Juvenile Offenders on Death Row

26 on Texas Death Row	
22 Minority	85%
11 Black	42%
10 Latino	39%
1 Asian	4%
4 White	15%

February, 2002

Table 6

U.S. Military Death Row

Total 7		
Minority	6	86%
Black	5	71%
Asian	1	14%
White	1	14%

Reinstated in 1984 by executive order of Pres. Ronald Reagan

Last military execution in 1963 (hanging)

Table 7

Federal Death Row

Total 19		
Minority	16	84%
Black	14	74%
Latino	2	10%
White	3	16%

(Four cases pending: 3 Black, 1 Asian)

January, 2002

Furthermore, if we look at other jurisdictions in addition to the thirty-eight states with death penalty statutes, the racial disparities are even more glaring. The United States military has its own death penalty statute, and 86 percent of the military prisoners on death row are minorities (Table 6). This statistic does not augur well for the military tribunals that President Bush has authorized by executive order to adjudicate capital cases in the wake of September 11. The federal government also has its own death penalty statute that authorizes the execution of prisoners in the name of every citizen in the nation. Eighty-seven percent of the prisoners on federal death row are minorities (Table 7). Because of these statistics, the federal government went to great lengths to ensure that McVeigh would precede Mexican-born Garza to the federal death chamber. The federal government had not put anyone to death in thirty-eight years, so whoever inaugurated the newly built state-of-the-art federal execution chamber in Terre Haute, Indiana—strategically chosen as the geographic "crossroads of America"—would attract extraordinary media attention. Garza originally had been scheduled to go to the gurney first, August 5, 2000, but two stays of execution pushed back his date to June 19, 2001, behind Timothy McVeigh who was scheduled for May 16, 2001. The shocking revelation on May 10 that the FBI had failed to turn over 4,400 documents of evidence to the McVeigh defense team, as they were required to do by law, threatened to derail McVeigh's timely execution. However, Attorney General John Ashcroft granted only a one-month reprieve, which kept McVeigh just in front of Garza, absorbing the full media spotlight as the "first" prisoner executed by the federal government in thirty-eight years. In this sense,

Table 10

Section V. "THE FINAL THIRTY MINUTES PRIOR TO THE EXECUTION"

A. Final Sequence of Events: Preparation

---

1. Bringing the Condemned Individual to the Execution Room: At a time determined by the warden, the condemned individual will be:

   a. removed from the Inmate Holding Cell by the Restraint Team

   b. strip-searched by the Restraint Team and then dressed in khaki pants, shirt, and slip-on shoes

   c. secured with restraints, if deemed appropriate by the Warden

   d. escorted to the Execution Room by the Restraint Team

2. *Restraint Team Procedures*

   In the execution room the ambulatory restraints, if any, will be removed, and the condemned individual will be restrained to the Execution Table. . . .

VI. FINAL SEQUENCE OF EVENTS: EXECUTION

A. Staff Witnesses

---

1. Staff participating in the preparation for the execution will exit the Execution Room but stand by in an adjacent area

2. Staff members remaining to participate in and observe the execution will include the:

   a. Designated United States Marshal

   b. Warden

   c. Executioner

   d. Other staff authorized by the Director of the Bureau of Prisons

B. Countdown

---

1. Once the condemned individual has been secured to the table, at the direction of the Warden, staff inside the execution room will open the drapes covering the windows of the witness room.

2. The Warden will ask the condemned individual if he/she has any last words, or wishes to make a statement. The condemned individual will have been advised in advance by the warden that this statement should be reasonably brief. . . .

3. At the conclusion of the remarks, or when the Warden determines it is time to proceed, the Warden will read documentation deemed necessary to the execution process. The Warden will then advise the Designated United States Marshal that, quote, "We are ready." Close quote. A prearranged signal will then be given by the Designated United States Marshal to the Warden, who will direct the executioner to administer the lethal injection.

4. If the execution is ordered delayed, the Designated United States Marshal will instruct the Executioner to step away from the execution equipment and will notify the condemned individual and all present that the execution has been stayed or delayed. The Warden will direct stand down procedures and return the institution to normal operations after the condemned individual has been returned to appropriate living quarters.

C. Execution

After receiving the signal from the Designated United States Marshal, the Warden will direct the executioner to administer the lethal injection.

His immediate predecessor, Harley Lappin, scored high marks for directing the June 2001 executions of McVeigh and Garza, again the first federal executions since 1963. By the time I was able to return to Terre Haute in September 2001 to tour the prison and talk with staff, Lappin already had been rewarded with a promotion and transfer. He is now the Director of the Mid-Atlantic Region, with twenty prisons under his supervision.

Even the demonstrators who come to protest the executions are carefully monitored and controlled. No one is permitted onto the prison grounds with his or her own transportation. At both the McVeigh and Garza executions, we had to meet at a designated park, walk down a fenced corridor, and get searched before being permitted to board the Bureau of Prisons buses. We were required to take a "Pledge of Nonviolence," which included: "we will not swear or use insulting language. We will not run in public or otherwise make threatening motions. We will honor the directions of the designated coordinators. In the event of serious disagreement, we will remove ourselves from the Vigil Action." Once on the bus, two guards with rifles accompanied us, one riding up front, the other in the back. Each bus was escorted to the prison by two police cars with flashing lights, one car in front, one in the rear.

"What is at stake," Sarat asks, "when the state imagines itself killing painlessly, humanely?"[110] When it invents new and improved technologies for putting people to death with "decency" and "dignity"? What do the shifting modes and methods of execution say about public standards of taste and thresholds of squeamishness? The quest for quick, efficient, and clean modes of execution that do not disfigure the corpse is for the sake of spectators more than the condemned. When Ronald Reagan was governor of California, he was one of the first government officials to imagine lethal injection. He observed, "as a former rancher and horse raiser, I know what it's like to eliminate an injured horse by shooting him," recommending instead, "a simple shot or tranquilizer."[111] Reagan's point was not to spare the defendant pain, but to shield the executioners—and by extension,

civil society—from the horror and anguish of exterminating a human being.

In 1977 Oklahoma reinvented capital punishment for the modern age by developing the new performance technology of "lethal injection." In 1982 in Texas, Charles Brooks became the first prisoner executed by lethal injection. Outside the United States, China first used lethal injection in 1997, which it deemed more scientific than shooting a kneeling prisoner in the back of the head at close range. When lethal injection was first discussed in the Oklahoma legislature, advocates argued the merits of: "No pain, no spasms, no smells or sounds—just sleep, then death." Governor David Boren pointed out that it provided "a nice clean exit plan."[112] Susan Blaustein, a media witness to a lethal injection in Texas, described the experience in a *Harper's Magazine* article titled, "Witness to Another Execution in Texas: Death Walks an Assembly Line." She wrote: "The lethal injection method has turned dying into a *still life*, thereby enabling the state to kill without anyone involved feeling anything at all. . . . We have perfected the art of institutional killing to the degree that it has deadened our natural, quintessentially human response to death."[113]

Tulsa Republican representative William Wiseman Jr. was the principal architect of Oklahoma's lethal injection bill. He argued that the needle would "make the death penalty more humane by eliminating the brutality and violence of electrocution"—Oklahoma's then-current method for executing criminals. In June 2001, Wiseman published an apologia in the *Christian Century*. He admitted: "The dramatic irony of my action as a legislator is that what purported to be a means of reducing violence became instead a means of increasing it. The moral burden I carry is that, if it were not for my *palatable technique* of death, many who have now been executed would likely have been spared by squeamish juries." He left politics and is now pursuing a Master's of Divinity degree at a theological seminary in Tulsa.[114]

Lethal injection, the favored method of modern capital punishment, borrows props from the medical profession and eerily mimics a therapeutic intervention. Missouri's lethal injection chamber at Potosi Correctional Center is right in the center of the prison hospital ward.[115] One of the uncanny consequences of this slippage between curing and killing is that there is a new emergent justification for executions: executions are justified so that the families of victims can heal and achieve "closure." This is a new development in the history of justifications for capital punishment. We have moved from support of capital punishment as a deterrent, as retribution, and now as an extension and necessary part of the grieving process and form of group therapy. This link between capital punishment and mourning is aligned with the politics of the powerful victims' rights movement: "By transforming courts into sites for the rituals of grieving, that movement seeks to make private experiences part of public discourse."[116] Appellate Judge Alex Kosinski says that when he reviews and signs off on executions, he "hear[s] the tortured voices of the victims calling out to [him] . . . for vindication."[117]

The execution of McVeigh demonstrates the political efficacy of mourning. The same group of mourning survivors and family and friends of victims who planned the Oklahoma City National Memorial also campaigned for passage of the 1996 Antiterrorism and Effective Death Penalty Act, legislation that restricts the right of appeal and habeas corpus in order to streamline and speed up the execution process. They also successfully lobbied Attorney General Ashcroft to telecast McVeigh's execution to an invited group of designated mourners in Oklahoma. In an unprecedented move, Attorney General Ashcroft authorized the closed circuit telecast of McVeigh's execution to an arena filled with relatives of victims and survivors of the Murrah Building bombing. He infamously said that survivors and families of victims need to be able to see McVeigh executed "to help them meet their need to close this chapter in their lives."[118] Over one thousand people were invited to the live telecast of McVeigh's execution, more than half declined, and on the morning of June 19, 2001, 232 showed up at the telecast site, a federal prison.[119]

Several of the invited people went directly from watching the telecast of McVeigh's execution to the Oklahoma City National Memorial Center, thus collapsing the execution into personal rituals of bereavement. One of them, Tom Kight, placed the blue federal badge identifying him as "Witness 223" at the execution telecast on the commemorative chair for his stepdaughter killed in the blast.[120] Several newspapers reinforced this conflation of capital punishment with rites of mourning by running full-color photographs of the Oklahoma City National Memorial Center underneath banner headlines announcing McVeigh's execution. On June 12, the *New York Times* ran "McVeigh Dies for Oklahoma City Blast" headline above a photograph of family members kneeling and grieving by the chair commemorating their mother at the Oklahoma City National Memorial Center. The caption explained that the family members had just come from watching the execution on closed-circuit TV.[121] The same day the *Chicago Tribune* ran "U.S. Executes Its Worst Terrorist" banner headline above a panoramic photograph of the Oklahoma City National Memorial Center likewise showing grieving family members just arrived from viewing the execution, kneeling at memorial chairs. On an inside page, there was another photograph of a woman holding a radio and listening intently while kneeling in front of one of the memorial chairs. The caption read: "Renee Pendley listens to a radio report on the execution as she kneels near the memorial chair for her friend Teresa Lauderdale."[122]

Two of the relatives of Oklahoma City bombing victims, who won the lottery to witness the McVeigh execution live in Terre Haute, pressed photographs of deceased loved ones against the window as they watched McVeigh die. What does it mean when the rituals of state killing are conflated and enfolded within rituals of mourning and bereavement? In the wake of September 11, 2001, with its massive trauma to the national psyche, we can expect to see the death penalty figure prominently in the politics of grief as executions are argued for and justified as necessary therapies of collective healing and closure.

ENDNOTES

1. These are the last words of Napoleon Beazley, a young African American man, who was executed in Huntsville, Texas, May 28, 2002. His last words are posted on the website of the Texas Department of Criminal Justice.

2. Albert Camus, "Reflections on the Guillotine," *Resistance, Rebellion, and Death* (New York: Vintage, 1995 [1960]), 234.

3. John Whitley, the warden responsible for directing executions at Louisiana's Angola State Prison, quoted in Ivan Solotaroff, *The Last Face You'll Ever See: The Private Life of the American Death Penalty* (New York: HarperCollins, 2001), 34.

4. Austin Sarat, *When the State Kills: Capital Punishment and the American Condition* (Princeton: Princeton University Press, 2001), 242.

5. Michel Foucault, *Discipline and Punish: The Birth of the Prison,* trans. Alan Sheridan (New York: Vintage, 1979 [1975]).

6. Ibid., 307.

7. Ibid., 302.

8. There are several excellent books that track this history: Stuart Banner, *The Death Penalty: An American History* (Cambridge: Harvard University Press, 2002); Hugo Bedau, ed., *The Death Penalty in America: Current Controversies* (New York: Oxford University Press, 1997); Jesse L. Jackson Sr., Jesse Jackson Jr., and Bruce Shapiro, *Legal Lynching: The Death Penalty and America's Future* (New York: New Press, 2001); Robert Jay Lifton and Greg Mitchell, *Who Owns Death?: Capital Punishment, the American Conscience, and the End of Executions* (New York: Morrow, 2000). See also Thomas Laqueur, "Festival of Punishment," *London Review of Books,* 5 October 2000: 17–24; Gary Wills, "The Dramaturgy of Death," *New York Review of Books,* 21 June 2001: 6–10.

9. The most authoritative source for updated data on the death penalty is the Death Penalty Information Center, Washington, D.C. Their excellent website address is http://www.deathpenaltyinfo.org/.

10. See John D. Bessler, *Death in the Dark: Midnight Executions in America* (Boston: Northeastern University Press, 1997), 146.

11. See especially Banner, *The Death Penalty.*

12. The White House, Office of the Press Secretary, *Military Order: Detention, Treatment, and Trial of Certain Non-Citizens in the War Against Terrorism,* 13 November 2001.

13. *The American Heritage Dictionary of the English Language,* 4th ed. (Boston: Houghton Mifflin, 2000).

14. See Mary Douglas, *Purity and Danger* (London: Routledge & Kegan Paul, 1966); Clifford Geertz, *The Interpretation of Cultures* (New York: Basic, 1973); Victor Turner, *The Ritual Process: Structure and Anti-Structure* (Ithaca: Cornell University Press, 1969) and *From Ritual to Theatre: The Human Seriousness of Play* (New York: Performing Arts Journal Publications, 1982); Roy Rappaport, *Ritual and Religion in the Making of Humanity* (Cambridge: Cambridge University Press, 1999). See also Catherine Bell, *Ritual Theory, Ritual Practice* (New York: Oxford University Press, 1992), and *Ritual: Perspectives and Dimensions* (New York: Oxford University Press, 1997). For important studies of political rituals, see Katherine A. Bowie, *Rituals of National Unity: An Anthropology of the State and the Village Scout Movement in Thailand* (New York: Columbia University Press, 1997); David I. Kertzer, *Ritual, Politics, and Power* (New Haven: Yale University Press, 1988); Richard J. Evans, *Rituals of Retribution: Capital Punishment in Germany, 1600–1987* (New York: Oxford University Press, 1996). For a historical case study of execution rituals, see Mark Fearnow, "Theatre for an Angry God: Public Burnings and Hangings in Colonial New York, 1741," *Drama Review* 40, T150 (1996): 15–36.

15. Victor Turner, *The Anthropology of Performance* (New York: Performing Arts Journal Publications, 1986), 48.

16. Robert Johnson, *Death Work: A Study of the Modern Execution Process,* 2nd ed. (Belmont, CA: Wadsworth, 1998), 20.

17. Richard Schechner, *Between Theater and Anthropology* (Philadelphia: University of Pennsylvania Press, 1985), 36–37. See also Schechner's *The Future of Ritual: Writings on Culture and Performance* (New York: Routledge, 1993).

18. For pathfinding analyses of the processual and improvisatory dynamics of ritual see Nicholas B. Dirks, "Ritual and Resistance: Subversion as a Social Fact," in *Culture/Power/History: A Reader in Contemporary Social Theory,* ed. Nicholas B. Dirks, Geoff Eley, and Sherry B. Ortner (Princeton: Princeton University Press, 1994), 483–503; Margaret Thompson Drewal, *Yoruba Ritual: Performers, Play, and Agency* (Bloomington: Indiana University Press, 1992).

19. Louis P. Masur, *Rites of Execution: Capital Punishment and the Transformation of American Culture, 1776–1865* (New York: Oxford University Press, 1989), 6. See also Norbert Elias, *The Civilizing Process: The History of Manners,* trans. Edmund Jephcott (New York: Urizen Books, 1978); John R. Kasson, *Rudeness and Civility: Manners in Nineteenth-Century Urban America* (New York: Hill & Wang, 1990); Lawrence W. Levine, *Highbrow/Lowbrow: The Emergence of Cultural Hierarchy in America* (Cambridge: Harvard University Press, 1988).

20. Cotton Mather, *Faithful Warnings to Prevent Fearful Judgments. Uttered in a Brief Discourse, Occasioned, by a Tragical Spectacle, In a Number of Miserables Under a Sentence of Death for Piracy* (Boston: printed and sold by Timothy Green, 1704).

21. John Dunston, quoted in Edwin Powers, *Crime and Punishment in Early Massachusetts, 1620–1692: A Documentary History* (Boston: Beacon, 1966), 295.

22. Ibid., 296.

23. Wayne Minnick, "The New England Execution Sermon, 1639–1800," *Speech Monographs* 35 (1968): 80.

24. Banner, *The Death Penalty*, 25. Theatre historian Peter G. Buckley concurs: "Of all colonial ritual, executions drew the largest crowds." See Peter G. Buckley, "Paratheatricals and Popular Stage Entertainments," in *The Cambridge History of American Theatre* I, ed. Don B. Wilmeth and Christopher Bigsby (Cambridge: Cambridge University Press, 1998), 428.

25. Cotton Mather, *A Sorrowful Spectacle. In Two Sermons, Occasioned by a Just Sentence of Death, on a Miserable Woman, for the Murder of a Spurious Offspring. The One Declaring, The Evil of an Heart Hardened, under and against all Means of Good. The Other Describing, The Fearful Case of Such as in a Suffering Time, and much more such as in a Dying Hour, are found without the Fear of God* (Boston: printed by T. Fleet & T. Crump, 1715).

26. See "Hanging Day" in Banner, *The Death Penalty*, 24–52 and "The Design of Public Executions in the Early American Republic" in Masur, *Rites of Execution*, 25–49. See also Ronald A. Bosco, "Lectures at the Pillory: The Early American Execution Sermon," *American Quarterly* 30 (1978): 156–76; Daniel E. Williams, "'Behold a Tragic Scene Strangely Changed into a Theater of Mercy': The Structure and Significance of Criminal Conversion Narratives in Early New England," *American Quarterly* 38 (1986): 827–47.

27. John Rogers, *Death the Certain Wages of Sin to the Impenitent: Life the Sure Reward of Grace to the Penitent: Together with the only Way for Youth To avoid the former, and attain the latter. Delivered in Three Lecture Sermons; Occasioned by the Imprisonment, condemnation and Execution, of a Young Woman, who was guilty of Murdering her infant begotten in Whoredom* (Boston: Printed by B. Green and T. Allen, 1701), 147.

28. See Peggy Phelan, *Unmarked: The Politics of Performance* (New York: Routledge, 1993).

29. Banner, *The Death Penalty*, 44.

30. Rogers, *Death the Certain*, 144.

31. Ibid., 2, 118. For important historical studies of Puritan culture, see Daniel A. Cohen, *Pillars of Salt, Monuments of Grace: New England Crime Literature and the Origins of American Popular Culture, 1674–1860* (New York: Oxford University Press, 1993); David D. Hall, *Worlds of Wonder, Days of Judgment: Popular Religious Belief in Early New England* (New York: Knopf, 1989).

32. Ibid., 153.

33. Ibid., 124.

34. Ibid., 123.

35. Ibid., 2.

36. Ibid., 2, 142.

37. Ibid., 3.

38. Ibid., 118.

39. Jonas Barish, *The Antitheatrical Prejudice* (Berkeley: University of California Press, 1981).

40. Rogers, *Death the Certain*, 118.

41. Samuel Danforth, *The Cry of Sodom Enquired Into: Upon Occasion of the Arraignment and Condemnation of Benjamin Goad, For his Prodigious Villany. Together with a Solemn Exhortation to Tremble at Gods Judgements, and to Abandon Youthful Lusts* (Cambridge: printed by Marmaduke Johnson, 1674).

42. Rogers, *Death the Certain*, 3.

43. Ibid., 119. On "performative metaphors," see James Fernandez, *Persuasions and Performances: The Play of Tropes in Culture* (Bloomington: Indiana University Press, 1986).

44. Rogers, *Death the Certain*, 2.

45. On "interpretive communities," see Stanley Fish, *Is There a Text in This Class?: The Authority of Interpretive Communities* (Cambridge: Harvard University Press, 1980).

46. John Williams, *Warnings to the Unclean: In a Discourse from Rev. XXXI. 8. Preacht at Springfield Lecture, August 25th. 1698. At the Execution of Sarah Smith* (Boston: Printed by B. Green and J. Allen, 1699), 7.

47. Rogers, *Death the Certain*, 118, emphasis added.

48. Ibid., 133.

49. Ibid., 115–16.

50. Ibid., 119, 144.

51. Ibid., 152.

52. Ibid., 132.

53. Williams, *Warnings*, 12, 37.

54. Rogers, *Death the Certain*, 3.

55. For important works on spectatorship see Jill Dolan, *The Feminist Spectator as Critic* (Ann Arbor: University of Michigan Press, 1988); Lisa Merrill, *When Romeo Was a Woman: Charlotte Cushman and Her Circle of Female Spectators* (Ann Arbor: University of Michigan Press, 1999).

56. Rogers, *Death the Certain*, 133.

57. Ibid., 153.

58. Ibid., 122.

59. Ibid., 114.

60. Ibid., 143.

61. Ibid., 144.

62. Ibid., 119.

63. Ibid., 146.

64. Ibid., 152.

65. See Thomas W. Laqueur, "Crowds, Carnival, and the State in Early English Executions, 1604–1868," in *The First Modern Society: Essays in English History in Honour of Lawrence Stone*, ed. A. L. Beier, David Cannadine, James M. Rosenheim (Cambridge: Cambridge University Press, 1989), 305–55.

66. Rogers, *Death the Certain*, 113.

67. Danforth, *The Cry of Sodom*, i.

68. Rogers, *Death the Certain*, 2.

69. Richard Godbeer, *Sexual Revolution in Early America* (Baltimore: Johns Hopkins University Press, 2002), 55.

70. Danforth, *The Cry of Sodom*, 10.

71. See Karen Halttunen, *Murder Most Foul: The Killer and the American Gothic Imagination* (Cambridge: Harvard University Press, 1998); Leigh B. Bienen, "A Good Murder," in *The Death Penalty in America*, ed. Hugo Bedau (New York: Oxford University Press, 1997), 319–32.

72. G. W. Peck, "On the Use of Chloroform in Hanging," *American Whig Review* 8 (1848): 283–97. Peck opens with an extended "essay on manners" and does not even mention capital punishment until page 292, ten pages into the essay. Peck is much more interested in the everyday performativity of class—manners, deportment, refinement, cultivation of speech and gesture—than he is in the cultural performance of executions. His essay resonates with other elocutionary texts of the period. For a discussion of the class and racial exclusions upon which the elocutionary movement was based, see my "Rethinking Elocution: The Trope of the Talking Book and Other Figures of Speech," *Text and Performance Quarterly* 20 (2000): 325–41.

73. Ibid., 295.

74. Ibid., 286.

75. Ibid., 291.

76. Ibid., 292.

77. Ibid., 296.

78. See Johnson, *Death Work*.

79. See Michael Taussig, *The Magic of the State* (New York: Routledge, 1997), 187. On the massive incarceration campaign and prison building boom, see Elliott Currie, *Crime and Punishment in America* (New York: Metropolitan Books, 1998); Joseph T. Hallinan, *Going Up the River: Travels in a Prison Nation* (New York: Random House, 2001); Marc Mauer and The Sentencing Project, *Race to Incarcerate* (New York: Free Press, 1999); Christian Parenti, *Lockdown America: Police and Prisons in the Age of Crisis* (New York: Verso, 1999).

80. Michel Foucault, *Power,* ed. James D. Faubion (New York: New Press, 1994), 435–36.

81. See David Johnston, "Ashcroft Delays Death of McVeigh Over FBI's Lapse," *New York Times,* 12 May 2001, A1.

82. See the Center On Wrongful Convictions website: http://www.law.northwestern.edu/depts/clinic/wrongful/index.htm.

83. Joseph Roach, *Cities of the Dead: Circum-Atlantic Performance* (New York: Columbia University Press, 1996), 36–41; Michael Taussig, *Mimesis and Alterity: A Particular History of the Senses* (New York: Routledge, 1993).

84. The Death Penalty Information Center is a reliable source for demographic data on the death penalty. See also, Deborah Fins, *Death Row USA,* Quarterly Report, NAACP Legal Defense and Educational Fund, 2002.

85. See William S. McFeely, *Proximity to Death* (New York: Norton, 2000), 69. Gary Gilmore was executed by a firing squad in Utah in 1977, making his the first post-Furman execution. But because he refused all appeals, he was considered a "volunteer."

86. See U.S. General Accounting Office, "Death Penalty Sentencing: Research Indicates Pattern of Racial Disparities," in *The Death Penalty in America*, ed. Hugo Bedau, 268–74. See also Bienen, "A Good Murder," 327.

87. Jackson, Jackson, and Shapiro, *Legal Lynching,* 75.

88. Mumia Abu-Jamal, quoted in ibid., 35. For an astute historical analysis of the codependent connection between capitalism and capital punishment, see Peter Linebaugh, *The London Hanged: Crime and Civil Society in the Eighteenth Century* (Cambridge: Cambridge University Press, 1992).

89. Stephen Bright, "Counsel for the Poor: The Death Sentence Not for the Worst Crime But for the Worst Lawyer," in *The Death Penalty in America*, ed. Hugo Bedau, 275–309.

90. http://www.tdcj.state.tx.us/stat/finalmeal.htm

91. See Mary Douglas, "Food as a System of Communication," in *The Active Voice* (London: Routledge & Kegan Paul, 1982), 82–124; Pierre Bourdieu, *Distinction: A Social Critique of the Judgment of Taste,* trans. Richard Nice (Cambridge: Harvard University Press, 1984).

92. Victoria Brownworth, "Dykes on Death Row," *The Advocate*, June 1992, 62–64. See also Victor Streib, "Death Penalty for Lesbians," *National Journal of Sexual Orientation Law* 1 (1995): 105–26; Richard Goldstein, "Queer on Death Row," *Village Voice*, March 2001.

93. Lifton and Mitchell, *Who Owns Death?*, 135.

94. Ibid., 101.

95. See Bessler, *Death in the Dark*, 142. For studies of the stress and trauma that executions wreak on the prison staff whose job it is to actually carry out this grisly work, see Donald A. Cabana, *Death at Midnight: The Confession of an Executioner* (Boston: Northeastern University Press, 1996); Johnson, *Death Work*, 109–16; Solotaroff, *Last Face You'll Ever See*.

96. Tonya McClary, "Sexuality and Capital Punishment: The Execution of Wanda Jean Allen," *Outfront: Amnesty International's Program for Lesbian, Gay, Bisexual, and Transgender Human Rights*, Winter, 2002, 1, 4, 6.

97. Robert Bork, quoted in Sarat, *When the State Kills*, 33.

98. Lou Michel and Dan Herbeck, *American Terrorist: Timothy McVeigh and the Oklahoma City Bombing* (New York: HarperCollins, 2001), 226.

99. Sarat, *When the State Kills*, 258.

100. Jackson, Jackson, and Shapiro, *Legal Lynching*, 110.

101. Sarat, *When the State Kills*, 17–18.

102. Timothy McVeigh's death certificate listed the cause of death as "Homicide." See "Coroner Prepares to Sign Death Certificate," *Terre Haute Tribune-Star*, 11 June 2001, A6.

103. See Johnson, *Death Work*.

104. See Jon McKenzie, *Perform or Else: From Discipline to Performance* (New York: Routledge, 2001).

105. See Frank Bruni and Jim Yardley, "Inmate Is Executed in Texas as 11th-Hour Appeals Fail," *New York Times*, 23 June 2000, A18. See also, Amy Dorsett, "Execution Day," *San Antonio Express-News*, 22 June 2000, 1A, 8A.

106. For scathing critiques of the hypocrisy of sanitized lethal injection as a modern and humane method, see Lifton and Mitchell, *Who Owns Death?*, 43–69; Sarat, *When the State Kills*, 60–84.

107. Lifton and Mitchell, *Who Owns Death?*, 44. For examples of botched lethal injections, see ibid., 65–66. Bungled executions are so commonplace that the Death Penalty Information Center documents them under the special topic, "Botched Executions." See http://www.deathpenaltyinfo.org/botched.html.

108. Modern executions conflate the three performance paradigms that Jon McKenzie identifies as "the efficacy of cultural performance," "the efficiency of organizational performance," and "the effectiveness of technological performance." See McKenzie, *Perform or Else*, 27–135.

109. A redacted version of the *Execution Protocol* is posted on the internet at http://www.thesmokinggun.com/archive/bopprotocol1.shtml.

110. Sarat, *When the State Kills*, 69.

111. Quoted in Jackson, Jackson, and Shapiro, *Legal Lynching*, 113. In 1984, Reagan issued an executive order that reinstated the Military Death Penalty.

112. William J. Wiseman, Jr., "Inventing Lethal Injection," *Christian Century*, 20 June 2001, 6.

113. Susan Blaustein, "Witness to Another Execution," in *Death Penalty in America*, ed. Hugo Bedau (New York: Oxford University Press, 1997), 387–400.

114. Wiseman Jr., "Inventing," 6. See also James Walsh, "The Medicine That Kills: Lethal Injection for Execution," *Lancet*, 7 February 1998, 441.

115. See Lifton and Mitchell, *Who Owns Death?*, 97.

116. Sarat, *When the State Kills*, 35. On the victims' rights movement, see Wendy Kaminer, *It's All the Rage: Crime and Culture* (New York: Addison-Wesley, 1995); for trenchant critique of the privatization of public discourse, especially the way victims are cast in the role of exemplary citizen, see Lauren Berlant, *The Queen of America Goes to Washington City: Essays on Sex and Citizenship* (Durham: Duke University Press, 1997).

117. Alex Kosinski, quoted in Lifton and Mitchell, *Who Owns Death?*, 162.

118. See Mike Dorning, "Hundreds Will Watch McVeigh Die," *Chicago Tribune*, 13 April 2001, 1, 20.

119. See Rick Bragg, "McVeigh Dies for Oklahoma City Blast," *New York Times*, 12 June 2001, A1, A19; Lisa Anderson, "In Oklahoma City, Some Feel Cheated by 'Easy' Death," *Chicago Tribune*, 12 June 2001, 1, 14.

120. Anderson, "In Oklahoma City, Some Feel Cheated," 14. For an excellent study of the politics of memory and how this played out in the contested process of planning, designing, and building the Oklahoma City National Memorial Center, see Edward T. Linenthal, *The Unfinished Bombing: Oklahoma City in American Memory* (New York: Oxford University Press, 2001).

121. Bragg, "McVeigh Dies," A1.

122. "The McVeigh Execution," *Chicago Tribune*, 12 June 2001, 14.

Reading Questions

1. What is Conquergood's position on the death penalty? What evidence can you provide from the opening paragraphs to support your contention concerning his position?

2. What does Conquergood mean to suggest when he quotes Robert Johnson, who wrote that "All of justice is a stage; it is the appearance—the ritual—that is the meaningful thing" (par. 6)?

3. According to Conquergood, why is it possible to see the spectator of executions in Puritan New England as "a deeply engaged, co-performative witness" (21)?

4. Conquergood argues that views of the criminal changed quite dramatically from Puritan America to the nineteenth century. What accounts for that change in views, according to Conquergood?

5. According to Conquergood, how does G. W. Peck's "On the Use of Chloroforming in Hanging" illustrate an important transition moment in our understanding of the execution ritual?

6. Provide a brief explanation of Conquergood's assertion that Timothy McVeigh's "high-profile execution was a perverse form of whiteface minstrelsy, a whiteout of the glaring racial inequities in the way capital punishment is meted out in America" (26).

7. What does Conquergood mean by "the circular absurdity of memetic violence" (32), and how is that absurdity illustrated in the following question: "Why Do We Kill People, Who Kill People, to Show That Killing People Is Wrong?" (32)?

8. Conquergood identifies four "troubling problems with capital punishment" (33). What are they?

Rhetoric Questions

9. Conquergood's article is prefaced by a number of epigraphs. What purpose do you believe they serve, and what is the effect of the epigraphs on you as a reader?

10. Conquergood references the work of Foucault numerous times at the beginning of his article. Describe Conquergood's purpose for referencing Foucault and his attitude toward Foucault's work.

11. Identify a single sentence in the opening paragraphs of Conquergood's article that you might describe as his thesis. Briefly explain why you chose the sentence you did.

12. Conquergood develops his arguments about capital punishment by narrating historical accounts of individuals who have been executed. What are the strengths of this strategy, and why is it appropriate for Conquergood's aims? Are there weaknesses in this strategy? If so, what are they, and where do they appear in Conquergood's article?

13. Conquergood's article includes a paragraph (19) that is made up of eleven questions. Provide a brief explanation for this paragraph in light of Conquergood's goals as a writer in the moment and in terms of the aims of his article more broadly.

14. Explain the central strategy Conquergood uses to organize his paragraphs in the section of his article titled "The Magical Realism of Modern Capital Punishment."

Response and Research Questions

15. Conquergood encourages his readers to visit the website of the Texas Department of Criminal Justice to view the last meal requests of individuals who have been put to death. Their meal requests, Conquergood suggests, reveal evidence "that people sentenced to death in this country are overwhelmingly impoverished and working class" (28). Research the last meals of individuals, as Conquergood asks. Do you agree or disagree that their meal requests reveal evidence of their class or social positioning? Why or why not?

16. Conquergood traces a number of parallels between the theatrical elements of modern execution ritual and the production of a play. How are these two things similar? How are they different?

17. Locate a news account of a recent execution. Identify the ways in which the report supports or challenges any of Conquergood's views or assertions about the modern execution ritual.

18. Conquergood ends his article with a question for his readers to ponder: "What does it mean when the rituals of state killing are conflated and enfolded within rituals of mourning and bereavement?" (47). In a paragraph, offer a response to Conquergood's question.

ACADEMIC CASE STUDY • CAPITAL PUNISHMENT   SOCIAL SCIENCES

Capital Punishment in Films: The Impact of Death Penalty Portrayals on Viewers' Mood and Attitude toward Capital Punishment

BENEDIKT TILL AND PETER VITOUCH

Benedikt Till is a research associate at the Department of General Practice and Family Medicine, Center for Public Health, Medical University of Vienna and lecturer at the Medical University of Vienna. The following study was published in the *International Journal of Public Opinion Research* in 2012 with co-author Peter Vitouch, a professor of media psychology in the Department of Communication and vice-dean of the Faculty of Social Science at the University of Vienna. The article examines the impact that filmic representations of capital punishments have on viewers' moods and attitudes.

INTRODUCTION

Since several decades there has been a lively debate on the legitimacy of the death penalty between those for and those against capital punishment (see e.g., Ellsworth & Gross, 1994; Fan, Keltner, & Wyatt, 2002; Niven, 2002). The entrance of capital punishment in the forefront of debate and consciousness at nearly all levels of society is due at least in part to the plethora of movies and books on this topic (Giles, 1995). But what is the effect of such media accounts on recipients?

Learn more about research questions in the social sciences on pages 189–91.

The Impact of Fictional and Nonfictional Death Penalty Portrayals

In a laboratory experiment, Howells, Flanagan, and Hagan (1995) demonstrated that the screening of tapes of executions leads to reduced support for the death penalty. A study by Holbert, Shah, and Kwak (2004) suggests that viewing police reality shows, crime drama, and TV news is related to the endorsement of capital punishment. Furthermore, press coverage was found to be a driving force for opinion about capital punishment (Fan et al., 2002; Niven, 2002). An association between media use and support for the death penalty was also reported by Sotirovic (2001).

Evidence for fictional portrayals is rather heterogeneous. Slater, Rouner, and Long (2006) found increased support for the death penalty among viewers of a television drama that endorsed capital punishment. Mutz and Nir (2010) demonstrated that viewers who watched a fictional television program emphasizing flaws in the justice system, exhibit a greater rejection of the death penalty than those who viewed a more positive portrayal of the criminal justice system. Other studies, however, found no change in attitude toward the death penalty among viewers of films focusing on capital punishment (e.g., Önder & Öner-Özkan, 2003; Peterson & Thurstone, 1970). Thus, the effects of fictional entertainment narratives dealing with capital punishment on viewers' attitudes toward the death penalty are still unclear and undetermined.

> The researchers review previous scholarship on the topic and establish a gap, or remaining question, that is unresolved by scholars.

Emotional Audience Responses to Dramas

According to affective disposition theory (Zillmann, 1996), viewers enjoy a film the most when the protagonist benefits from the story's outcome. If the heroes fail, we feel bad for them—this might lead to negative emotions. Evidence from several studies suggests that individuals exposed to sad film endings experience significantly higher degrees of emotional stress and a deterioration of mood (e.g., Hesse, Spies, Hänze, & Gerrards-Hesse, 1992; Tannenbaum & Gaer, 1965).

> Learn more about the role of theory in the social sciences on pages 185–96.

On the other hand, Festinger's (1954) social comparison theory proposes that humans tend to evaluate their values, abilities, and living conditions by comparing them with those of other people. A comparison with the undesirable situation of a person sentenced to death might improve an individual's mood. Also, people may use sad films to cope with some negative experience in their lives (see e.g., Mares & Cantor, 1992; Nabi, Finnerty, Domschke, & Hull, 2006; Tan, 2008). Till, Niederkrotenthaler, Herberth, Vitouch, and Sonneck (2010) discovered a deterioration of mood and an increase of depression in viewers of films featuring the suicide of the protagonist. Concurrently, the viewers also reacted with a rise in life satisfaction and a drop in suicidality. However, studies focusing on emotional audience reactions to films dealing with capital punishment are rare.

> The researchers stress the originality of their study and thus indicate its potential to contribute to theory development.

DETERMINANTS OF FILM EFFECTS

Audience reactions to motion pictures and television programs are partly based on the characters who populate them and on the viewers' engagement in the process of impression formation in getting to know the respective persona (Hoffner & Cantor, 1991). Identification with media characters is defined as "an imaginative process through which an audience member assumes the identity, goals, and perspective of a character" (Cohen, 2001, p. 261). Several studies provided evidence that identification has the potential to amplify media-induced reactions in terms of emotions (e.g., Slater & Rouner, 2002; Tannenbaum & Gaer, 1965; Till et al., 2010), attitude changes (e.g., Basil, 1996; Gau, James, & Kim, 2009; Greenwood, 2004), and behavior modifications (e.g., Brown & Basil, 1995; Niederkrotenthaler et al., 2009; Perry & Perry, 1976).

The impact of a motion picture can also be determined by the way certain actions are portrayed in key scenes of the movie. Print media guidelines—for example, recommended restrictions for newspaper reports on suicide—are known to influence readers' imitation behavior (Etzersdorfer & Sonneck, 1998; Niederkrotenthaler & Sonneck, 2007; Sonneck, Etzersdorfer, & Nagel-Kuess, 1994). Accordingly, removing scenes from a film has been discussed as a means to mitigate possible negative effects of movies and television programs on their viewers and has been used by television stations to moderate their broadcasts and thereby avoid public criticism (Worringham & Buxton, 1997). The effectiveness of such editing, however, has been questioned in the past, since most studies on this topic have failed to demonstrate a significant influence on film effects (e.g., Ferracuti & Lazzari, 1970; Tannenbaum, 1978; Till et al., 2010; Till & Vitouch, 2008).

The present study investigates the impact of two films featuring the portrayal of the protagonist's death via capital punishment on their viewers' mood and attitude toward the death penalty and compares the effects of these two movies to those of edited versions—thus being the first study to examine emotional, as well as cognitive, audience responses to different versions of such films. The importance of using emotional, as well as cognitive, parameters to assess the impact of a drama was recently highlighted by Till et al. (2010). The following hypotheses were formulated:

H1: The viewing of a film drama focusing on capital punishment has a negative influence on the viewers' mood.

H2: The viewing of a film drama focusing on the negative aspects of capital punishment reduces the viewers' approval of the death penalty.

H3: Excluding the protagonist's execution from a film that focuses on capital punishment reduces its impact on (a) the viewers' mood and (b) their attitudes toward the death penalty.

H4: The more a viewer identifies with the dying protagonist of a film focusing on capital punishment, the greater is (a) the deterioration of his or her mood and (b) the reduction of his or her approval of the death penalty.

The researchers assert four hypotheses: H1, H2, H3 (a and b), H4 (a and b). Learn more about hypotheses in the social sciences by reading pages 190–91.

METHODS

Design and Material

Group 1 viewed the movie *The Chamber* (United States, 1996), while group 2 watched *Dancer in the Dark* (Denmark/France, 2000). Both films portray the death penalty in a negative way and conclude with the explicit portrayal of (one of) the main character's execution. However, while *The Chamber* is a mainstream movie, in *Dancer in the Dark*, the plot and its depiction are rather unconventional due to the usage of different themes in the genres of the musical, the neo-realist film, and the melodrama. Furthermore, in *The Chamber* there is a certain amount of uncertainty regarding the convict's guilt, whereas in *Dancer in the Dark*, the crime—and thus the protagonist's innocence—is shown explicitly. Groups 3 and 4 saw an edited version of the respective film without the portrayal of the execution. However, it was still clear to the viewer that the protagonist was killed via death penalty. Only the execution itself was removed from the film, not the events immediately before and after the execution. The editing of the scenes was carried out in a manner one would expect from a television station to mitigate possible negative effects of its broadcasted program (see Worringham & Buxton, 1997).

In *The Chamber*, a young attorney seeks to appeal the death sentence of his grand- 10 father, a Ku Klux Klan bomber, for the murder of a lawyer and his two small boys. Despite the attorney's efforts and the proof that his grandfather did not have the intention to kill his victims, the Ku Klux Klan bomber is executed in the gas chamber.

The film *Dancer in the Dark* involves a woman, Selma, who works day and night to save her son from the same disease she suffers from, a disease that inevitably will make her blind. When her neighbor and friend, a police officer, steals money from her to pay his debts, Selma confronts him and tries to get her money back. In the resulting turmoil, Selma shoots the police officer in self-defense. Despite her innocence, Selma gets sentenced to death. The film concludes with her execution by hanging.

Subjects

Participants were 121 individuals living in Austria ($n = 121$)—49 men (40.5%), with mean age of 34.20 years, and 72 women (59.5%), with mean age of 41.25 years.

Measures

Mood. Mood was measured by the subscales *Sorrow* and *Positive Mood* of a German short version of the *Profile of Mood States* by McNair, Lorr, and Doppleman (1971) using three items (adjectives such as "unhappy" or "sad") for sorrow and six items (adjectives such as "happy" or "merry") for positive mood on a 7-point scale ranging from 1—"not at all" to 7—"very strong" (sorrow: Cronbach's $\alpha = .89$; positive mood: Cronbach's $\alpha = .71$).

Attitude toward Capital Punishment. Attitudes toward capital punishment were measured by a questionnaire based on analogous scales developed by Önder and Öner-Özkan (2003), as well as Peterson and Thurstone (1970), using 11 items (statements such as "Life imprisonment is more effective than capital punishment") on a 5-point scale ranging from 1—"disagree" to 5—"agree." However, one item was excluded from the analysis to improve the scale's reliability (Cronbach's $\alpha = .91$).

Identification with the Protagonist. Identification was measured by a questionnaire 15 based on an analogous scale developed by Cohen (2001) using 11 items (statements such as "I felt I knew exactly what character X was going through") on a 5-point scale ranging from 1—"disagree" to 5—"agree." However, one item was excluded from the analysis to improve the scale's reliability (Cronbach's $\alpha = .85$).

In computing the parameters, scores on the negative items were reversed, so that high scores indicated a high level of the respective variable. The scores were then added together according to the instructions given in the respective manual.

Procedure

Participation in the study was voluntary and anonymous. The subjects' allocation to the experimental groups was randomized. It was ensured that the subjects had not already seen the respective film in the past. Before the film, questionnaires on mood and attitudes toward capital punishment were completed by the participants. After the movie, these parameters were measured again, as well as the subjects' identification with the respective protagonist.

Data Analysis

Nonparametric tests were applied, since normal distribution could not be assumed within the given set of data. The subjects were disproportionately low on sorrow (skew ranging between 0.47 and 2.08, and kurtosis between -1.22 and 3.61) and approval of capital punishment (skew ranging between 0.48 and 2.18, and kurtosis between -0.78 and 5.23). An overview of the medians, percentiles, means, and standard deviations of the subjects' mood and attitudes toward capital punishment is shown in Table 1. Wilcoxon tests were performed to analyze the impact the films have on the subjects' mood and attitudes toward capital punishment. To examine to which extent identification influences the impact of the films, Spearman correlations were performed. An overview of the medians, percentiles, means, and standard deviations of the subjects' identification with the respective protagonist is shown in Table 2. For the Wilcoxon tests, the parameters' summarized scores before and after the movie screening were used to conduct the analysis. Change scores and the summarized score for identification were used for the correlations.

Learn more about quantitative methods and the use of statistical procedures in social science research by reading pages 191–93.

RESULTS

A summary of the results of the Wilcoxon tests can be found in Table 3. There was a significant deterioration of the subjects' positive mood in all four film groups (*The Chamber*: $Z = -4.06$, $n = 30$, $p < .001$; *The Chamber*, edited version: $Z = -4.27$, $n = 31$, $p < .001$; *Dancer in the Dark*: $Z = -4.61$, $n = 30$, $p < .001$; *Dancer in the Dark*, edited version: $Z = -3.57$, $n = 30$, $p < .001$). The screening of the movies also led to a significant increase of sorrow in all groups (*The Chamber*, edited version: $Z = -2.33$, $n = 31$, $p < .05$; *Dancer in the Dark*: $Z = -3.56$, $n = 30$, $p < .001$; *Dancer in the Dark*, edited version: $Z = -2.19$, $n = 30$, $p < .05$) except for the audience watching the original version of *The Chamber* ($Z = -0.70$, $n = 30$, $p = .47$). Thus, Hypothesis 1 was confirmed. Furthermore, there was a significant swing toward unfavorable assessments of capital punishment in the groups watching the edited versions of the two films (*The Chamber*: $Z = -2.95$, $n = 31$, $p < .01$; *Dancer in the Dark*: $Z = -2.78$, $n = 30$, $p < .01$), but surprisingly, not among viewers of the original versions (*The Chamber*: $Z = -1.67$, $n = 30$, $p = .09$; *Dancer in the Dark*: $Z = -0.96$, $n = 30$, $p = .33$). Therefore, Hypothesis 2 was partly

Results confirm hypothesis 1.

Table 1

Means (*M*), Standard Deviations (*SD*), Medians (μ), and Percentiles (P_{25}, P_{75}) for the Recipients' Mood and Attitudes toward Capital Punishment for Each Film before and after the Screening

		The Chamber (original)	Dancer in the Dark (original)	The Chamber (edited)	Dancer in the Dark (edited)
Positive mood					
Before	M (SD)	4.01 (1.24)	4.63 (1.35)	4.2 (1.26)	3.98 (1.29)
	P_{25}	3.25	3.45	3.5	2.95
	μ	4	4.66	4.33	4
	P_{75}	4.66	6	5.16	5.04
After	M (SD)	2.75 (1.41)	2.87 (1.59)	3.03 (1.37)	2.96 (1.42)
	P_{25}	1.62	1.33	1.83	1.5
	μ	2.58	2.58	3.16	3
	P_{75}	4	4.08	4	4.04
Sorrow					
Before	M (SD)	1.81 (1.38)	1.38 (0.69)	1.87 (1.3)	1.77 (1.17)
	P_{25}	1	1	1	1
	μ	1	1	1.33	1
	P_{75}	2.08	1.5	2.66	2.16
After	M (SD)	2 (1.25)	2.26 (1.37)	2.54 (1.37)	2.54 (1.68)
	P_{25}	1	1.25	1.33	1
	μ	1.5	2	2	2
	P_{75}	3	3.33	4	4
Attitudes toward capital punishment					
Before	M (SD)	2.41 (1.17)	2.12 (1.14)	2.18 (1.19)	1.98 (1.08)
	P_{25}	1.37	1.2	1.2	1.17
	μ	2.1	1.75	1.6	1.5
	P_{75}	3.32	2.92	3.3	2.85
After	M (SD)	2.28 (1.28)	2.06 (1.1)	1.96 (1.09)	1.67 (0.93)
	P_{25}	1	1	1	1
	μ	1.85	1.7	1.5	1.35
	P_{75}	3.07	2.7	2.5	2.05

Note. Values are means, standard deviations, medians, and percentiles of the parameters representing the subjects' positive mood, sorrow, and attitudes toward capital punishment based on the descriptive statistics analyzed via SPSS. The indices are based on means.

Learn more about the visual representation of data, including the use of tables, in social science research by reading pages 202–4.

Table 2

Means (*M*), Standard Deviations (*SD*), Medians (μ), and Percentiles (P_{25}, P_{75}) for the Recipients' Identification with the Protagonist of the Respective Film

	The Chamber (original)	Dancer in the Dark (original)	The Chamber (edited)	Dancer in the Dark (edited)
M (SD)	2.59 (0.72)	3.00 (0.94)	2.83 (0.56)	3.40 (0.98)
P_{25}	2.07	2.30	2.50	2.57
μ	2.50	3.00	2.80	3.40
P_{75}	3.05	3.80	3.20	4.30

Note. Values are means, standard deviations, medians, and percentiles of the parameters representing the subjects' identification based on the descriptive statistics analyzed via SPSS. The indices are based on means.

confirmed. Hypotheses 3a and 3b, on the other hand, were rejected—excluding the execution from the films did not reduce the impact on the viewers' mood and their attitudes toward the death penalty.

> Hypothesis 2 is "partly confirmed," but hypothesis 3 (a and b) is rejected.

For the correlations, the data across the four groups were collapsed and analyzed together, as only few differences were revealed between the respective films and film versions. Identification was significantly linked to the increase of sorrow (Spearman's $r = .39$, $r^2 = .15$, $n = 121$, $p < .001$) and the change of attitudes toward capital punishment (Spearman's $r = .21$, $r^2 = .04$, $n = 121$, $p < .05$), indicating that the more a viewer identified with the dying main character of the film, the more was the recipient's sadness increasing and the greater was his or her swing toward unfavorable assessments of the death penalty. Furthermore, there was a positive correlation between identification and the deterioration of positive mood close to statistical significance (Spearman's $r = .15$, $r^2 = .02$, $n = 121$, $p = .09$). Since identification was normally distributed, we performed regression analyses to

Table 3

Findings from Wilcoxon Tests Performed on the Recipients' Mood and Attitudes toward Capital Punishment for Each Film

	The Chamber (original)	Dancer in the Dark (original)	The Chamber (edited)	Dancer in the Dark (edited)
Positive mood	−4.06***	−4.61***	−4.27***	−3.57***
Sorrow	−0.70	−3.56***	−2.33*	−2.19*
Attitudes toward capital punishment	−1.67	−0.96	−2.95**	−2.78**

*$p < .05$. **$p < .01$. ***$p < .001$. (two-tailed)

Note. Values are *Z*-values from Wilcoxon Tests representing the change of the subjects' positive mood, sorrow, and attitudes toward capital punishment.

further examine the characteristics of the associations between the viewers' identification and the film effects. The influence of identification on the change of attitudes ($B = -3.01$, Standard error $= 1.46$, $p < .05$, $R^2 = .09$, adapted $R^2 = .08$, $F = 11.92$) and sorrow ($B = -4.27$, Standard error $= 1.18$, $p < .001$, $R^2 = .19$, adapted $R^2 = .19$, $F = 29.36$) was significant—and close to statistical significance in terms of the reduction of positive mood ($B = 3.51$, Standard error $= 2.49$, $p = .16$, $R^2 = .02$, adapted $R^2 = .01$, $F = 3.20$). In addition, Sobel-Tests with bootstrap estimates were conducted to verify mediation (see Preacher & Hayes, 2004). However, identification was not found to be a significant mediator variable for the film-induced attitude change ($Z = 1.17$, $n = 121$, $p = .23$, 95% CI $= -0.01$ to 0.04), the deterioration of positive mood ($Z = 1.21$, $n = 121$, $p = .22$, 95% CI $= -0.01$ to 0.08), and the increase of sorrow ($Z = -0.24$, $n = 121$, $p = .80$, 95% CI $= -0.09$ to 0.05). Thus, hypotheses 4a and b were rejected.

After performing additional statistical analyses, the researchers reject hypothesis 4 (a and b).

DISCUSSION

The results of the present study show that recipients of films featuring the portrayal of the protagonist's execution are less happy and sadder after the screening than before. This effect is concordant with Zillmann's (1996) affective disposition theory proposing that an outcome victimizing the protagonist is deplored by the viewers and fits well with previous research demonstrating a deterioration of the viewers' mood after the screening of a drama (Hesse et al., 1992; Tannenbaum & Gaer, 1965; Till et al., 2010). It is interesting to note that this effect occurred in all groups showing no differences between the two motion pictures and the different film versions. The ineffectiveness of excluding scenes from a film to alter its emotional impact is consistent with findings of earlier research (see Ferracuti & Lazzari, 1970; Till et al., 2010; Till & Vitouch, 2008).

The researchers discuss the meaning of their results and explore the implications of their findings for social science theory.

The negative portrayal of the death penalty in the two films also produced a diminished endorsement of capital punishment among the audience. This result is concordant with earlier research supporting the proposition that fictional television dramas can change people's opinion about the death penalty (Mutz & Nir, 2010; Slater et al., 2006). Given these results, it is plausible to assume that film dramas have the potential to affect viewers' political attitudes and influence their support not only for capital punishment, but also for other controversial public policies. However, a definite statement on this issue cannot be made based on our analyses.

The researchers identify how their study's findings contribute to the body of research on the topic.

It is important to point out that the viewers' attitudes toward the death penalty changed only in the groups watching the edited versions of the movies. Usually, the removal of such film scenes is meant to mitigate film effects (see Worringham & Buxton, 1997), but in this case it increased the influence on the audience's attitudes. This finding is surprising and very puzzling because of its counterintuitive nature. A possible explanation for this result may be that recipients complement missing details in a film by using their imagination; this can lead to a more brutal or gruesome picture of an event in the viewer's imagination than actually displayed on screen, which might aggravate the impact of a movie (see Till & Vitouch, 2008). The human mind and its imaginativeness should not be neglected or underestimated. After all, the sheer

The researchers identify and provide possible explanations for unexpected results.

imagination of an event can change attitudes and behavior (Anderson, 1983; Gregory, Burroughs, & Ainslie, 1985; Gregory, Cialdini, & Carpenter, 1982). This is in line with earlier findings that demonstrated a counterproductive impact of removing disturbing scenes from a film. Tannenbaum (1978), for example, reported higher physiological arousal when a violent scene of a film was deleted than without editing. He also found that some viewers believe to recall the deleted film scene, even though they never actually saw this particular scene. Therefore, simply removing a possibly disturbing scene from a film cannot be deemed to be an effective tool to mitigate potentially negative film effects.

Identification with the dying protagonist was not a significant mediator variable for the film-induced audience reactions. Various persuasion theories, such as the Elaboration Likelihood Model by Petty and Cacioppo (1986a, 1986b) or the Heuristic-Systematic Model by Chaiken (1980), suggest that absorption in a narrative and response to its characters enhance persuasive effects and suppress counter arguing, which is likely to be a necessary prerequisite for behavior change (Slater & Rouner, 2002). In this study, however, there is only limited evidence for identification to produce such effects. Maybe identification is not an adequate concept to comprehend the viewers' reception process, as suggested by Zillmann (1994, 1996). Other concepts, such as involvement (Krugman, 1965), transportation (Gerrig, 1993), modes of reception (Suckfüll & Scharkow, 2009), para-social interaction (Horton & Wohl, 1956), or empathy (Zillmann, 1991), might be more adequate to explore the psychological dynamics of how film messages may influence human emotions, attitudes, and behavior.

This study also has some limitations. First, most of our hypotheses were tested in a before–after quasi-experimental design with repetition of the exact measures within a 2-hr period. This approach might have attenuated the films' effects. Furthermore, the distribution of several variables was too skewed to assume normal distribution of the data. Therefore, nonparametric tests were applied that are known to have less statistical power than parametric tests (Hodges & Lehmann, 1956). The fact that the data was not normally distributed is not uncommon (Altman & Bland, 1995), but is certainly noteworthy and needs to be considered at the interpretation of the results, including their generalization to the general public. A reason for the skewed distribution of the data might be the relatively small sample size (Altman & Bland, 1995). Finally, both movies in our study featured a critical or negative portrayal of the death penalty, so our results do not refer necessarily to all films focusing on capital punishment. However, most films in today's mainstream do not glorify capital punishment (see e.g., Giles, 1995).

Our results provide no reason to believe that people will suffer emotional distress due to watching motion pictures featuring the execution of the protagonist, but these films certainly deteriorate the viewers' mood and have the potential to influence their social values and beliefs. It also challenges Tyler and Boeckmann's (1997) proposition that support for capital punishment is strongly linked to values that reflect stable and long-standing political orientations, and it supports the notion that approval of the death penalty is based on emotion rather than factual information (Ellsworth & Gross,

25 The researchers identify the limitations of their study. Learn more about the convention of reporting limitations in social science research on page 204.

The researchers conclude by identifying the broader implications of their study for the effects of movies on viewers' ideas about capital punishment.

The researchers note a possible area of interest for further investigation or future research.

1994). It seems that values and priorities communicated by television dramas have a nontrivial influence on public policies (Slater et al., 2006) by shaping people's political views through emotions (Mutz & Nir, 2010). Our study also clearly shows that the exclusion of death scenes is not an effective tool to mitigate the impact of a brutal or gruesome film. As we were able to demonstrate, that kind of editing may even lead to adverse effects. This finding highlights the need for new schemes to protect television viewers from harmful effects.

Learn more about the documentation style (APA) typical of research in the social sciences on page 209.

REFERENCES

Altman, D. G., & Bland, J. M. (1995). Statistics notes: The normal distribution. *British Medical Journal, 310,* 298.

Anderson, C. A. (1983). Imagination and expectation: The effect of imagining behavioral scripts on personal intentions. *Journal of Personality and Social Psychology, 45,* 293–305.

Basil, M. D. (1996). Identification as a mediator of celebrity effects. *Journal of Broadcasting & Electronic Media, 40,* 478–495.

Brown, W. J., & Basil, M. D. (1995). Media celebrities and public health: Responses to "Magic" Johnson's HIV disclosure and its impact on AIDS risk and high-risk behaviors. *Health Communication, 7*(4), 345–370.

Chaiken, S. (1980). Heuristic versus systematic processing and the use of source versus message cues in persuasion. *Journal of Personality and Social Psychology, 39,* 752–766.

Cohen, J. (2001). Defining identification: A theoretical look at the identification of audiences with media characters. *Mass Communication & Society, 4*(3), 245–264.

Ellsworth, P., & Gross, S. (1994). Hardening of the attitudes: Americans' views of the death penalty. *Journal of Social Issues, 50*(2), 19–52.

Etzersdorfer, E., & Sonneck, G. (1998). Preventing suicide by influencing mass-media reporting. The Viennese experience 1980–1996. *Archives of Suicide Research, 4,* 67–74.

Fan, D. P., Keltner, K. A., & Wyatt, R. O. (2002). A matter of guilt or innocence: How news reports affect support for the death penalty in the United States. *International Journal of Public Opinion Research, 14*(4), 439–452.

Ferracuti, F., & Lazzari, R. (1970). Indagine sperimentale sugli effetti immediati della presentazione di scene di violenza filmata [An experimental research on the immediate effects of the presentation of scenes of violence in motion pictures]. *Bollettino di Psicologia Applicata, 100–102,* 87–153.

Festinger, L. (1954). A theory of social comparison processes. *Human Relations, 7,* 117–140.

Gau, L.-S., James, J. D., & Kim, J.-C. (2009). Effects of team identification on motives, behavior outcomes, and perceived service quality. *Asian Journal of Management and Humanity Sciences, 4*(2–3), 76–90.

Gerrig, R. J. (1993). *Experiencing narrative worlds. On the psychological activities of reading.* New Haven, CT: Yale University Press.

Giles, J. E. (1995). Pop culture portrayals of capital punishment: A review of *Dead Man Walking* and *Among the Lowest of the Dead. American Journal of Criminal Justice, 20*(1), 137–146.

Greenwood, D. N. (2004). Transporting to TV-land: The impact of idealized character identification on self and body image. *Dissertation Abstracts International: Section B. Sciences and Engineering, 65*(6), 3222.

Gregory, W. L., Burroughs, W. J., & Ainslie, F. M. (1985). Self-relevant scenarios as an indirect means of attitude change. *Personality and Social Psychology Bulletin, 11*(4), 435–444.

Gregory, W. L., Cialdini, R. B., & Carpenter, K. M. (1982). Self-relevant scenarios as mediators of likelihood estimates and compliance: Does imagining make it so? *Journal of Personality and Social Psychology, 43,* 89–99.

Hesse, F. W., Spies, K., Hänze, M., & Gerrards-Hesse, A. (1992). Experimentelle Induktion emotionaler Zustände: Alternativen zur Velten-Methode [Experimental induction of mood states:

Alternatives to the Velten method]. *Zeitschrift für Experimentelle und Angewandte Psychologie, 39*, 559–580.

Hodges, J., & Lehmann, E. L. (1956). The efficiency of some nonparametric competitors of the t test. *Annals of Mathematical Statistics, 27*, 324–335.

Hoffner, C., & Cantor, J. (1991). Perceiving and responding to mass media characters. In J. Bryant & D. Zillmann (Eds.), *Responding to the screen: Reception and reaction processes* (pp. 63–101). Hillsdale, NJ: Erlbaum.

Holbert, R. L., Shah, D. V., & Kwak, N. (2004). Fear, authority, and justice: Crime-related TV viewing and endorsements of capital punishment and gun ownership. *Journalism & Mass Communication Quarterly, 81*(2), 343–363.

Horton, D., & Wohl, R. R. (1956). Mass communication and para-social interaction. Observations on intimacy at a distance. *Psychiatry, 19*, 215–224.

Howells, G. N., Flanagan, K. A., & Hagan, V. (1995). Does viewing a televised execution affect attitudes toward capital punishment? *Criminal Justice and Behavior, 22*(4), 411–424.

Krugman, H. E. (1965). The impact of television advertising: Learning without involvement. *Public Opinion Quarterly, 29*, 349–356.

Mares, M. L., & Cantor, J. (1992). Elderly viewers' responses to televised portrayals of old age. Empathy and mood management versus social comparison. *Communication Research, 19*, 459–478. doi:10.1177/009365092019004004

McNair, D. M., Lorr, M., & Doppleman, L. F. (1971). *EITS manual for the profile of mood states*. San Diego, CA: Educational and Industrial Testing Service.

Mutz, D. C., & Nir, L. (2010). Not necessarily the news: Does fictional television influence real-world policy preferences? *Mass Communication and Society, 13*, 196–217.

Nabi, R. L., Finnerty, K., Domschke, T., & Hull, S. (2006). Does misery love company? Exploring the therapeutic effects of TV viewing on regretted experiences. *Journal of Communication, 56*, 689–706.

Niederkrotenthaler, T., & Sonneck, G. (2007). Assessing the impact of media guidelines for reporting on suicides in Austria: Interrupted times series analysis. *Australian and New Zealand Journal of Psychiatry, 41*, 419–428.

Niederkrotenthaler, T., Till, B., Kapusta, N. D., Voracek, M., Dervic, K., & Sonneck, G. (2009). Copycat effects after media reports on suicide: A population-based ecologic study. *Social Science & Medicine, 69*(7), 1085–1090.

Niven, D. (2002). Bolstering an illusory majority: The effects of the media's portrayal of death penalty support. *Social Science Quarterly, 83*(3), 671–689.

Önder, Ö. M., & Öner-Özkan, B. (2003). Visual perspective in causal attribution, empathy and attitude change. *Psychological Reports, 93*, 1035–1046.

Perry, D. G., & Perry, L. C. (1976). Identification with film characters, covert aggressive verbalization, and reactions to film violence. *Journal of Research in Personality, 10*(4), 399–409.

Peterson, R. C., & Thurstone, L. L. (1970). *Motion pictures and the social attitudes of children*. New York: Arno Press & The New York Times.

Petty, R. E., & Cacioppo, J. T. (1986a). *Communication and persuasion: Central and peripheral routes to attitude change*. New York: Springer.

Petty, R. E., & Cacioppo, J. T. (1986b). The elaboration likelihood model of persuasion. *Advances in Experimental Social Psychology, 19*, 123–205.

Preacher, K. J., & Hayes, A. F. (2004). SPSS and SAS procedures for estimating indirect effects in simple mediation models. *Behavior Research Methods, Instruments, and Computers, 36*, 717–731.

Slater, M. D., & Rouner, D. (2002). Entertainment-education and elaboration likelihood: Understanding the processing of narrative persuasion. *Communication Theory, 12*(2), 173–191.

Slater, M. D., Rouner, D., & Long, M. (2006). Television dramas and support for controversial public policies: Effects and mechanisms. *Journal of Communication, 56*, 235–252.

Sonneck, G., Etzersdorfer, E., & Nagel-Kuess, S. (1994). Imitative suicide on the Viennese subway. *Social Science & Medicine, 38*, 453–457.

Sotirovic, M. (2001). Effects of media use on complexity and extremity of attitudes toward the death penalty and prisoners' rehabilitation. *Media Psychology, 3*, 1–24.

Suckfüll, M., & Scharkow, M. (2009). Modes of reception for fictional films. *Communications, 34*, 361–384.

Tan, E. S. (2008). Entertainment is emotion: The functional architecture of the entertainment experience. *Media Psychology, 11*, 28–51.

Tannenbaum, P. H. (1978). Emotionale Erregung durch kommunikative Reize. Der Stand der Forschung [Emotional arousal via communicative stimuli. State of the art]. *Fernsehen und Bildung, 12*(3), 184–195.

Tannenbaum, P. H., & Gaer, E. P. (1965). Mood change as a function of stress of protagonist and degree of identification in a film viewing situation. *Journal of Personality and Social Psychology, 2*, 612–616.

Till, B., Niederkrotenthaler, T., Herberth, A., Vitouch, P., & Sonneck, G. (2010). Suicide in films: The impact of suicide portrayals on non-suicidal viewers' well-being and the effectiveness of censorship. *Suicide & Life-Threatening Behavior, 40*(4), 319–327.

Till, B., & Vitouch, P. (2008). On the impact of suicide portrayal in films: Preliminary results. In A. Herberth, T. Niederkotenthaler, & B. Till (Eds.), *Suizidalität in den Medien/Suicidality in the media: Interdisziplinäre Betrachtungen/Interdisciplinary contributions* (pp. 69–77). Münster, Germany: LIT.

Tyler, T. R., & Boeckmann, R. J. (1997). Three strikes and you are out, but why? The psychology of public support for punishing rule breakers. *Law & Society Review, 31*, 237–265.

Worringham, R., & Buxton, R. A. (1997). Censorship. In H. Newcomb (Ed.), *The encyclopedia of television* (Vol. 1, pp. 331–334). Chicago: Fitzroy Dearborn.

Zillmann, D. (1991). Empathy: Affect from bearing witness to the emotions of others. In J. Bryant & D. Zillmann (Eds.), *Responding to the screen: Reception and reaction processes* (pp. 135–167). Hillsdale, NJ: Erlbaum.

Zillmann, D. (1994). Mechanisms of emotional involvement with drama. *Poetics, 23*, 33–51.

Zillmann, D. (1996). The psychology of suspense in dramatic exposition. In P. Vorderer, H. J. Wulff, & M. Friedrichsen (Eds.), *Suspense: Conceptualizations, theoretical analyses, and empirical explorations* (pp. 199–231). Mahwah, NJ: Erlbaum.

Reading Questions

1. What do the authors present as their central research question? Where is this question located in their research report?

2. Based on their review of previous scholarship, are Till and Vitouch able to discern any areas of clear consensus among scholars? If so, what are they?

3. According to Till and Vitouch, what makes their study groundbreaking?

4. What are the researchers' four hypotheses? What are their findings in terms of accepting or rejecting each of their hypotheses?

5. Till and Vitouch indicate that one of their findings is particularly "surprising and very puzzling because of its counterintuitive nature" (par. 23). What was the finding, and how do the researchers rationalize this result?

Rhetoric Questions

6. How does the section entitled "Emotional Audience Responses to Dramas" serve to enhance Till and Vitouch's work as social scientists? How does it foster meaning in their work?

7. Till and Vitouch discuss the results of their study in the Results section of their report, but they also provide results in the form of three different tables. Does one form of presentation provide something for the reader that the other does not? Which presentation method works best for you as a reader?

8. Analyze the structure of the study's Discussion section paragraph-by-paragraph. How is it organized, and what is the logic guiding the organization? Is this organization likely to be helpful to the intended audience? Why or why not?

9. The researchers note a number of limitations affecting their study's results. For you as a reader, what is the effect of the authors' identifying these limitations?

Response and Research Questions

10. Watch a creative film that directly concerns the death penalty. As you watch, track how your own mood and attitude shift. Evaluate Till and Vitouch's four hypotheses in light of your own experience.

11. Identify a film that has directly influenced the way you feel about a particular social issue or topic. What was the social issue or topic? In what ways were you affected? Explain why you believe the film was able to affect your beliefs or attitudes.

ACADEMIC CASE STUDY • CAPITAL PUNISHMENT   **NATURAL SCIENCES**

Lethal Injection for Execution: Chemical Asphyxiation?

TERESA A. ZIMMERS, JONATHAN SHELDON, DAVID A. LUBARSKY, FRANCISCO LÓPEZ-MUÑOZ, LINDA WATERMAN, RICHARD WEISMAN, AND LEONIDAS G. KONIARIS

Teresa A. Zimmers is an associate professor of surgery, anatomy, and cell biology at Indiana University's School of Medicine. "Lethal Injection for Execution: Chemical Asphyxiation?," a study co-written with six of her colleagues at the University of Miami Miller School of Medicine and published in the online access journal *PLoS Medicine* in 2007, offers evidence to challenge "the conventional view of lethal injection [as] leading to an invariably peaceful and painless death." According to the editor of the journal that published the study, the researchers' findings call into question the constitutionality of the current lethal injection protocol.

ABSTRACT

Background

Lethal injection for execution was conceived as a comparatively humane alternative to electrocution or cyanide gas. The current protocols are based on one improvised by a medical examiner and an anesthesiologist in Oklahoma and are practiced on an ad hoc basis at the discretion of prison personnel. Each drug used, the ultrashort-acting barbiturate thiopental, the neuromuscular blocker pancuronium bromide, and the electrolyte potassium chloride, was expected to be lethal alone, while the combination was intended to produce anesthesia then death due to respiratory and cardiac arrest. We sought to determine whether the current drug regimen results in death in the manner intended.

Methods and Findings

We analyzed data from two US states that release information on executions, North Carolina and California, as well as the published clinical, laboratory, and veterinary animal experience. Execution outcomes from North Carolina and California together with interspecies dosage scaling of thiopental effects suggest that in the current practice of lethal injection, thiopental might not be fatal and might be insufficient to induce surgical anesthesia for the duration of the execution. Furthermore, evidence from North Carolina, California, and Virginia indicates that potassium chloride in lethal injection does not reliably induce cardiac arrest.

Conclusions

We were able to analyze only a limited number of executions. However, our findings suggest that current lethal injection protocols may not reliably effect death through the mechanisms intended, indicating a failure of design and implementation. If thiopental and potassium chloride fail to cause anesthesia and cardiac arrest, potentially aware inmates could die through pancuronium-induced asphyxiation. Thus the conventional view of lethal injection leading to an invariably peaceful and painless death is questionable.

EDITORS' SUMMARY

Background

Lethal injection is a common form of execution in a number of countries, most prominently the United States and China. The protocols currently used in the United States contain three drugs: an ultrashort-acting barbiturate, thiopental (which acts as an anesthetic, but does not have any analgesic effect); a neuromuscular blocker, pancuronium bromide (which causes muscle paralysis); and an electrolyte, potassium chloride (which stops the heart from beating). Each of these drugs on its own was apparently intended by those who derived the protocols to be sufficient to cause death; the combination was intended to produce anesthesia then death due to respiratory and cardiac arrest. Following a number of executions in the United States, however, it has recently become apparent that the regimen as currently administered does not work as efficiently as intended. Some prisoners take many minutes to die, and others become very distressed.

Why Was This Study Done?

It is possible that one cause of these difficulties with 5 the injections is that the staff administering the drugs are not sufficiently competent; doctors and nurses in the United States are banned by their professional organizations from participating in executions and hence most personnel have little medical knowledge or skill. Alternatively, the drug regimens used might not be effective; it is not clear whether they were derived in any rational way. The researchers here wanted to investigate the scientific basis for the protocols used.

What Did the Researchers Do and Find?

They analyzed data from some of the few states (North Carolina and California) that release information on executions. They also assessed the regimens with respect to published data from clinical, laboratory, and veterinary animal studies. The authors concluded that in the current regimen thiopental might not be fatal and might be insufficient to induce surgical anesthesia for the duration of the execution, and that potassium chloride does not reliably induce cardiac arrest. They conclude therefore that potentially aware inmates could die through asphyxiation induced by the muscle paralysis caused by pancuronium.

What Do These Findings Mean?

The authors conclude that even if lethal injection is administered without technical error, those executed may experience suffocation, and therefore that "the conventional view of lethal injection as an invariably peaceful and painless death is questionable." The Eighth Amendment of the US Constitution prohibits cruel and unusual punishment. The results of this paper suggest that current protocols used for lethal injection in the United States probably violate this amendment.

Additional Information

Please access these Web sites via the online version of this summary at http://dx.doi.org/10.1371/journal .pmed.0040156.

• *In a linked editorial the PLoS Medicine editors discuss this paper further and call for the abolition of the death penalty.*

- *The Death Penalty Information Center is a rich resource on the death penalty both in the United States and internationally.*
- *Information on challenges to lethal injection in various states, including California and North Carolina, is available from the University of California, Berkeley, School of Law.*
- *Human Rights Watch monitors executions in the United States.*
- *Amnesty International campaigns against the death penalty.*
- *A compendium of death-penalty-related links are available from a pro-death-penalty site, the Clark County Prosecuting Attorney.*

INTRODUCTION

In the United States, lethal injection can be imposed in 37 states and by the federal government and military. The origin of the lethal injection protocol can be traced to legislators in Oklahoma searching for a less expensive and potentially more humane alternative to the electric chair [1]. Both the state medical examiner and a chairman of anesthesiology appear to have been consulted in the writing of the statute. The medical examiner has since indicated that no research went into his choice of drugs—thiopental, pancuronium bromide, and potassium chloride—but rather he was guided by his own experience as a patient [2]. His expectation was that the inmate would be adequately anesthetized, and that although each individual drug would be lethal in the dosage specified, the combination would provide redundancy. The anesthesiologist's input relating to thiopental was written into law as "the punishment of death must be inflicted by continuous, intravenous administration of a lethal quantity of an ultra-short-acting barbiturate in combination with a chemical paralytic agent" [3], although in practice Oklahoma uses bolus dosing of all three drugs [4,5]. Texas, the first state to execute a prisoner by lethal injection, and subsequently other jurisdictions copied Oklahoma's protocol without any additional medical consultation [1].

Although executioners invariably achieve death, the mechanisms of death and the adequacy of anesthesia are unclear. Used independently in sufficiently high doses, thiopental can induce death by respiratory arrest and/or circulatory depression, pancuronium bromide by muscle paralysis and respiratory arrest, and potassium chloride by cardiac arrest. When used together, death might be achieved by a combination of respiratory arrest and cardiac arrest due to one or more of the drugs used. Because thiopental has no analgesic effects (in fact, it can be antianalgesic) [6], and because pancuronium would prevent movement in response to the sensations of suffocation and potassium-induced burning, a continuous surgical plane of anesthesia is necessary to prevent extreme suffering in lethal injection.

Recently we reported that in most US executions, executioners have no anesthesia training, drugs are administered remotely with no monitoring for anesthesia, data are not recorded, and no peer review is done [7]. We suggested that such inherent procedural problems might lead to insufficient anesthesia in executions, an assertion supported by low postmortem blood thiopental levels and eyewitness accounts of problematic executions. Because of a current lack of data and reports of problems with lethal injection for executions, we sought to evaluate the three-drug protocol for its efficacy in producing a rapid death with minimal likelihood of pain and suffering.

METHODS

North Carolina lethal injection protocols were determined from Department of Corrections drug procurement records and testimony of prison personnel participating in the process. Times to death were determined from North Carolina Department of Corrections documents, including the Web site [8], official statements, and corroborating news and eyewitness reports. Start times were available for 33 executions, of which 19 could be independently confirmed.

The North Carolina warden pronounces death after a flat line is displayed on the electrocardiogram (ECG) monitor for 5 min, thus time to death was calculated from start time to pronouncement of death less 5 min. Dosages were calculated from postmortem body weights taken from Reports of Investigation by the North Carolina Office of the Chief Medical Examiner. Information regarding the California protocol and execution logs and Florida and Virginia executions were obtained through available court documents [9,10,11]. Data are expressed as mean ± standard deviation. One-way ANOVA with Tukey's multiple comparison test was used for statistical analysis.

RESULTS

Data from North Carolina Executions

Three lethal injection protocols have been used in North Carolina from the first execution in 1984 to the most recent at the time of this writing in August 2006 (Figure 1A). The initial use of serial, intravenous (IV) injections of 3 g of thiopental and 40 mg of pancuronium bromide (referred to here as "Protocol A," $n = 8$, Figure 1A) was superseded by Protocol B in 1998. Protocol B consisted of serial injections of 1.5 g of thiopental, 80 mEq of potassium chloride, 40 mg of pancuronium bromide, 80 mEq of potassium chloride, and finally 1.5 g of thiopental ($n = 21$) [1,12]. After criticism from expert witnesses [13], in 2004 the injection order was changed to the current protocol of serial injections of 3 g of thiopental, 40 mg of pancuronium bromide, and 160 mEq of potassium chloride (Protocol C, $n = 11$) [14]. Each injection is performed in rapid succession with intermittent saline flushes to avoid drug precipitation. Until the last two executions in 2007, no assessment or monitoring of anesthesia was performed.

According to the North Carolina Department of Corrections, once the ECG monitor displays a flat line for 5 min, the warden declares death and a physician certifies that death has occurred [7,12]. Execution start times and declaration times were available for 33 of the 42 lethal injections conducted in North Carolina

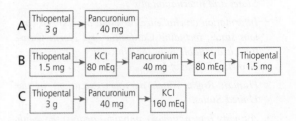

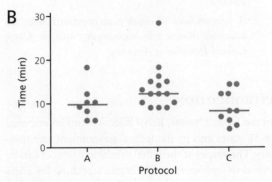

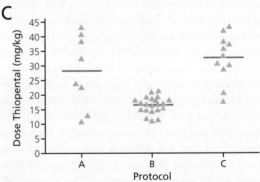

Figure 1 Lethal Injection Executions in North Carolina
(A) Schematic depicting quantity and order of drug administration in the three protocols.
(B) Time to death by protocol, calculated as the interval from execution start time to declaration of death, minus 5 min (see Methods).
(C) Actual dose of thiopental by body weight (not available for all inmates). In Protocol B, 1.5 g of thiopental was given after the pancuronium bromide and potassium chloride, once painful stimuli had been administered and death should have occurred; accordingly, only the first 1.5 g dose is plotted.

DOI:10.1371/JOURNAL.PMED.0040156.G001

(Figure 1B). Mean times to death were 9.88 ± 3.87 min for Protocol A, 13.47 ± 4.88 min for Protocol B, and 9.00 ± 3.71 min for Protocol C. The mean time to death for Protocol B was significantly longer than for Protocol C ($p < 0.05$, Tukey-Kramer test after one-way ANOVA). No other differences were statistically significant. These data indicate that the five-dose regimen of Protocol B slightly prolonged time to death, but more importantly, they indicate that the addition of potassium chloride did not hasten death overall.

In contrast to clinical use of these same drugs, jurisdictions invariably specify mass quantities for injection rather than dosing by body weight. We sought to determine the actual doses used in executions using postmortem body weights recorded by the Office of the Medical Examiner. North Carolina injects 3 g of thiopental; however, in Protocol B inmates were given half the thiopental at the end, once all painful stimuli were administered and death should have been achieved. Thus we considered only the first 1.5 g for Protocol B. Overall the median thiopental dose was 20.3 mg/kg (range 11.2–44 mg/kg, $n = 40$) (Figure 1C). Virtually all of the lowest doses were under Protocol B, although four very large individuals executed under Protocols A and C received less than the median dose. Eyewitness reports of inmate movement including convulsions and attempts to sit up in four executions [15] did not cluster in the lowest doses, but rather occurred at doses of 17.1, 18.9, 19.6, and 21 mg/kg, all performed under Protocol B. Calculated median doses of pancuronium bromide and potassium chloride were 0.46 mg/kg (range 0.28–0.46 mg/kg) and 1.83 mEq/kg (range 1.11–2.35 mEq/kg), respectively.

Data from California Executions

Executions in California provided a second insight into the methodologies and outcomes in lethal injections. The public version of the California protocol specifies injection of 5 g of thiopental, 100 mg of pancuronium bromide, and 100 mEq of potassium chloride [9]. California Department of Corrections from 226A, "Lethal Injection—Execution Record," consists of a table listing "operations," including injection

15

of each drug, cessation of respiration, flatlining of the cardiac monitor, and pronouncement of death, with columns for time, heart rate, and respiration rate. Such execution records were available for 9 of the 11 lethal injections performed in San Quentin California State Prison from 1996 to 2006 [9,10]. One record was incomplete and contradictory and is not reported here. In the remaining 8 executions, respiration rate ceased from 1 min (inmate WB1966) to 9 min (CA2006) after the injection of thiopental (Figure 2). Cessation of respiration was noted coincident with (WB1966, SW2005, CA2006) or up to 3 min after (SA2002) injection of pancuronium bromide. Flatlining of the cardiac monitor occurred 2 min (DR2000) to 8 min (JS1999) after the last injection of potassium chloride. The records indicate that a second dose of potassium chloride was used in the execution of SA2002, and the California warden has said that additional doses were used in two other executions, one being CA2006 and the other unknown [16]. Eyewitness reports document "sudden and extreme" convulsive movements 3–4 min into the execution of MB1999 [17] and more than 30 heaving, convulsive movements of the chest and abdomen of SA2002 [18].

DISCUSSION

Most US executions are beset by procedural problems that could lead to insufficient anesthesia in executions. This hypothesis has been supported by findings of low postmortem blood thiopental levels and eyewitness accounts of problematic executions. Herein we report evidence that the design of the drug scheme itself is flawed. Thiopental does not predictably induce respiratory arrest, nor does potassium chloride always induce cardiac arrest. Furthermore, on the basis of execution data and clinical, veterinary, and laboratory animal studies, we posit that the specified quantity of thiopental may not provide surgical anesthesia for the duration of the execution. Thus some inmates may experience the sensations of pancuronium-induced paralysis and respiratory arrest.

In the United States and Europe, techniques of animal euthanasia for clinical, laboratory, and

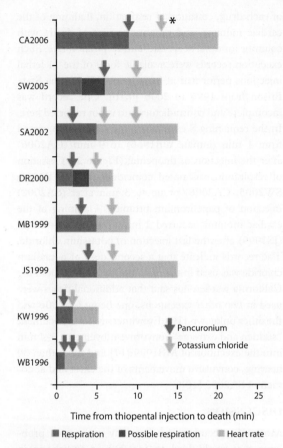

CA2006 *

SW2005

SA2002

DR2000

MB1999

JS1999

KW1996

Pancuronium

Potassium chloride

WB1996

0   5   10   15   20   25

Time from thiopental injection to death (min)

■ Respiration ■ Possible respiration ■ Heart rate

Figure 2 Lethal Injection Executions in California

Depicted are duration of respiration and heart rate after initiation of the thiopental injection at time 0. Injection of pancuronium bromide is indicated by the blue arrow, potassium chloride by the black arrow. Note that additional injections were given of potassium chloride in SA2002 and of pancuronium bromide in WB1996. SW2005 was noted to be breathing 3 min after thiopental, but not at the time of pancuronium bromide injection; the exact time respiration ceased was not recorded. DR2000 was noted to have chest movements 2 min after respiration was noted to have ceased. *A second dose of potassium chloride was administered to CA2006, but not noted on the log. A third, unidentified inmate was also given a second dose of potassium chloride, according to the warden (see text).

DOI:10.1371/JOURNAL.PMED.0040156.G002

agricultural applications are rigorously evaluated and governed by professional, institutional, and regulatory oversight. In university and laboratory settings,

local oversight bodies known as Animal Care and Use Committees typically follow the American Veterinary Medical Association's guidelines on euthanasia, which consider all aspects of euthanasia methods, including drugs, tools, and expertise of personnel in order to minimize pain and distress to the animal. Under those guidelines, lethal injections of companion or laboratory animals are limited to injection by qualified personnel of certain clinically tested, Food and Drug Administration–approved anesthetics or euthanasics, while monitoring for awareness.

In stark contrast to animal euthanasia, lethal injection for judicial execution was designed and implemented with no clinical or basic research whatsoever. To our knowledge, no ethical or oversight groups have ever evaluated the protocols and outcomes in lethal injection. Furthermore, there are no published clinical or experimental data regarding the safety and efficacy of the three-drug lethal injection protocol. Until the unprecedented and controversial use of bispectral index monitoring in the last two North Carolina lethal injections [19], no monitoring for anesthesia was performed. Given this paucity of knowledge and documentation, we sought to evaluate available data in order to determine the efficacy of the three-drug protocol.

The designers of lethal injection intended that each of the drugs be fatal independently and that the combination provide redundancy [2]. Moreover, in legal challenges to the death penalty, the leading expert witness testifying on behalf of the states routinely asserts that 3 g of thiopental alone is a lethal dose in almost all cases [14]. The data presented here, however, suggest that thiopental alone might not be lethal. First, extrapolating from clinical use, the lowest dosages used in some jurisdictions would not be expected to kill. Calculated dosages in North Carolina executions using 3 g of thiopental ranged from 10 to 45 mg/kg. Assuming inmates are roughly the same size across jurisdictions, the dose range would be 17–75 mg/kg in California, where 5 g of thiopental is used, and 6.6–30 mg/kg in Virginia and other jurisdictions, which use 2 g. Thus, at the lowest doses, thiopental would be given near the upper range of that recommended for clinical induction of anesthesia (3–6.6 mg/kg) — clearly not a dose designed to be fatal [20]. Second, the calculated doses used across lethal injections are only 0.1–2 times the LD_{50} (dose required to kill 50% of the tested population) of thiopental in dogs (37 mg/kg), rabbits (35 mg/kg), rats (57.8 mg/kg), and mice (91.4 mg/kg) [21, 22]. Third, intravenous delivery of thiopental alone is not recommended by the Netherlands Euthanasics Task Force, which concluded "it is not possible to administer so much of it that a lethal effect is guaranteed" [23], even in their population of profoundly ill patients.

The most compelling evidence that even 5 g of thiopental alone may not be lethal, however, is that some California inmates continued to breathe for up to 9 min after thiopental was injected. This observation directly contradicts testimony of that state's expert witness, who asserted that "this dose of thiopental sodium will cause virtually all persons to stop breathing within a minute of drug administration" and that "virtually every person given 5 grams of thiopental sodium will have stopped breathing prior to the administration of the pancuronium bromide" [24]. The witness has made identical statements regarding 3 g of thiopental [14]. Indeed, the clinical literature is replete with examples of patients experiencing respiratory failure after even low doses of thiopental [25]. Others, however, experience merely transient, nonfatal apnea. Of course, for inmates who did not stop breathing with thiopental alone, it is impossible to know whether the thiopental solution was correctly mixed, whether the entire dose was administered intravenously, or whether the apparent resistance was due to bolus dosing or individual variation. It remains possible, however, that bolus dosing of 5 g of thiopental alone might not be fatal in all persons. Indeed, nonhuman primates given as much as 60 mg/kg (the mass equivalent of 6 g for a 100 kg man) experienced prolonged sleep, but ultimately recovered [26].

If thiopental does not reliably kill the inmates, then perhaps death is effected by potassium chloride. Rapid intravenous or intracardiac administration of 1–2 mmol/kg potassium chloride under general anesthesia is considered acceptable for euthanasia of large animal species; thus the 1.11–2.35 mmol/kg doses given in North Carolina's lethal injections ought to be fatal. If potassium chloride contributes to death through cardiotoxicity, however, cardiac activity ought to cease more quickly when potassium is used than when it is not. Indeed, such is the principle behind the animal euthanasia agent, Beuthanasia-D Special, in which the cardiotoxic effects of phenytoin synergize with the central nervous system–depressive effects of pentobarbital, accelerating death over pentobarbital alone [27]. In contrast, our analysis shows that use of potassium chloride in North Carolina's Protocol C did not hasten death (defined as flatlining of the ECG) over Protocol A, which used thiopental and pancuronium alone. Moreover, in California executions, ECG flatlining was noted from 2 to 9 min after potassium chloride administration. This observation contrasts sharply with reports of accidental bolus IV administration of concentrated potassium chloride solution, in which patients experienced complete cardiopulmonary arrest almost immediately upon injection [28]. The North Carolina and California data together suggest that potassium chloride might not be the lethal agent in lethal injection.

Given that neither thiopental nor potassium chloride can be construed reliably to be the agent of death in lethal injection, death in at least some inmates might have been due to respiratory cessation from the use of pancuronium bromide. The typical use of 0.06–0.1 mg/kg pancuronium bromide under balanced anesthesia produces 100% neuromuscular blockade within 4 min, with approximately 100 min required for 25% recovery [29]. The doses used in North Carolina were some 3–11 times greater than the typical intubation dose, and thus would be expected to produce more rapid paralysis of many hours duration and complete respiratory arrest [30]. Indeed, pancuronium might have been the agent of death even in inmates who ceased breathing coincident with or shortly after injection of pancuronium, rendering permanent the thiopental-induced apnea. In addition, because pancuronium bromide is effective even when delivered subcutaneously or intramuscularly, pancuronium is likely the sole agent of death when IV catheter misplacement or blowout impairs systemic delivery of the other two drugs. In such cases death by suffocation would occur in a paralyzed inmate fully aware of the progressive suffocation and potassium-induced sensation of burning. This was likely the experience of Florida inmate Angel Diaz, whose eyes were open and mouth was moving 24 min into his execution and who was pronounced dead after 34 min. Findings of two 30-cm burns over both antecubital fossae prompted the medical examiner to conclude that the IV lines were misplaced and the drugs were delivered subcutaneously [31].

Executions such as Diaz's, in which additional drugs were required, constitute further evidence that the lethal injection protocols are not adequate to ensure a predictable, painless death. Court documents and news reports indicate that at least Virginia [32], California [10], and Florida [31] have administered additional potassium chloride in multiple executions when the inmate failed to die as expected. If a Virginia execution takes too long and if the inmate fails to die, the protocol indicates that additional pancuronium and potassium chloride should be injected, although there is no provision for additional thiopental [32]. In cases such as Diaz's, additional drugs may have been required due to technical problems with delivery, but it remains possible that in others, the standard drug protocol failed to kill.

Given the uncertainty surrounding the mechanism of death and low postmortem blood thiopental levels in some executed inmates [7], one must ask whether adequate anesthesia is maintained to prevent awareness and suffering. Medical experts on both sides of the lethal injection debate have asserted that 3 g of thiopental properly delivered should reliably result in either death or a long, deep surgical plane of anesthesia [13,14]. In support of this contention, continuous or intermittent thiopental administration was formerly used for surgical procedures lasting many hours. In one study, 3.3–3.9 g given to patients over 25–50 min resulted in sleep for 4–5.5 h [33]. Depth and duration of thiopental anesthesia depends

greatly upon dose and rate of administration, however, and bolus dosing results in significantly different pharmacokinetics and duration of efficacy than administration of the same quantity of drug at a lower rate [22].

In the modern practice of anesthesia, thiopental is used solely to induce a few moments of anesthesia prior to administering additional agents. Anesthesiologists are taught to administer a small test dose while assessing patient response and the need for additional doses [20]. Such stepwise administration and evaluation has been the practice from the first reports of thiopental usage in 1934, due to the known potential for barbiturate-induced respiratory arrest [34]. It was early recognized that age, body composition, health status, anxiety, premedication, and history of substance abuse clearly influence response to thiopental, with some individuals showing marked resistance to standard doses [35] and others fatal sensitivity [25]. Thus the historical and modern clinical use of thiopental results from its cautious application to prevent respiratory arrest both in the typical patient and the abnormally susceptible. In consequence, there is almost no information about duration of anesthesia following large bolus doses of thiopental in unpremedicated patients, and there are few living anesthesiologists with clinical experience relevant to lethal injection protocols.

Unlike in clinical medicine, however, bolus injection of thiopental is regularly practiced in laboratory animals and veterinary medicine. Standard texts specify from 6 to 50 mg/kg thiopental, depending on the species, for 5–10 min of anesthesia [36], including 18–22 mg/kg for 10–15 min of anesthesia in dogs, pigs, sheep, and swine [37]. Such dosages are conservative guidelines based on average responses of animals in experimental trials (Table 1), with the assumption that respiration and depth of anesthesia will be assessed in individual animals prior to onset of the procedure. (In addition, thiopental is not recommended for painful procedures in animals.) Withholding or administering additional dosages would compensate for individual variation in response.

Table 1

Reported Duration of Sleep or Anesthesia after Bolus IV Injections of Thiopental in Experimental Animals

Species	Dose (mg/kg)	n	Mean Duration of Sleep[a] (min)	Mean Duration of Anesthesia[b] (min)	Reference	Calculated HED[c] (mg/kg)
Mouse	30		4.7–6.4		[43]	2.4
Rat	20		4.0–7.0		[43]	3.2
	25		22.6		[43]	4
	18	32	9.3–10.5		[44]	2.88
	22	7	30.0 ± 6.0		[44]	3.52
Rabbit	20	1	0	0	[45]	6.4
	21	10	28		[21]	6.72
	22	16	14.8–15.2		[44]	7.04
Dog	10.2	5	10.8	1.8	[46]	5.51
	10.9	5	11.4	1.4	[46]	5.89
	15	8	26	8.5	[47]	8.1
	25	22	74.4 ± 7.1		[47]	13.5
Sheep	20	4		18.3 ± 5.10	[48]	18.1
	25		30–45	15	[49]	22.6
Goat	12.7–13.9	4		12.0 ± 5.20	[48]	8.8–9.6
Swine	13.8–25.0	4		5.5 ± 2.7	[48]	12.3–22.4
Cattle	20	4		32.25 ± 14.36	[46]	28.8
Nonhuman primate	60	1	95		[43]	16.5

[a] From loss to return of righting reflex or voluntary movement.

[b] Typically corneal areflexia.

[c] Human equivalent dose was calculated as HED = animal dose (mg/kg) × (animal weight [kg]/human weight [kg])$^{0.33}$ [35,36].

doi:10.1371/journal.pmed.0040156.t001

Although species differences complicate pharmacological comparisons from animals to humans, animal studies are the basis for virtually all human drug trials. According to FDA guidelines, toxicity endpoints for drugs administered systemically to animals are typically assumed to scale well across species when doses are normalized to body surface area (i.e., mg/m^2) [38]. Calculating the human equivalent dose (HED) as recommended by the FDA [39] gives a more conservative estimate of thiopental equivalencies across species than does using simple mg/kg comparisons (Table 1). Swine in particular are regarded as an excellent model of human cardiopulmonary and cerebrovascular physiology, with comparable size, body composition, and brain perfusion rates [40]. Comparing the HED for thiopental anesthesia in swine to lethal injection dosages, we conclude that at least some inmates at the lower end of the thiopental dose range might have experienced fleeting or no surgical anesthesia, while others at the higher end of the range might have received doses predicted to induce more prolonged anesthesia (Table 1). Such a prediction is impossible to evaluate, however, because any evidence of suffering would be masked by the effects of pancuronium.

Our study is necessarily limited in scope and interpretations. Given the secrecy surrounding lethal injections, we were able to analyze only a small fraction of the 891 lethal injections in the United States to date. Indeed, the majority of executions actually take place in states such as Texas and Virginia, where the protocols and procedural problems are likely similar to the ones described, but where the states are unwilling to provide information [7]. Not only are available data limited, however, medical literature addressing the effects of these drugs at high doses and in combination is nonexistent, emphasizing the failure of lethal injection practitioners to design and evaluate rigorously a process that ensures reliable, painless death, even in animals. In consequence, the adequacy of anesthesia and mechanism of death in the current lethal injection protocol remains conjecture.

Despite such limitations, our analysis of data from more forthcoming states along with reports of problematic executions and judicial findings [41] together indicate that the protocol of lethal injection for execution is deeply flawed. Technical difficulties are clearly responsible for some mishandled executions, such as Diaz's. Better training of execution personnel and altering delivery conditions may not "fix" the problem [41, 42], however, because the drug regimen itself is potentially inadequate. Our analysis indicates that as used, thiopental might be insufficient both to maintain a surgical plane of anesthesia and to predictably induce death. Consequently, elimination of pancuronium or both pancuronium and potassium, as has been suggested in California [41], could result in situations in which inmates ultimately awaken.

With the growing recognition of flaws in the lethal injection protocol, 11 states have now suspended the death penalty, with nine of those seeking resolution of issues surrounding the process [42]. In California and Florida, commissions of experts have been charged with evaluating and refining lethal injection protocols. As deliberations begin, we suggest that the secrecy surrounding protocol design and implementation should be broken. The available data or lack of data should be made public and deliberations should be open and transparent.

SUPPORTING INFORMATION

Alternative Language Abstract S1. Translation into Spanish by Francisco López-Muñoz

Found at doi:10.1371/journal.pmed.0040156 .sd001 (24 KB DOC)

ACKNOWLEDGMENTS

Author contributions. TAZ, JPS, DAL, and LGK conceived the study. TAZ and JPS obtained protocol information and execution data. TAZ, DAL, and LGK analyzed the data and published literature. DAL, LW, and RW provided clinical insights. TAZ, JPS, and FLM provided historical perspectives and references. All authors contributed to writing and editing the manuscript.

REFERENCES

[1] Denno D (2002) When legislatures delegate death: The troubling paradox behind state uses of electrocution and lethal injection and what it says about us. Ohio State Law J 63: 63–260. Available at: http://moritzlaw.osu .edu/lawjournal/issues/volume63/number1/denno.pdf. Accessed 16 March 2007.

[2] Fellner J, Tofte S (2006) So long as they die: Lethal injection in the United States. Human Rights Watch. Available at: http://hrw.org/reports/2006/us0406. Accessed 16 March 2007.

[3] Oklahoma Statute Title §22-1014(A) Available at: http://www.lsb.state.ok.us/osstatuestitle.html. Accessed 16 March 2007.

[4] United States District Court, Western District of Oklahoma (20 July 2005) Complaint and Motion to Dismiss, Anderson v. Evans. Case Number 5-825. Document Number 1, pp. 25–34.

[5] US District Court, Western District of Oklahoma (6 September 2005) Complaint and Motion to Dismiss, Anderson v. Evans. Case Number 5-825. Document Number 26, pp. 3–4.

[6] Dundee JW (1960) Alterations in response to somatic pain associated with anaesthesia. II. The effect of thiopentone and pentobarbitone. Br J Anaesth 32: 407–414.

[7] Koniaris LG, Zimmers TA, Lubarsky DA, Sheldon JP (2005) Inadequate anaesthesia in lethal injection for execution. Lancet 365: 1412–1414.

[8] North Carolina Department of Correction (2007) News regarding scheduled executions. Available at: http://www.doc.state.nc.us/dop/deathpenalty/execution__news.htm. Accessed 19 March 2007.

[9] United States District Court, Northern District of California (20 January 2006) Exhibit A to Motion for TRO, Morales v. Hickman. Case Number 6-219. San Quentin Operational Procedure No. 770. Available at: http://www.law.berkeley.edu/clinics/dpclinic/Lethal%20Injection%20Documents/California/Morales/Morales%20Dist%20Ct.Cp/Ex%20A%20to%20TRO%20motion%20(Procedure%20No.%20770).pdf. Accessed 16 March 2007.

[10] United States District Court, Northern District of California (20 January 2006) Exhibit 2 to Exhibit C in Motion for TRO, Morales v. Hickman. Case Number 6-219. Document Number 15-2. Available at: http://www.law.berkeley.edu/clinics/dpclinic/Lethal%20Injection%20Resource%20Pages/resources.ca.html. Accessed 16 March 2007.

[11] United States Supreme Court (6 March 2007) Brief for Amicus Habeas Corpus Resource Center, Hill v. McDonough. Case Number 05-8794. Available at: http://www.law.berkeley.edu/clinics/dpclinic/Lethal%20Injection%20Documents/Florida/Hill/2006.03.06%20amicus%20hcrc.pdf. Accessed 16 March 2007.

[12] United States District Court, Eastern District of North Carolina (31 October 2005) Polk Deposition, Page v. Beck. Case Number 5:04-CT-4. Document Number 98.

[13] United States District Court, Eastern District of North Carolina (3 November 2005) Second Heath Affidavit, Page v. Beck. Case Number 4-04. Document Number 102.

[14] United States District Court, Eastern District of North Carolina (27 September 2004) Affidavit of Dershwitz, Perkins v. Beck. Case Number 04-643. Document Number 7, pp. 22–31.

[15] United States District Court, Eastern District of North Carolina (7 April 2006) Order, Brown v. Beck. Case Number 5:06-CT-3018-H. Available at: http://deathpenaltyinfo.org/Brownorder.pdf. Accessed 16 March 2007.

[16] United States District Court, Northern District of California (25 January 2006) Second Declaration of Dr. Mark Heath, Morales v. Hickman. Case Number 06-219. Document Number 22-1.

[17] United States District Court, Northern District of California (20 January 2006) Declaration of Patterson, Morales v. Hickman. Case Number 06-219. Document Number 14. Available at: http://www.law.berkeley.edu/clinics/dpclinic/Lethal%20Injection%20Documents/California/Morales/Morales%20Dist%20Ct.Cp/Ex%20B%20to%20TRO%20Motion.pdf. Accessed 16 March 2007.

[18] United States District Court, Northern District of California (20 January 2006) Declaration of Rocconi, Morales v. Hickman. Case Number 06-219. Document Number 15-4. Available at: http://www.law.berkeley.edu/clinics/dpclinic/Lethal%20Injection%20Documents/California/Morales/Morales%20Dist%20Ct.Cp/Ex%203%20to%20Heath%20Decl%20(Rocconi%20Decl%20re.%20Anderson%20execution).pdf. Accessed 16 March 2007.

[19] Steinbrook R (2006) New technology, old dilemma—Monitoring EEG activity during executions. N Engl J Med 354: 2525–2527.

[20] Abbott Laboratories (1993 November) Pentothal for injection, USP (Thiopental Sodium) Reference 06-8965-R10. A similar document is available at: http://www.rxlist.com/cgi/generic/thiopental.htm. Accessed 16 March 2007.

[21] Werner HW, Pratt TW, Tatum AL (1937) A comparative study of several ultrashort-acting barbiturates, nembutal, and tribromethanol. J Pharmacol Exp Ther 60: 189–197.

[22] Robinson MH (1945) The effect of different injection rates upon the AD50, LD50 and anesthetic duration of pentothal in mice, and strength-duration curves of depression. J Pharmacol Exp Ther 85: 176–191.

[23] (1994) Administration and compounding of euthanasic agents. The Hague: Royal Dutch Society for the Advancement of Pharmacy.

[24] United States District Court, Northern District of California (20 January 2006) Declaration of Dershwitz, Morales v. Woodford. Case Number 06-219. Document Number 15.

[25] Harris WH (1943) Collapse under pentothal sodium. Lancet 242: 173–174.

[26] Taylor JD, Richards RK, Tabern DL (1951) Metabolism of ^{35}S thiopental (pentothal): Chemical and paper chromatographic studies of ^{35}S excretion by the rat and monkey. J Pharmacol Exp Ther 104: 93–102.

[27] (2005) Freedom of Information Summary. Original Abbreviated New Animal Drug Application. Euthanasia-III Solution. Rockville (Maryland): Food and Drug Administration. Available at: http://www.fda.gov/cvm/FOI/200-280020305.pdf. Accessed 6 March 2007.

[28] Wetherton AR, Corey TS, Buchino JJ, Burrows AM (2003) Fatal intravenous injection of potassium

in hospitalized patients. Am J Forensic Med Pathol 24: 128–131.

[29] Gensia Sicor Pharmaceuticals (2003 October) Pancuronium bromide injection (prescribing information and material safety data sheet). Available at: http://www.sicor.com/products/1044.html. Accessed 16 March 2007.

[30] Mehta MP, Sokoll MD, Gergis SD (1988) Accelerated onset of non-depolarizing neuromuscular blocking drugs: Pancuronium, atracurium and vecuronium. A comparison with succinylcholine. Eur J Anaesthesiol 5: 15–21.

[31] Tisch C, Krueger C (14 December 2006) Second dose needed to kill inmate. St Petersburg Times. State/Suncoast edition. St. Petersburg. p. 1A. Available at: http://www.sptimes.com/2006/12/14/State/Second__dose__needed__to.shtml. Accessed 16 March 2007.

[32] United States Supreme Court (6 March 2006) Brief for Amicus Curiae, Darick Demorris Walker, Hill v. McDonough. Case Number 05-8794. Available at: http://www.jenner.com/files/tbl__s69NewsDocumentOrder/FileUpload500/674/Brief__Amicus__Curiae__Walker.pdf. Accessed 16 March 2007.

[33] Brodie BB, Mark LC, Lief PA, Bernstein E, Papper EM (1951) Acute tolerance to thiopental. J Pharmacol Exp Ther 102: 215–218.

[34] Heard KM (1936) Pentothal: A new intravenous anesthetic. Can Med Assn J 34: 628–634.

[35] Mallison FB (1937) Pentothal sodium in intravenous anaesthesia. Lancet 230: 1070–1073.

[36] Kohn DF, Wixson SK, White WJ, Benson GJ, editors (1997) Anesthesia and analgesia in laboratory animals. New York: Academic Press. 426 p.

[37] Plumb DC (2005) Veterinary drug handbook. 5th Ed. Stockholm (Wisconsin): PharmaVet. 929 p.

[38] Mordenti J, Chappell W (1989) The use of interspecies scaling in toxicokinetics. In: Yacobi A, Kelly J, Batra V, editors. Toxicokinetics and new drug development. New York: Pergamon Press. pp. 42–96.

[39] Center for Drug Evaluation and Research (2005) Guidance for industry estimating the maximum safe starting dose in initial clinical trials for therapeutics in adult healthy volunteers. Rockville (Maryland): Food and Drug Administration. Available at: http://www.fda.gov/CDER/GUIDANCE/5541fnl.htm. Accessed 16 March 2007.

[40] Hannon JP, Bossone CA, Wade CE (1990) Normal physiological values for conscious pigs used in biomedical research. Lab Anim Sci 40: 293–298.

[41] United States District Court, Northern District of California (15 February 2006) Memorandum of Intended Decision; Request for Response from Defendants, Morales v. Tilton. Case Number C 06-219, C 06-926. Available at: http://www.deathpenaltyinfo.org/CalifLethalInjection.pdf. Accessed 16 March 2007.

[42] Koniaris LG, Sheldon JP, Zimmers TA (2007) Can lethal injection for execution really be "fixed"? Lancet 369: 352–353.

[43] Mirsky JH, Giarman NJ (1955) Studies on the potentiation of thiopental. J Pharmacol Exp Ther 114: 240–249.

[44] Richards RK, Taylor JD, Kueter KE (1953) Effect of nephrectomy on the duration of sleep following administration of thiopental and hexobarbital. J Pharmacol Exp Ther 108: 461–473.

[45] Gruber CM, Gruber JCM, Colosi N (1937) The effects of anesthetic doses of sodium thio-pentobarbital, sodium thio-ethamyl and pentothal sodium upon the respiratory system, the heart and blood pressure in experimental animals. J Pharmacol Exp Ther 60: 143–147.

[46] Ramsey H, Haag HB (1946) The synergism between the barbiturates and ethyl alcohol. J Pharmacol Exp Ther 88: 313–322.

[47] Wyngaarden JB, Woods LA, Ridley R, Seevers MH (1948) Anesthetic properties of sodium 5-allyl-5-(1-methyl-butyl)-2-thiobarbiturate (surital) and certain other thiobarbiturates in dogs. J Pharmacol Exp Ther 95: 322–327.

[48] Sharma RP, Stowe CM, Good AL (1970) Studies on the distribution and metabolism of thiopental in cattle, sheep, goats and swine. J Pharmacol Exp Ther 172: 128–137.

[49] Komar E (1991) Intravenous anaesthesia in the sheep. Proc Int Congr Vet Anesth, 4th. Utrecht (The Netherlands). pp. 209–210.

Reading Questions

1. As reported in the study, what three drugs, each supposedly administered in lethal quantities, are used as part of the execution protocol?

2. Based on your reading of the study's introduction, what is the researchers' primary concern about the effects of the lethal cocktail? On what do they base this concern?

3. The researchers suggest that the quantity of thiopental used in the execution protocol may not induce surgical anesthesia. What kinds of sensations might individuals experience during the execution process as a result?

4. What are the researchers able to suggest by comparing the human equivalent dose (HED) of thiopental anesthesia in swine to lethal injection doses?

5. According to the researchers, what does the lack of research concerning the effects of the drugs used as part of the execution protocol suggest about the protocol overall?

Rhetoric Questions

6. What elements of the study's structural components are designed to lessen any appearance of bias on the part of the researchers?

7. The study is published with an abstract and an editors' summary at the beginning. Why do you suppose both of these are offered to readers, and in what context is one likely more useful to readers than the other?

8. As part of the Discussion section, the authors include details of Angel Diaz's execution, suggesting that he was likely fully aware while experiencing suffocation and burning sensations. What is the purpose of providing this example? Is it effective? Why or why not?

9. Calculate the number of documented references in each of the study's sections — Introduction, Methods, Results, and Discussion. In what section do most of the references occur? Why do you suppose this is?

Response and Research Questions

10. According to the editors' summary, the study's results "suggest that current protocols used for lethal injection in the United States probably violate" (par. 7) the Eighth Amendment of the U.S. Constitution, which prohibits cruel and unusual punishment. Do you agree with the editors' assessment?

11. Identify three unique challenges you believe researchers face when they study controversial issues like capital punishment. How might researchers address those challenges?

ACADEMIC CASE STUDY • CAPITAL PUNISHMENT   APPLIED FIELDS

The Myth of Innocence

JOSHUA MARQUIS

Joshua Marquis is the district attorney for Clatsop County, Oregon. He is a former president of the Oregon District Attorneys Association and has served on the board of directors of the National District Attorneys Association as well as on the leadership council of the American Bar Association's Criminal Justice Section. Marquis is a contributing author to the book *Debating the Death Penalty* (2004). In his article below, published in *The Journal of Criminal Law and Criminology* in 2005, Marquis calls into question a number of the claims of anti-death-penalty activists and makes a call for an intellectually honest approach to the debate over capital punishment.

For decades in America, questions about the death penalty centered on philosophical and sometimes religious debate over the morality of the state-sanctioned execution of another human being. Public opinion ebbed and flowed with support for the death penalty, declining as civil rights abuses became a national concern in the 1960s and increasing along with a rapid rise in violent crime in the 1980s.[1]

Those who oppose capital punishment call themselves "abolitionists,"[2] clearly relishing the comparison to those who fought slavery in the 19th century. In the mid-1990s these abolitionists, funded by a cadre of wealthy supporters including George Soros and Roderick MacArthur, succeeded in changing the focus of the debate over the death penalty from the morality of executions to questions about the "fundamental fairness" or, in their minds, unfairness of the institution.[3] The abolitionists were frustrated by polling that showed that virtually all groups of Americans supported capital punishment in some form in some cases.[4]

Led by Richard Dieter of the neutral-sounding Death Penalty Information Center, opponents of capital punishment undertook a sweeping make-over of their campaign.[5] In addition to painting America as a rogue state—a wolf among the peaceful lambs of the European Union who had forsaken the death penalty—the latter-day abolitionists sought to convince America that, as carried out, the death penalty was inherently racist, that the unfortunates on death row received wretched and often incompetent defense counsel, and, most appalling, that a remarkable number of those sentenced to death were in fact innocent.[6]

Dieter and his allies pointed to the fact that while African-Americans make up only slightly more than 10 percent of the American population, they constitute more than 40 percent of those on death row.[7] In addition, they described some cases in which the appointed lawyers were nothing more than golfing pals with the judge making the appointment, that some of these lawyers had no previous experience with murder cases, and that in at least one case the lawyer appears to have slept through portions of the trial.[8]

Abolitionists painted a picture of massive prosecution, funded by the endless resources of the government and pitted against threadbare public defenders either barely out of law school or, if experienced, pulled from the rubbish heap of the legal profession.[9]

But most compelling of all the arguments that called capital punishment "fatally flawed" were the stories of men who had served years on death row, a few coming close to their scheduled execution only to be released because a court had determined that they were "exonerated." Television programs showed dramatic footage of Anthony Porter, freed from Illinois's death row, running into the arms of his savior, Northwestern University journalism professor David Protess.[10] A handful of other stories of "innocents on death row" filled magazines, television programs, and symposia on college campuses across the country.

In the face of horrific crimes like the murder of more than 160 people by Timothy McVeigh, death penalty opponents sought to recruit new converts. By the time of the 2000 presidential campaign, they had succeeded in moving the debate to a point where supporters of capital punishment felt beleaguered and outgunned.[11] A growing number of classic conservatives, from William F. Buckley to Pat Robertson, expressed their mistrust of capital punishment.[12] The arguments succeeded in driving down public support for the death penalty from a high of almost 80 percent in the late 1980s[13] to a low of around 65 percent in the year George W. Bush ran against Al Gore for president.[14]

Recognizing that the polls still showed majority support for the existence of the death penalty, abolitionists started advocating for a "moratorium," suggesting that short of abolition, a halt should be declared to executions while the issue was intensively studied.[15] They found an unlikely ally in then-Governor George Ryan of Illinois.[16]

Ryan, a conservative Republican, had just two years earlier, in 1998, won election in part by underlining his support for capital punishment.[17] But in 1999 the *Chicago Tribune* began running a hard-hitting series of lengthy articles, accusing Illinois prosecutors of serious misconduct and highlighting a number of cases in which men sentenced to death row had been released when appellate courts found serious errors in their trials or claims of misconduct by police or prosecutors.[18] Although prosecutors and at least one state Supreme Court justice questioned Ryan's authority simply to halt the death penalty process,[19] Ryan's action effectively prevented the execution of any of the 170 men on that state's death row.[20]

Ryan became a folk hero. He was lauded on college campuses across the country, cited as a profile in political courage by foreign politicians, and was even nominated for the Nobel Peace Prize.[21] Just before leaving office in 2003, Ryan stunned many when he announced a sweeping clemency, using his executive powers to release 164 men from death row and granting outright pardons to four more.[22]

Sensing a possible sea change in public sentiment, the abolitionists pushed for other states to follow Ryan's example. The moratorium became a leading campaign issue in the Maryland governor's race in 2002, following the outgoing governor's decision to place a moratorium on that state's use of the death penalty and commission a study to determine whether race plays a role in the application of the death penalty.[23]

After these apparent victories, the tide started to turn, but not in the way the abolitionists expected. Governor Ryan was dogged by a federal investigation into bribery and corruption charges that drove his approval rating to less than 25 percent.[24] His name became so toxic in Illinois politics that a Republican candidate for governor in 2004, whose last name was also Ryan but was no relation to the Governor, campaigned on first name.[25] After securing indictments and convictions against his top aides and even his campaign committee, federal prosecutors indicted Ryan on charges of bribery, corruption, and racketeering.[26]

In Maryland, Democratic gubernatorial candidate Kathleen Kennedy Townsend, who had pledged her continued support for the death penalty moratorium, suffered a defeat in the 2002 election in the wake of the Washington-area sniper shootings.[27] And, finally, the murder of 3,000 people on September 11, 2001, reminded many Americans that some crimes merited the ultimate punishment.

Having largely abandoned the moral arguments against capital punishment, the modern abolition movement is now based on a trio of urban legends: (1) the death penalty is racist at its core; (2) those accused of capital murder get grossly inadequate representation; and (3) a remarkable number of people on death row are innocent.

In the last ten years the violent crime rate in America, including the murder rate, has decreased dramatically.[28] A series of recent studies by economists showed an undeniable correlation between the death penalty and deterrence.[29]

One researcher who reported that pardons may have actually cost lives nonetheless added a postscript to the study, saying that despite the results of his study he personally believed that the death penalty remained biased against minorities.[30]

How could the death penalty not be racially biased given the disproportionate number of African-Americans convicted of murder? A Cornell University study issued in March of 2004 by law professors John Blume and Theodore Eisenberg and statistician Martin Wells[31]—all opponents of the death penalty[32]—showed that the conventional wisdom about the South's so-called "death belt," where blacks are said to be much more likely to die than whites convicted of similar murders, simply does not hold up. In the words of the authors, "[t]he conventional wisdom about the death penalty is incorrect in some respects and misleading in others."[33]

Until the Cornell study, the abolitionists had relied largely on the studies of David Baldus for their accusations of racism. Baldus, an Iowa law professor, claimed that race was a key factor in the imposition of death sentences.[34] The Cornell University study, however, drawn from statistics gathered by the U.S. Department of Justice's Bureau of Justice Statistics, showed that while African-Americans were convicted of committing 51.5 percent of all murders, they comprised only 41.3 percent of death row's population.[35] The study revealed that roughly 10 percent of the murders were cross-racial[36] and that in twenty-eight states, including Georgia, South Carolina and Tennessee, blacks were under-represented on death row.[37] States like Texas, which had the greatest number of people on death row, actually had a lower per capita rate of imposing the death penalty than Nevada, Ohio, and Delaware.[38]

The Cornell study thereby confirmed what many prosecutors had suspected: that a white murderer sentenced to death was twice as likely actually to be executed than a black person sentenced to death.[39]

It may be shockingly politically incorrect to say, but the fact is that the most horrific murders—serial killings, torture murders, and sex crimes against children—tend to be committed more frequently by white murderers than blacks.[40]

The next urban legend is that of the threadbare but plucky public defender fighting against all odds against a team of sleek, heavily funded prosecutors with limitless resources. The reality in the 21st century is startlingly different. There is no doubt that before the landmark 1963 decision in *Gideon v. Wainwright*,[41] appointed counsel was often inadequate. But the past few decades have seen the establishment of public defender systems that in many cases rival some of the best lawyers retained privately. The *Chicago Tribune*, while slamming the abilities of a number of individual defense counsel in Cook County capital cases in the 1980s, grudgingly admitted that the Cook County Public Defender's Office provided excellent representation for its indigent clients.[42]

Many giant silk-stocking law firms in large cities across America not only provide pro-bono counsel in capital cases, but also offer partnerships to lawyers whose sole job is to promote indigent capital defense.[43] In one recent case in Alabama, a Portland, Oregon, law firm spent hundreds of thousands of dollars of lawyer time on a post-conviction appeal for a death row inmate.[44] In Oregon, where I have both prosecuted and defended capital cases, it is common for attorneys to be paid hundreds of thousands of dollars by the state for their representation of indigent capital clients. And the funding is not limited to legal assistance. Expert witnesses for the defense often total tens of thousands of dollars each, resources far beyond the reach of individual district attorneys who prosecute the same cases.

As the elected prosecutor of what is considered a mid-sized county in Oregon, I have a set budget that rarely gives me more than $15,000 a year to cover the total expenses of expert witnesses for *all* of the hundreds of cases my office prosecutes each year. Yet in one recent murder trial, one witness in the mitigation phase admitted he had already billed the state indigent defense program for over $30,000. In a related case the investigators for the defense were paid over $100,000.

Finally, and perhaps most importantly, we come to discuss why it matters whether someone is "innocent," "exonerated," "acquitted," or merely let go. Words like "innocence" convey enormous moral authority and are intended to drive the public debate by appealing to a deep and universal revulsion at the idea that someone who is genuinely blameless could wrongly suffer for a crime in which he had no involvement. But in the practice of law, words matter enormously. To call someone "innocent" when all they managed to do was wriggle through some procedural cracks in the justice system cheapens the word and impeaches the moral authority of those who claim that a person has been "exonerated."

Scott Turow, the best-selling novelist, spent some time as a federal prosecutor before joining a high-end Chicago law firm. He became interested in the death penalty through pro-bono work that he and his firm performed for a group of death row defendants who were eventually released. Governor Ryan appointed Turow to a seventeen-member commission that sought to review Illinois's death penalty laws.[45] The commission was heavily laden with "former prosecutors" like Turow, who were now criminal defense lawyers. Only one commission member was a sitting prosecutor. That member, Mike Waller, was the lone dissenter on many of the recommendations that were adopted almost in their entirety by the Illinois legislature.[46]

Turow has written two recent books, one fictional—*Reversible Errors*,[47] already a TV movie-of-the-week[48]—and a slim, austere volume of his personal reflections, *Ultimate Punishment*.[49] The novel sold well, like most of Turow's other works. It paints the traditional urban myth of over-zealous and politically ambitious prosecutors and incompetent forensics resulting in a tragic miscarriage of justice, thwarted by a brave civil attorney who is dabbling in pro-bono capital defense work, aided by his love interest, a recovering addict who sold her office as a judge and fell from grace.[50]

Popular culture, most of it not as well-crafted as Turow's, has created an entire alternate universe that posits a legal system that regularly hurls doe-eyed innocents onto death row through the malevolent machinations of corrupt cops and district attorneys who either earn bonuses for the innocent people they convict or are so intent on advancing their careers that they disregard the truth and conceal evidence that might clear the defendant. These fantastic constructions are prominent in television programs like *The Practice*[51] (mercifully axed), in movies like *True Believer*[52] and *True Crime*,[53] as well as in popular fiction. There is an axiom in journalism that it's not news how many planes landed safely today. Accordingly, it's not surprising that the news articles that make the front page of major publications are about the exceedingly rare cases where the convicted defendant did not, in fact, commit the offense.

One of the most striking examples of truth and fiction blended in popular culture is a play called *The Exonerated*, which just finished a successful two-year run off-Broadway and is now touring the United States.[54] The play profiles six people who were once on death row and now walk free.[55] The clear implication is that they are innocent in the classic sense of that word—that they didn't do it, weren't there, didn't participate. Yet two of the six, Sonia "Sunny" Jacobs and Kerry Cook, stand convicted by their own guilty pleas[56] of the murders for which they were supposedly "exonerated."[57] A third, Robert Hayes, is currently serving a lengthy prison sentence for a crime eerily similar to the one for which the play claims he was exonerated.[58] Neither the script, nor the reviews of, nor most of the press for *The Exonerated* bear any resemblance to the stark facts of these cases.

> Imagine everything you did between the years of 1976 and 1992. Now remove all of it. Those sixteen years were taken away from Sunny Jacobs, convicted and sentenced to death for a crime she did not commit. But her story is not unique. And it could happen just as easily to you. *The Exonerated* tells the true stories of six innocent survivors of death row.
>
> —Advertisement for the play *The Exonerated*[59]

Susan Sarandon, Debra Winger, Mia Farrow, Vanessa Redgrave and other stars of stage and screen

have been pleased at the chance to read the words of a woman who stands convicted of two murders. *The Exonerated* was rated the third-best play of 2002 by *Time* magazine, and many reviewers (and, most likely, audiences) have accepted these effective theatrics as the truth. For example, veteran theater critic John Simon declared that "[d]ocudramas can take liberties with the truth in subtle, sometimes unintentional ways," but that he has "no reason to disbelieve" authors Erik Jensen and Jessica Blank's version of the truth.[60] Obviously Mr. Simon has only seen and read the play, not the trials involved. In fact, Sunny Jacobs, the main character in *The Exonerated*, is legally guilty, and contrary to claims made by the play, cannot be deemed factually innocent. Sunny Jacobs is a woman who has been exonerated only by theater critics or other glitterati who take these claims at face value.

During the off-Broadway run of *The Exonerated*, one reviewer recounted that, after Sunny and her children were kidnapped by the real killer, "Sunny and [her common law husband] were arrested for murder along with the killer, who made a deal with the state attorney and accused the couple."[61] In an English production of the play, Jacobs is described as "a yoga instructor" who calls herself "a hippie. I was a peace-and-love person. I'm a vegetarian."[62] No mention of her several arrests for gun and drug charges[63] or her admission that she participated in gunning down two men.[64] Another review calls her "a young mother trying to protect her children and her mate . . . caught in a police shooting . . ."[65]

Here are the facts, gained from the trial transcripts, published opinions of the Florida Supreme Court[66] and the U.S. Court of Appeals for the Eleventh Circuit,[67] and from reviewing the tapes and transcripts of police interrogations:[68]

Canadian constable Donald Irwin was on a "ride-along" with his friend Phillip Black, a trooper for the Florida State Police, on the morning of February 20, 1976.[69] Trooper Black had met Corporal Irwin of the Ontario Provincial Police and the two had visited each other's homes over the years.[70]

Black and Irwin were checking a car parked at a rest stop along I-95 near Pompano Beach.[71]

The Camaro was occupied by two men—Jesse Tafero (Jacobs's boyfriend and the father of their infant son) and a prison pal of Tafero's named Walter Rhodes[72]—and Jacobs and her two children.[73] Two truck drivers saw the trooper order the men out of the car, leaving only Jacobs and her two children in the car.[74] Jacobs admitted to firing one shot from inside the car.[75] The State's theory, which ultimately resulted in convictions, was that she then handed the gun, which she had purchased in North Carolina, to Tafero, who fired several more shots.[76]

Both Irwin and Black lay dying when the group stole the trooper's car and took off.[77] One of the truck drivers who witnessed the event saw a man later identified as Rhodes with his hands in full view (i.e., no gun in hand).[78] A TASER dart was discovered in the door of the cruiser.[79] In the Camaro, an empty container for a TASER weapon was found in the back seat near where Jacobs and her kids had been seated.[80] Expended shells from a semi-automatic pistol registered to Jacobs were found both outside and inside the car, consistent with some shots being fired from inside the car.[81]

After taking the trooper's car, the group then kidnapped an elderly man and his Cadillac, initially claiming they had to take a sick child to the hospital.[82] With Rhodes at the wheel and with the 9mm pistol (owned by Jacobs) strapped to a holster around Tafero's waist, they tried to run a roadblock.[83] Police opened fire and shot Rhodes in the leg.[84]

Officers initially were unclear about Jacobs's relationship to the men. She clarified it by kissing Tafero[85] and later telling her nine-year-old that she loved him and for him "to keep [his] mouth shut."[86] Shortly thereafter, officers asked Jacobs, "Do you like shooting troopers?"[87] "We had to," she said,[88] and while being transported she told officers that she had fired the first shot.[89]

Jacobs's version in the play? "It all happened so fast, you know. I just ducked down to cover the kids. . . . We were kidnapped at that point. . . . I know there must be a roadblock. 'Hey we're gonna be *rescued*! Help is on the way, you know, the cavalry!'"[90]

The prosecution gave Walter Rhodes, who denied firing any of the fatal shots, a lie detector test; when he passed they allowed him to plead guilty to murder in the second-degree.[91] He agreed to testify against Jesse Tafero and Sunny Jacobs.[92] Tafero was tried first, convicted, and sentenced to death.[93] Jacobs was tried next and also convicted.[94] Although gushing reviews of *The Exonerated* refer to readings from actual transcripts,[95] Jacobs never testified at trial before a jury. Her only testimony was before a judge' in a pre-trial motion, seeking to keep statements she made to investigators away from the trial jury. She chose to invoke her constitutional right not to testify, but now wants to be vindicated in the court of public opinion, where there is no Fifth Amendment.

The jury recommended life in prison but the judge overruled the jury and imposed a death sentence.[96] The Florida Supreme Court in turn overruled the trial judge and reduced the sentence to life.[97] Jacobs served five years on death row, not sixteen as the play would have the audience believe,[98] before being released into the prison's general population. Another decade went by and the case ended up before the federal appeals court that oversees Florida. In ordering a new trial, the Eleventh Circuit made no findings about Sunny Jacobs's factual innocence but held that a polygraph administered to Walter Rhodes contained answers that were inconsistent with some of Rhodes's testimony, and should have been turned over to the defense.[99] The court also ruled that some of Jacobs's statements should not have been admitted against her at trial (these did not include her statement that she had fired the first shot).[100] The appeals court ordered a new trial for Jacobs.[101]

Jacobs was represented by top-notch defense counsel who had become personally devoted to her cause.[102] She was released from prison in 1992 after entering an *Alford* guilty plea, allowing her to claim she didn't really commit the crime but still plead guilty to take advantage of the plea offer.[103] Jacobs pled guilty to two counts of Murder in the Second Degree, the same charges to which Rhodes pled.[104] At the plea and sentencing hearing, the prosecutor recited the facts the state could prove.[105] Jacobs and her lawyers agreed the state could prove those facts.[106] Witnesses had died, and Rhodes had recanted and then unrecanted at least twice.[107] (He now maintains that his original testimony was correct.)[108] After sixteen years of battling in the courts, the prosecutor decided that a plea to Murder in the Second Degree and seventeen years in prison was an acceptable result.[109]

In the play, the clear impression is that Sunny Jacobs was freed from prison by a guardian angel: "But after all that, one day, the guard came into my cell and told me I was getting out. I thought he was trying to trick me."[110]

No court ever "exonerated" Sonia Jacobs. She was convicted of the same crime as Walter Rhodes, who actually served more time than Jacobs. She is *legally guilty by virtue of a plea and sentence.*[111] But she came from a wealthy white family. Her background isn't what people expect from a murderer. The elegant Mimi Rogers played her in a made-for-TV movie, *In the Blink of an Eye,* which aired on ABC in 1996.[112] The inconvenient facts of her cold-blooded executions of two innocent men from the back seat of a Camaro while her nine-year-old son looked on were deleted from the movie, to make her release from prison palatable to the television audience.

The Jacobs case caught my attention a few years ago and I have spent hundreds of hours reading trial transcripts and appellate decisions, listening to tape recordings of Jacobs's questioning and conducting extensive interviews with several of those involved with the case. After such scrutiny, the claim of "exoneration" made by the eponymous play simply fails. The concept of "innocence" is cheapened when used to describe Jacobs, whose guilt is supported not only by her own plea, but more importantly the actual facts surrounding her case.

In an article published November 27, 2003, *Contra Costa Times* reporter Georgia Rowe glibly parroted, "American history is rife with people who were convicted of crimes they didn't commit."[113]

In 1998, Northwestern University sponsored a conference that celebrated a group of people it claimed were innocents on death row. One of the men on stage was Dr. Jay Smith, made infamous by Joseph Wambaugh's book *Echoes in the Darkness*[114] and one of the 118 men the Death Penalty Information Center fetes as having been "freed from death row."[115] The real story is not so festive.

Dr. Smith was convicted of the murder of high school English teacher Susan Reinert and her two children.[116] A jury concluded that Smith and another teacher had conspired to murder Reinert, and that her children were collateral damage of the murder scheme, killed because they might have given witness.[117] Reinert's body was recovered, but the children have never been found.[118]

A state appellate court held that prosecutors had failed to disclose the existence on the victim's body of a few grains of sand that might possibly have supported Smith's claim of innocence.[119] Smith's conviction was set aside and he was freed from a life sentence in prison.[120] Emboldened by his newfound freedom (and despite his undisturbed convictions for theft by deception, receiving stolen property, possession of a firearm without a license and possession of marijuana),[121] Smith filed lawsuits against the State of Pennsylvania, the officer who arrested him, and everyone connected with his prosecution.[122]

There was only one problem: Smith was not innocent. In its final decision throwing Smith's case out of court, the U.S. Court of Appeals for the Third Circuit concluded: "Our confidence in Smith's convictions for the murder of Susan Reinert and her two children is not the least bit diminished by consideration of the suppressed lifters and quartz particles, and Smith has therefore not established that he is entitled to compensation for the unethical conduct of some of those involved in the prosecution."[123]

Yes, there are a few people who actually did not do it. Some are true poster boys: Kirk Bloodsworth, a Maryland man who was convicted of murder and later exonerated by DNA testing.[124] Cases like Bloodsworth's show that the years and layers of appeals required in capital cases do in fact catch the rare mistake that wrongfully jails or condemns an innocent man.

Most have stories more akin to Anthony Porter, whose release was due in large part to the work of journalism students at Northwestern University. What doesn't make it into the stock footage of him running jubilantly into the arms of Professor Protess upon his release from prison is how he got to prison in the first place. Porter was committing an armed robbery in the same park, at the same time as a drug murder.[125] He ran from the park, gun in hand, in full view of witnesses who identified Porter to the police.[126] Porter denied not only the murder, but even being in the park, a lie he maintained until after his convictions were affirmed.[127]

The justice system is far from perfect and has made many mistakes, mostly in *favor* of the accused. Hundreds, if not thousands, have died or lost their livelihoods through embezzlement or rape because the American justice system failed to incarcerate people who were guilty by any definition.

Since the death penalty was re-authorized in 1976 by the Supreme Court,[128] there have been upwards of 500,000 murders.[129] About 7,000 murderers were sentenced to death and about 3,700 remain on death row today.[130] About 950 have been executed.[131] Appellate courts at the state and federal levels have imposed what one justice called "super due process"[132] for convicted capital murderers, overturning almost two-thirds of all death sentences, a rate far exceeding that in other cases.[133] Virtually none have been overturned because of "actual innocence."[134]

Some claim that a civilized society must be prepared to allow ten guilty men to walk free in order to spare one innocent. But the well-organized and even better-funded abolitionists cannot point to a single case of a demonstrably innocent person executed in the modern era of American capital punishment.

Instead, let's tally the *additional* victims of the freed: *Nine,* killed by Kenneth McDuff, who had been sentenced to die for child murder in Texas and then was freed on parole after the death penalty laws at the time were overturned.[135] *One,* by Robert Massie of California, also sentenced to die and also paroled. Massie rewarded the man who gave him a job on parole by murdering him less than a year after getting out of prison.[136] *One,* by Richard Marquette, in Oregon, sentenced to "life" (which until 1994 meant about eight years in Oregon) for abducting and then dismembering women.[137] He did so well in a woman-free environment (prison) that he was released—only to abduct, kill, and dismember women again.[138] *Two,* by Carl Cletus Bowles, in Idaho, guilty of kidnapping nine people and the murder of a police officer. Bowles escaped during a conjugal visit with a girlfriend, only to abduct and murder an elderly couple.[139]

The victims of these men didn't have "close calls" with death. They are dead. Murdered. Without saying goodbye to their loved ones. Without appeal to the state or the media or Hollywood or anyone's heartstrings.

Discouraged over polls that have consistently shown public support for capital punishment between 65 and 85 percent over the last quarter century,[140] proponents of the death penalty have decided to tap into an understandable horror that people who are truly innocent of the murder of which they stand convicted are on death row. They are turning into doe-eyed innocents the few murderers who have slipped through one of the countless cracks in the law afforded to capital defendants. They want us to believe that any one of us could be snatched at any time from our daily freedoms and sentenced to die because of a false and coerced confession, police corruption, faulty eyewitness identification, botched forensics, prosecutorial misconduct, and shoddy and ill-paid defense counsel.

There are a handful of people who have spent time, in some cases many years, on death row, for crimes they genuinely did not commit. The number bandied about by the abolitionists is just past the 100 mark.[141] But a closer examination using a more realistic definition of innocence—that is, had no involvement in the death, wasn't there, didn't do it—drops the number to thirty or even twenty-five.[142] At a seminar in February of 2004 held by the Federal Bar Council of New York, U.S. District Court Judge Jed Rakoff, who made history in 2001 by ruling the death penalty unconstitutional, acknowledged that his research showed the number to be closer to thirty.[143] The larger question is whether the problem of wrongful convictions in capital cases is an episodic or epidemic problem.

For those who believe that no rate of error is acceptable, the death penalty can never be "reformed" sufficiently, despite the claims that they are seeking only to insure a fairer system. Yet these same advocates urge the substitution of life without parole, claiming (as is sometimes true) that many inmates consider a life sentence to be worse than execution. Peel back the layers of this reckoning and you'll find these advocates claiming that it is just as horrible to threaten to take away the remaining days of a murderer's life, and therefore we must abolish all long prison sentences as well as the death penalty. In a debate at the American Bar Association's annual convention in Chicago in 2001, I confronted Nadine Strossen[144] of the American Civil Liberties Union on that very question. I asked her, if I would—for the sake of argument—abandon my support for capital punishment, would she, on behalf of the ACLU, affirm her support for sentences of life without possibility of parole? She honestly responded that she could not; that it was an ever-changing political and moral environment.[145] And therein lies the dilemma. If there are people so dangerous, so evil that they can never be trusted to walk among us, how will we answer to their next victims? What level of risk are the abolitionists willing to accept for those who will die at the hands of a McDuff, a Marquette, or a Massie?

The number of death sentences is, in fact, decreasing. Criminal sentences for crimes other than murder have become tougher, terms of imprisonment more certain, and perhaps more significantly, the rate of murder is down overall. Prosecutors and juries are properly and appropriately becoming even more discriminating about determining who should die for their crimes. It is a journey not taken lightly.

Likewise, casting the accused as true innocents caught up by a corrupt and uncaring system only discredits a movement that has legitimate moral arguments. Nothing excuses making the victims nameless and faceless, making martyrs out of murderers, and turning killers into victims.

Some may wonder why it should matter if the number of people who were genuinely exonerated is 30 or 150. Many will claim that even one innocent person put to death is an intolerable number, but those who make that argument are demanding an impossibility—a perfect system. Such errors are episodic, not epidemic, and merit the most rigorous review, precisely as occurs in 21st-century capital jurisprudence.

But if one of the primary engines in the debate over capital punishment is that wrongful capital convictions are rampant, then the devil is very much in the details. To call a man with blood on his hands innocent stains not only the truth, but calls into question the actual innocence of the fewer number who are truly exonerated.

In a subject as emotionally charged as the death penalty these claims must be made precisely—by all sides. Intellectual honesty is a critical ingredient to a meaningful discussion of this important subject. Death penalty opponents risk losing their credibility when they are reckless with the truth.

ENDNOTES

1. BUREAU OF JUSTICE STATISTICS, U.S. DEP'T OF JUSTICE, SELECTED FINDINGS, VIOLENT CRIME (1994), available at http://www.ojp.usdoj.gov/bjs/pub/pdf/viocrm.pdf; BUREAU OF JUSTICE STATISTICS, U.S. DEP'T OF JUSTICE, FEDERAL CRIMINAL CASE PROCESSING, 2002: WITH TRENDS 1982–2002, RECONCILED DATA 1 (2005), available at http://www.ojp.usdoj.gov/bjs/pub/pdf/fccp02.pdf.

2. See, e.g., Byron York, The Death of Death, AM. SPECTATOR, Apr. 2000, at 21.

3. Id. at 21–23.

4. Id. at 21.

5. Id.

6. Id. at 21–22.

7. Press Release, Amnesty International USA (Apr. 24, 2003) (cited in Associated Press, Death Penalty Discrimination, CBS News, Apr. 24, 2003, available at http://www.cbsnews.com/stories/2003/04/24/national/main550986.shtml).

8. Burdine v. Johnson, 262 F.2d 336 (5th Cir. 2001), cert., denied, 535 U.S. 1120 (2002).

9. *See* York, *supra* note 2, at 22.

10. *See id.; see also* Rob Warden, *Illinois Death Penalty Reform: How It Happened, What It Promises*, 95 J. CRIM. L. & CRIMINOLOGY 381 app. A (2005) (detailing the facts of the Porter case).

11. *See* York, *supra* note 2, at 23.

12. David Firestone, *Absolutely, Positively for Capital Punishment*, N.Y. TIMES, Jan. 19, 2003, § 4, at 5.

13. *See, e.g.,* The Gallup Organization, *Question: Do You Favor or Oppose the Death Penalty for Persons Convicted of . . . Murder* (Sept. 11, 1988) (78.94%).

14. *See, e.g.,* The Gallup Organization, *Question: Do You Favor or Oppose the Death Penalty for Persons Convicted of . . . Murder* (June 23, 2000) (65.63%).

15. *See* York, *supra* note 2, at 23.

16. *Id.* at 22–23.

17. *See, e.g.,* Ken Armstrong & Steve Mills, *The Failure of the Death Penalty in Illinois* (series), *Part One: Death Row Justice Derailed; Bias, Errors and Incompetence in Capital Cases Have Turned Illinois's Harshest Punishment into Its Least Credible*, CHI. TRIB., Nov. 14, 1999, at 1.

18. *See* Ken Armstrong & Maurice Possley, *The Verdict: Dishonor* (series), *Trial and Error: How Prosecutors Sacrifice Justice to Win*, CHI. TRIB., Jan. 10, 1999, at 1, *available at* http://www.soci.niu.edu/~criticism/wrong/tribpros10.html; *see also* Michael Miner, *Prosecutors v. Journalists: The Gloves Are Off*, CHI. READER, June 9, 2000, *available at* http://www.chireader.com/hottype/2000/000609_1.html.

19. *Heiple: Execution Moratorium Illegal; "System Hasn't Failed": Departing Justice Says Ryan Doesn't Have the Authority*, TELEGRAPH HERALD (Dubuque, IA), Oct. 4, 2000, at C5.

20. Ken Armstrong & Steve Mills, *Ryan Suspends Death Penalty*, CHI. TRIB., Jan. 31, 2000, at 1.

21. Debbie Howlett, *Ex-Illinois Gov. George Ryan Indicted on Corruption Charges*, USA TODAY, Dec. 17, 2003, *available at* http://www.usatoday.com/news/nation/2003-12-17-ryan _x.htm; *see also* DEADLINE (Big Mouth Productions 2004; NBC television broadcast, July 30, 2004) (reference material regarding former Governor Ryan at http://deadlinethe movie.com/characters/governor_george_h_ryan.php).

22. Maurice Possley & Steve Mills, *Clemency for All*, CHI. TRIB., Jan. 12, 2003, at 1.

23. Howard Libit, *Death Penalty Issue No. 1: Impact of Moratorium to be Felt in Races for Governor; Assembly: "It'll Be the Talk of the Town"; Sept. Deadline for Study Will Put Any Change in Law on Next Year's Agenda*, BALT. SUN, May 12, 2002, (Telegraph), at 1A; *see also Finally a Moratorium*, BALT. SUN, May 10, 2002, at 22A (Editorial) (republished in CAL. BAR JOURNAL (2000), *available at* http://www.calbar .ca.gov/calbar/2cbj/02jun/page8-2.htm).

24. Center for State Policy and Leadership (Univ. of Ill. at Springfield), Survey Research Office, *Approval of President Bush and Governor Ryan* (July 31, 2002), *available at* http://cspl.uis.edu/SurveyResearchOffice/Common/News /ApprovalPresident.htm.

25. *See* Dave McKinney, *Key Election Fight Looming in Illinois*, STATELINE.ORG, Mar. 26, 2002, *at* http://www.stateline .org/stateline/?pa=story&sa=showStoryInfo&id=229882 (regarding Jim Ryan).

26. Matt O'Connor & Ray Gibson, *Ryan Indicted*, CHI. TRIB., Dec. 18, 2003, at 1.

27. Jeff Barker, *Md. Moratorium Unlikely to Block the Death Penalty; Trial of Adult Suspect Is Expected to Finish After Study Completed; Search for the Sniper*, BALT. SUN, Oct. 26, 2002 (Telegraph), at 4A. While Townsend conceded on the campaign trail that the death penalty would be appropriate for "heinous cases" like the sniper killings, she would have continued to uphold the outgoing governor's moratorium on existing death sentences. *Id.* The Republican candidate, Robert Ehrlich, earned significant support due to his opposition to the death penalty moratorium. Tim Craig, *Police Union Backs Ehrlich, First Big Labor Group to Support GOP Candidate; Substantial Research Pledged; Opposition to Gun Control, Death Penalty Are Factors*, BALT. SUN, June 25, 2002, at 1. Interestingly, Governor-elect Ehrlich had also voiced support during his campaign for expanding the death penalty to juveniles in egregious cases, like the sniper shootings. Sarah Koenig & Ivan Penn, *Gubernatorial Campaigns Work in Sniper Issues: Ehrlich Might Widen Death Penalty, Townsend Limit Assault Weapons*, BALT. SUN, Oct. 30, 2002, at 1.

28. Phillipa Thomas, *U.S. Murder Rate Drops*, BBC NEWS, Oct. 15, 2000, *available at* http://news.bbc.co.uk/l/hi/world /americas/973814.stm; BUREAU OF JUSTICE STATISTICS, U.S. DEP'T OF JUSTICE, HOMICIDE TRENDS IN THE UNITED STATES: 2000 UPDATE (2003), *available at* http://www.ojp.usdoj.gov /bjs/pub/pdf/htus00.pdf.

29. Dale O. Cloninger & Roberto Marchesini, *Execution and Deterrence: A Quasi-Controlled Group Experiment*, 33 APPLIED ECON. 569 (2001); Hashem Dezhbakhsh et al., *Does Capital Punishment Have a Deterrent Effect? New Evidence from Post-moratorium Panel Data*, 5 AM. L. & ECON. REV. 344 (2003); H. Noci Mocan & R. Kaj Gittings, *Getting Off Death Row: Commuted Sentences and the Deterrent Effect of Capital Punishment*, 46 J.L. & ECON. 453 (2003); Joanna M. Shepherd, *Murders of Passion, Execution Delays, and the Deterrence of Capital Punishment*, 33 J. LEGAL STUD. 283 (2004).

30. Mocan & Gittings, *supra* note 29, at 474; *see also* John Blume et al., *Explaining Death Row's Population and Racial Composition*, 1 J. EMPIRICAL LEGAL STUD. 165, 167 (2004), *available at* http://www.deathpenaltyinfo.org/Blume_etal.pdf

(denying that their finding, that the death sentence is not disproportionately imposed on black murderers, is any proof of race-neutral application of the death penalty).

31. Blume et al., *supra* note 30.

32. *See, e.g.,* Theodore Eisenberg, Stephen P. Garvey, & Martin T. Wells, *The Deadly Paradox of Capital Jurors* (Aug. 28, 2000), *available at* http://ssrn.com/abstract=240285 (conveying Eisenberg's and Wells's view of the death penalty as a product of flawed democracy); *Jail Letter Led to Major Legal Test; Representation, State-Federal Questions Raised,* RICHMOND-TIMES DISPATCH, Jan. 8, 2000, *available at* http://www .truthinjustice.org/stone08.htm (quoting Blume as distrusting the accuracy of state capital convictions).

33. Blume et al., *supra* note 30, at 166.

34. *See e.g.,* David C. Baldus et al., *Racial Discrimination and the Death Penalty in the Post-Furman Era: An Empirical and Legal Overview, with Recent Findings from Philadelphia,* 83 CORNELL L. REV. 1638 (1998).

35. *See* Blume et al., *supra* note 30, at 189–90.

36. *Id.* at 192. The study indicated that 86 percent of white victims are killed by whites, and 94 percent of blacks are killed by blacks. Even accounting for some difference in the number of black and white murder victims, the number would fall somewhere between 8 and 12 percent of all murders as cross-racial.

37. *Id.* at 189 fig.3.

38. *Id.* at 172 tbl.1.

39. *Id.* at 197 tbl.8. Table 8 indicates that, in eight states with racial data, 39,356 blacks were convicted of murder, with 517 sentenced to death (giving a death sentence rate of 1.31 percent). The same table indicates that, of 20,650 whites convicted of murder, 575 were sentenced to death (yielding a 2.78 percent death sentence rate).

40. Sean Kelly, *This Time, Profiles Didn't Fit,* DENVER POST, Oct. 25, 2002, *available at* http://www.denverpost.com /Stories/0,1413,36%257E53%257E947729,00.html; Tanika White et al., *African-Americans Grapple With Race of Sniper Suspects: Relief at Capture, Worry About Repercussions,* BALT. SUN, Oct. 25, 2002, *available at* http://www.baltimoresun.com /news/local/bal-te.md.concern25oct25.story.

41. 372 U.S. 335 (1963).

42. Ken Armstrong & Steve Mills, *The Failure of the Death Penalty in Illinois* (series), *Part Two: Inept Defenses Cloud Verdict,* CHI. TRIB., Nov. 15, 1999, at 1, *available at* http://www.chicagotribune .com/news/specials/chi-991115deathillinois2,1,5386873 .story?coll=chi-newsspecials-hed&ctrack=3&cset=true/.

43. Series of telephone interviews with Clay Crenshaw, Assistant Attorney General, Alabama (2001).

44. *Id.*

45. *See* FORMER GOVERNOR RYAN'S COMM'N ON CAPITAL PUNISHMENT, FINAL REPORT (2002), *available at* http://www .idoc.state.il/us/ccp/reports/index.html.

46. FORMER GOVERNOR RYAN'S COMM'N ON CAPITAL PUNISHMENT, COMMISSION MEMBERS, *at* http://www.idoc.state.il.us /ccp/ccp/member_info.html (last visited Feb. 15, 2005).

47. Scott Turow, REVERSIBLE ERRORS (2002).

48. REVERSIBLE ERRORS (Hallmark Entertainment 2004). The movie version of the book starred William H. Macy and Tom Selleck.

49. Scott Turow, ULTIMATE PUNISHMENT: A LAWYER'S REFLECTIONS ON DEALING WITH THE DEATH PENALTY (2003).

50. *See generally* Turow, *supra* note 47.

51. *The Practice* (regular ABC television broadcasts).

52. TRUE BELIEVER (Columbia Pictures 1989).

53. TRUE CRIME (Warner Brothers 1999).

54. Jessica Blank & Erik Jensen, THE EXONERATED (2004); *see also* The Culture Project @ 45 Bleecker, *at* http:// www.45bleecker.com/exonerated.html (last visited Jan. 26, 2005).

55. Blank & Jensen, *supra* note 54, at xvi.

56. Entry of Plea at 17-33, State v. Jacobs (No. 76-1275CF) (Fla. Broward County Ct., Oct. 9, 1992); Stipulation of Evidence, State v. Cook, No. 1-77-179 (Tex. Smith County Ct., Feb. 16, 1999) (on file with author). When a defendant agrees in a plea bargain that the state could prove a certain set of facts, as occurred in both the Cook and Jacobs cases, that becomes the truth as much as it can ever be established in the eyes of the law. A stipulation is an agreement that certain facts are true. *See* BLACK'S LAW DICTIONARY 1269 (5th ed. 1979) ("An agreement, admission or confession made in a judicial proceeding by the parties thereto or their attorneys.") (citing Bourne v. Atchison, Topeka & Santa Fe Ry., 209 Kan. 511, 517 [1972]). A court record, complete with affirmation of counsel and signed by a judge, is tantamount to a guilty plea, and probably more compelling than a guilty verdict in the face of a defendant's contention they did not commit the act.

57. Although my article focuses on Sunny Jacobs in particular, *The Exonerated* makes equally astounding misrepresentations about Kerry Cook. Mr. Cook was not the victim he and *The Exonerated* portray him to be. Despite Cook's denial of any contact with Linda Joe Edwards — the woman for whose murder he was arrested and convicted — Cook told two different people that he had watched a woman undress through a window in Edwards's condominium. Defendant's Stipulation of Evidence at 2, State v. Cook, No. 1-77-179 (Tex. Smith County Dist. Ct., Feb. 16, 1999) (on file with author).

Police identified Cook's fingerprints both on the inside of the sliding glass door of the victim's condominium and on a statue believed to be the murder weapon. *Id.* at 1, 2. And during his 1978 trial, Cook confessed to a reserve deputy that he killed Edwards. *Id.* at 1. Moreover, the man Cook claims really killed Linda Jo Edwards passed a polygraph during which he attested to his own innocence. Report from Eric J. Holden, M.A., Behavioral Measures & Forensic Services, L.L.C., Polygraph Examination Administered to James Lee Mayfield on February 11, 1999 (Feb. 12, 1999) (on file with author).

58. Hayes is one of the exonerated that is honored in the play. Hayes was tried and convicted, but the case was sent back because some of the DNA evidence used to convict him was still in its infancy and therefore did not pass the scientific standard for admissible evidence. Hayes v. State, 660 So. 2d 257, 262–66 (Fla. 1995). In his second trial, without all of the DNA evidence, Hayes was acquitted. Thus, the play's representation of Hayes as exonerated is more accurate than that of Sonia Jacobs or Kerry Cook.

Nevertheless, it is worth telling the reader some more facts. Since his acquittal, Robert Hayes has been convicted of another crime, which occurred before and was nearly identical to the crime for which he had been acquitted. Wanda DeMarzo, *Murder-Rape Suspect Back in Jail After DNA Glitch*, MIAMI HERALD, Oct. 14, 2003, *available at* http://www.fadp .org/news/Herald-20031014.htm; Elizabeth Rinaldo, *Man Admits to Killing Woman in 1987*, ONEIDA DAILY DISPATCH (N.Y.), Nov. 17, 2004, *available at* www.oneidadispatch.com /site/news.cfm?newsid=13389710&BRD=1709&PAG =461&dept_id=68844&rfi=8.

The point is that yes, Robert Hayes was found not guilty by a jury for one crime, but he also pled guilty to a similar homicide, rendering it questionable whether his first jury trial "got it wrong."

59. *See, e.g.,* The Culture Project @ 45 Bleecker, *supra* note 54.

60. John Simon, *Bay Tripper: David Henry Hwang Takes on Flower Drum Song, Set in a San Francisco Nightclub, but It's Rodgers and Hammerstein Who'd Be Singing the Blues; A Play About the Death Penalty Is—Exhilarating*, N.Y. MAG., Oct. 28, 2002, *available at* http://newyorkmetro.com/nymetro/arts /theater/reviews/n_7880/.

61. Lucy Komisar, *"The Exonerated" Chills in Tales of Death Row Innocents*, TURBULA, Winter 2004, *at* http://turbula .net/2003-summer/theater-exonerated.html.

62. Michael Ellison, *Escape from the Electric Chair: How Wrongly Convicted Death Row Prisoners Made Theatre History*, GUARDIAN (U.K.), Jan. 3, 2001 (Arts Theatre), at 14, *available at* http://www.guardian.co.uk/arts/story/0,3604,417155,00 .html.

63. Entry of Plea, *supra* note 56, at 17–18; Arrest Report of Sonia Jacobs (on file with author).

64. Entry of Plea, *supra* note 56, at 29.

65. Jeannie Lieberman, *The Exonerated: But Are They?*, THEATERSCENE.NET, Nov. 15, 2002, *available at* http://www .theaterscene.net/ts%5Carticles.nsf/OBP/AB0F0F875FF 4057E85256C75002094E4?OpenDocument.

66. Jacobs v. Florida, 357 So. 2d 169 (Fla. 1978); Jacobs v. State, 396 So. 2d 713 (Fla. 1981).

67. Jacobs v. Singletary, 952 F.2d 1282 (11th Cir. 1992).

68. Statement of Sonia Jacobs on Feb. 20, 1976 (Complaint 76-2-3612; taken at Palm Beach County Sheriff's Office, in reference to Broward County Sheriff's Office Case), State v. Jacobs (Fla. Broward County Ct.) (No. 76-1275CF) (on file with author).

69. *Jacobs,* 952 F.2d at 1285.

70. Series of telephone interviews with Michael Satz, Trial Prosecutor of Sonia Jacobs and Current State Attorney of Broward County (2003–04); *see also Jacobs,* 396 So. 2d at 715; Entry of Plea, *supra* note 56, at 19.

71. Entry of Plea, *supra* note 56, at 20.

72. *Id.*

73. *Jacobs,* 952 F.2d at 1285.

74. Entry of Plea, *supra* note 56, at 24–25; Trial Transcript at 929–30, *Jacobs* (No. 76-1275CF) (testimony of Pierce Hyman, truck driver, on July 12, 1976); *id.* at 1076 (testimony of Robert McKenzie, truck driver, on July 12, 1976).

75. *Jacobs,* 952 F.2d at 1296; *see also* Entry of Plea, *supra* note 56, at 29; Trial Transcript at 931, *Jacobs* (No. 76-1275CF) (testimony of Pierce Hyman, truck driver, on July 12, 1976) (stricken testimony).

76. Telephone interview with Michael Satz, Trial Prosecutor of Sonia Jacobs and Current State Attorney of Broward County (Feb. 23, 2005) [hereinafter Satz Interview, 2005]; *see also* Entry of Plea, *supra* note 56, at 21–22.

77. Entry of Plea, *supra* note 56, at 22.

78. *Id.* at 25.

79. *Id.* at 32.

80. Satz Interview, 2005, *supra* note 76. The actual TASER weapon was found in an attaché case along with several personal effects, including Jacobs's passport and Jesse Tafero's baptismal certificate.

81. Entry of Plea, *supra* note 56, at 31.

82. *Jacobs,* 396 So. 2d at 715–16.

83. Entry of Plea, *supra* note 56, at 23.

84. *Id.*

85. *Jacobs,* 396 So. 2d at 717.

86. Trial Transcript at 2184, *Jacobs* (No. 76-1275CF) (testimony of Valjean Haley, Deputy, Palm Beach County Sheriff's Dep't, on July 12, 1976).

87. *Jacobs,* 396 So. 2d at 717; *Jacobs,* 952 F.2d at 1291.

88. *Jacobs,* 396 So. 2d at 717.

89. *Jacobs,* 952 F.2d at 1296.

90. Blank & Jensen, *supra* note 54, at 28.

91. *Jacobs,* 396 So. 2d at 716.

92. *Id.*

93. *Jacobs,* 952 F.2d at 1285.

94. *Id.*

95. Sharon Perlmutter, *The Exonerated,* Talkin'Broadway .com (Regional News and Review: Los Angeles), *available at* http://www.talkinbroadway.com/regional/la/la69 .html ("The play is not fiction. Its text was derived from trial transcripts, records of police interrogations, depositions, and interviews with some of the over 100 people who have been The Exonerated after conviction of capital murder."); *see also* Martin F. Kohn, *"Exonerated" Castigates the Death Penalty,* Detroit Free Press, Feb. 22, 2004, *at* http://www.freep.com/entertainment/newsandreviews /exon22_20040222.htm; Amy Goldwasser, *The Exonerated,* Salon.com, Oct. 20, 2000, *available at* http://dir.salon .com/news/feature/2000/10/20/exonerated/index.html?pn=l; Ernio Hernandez, *Unjust Prison Drama* The Exonerated *in Final Weeks Off-Broadway,* Playbill, Jan. 6, 2004, *at* http://www.playbill.com/news/article/print/84012.html; Richard Zoglin, *The Best Theater,*Time, Dec, 17, 2002, *available at* http://www.time.com/time/bestandworst/2002/theater.html.

96. *Jacobs,* 952 F.2d at 1285.

97. *Jacobs,* 396 So. 2d at 718.

98. Blank & Jensen, *supra* note 54, at 66. In *The Exonerated,* the character of Sunny Jacobs asks the audience to "reflect: From 1976 to 1992, just remove that entire chunk from your life, and that's what happened." *Id.* Blank and Jensen make no mention of the fact that, of those sixteen years, only five were actually spent on death row.

99. *Jacobs,* 952 F.2d at 1287–89.

100. *Id.* at 1291–96.

101. *Id.* at 1296.

102. Satz Interview, 2005, *supra* note 76.

103. *See* North Carolina v. Alford, 400 U.S. 25 (1970).

104. Entry of Plea, *supra* note 56, at 37.

105. *Id.* at 17–23.

106. *Id.* at 34.

107. *Id.* at 36.

108. Affidavit of Walter Norman Rhodes, Jr. (Mar. 28, 1991) (on file with author) ("I . . . was standing at the front of the police car with my back turned and hands raised when Sonia and Black exchanged shots with each other. I turned my head in time to see Tafero grab the gun from Sonia, turn, and fire four shots at Black and then two at Irwin."); telephone interview with Sara Estes, wife of Walter Rhodes (Feb. 27, 2005).

109. Entry of Plea, *supra* note 56, at 36; *see also* Satz Interview, 2005, *supra* note 76.

110. Blank & Jensen, *supra* note 54, at 66.

111. *See* Entry of Plea, *supra* note 56.

112. *In the Blink of an Eye* (ABC television broadcast, Mar. 24, 1996).

113. Georgia Rowe, *Curran Theatre Does "Exonerated" Justice,* Contra Costa Times (Cal.), Nov. 27, 2003, at Dl, *available at* http://www.realcities.com/mld/cctimes /entertainment/performing_arts/7362764.htm.

114. Joseph Wambaugh, Echoes in the Darkness (William Morrow & Co. ed., 1987).

115. Jayne Keedle, *Death of Innocents,* CUTV.com, *available at* http://www.cutv.com/dpenalty.htm (last visited Feb. 6, 2005); Death Penalty Information Center, Innocence: Freed From Death Row, *available at* http://www.deathpenaltyinfo .org/article.php?scid=6&did=l10 (last visited Feb. 23, 2005).

116. Commonwealth v. Smith, 568 A.2d 600, 602 (Pa. 1989).

117. *Id.* at 602–04.

118. *Id.* at 603.

119. Smith v. Holtz, 210 F.3d. 186, 193–194 (3d Cir. 2000). A state appellate court set aside Smith's conviction as a result of the admission of certain hearsay statements. The state was then prevented from retying Smith due to prosecutorial misconduct in withholding the "lifters."

120. *Smith,* 568 A.2d at 610.

121. *Smith,* 210 F.3d 186.

122. *Id.* at 194.

123. *Id.* at 201.

124. The Innocence Project, The Case of Kirk Bloodsworth, *available at* http://www.innocenceproject.org /case/display_profile.php?id=21 (last visited Feb. 6, 2005).

125. Monica Davey, *Porter's Convictions Upset,* Chi. Trib., Mar. 11, 1999 (Late Edition), at 1.

126. *Id.*

127. *Id.*

128. Gregg v. Georgia, 428 U.S. 153 (1976).

129. BUREAU OF JUSTICE STATISTICS, U.S. DEP'T OF JUSTICE, HOMICIDE TRENDS IN THE UNITED STATES (2004), *available at* http://www.ojp.usdoj.gov/bjs/pub/pdf/htius.pdf; FED. BUREAU OF INVESTIGATION, U.S. DEP'T OF JUSTICE, UNIFORM CRIME REPORTS, various years, *at* http://www.fbi.gov/ucr/ucr.htm (last visited May 12, 2004). Data is also available at National Archive of Criminal Justice Data, Institute for Social Research, University of Michigan, *at* http://www.icpsr.umich.edu/NACJD/ucr.html (last visited Jan. 11, 2005).

130. AMNESTY INTERNATIONAL, FACTS AND FIGURES ON THE DEATH PENALTY, *available at* http://web.amnesty.org/pages/deathpenalty-facts-eng (last visited Feb. 15, 2005); BUREAU OF JUSTICE STATISTICS, U.S. DEP'T OF JUSTICE, CAPITAL PUNISHMENT STATISTICS, *at* http://www.ojp.usdoj.gov/bjs/cp.htm (last visited Feb. 15, 2005); Marcia Coyle, *68 Percent Error Rate Found in Death Case Study*, NAT'L L.J., June 9, 2000, *available at* http://www.truthinjustice.org/68percent.htm.

131. AMNESTY INTERNATIONAL, *supra* note 130. As of February 15, 2005, Amnesty put the number at 944.

132. *Gregg*, 428 U.S. at 154 (Powell, J., concurring).

133. James Liebman et al., *A Broken System, Part I: Error Rates in Capital Cases, 1973–1995* (2000), *available at* http://www2.law.columbia.edu/instructionalservices/liebman/.

134. *See generally* DEBATING THE DEATH PENALTY: SHOULD AMERICA HAVE CAPITAL PUNISHMENT? THE EXPERTS ON BOTH SIDES MAKE THEIR BEST CASE (Hugo Adam Bedau & Paul G. Cassell eds., 2004).

135. Mike Cochran, *McDuff Likely to Take Grisly Secrets to Grave*, Nov. 24, 1996, ASSOCIATED PRESS, *available at* http://www.lubbockonline.com/news/112496/mcduff.htm.

136. Rob Rossi, *Capital Punishment and Voices from Death Row*, THE RECORDER, Jan. 19, 1996, *available at* http://www.courttv.com/archive/map/library/capital/voices.html; Jennifer C. Vergaras, *Death Penalty, Massie Execution Criticized at Justice Conference*, TIDINGS ONLINE, Mar. 23, 2001, *available at* http://www.the-tidings.com/2001/0323/deathpenalty.htm.

137. House Committee on Judiciary, Subcommittee on Criminal Law, March 27, 1997, Or. State Leg., *available at* http://arcweb.sos.state.or.us/legislative/legislativeminutes/1997%20LEGIS%20WEB/4th%201ayer/house.jud.html/hjudcr.327.html (statement of Rep. John Minnis); THE OREGONIAN, AN OREGON CENTURY, 1960s LIFE, *available at* http://www.oregonlive.com/century/1960_life.html (a statistical view of life in Oregon in the 1960s).

138. THE OREGONIAN, *supra* note 137.

139. Jim Redden, *Tumultuous Times Fattened the Files*, PORTLAND TRIB., Sept. 17, 2002, *available at* http://www.portlandtribune.com/archold.cgi?id=13719.

140. Joseph Caroll, *Americans and the Death Penalty*, The Gallup Polls, 1965–2002, *available at* http://www.gallup.com/poll/content/login.aspx?ci=14371; CLARK COUNTY PROSECUTING ATTORNEY (Indiana), A SUMMARY OF GALLUP POLLS RELATING TO THE DEATH PENALTY, *available at* http://www.clarkprosecutor.org/html/death/opinion.htm (last visited Feb. 6, 2005).

141. Kris Axtman, *US Milestone: 100th Death Row Inmate Exonerated*, CHRISTIAN SCI. MONITOR, Apr. 12, 2002, *available at* http://www.csmonitor.com/2002/0412/p01s02-usju.html; Stephen Bright, *Capital Punishment, Capital Crime?*, ALTERNATIVE RADIO, Mar. 2, 2002, *available at* http://www.altemativeradio.org/programs/BRIS001.shtml.

142. Comments by Judge Jed Rackoff (S.D.N.Y.), Federal Bar Council Conference in Manzanillo, Mexico, Feb. 19, 2004; *see also* Peter DuPont, *The Rakoff Rule*, WALL ST. J., July, 10, 2002, *available at* http://www.opinionjournal.com/columnists/pdupont/?id=110001967 (questioning the number of convicted persons that are actually "innocent").

143. Comments by Judge Jed Rackoff, *supra* note 142 (in response to a presentation by the author).

144. *See* Justice Talking, *available at* http://www.justicetalking.org/viewprogram.asp?progID=196 (last visited Jan. 14, 2005) (detailing a short biography of Nadine Strossen).

145. Nadine Strossen, American Civil Liberties Union, Comments at the American Bar Association Conference in Chicago, Ill. (2001) (responding to questions by the author).

Reading Questions

1. According to Marquis, what are three arguments put forth by the "abolitionists" of the Death Penalty Information Center who sought to end capital punishment in America?

2. In 1999, Governor George Ryan halted the death penalty process for those on death row in Illinois. What events, according to Marquis, led to the governor's decision to place a moratorium on executions?

3. Marquis argues that "the modern abolition movement is now based on a trio of urban legends" (par. 14). What are those urban legends, according to Marquis?

4. What does Marquis accomplish by comparing the play *The Exonerated* to the actual events it is based upon, according to his retelling of those events?

5. What is Marquis's "more realistic definition of innocence" (56)?

6. What is Marquis's purpose in differentiating between "episodic" and "epidemic" errors made by the criminal justice system?

Rhetoric Questions

7. Identify what you believe to be Marquis's central claim and explain how his article is organized to support the elements of his claim.

8. Marquis occasionally relies on personal experience as evidence to support his arguments. Identify one instance in which he employs personal experience and assess its effectiveness. Is it helpful to his argument? It is convincing? Why or why not?

9. How would you describe the tone of Marquis's article? Provide examples of his language from the text to support your answer.

10. At times, Marquis employs emotional appeals to move his audience. Identify an instance from the text when he employs such an appeal and assess its likely effectiveness in light of his intended audience.

11. Do you think Marquis offers adequate evidence to discredit those who would argue that "the death penalty is racist at its core" (14)? Why or why not?

12. Consider closely the final two paragraphs of Marquis's argument and answer the following questions: What does he achieve in these paragraphs? Are they effective as a conclusion to his argument? If not, what recommendations would you make to explain how these paragraphs might be improved?

Response and Research Questions

13. Marquis claims that "the well-organized and even better-funded abolitionists cannot point to a single case of a demonstrably innocent person executed in the modern era of American capital punishment" (52). Do you believe Marquis is correct? If not, what "case" could be made against his assertion?

14. Marquis suggests that the number of innocent people who have spent time on death row is somewhere around twenty-five to thirty. In your opinion, is any rate of error acceptable in capital punishment cases? Why or why not?

15. If you haven't done so already, read Dwight Conquergood's "Lethal Theatre: Performance, Punishment, and the Death Penalty" on pages 434–55. In a few paragraphs, explain which author's text is more convincing to you and why.

Writing a Brief Annotated Bibliography

The readings in this chapter raise and address a host of complex questions related to crime, punishment, and justice in America, although these questions are not always stated outright. Perhaps the chapter has caused you to formulate your own questions about the topics as well.

Begin this writing project by selecting a question related to crime, punishment, or justice that is appropriate for an academic research project. You might be interested in any of the following questions, for example: Is capital punishment really a deterrent to crime? What are the implications for sentencing in light of advances in criminal brain scanning? How does the presentation of capital punishment impact how we consider it as a culture? What role does race play in sentencing for minor drug offenses?

Once you have established a workable research question, locate three to five recent and scholarly journal articles from any academic field(s) you believe will help to build an answer to your research question. Remember that Chapter 5 offers helpful instruction on conducting this kind of research.

Study the articles you select carefully, and then compose a brief annotated bibliography that includes these three parts:

- An Introduction section that establishes appropriate background and context for your research question: What led you to your research question? What makes your question important or meaningful? Why does your question need to be answered?

- A section that specifically highlights your research question.

- Full bibliographic information for each of your scholarly sources. Compose a brief summary of each article directly under each of your bibliographic entries. As part of your summaries, explain the researchers' goals (hypothesis, thesis, etc.), outline their primary research methods and findings, and briefly explain how you believe the article can help to answer your research question.

Composing an Evaluative Rhetorical Analysis

Begin this assignment by locating a popular news article that explores an issue related to crime, punishment, or justice in America. Alternatively, you might choose to focus on one of the articles written for a popular audience included in the chapter offerings:

- Barbara Bradley Hagerty, "Inside a Psychopath's Brain: The Sentencing Debate"

- Sophia Kerby, "The Top 10 Most Startling Facts about People of Color and Criminal Justice in the United States: A Look at the Racial Disparities Inherent in Our Nation's Criminal-Justice System"

- Inimai Chettiar, "The Many Causes of America's Decline in Crime"
- Abigail Pesta, "I Survived Prison: What Really Happens behind Bars"

After carefully reading the article, compose an evaluative rhetorical analysis in which you assess the likely effectiveness of the article in light of its intended audience.

As part of your introduction, identify the source of publication for the piece you selected (Where was it published?) and its likely intended audience (Who is likely to read the piece, given its publication source?). Then identify the specific values, beliefs, or desires you think the intended audience members of the piece likely share with one another. With these common values in mind, offer your evaluation of the likely effectiveness of the rhetorical strategies used in the article as your thesis: How effective is the writer at crafting the text, via its rhetorical elements, specifically for the intended audience?

Develop the body of your analysis by addressing the following two questions as support for your position or evaluation of the writer's rhetorical decisions:

- What does the writer successfully do that likely appeals directly to the intended audience's values, beliefs, or desires?
- What other decisions could the writer have made to appeal even more directly or successfully to the intended audience's values, beliefs, or desires?

As part of your conclusion, reflect on the piece's overall potential for connecting with, or for moving, the intended audience. Given what you've shown, what effects do you think the piece will have on its intended audience?

CHAPTER

13

Food, Sustainability, and Class

The readings in this chapter offer a number of perspectives, both popular and academic, that consider both food and its sustainability, as well as their intersection with the politics of labor, economics, and class. The chapter begins with an article that explores Mexican food as a new metaphor for America, positioning it against the classic image of the melting pot. In so doing, the article broaches some of the complex economic, social, and political realities of American society. The second selection briefly traces the history of cooking to highlight its impact on the physical development of humans and their cultural practices. In the third selection, the author interrogates the language we use to describe food products and suggests that it often misrepresents the truth about the products we purchase and consume. The final popular reading in this chapter extols the virtues of cooking for ourselves in response to the question, "Why cook?"

These readings offer a wide range of perspectives on food and its various functions and meanings. We hope they inspire you to pose your own critical questions about the role of food in our lives. Such questions might include:

- What do an individual's food choices say about that person, if anything at all?

- What role should issues of sustainability play in our food purchase decisions?

- How does the food we eat relate to our personal identity, or how does it affect the ways we engage with other people?

- What does the food you eat mean to you?

The academic case study for this chapter provides a number of disciplinary perspectives on the topic of genetically modified (GM) foods:

- **Humanities** What are some of the ethical concerns regarding GM foods?

- **Social Sciences** Will consumers purchase GM food products? If so, what is their tolerance level for GM content in food products?

- **Natural Sciences**   What are the exposure levels of pesticides associated with GM foods among pregnant and non-pregnant women in eastern Canada?

- **Applied Fields**   How do middle school students negotiate complex scientific issues in a curriculum designed to foster their knowledge of the genetically modified foods controversy?

Taco USA: How Mexican Food Became More American Than Apple Pie

GUSTAVO ARELLANO

Gustavo Arellano is the former publisher and editor of *OC Weekly*, an alternative newspaper in Orange County, California. He is the author of two books, *Orange County: A Personal History* (2008) and *Taco USA: How Mexican Food Conquered America* (2012), as well as the writer behind ¡Ask a Mexican!, a nationally syndicated newspaper column. In the article below, published in 2012 in *Reason* magazine online, Arellano challenges misconceptions about the appropriation of Mexican food in America. Citing concoctions such as tater tot burritos and frozen margarita machines, Arellano uses personal narrative and historical research to argue that Mexican food has, in fact, conquered North America.

MAY 14, 2012, 12:00 PM—Exit 132 off Interstate 29 in Brookings, South Dakota, offers two possibilities. A right turn will take drivers through miles of farms, flatland that stretches to the horizon, cut up into grids by country roads and picturesque barns—a scenic route to nowhere in heartland America. But take a left at the light, and you wind up coasting through a college town of 19,000 that's more than 95 percent white. The city's small Latino minority—less than 1 percent of the population—is mostly students or faculty members passing through South Dakota State University. It was here, in late 2009, that I experienced an epiphany about Mexican food in the United States.

I had been visiting the campus and found myself desperate for a taste of home. For us Southern Californians, that means burritos. Google Maps found me four Mexican restaurants in town. One, named Guadalajara, is a small South Dakota chain with outposts in Pierre and Spearfish. The food there was fine: a mishmash of tacos, burritos, and bean-and-rice

pairings. But talk to the waiters in Spanish, and their faces brighten; they trot out the secret salsa they make for themselves but don't dare share with locals for fear of torching their tongues.

The most popular restaurant in town that day was Taco John's. I didn't know it then, but Taco John's is the third-largest taco chain in the United States, with nearly 500 locations. But what lured me that morning was a drive-through line snaking out from the faux-Spanish revival building (whitewashed adobe and all) and into the street. Once I inched my rental car next to the menu, I was offered an even more outrageous simulacrum* of the American Southwest: tater tots, that most midwestern of snacks, renamed "Potato Olés" and stuffed into a breakfast burrito, nacho cheese sauce slowly oozing out from the bottom of the flour tortilla.

There is nothing remotely Mexican about Potato Olés—not even the quasi-Spanish name, which has

simulacrum: the likeness or representation of a thing.

a distinctly Castilian accent. The burrito was more insulting to me and my heritage than casting Charlton Heston as the swarthy Mexican hero in *Touch of Evil*. But it was intriguing enough to take back to my hotel room for a taste. There, as I experienced all of the concoction's gooey, filling glory while chilly rain fell outside, it struck me: Mexican food has become a better culinary metaphor for America than the melting pot.

Back home, my friends did not believe that a tater 5 tot burrito could exist. When I showed them proof online, out came jeremiads about inauthenticity, about how I was a traitor for patronizing a Mexican chain that got its start in Wyoming, about how the avaricious *gabachos* had once again usurped our holy cuisine and corrupted it to fit their crude palates.

In defending that tortilla-swaddled abomination, I unknowingly joined a long, proud lineage of food heretics and lawbreakers who have been developing, adapting, and popularizing Mexican food in El Norte since before the Civil War. Tortillas and tamales have long left behind the moorings of immigrant culture and fully infiltrated every level of the American food pyramid, from state dinners at the White House to your local 7-Eleven. Decades' worth of attempted restrictions by governments, academics, and other self-appointed custodians of purity have only made the strain stronger and more resilient. The result is a market-driven mongrel cuisine every bit as delicious and all-American as the German classics we appropriated from Frankfurt and Hamburg.

IMPERIALISM AND ENCHILADAS

Food is a natural conduit of change, evolution, and innovation. Wishing for a foodstuff to remain static, uncorrupted by outside influence—especially in these United States—is as ludicrous an idea as barring new immigrants from entering the country. Yet for more than a century, both sides of the political spectrum have fought to keep Mexican food in a ghetto. From the right has come the canard that the cuisine is unhealthy and alien, a stereotype dating to the days of the Mexican-American War, when urban legend had it that animals wouldn't eat the corpses of fallen Mexican soldiers due to the high chile content in the decaying flesh. Noah Smithwick, an observer of the aftermath of the Battle of San Jacinto in 1836, claimed "the cattle got to chewing the bones [of Mexican soldiers], which so affected the milk that residents in the vicinity had to dig trenches and bury them."

Similar knocks against Mexican food can be heard to this day in the lurid tourist tales of "Montezuma's Revenge" and in the many food-based ethnic slurs still in circulation: *beaner, greaser, pepper belly, taco bender, roach coach*, and so many more. "Aside from diet," the acclaimed borderlands scholar Américo Paredes wrote in 1978, "no other aspect of Mexican culture seems to have caught the fancy of the Anglo coiner of derogatory terms for Mexicans."

Thankfully, the buying public has never paid much attention to those prandial *pendejos*. Instead, Americans have loved and consumed Mexican food in large quantities almost from the moment it was available—from canned chili and tamales in the early 20th century to fast-food tacos in the 1960s, sit-down eateries in the 1970s, and ultra-pricey hipster mescal bars today. Some staples of the Mexican diet have been thoroughly assimilated into American food culture. No one nowadays thinks of "chili" as Mexican, even though it long passed for Mexican food in this country; meanwhile, every Major League baseball and NFL stadium sells nachos, thanks to the invention of a fast-heated chips and "cheese" combination concocted by an Italian-American who was the cousin of Johnny Cash's first wife. Only in America!

In the course of this culinary blending, a 10 multibillion-dollar industry arose. And that's where leftist critics of Mexican food come in. For them, there's something inherently suspicious about a cuisine responsive to both the market and the *mercado*. Oh, academics and foodies may love the grub, but they harbor an atavistic view that the only "true" Mexican food is the just-off-the-grill carne asada found in the side lot of your local *abuelita* (never mind that it was the invading Spaniards who introduced beef to the New World). "Mexico's European-and-Indian soul," writes Rick Bayless, the high priest of the "authentic"

Mexican food movement, in his creatively titled book, *Authentic Mexican*, "feels the intuitions of neither bare-bones Victorianism nor Anglo-Saxon productivity"—a line reminiscent of dispatches from the Raj. If it were up to these authentistas, we'd never have kimchi tacos or pastrami burritos. Salsa would not outsell ketchup in the United States. This food of the gods would be locked in Mexican households and barrios of cities, far away from Anglo hands.

That corn-fed Americans love and profit from Mexican food is viewed as an open wound in Chicano intellectual circles, a gastronomic update of America's imperial taking of the Southwest. *Yanqui* consumption and enjoyment of quesadillas and margaritas, in this view, somehow signifies a weakness in the Mexican character. "The dialectic between representation and production of Mexican cuisine offers a critical means of gauging Latino cultural power, or, more precisely, the relative lack of such power," write scholars Victor Valle and Rudy Torres in their 2000 book *Latino Metropolis*. (Another precious thought from Valle and Torres concerns Mary Sue Milliken and Susan Feniger, two midwestern girls who came to Los Angeles and learned to love Mexican food during the 1980s, parlaying that fondness into a series of television shows and books under the billing "Two Hot Tamales." The academics claim the Tamales' success arose from "neocolonial appropriations of world cuisine by reviving a gendered variant of the Hispanic fantasy discourse." Um, yeah . . .)

With due respect to my fellow lefty professors, they're full of beans. I'm not claiming equal worth for all American interpretations of Mexican food; Taco Bell has always made me retch, and Mexican food in central Kentucky tastes like . . . well, Mexican food in central Kentucky. But when culinary anthropologists like Bayless and Diana Kennedy make a big show out of protecting "authentic" Mexican food from the onslaught of commercialized glop, they are being both paternalistic and ahistorical.

That you have a nation (and increasingly a planet—you can find Mexican restaurants from Ulan Bator to Sydney to Prague) lusting after tequila, guacamole, and *tres leches* cake isn't an exercise in culinary neocolonialism but something closer to the opposite. By allowing itself to be endlessly adaptable to local tastes, Mexican food has become a primary vehicle for exporting the culture of a long-ridiculed country to the far corners of the globe. Forget Mexico's imaginary *Reconquista* of the American Southwest; the *real* conquest of North America is a peaceful and consensual affair, taking place one tortilla at a time.

I'll never forget the delight I felt a couple of years ago when I worked on a series of investigative stories on Orange County neo-Nazis. One of the photos I unearthed showed two would-be Aryans scarfing down food from Del Taco, a beloved California chain best known for its cheap and surprisingly tasty burritos. The neo-colonizers have become the colonized, and no one even fired a shot.

TAMALES AND TRUNCHEONS

As long as Mexican food has existed in this country, 15 government has tried to legislate it out of existence. This is partly because of stereotypes but mostly because government is government. The resulting underground Mexican food economy, meanwhile, has birthed some of the cuisine's most innovative trends.

In 1880s San Antonio, so-called chili queens—Mexican women who brought the Alamo City national attention by setting up impromptu stalls in city squares to sell fiery bowls of what was then known as *chile con carne*—began a decades-long game of cat and mouse with local officials. The authorities would declare a certain neighborhood legally off-limits, and the chili queens would shrug and move their tents to the outdoor plaza across the street, bringing with them their legions of loyal customers. It took until the 1940s for San Antonio bureaucrats to formally legalize the street vendors, but only if they subjected themselves to rigorous health inspections and hawked their food from white tents with screens. The public scorned these bowdlerized* women, and the chili queens disappeared within years.

**bowdlerized:* stripped of offensive content.

The same story arc has played out nearly every-where in the United States where there has been a Mexican with food to sell. Wandering tamale men spread across the United States during the 1890s until competitors and not-in-my-backyard types convinced city councils to pass laws against them. A century later, *loncheras* peddling tacos and burritos—first to construction sites, then to anywhere workers take their lunches—have encountered the same protectionism and prejudice. As the public embraces the convenience, affordability, and taste of food trucks, restaurant owners and the city officials they lobby have repeatedly attempted to squash the competition.

Any new businesses in town will always make city planners and councilmen wary and greedy, of course. But the sad, surprising reality is that most of the resistance to *loncheras* comes from brick-and-mortar businesses. Instead of refining and broadening their offerings to keep up with their new competitors, the incumbents fall back on an argument straight out of a Mafia protection racket: Since we pay more taxes and business fees than food trucks, government should squash our competition so we can continue business as usual.

It's a strategy that has long worked. In 1992 tiny Pasco, Washington, set rules limiting where taco trucks could park and requiring them to pay $45 each month per parking spot. Pasco's restaurants, by contrast, paid only $35 a year for a license. Five street vendors took Pasco all the way up to the U.S. Court of Appeals for the 9th Circuit, arguing that the double standard was unconstitutional, but they ultimately lost. Similar crackdowns have taken place in Fresno (1995), Chicago (1997), Phoenix (1999), and Dallas (1999), where Planning Commissioner James Lee Fantroy sneered during a public hearing on the subject, "The proper preparation of food is one of those things that we must carefully watch. I don't think I could bring my family to one of these [trucks] and feel comfortable."

Even in Los Angeles, the second-largest Mexican metropolis in the world, the majority-Democrat L.A. County Board of Supervisors tried to ban food trucks as recently as four years ago. The city has destroyed carts selling unauthorized bacon dogs and even hauled off some entrepreneurs to jail, despite acknowledging that no bacon-dog customer has ever registered a complaint.

L.A. has a long history of putting the squeeze on Mexican-food peddlers. From 1900 to about 1925, the city council passed resolution after resolution trying to ban tamale wagons from downtown Los Angeles. The *tamaleros*, knowing what they meant to their legions of customers, fought back. In 1903, when the council tried to outlaw them altogether, tamale wagons formed a mutual-aid society and presented a petition with the signatures of more than 500 customers that read in part, "We claim that the lunch wagons are catering to an appreciative public and to deprive the people of these convenient eating places would prove a great loss to the many local merchants who sell the wagon proprietors various supplies." When the city council finally kicked the vendors out as part of the effort to create the sanitized, whitewashed ethnic fantasyland now known as Olvera Street, the vendors just went underground, where they flourished for decades and eventually transformed into *loncheras*.

In 2008 the L.A. County Board of Supervisors passed a resolution making parking a truck for longer than one hour in unincorporated communities such as East L.A. a misdemeanor with a maximum penalty of a $1,000 fine and six months in jail. The plan sparked a furious backlash—not only among the *loncheros*, who created La Asociación de Loncheros L.A. Familia Unida de California (Association of Loncheros Los Angeles United Family of California) to defend themselves, but among young bloggers and hipsters who had grown up patronizing *loncheras* after clubbing or working late. Soon black T-shirts emblazoned with a white *lonchera* and the statement "Carne Asada Is Not a Crime" flowered across Southern California, and a group of foodies helped the *loncheras* sue the board of supervisors. A Los Angeles Superior Court judge eventually overturned the supes' diktat.*

But it was mostly the will of the *loncheros*—almost all immigrants who initially came to the United States with no knowledge of English, let alone an understanding of our legal system—that earned the victory.

**diktat:* a mandate without consent from the populace.

In my homeland of Orange County, Roberto Guzmán led a group of *loncheros* in 2006 to sue the city of Santa Ana to be able to park on city streets from 9 A.M. until 9 P.M., seven days a week. His Cadillac-pink truck "Alebrije's" sells food from Mexico City—buttery, crepe-like quesadillas, massive chili-soaked sandwiches called *pambazos*, and a concoction of six tortillas covered with sautéed onions, bell peppers, jalapeños, and grilled ham, bacon, and carne asada called *alambres*.

When the city council (also majority Democrat, and all Latino, making Santa Ana the largest city in the United States with such leadership) sought to negotiate with the *loncheros* to install a lottery system giving rights to some food trucks but not all, they refused. "Please," Guzmán scoffs. "It would've been favoritism all the way. I felt as if they were going to take away the sustenance of so many families. It was going to be a huge economic loss. And it was too much a worry that, at any moment, [the city] could take away the parking spots from us." Today Santa Ana is a *lonchera* paradise—and Guzmán owns three of them, with plans for more.

MARGARITA MILLIONAIRES

The self-appointed guardians of Mexican food in this country are right on one point: The popularity of Mexican food has indeed allowed many non-Mexicans to build multimillion-dollar fortunes. German immigrant William Gebhardt created Eagle Brand Chili Powder from the basement of a bar in New Braunfels, Texas, in the early 1890s, parlaying that into a canned food empire that lasts to this day. Glen Bell, founder of Taco Bell, got his idea for hard-shelled tacos from Mitla Café, a San Bernardino Mexican restaurant that stood across the street from Bell's burger stand during the early 1950s. The Frito-Lay company developed its most iconic chips, Fritos and Doritos, by purchasing the rights to those crunchy treats from Mexican immigrants. And Steve Ells, founder of Chipotle, which has mainstreamed massive burritos during the last decade, openly admits he was "inspired" by the burritos sold in San Francisco's famously Latino Mission District.

The easy response to critics of appropriation is that it's the market that decides who gets rich, not ethnic politics. Besides, obsessing over the many *gabachos* who have become Mexican-food millionaires ignores the many success stories involving Mexicans who displayed the same guile as their pasty-skinned contemporaries.

Larry Cano, for example, started out as a dishwasher at a Polynesian-themed restaurant in the Los Angeles enclave of Encino, worked his way up enough to eventually buy the place, then renamed it El Torito—the chain that pioneered sit-down Mexican dining in the United States. In Texas, the Martinez and Cuellar families created empires with their El Fenix and El Chico chains, respectively, formalizing Mexican restaurants for the rest of the country and essentially creating the genre of Tex-Mex. In Southern California during the 1990s, the Lopez family, immigrants from the southern Mexico state of Oaxaca, helped popularize regional Mexican food in this country, fighting the double challenge of introducing Oaxacan food to both Americans *and* Southern California Mexicans who looked down on the cuisine as the domain of backward Indians. Today Mexican immigrants are following the Lopez/Oaxacan lead and selling their regional specialties nationwide.

And then there's the story of Mariano Martinez, scion of the Cuellars, who in 1971 created the frozen margarita machine. At his Dallas restaurant Mariano's, which serves heroic enchilada platters, Martinez birthed an empire off the slushy tequila drink, inventing an instant mix that has powered many a house party since. Nowadays Martinez disavows the frozen margarita— he prefers his fresh, with Cointreau. But Mariano's pride in his creation and his cuisine—long dismissed by "serious" food critics as forgettable—remains.

"I've seen them all over the years," he says. "They come in and do this upscale food. . . . Some of those places aren't there anymore. My little old place I have? Forty years later, we're still pumping the same food. Same phone number. Here I am plugging away at this little Tex-Mex peasant food that no one wanted to play with, that all the ivory tower critics made fun of. And with a drink that no one can resist."

Mariano's original frozen margarita machine is now in the Smithsonian. And Mexican food marches on, a combo plate of freedom giving indigestion to busybodies and authentistas everywhere.

Reading Questions

1. Describe Arellano's initial reaction to Taco John's Potato Olés.

2. According to Arellano, what "staples of the Mexican diet have been thoroughly assimilated into American food culture" (par. 9)?

3. How does Arellano respond to leftist academic critiques about the appropriation of Mexican food in America?

Rhetoric Questions

4. Arellano writes extensively about the history of local laws and ordinances that regulate Mexican food in America. Locate one of these laws or ordinances. How does the example work within his larger argument? What does the example illustrate?

5. How does Arellano use personal narrative in this essay? Are there genres in your discipline in which personal narrative would be appropriate? Why or why not?

6. Arellano's essay culminates in a description of the frozen margarita machine and its inventor. How does this example illustrate his main argument?

Response and Research Questions

7. Arellano says that a taste of home for Southern Californians like himself means burritos. What food would you consider as your "taste of home"? Explain your choice.

8. Arellano writes, "Food is a natural conduit of change, evolution, and innovation" (7). What other cultural products might be considered conduits of change? Provide and explain several examples.

9. How might researchers in other disciplines study the cultural adaptation of food? What specifically would they be looking for? How might they design their research?

10. Do you agree with Arellano's central position that "Mexican food has become a better culinary metaphor for America than the melting pot" (4)? Why or why not? If not, can you think of a better metaphor, culinary or otherwise?

How Cooking Has Changed Us

PATRICK J. KIGER

Patrick J. Kiger is an author and journalist who regularly publishes in a number of popular news and information outlets, including *Urban Land* magazine, *Orange Coast* magazine, and *Sierra* magazine. He is co-author of *Poplorica: A Popular History of the Fads, Mavericks, Inventions, and Lore That Shaped Modern America* (2004) and *Oops: 20 Life Lessons from the Fiascoes That Shaped America* (2006), both published by HarperCollins. Kiger is also a blogger for the National Geographic Channel (online), where "How Cooking Has Changed Us" was published in 2014. The article traces the history and development of cooking, from early human civilization to the twenty-first century, to highlight its paradoxical position in American society today.

In a cave in South Africa, archaeologists have unearthed the remains of a million-year-old campfire, and discovered tiny bits of animal bones and ash from plants. It's the oldest evidence of our ancient human ancestors — probably *Homo erectus*, a species that preceded ours — cooking a meal.

It's a long way, of course, from that primitive repast to preparing a multi-course meal on your kitchen stove, or sticking a quick snack into the microwave. But without our early ancestors' innovation, you might not be here now to enjoy that broiled chicken breast and side of sweet-potato fries. Cooking, some scientists believe, played a crucial role in the evolution, survival, and ascent of early humans, helping to transform them from a ragged, miniscule fringe of struggling hunter-gatherers into the animal that dominates the planet. Moreover, since then cooking has continued to exert a powerful influence upon human civilization in numerous ways — not just by filling our bellies, but by helping to nourish the culture and rituals that form humanity's social nature.

Early humans may have been motivated by a simple benefit. When food was cooked, it probably tasted better to them. But Harvard University professor of biological anthropology Richard Wrangham, author of the book *Catching Fire: How Cooking Made Us Human*, argues that cooking had far more profound benefits for humans. By using heat to chemically alter their food, human cooks softened the cell walls of plants to enable them to release their stores of starch and fat, and broke down the connective tissue in meat, making its nutrients more accessible as well. As a result, they got a greater caloric payoff from their food; a cooked portion of oats, wheat, or potatoes provided 30 percent more energy than the raw stuff.

As a result, Wrangham and others believe, human ancestors were able to consume enough energy to fuel the evolutionary development of successively larger brains. At the same time, because they didn't need big guts to digest all that raw stuff, their body shape evolved to become more slim and lithe. And by cooking and making their food easier to chew, they avoided having to spend four to seven hours a day on mastication, as other great apes have to do. That freed up enormous amounts of time that they could use for other purposes, such as learning and developing language.

Cooking, Wrangham has written, may also have 5 led to the division of labor along gender lines and mating practices. By providing quickly-produced calories, it enabled male hunters to get back into the wild and stalk more prey, while females stayed behind and concentrated upon cooking the meat and whatever plant foods they could gather. But that division also left the female cooks vulnerable to marauding, hungry males who might be attracted by the smell of the food. In order to protect themselves and ensure access to the food for themselves and their young, a female found it advantageous to bond with a single male protector and provider. That may have been a factor in development of the basic human pattern of monogamy that continues to this day—as well as gender inequality, he believes.

But that was just the start of cooking's influence upon civilization. In ancient Rome, fine dining became a status symbol, and the society developed a class of highly-sought-after slave cooks who competed against one another to provide the tastiest dishes to the rich, in addition to bakers, grinders, buyers, carvers, and others who worked beneath them.

In 14th- and 15th-century Europe, what people cooked in their kitchens became an even more pronounced dividing line between economic and social classes, and nobles even began to collect and publish books of recipes of dishes "which are more delicious than others and more suitable to the tables of kings and princes than the lowly and men of little property," as one culinary writer of the time explained.

In 19th-century America, the experience of cooking for ordinary people was altered by technology. The development of the mass-produced cast-iron cook stove, which provided a raised cooking surface that required less bending and heavy lifting than cooking at a hearth, enabled a cook to perform multiple tasks, such as boiling water while baking, on a single coal or wood fire.

At the same time, railroads enabled people in cities and towns to get relatively fresh food from farms that were many miles away, which gave people more good ingredients to cook—meat, poultry, fish, vegetables, and fruits—than ever before.

By the turn of the 20th century, new labor-saving 10 gadgetry such as egg beaters and mechanical apple peelers also became the vogue; one cookbook author, for example, recommended 139 different utensils that every homemaker supposedly needed. That undoubtedly made Americans healthier and happier.

In the decades that followed, kitchens shrank in size and cooking for the family, once a communal activity that often involved multiple generations, became increasingly the job of the lady of the house. Canned soups and packaged convenience foods became common, which undoubtedly drained some of the pleasure and feeling of achievement from cooking. But after World War II, things again began to change, according to food historians Elizabeth Demers and Victor Geraci. Americans visited Europe and brought back the French ideal of eating fresh foods and savoring meals. And immigrants from Central and South America and Asia introduced new foods to the American palate. As a result, Americans began to seek out new tastes and new cooking techniques, and more of us came to see cooking and eating as a sensual, artistic experience that was an important part of our lives.

That trend toward viewing cooking as a source of pleasure and enjoyment, rather than just a source of nourishment, has become even more prevalent in the 21st century. Food writer Michael Pollan notes that since the mid-1960s, the amount of time spent preparing meals in the typical American household has decreased by half, to just 27 minutes per day. But at the same time, paradoxically, "We're talking about cooking more—watching cooking, and reading about cooking, and going to restaurants designed so that we can watch the work performed live," he writes. Additionally, top chefs increasingly are household names who star in their own reality TV shows. Cooking, he argues, "Has somehow been elevated to a popular spectator sport."

Reading Questions

1. In your own words, explain how cooking may have made "the evolutionary development of successively larger brains" (par. 4) in humans possible.

2. Identify two technological advances Kiger traces that have altered cooking's influence on civilization, and briefly explain how each may have changed the trajectory of human civilization.

3. Kiger concludes his article by identifying a paradoxical trend in American society. In your own words, describe this paradoxical trend.

Rhetoric Questions

4. Read the article's first two paragraphs again. Then, identify a single sentence within those two paragraphs that you believe establishes Kiger's focus for the article. Explain why you chose that sentence.

5. Kiger relies heavily on the work of Wrangham at the beginning of his article. Briefly explain Kiger's strategy for crediting ideas to Wrangham when such crediting is necessary.

6. Read again the opening sentence of each of the article's paragraphs. Then, describe the organizational strategy Kiger employs to control the flow of information throughout his article.

Response and Research Questions

7. Kiger identifies a number of technological advances that have altered the way we cook. Identify a specific technology or invention that has changed how you cook and explain how your cooking has changed as a result of that technology.

8. The history of cooking, Kiger suggests, may have contributed to the division of labor along gender lines. Based on your personal experiences, would you agree or disagree with this position? Why?

9. Kiger notes that for many Americans today cooking and eating are a "sensual, artistic experience" (11). Would you agree or disagree with this position? Why?

No Food Is Healthy. Not Even Kale.

MICHAEL RUHLMAN

Michael Ruhlman is the author of more than twenty books, and much of his nonfiction work, including a collaboration with chef Thomas Keller, concerns food and cooking. Ruhlman is also a memoirist and fiction writer. His latest work of fiction, *In Short Measures: Three Novellas,* was published in 2015, and his most recent publication is *Grocery: The Buying and Selling of Food in America* (2017). In the article below, which appeared in the *Washington Post* in January 2016, Ruhlman demonstrates how the language often used to describe food products is far from accurate.

Not long ago, I watched a woman set a carton of Land O' Lakes Fat-Free Half-and-Half on the conveyor belt at a supermarket.

"Can I ask you why you're buying fat-free half-and-half?" I said. Half-and-half is defined by its fat content: about 10 percent, more than milk, less than cream.

"Because it's fat-free?" she responded.

"Do you know what they replace the fat with?" I asked.

"Hmm," she said, then lifted the carton and read 5 the second ingredient on the label after skim milk: "Corn syrup." She frowned at me. Then she set the carton back on the conveyor belt to be scanned along with the rest of her groceries.

The woman apparently hadn't even thought to ask herself that question but had instead accepted the common belief that fat, an essential part of our diet, should be avoided whenever possible.

Then again, why should she question it, given that we allow food companies, advertisers, and food researchers to do our thinking for us? In the 1970s, no one questioned whether eggs really were the heart-attack risk nutritionists warned us about. Now, of course, eggs have become such a cherished food that many people raise their own laying hens. Such examples of food confusion and misinformation abound.

"This country will never have a healthy food supply," said Harry Balzer, an NPD Group analyst and a gleeful cynic when it comes to the American food shopper. "Never. Because the moment something becomes popular, someone will find a reason why it's not healthy."

Here, Balzer used the most dangerous term of all: "healthy."

We are told by everyone, from doctors and nutri- 10 tionists to food magazines and newspapers, to eat healthy food. We take for granted that a kale salad is healthy and that a Big Mac with fries is not.

I submit to you that our beloved kale salads are not "healthy." And we are confusing ourselves by believing that they are. They are not healthy; they are nutritious. They may be delicious when prepared well, and the kale itself, while in the ground, may have been a healthy crop. But the kale on your plate is not healthy, and to describe it as such obscures what is most important about that kale salad: that it's packed with nutrients your body needs. But this is not strictly about nomenclature. If all you ate was kale, you would become sick. Nomenclature rather shows us where to begin.

"'Healthy' is a bankrupt word," Roxanne Sukol, preventive medicine specialist at the Cleveland Clinic, medical director of its Wellness Enterprise and a nutrition autodidact ("They didn't teach us anything about nutrition in medical school"), told me as we strolled the aisles of a grocery store. "Our food isn't healthy. We are healthy. Our food is nutritious. I'm all about the words. Words are the key to giving people the tools they need to figure out what to eat. Everyone's so confused."

Last March, the Food and Drug Administration sent the nut-bar maker Kind a letter saying their use of the word "healthy" on their packaging was a violation (too much fat in the almonds). Kind responded with a citizens' petition asking the FDA to reevaluate its definition of the word.

If I may rephrase the doctor's words: Our food is not healthy; we will be healthy if we eat nutritious food. Words matter. And those that we apply to food matter more than ever.

Kraft cheese slices cannot be called cheese but 15 must be labeled "cheese food" or a "cheese product." Pringles cannot be called "chips" but rather "crisps." Yet packaged foods can be labeled "natural" or "all-natural"—what exactly is the difference between the two, anyway?—with little regulation.

Here is a word we think we understand: protein. Protein is good, yes? Builds strong muscles, has positive health connotations. That's why "protein shakes" are a multibillion-dollar business. Pork cracklings do not have positive health connotations because we think of them as having a high fat content. But pork cracklings are little more than strips of fried pig skin. Skin is one of the many forms of connective tissue in all animal bodies and is composed almost entirely of protein, typically undergirded by a layer of fat. When these strips of pig skin are fried, most of the fat is rendered out and the connective tissue puffs, resulting in a delectable, crunchy, salty crackling. I therefore recommend them to you as a "protein snack" during your on-the-go day.

Given the infinitely malleable language of food, it's no wonder American food shoppers are confused.

What is "mechanically separated meat," a standard ingredient in the turkey bacon and chicken sausages popularized because of our low-fat love? "Do you know what that is?" a grocery store owner asked me. "They basically put poultry carcasses in a giant salad spinner." Whatever winds up on the walls of the spinner in addition to meat—bits of cartilage (protein!), nerves (I have enough of my own, thank you), vessels, bone fragments—is scraped off and added to the mixing bowl. "Mechanically separated meat" engages our imagination only when someone attaches new words to it, such as "pink slime."

"Refined" is another critical food word. Generally, refined means elegant and cultured in appearance, manner or taste, or with impurities removed. Yet that is what food companies have been calling wheat from which the germ and bran have been removed, leaving what is in effect pure starch, devoid of the fiber, oils, iron, and vitamins that make wheat nutritious.

That's not refined, Sukol said, "that's stripped." [20] Flour stripped of the nutrition that makes it valuable to our bodies but reduces shelf life.

Because it has been stripped, we must "enrich" it. "Enriched." "Fortified." Good, yes? To make rich, to make strong. Food companies added the iron they took out during the refining process, but not enough of what we need. "Refined flour—this resulted in B vitamin and iron deficiencies," Sukol said, "so they added vitamins and iron. And what do they call that?

Enriched and fortified. But they forgot to add folate, vitamin B9, until the 1990s."

What we don't know, Sukol said, is how those additions, not to mention the diglycerides and sulphates, combined with the lack of fiber, will affect our metabolism in the long run. So far, she said, "it has resulted in diabetes and metabolic syndrome."

We will be healthy if we eat nutritious food. Our food is either nutritious or not. We are healthy or we are not. If we eat nutritious food, we may enhance what health we possess.

This is not a judgment on what you choose to eat. If you hunger for a cheese product grilled between bread that's been stripped of its nutrition, along with a bowl of Campbell's tomato soup (made with tomato paste, corn syrup and potassium chloride), fine. It was one of my favorite childhood meals. Just be aware. Buy fat-free half-and-half if that's what you like; just know what it is you're putting in your body and why.

Because, and this is the judgment call, fat isn't [25] bad; stupid is bad. And until we have better information and clearer shared language defining our food, smart choices will be ever harder to make.

Reading Questions

1. According to Ruhlman, what is the most dangerous term often employed in discussions of what we should and should not eat?

2. In your own words, briefly explain the difference between "healthy" and "nutritious" foods, according to Ruhlman's point of view.

3. What, according to Ruhlman's argument, is the better way to understand the meaning of *refined* as a food word?

4. What solutions does Ruhlman provide to help us make smarter food choices?

Rhetoric Questions

5. Ruhlman opens his article with a story about a personal encounter with a shopper at a supermarket. What is the impact of this opening on you as a reader? Is it effective for his purpose as a writer? Why or why not?

6. How would you describe Ruhlman's tone throughout the article? Is it likely to be effective for his purpose as a writer and his intended audience? Why or why not?

7. Consider Ruhlman's concluding paragraph. How would you describe the strategy he employs to end his article? Is it an effective ending? Why or why not?

8. Ruhlman cites Harry Balzer, whom he refers to as an "NPD Group analyst" (par. 8). Research Harry Balzer and the NPD Group. Explain why Ruhlman might see Balzer as a valuable source of information for his article.

9. Ruhlman provides a number of examples of how the words we use to describe certain foods often do not convey the real value of those foods. Identify and describe an instance, from your personal experience with food purchases, when the language used by a food company or advertiser belied the reality of their product.

10. Overall, Ruhlman's argument might be summed up by this simple statement: "[F]at isn't bad; stupid is bad" (25). Consider Ruhlman's likely audience, and then identify another single sentence in his article that might be said to sum up his overall argument. Explain why you chose the sentence you did.

Why Cook?

MICHAEL POLLAN

Michael Pollan is one of the leading voices on food politics in America today. He is the author of numerous award-winning articles and books, including *The Omnivore's Dilemma: A Natural History of Four Meals* (2006) and *In Defense of Food: An Eater's Manifesto* (2008). In the essay below, an excerpt from *Cooked: A Natural History of Transformation* (2013), Pollan maintains that Americans are increasingly separated from the food they eat because of the industrialization and specialization of modern food production. Further, Pollan argues that we must reconnect with the act of cooking for ourselves. Then (and only then) will we reconnect with our health and happiness.

I.

At a certain point in the late middle of my life I made the unexpected but happy discovery that the answer to several of the questions that most occupied me was in fact one and the same.

Cook.

Some of these questions were personal. For example, what was the single most important thing we could do as a family to improve our health and general well-being? And what would be a good way to better connect to my teenage son? (As it turned out, this involved not only ordinary cooking but also the specialized form of it known as brewing.) Other questions were slightly more political in nature. For years I had been trying to determine (because I am often asked) what is the most important thing an ordinary person can do to help reform the American food system, to make it healthier and more sustainable? Another related question is, how can people living in a highly specialized consumer economy reduce their sense of dependence and achieve a greater degree of self-sufficiency? And then there were the more philosophical questions, the ones I've been chewing on since I first started writing books. How, in our everyday lives, can we acquire a deeper understanding of the natural world and our species' peculiar role in it? You can always go to the woods to confront such questions, but I discovered that even more interesting answers could be had simply by going to the kitchen.

I would not, as I said, ever have expected it. Cooking has always been a part of my life, but more like the furniture than an object of scrutiny, much less a passion. I counted myself lucky to have a parent—my mother—who loved to cook and almost every night made us a delicious meal. By the time I had a place of my own, I could find my way around a kitchen well enough, the results of nothing more purposeful than all those hours spent hanging around the kitchen while my mother fixed dinner. And though once I had my own place I cooked whenever I had the time, I seldom *made* time for cooking or gave it much consideration. My kitchen skills, such as they were, were pretty much frozen in place by the time I turned thirty. Truth be told, my most successful dishes leaned heavily on the cooking of others, as when I drizzled my incredible sage-butter sauce over store-bought ravioli. Every now and then I'd look at a cookbook or clip a recipe from the newspaper to add a new dish to my tiny repertoire, or I'd buy a new kitchen gadget, though most of these eventually ended up in a closet.

In retrospect, the mildness of my interest in cook- 5 ing surprises me, since my interest in every other link of the food chain had been so keen. I've been a gardener since I was eight, growing mostly vegetables, and I've always enjoyed being on farms and writing about agriculture. I've also written a fair amount about the opposite end of the food chain—the eating end, I mean, and the implications of our eating for our health. But to the middle links of the food chain, where the stuff of nature gets transformed into the things we eat and drink, I hadn't really given much thought.

Until, that is, I began trying to unpack a curious paradox I had noticed while watching television, which was simply this: How is it that at the precise historical moment when Americans were abandoning the kitchen, handing over the preparation of most of our meals to the food industry, we began spending so much of our time thinking about food and watching other people cook it on television? The less cooking we were doing in our own lives, it seemed, the more that food and its vicarious preparation fascinated us.

Our culture seems to be of at least two minds on this subject. Survey research confirms we're cooking less and buying more prepared meals every year. The amount of time spent preparing meals in American households has fallen by half since the mid-sixties when I was watching my mom fix dinner to a scant 27 minutes a day. (Americans spend less time cooking than people in any other nation, but the general downward trend is global.) And yet at the same time we're talking about cooking more—and watching cooking, and reading about cooking, and going to restaurants designed so that we can watch the work performed live. We live in an age when professional cooks are household names, some of them as famous as athletes or movie stars. The very same activity that many people regard as a form of drudgery has somehow been elevated to a popular spectator sport. When you consider that 27 minutes is less time than it takes to watch a single episode of *Top Chef* or *The Next Food Network Star*, you realize that there are now millions of people who spend more time watching food being cooked on television than they spend actually cooking it themselves. I don't need to point out that the food you watch being cooked on television is not food you get to eat.

This is peculiar. After all, we're not watching shows or reading books about sewing or darning socks or changing the oil in our cars, three other domestic chores that we have been only too happy to outsource—and then promptly drop from conscious awareness. But cooking somehow feels different. The work, or the process, retains an emotional or psychological power we can't quite shake, or don't want to. And in fact it was after a long bout of watching cooking programs on television that I began to wonder if this activity I had always taken for granted might be worth taking a little more seriously.

I developed a few theories to explain what I came to think of as the Cooking Paradox. The first and most obvious is that watching other people cook is not exactly a new behavior for us humans. Even when "everyone" still cooked, there were plenty of us who mainly watched: men for the most part, and children. Most of us have happy memories of watching our mothers in the kitchen, performing feats that sometimes looked very much like sorcery and typically resulted in something tasty to eat. In ancient Greece, the word for "cook," "butcher," and "priest" was the same—*mageiros*—and the word shares an etymological root with "magic." I would watch, rapt, when my mother conjured her most magical dishes, like the tightly wrapped packages of fried chicken Kiev that, when cut open with a sharp knife, liberated a pool of melted butter and an aromatic gust of herbs. But watching an everyday pan of eggs get scrambled was nearly as riveting a spectacle, as the slimy yellow goop suddenly leapt into the form of savory gold nuggets. Even the most ordinary dish follows a satisfying arc of transformation, magically becoming something more than the sum of its ordinary parts. And in almost every dish, you can find, besides the culinary ingredients, the ingredients of a story: a beginning, a middle, and an end.

Then there are the cooks themselves, the heroes 10 who drive these little dramas of transformation. Even as it vanishes from our daily lives, we're drawn to the rhythms and textures of the work cooks do, which seems so much more direct and satisfying than the more abstract and formless tasks most of us perform in our jobs these days. Cooks get to put their hands on real stuff, not just keyboards and screens but fundamental things like plants and animals and fungi. They get to work with the primal elements, too, fire and water, earth and air, using them—mastering them!—to perform their tasty alchemies. How many of us still do the kind of work that engages us in a dialogue with the material world that concludes—assuming the chicken Kiev doesn't prematurely leak or the soufflé doesn't collapse—with such a gratifying and delicious sense of closure?

So maybe the reason we like to watch cooking on television and read about cooking in books is that there are things about cooking we really miss. We might not feel we have the time or energy (or the knowledge) to do it ourselves every day, but we're not prepared to see it disappear from our lives altogether. If cooking is, as the anthropologists tell us, a defining

human activity—the act with which culture begins, according to Claude Lévi-Strauss—then maybe we shouldn't be surprised that watching its processes unfold would strike deep emotional chords.

The idea that cooking is a defining human activity is not a new one. In 1773, the Scottish writer James Boswell, noting that "no beast is a cook," called *Homo sapiens* "the cooking animal." (Though he might have reconsidered that definition had he been able to gaze upon the frozen-food cases at Walmart.) Fifty years later, in *The Physiology of Taste*, the French gastronome Jean Anthelme Brillat-Savarin claimed that cooking made us who we are; by teaching men to use fire, it had "done the most to advance the cause of civilization." More recently, Lévi-Strauss, writing in *The Raw and the Cooked* in 1964, reported that many of the world's cultures entertained a similar view, regarding cooking as the symbolic activity that "establishes the difference between animals and people."

For Lévi-Strauss, cooking was a metaphor for the human transformation of raw nature into cooked culture. But in the years since the publication of *The Raw and the Cooked*, other anthropologists have begun to take quite literally the idea that the invention of cooking might hold the evolutionary key to our humanness. A few years ago, a Harvard anthropologist and primatologist named Richard Wrangham published a fascinating book called *Catching Fire*, in which he argued that it was the discovery of cooking by our early ancestors—and not tool making or meat eating or language—that set us apart from the apes and made us human. According to the "cooking hypothesis," the advent of cooked food altered the course of human evolution. By providing our forebears with a more energy-dense and easy-to-digest diet, it allowed our brains to grow bigger (brains being notorious energy guzzlers) and our guts to shrink. It seems that raw food takes much more time and energy to chew and digest, which is why other primates our size carry around substantially larger digestive tracts and spend many more of their waking hours chewing—as much as six hours a day.

Cooking, in effect, took part of the work of chewing and digestion and performed it for us outside of the body, using outside sources of energy. Also, since cooking detoxifies many potential sources of food, the new technology cracked open a treasure trove of calories unavailable to other animals. Freed from the necessity of spending our days gathering large quantities of raw food and then chewing (and chewing) it, humans could now devote their time, and their metabolic resources, to other purposes, like creating a culture.

Cooking gave us not just the meal but also the occasion: the practice of eating together at an appointed time and place. This was something new under the sun, for the forager of raw food would have likely fed himself on the go and alone, like all the other animals. (Or, come to think of it, like the industrial eaters we've more recently become, grazing at gas stations and eating by ourselves whenever and wherever.) But sitting down to common meals, making eye contact, sharing food, and exercising self-restraint all served to civilize us. "Around that fire," Wrangham writes, "we became tamer."

Cooking thus transformed us, and not only by making us more sociable and civil. Once cooking allowed us to expand our cognitive capacity at the expense of our digestive capacity, there was no going back: Our big brains and tiny guts now depended on a diet of cooked food. (Raw-foodists take note.) What this means is that cooking is now obligatory—it is, as it were, baked into our biology. What Winston Churchill once said of architecture—"First we shape our buildings, and then they shape us"—might also be said of cooking. First we cooked our food, and then our food cooked us.

If cooking is as central to human identity, biology, and culture as Wrangham suggests, it stands to reason that the decline of cooking in our time would have serious consequences for modern life, and so it has. Are they all bad? Not at all. The outsourcing of much of the work of cooking to corporations has relieved women of what has traditionally been their exclusive responsibility for feeding the family, making it easier for them to work outside the home and have careers. It has headed off many of the conflicts and domestic arguments that such a large shift in gender roles and family dynamics was bound to spark. It has relieved all sorts of other pressures in the household, including longer workdays and overscheduled children, and saved us time that we can now invest in other pursuits. It has also allowed us to diversify our diets substantially, making it possible even for people with no cooking skills and little money to enjoy a whole different cuisine every night of the week. All that's required is a microwave.

These are no small benefits. Yet they have come at a cost that we are just now beginning to reckon. Industrial cooking has taken a substantial toll on our health and well-being. Corporations cook very differently from how people do (which is why we usually call what they do "food processing" instead of cooking). They tend to use much more sugar, fat, and salt than people cooking for people do; they also deploy novel chemical ingredients seldom found in pantries in order to make their food last longer and look fresher than it really is. So it will come as no surprise that the decline in home cooking closely tracks the rise in obesity and all the chronic diseases linked to diet.

The rise of fast food and the decline in home cooking have also undermined the institution of the shared meal, by encouraging us to eat different things and to eat them on the run and often alone. Survey researchers tell us we're spending more time engaged in "secondary eating," as this more or less constant grazing on packaged foods is now called, and less time engaged in "primary eating"—a rather depressing term for the once-venerable institution known as the meal.

The shared meal is no small thing. It is a foundation of family life, the place where our children learn the art of conversation and acquire the habits of civilization: sharing, listening, taking turns, navigating differences, arguing without offending. What have been called the "cultural contradictions of capitalism"—its tendency to undermine the stabilizing social forms it depends on—are on vivid display today at the modern American dinner table, along with all the brightly colored packages that the food industry has managed to plant there.

These are, I know, large claims to make for the centrality of cooking (and not cooking) in our lives, and a caveat or two are in order. For most of us today, the choice is not nearly as blunt as I've framed it: that is, home cooking from scratch versus fast food prepared by corporations. Most of us occupy a place somewhere between those bright poles, a spot that is constantly shifting with the day of the week, the occasion, and our mood. Depending on the night, we might cook a meal from scratch, or we might go out or order in, or we might "sort of" cook. This last option involves availing ourselves of the various and very useful shortcuts that an industrial food economy offers: the package of spinach in the freezer, the can of wild salmon in the pantry, the box of store-bought ravioli from down the street or halfway around the world. What constitutes "cooking" takes place along a spectrum, as indeed it has for at least a century, when packaged foods first entered the kitchen and the definition of "scratch cooking" began to drift. (Thereby allowing me to regard my packaged ravioli with sage-butter sauce as a culinary achievement.) Most of us over the course of a week find ourselves all over that spectrum. What is new, however, is the great number of people now spending most nights at the far end of it, relying for the preponderance of their meals on an industry willing to do *every*thing for them save the heating and the eating. "We've had a hundred years of packaged foods," a food-marketing consultant told me, "and now we're going to have a hundred years of packaged meals."

This is a problem—for the health of our bodies, our families, our communities, and our land, but also for our sense of how our eating connects us to the world. Our growing distance from any direct, physical engagement with the processes by which the raw stuff of nature gets transformed into a cooked meal is changing our understanding of what food is. Indeed, the idea that food has *any* connection to nature or human work or imagination is hard to credit when it arrives in a neat package, fully formed. Food becomes just another commodity, an abstraction. And as soon as that happens we become easy prey for corporations selling synthetic versions of the real thing—what I call edible foodlike substances. We end up trying to nourish ourselves on images.

Now, for a man to criticize these developments will perhaps rankle some readers. To certain ears, whenever a man talks about the importance of cooking, it sounds like he wants to turn back the clock, and return women to the kitchen. But that's not at all what I have in mind. I've come to think cooking is too important to be left to any one gender or member of the family; men and children both need to be in the kitchen, too, and not just for reasons of fairness or equity but because they have so much to gain by being there. In fact, one of the biggest reasons corporations were able to insinuate themselves into this part of our lives is because home cooking had for so long been denigrated as "women's work" and therefore not important enough for men and boys to learn to do.

Though it's hard to say which came first: Was home cooking denigrated because the work was mostly done by women, or did women get stuck doing most of the cooking because our culture denigrated the work? The gender politics of cooking are nothing if not complicated, and probably always have been. Since ancient times, a few special types of cooking have enjoyed considerable prestige: Homer's warriors barbecued their own joints of meat at no cost to their heroic status or masculinity. And ever since, it has been socially acceptable for men to cook in public and professionally—for money. (Though it is only recently that professional chefs have enjoyed the status of artists.) But for most of history most of humanity's food has been cooked by women working out of public view and without public recognition. Except for the rare ceremonial occasions over which men presided—the religious sacrifice, the July 4 barbecue, the four-star restaurant—cooking has traditionally been women's work, part and parcel of homemaking and child care, and therefore undeserving of serious—i.e., male—attention.

But there may be another reason cooking has not received its proper due. In a recent book called *The Taste for Civilization*, Janet A. Flammang, a feminist scholar and political scientist who has argued eloquently for the social and political importance of "food work," suggests the problem may have something to do with food itself, which by its very nature falls on the wrong side—the feminine side—of the mind-body dualism in Western culture.

"Food is apprehended through the senses of touch, smell, and taste," she points out, "which rank lower on the hierarchy of senses than sight and hearing, which are typically thought to give rise to knowledge. In most of philosophy, religion, and literature, food is associated with body, animal, female, and appetite — things civilized men have sought to overcome with knowledge and reason."

Very much to their loss.

. . .

III.

As I grew steadily more comfortable in the kitchen, I found that, much like gardening, most cooking manages to be agreeably absorbing without being too demanding intellectually. It leaves plenty of mental space for daydreaming and reflection. One of the things I reflected on is the whole question of taking on what in our time has become, strictly speaking, optional, even unnecessary work, work for which I am not particularly gifted or qualified, and at which I may never get very good. This is, in the modern world, the unspoken question that hovers over all our cooking: Why bother?

By any purely rational calculation, even everyday home cooking (much less baking bread or fermenting kimchi) is probably not a wise use of my time. Not long ago, I read an Op-Ed piece in the *Wall Street Journal* about the restaurant industry, written by the couple that publishes the Zagat restaurant guides, which took exactly this line. Rather than coming home after work to cook, the Zagats suggested, "people would be better off staying an extra hour in the office doing what they do well, and letting bargain restaurants do what they do best."

Here in a nutshell is the classic argument for the division of labor, which, as Adam Smith and countless others have pointed out, has given us many of the blessings of civilization. It is what allows me to make a living sitting at this screen writing, while others grow my food, sew my clothes, and supply the energy that lights and heats my house. I can probably earn more in an hour of writing or even teaching than I could save in a whole week of cooking. Specialization is undeniably a powerful social and economic force. And yet it is also debilitating. It breeds helplessness, dependence, and ignorance and, eventually, it undermines any sense of responsibility.

Our society assigns us a tiny number of roles: We're producers of one thing at work, consumers of a great many other things all the rest of the time, and then, once a year or so, we take on the temporary role of citizen and cast a vote. Virtually all our needs and desires we delegate to specialists of one kind or another — our meals to the food industry, our health to the medical profession, entertainment to Hollywood and the media, mental health to the therapist or the drug company, caring for nature to the environmentalist, political action to the politician, and on and on it goes. Before long it becomes hard to imagine doing much of anything for ourselves — anything, that is, except the work we do "to make a living." For everything else, we feel like we've lost the skills, or that there's someone who can do it better. (I recently heard about an agency that will dispatch a sympathetic someone to visit your elderly parents if you can't spare the time to do it yourself.) It seems as though we can no longer imagine anyone but a professional or an institution or a product supplying our daily needs or solving our problems. This learned helplessness is, of course, much to the advantage of the corporations eager to step forward and do all this work for us.

One problem with the division of labor in our complex economy is how it obscures the lines of connection, and therefore of responsibility, between our everyday acts and their real-world consequences. Specialization makes it easy to forget about the filth of the coal-fired power plant that is lighting this pristine computer screen, or the back-breaking labor it took to pick the strawberries for my cereal, or the misery of the hog that lived and died so I could enjoy my bacon. Specialization neatly hides our implication in all that is done on our behalf by unknown other specialists half a world away.

Perhaps what most commends cooking to me is that it offers a powerful corrective to this way of being in the world — a corrective that is still available to all of us.

To butcher a pork shoulder is to be forcibly reminded that this is the shoulder of a large mammal, made up of distinct groups of muscles with a purpose quite apart from feeding me. The work itself gives me a keener interest in the story of the hog: where it came from and how it found its way to my kitchen. In my hands its flesh feels a little less like the product of industry than of nature; indeed, less like a product at all. Likewise, to grow the greens I'm serving with this pork, greens that in late spring seem to grow back almost as fast as I can cut them, is a daily reminder of nature's abundance, the everyday miracle by which photons of light are turned into delicious things to eat.

Handling these plants and animals, taking back the production and the preparation of even just some part of our food, has the salutary effect of making visible again many of the lines of connection that the supermarket and the "home-meal replacement" have succeeded in obscuring, yet of course never actually eliminated. To do so is to take back a measure of responsibility, too, to become, at the very least, a little less glib in one's pronouncements.

Especially one's pronouncements about "the environment," which suddenly begins to seem a little less "out there" and a lot closer to home. For what is the environmental crisis if not a crisis of the way we live? The Big Problem is nothing more or less than the sum total of countless little everyday choices, most of them made by us (consumer spending represents nearly three-quarters of the U.S. economy) and the rest of them made by others in the name of our needs and desires. If the environmental crisis is ultimately a crisis of character, as Wendell Berry told us way back in the 1970s, then sooner or later it will have to be addressed at that level—at home, as it were. In our yards and kitchens and minds.

As soon as you start down this path of thinking, the quotidian* space of the kitchen appears in a startling new light. It begins to matter more than we ever imagined. The unspoken reason why political reformers from Vladimir Lenin to Betty Friedan sought to get women out of the kitchen was that nothing of

*quotidian: mundane; literally, a daily occurrence.

importance—nothing worthy of their talents and intelligence and convictions—took place there. The only worthy arenas for consequential action were the workplace and the public square. But this was before the environmental crisis had come into view, and before the industrialization of our eating created a crisis in our health. Changing the world will always require action and participation in the public realm, but in our time that will no longer be sufficient. We'll have to change the way we live, too. What that means is that the sites of our everyday engagement with nature—our kitchens, gardens, houses, cars—matter to the fate of the world in a way they never have before.

To cook or not to cook thus becomes a consequential question. Though I realize that is putting the matter a bit too bluntly. Cooking means different things at different times to different people; seldom is it an all-or-nothing proposition. Yet even to cook a few more nights a week than you already do, or to devote a Sunday to making a few meals for the week, or perhaps to try every now and again to make something you only ever expected to buy—even these modest acts will 35 constitute a kind of vote. A vote for what, exactly? Well, in a world where so few of us are obliged to cook at all anymore, to choose to do so is to lodge a protest against specialization—against the total rationalization of life. Against the infiltration of commercial interests into every last cranny of our lives. To cook for the pleasure of it, to devote a portion of our leisure to it, is to declare our independence from the corporations seeking to organize our every waking moment into yet another occasion for consumption. (Come to think of it, our nonwaking moments as well: Ambien, anyone?) It is to reject the debilitating notion that, at least while we're at home, production is work best done by someone else, and the only legitimate form of leisure is consumption. This dependence marketers call "freedom."

Cooking has the power to transform more than plants and animals: It transforms us, too, from mere consumers into producers. Not completely, not all the time, but I have found that even to shift the ratio between these two identities a few degrees toward the side of production yields deep and unexpected satisfactions. *Cooked* is an invitation to alter, however slightly, the ratio between production and consumption in your life. The regular exercise of these simple skills for producing some of the necessities of life increases self-reliance and freedom while reducing our dependence on distant corporations. Not just our money but our power flows toward them whenever we cannot supply any of our everyday needs and desires ourselves. And it begins to flow back toward us, and our community, as soon as we decide to take some responsibility for feeding ourselves. This has been an early lesson of the rising movement to rebuild local food economies, a movement that ultimately depends for its success on our willingness to put more thought and effort into feeding ourselves. Not every day, not every meal—but more often than we do, whenever we can.

Cooking, I found, gives us the opportunity, so rare in modern life, to work directly in our own support, and in the support of the people we feed. If this is not "making a living," I don't know what is. In the calculus of economics, doing so may not always be the most efficient use of an amateur cook's time, but in the calculus of human emotion, it is beautiful even so. For is there any practice less selfish, any labor less alienated, any time less wasted, than preparing something delicious and nourishing for people you love?

So let's begin.   40

At the beginning, with fire.

Reading Questions

1. Why, according to Pollan, do so many people enjoy watching others cook or reading about cooking?

2. Explain the connections Pollan makes between "the 'cooking hypothesis'" (par. 13) and advances in human sociability and civility.

3. According to Pollan, what are the effects, both positive and negative, of losing our connection to cooking?

4. Pollan writes briefly about the gender politics of food. What does he mean by this? How has cooking labor traditionally been divided between the sexes?

5. How does the division of labor apply to food preparation? What, according to Pollan, does this division of labor obscure? What benefits might we gain by cooking more food at home?

Rhetoric Questions

6. Pollan argues that cooking "transformed" (16) humans and is central to our identity. What does he mean by this? What type of evidence does he provide to support this argument? Do you find his argument effective?

7. In this excerpt, Pollan admits that some of his claims may seem very large. What caveats does he offer in an effort to hedge these claims? How might you use hedging in your own writing?

8. Pollan's conclusion is a call to action for readers to cook more often. Rhetorically, how does Pollan convince readers to heed his call?

Response and Research Question

9. Consider your own experiences with cooking. What motivates you to cook when you do? What do you get from it, besides nutrition? What keeps you from cooking (more often)?

Ethical Discourse on the Use of Genetically Modified Crops: A Review of Academic Publications in the Fields of Ecology and Environmental Ethics

DANIEL GREGOROWIUS, PETRA LINDEMANN-MATTHIES, AND MARKUS HUPPENBAUER

Daniel Gregorowius, first author of "Ethical Discourse on the Use of Genetically Modified Crops: A Review of Academic Publications in the Fields of Ecology and Environmental Ethics," is an affiliated staff member at the University of Zurich's Center for Ethics–Institute for Biomedical Ethics. Along with Petra Lindemann-Matthies, professor of biology and didactics at the Karlsruhe University of Education, and Markus Huppenbauer, also of the University of Zurich's Center for Ethics, the researchers' study presented here "provides a comprehensive overview of the moral reasoning on the use of GM [genetically modified] crops expressed in academic publications from 1975 to 2008." The article was published in the *Journal of Agricultural and Environmental Ethics* in 2012.

ABSTRACT

The use of genetically modified plants in agriculture (GM crops) is controversially discussed in academic publications. Important issues are whether the release of GM crops is beneficial or harmful for the environment and therefore acceptable, and whether the modification of plants is ethically permissible per se. This study provides a comprehensive overview of the moral reasoning on the use of GM crops expressed in academic publications from 1975 to 2008. Environmental ethical aspects in the publications were investigated. Overall, 113 articles from 15 ecology, environmental ethics, and multidisciplinary science journals were systematically reviewed. Three types of moral concerns were used to structure the normative statements, moral notions, and moral issues found in the articles: concerns addressing consequences of the use of GM crops, concerns addressing the act (the technique itself), and concerns addressing the virtues of an actor. Articles addressing consequences (84%) dealt with general ecological and risk concerns or discussed specific ecological issues about the use of GM crops. Articles addressing the act (57%) dealt with the value of naturalness, the value of biotic entities, and conceptual reductionism, whereas articles addressing the actor (43%) dealt with virtues related to the handling of risks and the application of GM crops. The results of this study may help to structure the academic debate and contribute to a better understanding of moral concerns that are associated with the key aspects of the ethical theories of consequentialism, deontology, and virtue ethics.

INTRODUCTION

The use of genetically modified plants[1] in agriculture (GM crops) is controversially discussed in academic publications. An important aspect of this controversy is whether the release of GM crops in agriculture is beneficial or harmful for the environment and therefore acceptable (Hails 2000; Wolfenbarger and Phifer 2000; Clark and Lehmann 2001). Arguments against GM crops include concerns that transgenes might escape into wild populations (e.g., Pilson and Prendeville 2004; Marvier and Van Acker 2005), that the use of herbicide-resistant GM crops might lead to an increase in spraying herbicides (e.g., Firbank and Forcella 2000; Watkinson et al. 2000), and that toxins produced by GM crops might enter the food web and thus affect non-target organisms (e.g., Marvier 2002; Harwood et al. 2005). Moreover, concerns have been raised over the spread of transgenic DNA by horizontal gene transfer to unrelated species (e.g., Ho et al. 1999).

[1] A GM plant is an organism whose genetic characteristics have been modified by the insertion of an altered plant gene of the same species (intragenic modification) or a gene from other organisms (transgenic modification) using genetic engineering (Von Wartburg and Liew 1999).

Arguments in favor of GM crops are, for instance, that they might be more suitable than traditional techniques to control certain pest species (e.g., Cowgill et al. 2004), that the use of herbicide-resistant GM crops might enhance agricultural biodiversity (e.g., Hails 2002), and that GM crops might require less pesticide use and reduce greenhouse gas emissions (e.g., Brookes and Barfoot 2005).

These scientific arguments are concerned with the potential consequences of the use of GM crops. In addition, it has been asked whether the modification of plants is morally permissible *per se* (Reiss and Straughan 2002). The modification of plants will be morally wrong, if it is regarded as an infringement of the integrity or dignity of plants (e.g., Balzer et al. 2000) or an interference with the natural order (e.g., Verhoog et al. 2003). Such concerns address the process of genetic modification itself. Moreover, there are concerns that are related to the character traits of an actor, such as the concerns that genetic modification is a disrespectful offense against the inherent wisdom of nature (e.g., Deane-Drummond 2002) or a sign of human hubris (e.g., Sandler 2007).

Several review articles have summed up and discussed different moral concerns in the debate on GM crops (e.g., Robinson 1999; Shelton et al. 2002; Weaver and Morris 2005). However, none so far provides a comprehensive overview of the ethical discourse in academic publications on ecological *and* environmental ethical aspects. In 2007 and 2008, we thus carried out a systematic literature review of 15 journals (seven ecology journals, five environmental ethics journals, three multidisciplinary science journals). Our aim was not to reflect the different opinions on gene technology, but to structure the academic discourse by relating the morally relevant concerns and issues expressed in the reviewed articles to established ethical theories. The structure will add a new viewpoint to ethical tools that had already been developed for the decision-making in biotechnology (e.g., Busch et al. 2002; Mepham 2008). Our article will also contribute to the current debate on the ethics of genetically modifying plants (e.g., Balzer et al. 2000).

METHODOLOGY

Preparation of the Literature Review

Before the actual literature review, we analyzed moral [5] concerns about GM crops found in various monographs, proceedings, and anthologies about gene technology, plant ethics, risk perception, and related issues (e.g., Runtenberg 1997; Balzer et al. 1998; Rolston 1999; Busch et al. 2002; Heaf and Wirz 2002; Kallhoff 2002; Reiss and Straughan 2002; Ammann et al. 2003; Stewart 2004; Deane-Drummond 2004; Sandler 2007; Stöcklin 2007). Three types of moral concerns were most prominent and thus used to structure the normative statements, moral notions, and moral issues found in the subsequent literature review: (1) concerns about the consequences of the use of GM crops in agriculture (in the following called "*moral concerns addressing consequences*"), (2) concerns about the moral permissibility of genetic modification as such ("*moral concerns addressing the act*"), and (3) concerns about human character traits and attitudes that either contribute to or are influenced by using gene technology ("*moral concerns addressing the actor*").

Relevant Ethical Theories

The three types of moral concerns can be linked to well-known theories in environmental ethics (cf. Brennan and Lo 2008)[2]: (1) moral concerns addressing consequences to *consequentialism*, (2) moral concerns addressing the act to *deontology*, and (3) moral concerns addressing the actor to *virtue ethics*.

CONSEQUENTIALISM

This normative theory states that the rightness or wrongness of an action has to be judged in light of the value of its consequences (von Kutschera 1999;

---

[2] Besides the three mentioned normative ethical theories, other theories exist that are discussed in context of gene technology, e.g., contractualism. However, contractualism as an ethical theory of social contract could hardly be applied to the ethics of GM crops, because plants cannot be part of a social contract. Therefore, deontology, consequentialism, and virtue ethics were chosen as an underlying basis for our analysis.

Brink 2006). A consequentialist concept has to define the values that are worth being promoted by the outcome of an action (Brink 2006), e.g., personal pleasure, satisfaction of personal interests, or perfection of personal essential capacities. In order to find the *best* outcome, alternative actions have to be evaluated and harms and benefits of the consequences of one's action have to be weighed against each other. The one action has to be chosen that promotes the defined value in the best way, which means that harms are outweighed by benefits. Consequentialism allows trade-offs between alternative actions with the aim of maximizing the overall good for the greatest number of morally relevant entities,[3] e.g., maximizing the happiness for the greatest number of people.

DEONTOLOGY

This normative theory states that the moral evaluation of an action depends on the action's quality, i.e., certain actions are right or wrong *per se* and thus either permitted or forbidden (von Kutschera 1999; McNaughton and Rawling 2006). The rightness of an action is judged based on the action's compliance with a certain rule or principle for the sake of this rule or principle. The balancing between advantages and disadvantages of an action as in consequentialism is not a prime concern. Moral absolutists would state that, as it is the action itself that is important, a morally good act must be performed even if it has a bad consequence (Herold 2008). In addition to this approach, there is a huge diversity of theories that have been described as deontological (Gaus 2001a; Gaus 2001b). For instance, many deontologists do not agree with a moral absolutism and argue that exceptions should be made to avoid catastrophic outcomes (McNaughton and Rawling 2006). Often, deontological theories include considerations of respect for morally relevant entities for their own sake, and considerations of justice.

VIRTUE ETHICS

This normative theory is centered on the individual actor who shows certain virtues. A virtue is a character trait, state, or disposition that allows a person to act in a way that individual and collective well-being is promoted. To be named as a virtue, a character trait has to embody a commitment to an ethical value such as justice or benevolence that will provide a built-in ethical guidance for a moral agent (Annas 2006). Virtue ethics implies that acting morally right is based on the actor's moral personal attitudes and convictions. This means that the value of an action can be judged by the value of the virtues leading to this act (Rippe and Schaber 1998). The aim of a virtuous person is to develop an excellent character. Therefore, in virtue ethics an action will be judged as morally good if the actor shows a virtuous character (Annas 2006). Apart from pure forms of virtue ethics various pluralistic forms exist that allow non-virtue-based reasons that also play a role in deontology or consequentialism (Hursthouse 2003; Crisp 2003).

Although the three classical normative theories form the basis of our analysis, we do not classify these concerns in the literature review as consequentialist, deontological, or virtue concerns. This would be problematic as there exist, for instance, forms of so-called non-teleological consequentialism that evaluate the outcome of an act in applying *deontological criteria* (cf. Birnbacher 2007). This means that the consequences of the act are morally judged by the number of individual rights that are respected or by the number of intrinsically right or wrong actions that result as further consequences from doing the act (Birnbacher 2007). Moreover, many deontologists include consequences in their moral reasoning. However, the normative statements, moral notions, and moral issues found in the articles can be assigned to the key issues of the normative theories, i.e., the moral concerns addressing consequences, the act itself, or the actor.

Review of the Academic Literature

We pre-selected 18 journals from the fields of ecology and environmental ethics as well as multidisciplinary science journals for review (see Table 1). The period reviewed was from 1975 (first conference on the safety of recombinant DNA research in Asilomar, California;

---

[3] Biotic entities can be single organisms, species, ecosystems, or the biotic community.

Table 1

Overview of Journals Reviewed and Number of Relevant Articles Found (in parentheses)

Ecology journals (15)	IF	Environmental ethics journals (74)	IF	Multidisciplinary science journals (24)	IF
Trends in Ecology & Evolution (5)	14.1	Journal of Agricultural and Environmental Ethics (55)	0.7	Science (8)	30.0
Annual Review of Ecology, Evolution, and Systematics (1)	9.8	Environmental Ethics (2)		Nature (11)	26.7
Ecology Letters (0)	7.6	Environmental Values (9)		GAIA (5)	
Ecological Monographs (0)	7.1	Ethics & the Environment (3)			
Frontiers in Ecology and the Environment (2)	4.8	Ethics in Science and Environmental Politics (5)			
Molecular Ecology (1)	4.8				
Ecology (2)	4.8				
Journal of Applied Ecology (3)	4.5				
Journal of Ecology (0)	4.2				
Ecological Applications (1)	3.5				

Note. If applicable, the impact factor (IF, 2006) is shown.

see Stewart 2004) to 2008. In the initial selection process, we asked colleagues from biology and philosophy to indicate suitable journals for the literature review. Based on this information, the ten ecology journals with the highest impact factor in 2006[4] (start of study) were selected. As for most journals in environmental ethics no impact factor was available at that time; those journals were chosen that were recommended by *all* colleagues, i.e., five renowned environmental ethics journals dealing specifically with ecological and agricultural topics. In addition, three important and well-renowned multidisciplinary science journals were selected (Table 1).

Environmental ethics journals were selected as we supposed that the ecological and environmental ethical debate about GM crops will primarily take place in this type of journal. Nevertheless, we also wanted to investigate whether moral concerns about GM crops are raised in ecology journals. As journals in this field focus primarily on mere empirical questions, we selected a larger number of journals to have a greater chance to find relevant articles dealing with ethical concerns. As our literature review focused on the debate on GM crops in an environmental ethics context, journals from the fields of microbiology, biotechnology, or general moral philosophy were not assessed.

Online search engines of the journals or of JSTOR (Journal Storage)[5] were used to identify relevant articles for the literature review. Different types of keywords were used that referred to the genetic nature

[4] The journals were selected in 2007. At this time, the most recent impact factor was from 2006.

[5] JSTOR (Journal Storage) is an online system for archiving academic journals and provides a full-text search of digitized issues of several hundred journals. See Homepage jstor.org.

Table 2

Keywords Used in the Search for Relevant Articles

Keywords 1	Keywords 2	Keywords 3
Gene(s)	Engineering	Plant(s)
Genetic(s)	Modification(s)	Crop(s)
Genetical(ly)	Modify/ied	
Transgene(s)	(Bio)technology/ies	
Transgenic(s)		
GM(O)		

Note. Keywords in the first column were used in all different combinations with those in the second and third columns.

of the modification, the modification or engineering itself, and to plants or crops (Table 2). Keywords of one type were used in all different combinations with those of the other two types. In order not to exclude too many articles, we did not refine our search by using keywords like "value," "respect," "dignity," "integrity," "justice," or "risk." For two journals (*Environmental Ethics, Environmental Values*) no online search engines were available. Articles in these journals were selected by studying titles and abstracts.

Initially, more than 3,300 articles from 18 journals were selected and their titles and abstracts briefly examined. Articles that only briefly mentioned ecological or ethical issues or that were book reviews, editorials, and short news articles were immediately excluded. The remaining 250 original research and review articles were studied in more detail. Those articles that actually dealt with ecological or environmental concerns about GM crops from an ethical point of view were identified. Original research articles in ecology journals that did not address the moral relevance of empirical findings they discussed were excluded from the subsequent analysis. Finally, 113 articles from 15 journals remained.[6]

From the normative statements, moral notions, [15] and issues found in the 113 articles, basic semantic units were extracted. These basic semantic units could be, for instance, morally qualified empirical findings such as "harmful impact of GM crops on non-target insects," normative statements such as "gene technology is morally problematic because it is playing God," moral notions such as "dignity of plants," or issues that were related to principles or concepts with underlying moral implications such as the precautionary principle, global justice, or sustainable development.[7] Basic semantic units were joined to form classes of similar content. For example, the empirical finding "harmful impact of GM crops on non-target insects" was sorted under the header of "impact on species" and the notion "dignity of plants" under "individual biotic entities." The classes of similar content were finally assigned to certain clusters of moral concerns that fell under the header of one of the three moral concerns mentioned above. In order to assign semantic units to one of these concerns, it was necessary to clarify in which conceptual context they were used in the article (e.g., in context of sustainable agriculture or of the character traits of a person).

Semantic units (and thus the articles using them) that dealt with the outcome of the release of GM crops were grouped under the header of *moral concerns addressing consequences*. Articles that addressed consequences in purely empirical ecological terms (e.g., that there is a certain probability that hybrids between wild plants and GM crops can establish in the landscape) were only included in the analysis if the moral relevance of the outcome was clearly expressed (e.g., certain consequences of the release of GM crops are beneficial or harmful for biodiversity). Articles that dealt with environmental consequences in general terms (e.g., that there are risks for the environment) were only included if their moral relevance was clarified, for instance, by relating this general concern about consequences to a concern with a normative implication (e.g., sustainability and

---

[6] Full list of all reviewed articles is available from author 1.

[7] Only ecological concerns underlying these concepts are relevant for our analysis.

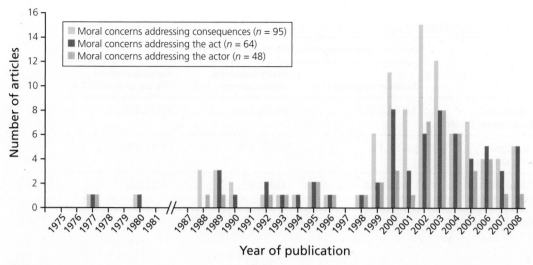

Figure 1. Number of Articles per Year in the Reviewed Period Sorted by the Three Different Types of Moral Concerns

its underlying concepts of global justice for recent and future generations). However, semantic units that questioned the permissibility of genetic modification *per se* (e.g., arguing against gene technology because of its "unnaturalness") were grouped under the header of *moral concerns addressing the act itself*. Semantic units that were related to personal motivations, states, dispositions, or character traits of a moral agent and thus to a virtue or vice were grouped under the header of *moral concerns addressing the actor*.

RESULTS

Overview of Results

The great majority of articles were published in journals in the field of environmental ethics and almost half of all even in one single journal (*Journal of Agricultural and Environmental Ethics*) (see Table 1). With the exception of two articles (Cohen 1977; Dickson 1980), the reviewed literature was published between 1988 and 2008 (Fig. 1). Since then, growing attention to the use of GM crops in agriculture was apparent in the scrutinized literature. Most articles were published between 1999 and 2008.

Almost all articles from ecology journals and most of those from the other two types dealt with moral concerns addressing consequences (Table 3). However, concerns addressing the act or the actor were also prominent in the literature, especially in journals in the field of environmental ethics.

Moral Concerns Addressing Consequences

More than 80% of all articles addressed consequences of the use of GM crops in agriculture. They dealt primarily with general ecological and risk concerns and also discussed specific ecological issues about the use of gene technology (Table 4). Overall, 50 articles dealt with both types of concerns, 42 articles only with general ecological and risk concerns, and three articles only with specific ecological concerns.

GENERAL ECOLOGICAL AND RISK CONCERNS
Under this header we grouped all concerns about risk 20 assessment principles or general concepts (e.g., the concept of sustainability) that have ethical implications. Moreover, concerns about ecological risks and benefits that did not further specify the morally relevant entities affected by the presence of GM crops were grouped here. Four groups of moral concerns

Table 3

Assignment of Articles That Express a Certain Moral Concern to Three Different Types of Journals

	Number and proportion of articles by journal type		
	Ecology journals (15)	Environmental ethics journals (74)	Multidisciplinary science journals (24)
Moral concerns addressing consequences	14/93.3%	64/86.5%	17/70.8%
Moral concerns addressing the act	5/33.3%	49/66.2%	10/41.7%
Moral concerns addressing the actor	4/26.7%	38/51.4%	6/25.0%

Note. Multiple assignments were possible. List of journals in Table 1.

Table 4

Assignment of Articles to Moral Concerns Addressing Consequences of the Use of GM Crops in Agriculture

I. Moral concerns addressing consequences (95/84.1%)

1. General ecological and risk concerns (92/81.4%)	1.1. Concerns related to risk assessment, risk management, and risk perception (65/57.5%)	
	1.2. Concerns about (scientific) uncertainty (43/38.1%)	
	1.3. Concerns about sustainable development (28/24.8%)	
	1.4. Unspecified concerns about ecological risk and benefits (58/51.3%)	1.4.1. Socio-economic concerns (35/31.0%)
		1.4.2. Unspecified risk concerns (31/27.4%)
		1.4.3. Unspecified moral concerns (7/6.2%)
2. Specific ecological concerns (53/46.9%)	2.1. Concerns about the consequences for species and individual plants (29/25.7%)	
	2.2. Concerns about the consequences for ecosystems (36/31.9%)	
	2.3. Concerns about the consequences for the environment in general (10/8.8%)	

Note. Multiple assignments of articles were possible. In parentheses: number and proportion of articles.

were present in the literature (see Table 4): concerns related to risk assessment, risk management, and risk perception, concerns about (scientific) uncertainty, concerns about sustainable development, and unspecified concerns about ecological risk and benefits.

Concerns related to risk assessment, risk management, and risk perception were often mentioned or discussed in the literature (see Table 4). Overall, 62 of these articles were related to risk assessment, 12 to risk management, and 21 to risk perception. In 21 articles concerns about risk assessment and risk management were discussed in detail, most often addressing the precautionary principle (e.g., Carr 2002; Mayer and Stirling 2002; Myhr and Traavik 2002; Skorupinski 2002).

Concerns about (scientific) uncertainty were frequently present (see Table 4), but discussed in detail in only nine articles (Kasanmoentalib 1996; Carr and Levidow 2000; Carr 2002; Myhr and Traavik 2002; Myhr and Traavik 2003a; Howard and Donnelly 2004; Böschen et al. 2006; Jensen 2006; Ramjoué 2007). Articles under this header were mostly published in environmental ethics journals ($n = 27$). Those articles that merely mentioned uncertainty ($n = 34$) did this most often in the context of discussing environmental risk assessment ($n = 29$) and consequences ($n = 24$). Those articles that dealt with uncertainty in detail discussed, for instance, the ethical implications of unknown risks or unpredictable side-effects of GM crops (e.g., Kasanmoentalib 1996) or the concept of "non-knowledge" (Böschen et al. 2006).

Concerns about sustainable development were identified in about a quarter of all articles (see Table 4) and addressed in detail in ten articles. Most articles addressed the contribution of gene technology to the future development of agriculture (e.g., Duvick 1995; Wenz 1999; Pouteau 2000; Snow 2003). The sustainable development of agriculture, including societal questions, was discussed in detail in ecology journals (e.g., Hoffman and Carroll 1995), environmental ethics journals (e.g., Duvick 1995), and multidisciplinary science journals (e.g., Altmann and Ammann 1992).

Unspecified concerns about ecological risk and benefits could be sorted into socio-economic, unspecified

risk, and unspecified moral concerns (see Table 4). However, socio-economic concerns were only relevant when they referred to ecological/environmental ethical issues. *Socio-economic concerns* were identified in 35 articles (see Table 4). They included, for instance, concerns about social and environmental justice (e.g., Osborn 2002), concerns about benefits or harms for future generations (e.g., Wambugu 1999), the acknowledgement of "non-scientific" concerns of the public (e.g., Devos et al. 2008), or the establishment of a societal contract with the public (e.g., Bruce 2002a).

Unspecified risk concerns addressed environmental concerns about the release of GM crops that were not further specified. They were identified in 31 articles (see Table 4) and dealt, for instance, with underlying scientific principles for ecologically based risk assessment (e.g., Regal 1994) or invoked the image of farmers as "stewards of the countryside" who are involved in environmental protection (e.g., Hails 2002). The notion "stewards of the countryside" is related to moral concerns about the actor and thus linked to virtue ethics.

Unspecified moral concerns were present in seven articles (see Table 4) that dealt with general normative aspects of consequences of gene technology. These articles discussed the consequentialist implication of the "harm principle" as such (Holtug 2001), referred to potential benefits or harms of GM crops in context of the "future benefits argument"[8] (e.g., Burkhardt 2001), or addressed ecological risks in the light of underlying research paradigms of science (e.g., Scott 2005).

SPECIFIC ECOLOGICAL CONCERNS

Articles under this header were quite common in the assessed literature and mentioned or discussed ecological consequences for individual plants as well as for species, ecosystems, or the environment in general (see Table 4). Consequences in light of the moral status of *individual plants* were of hardly any

[8]The "future benefits argument" (FBA) is a utilitarian ethical argument offered by proponents of agricultural biotechnology to justify continued research and development in gene technology.

interest, even in environmental ethics journals. Only two articles (Balzer et al. 2000; Holtug 2001) went into detail about consequences for single plant organisms. Balzer et al. (2000) pointed out that the dignity of individual plants (in this article a consequentialist interpretation is favored) is violated if plants are prevented from performing the functions that members of their species can normally perform. Holtug (2001) addressed the impact of gene technology on individual organisms (in context of the consequentialist "harm principle"), but denied that plants could be violated, because they cannot suffer. Other articles discussed whether the use of GM crops is a violation of the value of *species and ecosystems* (Comstock 1989; Comstock 1990). Articles in this group also stated that certain effects such as gene flow or non-target effects might have (harmful) consequences for the *environment* in general. These articles discussed the impact on agricultural biodiversity in general (e.g., Gura 2001; Hails 2002; Kotschi 2008) or pointed out that farmland biodiversity might be increased by the use of herbicide-resistant crops (e.g., Madsen and Sandøe 2001).

Articles that dealt with specific ecological concerns often discussed ecological risks for certain entities on the background of risk assessment and its underlying principles ($n = 36$), especially the precautionary principle (e.g., Mayer and Stirling 2002; Myhr and Traavik 2002; Howard and Donnelly 2004). They also discussed ecological issues in the context of general concerns about risk and benefits ($n = 36$), for instance, the question whether the use of GM crops and organic farming is incompatible or not (e.g., Bruce 2003). Moreover, unknown risks and unpredictable side-effects of GM crops on certain species or the environment in general were discussed ($n = 24$) (e.g., Kasanmoentalib 1996; Clark and Lehmann 2001; Scott 2005). Articles in this group also addressed specific consequences for the environment invoking the concept of sustainable development ($n = 16$) (e.g., Wenz 1999; Krebs et al. 1999).

Moral Concerns Addressing the Act

Articles under this header addressed concerns about the value of naturalness, the value of biotic entities, and about conceptual reductionism (Table 5).

Table 5

Assignment of Articles to Moral Concerns Addressing the Act of Genetic Modification

II. Moral concerns addressing the act (64/56.6%)		
1. Concerns about the value of naturalness (56/49.6%)	1.1. Nature as a safety mechanism (31/27.4%)	
	1.2. Nature as a guiding principle (29/25.7%)	1.2.1. Nature as a given order (18/15.9%)
		1.2.2. Nature as an autonomous identity (19/16.8%)
	1.3. Undefined concerns (9/8.0%)	
2. Concerns about the value of biotic entities (27/23.9%)	2.1. Intrinsic value of holistic biotic entities (22/19.5%)	2.1.1. Intrinsic value of species (11/9.7%)
		2.1.2. Intrinsic value of ecosystems (5/4.4%)
		2.1.3. Intrinsic value of the biotic community (14/12.4%)
	2.2. Intrinsic value of individual biotic entities (5/4.4%)	
	2.3. Undefined concerns (3/2.7%)	
3. Concerns about conceptual reductionism (11/9.7%)		

Note. Multiple assignments of articles were possible. In parentheses: number and proportion of articles.

Such concerns were articulated in order to question the permissibility of gene technology *per se*. Overall, 30 articles dealt only with the value of naturalness and six only with the value of biotic entities. Moreover, one article dealt only with conceptual reductionism. However, 27 articles dealt with two different concerns and three articles with all three concerns.

The term "value"—in this context—means "intrinsic value," i.e., that objects or actions have an end in themselves and cannot be reduced to a mere instrumental value for humans (O'Neill et al. 2006). Some environmental philosophers such as Taylor (1986) distinguished between intrinsic value and inherent worth. In the literature assessed both notions were used in the same sense. The term "intrinsic value," of course, is not limited to moral concerns addressing the act.

CONCERNS ABOUT THE VALUE OF NATURALNESS

Naturalness as a value implies that nature and its order is valuable and good *per se*. Thus, all forms of genetic modification are unnatural and therefore morally wrong. None of the articles from ecology journals or multidisciplinary science journals explicitly referred to the value of naturalness. Overall, 15 articles from the environmental ethics journals discussed concerns about the value of naturalness as such (e.g., Katz 1993; Karafyllis 2003; Verhoog et al. 2003; Siipi 2008). Articles in ecology journals only indirectly addressed concerns about naturalness. Authors argued, for instance, that gene technology just simulates a natural process (Tiedje et al. 1989). They stated that barriers that are crossed by biotechnology are comparable to those constantly crossed in nature (Tiedje et al. 1989). It was also discussed whether gene technology is unnatural in the sense that it is the ultimate manifestation of the cybernetic control of humans (Elliott and Cole 1989).

Nature as a safety mechanism was addressed in 31 articles (see Table 5). This type of concern implies that "nature knows best," because nature is the result of a long evolutionary process (cf. Reiss and Straughan 2002). Therefore, the inherent safety mechanisms of nature should be protected as otherwise there would be a violation of natural evolution (Madsen et al. 2002). The intrinsic value of nature lies in the inherent safety

mechanisms of natural evolution and these mechanisms would no longer function as an insurance against disastrous consequences if humans disturb them (e.g., Madsen et al. 2002). The safety net of nature is helpful in situations where humans' assumptions about the functioning of nature might be proved wrong (e.g., Karafyllis 2003). As far as the emphasis is on the avoidance of disastrous consequences, the concept of nature as a safety mechanism can be regarded as a "moral concern addressing consequences" and grouped there. However, if nature as a safety mechanism is subsumed under the header of "moral concerns addressing the act," the intrinsic value of the safety mechanism lies in nature as such, which invokes that the violation of this intrinsic value is morally problematic *per se*.

Nature as a guiding principle was addressed in 29 articles (see Table 5). These articles dealt either with *nature as a given order* or with *nature as an autonomous identity*. The concept of *nature as a given order* defines nature as a non-human domain or as God's order that humans have to respect. The more human actions or products resemble natural actions or products, the more natural they are, and the more respect humans show for the natural order (Siipi 2008). The natural order, which has an intrinsic value, can be understood in terms of harmony and balance (Lammerts van Bueren and Struik 2005), self-realization (Katz 1993), God's creation (Comstock 1989), or "something out there" that humans must obey and should not challenge (Madsen et al. 2002). The genetic modification of crops is therefore an infringement of the given order and thus morally wrong.

The concept of *nature as an autonomous identity* states that an inherent purpose can be ascribed to nature as a whole or to single natural entities. When humans intervene in nature and create artifacts, they destroy the autonomy of nature by imposing a system of domination (Katz 1993). By inserting foreign genes into a plant's genome, borders of species are crossed and their identity is infringed. GM crops are therefore unnatural and, in consequence, morally wrong. Human beings are called to respect the autonomy of nature. The concept of nature as an autonomous identity can be linked to the virtue of appreciation (cf. Katz 1993).

CONCERNS ABOUT THE VALUE OF BIOTIC ENTITIES[9]

Articles under this header regarded gene technology as a violation of the intrinsic value of biotic entities, i.e., a disrespect to organisms and life in general. The term "intrinsic value" was either mentioned directly or indirectly by using terms like "integrity" or "dignity." Integrity is defined as the intrinsic value of a biotic entity that accomplishes its natural aim (Lammerts van Bueren and Struik 2005), which includes both individual and holistic entities, whereas dignity is assigned only to individual organisms (Balzer et al. 2000).[10] No one article in the ecology journals or the multidisciplinary science journals dealt with concerns about the value of biotic entities. In six articles published in the *Journal of Agricultural and Environmental Ethics* and in two articles published in the journal *Environmental Values* concerns about the value of biotic entities were discussed in detail. Among these articles, three dealt with the concepts "integrity" and "dignity" (Balzer et al. 2000; Melin 2004; Lammerts van Bueren and Struik 2005), three with the concept of "integrity" (Verhoog et al. 2003; Dobson 1995; Westra 1998), and one with the concept of "dignity" (Heeger 2000). Another article discussed the intrinsic value of animals and also mentioned that of plants (Verhoog 1992).

The *intrinsic value of holistic biotic entities* was addressed in 22 articles (see Table 5). In these articles, an intrinsic value is ascribed to species, (agricultural) ecosystems, or the whole biotic community. The *intrinsic value of species* lies in the "wholeness" of species, their ability to fulfill species-specific characteristics, and their being in balance with the environment (Lammerts van Bueren and Struik 2005). Every human action that hinders species to fulfill their species-specific characteristics would be morally wrong. Overall, 11 articles addressed such concerns about the intrinsic value of species (see Table 5).

Only five articles addressed the *intrinsic value of ecosystems* (see Table 5), which lies in the harmony

and balance of their biotic and abiotic elements (Verhoog et al. 2003; Deckers 2005; Lammerts van Bueren and Struik 2005). Humans should follow the "ecological knowledge of nature" in cultivating the land (Verhoog et al. 2003). As "ecological integrity" results from natural, evolutionary processes, human-induced interferences such as gene technology must be banned (Westra 1998).

The *intrinsic value of the biotic community* was expressed in 14 articles (see Table 5). This value lies in the ability of life for self-regulation in order to accomplish a certain inherent purpose (Lammerts van Bueren and Struik 2005). In this context, integrity is understood as the state of "wholeness" or "completeness" of life allowing it to perform all the functions that are characteristic for the biotic community. Verhoog (1992) discussed this concept in terms of something (recognizable by phenomena such as homeostasis, stability, balance, and equilibrium) that can be disturbed by human actions. Dobson (1995) understood the intrinsic value of the biotic community in a similar way, stating that genetic engineering could be problematic because it is a technology that expresses a worldview of human mastery over the non-human world.[11] Overall, eight articles dealing with the value of the biotic community addressed the "land ethics" and cited the well-known notion about the "integrity, stability, and beauty of the biotic community" (Comstock 1989; Verhoog 1992; Dobson 1995; Saner 2000). This integrity can be irreversibly disturbed by human actions such as gene technology (Verhoog 1992).

The *intrinsic value of individual biotic entities* was addressed in five articles (see Table 5). Three articles dealt with both the *concept of integrity* and the *concept of dignity*. One article referred only to the *concept of integrity* and stated that integrity can only be guaranteed if the specific phenotype of an individual plant is in balance with its environment (e.g., Lammerts van Bueren and Struik 2005). Another article pointed to the *concept of dignity*: Balzer et al. (2000) critically discussed a deontological interpretation of dignity and

---

[9] The term "biotic entities" refers to individual organisms as well as to species, ecosystems, or the biotic community.

[10] Balzer *et al.* (2000) discussed different meanings and understanding of dignity, including deontological meanings. However, they favored a consequentialist meaning.

[11] Concerns about the human mastery over the non-human world are also topics within virtue concerns.

also an interpretation based on the concept of the "telos" (aim of an organism) that corresponds with the genetic make-up of an organism. This interpretation defines a plant's well-being as the potential of the individual (characterized by its genetic make-up) to develop to maturity. According to these meanings of dignity, changing the genome through genetic modification would collide with the integrity or dignity of an organism. This is in line with a deontological interpretation of dignity or integrity and was thus grouped under the header of "moral concerns addressing the act." However, Balzer et al. (2000) favored a consequentialist interpretation of the "dignity of plants."

CONCERNS ABOUT CONCEPTUAL REDUCTIONISM

Articles under this header addressed the reductionist perspective in handling gene technology. Two different types of reductionism can be distinguished (Woese 2004): a *methodological reductionism* that is the mode of scientific analysis, and a *conceptual reductionism* that is part of a worldview stating that the whole is no more than the sum of its parts. Concerns about conceptual reductionism represent a fundamental critique of the materialistic worldview and of the treatment of biotic entities only as a means to an end and not as ends in themselves. For opponents of gene technology, such a conceptual reductionism is inherent in the genetic

modification of plants. In consequence, they condemn gene technology *per se*.

Concerns about conceptual reductionism were rarely expressed in the literature (see Table 5). Articles that dealt with the concern often addressed naturalness or the intrinsic value of organisms. For instance, one article stated that in a "process of reduction" the distinctions between the living and the non-living and between the "nature" of plants, animals, and humans disappears at the molecular level (Verhoog 1992). As the idea of "crossing species barriers" seems to be irrelevant at the molecular level, humanity is getting further and further away from nature as given to humans (Verhoog 1992). This "reduction of life to the digital code of DNA" is critically related to the fictional character of Frankenstein (Scott 2000) and thus to concerns about the value of naturalness. Moreover, the critique of reductionism was addressed in context of the perception of risks and scientific uncertainties about risks (e.g., Verhoog et al. 2003; Deckers 2005). Linked to this conceptual reductionism were concerns about the moral status of biotic entities (Verhoog et al. 2003; Deckers 2005).

Moral Concerns Addressing the Actor

Articles under this header referred to virtues related to the handling of risks or to the application of GM crops (Table 6). Overall, 26 articles dealt only with virtues

Table 6

Assignment of Articles to Moral Concerns Addressing the Actor

III. Moral concerns addressing the actor (48/42.5%)		
1. Virtues related to the handling of risks (29/25.7%)	1.1. Virtues related to trust in actors to handle risks (22/19.5%)	1.1.1. Trustworthiness
	1.2. Virtues related to responsible behavior and awareness of consequences (12/10.6%)	1.2.1. Responsibility
2. Virtues related to the application of GM crops (22/19.5%)	2.1. Virtues related to temperance in application of GM crops (16/6.4%)	2.1.1. Humility (11/9.7%)
		2.1.2. Wisdom (6/5.3%)
	2.2. Virtues related to integration into nature (8/3.2%)	2.2.1. Care (5/4.4%)
		2.2.2. Justice (4/3.5%)
	2.3. Virtues related to respect for non-human life (7/2.8%)	2.3.1. Appreciation

Note. Multiple assignments of articles were possible. In parentheses: number and proportion of articles.

related to the handling of risks, 19 only with virtues related to the application of GM crops, and three with both types. As concerns addressing the actor are linked to a person's character traits and want to define what constitute a "good life" of humans, they are part of virtue ethics.

Most articles did not discuss virtues as such ($n = 34$), but dealt indirectly with concerns about the actor by speaking of trust, precaution, or responsibility in handling risks (e.g., Altmann and Ammann 1992; Segal 2001). Nevertheless, in 14 articles concerns about the actor were addressed in detail: five articles discussed different types of virtue concerns (Bruce 2002b; Deane-Drummond 2002; Pascalev 2003; Sandler 2004; Kirkham 2006) and nine articles dealt with certain virtues such as trustworthiness, precaution, respect, or humility (Scott 2000; Mayer and Stirling 2002; Myhr and Traavik 2002; Bruce 2002a; Bruce 2003; Vogel 2003; Scott 2003; Munnichs 2004; Paula and Birrer 2006).

VIRTUES RELATED TO THE HANDLING OF RISKS
Virtues related to the handling of risks are trustworthiness and responsibility (see Table 6). The virtue of *trustworthiness* referred to trust (or distrust) of the public toward scientific researchers, regulatory procedures, as well as political and economic institutions (e.g., Scott 2003; Munnichs 2004). The virtue of *responsibility* referred to a general awareness of humans of the outcomes of their work and research (Altmann and Ammann 1992), care for the environment (Myhr and Traavik 2002), and care for the future (Deblonde and du Jardin 2005). Virtues related to the handling of risks are only indirectly dealing with environmental concerns as they focus on how scientists should behave and what the public (as consumers) can expect from sciences, politics, and the market. Thus, they are linked to socio-economic questions.

VIRTUES RELATED TO THE APPLICATION OF GM CROPS
Virtues referring to the application of GM crops were humility, wisdom, care, justice, and appreciation (see Table 6). The virtues *humility* and *wisdom* call for *temperance in the application of GM crops*. Humility acknowledges that humans can never entirely know the outcomes of their actions (Vogel 2003). This

virtue is morally required for a proper understanding of humans' relationship with the natural environment (Sandler 2004) and implies a certain handling of scientific procedures and knowledge (Mayer and Stirling 2002). Seen this way, the precautionary principle embodies humility regarding scientific procedures and knowledge (Mayer and Stirling 2002). The virtue of wisdom acknowledges that humans have to interact cautiously with their environment to avoid a domination of nature. Wisdom is closely related to the virtues of prudence, temperance, precaution, and practical wisdom (Deane-Drummond 2002).[12]

The virtues of *care* and *justice* apply to motivations and attitudes concerning humans' *integration into nature*. Care is related, for instance, to questions regarding the technological development (Atkinson 2002) or the sustainable approach in agriculture (Osborn 2002; Verhoog et al. 2003). The virtue of justice is understood as a disposition that takes into account the importance of non-human species as part of the overall ecological community (e.g., Deane-Drummond 2002). Justice is said to embody questions dealing with the precautionary principle (Deane-Drummond 2002; Osborn 2002).

The virtue of *appreciation* is *related to the respect for non-human life*, e.g., the respect for the abilities and vulnerabilities of non-human life (Wenz 1999), the respect for the existence of individual life-projects and goals (Westra 1998), or the reverence for the autonomy of nature as a whole (Katz 1993; Dobson 1995). As appreciation is dealing with the relationship of humans with nature, it is linked to deontological questions concerning the value of nature and its biotic entities (cf. Westra 1998).

DISCUSSION

Overview of the Academic Debate on GM Crops

We have identified three types of moral concerns in the academic debate on GM crops: (1) *moral concerns about the consequences* of the modification or of the

---

[12] We agree with Celia Deane-Drummond (2002), who states that the virtue of wisdom includes the virtues of prudence, temperance, precaution, and practical wisdom. Therefore, as long as these virtues were mentioned, they were considered as the virtue of wisdom.

outcomes of GM crops in the environment (associated with *consequentialist ethics*), (2) *moral concerns addressing the act* of modifying the genome of plants *per se* (associated with *deontological ethics*), and (3) *moral concerns addressing the actor's character traits and attitudes* affected by applying gene technology (associated with *virtue ethics*).

The ethical literature on gene technology often conceives the discussion as a disagreement between two moral concerns: consequentialist and deontological concerns (e.g., Runtenberg 1997; Reiss and Straughan 2002). However, our study shows that virtue concerns were also present in the debate, especially since 2001. This might reflect the growing interest in virtue concerns in environmental ethics in general (cf. Deane-Drummond 2004; Sandler and Cafaro 2004; Sandler 2007). Nevertheless, our results have to be taken with care: they might not be representative for the entire academic debate on moral concerns about the release of GM crops in agriculture as we deliberately selected certain types of journals.

Moral Concerns about the Use of GM Crops in the Academic Debate

Moral concerns addressing consequences invoked rarely the impact on individual plants (but see Balzer et al. 2000). Holtug (2001) stated that in context of the "harm principle," which in his opinion has to be the moral basis for the regulation of GM food, holistic entities such as biotic communities and plants as non-sentient entities are often excluded as they cannot suffer. However, in recent years it is discussed how to ascribe a morally relevant value to certain characteristics of plants in a consequentialist sense. One example is the "value of flourishing"[13] by Kallhoff (2002). This concept implies that it is in the "interest" of a plant to develop and grow according to its species-specific characteristics, complete its life cycle, and flourish in a stress-free environment. In a similar way, Attfield (2003) ascribed an intrinsic value to individual plants, including GM crops, as they can grow, photosynthesize and respire, reproduce and self-repair.

[13] In German: "*Wert des pflanzlichen Gedeihens.*"

The lack of articles dealing with the intrinsic value of individual organisms in a consequentialist way might be due to our focus on plants. Plants have no interests as they lack the ability to feel and express pain, which is crucial for sentientist* consequentialism to assign the intrinsic value to a biotic entity. Reiss and Straughan (2002) pointed out that questions about the moral status of organisms are more important in the debate on transgenic animals. Regarding transgenic plants, socio-economic questions are said to be more prominent (cf. Reiss and Straughan 2002; Gonzalez 2007). This was also reflected by our finding that articles referring to general environmental consequences of GM crops often dealt with questions concerning socio-economic aspects (e.g., Goga and Clementi 2002; Bruce 2002; Bruce 2003). Even articles in natural sciences journals (*Science* and *Nature*) dealt with socio-economic concerns such as concerns about food security and living conditions of farmers in developing countries (e.g., Serageldin 1999; Wambugu 1999).

General ecological concerns were often directed to risk assessment and risk management. This can be explained by the controversial debate on the underlying principles of risk assessment, following the adoption of the Cartagena Protocol in 2000 (cf. Nisbet and Huge 2007). Since then, the ethical implications of the precautionary principle and of the concept of substantial equivalence[14] were broadly discussed (e.g., Pouteau 2000). This is also reflected in the increasing number of articles addressing risk assessment (especially the precautionary principle) after the turn of the century in our literature review (e.g., Mayer and Stirling 2002; Skorupinski 2002; Myhr and Traavik 2003a; Myhr and Traavik 2003b). One element of this discourse [involves] concerns about (scientific) uncertainty that are frequently addressed in the literature (e.g., Kasanmoentalib 1996; Carr and Levidow 2000; Myhr and Traavik 2002; Böschen et al. 2006). Uncertainty is closely related to questions about the acceptability of

sentientist: someone who believes that other creatures have sentience, or distinct thoughts.

[14] Sustainable equivalence is a concept that states that GM food should be considered the same as conventional food if it shows the same characteristics and composition as the conventional food.

certain risks, the trade-off between benefits and harms, and scientific research or risk assessment as such. In this context, questions arise with which scientists are unfamiliar, for example, how to define acceptable ecological risks, how to address different risk perceptions in a liberal society (e.g., Jensen 2006), or how to deal with different approaches in risk assessment in Europe and in the United States (e.g., Ramjoué 2007).

General ecological concern not only addressed risk assessment, but also the future of agriculture and the possible contribution of gene technology to a sustainable development. In articles discussing sustainable agriculture most often the safety of GM crops, the value of naturalness (used especially in context of organic farming), or socio-economic questions like the market concentration in global seed industry are addressed. However, the contribution of gene technology to a sustainable agriculture is a controversially discussed concern in the literature, i.e., whether gene technology is a sustainable approach or not. This controversy might be based on different understandings and definitions of sustainable agriculture. This is especially true if only organic farming is considered as a sustainable form of agriculture (cf. Verhoog 1997).

Moral concerns addressing the act, in particular those about naturalness, were common in the reviewed literature. Using naturalness in a normative sense either for or against gene technology is seen as a "naturalistic fallacy" (e.g., criticized by Comstock 1989 and Myskja 2006). A naturalistic fallacy is committed whenever a statement or argument attempts to prove that something *is* in a certain way natural and therefore *ought to be* that way. It has also been criticized that concerns about naturalness are quite meaningless, as there are many different meanings and types of naturalness (Cooley and Goreham 2004; Siipi 2008).

Concerns about the value of biotic entities were less prominent in the reviewed literature than concerns about the value of naturalness. Most often, an intrinsic value was assigned to holistic biotic entities such as species, ecosystems, or the biotic community, whereas only few articles assigned an intrinsic value to individual plants. Even among environmental ethicists

no consensus exists whether an intrinsic value can be assigned to individual plants (e.g., Melin 2004).

Moral concerns addressing the actor were linked in several articles to moral concerns addressing the act (pointing to deontological ethics) (e.g., Katz 1993; Westra 1998; Kirkham 2006). For instance, notions such as "vexing nature" or "playing God," which are used in context of act-orientated concerns, also have virtue-based implications invoking questions about the purpose of technology and the place of humanity within the natural environment (Kirkham 2006). Among actor-based concerns, *virtues that are related to the handling of risks* were important. Most often, the virtues of trustworthiness (of science as well as of politics and the market) and responsibility were mentioned. These virtues imply that actors are concerned about their actions and act in ways that promote or maintain environmental goods or values. When focusing on risks and benefits, i.e., on the outcome of gene technology, virtues like responsibility can be linked to concerns about consequences.

In the last decade, virtues such as humility, wisdom, care, justice, and appreciation have received increasing attention in environmental ethics. These virtues, which we grouped under the header of "*virtues related to the application of GM crops*," are justified by the worth of living organisms and humans' relationship with nature (cf. Sandler 2007). Because living organisms are valuable, humans have to behave prudently and respectfully toward them. Seen in this way, virtues related to the application of GM crops deal with the respect for living organisms and can overlap with act-orientated concerns. For example, the virtue of humility and the closely related virtue of caution can be linked to the concept of ecological integrity (Westra 1998). Moreover, virtues related to the application of GM crops can be linked to concerns addressing consequences. For instance, the precautionary principle with its aim to minimize ecological risks is based on consequentialist concerns. However, precaution is also related to attitudes of an actor, especially to the virtues of wisdom and care (cf. Deane-Drummond 2002; Mayer and Stirling 2002). To have such a virtue-based interpretation of the precautionary principle in mind is helpful to avoid misunderstandings in the public debate.

Virtue concerns can be linked to other types of moral concerns, i.e., concerns addressing the act and concerns addressing consequences. Moral concerns addressing the actor can thus help to overcome the often presupposed dichotomy of consequentialist and deontological concerns in the debate on the use of GM crops. Pluralistic forms of virtue ethics theories exist that integrate non-virtue-based reasons that play a role in deontology or consequentialism (Crisp 2003). For instance, it was stated by Hursthouse (2003) that virtue ethics appear to stand "shoulder to shoulder" with deontology. With the focus on the individual person's character traits, virtue ethics add a new viewpoint to the overall ethical debate, as the actor is not the prime focus in consequentialism or deontology.

In the reviewed literature, environmental concerns were closely linked to socio-economic concerns in several articles, for example, to questions about ecological and social justice or to the trustworthiness of science, politics, and the market (e.g., Wambugu 1999; Scott 2000; Scott 2003; Goga and Clementi 2002; Bruce 2002a; Bruce 2003). This shows that the debate about the ecological and environmental ethical aspects of GM crops is also a debate about the role of science, the role of politics and the market, and the role of laypersons in public as consumers. It is therefore doubtful whether the environmental debate on GM crops can be held separately from the debate on socio-economic aspects or whether they are mutually dependent.

Comparison of the Academic and Laypersons' Debate on the Use of GM Crops

Moral concerns of laypersons play an important role in the public debate on GM crops. Although moral concerns and arguments similar to those expressed by academics are put forward by laypersons in the public debate, laypersons' concerns do not only reflect scientific arguments associated with gene technology (cf. Harlander 1991), but also more fundamental personal beliefs (Hoban et al. 1992). Moreover, the risk perception between laypersons and scientific experts (in the field of biological sciences) differs in certain points: experts significantly and systematically perceive biotechnology as less risky than laypersons do (Savadori et al. 2004; Sjöberg 2008) and consider its applications in food production as more useful (Savadori et al. 2004). However, despite these dissimilarities *moral concerns addressing consequences* are prominent in the public debate on GM crops or GM food, too (e.g., Frewer et al. 1997a; Saba et al. 1998; Gaskell 2000; Gaskell et al. 2000; Magnusson and Koivisto Hursti 2002; Amin et al. 2007; Chen and Li 2007; Henson et al. 2008).

Moral concerns addressing the act are often invoked in the moral reasoning of laypersons (Hansen et al. 2003; Frewer et al. 2004; Siegrist 2008; Tanner et al. 2008). This is especially true for concerns about naturalness: about 65% of the participants in the 2002 Eurobarometer survey agreed that GM food threatens the natural order of things (Peters and Sawicka 2007). Concerns about the loss of naturalness have been recognized as important constituents of unease among the public (e.g., Reif and Melich 1996; Frewer et al. 1997b; Melich 2000). Naturalness concerns are often addressed by the public to express a desire for a world untouched by humans (Dürnberger 2008). However, laypersons are less concerned about the infringement of the intrinsic value in modifying plants than in the modification of animals (cf. Frewer et al. 1997a; Kinsey and Senauer 1997; Ganiere et al. 2006). In the academic debate, the moral status of plants appears to be less important.

In contrast to concerns addressing consequences of the act itself, *moral concerns addressing the actor* were rarely found in recent studies on the laypersons' perception of gene technology. However, several surveys have shown that trustworthiness is crucial for laypersons (Brown and Ping 2003; Frewer 2003; Gaskell et al. 2003; Hansen et al. 2003; Frewer et al. 2004; Savadori et al. 2004; Chen and Li 2007; Siegrist 2008). Therefore, virtues essential for handling risks are important for initiating and establishing a dialogue between academic experts and laypersons.

Similar to academic experts, laypersons base their moral reasoning about GM crops on concerns about perceived risks, unnaturalness, and personal ethical beliefs. However, conflicts within the public about GM crops are not likely to be solved by more knowledge about potential ecological risks. These conflicts are deeply rooted in personal ideas about life and nature, i.e., deontological and virtue concerns, which are important for the moral reasoning of laypersons, as recent psychological research showed (Tanner et al. 2008). Social and psychological scientists could help to identify factors that motivate and lead people to certain attitudes toward gene technology. Knowing the motivations of others makes it easier to take their position seriously, accepting that they do not act in bad faith but simply against a different normative backdrop. In this regard, ethicists are important for the dialogue between academic experts and laypersons in the public: they can discuss how moral concerns are used by laypersons and how a sound and well-grounded moral reasoning has to be established. Moreover, natural scientists can contribute to the debate with their expertise on ecological concerns. Knowledge of risks and benefits is fundamental for moral reasoning, especially for consequentialist ethics.

CONCLUSIONS

The literature review showed that there is no single dichotomy between moral concerns addressing consequences and the act, i.e., consequentialist and deontological concerns. Moral concerns addressing the actor, i.e., virtue concerns, were also present and linked with the other two concerns (cf. Crisp 2003; Hursthouse 2003). Environmental virtue ethics with its focus on the individual actor could help to bridge the split between deontological and consequentialist concerns. Psychological research on act choices (Tanner et al. 2008) indicates that deontological and consequentialist concerns are not mutually exclusive in the reasoning of laypersons: different types of moral concerns are often intertwined in laypersons' decision-making on act choices.

The perception of gene technology by academic experts, especially by natural scientists, differs from that of laypersons. The moral reasoning of academic experts is well founded on ecological concerns; their arguments are carefully considered and critically discussed. However, among laypersons, ecological concerns are more often associated with personal lifestyles and individual preferences (Korthals 2001; Meijboom et al. 2003). Ethics as the discipline that analyzes and justifies moral reasoning could help to take into account moral concerns of the general public in the debate on the use of GM crops by establishing an "empirically informed ethics" (cf. Musschenga 2005). Empirically informed ethics combines doing empirical research with philosophical analysis and reflection (Musschenga 2005). It could improve the context sensitivity in the debate on GM crops, for example, by addressing the personal lifestyles of laypersons. As consumers, laypersons are not only concerned with risk and safety of GM crops, but also follow personal preferences in their decisions (Korthals 2001). Ethicists could bridge the gap between the moral perception of (natural) scientists and laypersons with the help of an empirically informed ethics.

In moral philosophy, models are used that help to structure and analyze a moral debate. Moreover, practical tools for decision-making processes that integrate different moral concerns are provided. Such models and tools were developed, for instance, by Fraser (2001), Busch et al. (2002), Forsberg (2007), and Mepham (2008). The aim of such tools is to support a systematic public deliberation about the ethical aspects of agricultural biotechnologies (Beekman and Brom 2007). However, they rarely include virtue concerns and, if so, only address the virtue of justice. The present results exemplify the relevance of different virtues in the ecological discourse on the release of GM crops that should be integrated in the respective models and tools. They can help to overcome the focus in the debate on deontology and consequentialism. An example of how to integrate virtue concerns is the tool for ethical decision-making by Bleisch and Huppenbauer (2011).

Our study is the first to provide a comprehensive overview of the moral reasoning expressed in academic publications on the use of GM crops. It shows which types of moral concerns are expressed in the debate, how they are mutually linked, and could thus contribute to a better understanding of the academic debate on the release of GM crops. It would be helpful to investigate the public debate in the same way. To know the various types of moral concerns and their different usage in the academic as well as in the public debate would be a crucial starting point to develop a fruitful dialogue between sciences and the general public.

ACKNOWLEDGMENTS

We would like to thank the University Research Priority Programme Ethics (Universitärer Forschungsschwerpunkt Ethik) of the Ethics-Center, University of Zurich, for financial support, and Bernhard Schmid, Roger Busch, Marc Hall, and Oliver Jütersonke for providing valuable comments on the original manuscript. We would also like to thank the reviewers for helpful comments on a previous version of this manuscript.

REFERENCES

Altmann, M., & Ammann, K. (1992). Gentechnologie im gesellschaftlichen Spannungsfeld: Züchtung transgener Kulturpflanzen. *GAIA, 1*(4), 204–213.

Amin, L., Jahi, J., Nor, A. R., Osman, M., & Mahadi, N. M. (2007). Public acceptance of modern biotechnology. *Asia Pacific Journal of Molecular Biology and Biotechnology, 15*(2), 39–51.

Ammann, K., Jacot, Y., & Braun, R. (Eds.). (2003). *Methods for risk assessment of transgenic plants, IV. Biodiversity and biotechnology*. Basel: Birkhäuser Verlag.

Annas, J. (2006). Virtue ethics. In D. Copp (Ed.), *The Oxford handbook of ethical theory* (pp. 515–536). New York: Oxford University Press.

Atkinson, D. (2002). Agriculture—reconciling ancient tensions. *Ethics in Science and Environmental Politics, 2*(2002), 52–58.

Attfield, R. (2003). *Environmental ethics*. Cambridge: Polity Press.

Balzer, P., Rippe, K. P., & Schaber, P. (1998). *Menschenwürde vs. Würde der Kreatur*. München: Alber.

Balzer, P., Rippe, K. P., & Schaber, P. (2000). Two concepts of dignity for humans and non-human organisms in the context of genetic engineering. *Journal of Agricultural and Environmental Ethics, 13*(1), 7–27.

Beekman, V., & Brom, F. W. A. (2007). Ethical tools to support systematic public deliberations about the ethical aspects of agricultural biotechnologies. *Journal of Agricultural and Environmental Ethics, 20*(1), 3–12.

Birnbacher, D. (2007). *Analytische Einführung in die Ethik*. Berlin and New York: Walter de Gruyter.

Bleisch, B., & Huppenbauer, M. (2011). *Ethische Entscheidungsfindung. Ein Handbuch für die Praxis*. Zürich: Versus Verlag.

Böschen, S., Kastenhofer, K., Marschall, L., Rust, I., Soentgen, J., & Wehling, P. (2006). Scientific cultures of non-knowledge in the controversy over genetically modified organisms (GMO). *GAIA, 15*(4), 294–301.

Brennan, A., & Lo, Y.-S. (2008). Environmental ethics. In *Stanford encyclopedia of philosophy*, first published Mon Jun 3, 2002; substantive revision Thu Jan 3, 2008, plato.stanford.edu/entries/ethics-environmental/.

Brink, D. O. (2006). Some forms and limits of consequentialism. In D. Copp (Ed.), *The Oxford handbook of ethical theory* (pp. 380–423). New York: Oxford University Press.

Brookes, G., & Barfoot, P. (2005). GM crops: The global economic and environmental impact—the first nine years 1996–2004. *AgBioForum, 8*(2&3), 187–196.

Brown, J. L., & Ping, Y. (2003). Consumer perception of risk associated with eating genetically engineered soybeans is less in the presence of a perceived consumer benefit. *Journal of the American Dietetic Association, 103*(2), 208–214.

Bruce, D. (2002a). A social contract for biotechnology: Shared visions for risky technologies? *Journal of Agricultural and Environmental Ethics, 15*(3), 279–289.

Bruce, D. (2002b). GM ethical decision making in practice. *Ethics in Science and Environmental Politics, 2*(2002), 75–78.

Bruce, D. (2003). Contamination, crop trials, and compatibility. *Journal of Agricultural and Environmental Ethics, 16*(6), 595–604.

Burkhardt, J. (2001). Agricultural biotechnology and the future benefits argument. *Journal of Agricultural and Environmental Ethics, 14*(2), 135–145.

Busch, R. J., Knoepffler, N., Haniel, A., & Wenzel, G. (2002). *Grüne Gentechnik. Ein Bewertungsmodell*. München: Utz Verlag.

Carr, S. (2002). Ethical and value-based aspects of the European commission's precautionary principle. *Journal of Agricultural and Environmental Ethics, 15*(1), 31–38.

Carr, S., & Levidow, L. (2000). Exploring the links between science, risk, uncertainty, and ethics in regulatory controversies about genetically modified crops. *Journal of Agricultural and Environmental Ethics, 12*(1), 29–39.

Chen, M.-F., & Li, H.-L. (2007). The consumer's attitude toward genetically modified foods in Taiwan. *Food Quality and Preference, 18*(4), 662–674.

Clark, E. A., & Lehmann, H. (2001). Assessment of GM crops in commercial agriculture. *Journal of Agricultural and Environmental Ethics, 14*(1), 3–28.

Cohen, S. N. (1977). Recombinant DNA: Fact and fiction. *Science, 195*(4279), 654–657.

Comstock, G. (1989). Genetically engineered herbicide resistance, Part One. *Journal of Agricultural and Environmental Ethics, 2*(4), 263–306.

Comstock, G. (1990). Genetically engineered herbicide resistance, Part Two. *Journal of Agricultural and Environmental Ethics, 3*(2), 114–146.

Cooley, D. R., & Goreham, G. A. (2004). Are transgenic organisms unnatural? *Ethics and the Environment, 9*(1), 46–55.

Cowgill, S. E., Danks, C., & Atkinson, H. J. (2004). Multitrophic interactions involving genetically modified potatoes, nontarget aphids, natural enemies and hyperparasitoids. *Molecular Ecology, 13*(3), 639–647.

Crisp, R. (2003). Modern moral philosophy and the virtues. In R. Crisp (Ed.), *How should one live? Essays on the Virtues* (pp. 1–18). Oxford: Oxford University Press.

Deane-Drummond, C. E. (2002). Wisdom with justice. *Ethics in Science and Environmental Politics, 2*(2002), 65–74.

Deane-Drummond, C. E. (2004). *The ethics of nature.* Malden: Blackwell Publications.

Deblonde, M., & du Jardin, P. (2005). Deepening a precautionary European policy. *Journal of Agricultural and Environmental Ethics, 18*(4), 319–343.

Deckers, J. (2005). Are scientists right and non-scientists wrong? Reflections on discussions of GM. *Journal of Agricultural and Environmental Ethics, 18*(5), 451–478.

Devos, Y., Maeseele, P., Reheul, D., van Speybroeck, L., & de Waele, D. (2008). Ethics in the societal debate on genetically modified organisms: A (re)quest for sense and sensibility. *Journal of Agricultural and Environmental Ethics, 21*(1), 29–61.

Dickson, D. (1980). Patenting living organisms—how to beat the bug-rustlers. *Nature, 283*(5743), 128–129.

Dobson, A. (1995). Biocentrism and genetic engineering. *Environmental Values, 3*(4), 227–239.

Dürnberger, C. (2008). Der Mythos der Ursprünglichkeit: Landwirtschaftliche Idylle und ihre Rolle in der öffentlichen Wahrnehmung. *Forum TTN, 2008*(19), 45–52.

Duvick, D. N. (1995). Biotechnology is compatible with sustainable agriculture. *Journal of Agricultural and Environmental Ethics, 8*(2), 112–125.

Elliott, E. T., & Cole, C. V. (1989). A perspective on agroecosystem science. *Ecology, 6*(70), 1597–1602.

Firbank, L. G., & Forcella, F. (2000). Genetically modified crops and farmland biodiversity. *Science, 289*(5484), 1481–1482.

Forsberg, E.-M. (2007). Value pluralism and coherentist justification of ethical advice. *Journal of Agricultural and Environmental Ethics, 20*(1), 81–97.

Fraser, V. (2001). What's the moral of the GM food story? *Journal of Agricultural and Environmental Ethics, 14*(2), 147–159.

Frewer, L. J. (2003). Societal issues and public attitudes towards genetically modified foods. *Trends in Food Science and Technology, 14*(5–8), 319–332.

Frewer, L. J., Hedderley, D., Howard, C., & Shepherd, R. (1997a). "Objection" mapping in determining group and individual concerns regarding genetic engineering. *Agriculture and Human Values, 14*(1), 67–79.

Frewer, L. J., Howard, C., & Shepherd, R. (1997b). Public concerns in the United Kingdom about general and specific applications of genetic engineering: Risk, benefit, and ethics. *Science, Technology and Human Values, 22*(1), 98–124.

Frewer, L. J., Lassen, J., Kettlitz, B., Scholderer, J., Beekman, V., & Berdal, K. G. (2004). Societal aspects of genetically modified foods. *Food and Chemical Toxicology, 42*(7), 1181–1193.

Ganiere, P., Chern, W., & Hahn, D. (2006). A continuum of consumer attitudes toward genetically modified foods in the United States. *Journal of Agricultural and Resource Economics, 31*(1), 129–149.

Gaskell, G. (2000). Agricultural biotechnology and public attitudes in the European Union. *AgBioForum, 3*(2–3), 87–96.

Gaskell, G., Allum, N., Bauer, M., Durant, J., Allansdottir, A., Bonfadelli, H., et al. (2000). Biotechnology and the European public. *Nature Biotechnology, 18*(9), 935–938.

Gaskell, G., Allum, N., & Stares, S. (2003). Europeans and biotechnology in 2002—Eurobarometer 58.0 (2nd Edn. March 21st 2003). A report to the EC Directorate General for Research from the project "Life Sciences in European Society" QLG7-CT-1999-00286.

Gaus, G. F. (2001a). What is deontology? Part one: Orthodox views. *Journal of Value Inquiry, 35*(1), 27–42.

Gaus, G. F. (2001b). What is deontology? Part two: Reasons to act. *Journal of Value Inquiry, 35*(2), 179–193.

Goga, B. T. C., & Clementi, F. (2002). Safety assurance of foods: Risk management depends on good science but it is not a scientific activity. *Journal of Agricultural and Environmental Ethics, 15*(3), 305–313.

Gonzalez, C. G. (2007). Genetically modified organisms and justice: The international environmental justice implications of biotechnology. *Georgetown International Environmental Law Review, 19*(4), 583–610.

Gura, T. (2001). The battlefields of Britain. *Nature, 412*(6849), 760–763.

Hails, R. S. (2000). Genetically modified plants—the debate continues. *Trends in Ecology & Evolution, 15*(1), 14–18.

Hails, R. S. (2002). Assessing the risks associated with new agricultural practices. *Nature, 418*(6898), 685–688.

Hansen, J., Holma, L., Frewer, L. J., Robinson, P., & Sandøe, P. (2003). Beyond the knowledge deficit: Recent research into lay and expert attitudes to food risks. *Appetite, 41*(2), 111–121.

Harlander, S. K. (1991). Social, moral, and ethical issues in food biotechnology. *Food Technology, 45*(5), 152–159.

Harwood, J. D., Wallin, W. G., & Obrycki, J. J. (2005). Uptake of Bt endotoxins by nontarget herbivores and higher order arthropod predators: Molecular evidence from a transgenic corn agroecosystem. *Molecular Ecology, 14,* 2815–2823.

Heaf, D., & Wirz, J. (Eds.) (2002). *Genetic engineering and the intrinsic value and integrity of animals and plants.* Proceedings of a Workshop at the Royal Botanic Garden, Edinburgh. Hafan: Ifgene.

Heeger, R. (2000). Genetic engineering and the dignity of creatures. *Journal of Agricultural and Environmental Ethics, 13*(1), 43–51.

Henson, S., Annou, M., Cranfield, J., & Ryks, J. (2008). Understanding consumer attitudes toward food technologies in Canada. *Risk Analysis, 28*(6), 1601–1617.

Herold, N. (2008). Pflicht ist Pflicht! Oder nicht? Eine Einführung in die Deontologische Ethik. In J. S. Ach, K. Bayertz, & L. Siep (Eds.), *Grundkurs Ethik. Band 1: Grundlagen* (pp. 71–90). Paderborn: Mentis Verlag.

Ho, M.-W., Ryan, A., & Cummins, J. (1999). Cauliflower mosaic viral promoter—a recipe for disaster? *Microbial Ecology in Health and Disease, 11*(4), 194–197.

Hoban, T. J., Woodrum, E., & Czaja, R. (1992). Public opposition to genetic engineering. *Rural Sociology, 57*(4), 476–493.

Hoffman, C. A., & Carroll, C. R. (1995). Can we sustain the biological basis of agriculture? *Annual Review of Ecology, Evolution and Systematics, 26*(1995), 69–92.

Holtug, N. (2001). The harm principle and genetically modified food. *Journal of Agricultural and Environmental Ethics, 14*(2), 169–178.

Howard, J. A., & Donnelly, K. C. (2004). A quantitative safety assessment model for transgenic protein products produced in agricultural crops. *Journal of Agricultural and Environmental Ethics, 17*(6), 545–558.

Hursthouse, R. (2003). Normative virtue ethics. In R. Crisp (Ed.), *How should one live? Essays on the virtues* (pp. 19–36). Oxford: Oxford University Press.

Jensen, K. K. (2006). Conflict over risks in food production: A challenge for democracy. *Journal of Agricultural and Environmental Ethics, 19*(3), 269–283.

Kallhoff, A. (2002). *Prinzipien der Pflanzenethik. Die Bewertung pflanzlichen Lebens in Biologie und Philosophie.* New York and Frankfurt: Campus Verlag.

Karafyllis, N. C. (2003). Renewable resources and the idea of nature—what has biotechnology got to do with it? *Journal of Agricultural and Environmental Ethics, 16*(1), 3–28.

Kasanmoentalib, S. (1996). Science and values in risk assessment: The case of deliberate release of genetically engineered organisms. *Journal of Agricultural and Environmental Ethics, 9*(1), 42–60.

Katz, E. (1993). Artefacts and functions: A note on the value of nature. *Environmental Value, 2*(3), 223–232.

Kinsey, J., & Senauer, B. (1997). Food marketing in an electronic age: Implications for agriculture. *Choices, 12*(2nd Quarter), 32–35.

Kirkham, G. (2006). "Playing god" and "vexing nature": A cultural perspective. *Environmental Values, 15*(2), 173–195.

Korthals, M. (2001). Taking consumers seriously: Two concepts of consumer sovereignty. *Journal of Agricultural and Environmental Ethics, 14*(2), 201–215.

Kotschi, J. (2008). Transgenic crops and their impact on biodiversity. *GAIA, 17*(1), 36–41.

Krebs, J. R., Bradbury, R. B., Wilson, J. D., & Siriwardena, G. M. (1999). The second silent spring? *Nature, 400*(6753), 611–612.

Lammerts van Bueren, E., & Struik, P. (2005). Integrity and rights of plants: Ethical notions in organic plant breeding and propagation. *Journal of Agricultural and Environmental Ethics, 18*(5), 479–493.

Madsen, K. H., Holm, P. B., Lassen, J., & Sandøe, P. (2002). Ranking genetically modified plants according to familiarity. *Journal of Agricultural and Environmental Ethics, 15*(3), 267–278.

Madsen, K. H., & Sandøe, P. (2001). Herbicide resistant sugar beet—What is the problem? *Journal of Agricultural and Environmental Ethics, 14*(2), 161–168.

Magnusson, M. K., & Koivisto Hursti, U.-K. (2002). Consumer attitudes towards genetically modified foods. *Appetite, 39*(1), 9–24.

Marvier, M. (2002). Improving risk assessment for nontarget safety of transgenic crops. *Ecological Applications, 12*(4), 1119–1124.

Marvier, M., & Van Acker, R. C. (2005). Can crop transgenes be kept on a leash? *Frontiers in Ecology and Environment, 3*(2), 99–106.

Mayer, S., & Stirling, A. (2002). Finding a precautionary approach to technological developments—lessons for the evaluation of GM crops. *Journal of Agricultural and Environmental Ethics, 15*(1), 57–71.

McNaughton, D., & Rawling, P. (2006). Chapter 15. Deontology. In D. Copp (Ed.), *The Oxford handbook of ethical theory* (pp. 425–458). New York: Oxford University Press.

Meijboom, F. L. B., Verweij, M. F., & Brom, F. W. A. (2003). You eat what you are: Moral dimensions of diets tailored to one's genes. *Journal of Agricultural and Environmental Ethics, 16*(6), 557–568.

Melich, A. (2000). Modern biotechnology, quality of life, and consumers' access to justice—Eurobarometer 52.1 (Nov–Dec 1999). Conducted by INRA (Europe), Brussels. ICPSR02893-v4. Cologne, Germany: GESIS/Ann Arbor, MI. Inter-University Consortium for Political and Social Research [distributors].

Melin, A. (2004). Genetic engineering and the moral status of non-human species. *Journal of Agricultural and Environmental Ethics, 17*(6), 479–495.

Mepham, B. (2008). *Bioethics. An introduction for the biosciences* (2nd ed.). Oxford, New York: Oxford University Press.

Munnichs, G. (2004). Whom to trust? Public concerns, late modern risks, and expert trustworthiness. *Journal of Agricultural and Environmental Ethics, 17*(2), 113–130.

Musschenga, A. (2005). Empirical ethics, context-sensitivity, and contextualism. *Journal of Medicine and Philosophy, 30*(5), 467–490.

Myhr, A. I., & Traavik, T. (2002). The precautionary principle: Scientific uncertainty and omitted research in the context of GMO use and release. *Journal of Agricultural and Environmental Ethics, 15*(1), 73–86.

Myhr, A. I., & Traavik, T. (2003a). Genetically modified (GM) crops: Precautionary science and conflicts of interests. *Journal of Agricultural and Environmental Ethics, 16*(3), 227–247.

Myhr, A. I., & Traavik, T. (2003b). Sustainable development and Norwegian genetic engineering regulations: Applications, impacts, and challenges. *Journal of Agricultural and Environmental Ethics, 16*(4), 317–335.

Myskja, B. K. (2006). The moral difference between intragenic and transgenic modification of plants. *Journal of Agricultural and Environmental Ethics, 19*(3), 225–238.

Nisbet, M. C., & Huge, M. (2007). Where do science debates come from? Understanding attention cycles and framing. In D. Brossard, J. Shanahan, & T. C. Nesbitt (Eds.), *The media, the public and agricultural biotechnology* (pp. 193–230). London: CABI Publishing.

O'Neill, J., Holland, A., & Light, A. (2006). *Environmental values (Routledge Introductions to Environment)*. New York: Routledge Group.

Osborn, D. (2002). Stretching the frontiers of precaution. *Ethics in Science and Environmental Politics, 2*(2002), 37–41.

Pascalev, A. (2003). You are what you eat: Genetically modified foods, integrity, and society. *Journal of Agricultural and Environmental Ethics, 16*(6), 583–594.

Paula, L., & Birrer, F. (2006). Including public perspectives in industrial biotechnology and the biobased economy. *Journal of Agricultural and Environmental Ethics, 19*(3), 253–267.

Peters, H. P., & Sawicka, M. (2007). German reactions to genetic engineering in food production. In D. Brossard, J. Shanahan, & T. C. Nesbitt (Eds.), *The public, the media and agricultural biotechnology* (pp. 57–96). Wallingford (UK): CABI Publishing.

Pilson, D., & Prendeville, H. R. (2004). Ecological effects of transgenic crops and the escape of transgenes into wild populations. *Annual Review of Ecology, Evolution, and Systematics, 35*(1), 149–174.

Pouteau, S. (2000). Beyond substantial equivalence: Ethical equivalence. *Journal of Agricultural and Environmental Ethics, 13*(3–4), 271–291.

Ramjoué, C. (2007). The transatlantic rift in genetically modified food policy. *Journal of Agricultural and Environmental Ethics, 20*(5), 419–436.

Regal, P. J. (1994). Scientific principles for ecologically based risk assessment of transgenic organisms. *Molecular Ecology, 3*(1), 5–13.

Reif, K., & Melich, A. (1996). Biotechnology and genetic engineering: What Europeans think about biotechnology—Eurobarometer 39.1 (First ICPSR Edition, April 1996). Conducted by INRA (Europe), Brussels. ICPSR ed. Ann Arbor, MI. Interuniversity Consortium for Political and Social Research [producer], Köln. Zentralarchiv für Empirische Sozialforschung/Ann Arbor, MI. Inter-University Consortium for Political and Social Research [distributors].

Reiss, M. J., & Straughan, R. (2002). *Improving nature*. Cambridge: Cambridge University Press.

Rippe, K. P., & Schaber, P. (1998). Einleitung. In K. P. Rippe & P. Schaber (Eds.), *Tugendethik* (pp. 7–18). Stuttgart: Philipp Reclam jun.

Robinson, J. (1999). Ethics and transgenic crops: A review. *Electronic Journal of Biotechnology, 2*(2), 71–81.

Rolston, H., III. (1999). *Genes, genesis and god. Values and their origins in natural and human history*. Cambridge: Cambridge University Press.

Runtenberg, C. (1997). Argumentationen im Kontext angewandter Ethik: das Beispiel Gentechnologie. In N. Herold & S. Mischer (Eds.), *Philosophie: Studium, Text and Argument* (pp. 179–193). Münster: LIT-Verlag.

Saba, A., Moles, A., & Frewer, L. J. (1998). Public concerns about general and specific applications of genetic engineering: A comparative study between the UK and Italy. *Nutrition and Food Science, 98*(1), 19–29.

Sandler, R. (2004). An aretaic objection to agricultural biotechnology. *Journal of Agricultural and Environmental Ethics, 17*(3), 301–317.

Sandler, R. (2007). *Character and environment. A virtue-oriented approach to environmental ethics*. New York: Columbia University Press.

Sandler, R., & Cafaro, P. (2004). *Environmental virtue ethics*. Lanham: Rowman and Littlefield.

Saner, M. A. (2000). Biotechnology, the limits of Norton's convergence hypothesis, and implications for an inclusive concept of health. *Ethics and the Environment, 5*(2), 229–241.

Savadori, L., Savio, S., Nicotra, E., Rumiati, R., Finucane, M., & Slovic, P. (2004). Expert and public perception of risk from biotechnology. *Risk Analysis, 24*(5), 1289–1299.

Scott, D. (2003). Science and the consequences of mistrust: Lessons from recent GM controversies. *Journal of Agricultural and Environmental Ethics, 16*(6), 569–582.

Scott, D. (2005). The magic bullet criticism of agricultural biotechnology. *Journal of Agricultural and Environmental Ethics, 18*(3), 259–267.

Scott, I. M. (2000). Green symbolism in the genetic modification debate. *Journal of Agricultural and Environmental Ethics, 13*(3–4), 293–311.

Segal, H. P. (2001). Victor and victim. *Nature, 412*(6850), 861.

Serageldin, I. (1999). Biotechnology and food security in the 21st century. *Science, 285*(5426), 387–389.

Shelton, A. M., Zhao, J.-Z., & Roush, R. T. (2002). Economic, ecological, food safety, and social consequences of the deployment of Bt transgenic plants. *Annual Review of Entomology, 47*(2002), 845–881.

Siegrist, M. (2008). Factors influencing public acceptance of innovative food technologies and products. *Trends in Food Science and Technology, 19*(11), 603–608.

Siipi, H. (2008). Dimensions of naturalness. *Ethics and the Environment, 13*(1), 71–103.

Sjöberg, L. (2008). Genetically modified food in the eyes of the public and experts. *Risk Management, 10*(3), 168–193.

Skorupinski, B. (2002). Putting precaution to debate—about the precautionary principle and participatory technology assessment. *Journal of Agricultural and Environmental Ethics, 15*(1), 87–102.

Snow, A. (2003). Genetic engineering: Unnatural selection. *Nature, 424*(6949), 619.

Stewart, C. N. (2004). *Genetically modified planet. Environmental impacts of genetically engineered plants.* New York: Oxford University Press.

Stöcklin, J. (2007). Die Pflanze. Moderne Konzepte der Biologie. Eidgenössische Ethikkommission für die Biotechnologie im Ausserhumanbereich EKAH (Eds.). Beiträge zur Ethik und Biotechnologie, Band 2.

Tanner, C., Medin, D. L., & Iliev, R. (2008). Influence of deontological versus consequentialist orientations on act choices and framing effects: When principles are more important than consequences. *European Journal of Social Psychology, 38*(5), 757–769.

Taylor, P. (1986). *Respect for nature: A theory of environmental ethics.* Princeton: Princeton University Press.

Tiedje, J. M., Colwell, R. K., Grossman, Y. L., Hodson, R. E., Lenski, R. E., Mack, R. N., et al. (1989). The planned introduction of genetically engineered organisms: Ecological considerations and recommendations. *Ecology, 70*(2), 298–315.

Verhoog, H. (1992). The concept of intrinsic value and transgenic animals. *Journal of Agricultural and Environmental Ethics, 5*(2), 147–160.

Verhoog, H. (1997). Organic agriculture versus genetic engineering. *NJAS Wageningen Journal of Life Sciences, 54*(4), 387–400.

Verhoog, H., Matze, M., van Bueren, E. L., & Baars, T. (2003). The role of the concept of the natural (naturalness) in organic farming. *Journal of Agricultural and Environmental Ethics, 16*(1), 29–49.

Vogel, S. (2003). The nature of artifacts. *Environmental Ethics, 25*(2), 149–168.

von Kutschera, F. (1999). *Grundlagen der Ethik.* Berlin and New York: Walter de Gruyter.

Von Wartburg, W. P., & Liew, J. (1999). *Gene technology and social acceptance.* Lanham: University Press of America.

Wambugu, F. (1999). Why Africa needs agricultural biotech. *Nature, 400*(6739), 15–16.

Watkinson, A. R., Freckleton, R. P., Sutherland, W. J., & Robinson, R. A. (2000). Predictions of biodiversity response to genetically modified herbicide-tolerant crops. *Science, 289*(5484), 1554–1557.

Weaver, S. A., & Morris, M. C. (2005). Risks associated with genetic modification: An annotated bibliography of peer-reviewed natural science publications. *Journal of Agricultural and Environmental Ethics, 18*(2), 157–189.

Wenz, P. S. (1999). Pragmatism in practice: The efficiency of sustainable agriculture. *Environmental Ethics, 21*(4), 391–410.

Westra, L. (1998). Biotechnology and transgenics in agriculture and aquaculture: The perspective from ecosystem integrity. *Environmental Values, 7*(1), 79–96.

Woese, C. R. (2004). A new biology for a new century. *Microbiology and Molecular Biology Reviews, 68*(2), 173–186.

Wolfenbarger, L. L., & Phifer, P. R. (2000). The ecological risks and benefits of genetically engineered plants. *Science, 290*(5499), 2088–2093.

Reading Questions

1. The researchers identify three general types of moral concerns across the 113 articles that were ultimately analyzed as part of their final review of the scholarship. What are those three types of moral concerns?

2. The researchers analyzed the articles' content by a process of extracting and classifying "basic semantic units" (par. 15). In your own words, explain what this means.

3. According to Table 3 in the study, what percentage of environmental ethics journals expressed concern about the consequences of the use of genetically modified crops?

4. The researchers found the concept *nature as a safety mechanism* addressed in how many of the articles?

5. What are the three more specific "moral concerns addressing the act" (5) that are identified as part of this study?

Rhetoric Questions

6. In the report's Introduction, where do the authors switch from providing background and context for their study to presenting their specific aims? What makes the location of this switch appropriate?

7. In light of its central topic, the researchers' perspective, and the genre of presentation, could you make a case that this report should be classified as social science research? If so, on what basis would you make such an argument? If not, why not?

8. Look closely at the study's Results section. Explain the section's organizational logic. Account for the role of headings and subheadings.

Response and Research Questions

9. Do you find it surprising that moral concerns addressing the actor were identified least in the laypersons' debate on the use of genetically modified crops? Why or why not?

10. What are your personal concerns about the use of genetically modified crops? Do any of the specific moral concerns identified by the researchers as part of their literature review project intersect with your own concerns about genetically modified crops? If so, which ones?

ACADEMIC CASE STUDY • GENETICALLY MODIFIED FOOD   SOCIAL SCIENCES

Do Consumers Really Refuse to Buy Genetically Modified Food?*

CHARLES NOUSSAIR, STÉPHANE ROBIN, AND BERNARD RUFFIEUX

Charles Noussair is the Eller Professor of Economics and Director of the Economic Sciences Laboratory at the University of Arizona. He has published numerous research articles that apply experimental methods to economic questions. In the study report below, written with his colleagues Stéphane Robin and Bernard Ruffieux, Noussair examines the willingness of the French people to pay for genetically modified products, as well as their tolerance levels for genetically modified organisms in their products. The team's findings are applied to help manufacturers make various production decisions. Their report was published in the *Economic Journal* in 2004.

*The program "Pertinence économique et faisabilité d'une filière sans utilisation d'OGM" and the Institut National de la Recherche Agronomique (INRA) provided research support for this project. We would like to thank Isabelle Avelange, Yves Bertheau, Pierre Combris, Sylvie Issanchou, Egizio Valceschini, Steve Tucker and three anonymous referees for valuable comments and assistance.

The introduction of genetically modified organisms (GMOs) into food products has ignited a passionate debate, particularly in Europe. On the basis of recommendations from the scientific community, regulatory authorities such as the FSA in the UK, the FDA in the US and the DGAL in France, have recognized that the GMO products currently available are safe for the consumer and the environment. Moreover, there is a consensus among scientists that biotechnology has the potential to create products that will enhance nutrition, increase crop yields, and reduce the use of toxic pesticides and herbicides. Nevertheless, polling of European consumers consistently indicates a high degree of hostility[1] to the presence of GMOs in the food supply. The aversion to GMOs is based on both private considerations, such as potential health risk and a preference for natural foods, as well as social dimensions, such as environmental effects and ethical concerns. It appears that the unfavorable view has been aggravated by the spread of the "mad cow" epidemic, the lack of benefit that the first generation of GMOs provides to the consumer and the initial introduction of GMOs without the public's knowledge. The tension between scientific recommendations and public opinion has complicated the formulation of government policy with respect to GMOs,[2] because in a democratic system public opinion must be taken into account in addition to the scientific merits of the policy and the market pressures in the economy.

However, there is reason to question whether the anti-GMO sentiment expressed in surveys would be reflected in actual purchase behavior. It is known that individuals' decisions can differ drastically between when they are hypothetical, as in a contingent valuation study or other survey, and when they involve a real commitment to purchase; see for example Neill et al. (1994); Cummings et al. (1995); Brookshire and Coursey (1987); List and Shogren (1998); or List and Gallet (2001). Furthermore, most surveys do not inquire about actual purchase decisions at specific prices and, as Ajzen et al. (1996) note, subtle contextual cues or small changes in information provided to survey respondents may change results dramatically. More specific criticisms apply to surveys about preferences over public goods, such as the preservation of GMO-free crops. Sagoff (1988), Blamey et al. (1995) and Nyborg (2000) argue that survey and hypothetical contingent valuation measurement techniques for public goods do not reveal participants' willingness-to-pay. Surveys place respondents in the role of citizens, who make judgments from society's point of view, rather than consumers, who make actual purchase decisions. Thus the two instruments, surveys and purchase decisions, measure different variables. In addition, even if provision or preservation of a public good is valuable to an individual, it may not be reflected in his willingness-to-pay because of the free rider problem (Stevens et al., 1991; Krutilla, 1967).[3]

The focus of this paper is to consider, using experimental methods, the extent that actual decisions to purchase food products are affected by the presence of GMOs. We study purchasing behavior of consumers with a laboratory experiment designed to

[1] For example, Noussair et al. (2001) report that 79% of French respondents either agreed or mostly agreed with the statement "GMOs should simply be banned." 89% were opposed to the presence of GMOs in food products, 89% in livestock feed, 86% in medicine, 46% in food packaging and 46% in fuels. In the UK, surveys show a similar pattern (Moon and Balasubrimanian, 2001).

[2] Any food product sold in the European Union for human consumption that contains an ingredient that consists of more than 1% GMOs must be labelled "contains GMOs." There is no GM produce currently sold in Europe and the only GM products for sale appear as ingredients in processed foods. Currently there are three types of corn are authorized for cultivation in France. One type of corn and one type of soybean are authorized for importation. In the UK, in addition to corn and soybeans, one type of GM tomato is authorized for importation and use in tomato puree. No GM crops are grown commercially in the UK. In the US, as of early 2002, about two-dozen different GM fruits, vegetables, and grains were being cultivated. In the US, there are no specific regulations for biotech products, which are subject to the same regulations as other products. See Caswell (1998, 2000) for a discussion of policy issues relating to the labelling of GM products.

[3] A well-documented example of a dichotomy between surveys and consumer behavior was observed during the introduction of recombinant bovine somatropin (rbST), a bovine growth hormone, into milk production in the US in 1993. Surveys indicated that a majority of consumers had a negative opinion of the technique, primarily on ethical grounds. On the basis of the survey data, analysts predicted a 20% decline in total milk consumption. However, there was no decrease in actual milk consumption after the introduction of the technique; see Aldrich and Blisard (1998).

elicit and compare the willingness to pay for products that are traditional in content and labelling, that are explicitly guaranteed to be GMO-free, and that contain GMOs. We also consider buyer behavior with respect to different thresholds of maximum GMO content. The participants in our study are a demographically representative sample of residents of the Grenoble, France, area.

We use an experimental approach because of the absence of field data. The current policy of most major European retailers not to carry GM foods, which has resulted from pressure of activists and the media, means that it is very difficult to estimate product demand for foods containing GMOs using field data from European countries. For the few GM products that are available, there is experimental evidence that consumers are unaware of the labelling of GM content; see Noussair et al. (2002). Furthermore, in the US, where the vast majority of GM food is sold, demand for GMOs cannot be inferred from market data since GM content is not indicated on the labelling. We are unaware of any previous estimates of consumer demand for the GMO-free characteristic in food products. However, previous work suggests that experiments provide a good alternative method to study product demand in general, and that the artificial setting of the lab does not drastically alter consumer behavior.[4]

1. POLICY ISSUES: SEGREGATION AND THRESHOLDS

In response to the tension between scientific and 5 public opinion on the issue of GM foods, the policy adopted by most European governments has been to declare a moratorium on approval of new GM products for cultivation and sale. For the few products that have already been approved, their policy has been to segregate GM and GMO-free products at all stages of production, to require labelling of products containing GMOs, and to allow the market to determine how much of each type of product is sold. However, banning new GMOs may be inefficient if there are

welfare gains from the adoption of biotechnology that are foregone. In addition, although segregation and mandatory labelling is free-market-oriented[5] in that it offers consumers a choice, some economists might view it also as an inefficient policy.[6] Segregating the entire process of production is costly to farmers and firms throughout the production chain, especially in the upstream part of the chain, which consists of the seed producers, farmers, and primary processors.[7] Since there is no evidence that the GMOs that regulatory authorities have approved are harmful either to health or to the environment, it can be argued that the expenditure represents a deadweight loss.

On the other hand, if the production tracks are not segregated or labelling of GMO content is interdicted, as it is in the US, a "lemons" scenario may result (Akerlof, 1970). The GMOs currently on the market were introduced for agronomic reasons and the foods containing them are indistinguishable from conventional foods to the consumer in the absence of labelling information. Since GMOs lower production costs, producers have an incentive to insert them into the food supply. If consumers value foods containing GMOs less than foods that do not contain GMOs, they will be unwilling to pay more for an unlabelled product than an amount that reflects the

[5]Romer (2001) notes that the institutions of science and the market are the main engines of globalization. However, in some cases, the consensus of the scientific community and market pressures can clash with each other and with public opinion. The case of the first generation of GMOs in food products appears to constitute a prominent example of a situation where science, public opinion, and the market each exert pressure toward different outcomes. More generally, the current anti-globalization movement might be interpreted as a backlash against market or scientific forces. The "loss of sovereignty" lamented by some anti-globalization activists can be viewed as a decline in the ability of public opinion to influence outcomes when confronted by market forces or the scientific establishment.

[6]A few studies have estimated the gains from the adoption of biotechnology in farming in the US. See for example Anderson et al. (2000), Lin et al. (2001), Falk-Zepeda et al. (2000), Traxler et al. (2000), or Lence and Hayes (2001).

[7]In the US, segregation costs have been estimated at 12% of the current price of corn and 11% of the current price of soybeans (Economic Research Service/USDA, 2000). Buckwell et al. (1999) find that in general, identity preservation for specialty crops increases final costs by 5–15%.

[4]See for example Shogren et al. (1999).

presence of GMOs. This would cause the market for non-GMO varieties to disappear, reducing social welfare by eliminating potential gains from trade. Furthermore, it could potentially cause a market collapse for entire products. If a firm cannot disclose that its product uses no ingredients that contain GMOs, it might replace ingredients that consumers believe may contain GMOs with those that cannot contain GMOs. This could eliminate the entire market for many products, such as soy lecithin, corn syrup, and corn starch.

From an economist's point of view, the appropriate policy depends in part on whether the actual purchase behavior of consumers corresponds to the polling data. If, as suggested by the polls, a large majority of consumers are unwilling to purchase products containing GMOs, banning GMOs is probably the best option, as the expense of creating two tracks of production would not be justified. On the other hand, if the vast majority of consumers behave as if they are indifferent to GMOs, or would purchase products made with GMOs if they sold at lower prices, the production tracks could be safely integrated with little social cost. However, if a considerable segment of the market refuses to purchase products containing GMOs at any price, but another large segment would purchase GM products if they were cheaper, separation of the production tracks and the enforcement of mandatory labelling of products containing GMOs would be worth the expense.

Under a policy of segregation, the threshold level of GMO content, above which a product is considered to be bioengineered, must be specified. Because of the ease of contamination throughout the production chain, it is impossible intentionally to make any product, in whose manufacture GMOs are already authorized, without any trace of GMOs. This technological constraint requires the specification of a threshold above zero below which a product is to be considered as GMO-free and above which the product must be labelled as containing GMOs. The lower the threshold, the greater is the cost of production of GMO-free products. The increase involves the cost of producing very pure seeds, isolating parcels of land,

and cleaning storage and transportation containers. The marginal cost of lowering the threshold may be justified if consumers have a strong preference for a low threshold, as is suggested in surveys of public opinion. In our experiment, in addition to studying the willingness to pay for GMO relative to GMO-free products, we also investigate how consumers view the different thresholds.

2. METHODOLOGY

2.1. The Experiment

The experiment is designed to study the extent that consumers value the absence of GMOs in food products by measuring changes in willingness to pay in response to new information about GMO content. The protocol we use is new to the literature and can be readily applied to study the marginal value of different characteristics of many consumer goods. However, it is similar in spirit to several other experimental protocols in the literature such as the nth price auction technique used in Hoffman et al. (1993) and the CVM-X calibration method studied in Fox et al. (1998). See Shogren (2004) for a survey of experimental techniques of eliciting valuation information. Our protocol differs from many others that appear in the literature in three principal ways.

1. We train the subjects in the rules and incentive properties of the mechanism with auctions for goods with induced values.

2. During the training phase, there is an interactive dialogue between the subjects themselves.

3. When bidding for the products of interest, we do not make the bids public information at any time, so that privacy of valuations is safeguarded, no peer pressure can be mobilized to encourage systematic boycotting of the GMO products, and subjects cannot use others' bids to update their own valuations.

In our experiment, subjects bid for real consumer goods using the Becker-DeGroot-Marschak (BDM) mechanism (Becker et al., 1964). In the BDM, a type of auction, bidders have a dominant strategy in bidding an amount equal to their true valuations for the good. There are several advantages to using demand-revealing mechanisms to elicit willingness-to-pay information and other authors have already employed them to study potential consumer demand for food products before their introduction; see for example Fox *et al.* (1998) or Hoffman *et al.* (1993). The first advantage is that unlike survey data, the auction provides a common homogeneous unit, money, to measure preferences. Different respondents may interpret terms "strongly agree" and "agree" on a survey differently but the interpretation of £1 is common to all respondents. The use of money as a metric allows for comparisons of intensity of preferences between subjects, as well as between goods. Secondly, in the auction, the subject is committing himself to an actual purchase, unlike in a poll where there is no commitment. Thirdly, in a demand-revealing mechanism, there is a dominant strategy to indicate one's true valuation. In principle, this allows the willingness-to-pay to be directly measured, rather than inferred. The existence of a dominant strategy also simplifies calculation of a participant's best strategy since it is independent of own risk attitudes and beliefs about other players. Fourthly, the bid submitted in the auction weights each characteristic of the product, including GMO content, according to its importance for the purchase decision. Respondents to a survey may express a very strong preference for GMO-free products. However, the survey would not accurately reveal the weight the GMO-free characteristic carries compared to other dimensions such as taste, appearance, and price. As suggested earlier, a survey might be expected to accord greater weight to public dimensions, such as negative externalities that result from widespread use of the product, than a bid in an auction market.

Two previous experiments have directly studied willingness-to-pay for GMOs. Both employed subjects from the American Midwest, whose preferences on the GM issue may diverge sharply from European consumers. Lusk *et al.* (2000) study the decisions of American university students. They endow each subject with a bag of genetically modified corn chips and allow him to bid for the right to exchange it for a bag of non-genetically modified chips. Only 30% of subjects indicated a willingness to pay a positive amount for the GMO-free product, and the willingness-to-pay was on average 7 cents per ounce, with 20% willing to pay at least 20 cents per ounce. Huffman *et al.* (2001) investigate bidding behavior for GMO-containing and GMO-free types of vegetable oil, tortilla chips, and Russet potatoes of a sample of American consumers (mean age of 49 years). They used the random nth price auction, in which bidders simultaneously submit sealed bids and the n highest bidders each receive a unit of the good. The winners each pay a price equal to the $n + 1$th highest bid. The number n is chosen randomly after the bids are made. They found that for all three goods, the average bidder had a lower willingness to pay for the GM variety. The average premium for GMO-free food was 14%.

2.2. The Participants

The participants in our experiment were a demographically representative sample of consumers in the Grenoble area. Ninety-seven subjects participated, each taking part in exactly one of the ten sessions that comprised the experiment. The sessions took place between July 17th and 24th, 2000. Each session took approximately two hours. The ages of the subjects ranged between 18 and 75 years, and averaged 33 years. 52% were female. The socio-economic level of the sample was representative of the French urban population.

Subjects were recruited by sampling from the telephone directory of the city of Grenoble. The method of recruitment made it highly improbable that subjects communicated with others who participated in an earlier session. Over 1,000 telephone calls were necessary to recruit the 97 who participated in the study. Subjects were screened later in the recruiting process to make the sample more demographically representative after early recruiting attracted a disproportionate fraction of participants under age 25 and over age 60. At the time of recruitment, subjects received no indication that the experiment concerned GMOs or potential risks to the food supply. Subjects were invited to come to the laboratory to sample food products for a government research project which was not linked to private firms or marketing of any particular products. We invited only those respondents who indicated both that they were regular purchasers of biscuits* and that they made purchase decisions for their household.

2.3. The BDM Mechanism

We used the Becker-DeGroot-Marschak (BDM) mechanism to elicit willingness-to-pay information.[8] In the BDM, there is a dominant strategy to bid one's valuation. In other words, it is a best response, no matter what strategy other players adopt, and regardless of the risk attitude of the bidder, to bid truthfully an amount equal to his willingness-to-pay. Therefore in principle, the mechanism has the ability to reveal bidders' valuations.

The rules of the BDM mechanism are simple. Each subject simultaneously submits a bid to the experimenter in a closed envelope to purchase one unit of the good offered for sale. The experimenter then randomly draws a sale price from a pre-specified interval, from zero to a price greater than the maximum possible willingness to pay among bidders. Any subject who submits a bid greater than the sale price receives an item and pays an amount equal to the sale price. The others do not receive units and make no payment.

2.4. The Training Phase

Though previous studies of the BDM mechanism have shown it to be incentive compatible (Irwin et al., 1998),[9] we nevertheless included a training phase to ensure that subjects learned to use the dominant strategy. This training proceeded in the following manner. At the beginning of a session, each subject received 150 francs (roughly €23) in cash.

We started the training phase of each session with an auction of an actual consumer product, a bottle of orange juice, whose label was visible and that was previously tasted by the subjects. After bidding, all of the bids were posted, the sale price was drawn, the winners were announced, and the transactions were implemented immediately. There are two reasons that we introduced this first auction to the training phase. The first reason is that it made subjects aware that others' valuations for goods can differ from their own. The second reason was to provide an easier transition to the GMO phase of the experiment, where subjects would be placed in a situation that is different in three ways from typical market purchases. They buy products whose labels and packaging have been removed, taste products without knowledge of the information displayed on the label, and buy products without knowing the sale price beforehand. We believe it is better to make this leap into the unknown in two steps, with the first step being the auctioning of a product with visible packaging and labelling, which subjects do not taste but whose sale price is not known beforehand. This auction also serves to illustrate to subjects that they are spending real money for real products that they can keep after the experiment and that they are not in a simulation. To render this transparent, a bottle of orange juice is given to each winner, who is required to immediately pay the price determined by the auction from his current cash total.

---

*biscuits: cookies.

[8] Technically, the BDM procedure is not an auction, since agents are not competing with each other for the items for sale. However, because of their parsimony, we will use the term "bid" to refer to the submission of a limit price and the term "the auction" refer to the process as a whole. The BDM mechanism is theoretically equivalent to a second price sealed bid auction (Vickrey, 1961) where a bidder bids against one demand-revealing opponent.

[9] Rutstrom (1998) provides evidence that can be interpreted as suggesting that the BDM leads to bids closer to true valuations than the Vickrey auction. The two auctions both have dominant strategies of truthful bidding.

However, the second price auction yields bids that are too high in induced value auctions (Kagel et al., 1987). In auctions for a product with homegrown rather than induced value, chocolate truffles, Rutstrom finds that the BDM yields lower bids than the Vickrey auction, suggesting that it may be the case that the bias toward high bidding is less severe in the BDM than in the Vickrey auction. Bohm et al. (1997) point out that the BDM can fail to elicit true valuations when used to elicit willingness to sell information, if the maximum sale price is inappropriately set. Here we do not face this type of problem since we are eliciting willingness to pay information and we can specify the minimum purchase price equal to zero.

Subjects then participated in several BDM auctions in which they bid for fictitious items. The fictitious items had induced values; see Smith (1982) for an exposition of induced value theory. Before the auction took place, each subject received a sheet of paper that indicated an amount of money for which he could redeem a unit of the fictitious item from the experimenter, should he purchase it in the auction. The induced value differed from subject to subject and was private information. The ability to redeem an item from the experimenter induced a limit price in the auction, since a subject's payoff if he won the auction equalled the induced value minus the price he paid. The inclusion of the auctions with induced values had three objectives: to teach the subjects and verify their comprehension of the rules of the auction, to reduce the biases and noise that tend to arise in bidding behavior, and to show subjects that the auction involved transactions where real money was at stake.

The dominant strategy of bidding one's valuation in the auctions is not at first obvious to most subjects. We chose not to inform the subjects directly of the dominant strategy. Instead, we used a technique intended to encourage subjects to come to understand the strategies that constitute optimal behavior on their own. After subjects submitted their bids, the experimenter drew a selling price, wrote all of the valuations on the blackboard and asked subjects if they could identify their own valuations and predict which subjects would be receiving units of the good based on the valuations displayed. Then the experimenter recorded the submitted bids on the blackboard next to the corresponding valuations. He posed the following questions to the group of subjects, who were free to engage in open discussion on the topics.

a. Which subjects received units in the auction?

b. How much did the winners pay?

c. Did anyone regret the bid he submitted?

After the discussion, each of the winners received, in full view of all participants, an amount of money equal to his induced value minus the price he was required to pay. The cash was physically placed on the desk in front of the subject after the auction. A series of identical auctions was conducted using the same procedure.

The valuations in each period were randomly drawn from a uniform distribution whose endpoints differed in each period. The auctions continued until at least 80% of the bids were within 5% of valuations. This occurred within six periods in all sessions.

2.5. The GMO Phase

In the GMO phase we simultaneously auctioned four products, which we referred to as $S, L, C,$ and N during the sessions. All four products were biscuits that are typically available in grocery stores and supermarkets throughout France, and we informed subjects of that fact before bidding began. The products were different from each other, but were close substitutes. The GMO phase of the experiment consisted of five periods, as outlined in Table 1. At the beginning of this phase, subjects received a sample of each of the four products to taste, without its packaging or labelling. Before bidding in the first period, subjects were required to taste each product. They then marked down how much they liked the product on a scale where "I like it very much" and "I don't like it at all" were at the extremes of the rating scale (see Combris et al., 1997).[10] Then the auction for period 1 took place. The four products were auctioned simultaneously. Each of the following periods consisted of the revelation of some information about some or all of the products, followed by a simultaneous auction for the four products. The sale price was not drawn for any period until the end of period 5 and no information was given to participants about other players' bids.

Table 1 shows the information made available to subjects at the beginning of each period.[11] At the

[10] Results on the relationship between ratings and bids for these as well as other products are reported in Noussair et al. (forthcoming).

[11] We do not reveal bids publicly during the GMO phase, because it is possible that other players' bids might influence some individuals' willingness to pay, when the good being sold has homegrown rather than induced value. Also, in the GMO phase, we auction four goods simultaneously, whereas in the training phase, only one good was auctioned at a time. We felt that confronting the subjects too early in the session with bidding for multiple products simultaneously might have been overwhelming. On the other hand, once they had mastered the rules of the auction for one item, subjects seemed to have little difficulty with the multiple-good simultaneous auction.

Table 1

Sequence of Events in GMO Phase of an Experimental Session

Period 1	– Information: blind tasting of the four products S, L, C, and N – Recording of hedonic rating of the four products – Auction
Period 2	– Additional Information: "S contains GMOs" and "N is GMO free" – Auction
Period 3	– Additional Information: "No ingredient in L contains more than 1% GMOs," "No ingredient in C contains more than 1/10 of 1% GMOs," "One ingredient in S (soy) is derived from an authorized genetically modified product," and "No ingredient in N contains any detectable trace of GMOs" – Auction
Period 4	– Additional Information: general information about GMOs – Auction
Period 5	– Additional Information: the brand names of the four products and the designation "organically grown" for product N – Auction
Transactions	– Random draw of the auction that counts toward final allocations – Implementation of transactions for the period that counts

beginning of period 2, we informed the subjects that product S contained GMOs and that product N was GMO-free.[12] No information was given about products L and C in period 2. At the beginning of period 3, we informed the subjects that no ingredient in L contained more than 1% GMOs and that no ingredient in C contained more than 1/10 of 1% GMOs. We also indicated to subjects that no ingredient in N had any detectable trace of GM content, and that S contained a GM ingredient, soy, that was authorized in France. At the beginning of period 4, subjects received a four-page handout containing background information about GMOs. The information consisted of

a. the definition of a GMO

b. the criteria for classifying a product as containing GMOs

c. the list of GM plants authorized in France

d. the food products sold in France that contain GMOs, and

e. the current French law regarding GMOs.

Care was taken to provide an unbiased characterization because of the sensitivity of auction bids to favorable and unfavorable descriptions of the item sold. Before the last period, we revealed the brands of the four products and the label indicating that product N was organic.

3. RESULTS

3.1. The Impact of GMO Information

Figure 1 graphs the evolution of the average normalized bid over all subjects over the five periods of the GMO phase for the four products. The data in the figure are normalized by taking each individual's actual bid in period 1 as the base, set equal to 100, tracking that individual's bids over time relative to his

[12] See Fox *et al.* (2002) for another example of an experiment in which the impact of new information on willingness-to-pay is studied.

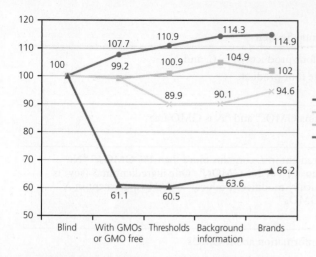

Figure 1. Average Bids for the
Four Biscuits in Periods 1–5

Legend:
- With GMOs (S)
- Thresholds 1% (L)
- Thresholds 0.1% (C)
- GMO Free (N)

bid in period 1, and averaging across all individuals in each period. Table 2 contains the unnormalized averages and variances of bids in each period for each product. The changes in individual bids between periods 1 and 3 are described in Table 3. Only the data from those who bid greater than 0 for the product in period 1 are included in Tables 2 and 3, as well as in Figure 1 (no subject who bid zero in period 1 ever submitted a positive bid in later periods).[13] The column entitled *Percentage Bidding Zero* indicates the percentage of subjects that bid 0 upon being informed of the product's GMO content. In the column labelled *Percentage Decreasing Bid,* the percentage of subjects that lower their bids for a product, while continuing to bid more than zero, is indicated. The *Percentage with Bid Unchanged* column is the percentage that does not change their bids after learning the GMO content. *Percentage Increasing Bid* is the percentage that increases their bids.

We observe that more consumers value the absence than the presence of GMOs and that the "average" consumer values the absence of GMOs. In period 2, we revealed that product N did not contain GMOs and product S did contain GMOs. The GMO-free guarantee raised the limit price for product N of the

[13]The number of subjects who bid zero in period 1 was 14 for products N and S, 13 for product L, and 29 for product C.

average consumer in our sample by 8%. Forty-one of the 83 subjects, who bid more than zero for product N in period 1, raised their bid in period 2 and only 7 lowered it. A sign test (eliminating the ties in which bids were the same in both periods) rejects the hypothesis that a bidder is equally likely to lower as to raise his bid at the $p < 0.001$ level. A pooled variance t-test also rejects the hypothesis that the mean bid for product N is equal in periods 1 and 2 at $p < 0.01$, indicating that the "average" consumer increased his bid in period 2. In contrast, revealing that product S contains GMOs lowered its average limit price by 39%. Only 4 participants increased their bid for S after learning that it contained GMOs while 64 lowered their bid. Both the sign test and the pooled variance t-test reject the hypothesis of equality at the $p < 0.001$ level. The relatively small increase for the GMO-free product suggests that in the absence of information, consumers typically act as if there is a low probability that products contain GMOs. The average premium for the GMO-free product over the product containing GMOs was 46.7%.

Our subjects appear to view a guarantee that no ingredient contains more than 0.1% GMOs as consistent with the typical GMO content of conventional products (the unlabelled product historically available). They value a 0.1% guarantee more highly than a 1% guarantee and the 1% threshold appears to be

Table 2

Average, Variance, and Median of Bids, Periods 1–5, All Products

	Period 1 Blind	Period 2 With GMOs or GMO-Free	Period 3 Thresholds	Period 4 Background Information	Period 5 Brands
N GMO Free	15.29FF	16.47FF	16.95FF	17.47FF	17.57FF
	(0.68)	(0.72)	(0.69)	(0.69)	(0.64)
		[+8%**]	[+3%**]	[+3%**]	[+1%]
	{13}	{15}	{15}	{15}	{16}
C Threshold 0.1%	15.02FF	14.96FF	15.16FF	15.75FF	15.32FF
	(0.65)	(0.63)	(0.69)	(0.65)	(0.66)
		[0%]	[+1%]	[+4%**]	[−3%**]
	{12}	{13}	{13}	{14}	{13}
L Threshold 1%	15.48FF	15.30FF	13.91FF	13.95FF	14.65FF
	(0.75)	(0.64)	(0.76)	(0.75)	(0.75)
		[−1%]	[−9%**]	[0%]	[+5%**]
	{14}	{15}	{12}	{12}	{15}
S With GMOs	17.85FF	10.90FF	10.80FF	11.35FF	11.81FF
	(0.69)	(1.03)	(0.96)	(0.93)	(0.91)
		[−39%**]	[−1%]	[+5%**]	[+4%**]
	{15}	{10}	{10}	{10}	{10}

(variance), [increase from previous period], {median}

**average significantly different at 1% level from previous period according to pooled-variance t-test.

seen as a higher level of GMO content than that of a conventional product. Furthermore, the 1% guarantee was viewed differently from the label "contains GMOs" and the 0.1% guarantee was viewed differently from "GMO-free." In period 3, we revealed that no ingredient in product *L* contained more than 1% GMOs and no ingredient in product *C* contained more than 0.1% GMOs. We observed no significant change in the median willingness to pay for product *C* between periods 2 and 3 (p = 0.38 for the sign test) but the average bid for product *L* declined by 10% and the decline was statistically significant (p < 0.05 for the sign test). A pooled variance t-test of the hypothesis that the mean normalized bids for products *L* and *C* are equal rejects the hypothesis at

a significance level of p < 0.01. There was no consensus among the participants about whether a product meeting the 0.1% threshold was valued more or less highly than a conventional product. Thirty-three percent increased their bid (by an average of 28%) after learning the maximum possible GMO content was 0.1% of any ingredient, while 27.9% reduced their bid, and 4.4% reduced their bid to zero. The bidding behavior for product *L* reveals that a product meeting a 1% threshold is viewed very differently from a product labelled as containing GMOs: 17.9% of subjects increased their bid when informed of the 1% threshold, and 40.5% left their bid unchanged. Thus over half of our participants considered a product satisfying the 1% threshold as no worse than the conventional product.

Table 3

Percentage Bidding Zero and Decreasing, Increasing, and Holding Constant Their Bids after Learning GMO Content

Product no. of subjects with a positive initial bid	Average initial bid for the product	Percentage bidding zero	Percentage decreasing bid	Percentage with bid unchanged	Percentage increasing bid
N GMO Free *83 subj.*		0%	8.4%	42.2%	49.4%
	(15.29FF)		(18.30FF)	(15.30FF)	(14.79FF)
			(−5.4F)	(−)	(+3.32)
			[−18.9%]	[0%]	[+22.4%]
C Threshold 0.1% *68 subj.*		4.4%	23.5%	38.2%	33.8%
	(15.02FF)	(8.63FF)	(18.71FF)	(13.51FF)	(14.99FF)
		(−8.63FF)	(−3.86FF)	(−)	(+4.24)
		[−100%]	[−20.6%]	[0%]	[+28.3%]
L Threshold 1% *84 subj.*		10.7%	31.0%	40.5%	17.9%
	(15.48FF)	(9.94FF)	(19.02FF)	(14.27FF)	(17.90FF)
		(−9.94FF)	(−3.98FF)	(−)	(+4.07FF)
		[−100%]	[−26.5%]	[0%]	[+20.9%]
S With GMOs *83 subj.*		34.9%	42.2%	18.1%	4.8%
	(17.85FF)	(13.09FF)	(22.37FF)	(18.04FF)	(12.13FF)
		(−13.09FF)	(−6.34FF)	(−)	(+6.10FF)
		[−100%]	[−28.3%]	[0%]	[+50.3%]

(Average bid in French Francs for observations in category), (*average absolute change in bid, in FF*), [average percentage change in bid, in FF].

The 1% guarantee was viewed as different from the 0.1% guarantee. The mean normalized bids in period 3 for products *N* and *C*, as well as for products *L* and *S*, were significantly different from each other at $p < 0.01$.

The distribution of background information about biotechnology in period 4 led to a slight increase in average limit prices, which was significant at $p < 0.05$ for three of the four products. The increase was greatest for the GMO-free product *N*. The information did not bring the prices of *L*, with a 1% threshold, or *S*, which contained GMOs, to their levels before any information was revealed. For all four products at least 57% of the bids were unchanged between periods 3 and 4. For product *N*, the GMO-free product, 20 bidders increased their bid while 9 lowered it

and we can reject the hypothesis that an individual was equally likely to raise and to lower his bid at the $p < 0.05$ level. However, we cannot reject the analogous hypotheses for the other three products. Thus for each of the products, though the pooled variance t-test indicates that the information increased the bid of the "average" consumer, the more conservative sign test is not significant and the majority of participants did not change their bids.

Revealing the brand names of the products in period 5 raised the average prices for three of the four products. The effect was significant at $p < 0.01$ for *L* and *S*. The average bid for product *C* was significantly lower in period 5 than in period 4 at $p < 0.01$. However, for all four products, we fail to reject the hypothesis that an equal number of bidders raised and lowered their bids in period 5 relative to period 4. There was no increase in price for product N from revealing that it was organically produced, perhaps because revealing its label exerted an offsetting negative effect.

3.2. Bidder Types and Demographics

Our consumers can be classified into four categories. In classifying the participants we consider only those who demonstrated a positive willingness to pay for product S before it was revealed to contain GMOs. In other words, the classification applies only to those for whom $b_1(S) > 0$, where $b_k(x)$ is the bid in period k for product x. We refer to those consumers whose bids satisfy $b_1(S) > 0$ and $b_2(S) = 0$, as *Unwilling* consumers. Unwilling consumers bid zero for product S after learning that it contained GMOs. They comprised 34.9% of our subjects. It is clear that they have lowered their bids in period 2 because of the information about GMO content, because only one of the Unwilling also lowered his bid for product N in period 2 after finding out it was GMO-free. Fourteen of the Unwilling consumers submitted $b_2(N) = b_1(N)$ and 13 submitted a bid satisfying $b_2(N) > b_1(N)$, indicating at least a weak preference for the GMO-free characteristic. However, the Unwilling were disproportionately likely to have a low opportunity cost of not purchasing the product, in that $1/3$ of them bid less than 50% of the average bid in period 1. We can also consider the percentage that bid zero for products L and C in period 3 in response to the availability of the threshold information. Specifying a threshold resulted in a lower incidence of zero bidding than the announcement "contains GMOs": 10.7% of the subjects bid zero for the product with a maximum of 1% GMO content in any ingredient, and only 4.4% bid zero at 0.1%. That means that over 95% of our participants were willing to accept a level of GMO content that typically results from inadvertent co-mingling if the product is sufficiently inexpensive.

For 18.1% of our consumers, $b_2(N) = b_1(S)$. That is, they did not change their bid for product S upon finding out that it contained GMOs. We classify them as *Indifferent* consumers. Sixty percent of these Indifferent consumers were indifferent for all goods. That is they set $b_2(S) = b_1(S)$, $b_2(N) = b_1(N)$, $b_3(L) = b_1(L)$ and $b_3(C) = b_1(C)$. Another 4.9% of participants were Favorable, in that their choices satisfied $b_2(S) > b_1(S)$, demonstrating behavior consistent with having a preference for GM foods. However only one of the four Favorable consumers satisfied $b_2(N) < b_1(N)$—whereas two submitted $b_2(N) = b_1(N)$ and one submitted $b_2(N) > b_1(N)$, suggesting possible confusion on his part about the decision situation)—which is consistent with a negative value for the GMO-free characteristic. Thus a full 23% of bidders were willing to accept GMOs in their food at the same price as the conventional product. Despite the current unpopularity of GMOs in food, there is still a group of consumers willing to buy them and to allow them to establish a foothold in the marketplace.

Of our pool of subjects, 44.2% submitted bids that satisfied $0 < b_2(S) < b_1(S)$. They lowered their bid for product S but did not go so far as to bid zero. The average percentage of the decrease was 28.3%. We call this group the *Reluctant* consumers. This group places negative value on GMO content and will lower (raise) its bid prices when faced with products with higher (lower) GMO content. They are willing to trade off GMO content and the price they pay. Of the Reluctant consumers, 36.1% also exhibited behavior satisfying $b_3(S)/b_1(S) < b_3(L)/b_1(L) < b_3(C)/b_1(C) < b_3(N)/b_1(N)$. This indicates that their willingness to pay is monotonic in the strength of the guarantee of the maximum GMO content.

We explore the relationship between acceptance of genetically modified organisms and certain demographic characteristics of our subjects. We estimate the following probit model:

$$Y_i = \beta_0 + \beta_1 \text{ Gender} + \beta_2 \text{ Age} + \beta_3 \text{ Food-health} + \beta_4 \text{ Diploma} + \beta_5 \text{ 1st cycle} + \beta_6 \text{ 2nd cycle} + \beta_7 \text{ 3rd cycle}$$

Y_i is a dummy variable that equals 1 if consumer i is classified as Unwilling or Reluctant, and equals 0 if the consumer is Favorable or Indifferent. Therefore Y_i can be interpreted as hostility to GMOs and a positive coefficient on an independent variable as a

Table 4

Relationship between Aversion to GM-Food and Demographic Variables

Ind Var.	Intercept	Gender (female = 1)	Age	Food-health	Bac.	1st Cycle	2nd Cycle	3rd Cycle
Coefficient	1.113	0.068	−0.013	−0.055	0.345	−0.301	−0.200	0.560
(std. error)	(0.577)	(0.171)	(0.015)	(0.411)	(0.391)	(0.344)	(0.317)	(0.371)

characteristic that is associated with a preference for consuming foods that do not contain GMOs. The results of the analysis are given in Table 4. The independent variable *Gender* equals 1 if the consumer is female and zero if male. *Age* is given in years. *Food-health* equals 1 if the consumer works in the food or health care industries, and therefore might be better informed about GMOs than the average person. The other four variables are dummy variables that indicate the highest level of education the individual has completed. *Diploma* equals 1 if the Baccalaureate is the highest degree completed. The variables *1st cycle, 2nd cycle,* and *3rd cycle* are increasing levels of university education, where *3rd cycle* is roughly equivalent to a Master's degree. All educational variables equal zero for those who have not completed their Baccalaureate. The probit estimates of the model, given in Table 4, show that none of the variables is significant. There is some tendency for those with the highest level of education to demonstrate a stronger preference for GMO-free products and weaker tendencies for younger people, those who work in the food or health industry and for men to be more willing to consume GM food. The individual level data reveal that the incidence of Unwilling consumers is not highly dependent on demographics. Thirty-five percent of men and 34.9% of women were classified as Unwilling. Profession was not a good predictor of refusal to purchase GMOs. For example, 33.3% of workers in service industries, 33.3% of manual laborers, and 35.9% of students bid zero for the product after finding out that it contained GMOs. The most pronounced difference was between consumers with different educational levels. Twenty percent of those who had not completed a Diploma but 52.6% of 3rd Cycle graduates were classified as Unwilling to purchase the GM product. In general,

demographic variables are not strongly related to bidding behavior and our results are not specific to certain demographic groups.

4. DISCUSSION

Our results show a sharp contrast to the predominantly negative views of French survey respondents toward genetically modified organisms in food products. In our experiments, we observe a wide range of revealed preferences. Whereas 35% of our subjects refused to purchase a product containing GMOs, the remaining 65% of our subjects were willing to purchase a GM product if it was sufficiently inexpensive. Nearly one-quarter of participants showed no decrease in their willingness to pay in response to learning that a product contained GMOs.

The two different thresholds, 0.1% and 1%, generated significantly different bids and thus were clearly perceived as meaningfully different. Furthermore, the 0.1% threshold was not considered to be GMO-free and the 1% threshold generated higher bids than the classification "contains GMOs." This indicates that demand is decreasing in GMO content. Eighty-nine percent of our participants were willing to purchase a product satisfying the 1% threshold, the maximum content that the European Union exempts from labelling. Lowering the threshold to 0.1% would make another 7% of participants willing to purchase products satisfying the threshold, as 96% of our participants were willing to purchase a product, in which no ingredient contained more than 0.1% GMOs, if it were sufficiently inexpensive.

The price patterns we observe underscore the importance of GMOs to many consumers. Changes in prices observed when GM content or thresholds were revealed overwhelm those observed when brand names were revealed. The data also indicate that revealing background information about GMOs had little effect on the behavior of our consumers. Their prior beliefs overwhelmed the content of the information. This suggests that a public information campaign intended to lead to a greater acceptance of GMOs may face considerable challenges.

One possible source of differences between the results from survey data and the consumer behavior observed in the experiment is a configuration of private and public dimensions of preference for GM food in which individuals are willing to consume it but opposed to it in general. For example, this might be the case if GMOs were viewed as carrying an environmental risk but also as safe for human consumption. A consumer's market behavior would neglect the externality his consumption imposes, whereas his response to a survey would not. This is analogous to the consumer of electricity who is opposed to nuclear power but uses the electricity from the power grid, despite the fact that some of the electricity is generated with nuclear power. This effect is consistent with negative responses to the question "are you in favor of the use of GM ingredients in food?" or "are you in favor of the cultivation of GM crops?" combined with a willingness to consume GM food. However, there are also differences between surveys and the experimental results that are inconsistent with this interpretation. For example, the Noussair *et al.* (2001) survey, conducted in the Grenoble area with a sample of participants with similar demographics as those in our study, asked specifically "would *you* buy [the product] if it contained GMOs?": 91.7% responded negatively for French fries, and 91.7% did so for tomatoes.[14] Therefore, there does appear to be a major difference in the results of hypothetical surveys and consumer behavior, even when the questions posed ask directly about the consumption decision.

The policy options available to address the arrival of biotechnology in food production can be grouped into three types. The first option is to ban the use of GMOs in food products. The second is to integrate conventional and biotech varieties into one production stream. The third is to create two production tracks and introduce a labelling system (which could be voluntary or mandatory) to allow the consumer to identify the two varieties. Based merely on polls, we would have concluded that the only policy action that would be feasible in France given current public opinion would be the complete interdiction of GMOs in food, or at least a temporary moratorium on their use. However, our results indicate that only slightly more than a third of the population would be unwilling to purchase GMOs. The remainder is willing to purchase GMOs even when no threshold is specified and could receive a welfare gain if GMOs make products cheaper. The data thus argue against the banning of GMOs, which would cause gains from trade to be foregone.

The data also reveal potential welfare costs to consumers from integrating the two production streams. The consumers who are willing to purchase GMOs if they are sold at a discount might be made better off. However, the segment that refuses to purchase GM-products at any price (35% of participants in our sample) would experience a decrease in their welfare, and would have to switch to products with ingredients that have no GM varieties.

In our view, our results weigh in favor of segmenting the market between products containing GMOs and products that are GMO-free. In this way, the Unwilling consumers could be assured of GMO-free varieties, while price sensitive consumers could benefit from the cost reductions that the first generation of GMOs provides. As long as the segregation costs are not greater than the welfare gains from market segmentation, the sizes of each of the markets appear to justify the establishment of two separate production tracks. The separation and labelling policy gives the

[14] Surveys that ask specifically about consumption decisions also indicate that some of the opposition to GMOs is based on concerns about personal consumption of GMOs. A poll conducted by Market and Opinion Research International in 1999 found that 77% of French consumers agreed with the statement "I would be unhappy to eat GM foods." In a *Sunday Independent* poll of consumers in the UK in early 1999, 68% indicated that they were "fearful of eating GM foods." An ABC News poll conducted in June 2001 found that 52% of Americans believed that GM foods were not safe to eat.

market the role of transmitting information about the safety of GM products, by providing an opportunity and an incentive for consumers to sample the lower cost products made with GMOs voluntarily. Our data indicate that a large fraction of consumers would do so.

We conclude with some thoughts about the future of GM foods in Europe. Following the framework of Nelson (1970) and Darby and Karni (1973) we can divide the characteristics of a product into three groups. A search characteristic is a property, such as color or shape, which the buyer can identify before purchase. An experience characteristic, such as taste, is only identified at the time the product is consumed, and a credence characteristic, such as nutritional value or chemical content, can never be identified, other than from information provided by a third party. Under a mandatory labelling system, the GMO content of a product is a search characteristic for products labelled "containing GMOs" and a credence characteristic for an unlabelled product. During the introduction of GM foods on the market, their safety and their equivalence to conventional products are also credence characteristics.

We believe that the experience of the segment of the market that purchased and consumed GM products would in time convince a greater percentage of consumers of the safety of GMOs and of the equivalence of products containing GMOs with conventional products. Safety and equivalence would become experience characteristics rather than credence characteristics. If this occurs, the threshold issue would become irrelevant in the long run. This argues for a fairly loose standard of what can be considered GMO-free that is not very costly to meet (such as 1% of any ingredient). Though the actual level of GMO content in a "GMO-free" product would remain a credence characteristic, who would care?

REFERENCES

Ajzen, I., Brown, T. and Rosenthal, C. (1996). Information bias in contingent valuation: effects of personal relevance, quality of information and motivational orientation, *Journal of Environmental Economics and Management*, vol. 30 (January), pp. 43–57.

Akerlof, G. (1970). The market for lemons: qualitative uncertainty and the market mechanism, *Quarterly Journal of Economics*, vol. 89 (August), pp. 488–500.

Aldrich, L. and Blisard, N. (1998). Consumer acceptance of biotechnology: lessons from the rbST experience, *Current Issues in Economics of Food Markets*, (December), pp. 1–6.

Anderson, K., Neilson, C. and Robinson, S. (2000). Estimating the economic effects of GMOs: the importance of policy choices and preferences, CIES Policy Discussion paper 35, University of Adelaide.

Becker, G., DeGroot, M. and Marschak, J. (1964). Measuring utility by a single-response sequential method, *Behavioral Science*, vol. 9 (July), pp. 226–32.

Blamey, R., Common, M. and Quiggin, J. (1995). Respondents to contingent valuation surveys: consumers or citizens? *Australian Journal of Agricultural Economics*, vol. 39 (December), pp. 263–88.

Bohm, P., Lindén, J. and Sonnegård J. (1997). Eliciting reservation prices: Becker-Degroot-Marschak mechanisms *vs.* markets, *Economic Journal*, vol. 107 (July), pp. 1079–89.

Brookshire, D. and Coursey, D. (1987). Measuring the value of a public good: an empirical comparison of elicitation procedures, *American Economic Review*, vol. 77 (September), pp. 554–66.

Buckwell, A., Brookes, G. and Bradley, D. (1999). Economics of identity preservation for genetically modified crops, *Food Biotechnology Communications Initiative Report*.

Caswell, J. (1998). Should use of genetically modified organisms be labelled?, *AgBioForum*, vol. 1(1), pp. 22–4.

Caswell, J. (2000). Labelling policy for GMOs: to each his own?, *AgBioForum*, vol. 3(1), pp. 305–9.

Combris, P., Lecocq, S. and Visser, M. (1997). Estimation of a hedonic price equation for Bordeaux wine: does quality matter?, *Economic Journal*, vol. 107 (March), pp. 390–402.

Cummings, R., Harrison, G. and Rutstrom, E. (1995). Homegrown values and hypothetical surveys: is the dichotomous choice approach incentive compatible?, *American Economic Review*, vol. 85 (March), pp. 260–6.

Darby, M. and Karni, E. (1973). Free competition and the optimal amount of fraud, *Journal of Law and Economics*, vol. 16 (April), pp. 67–88.

Falk-Zepeda, J., Traxler, G. and Nelson, R. (2000). Surplus distribution from the introduction of a biotechnology innovation, *American Journal of Agricultural Economics*, vol. 82 (May), pp. 360–9.

Fox, J., Hayes, D. and Shogren, J. (2002). Consumer preferences for food irradiation: how Favorable and unfavorable descriptions affect preferences for irradiated pork in experimental auctions, *Journal of Risk and Uncertainty,* vol. 24(1) (January), pp. 75–95.

Fox, J., Shogren, J., Hayes, D. and Kliebenstein, J. (1998). CVM-X: calibrating contingent values with experimental auction markets, *American Journal of Agricultural Economics,* vol. 80 (August), pp. 455–65.

Hoffman, E., Menkhaus, D., Chakravarti, D., Field, R. and Whipple, G. (1993). Using laboratory experimental auctions in marketing research: a case study of new packaging for fresh beef, *Marketing Science,* vol. 12(3), pp. 318–38.

Huffman, W., Shogren, J., Rousu, M. and Tegene, A. (2001). The value to consumers of GM foods in a market with asymmetric information: evidence from experimental auctions, mimeo, Iowa State University.

Irwin, J., McClelland, G., McKee, M., Schulze, W. and Norden, N. (1998). Payoff dominance vs. cognitive transparency in decision making, *Economic Inquiry,* vol. 36 (April), pp. 272–85.

Kagel, J., Harstad, R and Levin, D. (1987). Information impact and allocation rules in auctions with affiliated private values: a laboratory study, *Econometrica,* vol. 55 (November), pp. 1275–304.

Krutilla, J. (1967). Conservation reconsidered, *American Economic Review,* vol. 57 (September), pp. 777–86.

Lence, S. and Hayes, D. (2001). Response to asymmetric demand for attributes: an application to the market for genetically modified crops, mimeo, Iowa State University.

Lin, W., Price, G. and Fernandez-Cornejo, J. (2001). Estimating farm level effects of adopting herbicide-tolerant soybeans, *Oil Crops Situation and Outlook,* Economic Research Service, USDA, (October), pp. 25–34.

List, J. and Gallet, C. (2001). What experimental protocol influence disparities between actual and hypothetical stated values? Evidence from a meta-analysis, *Environmental and Resource Economics,* vol. 20 (November), pp. 241–54.

List, J. and Shogren, J. (1998). Calibration between actual and hypothetical bids in a field experiment, *Journal of Economic Behavior and Organisation,* vol. 37 (October), pp. 193–205.

Lusk, J., Daniel, M., Mark, D. and Lusk, C. (2000). Alternative calibration and auction institutions for predicting consumer willingness-to-pay for non-genetically modified corn chips, mimeo, Mississippi State University.

Moon, W. and Balasubrimanian, S. (2001). A multi-attribute model of public acceptance of genetically modified organisms, mimeo, Southern Illinois University.

Neill, H., Cummings, R., Ganderton, P., Harrison, G, and McGuckin, T. (1994). Hypothetical surveys and real economic commitments, *Land, Economics,* vol. 70 (May), pp. 145–54.

Nelson, P. (1970). Information and consumer behavior, *Journal of Political,* vol. 78 (March–April), pp. 311–29.

Noussair, C., Robin, S. and Ruffieux, B. (2001). Genetically modified organisms in the food supply: public opinion vs. consumer behavior, mimeo, Purdue University.

Noussair, C., Robin, S. and Ruffieux, B. (2002). Do consumers not care about biotech foods or do they just not read the labels?, *Economics Letters,* vol. 75 (March), pp. 47–53.

Noussair, C., Robin, S. and Ruffieux, B. (Forthcoming). A comparison of hedonic rating and demand revealing auctions, *Food Quality and Preference.*

Nyborg, K. (2000). Homo Economicus and Homo Politicus: interpretation and aggregation of environmental values, *Journal of Economic Behavior and Organisation,* vol. 42 (July), pp. 305–22.

Romer, P. (2001). Lecture at the American Economic Association Meetings, New Orleans.

Rutstrom, E. (1998). Home-grown values and incentive compatible auction design, *International Journal of Game Theory,* vol. 27 (October), pp. 427–41.

Sagoff, M. (1988). *The Economy of the Earth,* Cambridge: Cambridge University Press.

Shogren, J. (2004). Experimental methods and valuation, in (K.-G. Mäler and J. Vincent, eds.), *Handbook of Environmental Economics,* vol. 2, *Valuing Environmental Changes,* Amsterdam: North Holland.

Shogren, J., Fox, J., Hayes, D. and Roosen, J. (1999). Observed choices for food safety in retail, survey, and auction markets, *American Journal of Agricultural Economics,* vol. 81(5), (December), pp. 192–99.

Smith, V. (1982). Microeconomic systems as an experimental science, *American Economic Review,* vol. 72 (December), pp. 923–55.

Stevens, T., Echeverria, J., Glass, R., Hager, T. and More, T. (1991). Measuring the existence value of wildlife: what do CVM estimates really show?, *Land Economics,* vol. 67 (November), pp. 390–400.

Traxler, G., Falck-Zepeda, J. and Nelson, R. (2000). Rent creation and distribution from biotechnology innovations: the case of Bt cotton and herbicide-tolerant soybeans in 1997, *Agribusiness,* no. 1 (Winter).

Vickrey, W. (1961). Counter speculation, auctions, and competitive sealed tenders, *Journal of Finance,* vol. 16 (March), pp. 8–37.

Reading Questions

1. According to the authors of the study, what factors seem to account for customers' aversion to genetically modified foods in Europe?

2. Explain the researchers' rationale for using an experimental method, instead of relying on survey data, to determine the "extent that actual decisions to purchase food products are affected by the presence of GMOs" (par. 3).

3. According to the researchers, under what circumstances would it be economically advisable to separate the production tracks of products that contain GMOs and those that do not and to enforce "mandatory labelling of products containing GMOs" (7)?

4. What steps did the researchers take to ensure that their study participants accurately represented the population demographics of Grenoble?

5. The researchers classify their study participants into four categories, based on their findings. What are the four categories of participants, and what percentage of participants fell into each of the four categories?

6. What finding led the researchers to conclude that "a public information campaign intended to lead to a greater acceptance of GMOs may face considerable challenges" (32)?

7. According to the researchers, polling data in France indicates that GMOs should be banned from food. However, their experimental research indicates otherwise. How do the researchers explain this difference?

8. Based on their findings overall, what recommendation do the researchers make for the separation and labeling of products that do and do not contain GMOs in France?

Rhetoric Questions

9. In a brief paragraph, explain the purpose of section 1 of the study report, "Policy Issues: Segregation and Thresholds," in terms of the overall design of the report. What function does it serve in the overall design of the report?

10. The researchers provide four distinct reasons why they chose to use the Becker-DeGroot-Marschak (BDM) protocol for eliciting responses from their subjects. Why do you believe the researchers need to spend so much time offering a rationale for this particular research protocol, in light of the study's overall aims?

11. Look closely at the five paragraphs that make up section 3.1 of the report, "The Impact of GMO Information." What can you determine about the organizational strategy used to compose these paragraphs? Is there a consistent strategy? If so, what is it?

12. In what parts of the study report do you find use of first-person pronouns? Why do you suppose the authors use first-person pronouns in those parts of the study?

Response and Research Questions

13. As the authors of this study indicate, there is much variation in the use and labeling of GMOs in products between the United States and France. Do you consider the GMO content of a product when you are making a purchase? If so, how does the GMO content level affect your purchase decision? How does the purchase price affect your decision, if the cost is different from a non-GMO product?

14. Visit your local grocery store and try to locate a product with a brand that includes a GMO and a brand of the product that does not. What are the differences in cost? What are the differences in their labeling?

15. Noussair et al. rely on a number of sophisticated statistical procedures in their study, and they summarize large quantities of data in graphs. Design a graph to visually represent the findings the researchers present in section 3.2 of the report, "Bidder Types and Demographics." Be sure to include the four classifications of customers: Unwilling, Indifferent, Favorable, and Reluctant.

ACADEMIC CASE STUDY · GENETICALLY MODIFIED FOOD **NATURAL SCIENCES**

Maternal and Fetal Exposure to Pesticides Associated to Genetically Modified Foods in Eastern Townships of Quebec, Canada

AZIZ ARIS AND SAMUEL LEBLANC

Aziz Aris is an investigator for the Mother and Child Axis at the Clinical Research Center and associate professor of obstetrics and gynecology at the University of Sherbrooke Hospital in Quebec, Canada. With Samuel Leblanc, co-author of the study below, the researchers report on their investigation into the presence of pesticides associated with genetically modified foods in women (pregnant and nonpregnant) in eastern Canada. As the authors indicate, one of the goals of their research is to help "develop procedures to avoid environmentally induced disease in susceptible populations such as pregnant women and their fetuses." This article first appeared in the journal *Reproductive Toxicology* in 2011.

> Learn more about the use of non-rhetorical titles in the sciences on pages 253 and 281.

> Learn more about the presentation of researchers' names and the value of collaboration in the sciences on page 257.

ABSTRACT

> Learn more about the conventional expectations for abstracts on pages 205–6.

Pesticides associated to genetically modified foods (PAGMF) are engineered to tolerate her-bicides such as glyphosate (GLYP) and gluphosinate (GLUF) or insecticides such as the bacterial toxin bacillus thuringiensis (Bt). The aim of this study was to evaluate the correla-tion between maternal and fetal exposure, and to determine exposure levels of GLYP and its metabolite aminomethyl phosphoric acid (AMPA), GLUF and its metabolite 3-methylphos-phinicopropionic acid (3-MPPA), and Cry1Ab protein (a Bt toxin) in Eastern Townships of Quebec, Canada. Blood of thirty pregnant women (PW) and thirty-nine nonpregnant women (NPW) was studied. Serum GLYP and GLUF were detected in NPW and not detected in PW. Serum 3-MPPA and CryAb1 toxin were detected in PW, their fetuses, and NPW. This is the first study to reveal the presence of circulating PAGMF in women with and without pregnancy, paving the way for a new field in reproductive toxicology including nutrition and uteroplacental toxicities.

Learn more about the IMRaD format commonly used in research reports in the sciences on pages 197–204.

1. INTRODUCTION

An optimal exchange across the maternal-fetal unit (MFU) is necessary for a successful pregnancy. The placenta plays a major role in the embryo's nutrition and growth, in the regulation of the endocrine functions, and in drug biotransformation [1–3]. Exchange involves not only physiological constituents, but also substances that represent a pathological risk for the fetus such as xenobiotics that include drugs, food additives, pesticides, and environmental pollutants [4]. The understanding of what xenobiotics do to the MFU and what the MFU does to the xenobiotics should provide the basis for the use of the placenta as a tool to investigate and predict some aspects of developmental toxicity [4]. Moreover, pathological conditions in the placenta are important causes of intrauterine or perinatal death, congenital anomalies, intrauterine growth retardation, maternal death, and a great deal of morbidity for both mother and child [5].

Aris and Leblanc establish necessary background information for their study, including the identification of a specific problem: the possible threat of pesticides-associated GM foods to human health.

Genetically modified plants (GMP) were first approved for commercialization in Canada in 1996 then became distributed worldwide. Global areas of these GMP increased from 1.7 million hectares in 1996 to 134 million hectares in 2009, an 80-fold increase [6]. This growth rate makes GMP the fastest-adopted crop technology [6]. GMP are plants in which genetic material has been altered in a way that does not occur naturally. Genetic engineering allows gene transfer (transgenesis) from an organism into another in order to confer them new traits. Combining GMP with pesticides-associated GM foods (PAGMF) allows the protection of desirable crops and the elimination of unwanted plants by reducing the competition for nutrients or by providing insect resistance. There is a debate on the direct threat of genes used in the preparation of these new foods on human health, as they are not detectable in the body, but the real danger may come from PAGMF [6–10]. Among the innumerable PAGMF, two categories are largely used in our agriculture since their introduction in 1996: (1) residues derived from herbicide-tolerant GM crops such as glyphosate (GLYP) and its metabolite aminomethyl phosphoric acid (AMPA) [11], and gluphosinate ammonium (GLUF) and its metabolite 3-methylphosphinicopropionic acid (MPPA) [12]; and (2) residues derived from insect-resistant GM crops such as Cry1Ab protein [13,14].

Among herbicide-tolerant GM crops, the first to be grown commercially were soybeans which were modified to tolerate glyphosate [11]. Glyphosate [*N*-(Phosphonomethyl) glycine] is a nonselective, post-emergence herbicide used for the control of a wide range of weeds [15]. It can be used on non-crop land as well as in a great variety of crops. GLYP is the active ingredient in the commercial herbicide Roundup®. Glyphosate is an acid, but usually used in a salt form, most commonly the isopropylamine salt. The target of glyphosate is 5-enolpyruvoylshikimate 3-phosphate synthase (EPSPS), an enzyme in the shikimate pathway that is required for the synthesis of many aromatic plant metabolites, including some amino acids. The gene that confers tolerance of the herbicide is from the soil bacterium *Agrobacterium tumefaciens* and makes an EPSPS that is not affected by glyphosate. Few studies have examined the kinetics of absorption, distribution, metabolism, and elimination (ADME) of glyphosate in humans [15,16]. Curwin et al. [17] reported detection of urinary GLYP concentrations among children, mothers, and fathers living in farm and nonfarm households in Iowa. The ranges of detection were 0.062–5.0 ng/ml and 0.10–11 ng/ml for nonfarm and farm mothers, respectively. There was no significant difference between farm and nonfarm mothers and no positive association between the mothers' urinary glyphosate levels and glyphosate dust concentrations. These findings suggest that other sources of exposure such as diet may be involved.

Gluphosinate (or glufosinate) [ammonium dl-homoalanin-4-(methyl) phosphinate] 5 is a broad-spectrum, contact herbicide. Its major metabolite is 3-methylphosphinicopropionic acid (MPPA), with which it has similar biological and toxicological effects [18]. GLUF is used to control a wide range of weeds after the crop emerges or for total vegetation control on land not used for cultivation. Gluphosinate herbicides are also used to desiccate (dry out) crops before harvest. It is a phosphorus-containing amino acid. It inhibits the activity of an enzyme, glutamine synthetase, which is necessary for the production of the amino acid glutamine and for ammonia detoxification [12]. The application of GLUF leads to reduced glutamine and increased ammonia levels in the plant's tissues. This causes photosynthesis to stop and the plant dies within a few days. GLUF also inhibits the same enzyme in animals [19]. The gene used to make plants resistant to gluphosinate comes from the bacterium *Streptomyces hygroscopicus* and encodes an enzyme called phosphinothricine acetyl transferase (PAT). This enzyme detoxifies GLUF. Crop varieties carrying this trait include varieties of oilseed rape, maize, soybeans, sugar beet, fodder beet, cotton, and rice. As for GLYP, its kinetics of absorption, distribution, metabolism, and elimination (ADME) is not well studied in humans, except for a few poisoned-case studies [16,20,21]. Hirose et al. reported the case of a 65-year-old male who ingested BASTA, which contains 20% (w/v) of GLUF ammonium, about 300 ml, more than the estimated human toxic dose [20]. The authors studied the serial change of serum GLUF concentration every 3–6 h and assessed the urinary excretion of GLUF every 24 h. The absorbed amount of GLUF was estimated from the cumulative urinary excretion. The changes in serum GLUF concentration exhibited $T_{1/2\alpha}$ of 1.84 and $T_{1/2\alpha}$ of 9.59 h. The apparent distribution volume at b-phase and the total body clearance were 1.44 1/kg and 86.6 ml/min, respectively. Renal clearance was estimated to be 77.9 ml/min.

The Cry1Ab toxin is an insecticidal protein produced by the naturally occurring soil bacterium *Bacillus thuringiensis* [22,23]. The gene (truncated *cry1Ab* gene) encoding this insecticidal protein was genetically transformed into maize genome to produce a transgenic insect-resistant plant (Bt-maize; MON810) and, thereby, provide specific protection against Lepidoptera infestation [13,14]. For more than 10 years, GM crops have been commercialized and approved as an animal feed in several countries worldwide. The Cry toxins (protoxins) produced by GM crops are solubilized and activated to Cry toxins by gut proteases of susceptible insect larvae. Activated toxin binds to specific receptors localized in the midgut epithelial cells [24,25], invading the cell membrane and forming cation-selective ion channels that lead to the disruption of the epithelial barrier and larval death by osmotic cell lysis [26–28].

> Learn more about the use of jargon in scientific communication on page 254.

> Aris and Leblanc review the current state of scholarship on residues from herbicide-tolerant (GLYP, GLUF) and insect-resistant GM crops (Cry1Ab) that are the focus of this study. Learn more about literature reviews on pages 211–26.

Since the basis of better health is prevention, one would hope that we can develop procedures to avoid environmentally induced disease in susceptible populations such as pregnant women and their fetuses. The fetus is considered to be highly susceptible to the adverse effects of xenobiotics. This is because environmental agents could disrupt the biological events that are required to ensure normal growth and development [29,30]. PAGMF are among the xenobiotics that have recently emerged and extensively entered the human food chain [9], paving the way for a new field of multidisciplinary research, combining human reproduction, toxicology, and nutrition, but not as yet explored. Generated data will help regulatory agencies responsible for the protection of human health to make better decisions. Thus, the aim of this study was to investigate whether pregnant women are exposed to PAGMF and whether these toxicants cross the placenta to reach the fetus.

Aris and Leblanc establish the focus for their study: "to investigate whether pregnant women are exposed to PAGMF and whether these toxicants cross the placenta to reach the fetus."

2. MATERIALS AND METHODS

2.1. Chemicals and reagents

For the analytical support (Section 2.3), GLYP, AMPA, GLUF, APPA, and N-methyl-N-(tert-butyldimethylsilyl) trifluoroacetamide (MTBSTFA) + 1% tertburyldimethyl-chlorosilane (TBDMCS) were purchased from Sigma (St. Louis, MO, USA). 3-MPPA was purchased from Wako Chemicals USA (Richmond, VA, USA), and Sep-Pak Plus PS-2 cartridges, from Waters Corporation (Milford, MA, USA). All other chemicals and reagents were of analytical grade (Sigma, MO, USA). The serum samples for validation were collected from volunteers.

Learn more about the detailed reporting of methods and its relationship to replicability in the sciences on pages 255–56.

2.2. Study subjects and blood sampling

At the Centre Hospitalier Universitaire de Sherbrooke (CHUS), we formed two groups of subjects: (1) a group of healthy pregnant women ($n = 30$), recruited at delivery; and (2) a group of healthy fertile nonpregnant women ($n = 39$), recruited during their tubal ligation of sterilization. As shown in Table 1 of clinical characteristics of subjects, eligible groups were matched for age and body mass index (BMI). Participants were not known for cigarette or illicit drug use or for medical condition (i.e., diabetes, hypertension, or metabolic disease). Pregnant women had vaginal delivery and did not have any adverse perinatal outcomes. All neonates were of appropriate size for gestational age (3423 ± 375 g).

Learn more about the use of passive voice and its relationship to the appearance of objectivity on pages 207–8.

Blood sampling was done before delivery for pregnant women or at tubal ligation for nonpregnant women and was most commonly obtained from the median cubital vein, on the anterior forearm. Umbilical cord blood sampling was done after birth using the syringe method. Since labor time can take several hours, the time between taking the last meal and blood sampling is often a matter of hours. Blood samples were collected in BD Vacutainer 10 ml glass serum tubes (Franklin Lakes, NJ, USA). To obtain serum, whole blood was centrifuged at 2000 rpm for 15 min within 1 h of collection. For maternal samples, about 10 ml of blood was collected, resulting in 5–6.5 ml of serum. For cord blood samples, about 10 ml of blood was also collected by syringe, giving 3–4.5 ml of serum. Serum was stored at $-20°C$ until assayed for PAGMF levels.

Table 1

Characteristics of subjects

	Pregnant women (*n* = 30)	Nonpregnant women (*n* = 39)	*P* value[a]
Age (year, mean ± SD)	32.4 ± 4.2	33.9 ± 4.0	NS
BMI (kg/m², mean ± SD)	24.9 ± 3.1	24.8 ± 3.4	NS
Gestational age (week, mean ± SD)	38.3 ± 2.5	N/A	N/A
Birth weight (g, mean ± SD)	3364 ± 335	N/A	N/A

BMI, body mass index; N/A, not applicable; data are expressed as mean ± SD; NS, not significant.

[a]*P* values were determined by Mann-Whitney test.

Subjects were pregnant and nonpregnant women living in Sherbrooke, an urban area of Eastern Townships of Quebec, Canada. No subject had worked or lived with a spouse working in contact with pesticides. The diet taken is typical of a middle-class population of Western industrialized countries. A food market-basket, representative for the general Sherbrooke population, contains various meats, margarine, canola oil, rice, corn, grain, peanuts, potatoes, fruits and vegetables, eggs, poultry, meat, and fish. Beverages include milk, juice, tea, coffee, bottled water, soft drinks, and beer. Most of these foods come mainly from the province of Quebec, then the rest of Canada and the United States of America. Our study did not quantify the exact levels of PAGMF in a market-basket study. However, given the widespread use of GM foods in the local daily diet (soybeans, corn, potatoes, . . .), it is conceivable that the majority of the population is exposed through their daily diet [31,32].

The study was approved by the CHUS Ethics Human Research Committee on Clinical Research. All participants gave written consent.

Learn more about the IRB process and the use of human subjects in research on page 196.

2.3. Herbicide and metabolite determination

Levels of GLYP, AMPA, GLUF, and 3-MPPA were measured using gas chromatography-mass spectrometry (GC–MS).

2.3.1. CALIBRATION CURVE

According to a method described by Motojyuku et al. [16], GLYP, AMPA, GLUF, and 3-MPPA (1 mg/ml) were prepared in 10% methanol, which is used for all standard dilutions. These solutions were further diluted to concentrations of 100 and 10 μg/ml and stored for a maximum of 3 months at 4°C. A 1 μg/ml solution from previous components was made prior to herbicide extraction. These solutions were used as calibrators. A stock solution of DL-2-amino-3-phosphonopropionic acid (APPA) (1 mg/ml) was prepared and used as an internal standard (IS). The IS stock solution was further diluted to a concentration of 100 μg/ml. Blank serum samples (0.2 ml) were spiked with 5 μl of IS (100 μg/ml), 5 μl of each calibrator solution (100 μg/ml), or 10, 5 μl of 10 μg/ml solution, or 10, 5 μl of 1 μg/ml solution, resulting in calibration samples containing 0.5 μg of IS (2.5 μg/ml), with 0.5 μg (2.5 μg/ml), 0.1 μg (0.5 μg/ml), 0.05 μg (0.25 μg/ml), 0.01 μg (0.05 μg/ml), or 0.005 μg (0.025 μg/ml) of each compound (i.e., GLYP, AMPA, GLUF, and 3-MPPA). Concerning extraction development, spiked serum with 5 μg/ml of each compound was used as a control sample.

2.3.2. EXTRACTION PROCEDURE

The calibration curves and serum samples were extracted by employing a solid phase extraction (SPE) technique, modified from manufacturers' recommendations and from Motojyuku et al. [16]. Spiked serum (0.2 ml), prepared as described above, and acetonitrile (0.2 ml) were added to centrifuge tubes. The tubes were then vortexed (15 s) and centrifuged (5 min, 1600 $\times$ g). The samples were purified by SPE using 100 mg Sep-Pak Plus PS-2 cartridges, which were conditioned by washing with 4 ml of acetonitrile followed by 4 ml of distilled water. The samples were loaded onto the SPE cartridges, dried (3 min, 5 psi), and eluted with 2 ml of acetonitrile. The solvent was evaporated to dryness under nitrogen. The samples were reconstituted in 50 μl each of MTBSTFA with 1% TBDMCS and acetonitrile. The mixture was vortexed for 30 s every 10 min, 6 times. Samples of solution containing the derivatives were used directly for GC–MS (Agilent Technologies 6890N GC and 5973 Invert MS).

2.3.3. GC–MS ANALYSIS

Chromatographic conditions for these analyses were as follows: a 30 m $\times$ 0.25 mm Zebron ZB-5MS fused-silica capillary column with a film thickness of 0.25 μm from Phenomenex (Torrance, CA, USA) was used. Helium was used as a carrier gas at 1.1 ml/min. A 2 μl extract was injected in a split mode at an injection temperature of 250°C. The oven temperature was programmed to increase from an initial temperature of 100°C (held for 3 min) to 300°C (held for 5 min) at 5°C/min. The temperatures of the quadrupode, ion source, and mass-selective detector interface were respectively 150, 230, and 280°C. The MS was operated in the selected-ion monitoring (SIM) mode. The following ions were monitored (with quantitative ions in parentheses): GLYP (454), 352; AMPA (396), 367; GLUF (466); 3-MPPA (323); IS (568), 466.

The limit of detection (LOD) is defined as a signal of three times the noise. For 0.2 ml serum samples, LOD was 15, 10, 10, and 5 ng/ml for GLYP, GLUF, AMPA, and 3-MPPA, respectively.

2.4. Cry1Ab protein determination

Cry1Ab protein levels were determined in blood using a commercially available double antibody sandwich (DAS) enzyme-linked immunosorbent assay (Agdia, Elkhart, IN, USA), following manufacturer's instructions. A standard curve was prepared by successive dilutions (0.1–10 ng/ml) of purified Cry1Ab protein (Fitzgerald Industries International, North Acton, MA, USA) in PBST buffer. The mean absorbance (650 nm) was calculated and used to determine samples concentration. Positive and negative controls were prepared with the kit Cry1Ab positive control solution, diluted 1/2 in serum.

2.5. Statistical analysis

PAGMF exposure was expressed as number, range, and mean $\pm$ SD for each group. Characteristics of cases and controls and PAGMF exposure were compared using the

Learn more about the use of numbers and other symbol systems in the sciences on page 254.

Mann–Whitney U-test for continuous data and by Fisher's exact test for categorical data. Wilcoxon matched pairs test compared two dependent groups. Other statistical analyses were performed using Spearman correlations. Analyses were realized with the software SPSS version 17.0. A value of $P < 0.05$ was considered as significant for every statistical analysis.

3. RESULTS

As shown in Table 1, pregnant women and nonpregnant women were similar in terms of age and body mass index. Pregnant women had normal deliveries and birth-weight infants (Table 1).

GLYP and GLUF were non-detectable (nd) in maternal and fetal serum, but detected in nonpregnant women (Table 2, Fig. 1). GLYP was [2/39 (5%), range (nd-93.6 ng/ml), and mean ± SD (73.6 ± 28.2 ng/ml)] and GLUF was [7/39 (18%), range (nd-53.6 ng/ml), and mean ± SD (28.7 ± 15.7 ng/ml)]. AMPA was not detected in maternal, fetal,

Learn more visual representation of data and findings from statistical procedures in scientific research on pages 202–4.

Table 2
Concentrations of GLYP, AMPA, GLUF, 3-MPPA, and Cry1Ab protein in maternal and fetal cord serum

	Maternal ($n = 30$)	Fetal cord ($n = 30$)	P value[a]
GLYP			
Number of detection	nd	nd	nc
Range of detection (ng/ml)			
Mean ± SD			
AMPA			
Number of detection	nd	nd	nc
Range of detection (ng/ml)			
Mean ± SD (ng/ml)			
GLUF			
Number of detection	nd	nd	nc
Range of detection (ng/ml)			
Mean ± SD (ng/ml)			
3-MPPA			
Number of detection	30/30 (100%)	30/30 (100%)	$P < 0.001$
Range of detection (ng/ml)	21.9-417	8.76-193	
Mean ± SD (ng/ml)	120 ± 87.0	57.2 ± 45.6	
Cry1Ab			
Number of detection	28/30 (93%)	24/30 (80%)	$P = 0.002$
Range of detection (ng/ml)	nd-1.50	nd-0.14	
Mean ± SD (ng/ml)	0.19 ± 0.30	0.04 ± 0.04	

GLYP, glyphosate; AMPA, aminomethyl phosphoric acid; GLUF, gluphosinate ammonium; 3-MPPA, 3-methylphosphinicopropionic acid; Cry1Ab, protein from *Bacillus thuringiensis*; nd, not detectable; nc, not calculable because not detectable. Data are expressed as number (n, %) of detection, range, and mean ± SD (ng/ml).
[a]P values were determined by Wilcoxon matched pairs test.

and nonpregnant women samples. The metabolite 3-MPPA was detected in maternal serum [30/30 (100%), range (21.9-417 ng/ml), and mean ± SD (120 ± 87.0 ng/ml)], in fetal cord serum [30/30 (100%), range (8.76-193 ng/ml), and mean mean ± SD (57.2 ± 45.6 ng/ml)], and in nonpregnant women serum [26/39 (67%), range (nd-337 ng/ml), and mean ± SD (84.1 ± 70.3 ng/ml)]. A significant difference in 3-MPPA levels was evident between maternal and fetal serum ($P < 0.001$, Table 2, Fig. 1), but not between maternal and nonpregnant women serum ($P = 0.075$, Table 3, Fig. 1).

Serum insecticide Cry1Ab toxin was detected in: (1) pregnant women [28/30 (93%), range (nd-1.5 ng/ml), and mean ± SD (0.19 ± 0.30 ng/ml)]; (2) nonpregnant women [27/39 (69%), range (nd-2.28 ng/ml), and mean ± SD (0.13 ± 0.37 ng/ml)]; and (3) fetal cord [24/30 (80%), range (nd-0.14 ng/ml), and mean ± SD (0.04 ± 0.04

Aris and Leblanc present only the findings of their research in this section of their report. Learn more about Results sections in scientific research on pages 200–201.

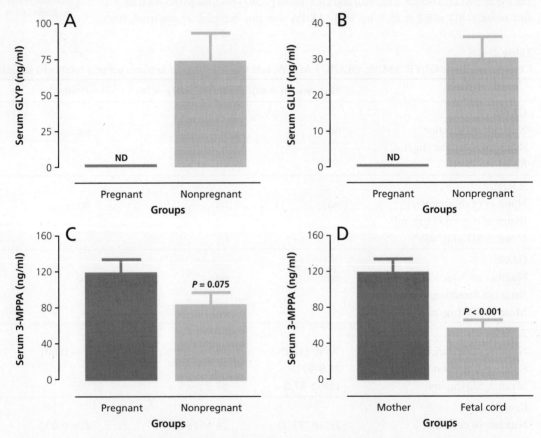

Figure 1. Circulating concentrations of glyphosate (GLYP: A), gluphosinate (GLUF: B), and 3-methylphosphinicopropionic acid (3-MPPA: C and D) in pregnant and nonpregnant women (A–C) and in maternal and fetal cord blood (D). Blood sampling was performed from 30 pregnant women and 39 nonpregnant women. Chemicals were assessed using GC-MS. *P* values were determined by Mann-Whitney test in the comparison of pregnant women to nonpregnant women (A–C). *P* values were determined by Wilcoxon matched pairs test in the comparison of maternal to fetal samples (D). A *P* value of 0.05 was considered as significant.

Table 3

Concentrations of GLYP, AMPA, GLUF, 3-MPPA, and Cry1Ab protein in serum of pregnant and nonpregnant women

	Pregnant women (*n* = 30)	Nonpregnant women (*n* = 39)	*P* value[a]
GLYP			
Number of detection	nd	2/39 (5%)	nc
Range of detection (ng/ml)		nd-93.6	
Mean ± SD		73.6 ± 28.2	
AMPA			
Number of detection	nd	nd	nc
Range of detection (ng/ml)			
Mean ± SD (ng/ml)			
GLUF			
Number of detection	nd	7/39 (18%)	nc
Range of detection (ng/ml)		nd-53.6	
Mean ± SD (ng/ml)		28.7 ± 15.7	
3-MPPA			
Number of detection	30/30 (100%)	26/39 (67%)	*P* = 0.075
Range of detection (ng/ml)	21.9-417	nd-337	
Mean ± SD (ng/ml)	120 ± 87.0	84.1 ± 70.3	
Cry1Ab			
Number of detection	28/30 (93%)	27/39 (69%)	*P* = 0.006
Range of detection (ng/ml)	nd-1.50	nd-2.28	
Mean ± SD (ng/ml)	0.19 ± 0.30	0.13 ± 0.37	

GLYP, glyphosate; AMPA, aminomethyl phosphoric acid; GLUF, gluphosinate ammonium; 3-MPPA, 3-methylphosphinicopropionic acid; Cry1Ab, protein from *Bacillus thuringiensis*; nd, not detectable; nc, not calculable because not detectable. Data are expressed as number (*n*, %) of detection, range, and mean ± SD (ng/ml).

[a]*P* values were determined by Mann-Whitney test.

ng/ml)]. A significant difference in Cry1Ab levels was evident between pregnant and nonpregnant women's serum (*P* = 0.006, Table 3, Fig. 2) and between maternal and fetal serum (*P* = 0.002, Table 2, Fig. 2).

We also investigated a possible correlation between the different contaminants in the same woman. In pregnant women, GLYP, its metabolite AMPA, and GLUF were undetectable in maternal blood and therefore impossible to establish a correlation between them. In nonpregnant women, GLYP was detected in 5% of the subjects, its metabolite AMPA was not detected, and GLUF was detected in 18%; thus, no significant correlation emerged from these contaminants in the same subjects. Moreover,

Aris and Leblanc explain the implications of their findings. Learn more about Discussion sections in IMRaD reports on page 204.

there was no correlation between 3-MPPA and Cry1AB in the same women, both pregnant and not pregnant.

4. DISCUSSION

Our results show that GLYP was not detected in maternal and fetal blood, but present in the blood of some nonpregnant women (5%), whereas its metabolite AMPA was not detected in all analyzed samples. This may be explained by the absence of exposure, the efficiency of elimination, or the limitation of the method of detection. Previous studies report that glyphosate and AMPA share similar toxicological profiles. Glyphosate toxicity has been shown to be involved in the induction of developmental retardation of fetal skeleton [33] and significant adverse effects on the reproductive system of male Wistar rats at puberty and during adulthood [34]. Also, glyphosate was harmful to human placental cells [35,36] and embryonic cells [36]. It is interesting to note that all of these animal and *in vitro* studies used very high concentrations of GLYP compared to the human levels found in our studies. In this regard, our results represent actual concentrations detected in humans and therefore they constitute a referential basis for future investigations in this field.

GLUF was detected in 18% of nonpregnant women's blood and not detected in maternal and fetal blood. As for GLYP, the non-detection of GLUF may be explained by the absence of exposure, the efficiency of elimination, or the limitation of the method of detection. Regarding the non-detection of certain chemicals in pregnant women compared with nonpregnant women, it is assumed that the hemodilution caused by pregnancy may explain, at least in part, such non-detection. On the other hand, 3-MPPA (the metabolite of GLUF) was detected in 100% of maternal and umbilical cord blood samples, and in 67% of the nonpregnant women's blood samples. This highlights that this metabolite is more detectable than its precursor and seems to easily cross the placenta to reach the fetus. Garcia et al. [37] investigated the potential teratogenic effects of GLUF in humans and found increased risk of congenital malformations with exposure to GLUF. GLUF has also been shown in mouse embryos to cause growth retardation, increased death, or hypoplasia [18]. As for GLYP, it is interesting to note that the GLUF concentrations used in these tests are very high (10 ug/ml) compared to the levels we found in this study (53.6 ng/ml). Hence, our data,

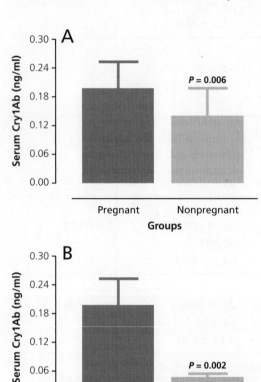

Figure 2. Circulating concentrations of Cry1Ab toxin in pregnant and nonpregnant women (A), and maternal and fetal cord (B). Blood sampling was performed from 30 pregnant women and 39 nonpregnant women. Levels of Cry1Ab toxin were assessed using an ELISA method. *P* values were determined by Mann-Whitney test in the comparison of pregnant women to nonpregnant women (A). *P* values were determined by Wilcoxon matched pairs test in the comparison of maternal to fetal samples (B). A *P* value of 0.05 was considered as significant.

which provide the actual and precise concentrations of these toxicants, will help in the design of more relevant studies in the future.

On the other hand, Cry1Ab toxin was detected in 93% and 80% of maternal and fetal blood samples, respectively, and in 69% of tested blood samples from nonpregnant women. There are no other studies for comparison with our results. However, trace amounts of the Cry1Ab toxin were detected in the gastrointestinal contents of livestock fed on GM corn [38–40], raising concerns about this toxin in insect-resistant GM crops: (1) that these toxins may not be effectively eliminated in humans and (2) there may be a high risk of exposure through consumption of contaminated meat.

Aris and Leblanc repeatedly note the need for additional research, laying the groundwork, based on their contribution, for additional studies.

5. CONCLUSIONS

To our knowledge, this is the first study to highlight the presence of pesticides-associated genetically modified foods in maternal, fetal, and nonpregnant women's blood. 3-MPPA and Cry1Ab toxin are clearly detectable and appear to cross the placenta to the fetus. Given the potential toxicity of these environmental pollutants and the fragility of the fetus, more studies are needed, particularly those using the placental transfer approach [41]. Thus, our present results will provide baseline data for future studies exploring a new area of research relating to nutrition, toxicology, and reproduction in women. Today, obstetric-gynecological disorders that are associated with environmental chemicals are not known. This may involve perinatal complications (i.e., abortion, prematurity, intrauterine growth restriction, and preeclampsia) and reproductive disorders (i.e., infertility, endometriosis, and gynecological cancer). Thus, knowing the actual PAGMF concentrations in humans constitutes a cornerstone in the advancement of research in this area.

Learn more about conclusions in IMRaD reports in the sciences on page 205.

CONFLICT OF INTEREST STATEMENT

The authors declare that they have no competing interests.

ACKNOWLEDGMENTS

This study was supported by funding provided by the Fonds de Recherche en Santé du Québec (FRSQ). The authors wish to thank Drs. Youssef AinMelk, Marie-Thérèse Berthier, Krystel Paris, François Leclerc, and Denis Cyr for their material and technical assistance.

Learn more about Acknowledgments sections in IMRaD reports in the sciences. Note, especially, the importance of understanding a study's funding source on page 206.

REFERENCES

[1] Sastry BV. Techniques to study human placental transport. Adv Drug Deliv Rev 1999;38:17–39.

[2] Haggarty P, Allstaff S, Hoad G, Ashton J, Abramovich DR. Placental nutrient transfer capacity and fetal growth. Placenta 2002;23:86–92.

[3] Gude NM, Roberts CT, Kalionis B, King RG. Growth and function of the normal human placenta. Thromb Res 2004;114:397–407.

[4] Myllynen P, Pasanen M, Pelkonen O. Human placenta: a human organ for developmental toxicology research and biomonitoring. Placenta 2005;26:361–71.

Learn more about reference selection and the value of recency in scientific writing on page 256.

[5] Guillette EA, Meza MM, Aquilar MG, Soto AD, Garcia IE. An anthropological approach to the evaluation of preschool children exposed to pesticides in Mexico. Environ Health Perspect 1998;106:347–53.

[6] Clive J. Global status of commercialized biotech/GM crops. In: ISAAA 2009. 2009.

[7] Pusztai A. Can science give us the tools for recognizing possible health risks of GM food? Nutr Health 2002;16:73–84.

[8] Pusztai A, Bardocz S, Ewen SW. Uses of plant lectins in bioscience and biomedicine. Front Biosci 2008; 13:1130–40.

[9] Magana-Gomez JA, de la Barca AM. Risk assessment of genetically modified crops for nutrition and health. Nutr Rev 2009;67:1–16.

[10] Borchers A, Teuber SS, Keen CL, Gershwin ME. Food safety. Clin Rev Allergy Immunol 2010;39:95–141.

[11] Padgette SR, Taylor NB, Nida DL, Bailey MR, MacDonald J, Holden LR, et al. The composition of glyphosate-tolerant soybean seeds is equivalent to that of conventional soybeans. J Nutr 1996;126:702–16.

[12] Watanabe S. Rapid analysis of glufosinate by improving the bulletin method and its application to soybean and corn. Shokuhin Eiseigaku Zasshi 2002;43:169–72.

[13] Estruch JJ, Warren GW, Mullins MA, Nye GJ, Craig JA, Koziel MG. Vip3A, a novel *Bacillus thuringiensis* vegetative insecticidal protein with a wide spectrum of activities against lepidopteran insects. Proc Natl Acad Sci USA 1996;93:5389–94.

[14] de Maagd RA, Bosch D, Stiekema W. Toxin-mediated insect resistance in plants. Trends Plant Sci 1999;4:9–13.

[15] Hori Y, Fujisawa M, Shimada K, Hirose Y. Determination of the herbicide glyphosate and its metabolite in biological specimens by gas chromatography–mass spectrometry. A case of poisoning by roundup herbicide. J Anal Toxicol 2003;27:162–6.

[16] Motojyuku M, Saito T, Akieda K, Otsuka H, Yamamoto I, Inokuchi S. Determination of glyphosate, glyphosate metabolites, and glufosinate in human serum by gas chromatography-mass spectrometry. J Chromatogr B: Anal Technol Biomed Life Sci 2008;875:509–14.

[17] Curwin BD, Hein MJ, Sanderson WT, Striley C, Heederik D, Kromhout H, et al. Urinary pesticide concentrations among children, mothers and fathers living in farm and non-farm households in Iowa. Ann Occup Hyg 2007;51:53–65.

[18] Watanabe T, Iwase T. Developmental and dysmorphogenic effects of glufosinate ammonium on mouse embryos in culture. Teratog Carcinog Mutagen 1996;16:287–99.

[19] Hoerlein G. Glufosinate (phosphinothricin), a natural amino acid with unexpected herbicidal properties. Rev Environ Contam Toxicol 1994;138:73–145.

[20] Hirose Y, Kobayashi M, Koyama K, Kohda Y, Tanaka T, Honda H, et al. A toxicokinetic analysis in a patient with acute glufosinate poisoning. Hum Exp Toxicol 1999;18:305–8.

[21] Hori Y, Fujisawa M, Shimada K, Hirose Y. Determination of glufosinate ammonium and its metabolite, 3-methylphosphinicopropionic acid, in human serum by gas chromatography–mass spectrometry following mixed-mode solid-phase extraction and t-BDMS derivatization. J Anal Toxicol 2001;25:680–4.

[22] Hofte H, Whiteley HR. Insecticidal crystal proteins of *Bacillus thuringiensis*. Microbiol Rev 1989;53:242–55.

[23] Schnepf E, Crickmore N, Van Rie J, Lereclus D, Baum J, Feitelson J, et al. *Bacillus thuringiensis* and its pesticidal crystal proteins. Microbiol Mol Biol Rev 1998;62:775–806.

[24] Van Rie J, Jansens S, Hofte H, Degheele D, Van Mellaert H. Receptors on the brush border membrane of the insect midgut as determinants of the specificity of *Bacillus thuringiensis* delta-endotoxins. Appl Environ Microbiol 1990;56:1378–85.

[25] Aranda E, Sanchez J, Peferoen M, Guereca L, Bravo A. Interactions of *Bacillus thuringiensis* crystal proteins with the midgut epithelial cells of Spodoptera frugiperda (Lepidoptera: Noctuidae). J Invertebr Pathol 1996;68:203–12.

[26] Slatin SL, Abrams CK, English L. Delta-endotoxins form cation-selective channels in planar lipid bilayers. Biochem Biophys Res Commun 1990;169:765–72.

[27] Knowles BH, Blatt MR, Tester M, Horsnell JM, Carroll J, Menestrina G, et al. A cytolytic delta-endotoxin from *Bacillus thuringiensis* var. israelensis forms cation-selective channels in planar lipid bilayers. FEBS Lett 1989;244:259–62.

[28] Du J, Knowles BH, Li J, Ellar DJ. Biochemical characterization of *Bacillus thuringiensis* cytolytic toxins in association with a phospholipid bilayer. Biochem J 1999;338(Pt 1):185–93.

[29] Dietert RR, Piepenbrink MS. The managed immune system: protecting the womb to delay the tomb. Hum Exp Toxicol 2008;27:129–34.

[30] Dietert RR. Developmental immunotoxicity (DIT), postnatal immune dysfunction and childhood leukemia. Blood Cells Mol Dis 2009;42:108–12.

[31] Chapotin SM, Wolt JD. Genetically modified crops for the bioeconomy: meeting public and regulatory expectations. Transgenic Res 2007;16:675–88.

[32] Rommens CM. Barriers and paths to market for genetically engineered crops. Plant Biotechnol J 2010;8:101–11.

[33] Dallegrave E, Mantese FD, Coelho RS, Pereira JD, Dalsenter PR, Langeloh A. The teratogenic potential of the herbicide glyphosate-roundup in Wistar rats. Toxicol Lett 2003;142:45–52.

[34] Dallegrave E, Mantese FD, Oliveira RT, Andrade AJ, Dalsenter PR, Langeloh A. Pre- and postnatal toxicity of the commercial glyphosate formulation in Wistar rats. Arch Toxicol 2007;81:665–73.

[35] Richard S, Moslemi S, Sipahutar H, Benachour N, Seralini GE. Differential effects of glyphosate and roundup on human placental cells and aromatase. Environ Health Perspect 2005;113:716–20.

[36] Benachour N, Seralini GE. Glyphosate formulations induce apoptosis and necrosis in human umbilical, embryonic, and placental cells. Chem Res Toxicol 2009;22:97–105.

[37] Garcia AM, Benavides FG, Fletcher T, Orts E. Paternal exposure to pesticides and congenital malformations. Scand J Work Environ Health 1998;24:473–80.

[38] Chowdhury EH, Shimada N, Murata H, Mikami O, Sultana P, Miyazaki S, et al. Detection of Cry1Ab protein in gastrointestinal contents but not visceral organs of genetically modified Bt11-fed calves. Vet Hum Toxicol 2003;45:72–5.

[39] Chowdhury EH, Kuribara H, Hino A, Sultana P, Mikami O, Shimada N, et al. Detection of corn intrinsic and recombinant DNA fragments and Cry1Ab protein in the gastrointestinal contents of pigs fed genetically modified corn Bt11. J Anim Sci 2003;81:2546–51.

[40] Lutz B, Wiedemann S, Einspanier R, Mayer J, Albrecht C. Degradation of Cry1Ab protein from genetically modified maize in the bovine gastrointestinal tract. J Agric Food Chem 2005;53:1453–6.

[41] Myren M, Mose T, Mathiesen L, Knudsen LE. The human placenta—an alternative for studying foetal exposure. Toxicol in Vitro 2007;21:1332–40.

Reading Questions

1. The researchers establish early in the introduction that their focus is not concerned with the effects of genetically modified (GM) foods on humans; instead, their focus is on the effects of pesticides associated with GM foods (PAGMF): "There is a debate on the direct threat of genes used in the preparation of these new foods on human health, as they are not detectable in the body, but the real danger may come from PAGMF" (par. 3). What are the two categories of pesticides the researchers focus on?

2. According to the researchers, what are the potential benefits of their findings for the general public as well as for other academic researchers?

3. Describe the two study groups created by the researchers. What characteristics of each group did the researchers consider as they created these two groups?

4. In the Discussion section, the researchers report that they detected 3-MPPA (a metabolite of gluphosinate, or GLUF, an herbicide) "in 100% of maternal and umbilical cord blood samples" (25). However, they also take caution to note the concentration levels of the detected herbicide. Why is the detected concentration important?

5. In light of their findings regarding the insecticide Cry1Ab toxin, what are two concerns that the researchers express?

Rhetoric Questions

6. The researchers frequently take caution not to overstate the implications of their findings. What strategies do the researchers use to hedge these implications?

7. The study's Introduction reviews previous research conducted on the pesticides under investigation. On average, how many previous studies are referenced in each paragraph of the introduction? What, if anything, might this number suggest about previous research in this area?

8. This research report includes a number of tables and figures. What are the main differences between the ways these visual elements are labeled? Do you find the tables or the figures easier to navigate and understand? Why?

9. What features of the study (structure, language, and reference) contribute to the appearance of objectivity or otherwise serve to enhance the researchers' credibility (ethos)? Explain your choices.

Response and Research Question

10. The researchers suggest that their work could "pav[e] the way for a new field of multidisciplinary research, combining human reproduction, toxicology, and nutrition" (7). In your estimation, what could each of these fields likely contribute to the continued study of the potential toxicity of pesticides associated with GM foods?

ACADEMIC CASE STUDY • GENETICALLY MODIFIED FOOD   APPLIED FIELDS

Genetically Modified Food in Perspective: An Inquiry-Based Curriculum to Help Middle School Students Make Sense of Tradeoffs

SHERRY SEETHALER AND MARCIA LINN

Sherry Seethaler holds a PhD in math and science education. She is a science writer and educator at the University of California–San Diego and the author of *Lies, Damned Lies, and Science: How to Sort through the Noise around Global Warming, the Latest Health Claims, and Other Scientific Controversies* (2009), along with other books aimed at translating the work of science for a general readership. Marcia Linn is a professor of development and cognition at the University of California–Berkeley Graduate

School of Education. She specializes in math, science, and technology education and has published a number of books and articles on the topics. In the following article, Seethaler and Linn report on a study they conducted to understand how middle school students learn about a controversial scientific issue, genetically modified foods. The article was published in the November 2004 issue of the *International Journal of Science Education.*

To understand how students learn about science controversy, this study examines students' reasoning about tradeoffs in the context of a technology-enhanced curriculum about genetically modified food. The curriculum was designed and refined based on the Scaffolded Knowledge Integration Framework to help students sort and integrate their initial ideas and those presented in the curriculum. Pre-test and post-test scores from 190 students show that students made significant (p < 0.0001) gains in their understanding of the genetically modified food controversy. Analyses of students' final papers, in which they took and defended a position on what type of agricultural practice should be used in their geographical region, showed that students were able to provide evidence both for and against their positions, but were less explicit about how they weighed these tradeoffs. These results provide important insights into students' thinking and have implications for curricular design.

INTRODUCTION

Making sound political and personal decisions about cloning, gene therapy, stem cell research, genetic engineering of food, and a vast array of other issues entails understanding and weighing complex tradeoffs involving economics, human health and safety, the environment, and ethics. Since science will continue to play an ever-increasing role in our lives, science educators face the challenging task of preparing students who will be autonomous learners of science even after they have completed their formal science education. This study examines how eighth-grade students learn about a complex scientific controversy, the genetically modified food[1] (GMF) controversy, including how these students synthesize evidence to evaluate tradeoffs.

Motivation for the curriculum

Classroom studies have shown that students are rarely called upon to engage in reflective thinking about mathematics and science (Driver et al. 2000; Stigler and Hiebert 1999). Furthermore, only about 1% of space in science textbooks is devoted to any discussion of science controversy, and science textbooks dominate instruction (Champagne 1998; Knain 2001; Schmidt et al. 1996). Most children and adults, including science teachers, hold the perspective that scientific knowledge is unchanging and uncontroversial, other than the accumulation of new knowledge (Driver et al. 1996). This would make people less likely to seek out competing viewpoints of scientists when making science-based decisions. On the other hand, over the past half-century, there has been a shift among philosophers and sociologists of science, away from seeing science as a purely empirical process, to seeing it as a social process of knowledge construction in which imagination and argument play an important role (Driver et al. 2000; Latour and Woolgar 1986). Science standards have called for changes in the way science is taught; in particular, drawing attention to the centrality of debate in science, the importance of the interactions between science and society, and the need for students to understand and apply the concept of a tradeoff in making decisions (American Association for the Advancement of Science 1993; National Committee on Science Education Standards and Assessment 1996).

Context for the curriculum

The GMF controversy generates a great deal of media attention, and has direct relevance to the daily lives of students because we are all eating GMF.[2] The topic also fits well with key content standards including: sexual reproduction in plants, the role of genes in inheritance, the interdependence of organisms in ecosystems (National Committee on Science Education Standards and Assessment 1996), the idea that technologies have side effects, and agriculture and the impact humans have on the environment (American Association for the Advancement of Science 1993). It was also possible to frame the final assignment (paper) in terms of a "decision" about whether to grow GMF or use another form of agriculture. This asked students to integrate what they had learned in a coherent way in order to choose and defend a position, in keeping with the goal of helping students develop a rich, connected set of ideas about the controversy.

The GMF controversy involves a complex set of tradeoffs, because it is difficult to predict the long-term impact of GMF, and because different genetically modified crops have different risks and benefits. Not including the ethical questions, there are three main themes of tradeoffs in the controversy:

- *Human health.* Genetic engineering of food has been touted as a way of growing enough food for an increasing world population, and improving the nutrient intake of populations at risk for deficiencies—as in the case of golden rice, which contains a precursor to vitamin A (Ye et al. 2000). Genetic engineering also has the power to remove allergens in food, and while research shows that this is feasible (Tada et al. 1996) critics contend that genetic engineering, by allowing us to introduce genes from completely unrelated species, could result in the introduction of novel allergens into the human food chain (Holdredge and Talbott 2001).

- *The environment.* Proponents of genetic engineering believe that crops engineered to express their own pesticides could reduce the use of chemicals on crops (Thayer 1999). Others are concerned that these crops may increase insecticide resistance in insect pests, lead to herbicide resistance in weeds, and may harm beneficial insects such as monarch butterflies (Losey et al. 1999; Wolfenbarger and Phifer 2000).

- *Economics.* Disease-resistant crops could benefit farmers; for example, a genetically modified disease-resistant papaya variety is credited with saving the livelihood of Hawaiian papaya farmers whose crops were being destroyed by a virus (Yoon 1999). On the other hand, opponents point to increasing difficulties exporting GMF to certain countries, and to the risks of corporate control of agriculture.

Further complicating the issue is what to use as the basis to compare the risks and benefits of genetically modified crops. All farming impacts the environment, so it is not fair to compare the impact of these crops with "virgin land," or even with idealized forms of organic farming. In reality, even organic farmers use chemicals on their crops to control insects, weeds, and plant diseases.[3] Furthermore, most food is grown using intensive (also called conventional) farming in large monocultures with use of synthetic pesticides and fertilizers. Moving away from use of these pesticides usually comes with a price; organic farmers often get lower yields, thus requiring more land to grow the same amount of food (Munn et al. 1998). While this is far from an exhaustive list of the issues in this debate, it makes it clear that the GMF controversy offers a meaningful and substantive context for science learning.

How do students learn about complex scientific issues?

We need to better understand how to scaffold students as they compare and combine "pieces" of knowledge about an issue to form an integrated understanding. We have gained some understanding of how students learn to make connections between ideas in areas such as Newtonian mechanics, heat and temperature, and plate tectonics, but our knowledge remains tentative (diSessa 1988; Gobert 2000; Linn and Hsi 2000). Even less is known about how students integrate sets of ideas, like those in the GMF controversy, which cut across different scientific domains and connect to social issues.

In this curriculum, students must sift through and synthesize what they have learned about GMF and agriculture to take a position on what agricultural method they think should be used in their geographical region. This requires students to make use of evidence to defend their position. There is research that has yielded insight into some of the difficulties people of all ages have in constructing arguments about everyday issues (Driver et al. 1996; Kuhn 1991; Means and Voss 1996; Ranney and Schank 1998; Voss and Means 1991). For example, they are often unable to use evidence appropriately or to generate counter-arguments. However, in these studies subjects were not usually given the opportunity to learn about the domain in question. Bell (1998, 2000) has shown that in the context of a curriculum about light, when students were given specific prompts and the debate was framed in terms of two alternative theories, students were able to make appropriate use of evidence to evaluate a theory. Thus, in a rich context, with appropriate scaffolding, students may be better at using evidence appropriately.

The findings reported here provide insight into how students grapple with complex, multidisciplinary scientific issues. Specifically, this study addresses the question: How successful are students in the eighth grade at learning to weigh the tradeoffs involved in using one method of agriculture or another, and supporting their position with appropriate evidence?

Overview of the curriculum

The curriculum described in this paper was designed to help students come to an integrated understanding of the GMF controversy. In other words, the curriculum should help students develop a rich, well-connected network of ideas about the controversy. The Scaffolded Knowledge Integration (SKI) Framework was used to guide the design of the GMF curriculum. SKI is a result of nearly 20 years of classroom research (Linn 1995; Linn and Hsi 2000). The overarching goal of SKI is to promote knowledge integration. SKI consists of four meta-principles that guide the development of new curricula: (1) to make science accessible; (2) to make thinking visible; (3) to help students learn from others; and (4) to promote autonomous lifelong science learning.

A team of educational researchers, teachers, and 10 scientists designed the curriculum. The curriculum was built in the Web-based Inquiry Science Environment (WISE) (http://wise.berkeley.edu/), which was created to support students based on the principles and philosophy of the SKI Framework (Linn and

Slotta 2000). (The GMF curriculum is available online at http.//wise.berkeley.edu). The WISE environment provides students with an inquiry map to keep track of what step they are on in the overall flow of the project, hints on demand, links to web pages, tools like the online discussion tool, and prompts to take notes.

At the beginning of the curriculum, students were asked whether or not they would eat GMF or plant it in their garden, to encourage them to think about what they had already heard regarding this food, and record their initial beliefs about it. In the next activity, students learned the history of corn, which introduced them to the importance of crosses in crop development. Next they learned what it means to genetically engineer a plant, and they investigated the differences between crosses and genetic engineering. Students participated in an in-class activity where they tasted genetically engineered food (pilot run only) and/or examined ingredient labels from common food products, and discussed how many foods were likely to contain genetically engineered ingredients. Students also read and discussed a short article on an anti-GMF incident in their local area. In the next part of the project, a variant of the jigsaw approach was used to allow students to explore the evidence for or against GMF, and for or against organic food (Aronson 1978; Brown and Palincsar 1989). (See Table 1 for a summary of the evidence students explored in the jigsaw.) The curriculum designers sought to present as balanced a view of GMF and agriculture as possible. We presented GMF in the context of other methods of agriculture to help students understand that all agricultural practices have both risks and benefits.

After they researched one of four positions (for or against GMF, for or against organic), pairs or groups of students prepared posters and short oral presentations to teach their classmates about the evidence they explored. As students listened to the presentations, they took notes on a form designed to scaffold their note taking and promote reflection. After each presentation, there was opportunity for discussion and debate. Once students heard all of the evidence for and against each position, they chose what type of agriculture they thought should be used in their geographical region—GMF, organic agriculture, or

Table 1

The four pieces of the jigsaw

Position	Evidence
For GMF	GMF saves Hawaiian papaya crop
	GMF can reduce allergens in food
	GMF can improve nutrient content of food: golden rice example
Against GMF	GMF insecticide-producing corn may harm monarch butterflies
	GMF could introduce novel allergens into food
	GMF could lead to herbicide-resistant superweeds
For organic	Organic farmers use crop rotation to enrich soil
	Organic farmers do not use synthetic chemicals
	Organic farms must undergo a rigorous certification procedure
Against organic	Organic farmers must still combat weeds and insects (practical issues)
	Organic farmers do use chemicals on their crops
	Organic farmers often get lower yields

conventional (intensive) farming methods—and they each wrote a paper defending their position. Students were scaffolded in writing their paper by the use of pages designed to help them organize arguments and evidence for the position they had chosen (handouts can be downloaded from http://wise.berkeley.edu). The curriculum took about 10 class periods each of 45 minutes. For a more detailed description of how the curriculum was designed in accordance with the SKI principles, see Seethaler (2003).

The curriculum was refined following a pilot run with one class, as described in Seethaler (2002). The changes were modest with the basic structure of the project remaining the same between runs. To increase the generalizability of our findings on students' reasoning about tradeoffs, results from both runs were pooled in the detailed analysis of students' reasoning.

METHODS

Participants

The pilot run of the curriculum took place in an eighth-grade classroom (17 students) in a school in an urban, middle-class neighborhood with an ethnically diverse student body. After the redesign of the curriculum (about two months later), it was run again by a different teacher in her six eighth-grade classrooms (173 students) in a moderately diverse, suburban, middle-class neighborhood. Both teachers have a strong scientific background: the teacher of the pilot class has a PhD in environmental science, and the teacher at the second school has a Bachelor's degree in biology. However, since the initial runs of the curriculum reported here, many other teachers with a variety of science backgrounds have reported success using this curriculum in their classrooms.

Sources of data

Data sources include students' written work, pre-tests and post-tests consisting of short-answer questions designed to promote reflective thinking, online notes that the students took as they were working through the project, offline notes taken during the poster presentations, and the position paper. Since students worked in pairs in the online portion of the project, notes were generated by pairs of students. All other written work was individual. Additional data includes classroom observations (pilot run), and audiotapes of interviews with individual students (pilot), with the teacher (pilot), and of whole class discussions (second run).

Scoring

Pre-tests and post-tests. The pre-tests and post-tests were used to assess changes in students' understanding of GMF and agriculture before and after the curriculum. They consisted of eight short-answer questions designed to encourage students to reflect on the risks and benefits of agricultural practices. For example, the questions "Why might an organic farmer think that organic food is safer for the environment than genetically engineered food?" and "Why might a farmer planting genetically engineered seeds choose to grow genetically modified food?" ask students to consider the benefits and risks of two different agricultural methods.

The marking scheme assigned points for each unique, correct (normative) response that a student generated. For most questions, there were a number of possible normative answers that a student could give. This meant that the total number of points that could be assigned was quite high, but not even an expert would be expected to get a perfect score since one respondent is unlikely to give every possible example or argument. The scoring scheme was set up this way to minimize the ceiling effect and to make sure that all possible normative responses were valued. Partial points were allotted if a response was consistent with a scientifically accepted response but was only partially elaborated. If a response contained one normative idea and one non-normative idea, students would receive points for the normative idea, as long as the non-normative idea given did not contradict it. A second coder graded a subset of the tests, with a greater than 85% inter-rater reliability. The following is an example of the coding scheme for one of the questions.

Why might an organic farmer think that organic food is safer for the environment than genetically engineered food? (10 points possible)

- Some genetically modified food that produces its own insecticides (1) is harmful to beneficial insects (1).

- Organic farmers do not use synthetic chemicals (1). Some synthetic pesticides have been shown to harm wildlife (1). For example, DDT got into the food chain (1) and caused some birds to lay soft-shelled eggs/die off (1).

- Organic food does not lead to superweeds (Other examples of benefits of organic food are allowed.) (1). Superweeds may occur when genetically modified food crosses with weeds (1).

- Most genetically modified food contains antibiotic resistance genes (1). Some people think that the presence of these genes in the environment could lead to the antibiotic resistance of disease-causing bacteria (1).

- (It is more natural (0). Organic farmers do not use pesticides (0).)

Position papers. Position papers were analyzed to better understand how students were using evidence in their arguments and making sense of tradeoffs in the controversy. In their papers, students were to decide what form of agriculture they thought should be used in California: organic farming, intensive farming of non-GMF, or farming of GMF. They were instructed to give evidence to support their positions, and explain what evidence someone with an opposing viewpoint might use.

Seven aspects of students' position papers were considered: (1) the number of pieces of evidence used; (2) the themes (topics) of evidence used; (3) scientific normativity; (4) the degree of elaboration of evidence students presented *in favor* of their position; (5) the degree of elaboration of evidence students presented *against* their position; (6) the degree of elaboration of the evidence used by the students to *address the evidence against* their position; and (7) the quality of students' conclusions.

To study the first two of these aspects of students' [20] position papers, each piece of evidence students used in their position papers was tabulated, and classified as either one of the 12 corresponding to those in the jigsaw (see Table 1) or as "other." The other category is an umbrella category that contains evidence that came up in the class discussion, or was derived from the curriculum (by students following additional web links), or came from students' experiences and discussions outside the classroom. Evidence in the "other" category was listed and then grouped into global categories based on the themes that arose from the analysis of students' responses.

To assess the remaining five aspects of students' position papers, each position paper was scored according to a 10-point knowledge integration (KI) scale. The presence or absence of non-normative conceptions was scored on a binary (0, 1) scale. If there were any non-normative ideas present in the paper, the normativity score was zero. Three-point KI scales were used to score: the evidence students presented in favor of their position, evidence against their position (i.e., possible challenges), and evidence to counter the challenges to their position. Usually, there was more than one of each of these three types of evidence presented, and students were assigned a score based on the best (most normative, most elaborated) piece of each type of evidence presented. Students could receive a score of 0, 1, or 2 (highest). Evidence was classified as present but not elaborated (KI = 1) or as present and elaborated (KI = 2). If it was absent entirely, or confusing, it was assigned a score of 0.

This scoring scheme for the position papers was inspired by the work of Toulmin (1958). Toulmin was the first and most influential individual to make a distinction between the idealized notion of arguments employed in logic and mathematics, and the everyday practice of arguments in a wide range of contexts. Toulmin's scheme for analyzing arguments identifies four major components of an argument: data, claim, warrant, and backing. Data are used to support a claim. A warrant is the justification stating why that data can be used to support the claim. The warrant thus functions as a bridge between the data and the claim. The warrant may be implicit in an argument, to be made explicit if there are challenges to the validity of using a particular piece of data to support the claim. Often drawing a sharp distinction between the data and the warrant is impossible, but, in general, the data is factual information, and the warrant contains more general rule-like statements (van Eemeren et al. 1996). If the authority of the warrant is not accepted right away, a backing may be required. The backing is not general

like the warrant; rather, it is more like data in that it consists of specific facts, incidences, or examples. For example, in a legal argument it would consist of a citation of a specific piece of legislation (Toulmin 1958). While the components are common to arguments in different domains, what counts as data, warrant, backing, and claims is field-dependent.

In our scoring scheme, evidence considered elaborated contained an explicit warrant or backing, or both, as well as data and claim; whereas "unelaborated" evidence consisted of data and claim only. An example of this coding scheme applied to students' "Con Evidence" (evidence against their chosen position) is shown in the following (bold type indicates **data**, claims are underlined, *warrants* are in italics, and ***backings*** are in bold italics). More examples are provided later (see Results).

Con KI = 0
Absent or non-scientific.
3MF (Paper is pro GMF): ". . . You are not letting the plant be natural, you could start a wipe out, and you could mess up the food."

Con KI = 1
Gives one or more normative pieces of evidence, but does not really elaborate on any of them.
1DT (Paper is pro GMF): GM foods "could cause allergic reactions to people [claim] because **the gene put in it could be from something that they are allergic to [data].**"

Con KI = 2
Elaborates on at least one of the pieces of evidence given.
4KB (Paper is pro GMF): "GM foods are important [claim] because they **keep the papaya crop in Hawaii healthy [data]**. *It is important to keep the papaya crop health [sic] and free of diseases because it is one large part of Hawaii's economy, and food source [warrant].* ***If we had GM the potato crops in Ireland there would not have been such devastation [sic]. What happened was around the 1940's [sic] the potato crops in Ireland all died from a disease and lots of people died of starvation . . .*** [backing]" (pro, KI = 2).

Finally, a four-point scale was used to assess the conclusion students gave to their essays. A maximum conclusion score meant that the student gave an explicit rationale that was completely normative from a scientific standpoint, of why the evidence in favor of their position outweighed the evidence against. Since the conclusion should not involve the presentation of any new evidence, but rather the weighing of evidence already presented, Toulmin's scheme was not applied to the conclusion. A score of zero was assigned when the conclusion was absent. One point was assigned if the student simply stated that there was more or better evidence for than against their position. A conclusion that merited a score of two points contained an indication that the student realized there were tradeoffs and offered some rationale as to why the evidence for their position outweighed the evidence against, but may have had some minor misconceptions. To merit a score of three the student would have to weigh only evidence that would be considered valid from a scientific or public policy standpoint.

In summary, students could receive a total of five points for the evidence in favor of, and against, their positions, and normativity. There were another five points possible for the evidence countering the challenges to their position, and the conclusion. Thus, this scheme treats students' papers as an extended argument, where the scoring of the evidence is based on Toulmin's scheme. The structure of the KI scheme is presented in Table 2. A second coder scored a subset of students' position papers. Initially, the second

Table 2

KI scoring scheme

Element of argument	Possible scores
Evidence in favor of chosen position	0, 1, 2
Evidence against chosen position	0, 1, 2
Normativity (presence/absence of non-normative ideas)	0/1
Counter-evidence to evidence against their position	0, 1, 2
Conclusions to overall argument	0, 1, 2, 3
Total possible Knowledge Integration points	10

coder agreed with the primary coder greater than 70% of the time. Following discussion, particularly regarding what ideas about agriculture should be considered non-normative, the second coder agreed with the primary coder greater than 90% of the time.

RESULTS

Changes in students' conceptions and attitudes over the course of the curriculum

Students came to the curriculum with a variety of ideas about GMF and agriculture. Some of their non-normative pre-test conceptions are presented in Table 3.

The overall pre-test to post-test gains for each school are presented in Table 4. As shown by a paired *t*-test, students had significant pre-test to post-test gains at each school. There were no significant gender differences in pre-test to post-test gains at either school (not shown).

The following pre-test and post-test responses show how one student, Sam, developed a more elaborated understanding of GMF over the course of the curriculum. The statements are Sam's responses to "Why might some people be afraid to eat food which comes from a plant that has been genetically engineered?"

> Some people are afraid to eat food from G.E. plants because they think there might be a bad chemical in them. (Sam, pre-test)

> Some people are afraid to eat GM foods because they think that there will be some effect on their body from genes that have been put into the plant. They could also have an allergic reaction because of a new gene in the plant. (Sam, post-test)

Sam's post-test response cited a more specific risk than his pre-test response, and it indicates that Sam understood that genetic engineering involves the transfer of new genes to the plant. Overall, students' pre-test and post-test responses tended to be brief, possibly because they are not accustomed to being required to provide extensive detail in test situations. However, in general, their responses moved to being more normative and less vague from the pre-test to post-test, indicating that they had come to

Table 3

Examples of students' non-normative pre-test conceptions

To genetically engineer a plant means:

"It is to grow something un-naturaly [*sic*]. To be grown with chemicals"

". . . a plant is artificially grown in a sense. . . . Plants are crossbred that don't usually do"

". . . I guess to make plants grow faster, become alive like in the movies!"

". . . To grow a plant with other parts of plants. It isn't grown outside with water and sun but they are grown with chemicals to make it grow faster"

"Maybe it means that you inject it with hormones or make its growing process different [*sic*]"

"See what kind of water or inviorment [*sic*] it can live in"

". . . When people take plants to make food from them, like corn chips for example [. . .] These chips don't look like corn kernels"

An organic farmer might think that organic food is safer for the environment (than GMF) because:

"Because organic food has no chemicals and stuff like that"

"Because organic food is grown safely and without any chemicals or breeding . . ."

"It's all natural"

"Nature has always grown the food that way and humans have never tampered with them"

a better understanding of GMF and agriculture over the course of the curriculum.

Students' attitudes about agricultural methods. Overall, students' attitudes toward GMF tended toward positive both before the curriculum (as indicated by the notes they took initially) and after (as indicated by the position they chose for the final paper). Initially, 80% of students said that they would eat GMF and 70% said they would grow it. At the end of the curriculum, 62% of students wrote papers in favor of GMF. In their final papers, students gave a much more extensive rationale for their stance than they did in these initial notes. For a more detailed discussion of students' attitudes, see Seethaler (2003).

How do students construct arguments in the context of this debate, and how successful are students in the eighth grade at learning to support their position with appropriate evidence and weighing the tradeoffs involved in using one method of agriculture or another?

Numbers and themes of evidence used. In their final papers, students in the pilot run used an average of 2.5 (standard deviation [SD], 1.3) pieces of evidence of the 12 they explored in the jigsaw (14 papers), and students in the second run used 3.7 (SD, 1.7) of these pieces of evidence (147 papers). These averages include only normative uses of the evidence. Very few students used "jigsaw" evidence inappropriately, or cited it incorrectly. There were only 26 instances of

Table 4

Pre-test to post-test gains for each run of the eighth-grade GMF curriculum

School	Number of students	Pre-test	Post-test	t-value	p-value
1. Pilot	17 (one class)	5.3, SD = 4.0	10.5, SD = 4.6	6.527	<0.0001
2. Second run	173 (six classes)	7.6, SD = 3.3	11.2, SD = 3.5	12.794	<0.0001

incorrect evidence use/misquoting of evidence, compared with more than 500 correct uses, suggesting that students understood the ideas presented in the curriculum. The most commonly cited incorrect evidence was that organic farmers do not use chemicals on their crops (12 students).

A little more than one-half of the evidence students used in their papers was presented as evidence in favor of their position, while just under one-half was described as possible counter-evidence to their position. This shows that, in a content-rich context, where students are given appropriate scaffolds, they can provide counter-evidence to their position. Furthermore, this observation, and the fact that nearly one-third of students wrote their paper in favor of a position other than the one they explored in the jigsaw, shows that students learned from their peers. The breakdown of the evidence used by students depending on their position on agriculture is presented in Table 5.

Some evidence was important for students independent of what position on agriculture they chose. For example, over one-half of the students used evidence about yield in their papers. Students who wrote papers in favor of genetic engineering or intensive farming could cite "increasing yields" in favor of their position, and this was especially common among students choosing intensive agriculture. However, well over one-half of the students writing papers about organic farming also addressed the yield issue (as evidence against their position). On the other hand, some evidence was not used very frequently, regardless of what position students chose. For example, only one in 20 students made use of the fact that organic agriculture is carefully regulated. Even students who wrote position papers in favor of organic farming did not usually make use of this evidence.

Another trend that can be observed is that while students made use of evidence both in favor of and against their positions, they usually did not draw from

Table 5

Percentage of students using each piece of evidence by position chosen for final paper

Evidence		Position chosen			Overall % of students using this evidence
		Pro organic	Pro intensive	Pro GMF	
Pro GMF	Papayas	*21*	*8*	**59**	45
	Reduce allergens	*13*	*17*	**40**	31
	Vitamin A rice	*26*	*0*	**57**	45
Against GMF	Risks to other insects	**18**	**8**	*43*	34
	Introduce allergens	**34**	**25**	*46*	41
	Superweeds	**21**	**0**	*35*	29
Pro organic	Crop rotation	**32**	*17*	*5*	13
	Synthetic chemicals	**55**	*92*	*12*	29
	Regulations	**13**	*0*	*3*	5
Against organic	Weeds and insects	*29*	**67**	**21**	26
	Chemicals are used	*42*	**42**	**10**	21
	Yields	*63*	**92**	**46**	54

Italics, evidence against position; **bold**, evidence in favor of position.

evidence presented about *another* agricultural method. For example, students writing position papers in favor of GMF drew on evidence presented in favor of this method and evidence presented against this method. However, with the exception of yield, they did not draw from evidence presented in favor of, or against, organic agriculture. This same trend is also observed for students writing papers in favor of intensive farming, but is slightly less prevalent among students defending organic methods of farming. Evidence about other agricultural methods was relevant to their position. For example, the fact that insects and weeds are difficult to control is a perfectly valid reason to give for choosing to grow GMF, but less than one-quarter of pro-GMF students used this to support their position. Like the observation that only a relatively small number of students wrote papers in favor of intensive farming, this observation also seems to indicate that students find it challenging to take evidence presented in one context and restate it in another. The evidence on yield is an exception, suggesting that students can do this under certain circumstances. Yield came up frequently in class discussions, possibly increasing connections across contexts.

In addition to the pieces of evidence from the jigsaw, students also cited evidence that had come up in class discussions, that they had learned from following other links to the web in the project, or that they had learned outside the classroom. On average, students used 1.8 (SD, 1.3) pieces of "other" evidence. This number includes only evidence that was normative and was not just a matter of opinion, or ethics. This evidence fell roughly into four broad categories: quality of food and cost to consumer, safety of the food, environmental risks and benefits of the method, and benefits and disadvantages to the farmer. The overwhelmingly most popular arguments used by students were about using genetic engineering to improve quality of the food, such as the taste of the food (37 students) or the size or shape of the food (44 students). Students also gave, on average, 1.3 (SD, 0.96) pieces of ethical/opinion-based evidence. ("Evidence" that was actually non-normative, not just a matter of opinion, was not counted.) Most

cited in the ethical/opinion-based category is "organic food is natural" or more natural than other food (used by 33 students), and genetic engineering is morally wrong or is playing God (used by 23 students). Students used these both in favor of their position, and as counter-arguments someone might give.

Normativity. About one-third of students had non-normative ideas in their final papers. It was rare for there to be more than one or two non-normative ideas in a student's paper. Note that the non-normative ideas were not included in statistics presented earlier of total evidence used by students. (Thus, in reality, students actually gave more evidence than we counted.) Non-normative ideas included: the belief that organic farmers do not use chemicals on their crops, that GMF may give you cancer, that you can (physically) remove genes from food, that no pesticides are used on genetically modified crops, and so on. There were a wide range of these sorts of ideas, and some students' ideas were the opposite of others (GMF may give you cancer/has made us healthier). Recall that students rarely used evidence from the jigsaw incorrectly. Thus, the non-normative ideas appearing in students' papers are not usually ideas that were a major focus of the curriculum. Some may have been ideas that students brought with them to the curriculum (like GMF giving you cancer); others may be due to students extrapolating from something that they learned in the curriculum (if you can remove toxins from food, this must mean you excise the genes). An unpaired t-test on the total KI scores not including the normativity score, grouped by the normativity score, indicated that otherwise the quality of students' papers was similar whether or not they included non-normative ideas ($t = 1.7$, $p = 0.08$). This is not surprising since non-normative ideas tended to be listed as additional evidence for or against a student's position rather than being a central idea in their argument. Thus, over the course of the curriculum, students gained a more integrated understanding of the controversy, but will need more experience with it to continue to refine their network of ideas.

Level of integration of evidence used by students. The KI [35] analysis based on Toulmin's scheme reveals how students were using evidence and comparing tradeoffs in the controversy. In the following excerpts, bold type indicates **data**, claims are underlined, *warrants* are in italics, and ***backings*** are in bold italics. (Note: evidence considered in favor of a student's position may be evidence against a competing position.)

The following is an example of normative, but less integrated evidence:

> We should grow GMF. "**GM foods can keep away disease, viruses, and even harmful bugs that destroy crops**" (pro, KI = 1).

All students achieved at least one on the KI scale for evidence in favor of their position, and most (90%) achieved at least one for the evidence against their position. Many students (nearly one-half) also elaborated, showing that they had a detailed understanding of what the consequences/benefits of using a particular technology could be.

> 4AG (Paper is pro organic): We should not use genetically modified food. ". . . **Superweeds occur when a food that has been given immunity to a certain type of herbicide, crosses with nearby weeds. The weeds then produce offspring that contain the same immunity to herbicides.** This produces a problem for the farmers. *They are forced to use a more powerful herbicide to kill weeds. That poses a threat to the environment and it can create a serious economic problem. . .*" (pro, KI = 2).

> 2DD (Paper is pro organic): ". . . Another argument that would make [. . .] intensively grown food worse than organically grown food is that **the pesticides they use have endangered two types of birds one of them was the Brown Pelican**. The pesticide that caused this was called DDT although it is no longer legal in the United States the bird's population is still just starting to recover. *Pesticides cause a sort of chain reaction.* ***For example worms eat the infected dirt then a fish eats the worms and then a bigger fish eats the smaller fish and then a human eats the fish. Now all of the pesticide combined is in the human . . .***" (pro, KI = 2).

Fewer students were able to give good counter-evidence to the evidence against their positions. The following quotations show how some students did effectively address counter-evidence to their positions.

2CH: "Another argument against genetically modified food is that if you put pesticides into it, it would kill beneficial bugs as well as harmful ones. **My response is that other external pesticides do that too.** So that isn't really a good argument" (counter to evidence against position, KI = 1).

3CN (Paper is pro intensive): ". . .The assumption that natural chemicals are safer than synthetic ones is the premise on which the argument against intensive farming is based. In most cases, however, it is the opposite. **For example, one chemical organic farmers use is copper sulfate, which kills honeybees.** *Many arguments have been made that synthetic chemicals kill all bugs, whereas organic chemicals kill only the bad insects. Clearly this isn't the case . . .*" (KI = 2).

Both of these quotations also reveal that students were evaluating agricultural methods in relation to one another. For example, the first student recognized that dangers to beneficial insects are not specific to insecticide-producing plants. In fact, as the student pointed out, traditional insect sprays have these risks as well.

Students' papers also yield some insights into how students weighed specific risks and benefits of each agricultural method to conclude their argument. For example:

7WB: "I think that the arguments for my position outweighs the opposing arguments because not only do I prove that genetically modified foods cost a significant amount of money, they also require a lot of experiment time and research. All arguments that I proposed against GM foods gave examples of situations that would be hard to resolve if they happened. They were all slim chances that something could go wrong, such as the superweeds, or allergic reactions, but we cannot afford to take these chances when human lives are involved" (conclusion, KI = 2).

1CW: "I am for the genetic manipulation of these crops to serve our purposes. I believe this because of what it has done for the people of Europe with the European Corn Borer, in Asia for its role with Gold Rice and for helping the agricultural economy with lower prices for foods everywhere. I know of the problems with the Tomato with the Peanut allergens, and the Monarch Butterflies being destroyed, but I still believe that Genetic Engineering is a good way to help ailing people around the world by improving their diet" (conclusion, KI = 2).

Both of these students gave some rational comment as to how they weighed the risks and benefits of GMF

Table 6

Distribution of knowledge integration scores

Element of argument	Percentage of students achieving each KI score and average scores for each element
Evidence in favor of chosen position	KI = 0, 0%
	KI = 1, 57%
	KI = 2, 43%
	Mean = 1.4, SD = 0.5
Evidence against chosen position	KI = 0, 10%
	KI = 1, 60%
	KI = 2, 30%
	Mean = 1.2, SD = 0.6
Normativity	KI = 0, 36%
	KI = 1, 64%
	Mean = 0.6, SD = 0.5
Counter-evidence to evidence against their position	KI = 0, 78%
	KI = 1, 20%
	KI = 2, 2%
	Mean = 0.2, SD = 0.5
Conclusions to overall argument	KI = 0, 15%
	KI = 1, 58%
	KI = 2, 27%
	KI = 3, 0%
	Mean = 1.1, SD = 0.6

in their conclusions. For example, the first student decided on his position as a way of minimizing risk. These conclusions contain some misconceptions about GMF; for example, GMF has helped with the European corn borer in the United States and other countries, but not in Europe (where GMF is not commercially grown). None of the students provided a conclusion that achieved a KI score of 3.

Table 6 presents the number of students achieving a given KI score for each element of their position paper.

Overall, students had a KI score of 4.6 (SD, 1.3). Their KI score was 3.3 (SD, 0.9) out of 5 for their pro and con evidence, and 1.4 (SD, 0.8) out of 5 for their conclusions and the rebuttals. In other words, students were able to identify and explain specific benefits and risks of a particular method of agriculture. However, in general, they tended to list these benefits and risks without explicitly concluding *why* they thought the benefits outweighed the risks. It seems that students either tended not to see the importance of giving an elaborated conclusion and rebuttals once they had detailed the evidence for and against their positions, or that they find giving an integrated conclusion rather challenging.

DISCUSSION

This study provides important insight into students' 40 thinking about multi-domain, multi-faceted, problematic science. In addition, the in-depth analysis of students' reasoning in the context of the curriculum can be used to re-inform the pedagogical principles used in the initial design.

Students' use of evidence

Over the course of the GMF curriculum, as shown by the analysis of students' work, students developed a more sophisticated understanding of GMF and agricultural methods. Furthermore, students were able to make appropriate use of evidence to argue for their positions on agriculture. On average, students used between three and four pieces of evidence gleaned from the curriculum in their papers, plus another three from various other sources. Importantly, they did not ignore evidence counter to their position. In fact, this accounted for almost one-half of the evidence students presented in their papers. This is an especially significant finding because others have found that students tend to fixate on one or two claims and have particular difficulty coming up with counter-evidence to their position (Driver et al. 1996; Kuhn 1991, 1992, 1993; Voss and Means 1991). People often ignore evidence that is not consistent with their own position (Chinn and Brewer 1993).

There are at least three possible reasons for the differences in our results regarding students' use of evidence. First, here the students wrote their position papers in the context of a curriculum where they were learning about agricultural methods, and were specifically challenged by the teacher and other students, who exposed them to new arguments and evidence. In other words, students were not being asked to come up with evidence "out of the blue," as in many studies that examine students' ability to use evidence (Kuhn 1991; Voss and Means 1991). Rather, they were synthesizing their ideas at the culmination of a set of activities designed to challenge them to come to a more integrated understanding about GMF and agriculture. In these activities, students were scaffolded as they learned new ideas and compared and sifted through them.

Second, the expectations for the position paper were made completely explicit to students, and students were provided with a number of scaffolds.

Instructions for the paper showed students how to structure their papers and gave them some sentence starter prompts. To help them plan their papers, they were also given idea-organizing pages, and were encouraged to list all the arguments and evidence about agriculture they had heard. Students were free to choose the agricultural method that seemed most ideal to them, and the evidence they thought best supported their position. However, they were reminded on a number of occasions that a scientific paper cannot be written solely "from the heart," but that opinions must be supported by evidence.

Third, in many of the studies that found students had difficulty using evidence appropriately, students were asked to generate evidence "on the spot," often orally (Kuhn 1991; Voss and Means 1991). Here, the students had time to reflect as they were writing their position papers. The generation of evidence to support a position requires time and reflection, and it seems unrealistic to think that students could generate good evidence in a short period of time about something they may never previously have given much thought.

The fact that students' papers contained evi- 45 dence both for and against their position on agriculture shows that students recognized that there are tradeoffs in the controversy, and could give examples of them. However, in general, students tended not to be explicit about how they were weighing the tradeoffs in the controversy (as indicated by the low conclusion KI scores). From the data we have collected thus far, it is not possible to say whether this is because students find it particularly challenging to weigh tradeoffs or because they believe that just laying out the evidence for and against their position is sufficient for making their point. Students may need further instruction about what is a good conclusion to an argument.

Design principles

Three principles might be derived from these observations. First, a subprinciple could be added to the SKI principle "help students learn from others." In order to help students learn to support their arguments with evidence, give students exposure to building arguments in a content-rich domain where they are exposed to multiple forms of evidence and have the opportunity to discuss the evidence with a community of peers and teachers. Ideally, over the course of multiple curricula like that described here, these communities would develop criteria for the evaluation of evidence in multiple domains.

Second, a subprinciple under the SKI principle "make science accessible" could be added: make goals for students explicit. Students need to understand the expectations placed on them in particular contexts. For example, an English teacher might want students to write "from the heart" on a creative writing assignment, but may have different expectations when students are writing a critique. This difference is not obvious to someone inexperienced in different forms of writing. Furthermore, many students are completely unaccustomed to "writing" in science class. In fact, Seethaler recently found that the undergraduate science students in her class at a major university (juniors and seniors) had minimal experience writing in their science classes, and they were not certain how to structure their papers (2001, unpublished data).

Third, to elaborate the principle "make thinking visible," it is important to note that students need to be given time to engage in the act of reflecting. Scaffolds can both prompt such reflection and sustain reasoning.

While these principles are derived from a study examining a single subject matter domain, and a single grade level, we believe that they will transfer to other contexts as well. The biggest challenge is in translating these principles into effective classroom practice. The teachers of the classes studied here both had strong domain knowledge, and were very self-motivated to bring science controversy into the classroom. Many teachers have since used this curriculum and reported success. Some had minimal subject matter preparation, but all chose to bring the genetically modified food controversy into their classrooms because they believed it was something their students should learn about. These are most likely to be the teachers who work to create a classroom culture where students engage in reflective thinking. Curricula like the one described here can give students the opportunity to learn to construct arguments and use evidence, but the generalizability of these results is likely to depend on classroom culture.

Students' use of warrants

It is difficult to compare our students' use of warrants with other researchers' findings, because studies in the literature tend to differ along multiple lines. Jiménez-Aleixandre et al. (2000) studied a ninth-grade classroom where students were engaged in small group discussions trying to explain the reason for the differences observed between wild and domesticated chicks' coloration. Students had time to reflect, but they were not given specific scaffolds in the discussion, other than the problem scenario, and the instruction to give reasons for their answer. In their study, warrants were used for about one-third of claims, but two students really dominated the group discussion, so it is not possible to generalize. Chinn and Anderson (1998) studied fourth-grade students' argumentative discourse about issues raised in stories the students had read. In general, they found that students' arguments were logical, but that warrants were not generally made explicit. Students may have different norms for the construction of arguments in conversation versus in written work; however, there are not enough data on this to make a definitive statement. In a study by Bell (2000), where students were scaffolded to provide warrants, specifically an explanation of *why* a particular piece of evidence could be used to support or challenge one of two theories about how light travels, students included warrants in over 70% of argument explanations. Bell's students were providing written explanations in the form of notes. We did not specifically prompt our students to use warrants in their position papers, and just under one-half of our students made use of warrants in their papers. In Toulmin's (1958) work on argumentation, he posited that warrants may only be made explicit if there are challenges to the validity of using particular data to support a claim; thus, getting students to use warrants even more consistently may require specific explicit challenges to their positions.

The role of context in students' reasoning

Despite our students' ability to use evidence appropriately and provide warrants spontaneously in nearly one-half of the papers, there are three lines of observations that show limits in their flexible use of evidence across contexts, suggesting that the students would benefit from more support to understand how evidence could be used in different ways to support or challenge various positions. First, students here used evidence for and against their positions, but tended not to use relevant evidence presented in the context of another position. For example, students writing a paper in favor of GMF used evidence from the curriculum that was presented in the context of arguments for and against GMF, but rarely used evidence that came up in discussions of organic food. Second, the fact that very few students wrote papers on intensive farming may reflect the lack of visibility to students of the evidence for this position, rather than students' dislike of this method of farming. (Recall that the jigsaw categories were for and against organic and for and against GMF, so the evidence in favor of intensive farming would have to be drawn from evidence against the other methods.) Finally, an observation that students in the pilot run had trouble deciding what to put on their posters, in particular a pair of students who had no difficulty explaining the papaya evidence (see Table 1), but still did not understand why it could be used by supporters of GMF, also illustrates this (Seethaler 2002). This difficulty on the part of students in using evidence flexibly is consistent with the literature on transfer (for a review, see Bransford and Schwartz 1999). Studies suggest that transfer is an active rather than passive process (Gick and Holyoak 1980). This implies that asking students to think more about *why* a particular piece of evidence can be used to support or challenge a position might help them use evidence more flexibly across contexts. An anecdotal observation that students seemed to have less trouble deciding what evidence to present

in their poster presentations in the second run of the project, after we had added prompts for them to think about why pieces of evidence were good support for a particular position, could be explained by viewing transfer as an active process (Seethaler 2002). The recommendation that students discuss evidence with their peers and the teacher, and work together as a community to develop criteria for the evaluation of evidence in various contexts, is also consistent with the goal of helping students to use evidence more flexibly, since it is known that presenting concepts in multiple contexts can increase transfer. This would argue for the inclusion of projects like the WISE GMF controversy project at various points in students' educational trajectories.

In summary, our results show that students made gains in their understanding of GMF over the course of the curriculum. Eighth-grade students constructed arguments with evidence to support their positions. These students also presented evidence counter to their positions, which shows that they understood both the risks and benefits of agriculture and thus that there were tradeoffs involved with their chosen method of agriculture. However, students were generally not explicit about how they weighed the tradeoffs they had identified, and this is an area that needs future work. Indeed, there is little research into how students make sense of tradeoffs, despite the fact that being able to identify and assess risks and benefits of technologies is so important in our daily lives. Having students construct arguments about scientific issues is important because it means that students are using what they know, rather than just recalling it piecemeal. The inclusion of science controversy into the middle school curriculum can help students start to become autonomous science learners by assisting them to think critically about important issues that will affect their lives.

ACKNOWLEDGMENTS

This work was supported by the National Science Foundation under grant numbers 9873180 and 9805420. The data and opinions expressed here are those of the authors and do not necessarily reflect those of the National Science Foundation. Special thanks to Professor Andrea diSessa, Stephanie Sisk-Hilton, Michelle Williams, and Timothy Zimmerman for their feedback on drafts of this manuscript.

NOTES

This work was completed while Seethaler was at U.C. Berkeley.

1. In reality, nearly all of the food we eat is "genetically modified" by cross-breeding. However, in this paper, as is general practice in the media, the term *genetically modified* is used more restrictively to describe food derived from plants altered using biotechnological techniques to directly manipulate genes or gene expression.

2. A number of food crops in the United States are now genetically modified, including well over one-half of the nation's soybean crop and about one-third of the corn (Kaeppler 2000). Other modified foods include potatoes, canola, papaya, and squash (*Wall Street Journal*, Tuesday, 12 October 1999). This genetically modified food, especially soybeans and corn, is found in a wide array of processed foods; for example, soy and corn oils, soy flour, and corn starch are added to cakes, crackers, candies, and so on.

3. For a list of chemicals approved for use on organic crops, see http://www.ams.usda.gov/nop/NationalList/FinalRule .html.

REFERENCES

American Association for the Advancement of Science (1993). *Benchmarks for Science Literacy* (New York: Oxford University Press).

Aronson, E. (1978). *The Jigsaw Classroom* (Beverly Hills, CA: Sage Publications).

Bell, P. (1998). Designing for students' conceptual change in science using argumentation and classroom debate. Unpublished doctoral dissertation, University of California at Berkeley, Berkeley, CA.

Bell, P. (2000). Scientific arguments as learning artifacts: Designing for learning from the web with KIE. *International Journal of Science Education*, 22(8), 797–817.

Bransford, J.D., and Schwartz, D.L. (1999). Rethinking transfer. A simple proposal with multiple implications. In A. Iran-Nejad and P.D. Peason (eds.), *Review of Research in Education* (vol. 24) (Washington, DC: AERA), 61–100.

Brown, A.L., and Palinscar, A.S. (1989). Guided, cooperative learning and individual knowledge acquisition. In L.B. Resnick (ed.), *Knowing, Learning, and Instruction: Essays in*

Honor of Robert Glaser (Hillsdale, NJ: Lawrence Erlbaum Associates), 393–451.

Champagne, A. (1998). Kill all the mosquitoes or cure malaria. Symposium conducted at the meeting of the American Association for the Advancement of Science (AAAS), Philadelphia, PA.

Chinn, C.A., and Anderson, R.C. (1998). The structure of discussions that promote reasoning. *Teachers College Record*, 100(2), 315–368.

Chinn, C., and Brewer, W. (1993). The role of anomalous data in knowledge acquisition: A theoretical framework and implications for science instruction. *Review of Educational Research*, 63(1), 1–49.

diSessa, A. (1988). Knowledge in pieces. In G. Forman and P. Pufall (eds.), *Constructivism in the Computer Age* (Hillsdale, NJ: Lawrence Erlbaum Associates), 49–70.

Driver, R., Leach, J., Millar, R., and Scott, P. (1996). *Young People's Images of Science* (Buckingham: Open University Press).

Driver, R., Newton, P., and Osborne, J. (2000). Establishing the norms of scientific argumentation in classrooms. *Science Education*, 84, 287–312.

Gick, M., and Holyoak, K. (1980). Analogical problem solving. *Cognitive Psychology*, 12(3), 306–355.

Gobert, J. (2000). A typology of causal models for plate tectonics: Inferential power and barriers to understanding. *International Journal of Science Education*, 22(9), 937–977.

Holdredge, C., and Talbott, S. (2001). Sowing technology: The ecological argument against genetic engineering down on the farm. *Sierra: The Magazine of the Sierra Club*, 24–72.

Jiménez-Aleixandre, M., Pilar, R., Anxela, B., and Duschl, R.A. (2000). Doing the lesson or doing science: Argument in high school genetics. *Science Education*, 84(6), 757–792.

Kaeppler, H. (2000). Food safety assessment of genetically modified crops. *Agronomics Journal*, 92, 793–797.

Knain, E. (2001). Ideologies in school science textbooks. *International Journal of Science Education*, 23(3), 319–329.

Kuhn, D. (1991). *The Skills of Argument* (Cambridge: Cambridge University Press).

Kuhn, D. (1992). Thinking as argument. *Harvard Educational Review*, 62(2), 155–178.

Kuhn, D. (1993). Science as argument: Implications for teaching and learning scientific thinking. *Science Education*, 77(3), 319–337.

Latour, B., and Woolgar, S. (1986). *Laboratory Life: The Construction of Scientific Facts* (Princeton, NJ: Princeton University Press).

Linn, M. (1995). Designing computer learning environments for engineering and computer science: The Scaffolded Knowledge Integration Framework. *Journal of Science Education and Technology*, 4(2), 103–126.

Linn, M.C., and Hsi, S. (2000). *Computers, Teachers, Peers: Science Learning Partners* (Mahwah, NJ: Lawrence Erlbaum Associates).

Linn, M., and Slotta, J. (2000). WISE Science. *Educational Leadership*, 58(2), 29–32.

Losey, J., Raylor, R., and Carter, M. (1999). Transgenic pollen harms monarch larvae. *Nature*, 399, 214.

Means, M., and Voss, J. (1996). Who reasons well? Two studies of informal reasoning among children of different grade, ability and knowledge levels. *Cognition and Instruction*, 14(2), 139–178.

Munn, D.A., Coffing, G., and Sautter, G. (1998). Response of corn, soybean and wheat crops to fertilizer and herbicides in Ohio compared with low-input production practices. *American Journal of Alternative Agriculture*, 13(4), 181–189.

National Committee on Science Education Standards and Assessment (1996). *National Science Education Standards: 1996* (Washington, DC: National Academy Press).

Ranney, M., and Schank, P. (1998). Toward an integration of the social and the scientific: Observing, modeling, and promoting the explanatory coherence of reasoning. In S.J. Read and L.C. Miller (eds.), *Connectionist Models of Social Reasoning and Social Behavior* (Mahwah, NJ: Lawrence Erlbaum Associates), 245–274.

Schmidt, W., McKnight, C., and Raizen, S. (1996). Splintered vision: An investigation of U.S. mathematics and science education. U.S. National Research Center for the Third International Mathematics and Science Study, Michigan State University.

Seethaler, S. (2002). Can middle school students learn to construct arguments that balance tradeoffs in the genetically modified food controversy? Paper presented at the annual meeting of the American Educational Research Association, New Orleans, LA.

Seethaler, S. (2003). Controversy in the classroom: How eighth-grade and undergraduate students reason about tradeoffs of genetically modified food. Unpublished doctoral dissertation, University of California at Berkeley, CA.

Stigler, J.W., and Hiebert, J. (1999). *The Teaching Gap: Best Ideas from the World's Teachers for Improving Education in the Classroom* (New York: The Free Press).

Tada, Y., Nakase, M., Adachi, T., Nakamura, R., Shimoda, H., Takahashi, M., Fujimura, T., and Matsuda, T. (1996). Reduction of 14–16 kDa allergenic proteins in transgenic rice plants by antisense gene. *FEBS Letters*, 391, 341–345.

Thayer, A. (1999). Transforming agriculture: Transgenic crops and the application of discovery technologies are altering the agrochemical and agricultural business. *Chemical and Engineering News*, 19 April, pp. 21–35.

Toulmin, S. (1958). *The Uses of Argument* (Cambridge: Cambridge University Press).

van Eemeren, F.H., Grootendorst, R., Henkemans, F.S., Blair, J.A., Johnson, R.H., Krabbe, E.C.W., Plantin, C., Walton, D.N., Willard, C.A., et al. (1996). *Fundamentals of Argumentation Theory: A Handbook of Historical Backgrounds and Contemporary Developments* (Hillsdale, NJ: Lawrence Erlbaum Associates).

Voss, J., and Means, M. (1991). Learning to reason via instruction in argumentation. *Learning and Instruction*, 1, 337–350.

Wolfenbarger, L., and Phifer, P. (2000). The ecological risks and benefits of genetically engineered plants. *Science*, 290, 2088–2093.

Ye, X., Al-Babali, S., Klöti, A., Zhang, J., Lucca, P., Beyer, P., and Potrykus, I. (2000). Engineering the provitamin-A (β-carotene) biosynthetic pathway into (carotenoid-free) rice endosperm. *Science*, 287(5451), 303–305.

Yoon, C. (1999). Stalked by deadly virus, papaya lives to breed again. *The New York Times*, 20 July.

Reading Questions

1. What do the researchers mean by their use of the term *tradeoff* when it comes to making decisions about scientific controversies?

2. In the Scoring section of their report, the researchers provide details about what two forms of data used to assess students' learning?

3. According to the researchers, what incorrect piece of evidence did students cite most often in their papers?

4. What three reasons do the researchers provide as possible supporting explanations for why, in their papers, students did not ignore evidence counter to their position?

5. In response to the problem of transfer, what do the researchers suggest instructors should have students do?

Rhetoric Questions

6. Where do the researchers present their central research question? What makes this placement appropriate in the overall design of their research report?

7. What role does the discussion of Sam's responses on the pre-test and post-test play in the reporting of the results? How does it figure into the discussion of "Changes in students' conceptions and attitudes over the course of the curriculum" covered in the Results section of the report?

8. Carefully read the section labeled "Design Principles," and make a note of every instance of hedging that appears in the authors' reporting. Looking specifically at those instances, offer an explanation for why the writers hedge when they do.

Response and Research Questions

9. The researchers report that "there has been a shift among philosophers and sociologists of science, away from seeing science as a purely empirical process, to seeing it as a social process of knowledge construction in which imagination and argument play an important role" (par. 3). In your opinion, what roles do imagination and argument play in the construction of scientific knowledge?

10. The researchers suggest that "many students are completely unaccustomed to 'writing' in science class" (47). What kinds of writing have you done in science classes? What kinds of writing do you feel you should do in those classes?

11. The researchers conclude that exploration of scientific controversies "can help students start to become autonomous science learners by assisting them to think critically about important issues that will affect their lives" (52). Make a list of scientific controversies with which you are familiar. Choose one, and briefly explain the sides of the controversy.

WRITING PROJECT

Writing a Persuasive Narrative

Many of the writers whose work for popular audiences is presented in this chapter offer compelling stories about their own and others' experiences as support for their larger claims about food, sustainability, and/or class, among other concerns. Gustavo Arellano, in "Taco USA: How Mexican Food Became More American Than Apple Pie," for instance, explains how he came to experience an "epiphany about Mexican food in the United States." Michael Pollan, in the introduction to his book *Cooked*, recounts his own "magical" experiences watching others prepare food to support his contention about the importance of returning to the practice of cooking for ourselves. In both cases, these personal narratives serve powerful persuasive purposes.

For this project, we invite you to craft a personal narrative that explores your own experience(s) with food in order to make a larger point or to support a claim about food, its sustainability, and/or its connections to larger concerns for American culture or society.

Consider first what you want to suggest to your readers, as you'll want to craft your text with that persuasive intent in mind: What is the overall point you want to emphasize in your narrative? For example, you might choose to make a case that we should eat organically as much as possible, or you might argue that we need to do more to support community gardens. You'll also need to decide if you want to state your position or argument outright or, instead, merely imply the position you're taking. Make the decision that best suits your needs.

Since your evidence for this argument is your personal experience(s), you'll want to consider carefully the structure of your narrative: Will you focus on a single event or experience? Will you focus on your engagement with food more broadly over a span of years? Regardless of the final organizational scheme you employ, remember that your experiences are meant to serve as evidence to support a claim.

Translating a Scholarly Work for a Popular Audience

WRITING PROJECT

For this project, we ask you to "translate" one of the academic, or scholarly, works included in the chapter for a popular audience. In order to do this, you'll first need to choose the work you'd like to be the focus of your translation:

- Daniel Gregorowius, Petra Lindemann-Matthies, and Markus Huppenbauer's "Ethical Discourse on the Use of Genetically Modified Crops: A Review of Academic Publications in the Fields of Ecology and Environmental Ethics" *(Humanities)*

- Charles Noussair, Stéphane Robin, and Bernard Ruffieux's "Do Consumers Really Refuse to Buy Genetically Modified Food?" *(Social Sciences)*

- Aziz Aris and Samuel Leblanc's "Maternal and Fetal Exposure to Pesticides Associated to Genetically Modified Foods in Eastern Townships of Quebec, Canada" *(Natural Sciences)*

- Sherry Seethaler and Marcia Linn's "Genetically Modified Food in Perspective: An Inquiry-Based Curriculum to Help Middle School Students Make Sense of Tradeoffs" *(Applied Fields)*

Once you've selected your target text for translation, you'll need to decide on the form your translation will take. For example, you might choose to translate Noussair et al.'s social science report for a popular audience by composing a news article about it. Or you might choose to translate the substance of Aris and Leblanc's natural science report into the form of a press release.

Regardless of the public, or popular, genre you choose (news article, press release, etc.), you'll likely want to study examples of that form of writing to become more aware of the conventional rhetorical features associated with the genre.

As you review each example, take care to note the structural, language, and reference features of the public genre:

- What kind of title does the example have?
- Can you discern a patterned presentation of information throughout the example?
- In what ways does the example attempt to connect to its intended audience?
- Typically, how long are the paragraphs? How long is the typical sentence?
- How would you assess the level of diction used in the piece? Is jargon employed?
- Are visuals typically used? If so, what kind?
- How does the writer of the example reference outside research?
- Are quotations used? If so, how often? Are they documented? If so, how?

Your final product should look and read as much as possible like a professional example of the genre you're producing.

CHAPTER

14

Writing, Identity, and Technology

The readings in this chapter explore what writing means to us as people and highlight how critical writing is to scholars in every discipline. The chapter opens with selections from popular sources that address the topic of writing. Stephen King's "Reading to Write," for instance, considers how reading serves writing, and makes the compelling point that the more we read, the more our common understanding of humanity helps to develop our voice and identity as writers. In "Writing as an Act of Hope," novelist Isabel Allende answers two central questions: why does she write, and for whom does she write? Jimmy Baca's "Coming into Language" exemplifies a poet's use of the literacy narrative genre, sharing how writing can be a form of freedom. Finally, in "Is Google Making Us Stupid?" Nicholas Carr critically examines the use of technology in our lives and asks how technology has shaped what we read, how we read, and how we think about and access the world around us.

Our purpose in providing these articles is to offer a context for engaging in discussion about what writing is, what it means to us as individuals and as scholars, and how writing and reading both contribute to shaping our identity and our sense of community and provide a means through which we can critically examine our lives. Questions to consider as you read these popular articles may include:

- How does writing contribute to your understanding of who you are?
- How does literacy affect conversations about our shared and disparate goals in society?
- What is knowledge? How does literacy contribute to our knowledge?
- What is the purpose of education for you personally and what is the purpose of education in our society?
- How does literacy impact freedom and access to freedom for all members of society?
- What roles do writing, reading, and education play in contributing to social and economic equality or inequality?

591

In the academic casebook section of this chapter, we feature scholarship on writing from a variety of academic disciplines to reveal the impact and value of writing in those disciplines:

- **Humanities**   What is the difference between being a writer and being an academic? What roles do personal and academic writing serve in the development of writers? What is and what should be their functions in the classroom?

- **Social Sciences**   How effective are particular psychological interventions, including various writing tasks, at increasing happiness?

- **Natural Sciences**   To what degree should we allow the marketplace (i.e., demands of employers) to determine the skills college students need in order to succeed?

- **Applied Fields**   How might the use of storytelling impact the efficacy of nursing research?

Reading to Write

STEPHEN KING

Stephen King is one of America's most prolific and popular writers of horror and science fiction, among other genres. Many of his books, short stories, and novellas have been adapted for film and television, including *Carrie* (1974), *The Shining* (1977), *Rita Hayworth and Shawshank Redemption* (1982), *Pet Cemetery* (1983), *It* (1986), and *1922* (2010), just to name a few. In the essay below, first published in *On Writing: A Memoir of the Craft* (2000), King offers advice, situated in his personal experiences, to those who want to write seriously, encouraging them "to read a lot and write a lot."

If you want to be a writer, you must do two things above all others: read a lot and write a lot. There's no way around these two things that I'm aware of, no shortcut.

I'm a slow reader, but I usually get through seventy or eighty books a year, mostly fiction. I don't read in order to study the craft; I read because I like to read. It's what I do at night, kicked back in my blue chair. Similarly, I don't read fiction to study the art of fiction, but simply because I like stories. Yet there is a learning process going on. Every book you pick up has its own lesson or lessons, and quite often the bad books have more to teach than the good ones.

When I was in the eighth grade, I happened upon a paperback novel by Murray Leinster, a science fiction pulp writer who did most of his work during the forties and fifties, when magazines like *Amazing Stories* paid a penny a word. I had read other books by Mr. Leinster, enough to know that the quality of his writing was uneven. This particular tale, which was about mining in the asteroid belt, was one of his less successful efforts. Only that's too kind. It was terrible, actually, a story populated by paper-thin characters and driven by outlandish plot developments. Worst of all (or so it seemed to me at the time), Leinster had fallen in love with the word *zestful*. Characters watched the approach of ore-bearing asteroids with *zestful smiles.* Characters sat down to supper aboard their mining ship with *zestful anticipation.* Near the end of the book, the hero swept the large-breasted, blonde heroine into a *zestful embrace.* For me, it was the literary equivalent of a smallpox vaccination: I have never, so far as I know, used the word *zestful* in a novel or a story. God willing, I never will.

Asteroid Miners (which wasn't the title, but that's close enough) was an important book in my life as a reader. Almost everyone can remember losing his or her virginity, and most writers can remember the first book he/she put down thinking: *I can do better than this. Hell, I am doing better than this!* What could be more encouraging to the struggling writer than to realize his/her work is unquestionably better than that of someone who actually got paid for his/her stuff?

One learns most clearly what not to do by reading 5 bad prose — one novel like *Asteroid Miners* (or *Valley of the Dolls, Flowers in the Attic,* and *The Bridges of Madison County,* to name just a few) is worth a semester at a good writing school, even with the superstar guest lecturers thrown in.

Good writing, on the other hand, teaches the learning writer about style, graceful narration, plot development, the creation of believable characters, and truth-telling. A novel like *The Grapes of Wrath* may fill a new writer with feelings of despair and good old-fashioned jealousy — "I'll never be able to write anything that good, not if I live to be a thousand" — but such feelings can also serve as a spur, goading the writer to work harder and aim higher. Being swept away by a combination of great story and great writing — of being flattened, in fact — is part of every writer's necessary formation. You cannot hope to sweep someone else away by the force of your writing until it has been done to you.

So we read to experience the mediocre and the outright rotten; such experience helps us to recognize those things when they begin to creep into our own work, and to steer clear of them. We also read in order to measure ourselves against the good and the great, to get a sense of all that can be done. And we read in order to experience different styles.

You may find yourself adopting a style you find particularly exciting, and there's nothing wrong with that. When I read Ray Bradbury as a kid, I wrote like Ray Bradbury — everything green and wondrous and seen through a lens smeared with the grease of nostalgia. When I read James M. Cain, everything I wrote came out clipped and stripped and hard-boiled. When I read Lovecraft, my prose became luxurious and Byzantine. I wrote stories in my teenage years where all these styles merged, creating a kind of hilarious stew. This sort of stylistic blending is a necessary part of developing one's own style, but it doesn't occur in a vacuum. You have to read widely, constantly refining (and redefining) your own work as you do so. It's hard for me to believe that people who read very little (or not at all in some cases) should presume to write and expect people to like what they have written, but I know it's true. If I had a nickel for every person who ever told me he/she wanted to become a writer but "didn't have time to read," I could buy myself a pretty good steak dinner. Can I be blunt on this subject? If you don't have time to read, you don't have the time (or the tools) to write. Simple as that.

Reading is the creative center of a writer's life. I take a book with me everywhere I go, and find there are all sorts of opportunities to dip in. The trick is to teach yourself to read in small sips as well as in long swallows. Waiting rooms were made for books — of course! But so are theater lobbies before the show, long and boring checkout lines, and everyone's favorite, the john. You can even read while you're driving, thanks to the audiobook revolution. Of the books I read each year, anywhere from six to a dozen are on tape. As for all the wonderful radio you will be missing, come on — how many times can you listen to Deep Purple sing "Highway Star"?

Reading at meals is considered rude in polite 10 society, but if you expect to succeed as a writer, rudeness should be the second-to-least of your concerns. The least of all should be polite society and what it expects. If you intend to write as truthfully as you can, your days as a member of polite society are numbered, anyway.

Where else can you read? There's always the treadmill, or whatever you use down at the local health club to get aerobic. I try to spend an hour doing that every day, and I think I'd go mad without a good novel to keep me company. Most exercise facilities (at home as well as outside it) are now equipped with TVs, but TV—while working out or anywhere else—really is about the last thing an aspiring writer needs. If you feel you must have the news analyst blowhards on CNN while you exercise, or the stock market blowhards on MSNBC, or the sports blowhards on ESPN, it's time for you to question how serious you really are about becoming a writer. You must be prepared to do some serious turning inward toward the life of the imagination, and that means, I'm afraid, that Geraldo, Keith Olbermann, and Jay Leno must go. Reading takes time, and the glass teat takes too much of it.

Once weaned from the ephemeral craving for TV, most people will find they enjoy the time they spend reading. I'd like to suggest that turning off that endlessly quacking box is apt to improve the quality of your life as well as the quality of your writing. And how much of a sacrifice are we talking about here? How many *Frasier* and *ER* reruns does it take to make one American life complete? How many Richard Simmons infomercials? How many whiteboy/fatboy Beltway insiders on CNN? Oh man, don't get me started. Jerry-Springer-Dr.-Dre-Judge-Judy-Jerry-Falwell-Donny-and-Marie, I rest my case.

When my son Owen was seven or so, he fell in love with Bruce Springsteen's E Street Band, particularly with Clarence Clemons, the band's burly sax player. Owen decided he wanted to learn to play like Clarence. My wife and I were amused and delighted by this ambition. We were also hopeful, as any parent would be, that our kid would turn out to be talented, perhaps even some sort of prodigy. We got Owen a tenor saxophone for Christmas and lessons with Gordon Bowie, one of the local music men. Then we crossed our fingers and hoped for the best.

Seven months later I suggested to my wife that it was time to discontinue the sax lessons, if Owen concurred. Owen did, and with palpable relief—he hadn't wanted to say it himself, especially not after asking for the sax in the first place, but seven months had been long enough for him to realize that, while he might love Clarence Clemons's big sound, the saxophone was simply not for him—God had not given him that particular talent.

I knew, not because Owen stopped practicing, but because he was practicing only during the periods Mr. Bowie had set for him: half an hour after school four days a week, plus an hour on the weekends. Owen mastered the scales and the notes—nothing wrong with his memory, his lungs, or his eye-hand coordination—but we never heard him taking off, surprising himself with something new, blissing himself out. And as soon as his practice time was over, it was back into the case with the horn, and there it stayed until the next lesson or practice time. What this suggested to me was that when it came to the sax and my son, there was never going to be any real playtime; it was all going to be rehearsal. That's no good. If there's no joy in it, it's just no good. It's best to go on to some other area, where the deposits of talent may be richer and the fun quotient higher.

Talent renders the whole idea of rehearsal meaningless; when you find something at which you are talented, you do it (whatever *it* is) until your fingers bleed or your eyes are ready to fall out of your head. Even when no one is listening (or reading, or watching), every outing is a bravura performance, because you as the creator are happy. Perhaps even ecstatic. That goes for reading and writing as well as for playing a musical instrument, hitting a baseball, or running the four-forty. The sort of strenuous reading and writing program I advocate—four to six hours a day, every day—will not seem strenuous if you really enjoy doing these things and have an aptitude for them; in fact, you may be following such a program already. If you feel you need permission to do all the reading and writing your little heart desires, however, consider it hereby granted by yours truly.

The real importance of reading is that it creates an ease and intimacy with the process of writing; one comes to the country of the writer with one's papers and identification pretty much in order. Constant reading will pull you into a place (a mind-set, if you like the phrase) where you can write eagerly and without self-consciousness. It also offers you a constantly growing knowledge of what has been done and what hasn't, what is trite and what is fresh, what works and what just lies there dying (or dead) on the page. The more you read, the less apt you are to make a fool of yourself with your pen or word processor.

Reading Questions

1. What does Stephen King say motivates his desire to read?

2. King suggests that talent "renders the whole idea of rehearsal meaningless" (par. 16). Is he suggesting that if you are talented, you don't ever need to rehearse or practice? What does he mean?

3. King writes: "If you expect to succeed as a writer, rudeness should be the second-to-least of your concerns" and that the "least of all should be polite society and what it expects" (10). How do you reconcile King's statement with the need as a student to be polite with teachers and peers in order to succeed?

Rhetoric Questions

4. How does King's use of the "I" point of view impact his connection with his audience?

5. What rules have you been taught about using the "I" point of view? What reasons were given for using or not using the "I" point of view?

6. Why do you think King juxtaposes the story about how he read voraciously as a youth with the story about his son Owen not practicing his saxophone? What is the purpose of these stories within his narrative?

Response and Research Questions

7. King writes about the "style" of writing. What does he mean by style? What does "good writing" consist of, according to King?

8. King writes: "One comes to the country of the writer with one's papers and identification pretty much in order" (17). Read the article "Culture Shock: Adjustments to New Cultural Environments" by Kalervo Oberg on pages 186–89 and compare what Oberg describes as "culture shock" to experiences you have writing in an unfamiliar genre. How is writing in a new genre like experiencing culture shock? How is it different?

9. Look at a piece of writing you have completed in the past (perhaps even your answers to these questions so far, if that's most convenient) and compare your own personal style of writing to King's style. What similarities in style do you notice? What differences?

Writing as an Act of Hope

ISABEL ALLENDE

Isabel Allende is an award-winning novelist. Since the publication of her first book, *The House of the Spirits*, in 1982, Allende has written more than twenty novels, including, most recently, *In the Midst of Winter* (2017). The following standalone essay was published online in *Peace Review* on December 4, 2007. In it, Allende explores her own relationship to writing, family, and her Latin American heritage. She laments the violence and inequality that have plagued Latin America and uses a literacy narrative of her own development as a novelist to present writing as an avenue of hope, giving voice to the troubles of a people.

In every interview during the last few years I encountered two questions that forced me to define myself as a writer and as a human being: why do I write? And who do I write for? Tonight I will try to answer those questions. In 1981, in Caracas, I put a sheet of paper in my typewriter and wrote the first sentence of *The House of the Spirits*: "Barrabas came to us by sea." At that moment I didn't know why I was doing it, or for whom.

In fact, I assumed that no one would ever read it except my mother, who reads everything I write. I was not even conscious that I was writing a novel. I thought I was writing a letter—a spiritual letter to my grandfather, a formidable old patriarch, whom I loved dearly. He had reached almost one hundred years of age and decided that he was too tired to go on living, so he sat in his armchair and refused to drink or eat, calling for Death, who was kind enough to take him very soon.

I wanted to bid him farewell, but I couldn't go back to Chile, and I knew that calling him on the telephone was useless, so I began this letter. I wanted to tell him that he could go in peace because all his memories were with me. I had forgotten nothing. I had all his anecdotes, all the characters of the family, and to prove it I began writing the story of Rose, the fiancée my grandfather had had, who is called Rose the Beautiful in the book. She really existed; she's not a copy from Garcia Marquez, as some people have said.

For a year I wrote every night with no hesitation or plan. Words came out like a violent torrent. I had thousands of untold words stuck in my chest, threatening to choke me. The long silence of exile was turning me to stone; I needed to open a valve and let the river of secret words find a way out. At the end of that year there were five hundred pages on my table; it didn't look like a letter anymore. On the other hand, my grandfather had died long before, so the spiritual message had already reached him. So I thought, "Well, maybe in this way I can tell some other people about him, and about my country, and about my family and myself." So I just organized it a little bit, tied the manuscript with a pink ribbon for luck, and took it to some publishers.

The spirit of my grandmother was protecting 5 the book from the very beginning, so it was refused everywhere in Venezuela. Nobody wanted it—it was too long; I was a woman; nobody knew me. So I sent it by mail to Spain, and the book was published there. It had reviews, and it was translated and distributed in other countries.

In the process of writing the anecdotes of the past, and recalling the emotions and pains of my fate, and telling part of the history of my country, I found that life became more comprehensible and the world more tolerable. I felt that my roots had been recovered and that during that patient exercise of daily writing I had also recovered my own soul. I felt at that time that writing was unavoidable—that I couldn't keep away from it. Writing is such a pleasure; it is always a private orgy, creating and recreating the world according to my own laws, fulfilling in those pages all my dreams and exorcising some of my demons.

But that is a rather simple explanation. There are other reasons for writing.

Six years and three books have passed since *The House of the Spirits.* Many things have changed for me in that time. I can no longer pretend to be naive, or elude questions, or find refuge in irony. Now I am constantly confronted by my readers, and they can be very tough. It's not enough to write in a state of trance, overwhelmed by the desire to tell a story. One has to be responsible for each word, each idea. Be very careful: the written word cannot be erased. . . .

Maybe the most important reason for writing is to prevent the erosion of time, so that memories will not be blown away by the wind. Write to register history, and name each thing. Write what should not be forgotten. But then, why write novels? Probably because I come from Latin America, a land of crazy, illuminated people, of geological and political cataclysms—a land so large and profound, so beautiful and frightening, that only novels can describe its fascinating complexity. A novel is like a window, open to an infinite landscape. In a novel we can put all the interrogations, we can register the most extravagant, evil, obscene, incredible, or magnificent facts—which, in Latin America, are not hyperbole, because that is the dimension of our reality. In a novel we can give an illusory order to chaos. We can find the key to the labyrinth of history. We can make excursions into the past, to try to understand the present and dream the future. In a novel we can use everything: testimony, chronicle, essay, fantasy, legend, poetry, and other devices that might help us to decode the mysteries of our world and discover our true identity.

For a writer who nourishes himself or herself on ¹⁰ images and passions, to be born in a fabulous continent is a privilege. In Latin America we don't have to stretch our imaginations. Critics in Europe and the United States often stare in disbelief at Latin American books, asking how the authors dare to invent those incredible lies of young women who fly to heaven wrapped in linen sheets; of black emperors who build fortresses with cement and the blood of emasculated bulls; of outlaws who die of hunger in the Amazon with bags full of emeralds on their backs; of ancient tyrants who order their mothers to

be flogged naked in front of the troops and modern tyrants who order children to be tortured in front of their parents; of hurricanes and earthquakes that turn the world upside down; of revolutions made with machetes, bullets, poems, and kisses; of hallucinating landscapes where reason is lost.

It is very hard to explain to critics that these things are not a product of our pathological* imaginations. They are written in our history; we can find them every day in our newspapers. We hear them in the streets; we suffer them frequently in our own lives. It is impossible to speak of Latin America without mentioning violence. We inhabit a land of terrible contrasts and we have to survive in times of great violence. Contrast and violence, two excellent ingredients for literature, although for us, citizens of that reality, life is always suspended from a very fragile thread.

The first, the most naked and visible form of violence, is the extreme poverty of the majority, in contrast with the extreme wealth of the very few. In my continent two opposite realities coexist. One is a legal face, more or less comprehensible and with a certain pretension to dignity and civilization. The other is a dark and tragic face, which we do not like to show but which is always threatening us. There is an apparent world and a real world—nice neighborhoods where blond children play on their bicycles and servants walk elegant dogs, and other neighborhoods, of slums and garbage, where dark children play naked with hungry mutts. There are offices of marble and steel where young executives discuss the stock market, and forgotten villages where people still live and die as they did in the Middle Ages. There is a world of fiction created by the official discourse, and another world of blood and pain and love, where we have struggled for centuries.

In Latin America we all survive on the borderline of those two realities. Our fragile democracies exist as long as they don't interfere with imperialist interests. Most of our republics are dependent on submissiveness. Our institutions and laws are inefficient. Our

pathological: diseased; unhealthy.

armed forces often act as mercenaries for a privileged social group that pays tribute to transnational enterprises. We are living in the worst economic, political, and social crisis since the conquest of America by the Spaniards. There are hardly two or three leaders in the whole continent. Social inequality is greater every day, and to avoid an outburst of public rancor, repression also rises day by day. Crime, drugs, misery, and ignorance are present in every Latin American country, and the military is an immediate threat to society and civil governments. We try to keep straight faces while our feet are stuck in a swamp of violence, exploitation, corruption, the terror of the state, and the terrorism of those who take arms against the status quo. Our Latin America is also a land of hope and friendship and love. Writers navigate in these agitated waters. They don't live in ivory towers; they cannot remove themselves from this brutal reality. In such circumstances there is no time and no wish for narcissistic* literature. Very few of our writers contemplate their navel in self-centered monologue. The majority want desperately to communicate.

I feel that writing is an act of hope, a sort of communion with our fellow men. The writer of good will carries a lamp to illuminate the dark corners. Only that, nothing more—a tiny beam of light to show some hidden aspect of reality, to help decipher and understand it and thus to initiate, if possible, a change in the conscience of some readers. This kind of writer is not seduced by the mermaid's voice of celebrity or tempted by exclusive literary circles. He has both feet planted firmly on the ground and walks hand in hand with the people in the streets. He knows that the lamp is very small and the shadows are immense. This makes him humble.

*narcissistic: pathologically self-centered; compulsively self-obsessed.

Reading Questions

1. What reasons does Isabel Allende give for why she writes?

2. How does she describe the process she used to write *The House of the Spirits*? How did she work on the novel?

3. How does Allende describe Latin America? How would you describe the land that served as the backdrop for your childhood?

Rhetoric Questions

4. Who does Isabel Allende see as her audience? What references from her past indicate who she sees as her audience?

5. How would you describe Allende's prose style? Give one or two specific examples that illustrate your point.

Response and Research Questions

6. How is Isabel Allende's political history reflected in her essay? To give yourself some additional context, do some research to determine what Allende's relationship was to the thirtieth president of Chile, Salvadore Allende. What happened to Salvadore Allende during his presidency?

7. How does understanding what happened to Salvadore Allende shed light on why Isabel writes the way she does of her family and her national history? What in your own family history would you find most compelling to write about?

8. If you were to write a letter to someone from your family who is no longer with you, as Allende did when writing *The House of the Spirits*, who would you write to, and what would you want to tell them?

9. How does Allende describe the social inequalities of Latin America? What are the major social inequalities facing your generation?

Coming into Language

JIMMY SANTIAGO BACA

Jimmy Santiago Baca is an American poet of Apache and Chicano descent. Orphaned as a child, Baca eventually became homeless and spent five years in a maximum-security prison on drug possession charges. While in prison, Baca taught himself to read and write. There, he also began to write poetry. Baca has since published numerous books of poetry, including, most recently, *Singing at the Gates: Selected Poems* (2014) and *The Face* (2013). His memoir, *A Place to Stand*, was published in 2001. In the essay below, published in 1991 in *Working in the Dark: Reflections of a Poet of the Barrio*, Baca recounts his experience of prison and traces his transformational journey toward literacy and self-empowerment.

On weekend graveyard shifts at St. Joseph's Hospital I worked the emergency room, mopping up pools of blood and carting plastic bags stuffed with arms, legs, and hands to the outdoor incinerator. I enjoyed the quiet, away from the screams of shotgunned, knifed, and mangled kids writhing on gurneys outside the operating rooms. Ambulance sirens shrieked and squad car lights reddened the cool nights, flashing against the hospital walls: gray—red, gray—red. On slow nights I would lock the door of the administration office, search the reference library for a book on female anatomy and, with my feet propped on the desk, leaf through the illustrations, smoking my cigarette. I was seventeen.

One night my eye was caught by a familiar-looking word on the spine of a book. The title was *450 Years of Chicano History in Pictures*. On the cover were black-and-white photos: Padre Hidalgo exhorting Mexican peasants to revolt against the Spanish dictators; Anglo vigilantes hanging two Mexicans from a tree; a young Mexican woman with rifle and ammunition belts crisscrossing her breast; César Chávez and field workers marching for fair wages; Chicano railroad workers laying creosote ties; Chicanas laboring at machines in textile factories; Chicanas picketing and hoisting boycott signs.

From the time I was seven, teachers had been punishing me for not knowing my lessons by making me stick my nose in a circle chalked on the blackboard. Ashamed of not understanding and fearful of asking questions, I dropped out of school in the ninth grade. At seventeen I still didn't know how to read, but those pictures confirmed my identity. I stole the book that night, stashing it for safety under the slop sink until I got off work. Back at my boardinghouse, I showed the book to friends. All of us were amazed; this book told us we were alive. We, too, had defended ourselves with our fists against hostile Anglos, gasping for breath in fights with the policemen who outnumbered us. The book reflected back to us our struggle in a way that made us proud.

Most of my life I felt like a target in the crosshairs of a hunter's rifle. When strangers and outsiders questioned me I felt the hang-rope tighten around my neck and the trapdoor creak beneath my feet. There was nothing so humiliating as being unable to express myself, and my inarticulateness increased my sense of jeopardy. Behind a mask of humility, I seethed with mute rebellion.

Before I was eighteen, I was arrested on suspicion of murder after refusing to explain a deep cut on my forearm. With shocking speed I found myself handcuffed to a chain gang of inmates and bused to a holding facility to await trial. There I met men, prisoners, who read aloud to each other the works of Neruda, Paz, Sabines, Nemerov, and Hemingway. Never had I felt such freedom as in that dormitory. Listening to the words of these writers, I felt that invisible threat from without lessen—my sense of teetering on a rotting plank over swamp water where famished alligators clapped their horny snouts for my blood. While I listened to the words of the poets, the alligators slumbered powerless in their lairs. The language of poetry was the magic that could liberate me from myself, transform me into another person, transport me to places far away.

And when they closed the books, these Chicanos, and went into their own Chicano language, they made barrio life come alive for me in the fullness of its vitality. I began to learn my own language, the bilingual words and phrases explaining to me my place in the universe.

Months later I was released, as I had suspected I would be. I had been guilty of nothing but shattering the windshield of my girlfriend's car in a fit of rage.

Two years passed. I was twenty now, and behind bars again. The federal marshals had failed to provide convincing evidence to extradite me to Arizona on a drug charge, but still I was being held. They had ninety days to prove I was guilty. The only evidence against me was that my girlfriend had been at the scene of the crime with my driver's license in her purse. They had to come up with something else. But there was nothing else. Eventually they negotiated a deal with the actual drug dealer, who took the stand against me. When the judge hit me with a million-dollar bail, I emptied my pockets on his booking desk: twenty-six cents.

One night in my third month in the county jail, I was mopping the floor in front of the booking desk. Some detectives had kneed an old drunk

and handcuffed him to the booking bars. His shrill screams raked my nerves like a hacksaw on bone, the desperate protest of his dignity against their inhumanity. But the detectives just laughed as he tried to rise and kicked him to his knees. When they went to the bathroom to pee and the desk attendant walked to the file cabinet to pull the arrest record, I shot my arm through the bars, grabbed one of the attendant's university textbooks, and tucked it in my overalls. It was the only way I had of protesting.

It was late when I returned to my cell. Under my blanket I switched on a pen flashlight and opened the thick book at random, scanning the pages. I could hear the jailer making his rounds on the other tiers. The jangle of his keys and the sharp click of his boot heels intensified my solitude. Slowly I enunciated the words . . . p-o-n-d, ri-pple. It scared me that I had been reduced to this to find comfort. I always had thought reading a waste of time, that nothing could be gained by it. Only by action, by moving out into the world and confronting and challenging the obstacles, could one learn anything worth knowing.

Even as I tried to convince myself that I was merely curious, I became so absorbed in how the sounds created music in me and happiness, I forgot where I was. Memories began to quiver in me, glowing with a strange but familiar intimacy in which I found refuge. For a while, a deep sadness overcame me, as if I had chanced on a long-lost friend and mourned the years of separation. But soon the heartache of having missed so much of life, that had numbed me since I was a child, gave way, as if a grave illness lifted itself from me and I was cured, innocently believing in the beauty of life again. I stumblingly repeated the author's name as I fell asleep, saying it over and over in the dark: Words-worth, Words-worth.

Before long my sister came to visit me, and I joked about taking her to a place called Xanadu and getting her a blind date with this *vato*[1] named Coleridge who lived on the seacoast and was *malias*[2] on morphine. When I asked her to make a trip into enemy territory

[1] In Chicano dialect: dude. (JSB)
[2] In Chicano dialect: strung out. (JSB)

to buy me a grammar book, she said she couldn't. Bookstores intimidated her, because she, too, could neither read nor write.

Days later, with a stub pencil I whittled sharp with my teeth, I propped a Red Chief notebook on my knees and wrote my first words. From that moment, a hunger for poetry possessed me.

Until then, I had felt as if I had been born into a raging ocean where I swam relentlessly, flailing my arms in hope of rescue, of reaching a shoreline I never sighted. Never solid ground beneath me, never a resting place. I had lived with only the desperate hope to stay afloat; that and nothing more.

But when at last I wrote my first words on the page, I felt an island rising beneath my feet like the back of a whale. As more and more words emerged, I could finally rest: I had a place to stand for the first time in my life. The island grew, with each page, into a continent inhabited by people I knew and mapped with the life I lived. 15

I wrote about it all—about people I had loved or hated, about the brutalities and ecstasies of my life. And, for the first time, the child in me who had witnessed and endured unspeakable terrors cried out not just in impotent despair, but with the power of language. Suddenly, through language, through writing, my grief and my joy could be shared with anyone who would listen. And I could do this all alone; I could do it anywhere. I was no longer a captive of demons eating away at me, no longer a victim of other people's mockery and loathing, that had made me clench my fist white with rage and grit my teeth to silence. Words now pleaded back with the bleak lucidity of hurt. They were wrong, those others, and now I could say it.

Through language I was free. I could respond, escape, indulge; embrace or reject earth or the cosmos. I was launched on an endless journey without boundaries or rules, in which I could salvage the floating fragments of my past, or be born anew in the spontaneous ignition of understanding some heretofore concealed aspect of myself. Each word steamed with the hot lava juices of my primordial making, and I crawled out of stanzas dripping with birth-blood, reborn and freed from the chaos of my life. The child in the dark room of my heart, who had never been able to find or reach the light switch, flicked it on now; and I found in the room a stranger, myself, who had waited so many years to speak again. My words struck in me lightning crackles of elation and thunderhead storms of grief.

When I had been in the county jail longer than anyone else, I was made a trustee. One morning, after a fistfight, I went to the unlocked and unoccupied office used for lawyer-client meetings, to think. The bare white room with its fluorescent tube lighting seemed to expose and illuminate my dark and worthless life. When I had fought before, I never gave it a thought. Now, for the first time, I had something to lose—my chance to read, to write; a way to live with dignity and meaning, that had opened for me when I stole that scuffed, second-hand book about the Romantic poets.

"I will never do any work in this prison system as long as I am not allowed to get my G.E.D." That's what I told the reclassification panel. The captain flicked off the tape recorder. He looked at me hard and said, "You'll never walk outta here alive. Oh, you'll work, put a copper penny on that, you'll work."

After that interview I was confined to deadlock maximum security in a subterranean dungeon, with ground-level chicken-wired windows painted gray. Twenty-three hours a day I was in that cell. Then, just before Christmas, I received a letter from Harry, a charity house Samaritan who doled out hot soup to the homeless in Phoenix. He had picked my name from a list of cons who had no one write to them. I wrote back asking for a grammar book, and a week later received one of Mary Baker Eddy's treatises on salvation and redemption, with Spanish and English on opposing pages. Pacing my cell all day and most of each night, I grappled with grammar until I was able to write a long true-romance confession for a con to send to his pen pal. He paid me with a pack of smokes. Soon I had a thriving barter business, exchanging my poems and letters for novels, commissary pencils, and writing tablets. 20

One day I tore two flaps from the cardboard box that held all my belongings and punctured holes along the edge of each flap and along the border of a ream of state-issue paper. After I had aligned them to form a spine, I threaded the holes with a shoestring, and sketched on the cover a hummingbird fluttering above a rose. This was my first journal.

Whole afternoons I wrote, unconscious of passing time or whether it was day or night. Sunbursts exploded from the lead tip of my pencil, words that grafted me into awareness of who I was; peeled back to a burning core of bleak terror, an embryo floating in the image of water, I cracked out of the shell wide-eyed and insane. Trees grew out of the palms of my hands, the threatening otherness of life dissolved, and I became one with the air and sky, the dirt and the iron and concrete. There was no longer any distinction between the other and I. Language made bridges of fire between me and everything I saw. I entered into the blade of grass, the basketball, the con's eye and child's soul.

At night I flew. I conversed with floating heads in my cell, and visited strange houses where lonely women brewed tea and rocked in wicker rocking chairs listening to sad Joni Mitchell songs.

Before long I was frayed like rope carrying too much weight, that suddenly snaps. I quit talking. Bars, walls, steel bunk and floor bristled with millions of poem-making sparks. My face was no longer familiar to me. The only reality was the swirling cornucopia of images in my mind, the voices in the air. Midair a cactus blossom would appear, a snake-flame in blinding dance around it, stunning me like a guard's fist striking my neck from behind. The prison administrators tried several tactics to get me to work. For six months, after the next monthly prison board review, they sent cons to my cell to hassle me. When the guard would open my cell door to let one of them in, I'd leap out and fight him—and get sent to thirty-day isolation. I did a lot of isolation time. But I honed my image-making talents in that sensory-deprived solitude. Finally they moved me to death row, and after that to "nut-run," the tier that housed the mentally disturbed.

As the months passed, I became more and more 25 sluggish. My eyelids were heavy, I could no longer write or read. I slept all the time.

One day a guard took me out to the exercise field. For the first time in years I felt grass and earth under my feet. It was spring. The sun warmed my face as I sat on the bleachers watching the cons box and run, hit the handball, lift weights. Some of them stopped to ask how I was, but I found it impossible to utter a syllable. My tongue would not move, saliva drooled from the corners of my mouth. I had been so heavily medicated I could not summon the slightest gestures. Yet inside me a small voice cried out, I am fine! I am hurt now but I will come back! I'm fine!

Back in my cell, for weeks I refused to eat. Styrofoam cups of urine and hot water were hurled at me. Other things happened. There were beatings, shock therapy, intimidation.

Later, I regained some clarity of mind. But there was a place in my heart where I had died. My life had compressed itself into an unbearable dread of being. The strain had been too much. I had stepped over that line where a human being has lost more than he can bear, where the pain is too intense, and he knows he is changed forever. I was now capable of killing, coldly and without feeling. I was empty, as I have never, before or since, known emptiness. I had no connection to this life.

But then, the encroaching darkness that began to envelop me forced me to re-form and give birth to myself again in the chaos. I withdrew even deeper into the world of language, cleaving the diamonds of verbs and nouns, plunging into the brilliant light of poetry's regenerative mystery. Words gave off rings of white energy, radar signals from powers beyond me that infused me with truth. I believed what I wrote, because I wrote what was true. My words did not come from books or textual formulas, but from a deep faith in the voice of my heart.

I had been steeped in self-loathing and rejected by everyone and everything—society, family, cons, God, and demons. But now I had become as the burning ember floating in darkness that descends on a dry leaf and sets flame to forests. The word was the ember and the forest was my life . . .

Writing bridged my divided life of prisoner and free man. I wrote of the emotional butchery of prisons, and my acute gratitude for poetry. Where my blind doubt and spontaneous trust in life met, I discovered empathy and compassion. The power to express myself was a welcome storm rasping at tendril roots, flooding my soul's cracked dirt. Writing was water that cleansed the wound and fed the parched root of my heart.

I wrote to sublimate my rage, from a place where all hope is gone, from a madness of having been damaged too much, from a silence of killing rage. I wrote to avenge the betrayals of a lifetime, to purge the bitterness of injustice. I wrote with a deep groan of doom in my blood, bewildered and dumbstruck; from an indestructible love of life, to affirm breath and laughter and the abiding innocence of things. I wrote the way I wept, and danced, and made love.

Reading Questions

1. In what ways was Jimmy Baca's writing a source of freedom in his life?

2. How did Baca's Chicano history play a role in how he perceived his identity, and how does he indicate that his identity has shaped his writing?

3. What would you say the effect of prison was on Baca?

Rhetoric Questions

4. Using dialogue, Baca describes a conversation with the captain of his reclassification panel. Read that dialogue and explain how it makes you feel. Have you ever had someone tell you something that stuck with you in similar way? What was it?

5. What imagery from Baca's essay evokes the most emotion in you and why?

6. Consider Baca's audience and purpose. Who does he see as his audience, and what does he want them to do?

Response and Research Questions

7. Baca writes: "I always had thought reading a waste of time, that nothing could be gained by it. Only by action, by moving out into the world and confronting and challenging the obstacles, could one learn anything worth knowing" (par. 10). To what degree do you agree with this perspective? What experiences of "moving out into the world and confronting and challenging the obstacles" have you learned from the most in your lifetime?

8. Search online to see if you can find a video of Jimmy Baca talking about "Coming into Language." Watch the video and explain how Baca describes his experiences with reading and writing. How does his early childhood experience compare with your own?

Is Google Making Us Stupid?

NICHOLAS CARR

Nicholas Carr is an essayist, blogger, and a former member of *Encyclopedia Britannica*'s editorial board. He has published writing in *Wired*, *Nature*, the *New York Times*, and the *Atlantic*, and has authored several books, including his latest title, *Utopia Is Creepy* (2016). The essay below originally appeared in the *Atlantic*, before Carr expanded it into the 2011 Pulitzer Prize finalist *The Shallows: What the Internet Is Doing to Our Brains*. In it, Carr questions the impact of technology, encouraging readers to consider how digital composition creates not just another way of reading but another way of living.

"Dave, stop. Stop, will you? Stop, Dave. Will you stop, Dave?" So the supercomputer HAL pleads with the implacable astronaut Dave Bowman in a famous and weirdly poignant scene toward the end of Stanley Kubrick's *2001: A Space Odyssey*. Bowman, having nearly been sent to a deep-space death by the malfunctioning machine, is calmly, coldly disconnecting the memory circuits that control its artificial "brain." "Dave, my mind is going," HAL says, forlornly. "I can feel it. I can feel it."

I can feel it, too. Over the past few years I've had an uncomfortable sense that someone, or something, has been tinkering with my brain, remapping the neural circuitry, reprogramming the memory. My mind isn't going—so far as I can tell—but it's changing. I'm not thinking the way I used to think. I can feel it most strongly when I'm reading. Immersing myself in a book or a lengthy article used to be easy. My mind would get caught up in the narrative or the turns of the argument, and I'd spend hours strolling through long stretches of prose. That's rarely the case anymore. Now my concentration often starts to drift after two or three pages. I get fidgety, lose the thread, begin looking for something else to do. I feel as if I'm always dragging my wayward brain back to the text. The deep reading that used to come naturally has become a struggle.

I think I know what's going on. For more than a decade now, I've been spending a lot of time online, searching and surfing and sometimes adding to the great databases of the Internet. The Web has been a godsend to me as a writer. Research that once required days in the stacks or periodical rooms of libraries can now be done in minutes. A few Google searches, some quick clicks on hyperlinks, and I've got the telltale fact or pithy quote I was after. Even when I'm not working, I'm as likely as not to be foraging in the Web's info-thickets, reading and writing e-mails, scanning headlines and blog posts, watching videos and listening to podcasts, or just tripping from link to link to link. (Unlike footnotes, to which they're sometimes likened, hyperlinks don't merely point to related works; they propel you toward them.)

For me, as for others, the Net is becoming a universal medium, the conduit for most of the information that flows through my eyes and ears and into my mind. The advantages of having immediate access to such an incredibly rich store of information are many, and they've been widely described and duly applauded. "The perfect recall of silicon memory," *Wired*'s Clive Thompson has written, "can be an enormous boon to thinking." But that boon comes at a price. As the media theorist Marshall McLuhan pointed out in the 1960s, media are not just passive channels of information. They supply the stuff of thought, but they also shape the process of thought. And what the Net seems to be doing is chipping away my capacity for concentration and contemplation. My mind now expects to take in information the way the Net distributes it: in a swiftly moving stream of particles. Once I was a scuba diver in the sea of words. Now I zip along the surface like a guy on a Jet Ski.

I'm not the only one. When I mention my troubles 5 with reading to friends and acquaintances—literary types, most of them—many say they're having similar experiences. The more they use the Web, the more they have to fight to stay focused on long pieces of writing. Some of the bloggers I follow have also begun mentioning the phenomenon. Scott Karp, who writes a blog about online media, recently confessed that he has stopped reading books altogether. "I was a lit major in college, and used to be [a] voracious book reader," he wrote. "What happened?" He speculates on the answer: "What if I do all my reading on the Web not so much because the way I read has changed, i.e., I'm just seeking convenience, but because the way I THINK has changed?"

Bruce Friedman, who blogs regularly about the use of computers in medicine, also has described how the Internet has altered his mental habits. "I now have almost totally lost the ability to read and absorb a longish article on the Web or in print," he wrote earlier this year. A pathologist who has long been on the faculty of the University of Michigan Medical School, Friedman elaborated on his comment in a telephone conversation with me. His thinking, he said, has taken on a "staccato" quality, reflecting the way he quickly scans short passages of text from many sources online. "I can't read *War and Peace* anymore," he admitted. "I've lost the ability to do that. Even a blog post of more than three or four paragraphs is too much to absorb. I skim it."

Anecdotes alone don't prove much. And we still await the long-term neurological and psychological experiments that will provide a definitive picture of how Internet use affects cognition. But a recently published study of online research habits, conducted by scholars from University College London, suggests that we may well be in the midst of a sea change in the way we read and think. As part of the five-year research program, the scholars examined computer logs documenting the behavior of visitors to two popular research sites, one operated by the British Library and one by a U.K. educational consortium, that provide access to journal articles, e-books, and other sources of written information. They found that people using the sites exhibited "a form of skimming activity," hopping from one source to another and rarely returning to any source they'd already visited. They typically read no more than one or two pages of an article or book before they would "bounce" out to another site. Sometimes they'd save a long article, but there's no evidence that they ever went back and actually read it. The authors of the study report:

> It is clear that users are not reading online in the traditional sense; indeed there are signs that new forms of "reading" are emerging as users "power browse" horizontally through titles, contents pages and abstracts going for quick wins. It almost seems that they go online to avoid reading in the traditional sense.

Thanks to the ubiquity of text on the Internet, not to mention the popularity of text-messaging on cell phones, we may well be reading more today than we did in the 1970s or 1980s, when television was our medium of choice. But it's a different kind of reading, and behind it lies a different kind of thinking—perhaps even a new sense of the self. "We are not only *what* we read," says Maryanne Wolf, a developmental psychologist at Tufts University and the author of *Proust and the Squid: The Story and Science of the Reading Brain.* "We are *how* we read." Wolf worries that the style of reading promoted by the Net, a style that puts "efficiency" and "immediacy" above all else, may be weakening our capacity for the kind of deep reading that emerged when an earlier technology, the printing press, made long and complex works of prose commonplace. When we read online, she says, we tend to become "mere decoders of information." Our ability to interpret text, to make the rich mental connections that form when we read deeply and without distraction, remains largely disengaged.

Reading, explains Wolf, is not an instinctive skill for human beings. It's not etched into our genes the way speech is. We have to teach our minds how to translate the symbolic characters we see into the language we understand. And the media or other technologies we use in learning and practicing the craft of reading play an important part in shaping the neural circuits inside our brains. Experiments demonstrate that readers of ideograms, such as the Chinese, develop a mental circuitry for reading that is very different from the circuitry found in those of us whose written language employs an alphabet. The variations extend across many regions of the brain, including those that govern such essential cognitive functions as memory and the interpretation of visual and auditory stimuli. We can expect as well that the circuits woven by our use of the Net will be different from those woven by our reading of books and other printed works.

Sometime in 1882, Friedrich Nietzsche bought 10 a typewriter—a Malling-Hansen Writing Ball, to be precise. His vision was failing, and keeping his eyes focused on a page had become exhausting and painful, often bringing on crushing headaches. He had been forced to curtail his writing, and he feared that he would soon have to give it up. The typewriter rescued him, at least for a time. Once he had mastered touch-typing, he was able to write with his eyes closed, using only the tips of his fingers. Words could once again flow from his mind to the page.

But the machine had a subtler effect on his work. One of Nietzsche's friends, a composer, noticed a change in the style of his writing. His already terse prose had become even tighter, more telegraphic. "Perhaps you will through this instrument even take to a new idiom," the friend wrote in a letter, noting that, in his own work, his "'thoughts' in music and language often depend on the quality of pen and paper."

"You are right," Nietzsche replied, "our writing equipment takes part in the forming of our thoughts." Under the sway of the machine, writes the German media scholar Friedrich A. Kittler, Nietzsche's prose "changed from arguments to aphorisms, from thoughts to puns, from rhetoric to telegram style."

The human brain is almost infinitely malleable. People used to think that our mental meshwork, the dense connections formed among the 100 billion or so neurons inside our skulls, was largely fixed by the time we reached adulthood. But brain researchers have discovered that that's not the case. James Olds, a professor of neuroscience who directs the Krasnow Institute for Advanced Study at George Mason University, says that even the adult mind "is very plastic." Nerve cells routinely break old connections and form new ones. "The brain," according to Olds, "has the ability to reprogram itself on the fly, altering the way it functions."

As we use what the sociologist Daniel Bell has called our "intellectual technologies"—the tools that extend our mental rather than our physical capacities— we inevitably begin to take on the qualities of those technologies. The mechanical clock, which came into common use in the 14th century, provides a compelling example. In *Technics and Civilization,* the historian and cultural critic Lewis Mumford described how the clock "disassociated time from human events and helped create the belief in an independent world of mathematically measurable sequences." The "abstract framework of divided time" became "the point of reference for both action and thought."

The clock's methodical ticking helped bring into 15 being the scientific mind and the scientific man. But it also took something away. As the late MIT computer scientist Joseph Weizenbaum observed in his 1976 book, *Computer Power and Human Reason: From Judgment to Calculation,* the conception of the world that emerged from the widespread use of timekeeping instruments "remains an impoverished version of the older one, for it rests on a rejection of those direct experiences that formed the basis for, and indeed constituted, the old reality." In deciding when to eat, to work, to sleep, to rise, we stopped listening to our senses and started obeying the clock.

The process of adapting to new intellectual technologies is reflected in the changing metaphors we use to explain ourselves to ourselves. When the mechanical clock arrived, people began thinking of their brains as operating "like clockwork." Today, in the age of software, we have come to think of them as operating "like computers." But the changes, neuroscience tells us, go much deeper than metaphor. Thanks to our brain's plasticity, the adaptation occurs also at a biological level.

The Internet promises to have particularly far-reaching effects on cognition. In a paper published in 1936, the British mathematician Alan Turing proved that a digital computer, which at the time existed only as a theoretical machine, could be programmed to perform the function of any other information-processing device. And that's what we're seeing today. The Internet, an immeasurably powerful computing system, is subsuming most of our other intellectual technologies. It's becoming our map and our clock, our printing press and our typewriter, our calculator and our telephone, and our radio and TV.

When the Net absorbs a medium, that medium is re-created in the Net's image. It injects the medium's content with hyperlinks, blinking ads, and other digital gewgaws, and it surrounds the content with the content of all the other media it has absorbed. A new e-mail message, for instance, may announce its arrival as we're glancing over the latest headlines at a newspaper's site. The result is to scatter our attention and diffuse our concentration.

The Net's influence doesn't end at the edges of a computer screen, either. As people's minds become attuned to the crazy quilt of Internet media, traditional media have to adapt to the audience's new expectations. Television programs add text crawls and pop-up ads, and magazines and newspapers shorten their articles, introduce capsule summaries, and crowd their pages with easy-to-browse info-snippets. When, in March of this year, the *New York Times* decided to devote the second and third pages of every edition to article abstracts, its design director, Tom Bodkin, explained that the "shortcuts" would give harried readers a quick "taste" of the day's news, sparing them the "less efficient" method of actually turning the pages and reading the articles. Old media have little choice but to play by the new-media rules.

Never has a communications system played 20 so many roles in our lives—or exerted such broad influence over our thoughts—as the Internet does today. Yet, for all that's been written about the Net, there's been little consideration of how, exactly,

it's reprogramming us. The Net's intellectual ethic remains obscure.

About the same time that Nietzsche started using his typewriter, an earnest young man named Frederick Winslow Taylor carried a stopwatch into the Midvale Steel plant in Philadelphia and began a historic series of experiments aimed at improving the efficiency of the plant's machinists. With the approval of Midvale's owners, he recruited a group of factory hands, set them to work on various metalworking machines, and recorded and timed their every movement as well as the operations of the machines. By breaking down every job into a sequence of small, discrete steps and then testing different ways of performing each one, Taylor created a set of precise instructions—an "algorithm," we might say today—for how each worker should work. Midvale's employees grumbled about the strict new regime, claiming that it turned them into little more than automatons, but the factory's productivity soared.

More than a hundred years after the invention of the steam engine, the Industrial Revolution had at last found its philosophy and its philosopher. Taylor's tight industrial choreography—his "system," as he liked to call it—was embraced by manufacturers throughout the country and, in time, around the world. Seeking maximum speed, maximum efficiency, and maximum output, factory owners used time-and-motion studies to organize their work and configure the jobs of their workers. The goal, as Taylor defined it in his celebrated 1911 treatise, *The Principles of Scientific Management*, was to identify and adopt, for every job, the "one best method" of work and thereby to effect "the gradual substitution of science for rule of thumb throughout the mechanic arts." Once his system was applied to all acts of manual labor, Taylor assured his followers, it would bring about a restructuring not only of industry but of society, creating a utopia of perfect efficiency. "In the past the man has been first," he declared; "in the future the system must be first."

Taylor's system is still very much with us; it remains the ethic of industrial manufacturing. And now, thanks to the growing power that computer engineers and software coders wield over our intellectual lives, Taylor's ethic is beginning to govern the realm of the mind as well. The Internet is a machine designed for the efficient and automated collection, transmission, and manipulation of information, and its legions of programmers are intent on finding the "one best method"—the perfect algorithm—to carry out every mental movement of what we've come to describe as "knowledge work."

Google's headquarters, in Mountain View, California—the Googleplex—is the Internet's high church, and the religion practiced inside its walls is Taylorism. Google, says its chief executive, Eric Schmidt, is "a company that's founded around the science of measurement," and it is striving to "systematize everything" it does. Drawing on the terabytes of behavioral data it collects through its search engine and other sites, it carries out thousands of experiments a day, according to the *Harvard Business Review*, and it uses the results to refine the algorithms that increasingly control how people find information and extract meaning from it. What Taylor did for the work of the hand, Google is doing for the work of the mind.

The company has declared that its mission is "to organize the world's information and make it universally accessible and useful." It seeks to develop "the perfect search engine," which it defines as something that "understands exactly what you mean and gives you back exactly what you want." In Google's view, information is a kind of commodity, a utilitarian resource that can be mined and processed with industrial efficiency. The more pieces of information we can "access" and the faster we can extract their gist, the more productive we become as thinkers.

Where does it end? Sergey Brin and Larry Page, the gifted young men who founded Google while pursuing doctoral degrees in computer science at Stanford, speak frequently of their desire to turn their search engine into an artificial intelligence, a HAL-like machine that might be connected directly to our brains. "The ultimate search engine is something as smart as people—or smarter," Page said in a speech a few years back. "For us, working on search is a way to work on artificial intelligence." In a 2004 interview with *Newsweek*, Brin said, "Certainly if you had all the world's information directly attached to your brain, or an artificial brain that was smarter than your brain, you'd be better off." Last year, Page told a convention of scientists that Google is "really trying to build artificial intelligence and to do it on a large scale."

Such an ambition is a natural one, even an admirable one, for a pair of math whizzes with vast quantities of cash at their disposal and a small army of computer scientists in their employ. A fundamentally scientific enterprise, Google is motivated by a desire to use technology, in Eric Schmidt's words, "to solve problems that have never been solved before," and artificial intelligence is the hardest problem out there. Why wouldn't Brin and Page want to be the ones to crack it?

Still, their easy assumption that we'd all "be better off" if our brains were supplemented, or even replaced, by an artificial intelligence is unsettling. It suggests a belief that intelligence is the output of a mechanical process, a series of discrete steps that can be isolated, measured, and optimized. In Google's world, the world we enter when we go online, there's little place for the fuzziness of contemplation. Ambiguity is not an opening for insight but a bug to be fixed. The human brain is just an outdated computer that needs a faster processor and a bigger hard drive.

The idea that our minds should operate as high-speed data-processing machines is not only built into the workings of the Internet, it is the network's reigning business model as well. The faster we surf across the Web—the more links we click and pages we view—the more opportunities Google and other companies gain to collect information about us and to feed us advertisements. Most of the proprietors of the commercial Internet have a financial stake in collecting the crumbs of data we leave behind as we flit from link to link—the more crumbs, the better. The last thing these companies want is to encourage leisurely reading or slow, concentrated thought. It's in their economic interest to drive us to distraction.

Maybe I'm just a worrywart. Just as there's a tendency to glorify technological progress, there's a countertendency to expect the worst of every new tool or machine. In Plato's *Phaedrus*, Socrates bemoaned the development of writing. He feared that, as people came to rely on the written word as a substitute for the knowledge they used to carry inside their heads, they would, in the words of one of the dialogue's characters, "cease to exercise their memory and become forgetful." And because they would be able to "receive a quantity of information without proper instruction," they would "be thought very knowledgeable when they are for the most part quite ignorant." They would be "filled with the conceit of wisdom instead of real wisdom." Socrates wasn't wrong—the new technology did often have the effects he feared—but he was shortsighted. He couldn't foresee the many ways that writing and reading would serve to spread information, spur fresh ideas, and expand human knowledge (if not wisdom).

The arrival of Gutenberg's printing press, in the 15th century, set off another round of teeth gnashing. The Italian humanist Hieronimo Squarciafico worried that the easy availability of books would lead to intellectual laziness, making men "less studious" and weakening their minds. Others argued that cheaply printed books and broadsheets would undermine religious authority, demean the work of scholars and scribes, and spread sedition and debauchery. As New York University professor Clay Shirky notes, "Most of the arguments made against the printing press were correct, even prescient." But, again, the doomsayers were unable to imagine the myriad blessings that the printed word would deliver.

So, yes, you should be skeptical of my skepticism. Perhaps those who dismiss critics of the Internet as Luddites or nostalgists will be proved correct, and from our hyperactive, data-stoked minds will spring a golden age of intellectual discovery and universal wisdom. Then again, the Net isn't the alphabet, and although it may replace the printing press, it produces something altogether different. The kind of deep reading that a sequence of printed pages promotes is valuable not just for the knowledge we acquire from the author's words but for the intellectual vibrations those words set off within our own minds. In the quiet spaces opened up by the sustained, undistracted reading of a book, or by any other act of contemplation, for that matter, we make our own associations, draw our own inferences and analogies, foster our own ideas. Deep reading, as Maryanne Wolf argues, is indistinguishable from deep thinking.

If we lose those quiet spaces, or fill them up with "content," we will sacrifice something important not only in our selves but in our culture. In a recent essay, the playwright Richard Foreman eloquently described what's at stake:

> I come from a tradition of Western culture, in which the ideal (my ideal) was the complex, dense and "cathedral-like" structure of the highly educated and articulate personality—a man or woman who carried inside themselves a personally constructed and unique version of the entire heritage of the West. [But now] I see within us all (myself included) the replacement of complex inner density with a new kind of self—evolving under the pressure of information overload and the technology of the "instantly available."

As we are drained of our "inner repertory of dense cultural inheritance," Foreman concluded, we risk turning into "'pancake people'—spread wide and thin as we connect with that vast network of information accessed by the mere touch of a button."

I'm haunted by that scene in *2001*. What makes it so poignant, and so weird, is the computer's emotional response to the disassembly of its mind: its despair as one circuit after another goes dark, its childlike pleading with the astronaut—"I can feel it. I can feel it. I'm afraid"—and its final reversion to what can only be called a state of innocence. HAL's outpouring of feeling contrasts with the emotionlessness that characterizes the human figures in the film, who go about their business with an almost robotic efficiency. Their thoughts and actions feel scripted, as if they're following the steps of an algorithm. In the world of

2001, people have become so machinelike that the most human character turns out to be a machine. That's the essence of Kubrick's dark prophecy: as we come to rely on computers to mediate our understanding of the world, it is our own intelligence that flattens into artificial intelligence.

Reading Questions

1. Carr quotes Scott Karp, who writes "the way I *think* has changed" (par. 5), and Bruce Friedman, who describes how the Internet has "altered his mental habits" (6). What are the ways that the Internet affects your friendships, interactions with your family, and your own mental habits?

2. What does Carr mean when he references the phrase "We are *how* we read" (8)? Why does he italicize the word *how* for emphasis?

3. Carr claims that technologies "play an important part in shaping the neural circuits in our brains" (10). What does he mean?

Rhetoric Questions

4. Consider what Carr's main points are in his essay and explain who he sees as his audience. What is he trying to convince his audience to do?

5. Discuss Carr's ethos. How does he attempt to establish his credibility, and how effective is he? Do you find his argument credible? Why or why not?

6. What is the purpose for Carr using the story of Socrates in his essay? What point does Carr make about the views Socrates held regarding the written word?

Response and Research Questions

7. Carr tells a story about Friedrich Nietzsche buying a typewriter in 1882. Who was Nietzsche, what kinds of things did Nietzsche believe, and what does Carr claim happened to Nietzsche's writing after he started using a typewriter?

8. Carr makes use of Stanley Kubrick's movie *2001: A Space Odyssey* throughout his essay. Why is *2001: A Space Odyssey* emblematic to Carr regarding his claims about how we think and read in a digital age?

9. Carr compares the invention of the printing press to that of the Internet as a similar change regarding how people read and process information. When was the printing press invented and how did society respond to its use in the first few decades afterward?

10. What would technology look like in a society not based on capitalism? How might companies like Google serve the public differently if money were not a motivating force behind what they do?

Writing with Teachers: A Conversation with Peter Elbow; Being a Writer vs. Being an Academic: A Conflict in Goals

DAVID BARTHOLOMAE, PETER ELBOW

David Bartholomae is a professor of English at the University of Pittsburgh. He has published numerous books and articles in the area of composition studies. Among other awards he has received, he was named the 2014 Pennsylvania Professor of the Year. Peter Elbow is a professor emeritus at the University of Massachusetts Amherst. He is the author of several books, including *Vernacular Eloquence: What Speech Can Bring to Writing* (2012). At the Conference on College Composition & Communication (CCCC) in 1989 and again in 1991, Bartholomae and Elbow entered into a public scholarly conversation about the nature and impact of personal and academic writing. The selections that follow are taken from the text of the presentations each gave at the 1991 conference. This type of collaborative exploration of (and even disagreement about) a topic is a relatively common occurrence in the humanities.

David Bartholomae:

WHERE TO BEGIN?

Most discussions like the one we are about to have begin or end by fretting over the central term *academic writing*. It is clear that this is not just a contested term, but a difficult one to use with any precision. If, for example, it means the writing that is done by academics, or the writing that passes as currency in the academy, then it is a precise term only when it is loaded: academic writing—the unreadable created by the unspeakable; academic writing—stuffy, pedantic, the price of a career; academic writing—pure, muscular, lean, taut, the language of truth and reason; academic writing—language stripped of the false dressings of style and fashion, a tool for inquiry and critique.

And so on. I don't need to belabor this point. Academic writing is a single thing only in convenient arguments. If you collect samples of academic writing, within or across the disciplines, it has as many types and categories, peaks and valleys, as writing grouped under any other general category: magazine writing, business writing, political writing, sports writing. Or, I could put it this way: Within the writing performed in 1990 under the rubric of English studies, writing by

English professors, you can find writing that is elegant, experimental, sentimental, autobiographical, spare, dull, pretentious, abstract, boring, dull, whatever.

If I am here to argue for academic writing as part of an undergraduate's training, or as a form or motive to be taught/examined in the curriculum, I need to begin by saying that I am not here to argue for stuffy, lifeless prose or for mechanical (or dutiful) imitations of standard thoughts and forms. We need a different set of terms to frame the discussion. It is interesting, in fact, to consider how difficult it is to find positive terms for academic writing when talking to a group of academics, including those who could be said to do it for a living. It is much easier to find examples or phrases to indicate our sense of corporate shame or discomfort.

I don't have time to pursue this line of argument here, but I think it is part and parcel of the anti-professionalism Fish argues is a pose of both the academic right (for whom the prose in our journals is evidence of bad faith, of the pursuit of trends, an abandonment of the proper pursuit of humane values, great books), but also for the academic left (for whom professional practice is the busy work we do because we are co-opted). For both, academic writing is what you do when you are not doing your "real" work.

MY POSITION, I THINK

I want to argue that academic writing is the real work 5
of the academy. I also want to argue for academic
writing as a key term in the study of writing and the
practice of instruction. In fact, I want to argue that
if you are teaching courses in the university, courses
where students write under your supervision, they
can't not do it and you can't not stand for it (academic writing, that is) and, therefore, it is better that
it be done out in the open, where questions can be
asked and responsibilities assumed, than to be done
in hiding or under another name.

To say this another way, there is no writing that is
writing without teachers. I think I would state this as
a general truth, but for today let me say that there is
no writing done in the academy that is not academic
writing. To hide the teacher is to hide the traces of
power, tradition, and authority present at the scene
of writing (present in allusions to previous work, in
necessary work with sources, in collaboration with
powerful theories and figures, in footnotes and quotations and the messy business of doing your work in the
shadow of others). Thinking of writing as academic
writing makes us think of the page as crowded with
others—or it says that this is what we learn in school,
that our writing is not our own, nor are the stories we
tell when we tell the stories of our lives—they belong
to TV, to Books, to Culture and History.

To offer academic writing as something else is
to keep this knowledge from our students, to keep
them from confronting the power politics of discursive practice, or to keep them from confronting the
particular representations of power, tradition, and
authority reproduced whenever one writes.

Now—I say this as though it were obvious.
Students write in a space defined by all the writing
that has preceded them, writing the academy insis-
tently draws together: in the library, in the reading list,
in the curriculum. This is the busy, noisy, intertextual
space—one usually hidden in our representations of
the classroom; one that becomes a subject in the
classroom when we ask young writers to think about,
or better yet, confront, their situatedness.

And yet, it is also obvious that there are many
classrooms where students are asked to imagine
that they can clear out a space to write on their
own, to express their own thoughts and ideas, not to
reproduce those of others. As I think this argument
through, I think of the pure and open space, the frontier classroom, as a figure central to composition as
it is currently constructed. The open classroom; a
free writing. This is the master trope. And, I would
say, it is an expression of a desire for an institutional
space free from institutional pressures, a cultural process free from the influence of culture, an historical
moment outside of history, an academic setting free
from academic writing.

Whose desire? That is a hard question to answer, 10
and I will finesse it for the moment. I don't want to say
that it is Peter's; I think it is expressed in Peter's work.

I can, however, phrase this question: "Whose
desire is this, this desire for freedom, empowerment,
an open field?"—I think I can phrase the question in
terms of the larger debate in the academy about the
nature of discourse and the humanities. The desire
for a classroom free from the past is an expression of
the desire for presence or transcendence, for a common language, free from jargon and bias, free from
evasion and fear; for a language rooted in common
sense rather than special sense, a language that renders (makes present) rather than explains (makes
distant). It is a desire with a particularly American
inflection and a particular resonance at a moment in
the academy when it has become harder and harder
to cast any story, let alone the story of education, in a
setting that is free, Edenic, or Utopian.

"I have learned to relinquish authority in my classroom." How many times do we hear this now as the
necessary conclusion in an argument about the goals
of composition? "I want to empower my students." "I
want to give my students ownership of their work."
What could it mean—to have this power over language, history, and culture? to own it?

Unless it means stepping outside of the real time
and place of our writing—heading down the river,
heading out to the frontier, going nowhere. Unless

it means stepping out of language and out of time. I am arguing for a class *in* time, one that historicizes the present, including the present evoked in students' writing. Inside this linguistic present, students (with instruction—more precisely, with lessons in critical reading) can learn to feel and see their position inside a text they did not invent and can never, at least completely, control. Inside a practice: linguistic, rhetorical, cultural, historical.

As I am thinking through this argument, I read Peter's work as part of a much larger project to preserve and reproduce the figure of the author, an independent, self-creative, self-expressive subjectivity. I see the argument against academic writing, and for another writing, sometimes called personal or expressive writing, as part of a general argument in favor of the author, a much beleaguered figure in modern American English departments. This is one way that the profession, English, has of arguing out the nature and role of writing as a subject of instruction— personal writing/academic writing—this opposition is the structural equivalent to other arguments, arguments about authorship and ownership, about culture and the individual, about single author courses, about the canon.

And these arguments are part of still other arguments, with different inflections, about production and consumption, about reading and writing, about presence and transcendence, culture and individualism—arguments working themselves out in particular ways at conferences and in papers in many settings connected to the modern academy. The desire for an open space, free from the past, is a powerful desire, deployed throughout the discourses of modern life, including the discourses of education.

THE CONTACT ZONE

When we talk about academic writing at CCCC, I don't think we are talking about discourse—at least, after Foucault, as *discourse* is a technical term. We are not, in other words, talking about particular discursive practices and how they are reproduced or policed within the academic disciplines.

I would say that we are talking about sites, possible scenes of writing, places, real and figurative, where writing is produced. This is why so much time is spent talking about the classroom and its literal or metaphorical arrangement of power and authority—where do we sit, who talks first, who reads the papers. Whether we rearrange the furniture in the classroom or rearrange the turns taken by speakers in a discussion, these actions have no immediate bearing on the affiliations of power brought into play in writing. At worst, the "democratic" classroom becomes the sleight of hand we perfect in order to divert attention for the unequal distribution of power that is inherent in our positions as teachers, as figures of institutional/disciplinary authority, and inherent in the practice of writing, where one is always second, derivative, positioned, etc.

I am trying to think about the scene of writing as a discursive space. So let me say that we shouldn't think of ourselves as frontier guides but as managers, people who manage substations in the cultural network, small shops in the general production of readers and writers. We don't choose this; it is the position we assume as teachers. If, from this position, we are going to do anything but preside over 15 the reproduction of forms and idioms, we have to make the classroom available for critical inquiry, for a critique that is part of the lesson of practice. We have to do more, that is, than manage.

If our goal is to make a writer aware of the forces at play in the production of knowledge, we need to highlight the classroom as a substation—as a real space, not as an idealized utopian space. There is no better way to investigate the transmission of power, tradition, and authority than by asking students to do what academics do: work with the past, with key texts (we have been teaching Emerson, Rich, Simon Frith on rock and roll); working with other's terms (key terms from Rich, like *patriarchy*, for example); struggling with the problems of quotation, citation, and paraphrase, where one version of a student's relationship to the past is represented by how and where he quotes Rich (does he follow the block quotation with commentary of his own? can Rich do more than "support" an argument, can a student argue with Rich's words, use them as a point to push off from?).

I want this issue to be precise as well as abstract. 20 You can teach a lot about a writer's possible relations with the past by looking at how and why she uses a passage from an assigned text. This is not, in other words, simply a matter of reproducing standard texts, but of using them as points of deflection, appropriation, improvisation, or penetration (those are Mary Louise Pratt's terms). But you can't do this without making foremost the situatedness of writing, without outlining in red the network of affiliations that constitute writing in the academy.

Let me do this another way. There is a student in my class writing an essay on her family, on her parents' divorce. We've all read this essay. We've read it because the student cannot invent a way of talking about family, sex roles, separation. Her essay is determined by a variety of forces: the genre of the personal essay as it has shaped this student and this moment; attitudes about the family and divorce; the figures of "Father" and "Mother" and "Child" and so on. The moment of this essay is a moment of the general problematics of writing—who does what to whom, who does the writing, what can an individual do with the cultural field? Of course we can help the student to work on this essay by letting her believe it is hers—to think that the key problem is voice, not citation; to ask for realistic detail rather than to call attention to figuration. Almost two hundred years of sentimental realism prepares all of us for these lessons. We can teach students to be more effective producers of this product. We can also teach them its critique. Perhaps here is a way of talking about the real issues in the debate over academic writing? How can you not reproduce the master narrative of family life? How might a student writer negotiate with the professional literature? How and what might it mean to talk back to (or to talk with) Adrienne Rich about family life? What does it mean for a student to claim that her own experience holds equivalent status with Rich's memories as material to work on?

TEACHERS AS WRITERS

We have several examples of academics announcing that they are now abandoning academic writing. I am thinking of Jane Tompkins's recent article, "Me and My Shadow." I am thinking of other similar moments of transcendence: Mina Shaughnessy's use of Hoggart and Baldwin as writers who could use autobiography to do intellectual work. I am thinking of Mike Rose's book, *Lives on the Boundary.* I am thinking of the recent issue of *PRE/TEXT* devoted to "expressive writing." I am thinking of the roles Gretel Ehrlich or Richard Selzer have played at this conference, or scholars like Peter and Chuck Schuster. Or that wonderful session of CCCC where Nancy Sommers and Pat Hoy presented extended personal essays as conference papers. I am thinking of Don McQuade's chair's address at the 1989 CCCC. I am thinking of some of Peter's prose. And some of my own.

I seem to be saying that one cannot not write academic discourse, and yet here are examples of the academics pushing at the boundaries in decidedly academic settings. I don't see this as a contradiction. I would say that these are not examples of transcendence but of writers calling up, for a variety of purposes, different (but highly conventional) figures of the writer. These are writers taking pleasure in (or making capital of) what are often called "literary devices"—dialogue, description, the trope of the real, the figure of the writer at the center of sentimental realism. There is great pleasure in writing this way (making the world conform to one's image, exalting one's "point of view"), and there are strategic reasons for not doing academic writing when it is expected—I would say all great academic writers know this. I would call the writing I cited above examples of blurred genres, not free writing, and both genres represent cultural interests (in reproducing the distinct versions of experience and knowledge). In my department, this other form of narrative is often called "creative non-fiction" or "literary non-fiction"—it is a way to celebrate individual vision, the detail of particular worlds. There is an argument in this kind of prose too, an argument about what is real and what it means to inhabit the real. The danger is assuming that one genre is more real than the other (a detailed, loving account of the objects in my mother's kitchen is more "real" than a detailed loving account of the discourse on domesticity found in 19th-century American women's magazines)—in assuming that one is real writing and the other is only a kind of game academics play. The danger lies in letting these tendentious terms guide the choices we make in designing the curriculum.

A BRIEF HISTORY

Why, we might ask, do we have such a strong desire to talk about schooling as though it didn't have to be schooling, a disciplinary process? I have started one answer—it is part of a general desire to erase the past and its traces from the present.

I would also say that our current conversations are very much a product of an important moment in composition in the early 1970s—one in which Peter played a key role. At a time when the key questions facing composition could have been phrased as questions of linguistic difference—what is good writing and how is that question a question of race, class, or gender?—at a time when composition could have made the scene of instruction the object of scholarly inquiry, there was a general shift away from questions of value and the figure of the writer in a social context of writing to questions of process and the figure of the writer as an individual psychology. If you turn to work by figures who might otherwise be thought of as dissimilar—Britton, Moffett, Emig, Northrop Frye, Jerome Bruner—you will find a common displacement of the social and a celebration of the individual as fundamentally (or ideally) congruent with culture and history. Here is how it was phrased: There is no real difference between the child and the adult (that's Bruner); the curriculum is in the learner (that's Moffett and Britton); we find the universal mind of man in the work of individuals (that's Frye). All find ways of equating change with growth, locating both the process and the mechanism within an individual psychology, equating the

learner with that which must be learned. And, as a consequence, schooling becomes secondary, not the primary scene of instruction, but a necessary evil in a world that is not well-regulated, where people would naturally mature into myth or prose or wisdom. School is secondary, instrumental, something to be overcome. And, in a similar transformation, writing becomes secondary, instrumental (to thinking or problem solving or deep feeling or unconscious imaginative forces).

I would say that the argument that produces archetypal criticism produces cognitive psychology, free writing, and new journalism: I've got Bruner, Linda Flower, Peter, Tom Wolfe, and John McPhee all lined up in this genealogy, this account of the modern curricular production of the independent author, the celebration of point-of-view as individual artifact, the promotion of sentimental realism (the true story of what I think, feel, know, and see).

CONCLUSION, OR, SO HOW DO I GET OUT OF THIS?

I am at the point where I should have a conclusion, but I don't. I could say this is strategic. Peter and I are having a conversation, and so it would be rude to conclude. Let me reimagine my position by rephrasing the questions that allow me access to it. Here is how I would now phrase the questions that I take to be the key questions in the debate on academic writing:

Should we teach new journalism or creative non-fiction as part of the required undergraduate curriculum? That is, should all students be required to participate in a first person, narrative or expressive genre whose goal it is to reproduce the ideology of sentimental realism—where a world is made in the image of a single, authorizing point of view? a narrative that celebrates a world made up of the details of private life and whose hero is sincere?

I don't have an easy answer to this question. It is like asking, should students be allowed to talk about their feelings after reading *The Color Purple*? Of course they should, but where and when? and under whose authority?

I think it is possible to say that many students will not feel the pleasure or power of authorship unless we make that role available. Without our classes, students will probably not have the pleasure or the power of believing they are the figure that they have seen in pieces they have read: the figure who is seeing the world for the first time, naming it, making their thoughts the center of the world, feeling the power of their own sensibilities. This has been true for teachers in the Writing Projects, it will be true in our classes. Unless we produce this effect in our classroom, students will not be Authors.

There is no question but that we can produce these effects. The real question is, should we?

In a sense, I feel compelled to argue that we should. We should teach students to write as though they were not the products of their time, politics, and culture, not our products, as though they could be free, elegant, smart, independent, the owners of all that they say. Why should they be denied this pleasure; or, why should it be reserved for some writers in our culture and not for others?

But I can also phrase the question this way: Why should I or a program I stand for be charged to tell this lie, even if it is a pleasant and, as they say, empowering one for certain writers or writers at a certain stage of their education? Why am I in charge of the reproduction of this myth of American life?

Or—is it a matter of stages in a writer's education? Should we phrase it this way: A nineteen-year-old has to learn to be a committed realist in order later to feel the potential for the critique of this position. People used to say something like this about traditional forms of order in the essay: You have to learn to write like E. B. White before you can learn to write like Gertrude Stein. Picasso couldn't have been a cubist if he hadn't learned to draw figures.

Learn to be logocentric? Learn to celebrate individualism? Learn to trust one's common sense point of view? Who needs to learn this at eighteen? Well, one might argue that students need to learn to do it well, so that it seems like an achievement. That is, students should master the figures and forms, learn to produce an elegant, convincing, even professional quality narrative before learning its critique and imagining its undoing.

I could phrase the question this way: Should composition programs self-consciously maintain a space for the "author" in a university curriculum that has traditionally denied students the category of author (by making students only summarizers or term paper writers)?

But it is too easy to say yes if I phrase the question like that. What if I put it this way? Should composition programs maintain a space for, reproduce the figure of, the author at a time when the figure of the author is under attack in all other departments of the academy. That is, should we be conservative when they are radical? Should we be retrograde in the face of an untested avant-garde?

Or—are we (should we be) a part of the critique, given our privileged role in the production of authors in the university curriculum, our positions in charge of sub-stations in the culture's determined production of readers and writers?

When I phrase the question that way, the answers become easy. I don't think I need to teach students to be controlled by the controlling idea, even though I know my students could write more organized texts. I don't think I need to teach sentimental realism, even though I know my students could be better at it than they are. I don't think I need to because I don't think I should. I find it a corrupt, if extraordinarily tempting genre. I don't want my students to celebrate what would then become the natural and inevitable details of their lives. I think the composition course should be part of the general critique of traditional humanism. For all the talk of paradigm shifting, the composition course, as a cultural force, remains fundamentally unchanged from the nineteenth century. I would rather teach or preside over a critical writing, one where the critique is worked out in practice, and for lack of better terms I would call that writing "academic writing."

Peter Elbow:

Perhaps David and others can persuade me that I am wrong, but I fear that there is a conflict between the role of writer and that of academic. I wish there were not. In this essay I will explore how this conflict plays out in a first-year writing class. But it will be obvious that I see the issue lurking in a larger dimension—even autobiographically. I am an academic and I am a writer. I've struggled to be able to make those claims, and I am proud of both identities—but I sometimes feel them in conflict. Thus I'm talking here about the relationship between two roles—two ways of being in the world of texts. It is my wish that students should be able to inhabit both roles comfortably.

Note that I'm talking here about roles, not professions. That is, I'm not trying to get first-year students to commit to making their living by writing—nor to get a Ph.D. and join the academy. But I would insist that it's a reasonable goal for my students to end up saying, "I feel like I *am* a writer: I get deep satisfaction from discovering meanings by writing—figuring out what I think and feel through putting down words; I naturally turn to writing when I am perplexed—even when I am just sad or happy; I love to explore and communicate with others through writing; writing is an important part of my life." Similarly, I would insist that it's a reasonable goal for my students to end up saying, "I feel like I *am* an academic: reading knowledgeable books, wrestling my way through important issues with fellows, figuring out hard questions—these activities give me deep satisfaction and they are central to my sense of who I am." In short, I want my first-year students to feel themselves as writers and feel themselves as academics.

Of course these are idealistic goals; many students will not attain them. But I insist on them as reasonable goals for my teaching, because if I taught well and if all the conditions for learning were good, I believe all my students *could* achieve them. I don't mind high or distant goals. But I'm troubled by a sense that they conflict with each other—that progress toward one could undermine progress toward the other. A distant mountain is a good guide for walking—even if I know I won't get to the top. But I feel as though I am trying to walk toward two different mountains.

In this dilemma, my first and strongest impulse is to be adversarial and fight for the role of the writer against the role of the academic. And I can't pretend I am doing otherwise here. But I'm also trying to resist that adversarial impulse. I'd like to celebrate academics—the other half of my own identity. If *we* don't celebrate academics, no one else will. Therefore I'll try to hold myself open so David or others of you can persuade me that I am misguided in my sense of conflict. Perhaps you can persuade me that if I would only make certain changes I could serve both goals well. Or better yet, perhaps you can assure me that I'm already serving both goals now and my only problem is my feeling of conflict. For I wish I didn't see things this way. Everyone says, "Don't give in to binary thinking. Take a cold shower, take a walk around the block." But I see specific conflicts in how to design and teach my first-year writing course. And since I feel forced to choose—I choose the goal of writer over that of academic.

Let me now explore specific points of conflict in my designing and teaching of a first-year writing course—conflicts between my attempts to help students see themselves as academics and see themselves as writers. But my first two points will be false alarms: places where I and others have sometimes been *tempted* to see a conflict but where careful examination shows me there is none. Perhaps some of the other conflicts can be similarly diffused.

(1) Sometimes I've felt a conflict about *what we should read* in the first-year writing course. It would seem as though in order to help students see themselves as academics I should get them to read "key texts": good published writing, important works of cultural or literary significance; strong and important works. However if I want them to see themselves as writers, we should primarily publish and read their own writing.

In my first-year writing class I take the latter path. I publish a class magazine about four times a semester, each one containing a finished piece by all the students. (I'm indebted to Charlie Moran for showing me how to do this—supporting the practice with a lab fee for the course.) We often discuss and write about these magazines. This may be the single most important feature of the course that helps students

45

begin to experience themselves as members of a community of writers.

But on reflection, I don't think there is any conflict here. It's not an either/or issue. To read both strong important published texts and the writing of fellow students serves both my goals. Academics read key texts and the writing of colleagues; so do writers. In short, I think I could and probably should read some strong important published works in my first-year course. I would never give up using the magazines of students' own writing, but that needn't stop me from also reading at least some of the other kind of texts.

(2) Just as I see no conflict about what to read in my first-year course, so too about *how to read* these texts. That is, whether I want my students to be academics or writers, it seems crucial to avoid coming at key texts (or at student texts) as models. That is, I must fight the tradition of treating these readings as monuments in a museum, pieces under glass. We must try to come at these strong important texts — no matter how good or hallowed they may be — as much as possible as fellow writers — as fully eligible members of the conversation: not treat them as sacred; not worry about "doing justice" to them or getting them dirty. To be blunt, I must be sure not to "teach" these texts (in the common sense of that term), but rather to "have them around" to wrestle with, to bounce off of, to talk about and talk from, to write about and write from. Again: not feel we must be polite or do them justice. In taking this approach I think we would be treating texts the way academics and writers treat them: *using* them rather than *serving* them. (I take this as one of the lessons of David's *Facts, Artifacts, and Counterfacts*.)

(3) But even if there is no conflict about what to read and how to read, I do see a problem when it comes to the question of *how much to read*. If my goal is to help my students experience themselves as academics, surely I should spend at least as much time reading as writing. Academics are readers. But I don't. I always spend much more of our time writing than reading. I even spend a significant amount of class time writing. Writing in class helps me not just sanction, dignify, and celebrate writing; it helps me frankly *coach* students in various concrete practices and techniques and approaches toward getting words on paper. I could weasel and say that writing *is* reading — what with all that crucial reading over what you write — and so I'm really serving both goals by emphasizing writing. But academics don't just read over what they write. This is a blunt issue of emphasis: In my course there is a clear emphasis on writing over reading.

It's not that I care absolutely more about writing than reading. I'm simply saying that virtually every other course privileges reading over writing — treats input as central and output as serving input. My only hope, it seems to me, of making students experience themselves as writers while they are in the academy — and a slim hope at that — means hanging on to at least one course where writing is at the center. When other courses in the university make writing as important as reading, I'll respond with a comparable adjustment and give reading equal spotlight in my first-year course. I might even make that adjustment if only English department courses made writing as important as reading, but of course they don't. Isn't it odd that most English courses study and honor writing (literature), but seldom treat the act of writing as central? The only course that tends to make writing central is the one course that most English faculty don't want to teach.

(4) But let me tighten the screw a bit. I've been talking as though everything would be dandy if only we had more time, or at least divided up the time equally — as though the interests of reading and writing do not inherently conflict. But I can't help sensing that they do. And I would contend that academics have come to identify with the interests of reading — often identifying themselves against writing.

Let me spell out some of the conflicts I see between the interests of writers and the interests of academics-as-readers.[1] To put it bluntly, readers and

[1] I am indebted here to a valuable unpublished paper about Polanyi by Elizabeth Wallace at Oregon State University.

writers have competing interests over who gets to control the text. It's in the interests of readers to say that the writer's intention doesn't matter or is unfindable, to say that meaning is never determinate, always fluid and sliding, to say that there is no presence or voice behind a text; and finally to kill off the author! This leaves the reader in complete control of the text.

It's in the interests of writers, on the other hand, to have readers actually interested in what was on their mind, what they intended to say, reading for intention. As writers we often fail to be clear, but it helps us if readers will just have some faith that our authorial meanings and intentions can be found. It helps to listen caringly. If we are lost in the woods, we have a better chance of being found if the searchers think we exist, care deeply about us, and feel there is hope of finding us. And it goes without saying, writers are interested in staying alive. Writers also have interest in *ownership* of the text—and, as with "killing," I want to take this metaphor seriously: Writers have a concrete interest in monetary payment for their labor. But of course the metaphorical meaning is important too. Writers usually want some "ownership," some say, some control over what a text means. Almost all writers are frustrated when readers completely misread what they have written. It doesn't usually help if the readers say, "But the latest theory says that we get to construct our own meaning." Of course there are exceptions here: Some writers say, "I don't care what meaning readers see in my words," but more often it is writers who celebrate presence and readers absence.

Let me be more concrete by using this very text as illustration. I get to decide what I *intended* with my words; you get to decide what you *heard*. But the question of what I "said," what meanings are "in" my text—that is a site of contention between us. And we see this fight everywhere, from the law courts to the bedrooms: "But I said . . ." "No you didn't, you said . . ." Academics in English are the only people I know who seem to think that the speaker/writer has no party in such discussions.

We see this contest between readers and writers 55 played out poignantly in the case of student texts.

The academic is reader and grader and always gets to decide what the student text means. No wonder students withdraw ownership and commitment. I can reinforce my point by looking at what happens when the tables are turned and academics produce text for a student audience—that is, lecturing extensively in class. Here the academic also turns the ownership rules upside down and declares that in this case the writer-lecturer gets to decide what the text means.

Is this just a story of readers being mean and disrespectful to writers? No, it goes both ways. Among writers, there is perhaps even a longer tradition of disdain for readers. (And also, of course, of disdain for academics.) Writers often say, "Readers are not my main audience. Sometimes the audience that I write for is me. For some pieces I don't even *care* whether readers always understand or appreciate everything I write. Sometimes I even write privately. What do readers know!" In response, readers often say, "What do writers know? We're in a much better position than they are to read the text. Let's not be put off by writers' wishful thinking. Intention is a will o' the wisp. Never trust the teller, trust the tale."

In short, where writers are tempted to think they are most important, readers and academics are tempted to think they are the most important party. Readers and academics like to insist that there is no such thing as private writing or writing only for the self. (See, for example, Jeanette Harris, *Expressive Writing*, SMU Press, 1990, 66.) Readers like to imagine that writers are always thinking about them; they are like children who naturally think their parents always have them in mind. Some readers even want to *see* everything that writers write. But writers, like parents, need some time away from the imperious demands of readers—need some time when they can just forget about readers and think about themselves. Yes, writers must acknowledge that in the end readers get to decide whether their words will be read or bought—just as parents know that in the end the child's interests must come first. But smart writers and parents know that they do a better job of serving these demanding creatures if they take some time for themselves.

(5) Another collision of interests between writers and readers. Writers testify all the time to the experience of knowing more than they can say, of knowing things that they haven't yet been able to get into words. Paying attention to such intuitions and feelings often leads them to articulations they couldn't otherwise find. Readers (and teachers and academics), on the other hand, being on the receiving end of texts, are more tempted to say, "If you can't say it, you don't know it"—and to celebrate the doctrine that all knowledge is linguistic. (Painters, musicians, and dancers also have the temerity to question academics who proclaim that if you can't say it in language you don't know it and it doesn't count as knowledge.)

In my first-year writing course I feel this conflict between the interests of readers and writers. Yes, my larger self wants them to feel themselves as readers and academics, but this goal seems to conflict with my more pressing hunger to help them feel themselves as writers. That is, I can't help wanting my students to have some of that uppitiness of writers toward readers. I want them to be able to say, "I'm not just writing for teachers or readers, I'm writing as much for me—sometimes even *more* for me." I want them to fight back a bit against readers. I want them to care about their intentions and to insist that readers respect them. I try to respect those intentions and see them—and assume I often can. Yes, I'll point out where these intentions are badly realized, but if my goal is to make students feel like writers, my highest priority is to show that I've *understood* what they're saying. It's only my second priority to show them where I had to struggle.

I want to call attention to this central pedagogical point that writers often understand and readers and academics and teachers often don't: The main thing that helps writers is to be understood; pointing out misunderstandings is only the second need. Thus—and this is a crucial consequence—I assume that students *know* more than they are getting into words. Most of my own progress in learning to write has come from my gradually learning to listen more carefully to what I haven't yet managed to get into words—and respecting the idea that I know more

than I can say. This stance helps me be willing to find time and energy to wrestle it into words. The most unhelpful thing I've had said to me as a student and writer is, "If you can't say it, you don't know it."

Imagine, then, how different our classrooms would be if all academics and teachers felt themselves to be writers as much as readers.

(6) Here is a related point of conflict between the role of academic and writer. What kind of attitude about language shall I try to instill in first-year students in a writing course? If my goal is to get them to take on the role of academic, I should get them to distrust language. It is a central tenet of academic thinking in this century that language is not a clear and neutral medium through which we can see undistorted non-linguistic entities.

But in my desire to help my students experience themselves as writers I find myself in fact trying to help them *trust* language—not to question it—or at least not to question it for long stretches of the writing process: to hold off distrust till they revise. Some people say this is good advice only for inexperienced and blocked writers, but I think I see it enormously helpful to myself and to other adult, skilled, and professional writers. Striking benefits usually result when people learn that decidedly unacademic capacity to turn off distrust or worry about language and learn instead to forget about it, not see it, look through it as through a clear window, and focus all attention on one's experience of what one is trying to say. Let me quote a writer, William Stafford, about the need to *trust* language and one's experience:

My main plea is for the value of an unafraid, face-down, flailing, and speedy process in using the language.

Just as any reasonable person who looks at water, and passes a hand through it, can see that it would not hold a person up; so it is the judgment of common sense people that reliance on the weak material of students' experiences cannot possibly sustain a work of literature. But swimmers know that if they relax on the water it will prove to be miraculously buoyant; and writers know that a succession of little strokes on the material nearest them—without any prejudgments about the specific gravity of the topic or the reasonableness of their expectations—will result in creative progress.

Writers are persons who write; swimmers are (and from teaching a child I know how hard it is to persuade a reasonable person of this) — swimmers are persons who relax in the water, let their heads go down, and reach out with ease and confidence. (*Writing the Australian Crawl: Views on the Writer's Vocation.* Ann Arbor: U of Michigan P, 1978, 22-23.)

(7) A large area of conflict: How shall I teach my students to *place themselves* in the universe of other writers? Insofar as I want them to internalize the role of academic, I should teach my students always to situate themselves and what they have to say in the context of important writers who have written on the subject: to see the act of writing as an act of finding and acknowledging one's place in an ongoing intellectual conversation with a much larger and longer history than what goes on in this classroom during these ten or fourteen weeks. In short, I should try to enact and live out in my classroom the Burkean metaphor of intellectual life as an unending conversation. This is what we academics do: carry on an unending conversation not just with colleagues but with the dead and unborn.

But the truth is (should I hang my head?) I don't give this dimension to my first-year writing classroom. I don't push my first-year students to think about what academics have written about their subject; indeed much of my behavior is a kind of invitation for them to *pretend* that no authorities have ever written about their subject before.

It might sound as though I invite only *monologic* discourse and discourage *dialogic* discourse. That's not quite right. I do invite monologic discourse (in spite of the current fashion of using "monologic" as the worst moral slur we can throw at someone), but I invite and defend dialogic discourse just as much. That is, I encourage students to situate what they write into the conversation of other members of the classroom community to whom they are writing and whom they are reading. Let me mention that the regular publication of the class magazine does more for this dialogic dimension than any amount of theoretical talk. I often assign papers *about* the class publication. In short, I find it helpful to invite students to see their papers as dialogic — parts of a conversation or dialogue; and I also find it crucial to assign dialogues and collaborative papers. But I also find it helpful to invite them to see their papers as monologues or soliloquies. My point here is that both academics and writers seem to me to engage in both monologic and dialogic discourse. (By the way, the classroom publication of student writing also helps me with another kind of "situating" — that is, I try quietly to find moments where I can invite students to be more aware of the positions from which they write — as men or women — as members of a race or class, or as having a sexual orientation.)[2]

In short, the real question or point of conflict here, then, is not so much about whether I should get my first-year students to feel their writing as monologue or dialogue, whether to get them to speak to other voices or not, or to recognize their own positions or not. I'm working for both sides in each case. Rather it's a larger more general question: Whether I should invite my first-year students to be self-absorbed and see themselves at the center of the discourse — in a sense, credulous; or whether I should invite them to be personally modest and intellectually scrupulous and to see themselves as at the periphery — in a sense, skeptical and distrustful. I recently read an academic critique of a writer for being too self-absorbed, of reading his subjectivity too much into the object he was allegedly examining, of being imperial, arrogant — practicing analysis by means of

[2] It might sound as though my emphasis on student writing means that I'm keeping *authoritative* voices out of the classroom, but I'm not. It's only *academic* voices I don't particularly invite in. For I bring in a *bit* of outside reading. My point is that even timid students find it relatively easy to speak back with conviction to President Bush, to the Pope, to Adrienne Rich, to the *New York Times*; but not to academic or scholarly writers. It's interesting to ask why this should be. It's not because academics and scholars have more authority — especially in the eyes of most students. It must be something about academic discourse. Of course it may be that I should spend more time teaching my students to talk back with authority to academics, and David gives good direction here in his *Facts, Counterfacts, and Artifacts*, but so far I haven't felt it as a high enough priority to give it the time it requires.

autobiography. I have to admit that I *want* first-year students in my writing class to do that. I think autobiography is often the best mode of analysis. I'm afraid that I invite first-year students to fall into the following sins: to take their own ideas too seriously; to think that they are the first person to think of their idea and be all wrapped up and possessive about it—even though others might have already written better about it—I invite them to write as though they are a central speaker at the center of the universe—rather than feeling, as they often do, that they must summarize what others have said and only make modest rejoinders from the edge of the conversation to all the smart thoughts that have already been written. (By the way, I was trained by good New Critics in the 1950s who often tried to get me to write as though no one else had ever written about the work I was treating. Therefore we cannot call this intellectual stance "nonacademic." New Critics may be out of fashion but no one could call them anything but full fledged academics—indeed their distinguishing mark in comparison to their predecessors was heightened professionalism in literary studies.)

Perhaps this sounds condescending—as though I am not treating my students seriously enough as smart adults. I hope not. When I come across a really strong and competent first-year writer who is being too arrogant and full of himself or herself and unwilling to listen to other voices—then in my feedback I instinctively lean a bit on that student: "Wait a minute. You're talking as though yours are the only feelings and thoughts on this matter; have you ever considered looking to see what X and Y have said? You will have no credibility till you do." And obviously, when students start to work in their disciplinary major, of course I am happy to force them to situate their writing among all the key positions in the conversation of that discipline. But grandstanding, taking themselves too seriously, and seeing themselves as the center of everything—I don't see these as the characteristic sins of first-year students.

Admittedly, first-year students often suffer from a closely related sin: naiveté. For being naive and taking oneself too seriously can look alike and can take

the same propositional form: implying simultaneously, "Everyone else is just like me" and "No one else in the universe has ever thought my thoughts or felt my feelings." But when we see a paper with these problematic assumptions, we should ask ourselves: Is this really a problem of the writer taking herself too seriously and being too committed and self-invested in her writing? or is it a problem of the writer, though perhaps glib, being essentially timid and tapping only a small part of her thinking and feeling? When I get a strongly felt, fully committed, arrogant paper I am happy to wrestle and try to get tough with the writer. But so often with first-year students it is the latter: timidity and lack of deep entwinement in what they are writing.

Am *I* just being naive? Maybe. In any case let me 70 openly acknowledge an arguable assumption underneath all this. I sense it is the distinguishing feature of writers to take themselves too seriously. Writing is a struggle and a risk. Why go to the bother unless what we say feels important? None of us who has a full awareness of all the trouble we can get into by writing would ever write by choice unless we also had a correspondingly full sense of pride, self-absorption, even arrogance. Most first-year students have a strong sense of the trouble they can get into with writing, but they tend to lack that writer's corresponding gift for taking themselves too seriously—*pride* in the importance of what they have to say. Look at our experience parenting: Most parents know instinctively that their job is to help their children take themselves more seriously, not less seriously. Once a student can really begin to own and care about her ideas, that will lead naturally to the necessary combat—which will lead to some cultural sophistication in itself.

(8) Here is my last brief point of conflict between the role of writer and academic. We all know that when students write to teachers they have to write "up" to an audience with greater knowledge and authority than the writer has about her own topic. The student is analyzing "To His Coy Mistress" for a reader who understands it better than she does. (Worse yet, the teacher/reader is often looking for a specific conclusion and form in the paper.) Even if

the student happens to have a better insight or understanding than the teacher has, the teacher gets to define her own understanding as right and the student's as wrong. Thus the basic subtext in a piece of student writing is likely to be, "Is this okay?"

In contrast to students, the basic subtext in a writer's text is likely to be, "Listen to me, I have something to tell you," for writers can usually write with more authority than their readers. Therefore, unless we can set things up so that our first-year students are often telling us about things that they know better than we do, we are sabotaging the essential dynamic of writers. We are transforming the process of "writing" into the process of "being tested." Many of the odd writing behaviors of students make perfect sense once we see that they are behaving as test-takers rather than writers.

How about academics on this score? It would seem as though they would have at least as strong an authority stance as writers do. After all, the academic in her writing has done a piece of research or reflection as a professional and is usually saying things that her readers do not know. But look again. I think you'll notice a curious resemblance between how students write to their teacher-readers and how academics write to their colleague-readers — even if the academic is a tenured professor. Yes, the academic may have data, findings, or thoughts that are news; yet the paradigm transaction in academic writing is one where the writer is conveying those data, findings, or thoughts to authorities in the field whose job is to decide whether they are acceptable. These authorities get to decide whether the writing counts as important or true — whether it is valid — and ultimately whether it counts as knowledge. Have you ever noticed that when we write articles or books as academics, we often have the same feeling that students have when they turn in papers: "Is this okay? Will you accept this?" But damn it, I want my first-year students to be saying in their writing, "Listen to me, I have something to tell you" not "Is this okay? Will you accept this?"

Of course some academics manage to send the strong perky message, "Listen to me, I have something to tell you." But the structure of the academy tends to militate against that stance. And of course the structure of the classroom and the grading situation militate even more heavily against it. Therefore, I feel I have a better chance of getting my students to take that forthright stance toward readers and their material if I do what I can to make them feel like writers, and avoid setting things up to make them feel like academics.

Conclusion. Behind this paper, then, I'm really asking a larger cultural question: Is there a conflict in general — apart from first-year students or students in general — between the role of writer and the role of academic? Perhaps my categories are oversimple, but I confess I'm talking also about my own experience. I'm proud of being both an academic and a writer, partly because I've had to struggle on both counts. I'd like to inhabit both roles in an unconflicted way, but I feel a tug of war between them.

I suspect that if we could be more sensible about how we create and define the roles of academic and writer in our culture, the conflict might not be necessary. I have the feeling that the role of academic as we see it suffers narrowness for not containing more of what I have linked to the role of writer. Frankly, I think there are problems with what it means to be an academic. If academics were more like writers — wrote more, turned to writing more, enjoyed writing more — I think the academic world would be better. David, on the other hand, probably believes that the role of writer suffers narrowness for not containing more of what I have associated with the role of academic. So the conflict plays itself out. I am ready to try to be more wise about these roles. I suppose the obvious problem is that I define writer in too "romantic" a fashion. I stand by — nervously — trying to hold myself open to correction on this point. But are you going to make me give up all the features of the role of writer that seem helpful and supportive? I hope you won't make the role of writer more astringent and trying than it already is.[3]

[3] Not knowing that David and I were going to publish these talks till fairly recently, I used points numbered 4–6 in my essay, "The War Between Reading and Writing — and How to End It." *Rhetoric Review* 12.1 (Fall 1993).

Reading Questions

1. According to Elbow, what is the difference between a scholar and a writer? What is Bartholomae's stance on the topic?

2. What does Bartholomae mean by "scenes of writing" (par. 17)?

3. What tension does Elbow identify between the process of "writing" and the process of "being tested"? Why does this tension cause problems for student writers?

4. How can the words a writer chooses be a point of conflict between the identity of students as academics and students as writers?

Rhetoric Questions

5. Bartholomae notes at the end of his essay that he cannot make a conclusion because he is engaging in a conversation. Elbow, on the other hand, does draw a conclusion. How do these different choices impact your perception of Bartholomae and Elbow as academics? How do they impact the strength of each scholar's argument?

6. In paragraphs 6–9, Elbow presents two points of perceived conflict before arguing that they are not conflicts after all. Why might he choose to do this? How does it impact your perception of his other six conflicts between students as academics and students as writers?

7. Consider the purpose of this scholarly debate. What do Bartholomae and Elbow want their audiences to do? What passages in their essays support this call to action?

8. These essays were originally presented orally at the Conference on College Composition & Communication and are part of a larger discussion between the two scholars. How does the writing benefit from being part of that ongoing conversation? How did that context make them more difficult to engage with as a reader?

Response and Research Questions

9. Bartholomae states that "[s]tudents write in a space defined by all the writing that has preceded them . . . : in the library, in the reading list, in the curriculum" (8). What writing has "preceded" you that most impacts your understanding of yourself as a writer? What writing particularly impacts how you view academic writing in particular? Why or how has this writing been so influential?

10. How does the grading of your writing make you feel about the writing you do? Would you write differently if grades were not given? How would that change what you write, how you write, and how you feel about writing?

Positive Psychology Progress: Empirical Validation of Interventions

MARTIN E. P. SELIGMAN, TRACY A. STEEN, NANSOOK PARK, AND CHRISTOPHER PETERSON

Martin E. P. Seligman is the Zellerbach Family Professor of Psychology and director of the University of Pennsylvania's Positive Psychology Center. He served as president of the American Psychological Association in 1998. With more than three hundred scholarly articles and twenty-five books to his credit, Seligman is a renowned authority in the area of positive psychology. In the following article, Seligman and his research team review developments in the area of positive psychology and report on the effectiveness of a number of psychological interventions, including various writing tasks, that may be used to increase happiness.

Positive psychology has flourished in the last five years. The authors review recent developments in the field, including books, meetings, courses, and conferences. They also discuss the newly created classification of character strengths and virtues, a positive complement to the various editions of the Diagnostic and Statistical Manual of Mental Disorders *(e.g., American Psychiatric Association, 1994), and present some cross-cultural findings that suggest a surprising ubiquity of strengths and virtues. Finally, the authors focus on psychological interventions that increase individual happiness. In a six-group, random-assignment, placebo-controlled Internet study, the authors tested five purported happiness interventions and one plausible control exercise. They found that three of the interventions lastingly increased happiness and decreased depressive symptoms. Positive interventions can supplement traditional interventions that relieve suffering and may someday be the practical legacy of positive psychology.*

Five years have passed since the *American Psychologist* devoted its millennial issue to the emerging science of positive psychology: the study of positive emotion, positive character, and positive institutions (Seligman & Csikszentmihalyi, 2000). Drawing on methods effectively used to advance the science of mental disorders, positive psychologists have been studying mental health and well-being. Building on pioneering work by Rogers (1951), Maslow (1954, 1962), Jahoda (1958), Erikson (1963, 1982), Vaillant (1977), Deci and Ryan (1985), and Ryff and Singer (1996)—among many others—positive psychologists have enhanced our understanding of how, why, and under what conditions positive emotions, positive character,

and the institutions that enable them flourish (e.g., Cameron, Dutton, & Quinn, 2003; Easterbrook, 2003; Gardner, Csikszentmihalyi, & Damon, 2001; Kahneman, Diener, & Schwarz, 1999; Murray, 2003; Vaillant, 2000).

Positive psychologists do not claim to have invented the good life or to have ushered in its scientific study, but the value of the overarching term *positive psychology* lies in its uniting of what had been scattered and disparate lines of theory and research about what makes life most worth living (Peterson & Park, 2003). As the basic science continues, other lines of work are moving into the realm of application (Linley & Joseph, 2004). Can psychologists take what they have learned about the science and practice of treating mental illness and use it to create a practice of making people lastingly happier? That is, can they create an evidence-based practice of positive psychology?

In this article, we first review the recent growth within positive psychology. Next, we describe basic research that bears on whether people can become lastingly happier, and then we present the results of our own happiness interventions that we rigorously tested with a randomized, placebo-controlled design.

PROGRESS REPORT

Positive psychology is an umbrella term for the study of positive emotions, positive character traits, and enabling institutions. Research findings from positive psychology are intended to supplement, not remotely to replace, what is known about human suffering, weakness, and disorder. The intent is to have a more complete and balanced scientific understanding of the human experience—the peaks, the valleys, and everything in between. We believe that a complete science and a complete practice of psychology should include an understanding of suffering and happiness, as well as their interaction, and validated interventions that both relieve suffering and increase happiness—two separable endeavors.

Books

In the last five years, aside from a special issue and a special section of the *American Psychologist* (January 2000 and January 2001, respectively), literally hundreds of articles have appeared in the scholarly and popular press on the topics of positive psychology. Books have begun to appear, for example, *The Handbook of Positive Psychology* (Snyder & Lopez, 2002), *Authentic Happiness* (Seligman, 2002), *A Psychology of Human Strengths* (Aspinwall & Staudinger, 2003), *Flourishing* (Keyes & Haidt, 2003), *Positive Psychological Assessment: A Handbook of Models and Measures* (Lopez & Snyder, 2004), *Positive Psychology in Practice* (Linley & Joseph, 2004), and *Handbook of Methods in Positive Psychology* (Ong & van Dulmen, in press). These volumes summarize the empirical findings and the methods used in the science.

We want to highlight our own *Character Strengths and Virtues: A Handbook and Classification* (*CSV*; Peterson & Seligman, 2004). The *CSV* represents the most ambitious project self-consciously undertaken from the perspective of positive psychology, and we intend it to do for psychological well-being what the *Diagnostic and Statistical Manual of Mental Disorders* (*DSM*) of the American Psychiatric Association (1994) does for the psychological disorders that disable human beings. The *CSV* describes and classifies strengths and virtues that enable human thriving. Although we were respectful of the *DSM*, we attempted to avoid some of its problems by making

clear why some entries were included in the *CSV* and others excluded, by regarding positive traits as individual differences that exist in degrees rather than as all-or-nothing categories, and by developing reliable and valid assessment strategies (questionnaires, surveys, interviews, and informant reports; Peterson, Park, & Seligman, 2005a).

The general scheme of the *CSV* relies on six overarching virtues that almost every culture across the world endorses: wisdom, courage, humanity, justice, temperance, and transcendence (Dahlsgaard, Peterson, & Seligman, in press). Under each virtue, we identified particular strengths that met the following criteria:

- ubiquity—is widely recognized across cultures
- fulfilling—contributes to individual fulfillment, satisfaction, and happiness broadly construed
- morally valued—is valued in its own right and not as a means to an end
- does not diminish others—elevates others who witness it, producing admiration, not jealousy
- nonfelicitous opposite—has obvious antonyms that are "negative"
- traitlike—is an individual difference with demonstrable generality and stability
- measurable—has been successfully measured by researchers as an individual difference
- distinctiveness—is not redundant (conceptually or empirically) with other character strengths
- paragons—is strikingly embodied in some individuals
- prodigies—is precociously shown by some children or youths
- selective absence—is missing altogether in some individuals
- institutions—is the deliberate target of societal practices and rituals that try to cultivate it

Table 1 lays out the classification, which includes 24 strengths of character. Although we avoid a claim of

Table 1

Classification of 6 Virtues and 24 Character Strengths (Peterson & Seligman, 2004)

Virtue and strength	Definition
1. Wisdom and knowledge	Cognitive strengths that entail the acquisition and use of knowledge
Creativity	Thinking of novel and productive ways to do things
Curiosity	Taking an interest in all of ongoing experience
Open-mindedness	Thinking things through and examining them from all sides
Love of learning	Mastering new skills, topics, and bodies of knowledge
Perspective	Being able to provide wise counsel to others
2. Courage	Emotional strengths that involve the exercise of will to accomplish goals in the face of opposition, external or internal
Authenticity	Speaking the truth and presenting oneself in a genuine way
Bravery	*Not* shrinking from threat, challenge, difficulty, or pain
Persistence	Finishing what one starts
Zest	Approaching life with excitement and energy
3. Humanity	Interpersonal strengths that involve "tending and befriending" others
Kindness	Doing favors and good deeds for others
Love	Valuing close relations with others
Social intelligence	Being aware of the motives and feelings of self and others
4. Justice	Civic strengths that underlie healthy community life
Fairness	Treating all people the same according to notions of fairness and justice
Leadership	Organizing group activities and seeing that they happen
Teamwork	Working well as member of a group or team
5. Temperance	Strengths that protect against excess
Forgiveness	Forgiving those who have done wrong
Modesty	Letting one's accomplishments speak for themselves
Prudence	Being careful about one's choices; not saying or doing things that might later be regretted
Self-regulation	Regulating what one feels and does
6. Transcendence	Strengths that forge connections to the larger universe and provide meaning
Appreciation of beauty and excellence	Noticing and appreciating beauty, excellence, and/or skilled performance in all domains of life
Gratitude	Being aware of and thankful for the good things that happen
Hope	Expecting the best and working to achieve it
Humor	Liking to laugh and tease; bringing smiles to other people
Religiousness	Having coherent beliefs about the higher purpose and meaning of life

universality, a claim of ubiquity seems warranted by the evidence presented below.

Each chapter in the *CSV* describes what is known and what is not known about each of the included strengths: paradigm cases, consensual definition, historical and cross-cultural background, measurement, correlations and consequences of having or lacking the strength, development, enabling and disabling conditions, gender differences, and interventions that build the strength. We intend this volume to be a framework for conducting future research and creating new interventions.

Three surprising empirical findings have already emerged. First, we have discovered a remarkable similarity in the relative endorsement of the 24 character strengths by adults around the world and within the United States (Park, Peterson, & Seligman, 2005a). The most commonly endorsed ("most like me") strengths, in 40 different countries, from Azerbaijan to Venezuela, are kindness, fairness, authenticity, gratitude, and open-mindedness, and the lesser strengths consistently include prudence, modesty, and self-regulation. The correlations of the rankings from nation to nation are very strong, ranging in the .80s, and defy cultural, ethnic, and religious differences. The same ranking of greater versus lesser strengths characterizes all 50 U.S. states — except for religiousness, which is somewhat more evident in the South — and holds across gender, age, red versus blue states, and education. Our results may reveal something about universal human nature and/or the character requirements minimally needed for a viable society (cf. Bok, 1995).

Second, a comparison of the strengths profiles of U.S. adults and U.S. adolescents revealed overall agreement on ranking yet a noticeably lower agreement than that found between U.S. adults and adults in any other nation we have studied (Park, Peterson, & Seligman, 2005b). Hope, teamwork, and zest were more common among U.S. youths than U.S. adults, whereas appreciation of beauty, authenticity, leadership, and open-mindedness were more common among adults. As we turn our attention to the deliberate cultivation of character strengths, we should be as concerned with how to keep certain strengths from

eroding on the journey to adulthood as we are with how to build others from scratch (Park & Peterson, in press-b).

Third, although part of the definition of a character strength is that it contributes to fulfillment, strengths "of the heart" — zest, gratitude, hope, and love — are more robustly associated with life satisfaction than are the more cerebral strengths such as curiosity and love of learning (Park, Peterson, & Seligman, 2004). We find this pattern among adults and among youths as well as longitudinal evidence that these "heart" strengths foreshadow subsequent life satisfaction (Park et al., 2005b). One more finding to note: Self-regulation among parents, although not strongly associated with parental life satisfaction, is positively linked to the life satisfaction of their children (Park & Peterson, in press-a).

Meetings, Centers, and Courses

Well-attended scholarly meetings on positive psychology occur regularly. For example, in October 2004, over 390 positive psychologists from 23 countries attended the Third Annual International Positive Psychology Summit in Washington, DC. The European Network of Positive Psychology sponsored its second conference in July 2004 in Italy, which was attended by 300 people from all over the world. Young researchers apply to attend the annual summer Positive Psychology Institute, a week-long program in which researchers at an early stage in their careers exchange ideas and receive guidance from more senior figures in positive psychology. From May 15 to June 30 of 2005, 2006, and 2007, Medici II will be held at the University of Pennsylvania; there, dozens of scientists and scholars will gather to work together on five projects: (a) productivity and health as a function of happiness; (b) national well-being indices; (c) spirituality and successful aging; (d) psychological capital; and (e) positive psychology Web sites in Chinese and Spanish and ultimately for all major language groups.

The Positive Psychology Network funds more than 50 research groups involving more than 150 scientists from universities all over the world. The first Positive

Psychology Centers (at the University of Pennsylvania, the University of Michigan, the University of Illinois, and Claremont Graduate University) now exist.

Positive psychology courses at both the undergraduate and graduate levels are now offered at several dozen U.S. universities and in Europe, exposing students to the idea that it makes sense to study what is right about people in addition to what is wrong. Martin Seligman and Ben Dean offered a 48-hour telephone course, Authentic Happiness Coaching, on the principles, tests, and interventions in positive psychology. More than 1,000 people participated, including clinical and counseling psychologists, coaches, educators, psychiatrists, physicians, and personnel managers. The first master's degree will be offered by the University of Pennsylvania, a Master of Applied Positive Psychology, starting in September 2005. Within one month of announcing the existence of the degree, over 200 applications were filed.

Widespread dissemination of positive psychology research means that the general psychological community is beginning to understand that respectable science can be conducted on the positive side of life. Web sites devoted to positive psychology are burgeoning, and some of the most popular include www.apa.org/science/positivepsy.html, www.bus.umich.edu/Positive/, www.reflectivehappiness.com, and www.positivepsychology.org/. A positive psychology listserv can be joined at www.positivepsychology.org/pospsy.htm#PP%20Listserve. There has been strong media interest in positive psychology, with hundreds of newspaper and magazine articles appearing all over the world. *Time Magazine* devoted its cover and almost its entire January 17, 2005, issue to the scientific advances and practice implications of the field.

Funders have been generous. Atlantic Philanthropies, the Annenberg Foundation, Sunnylands Trust, the Mayerson Foundation, the Templeton Foundation, the Hovey Foundation, the Gallup Foundation, the U.S. Department of Education, and others have made substantial grants to support the scientific research and the dissemination of the findings.

Interventions

We focus the rest of this article on the efficacy of psychological interventions to increase individual happiness, in many ways the bottom line of work in positive psychology. First, a caveat about the word *happiness* itself: We work under the assumption that *happiness* is a scientifically unwieldy term and that its serious study involves dissolving the term into at least three distinct and better-defined routes to "happiness" (Seligman, 2002): (a) positive emotion and pleasure (the pleasant life); (b) engagement (the engaged life); and (c) meaning (the meaningful life). Our recent research suggests that people reliably differ according to the type of life that they pursue and, further, that the most satisfied people are those who orient their pursuits toward all three, with the greatest weight carried by engagement and meaning (Peterson, Park, & Seligman, 2005b). We continue to use the word *happiness*, but only in the atheoretical sense of labeling the overall aim of the positive psychology endeavor and referring jointly to positive emotion, engagement, and meaning.

One nonobvious reason to be interested in interventions that build happiness is that happiness is not an epi-phenomenon. An important fact that has emerged in the last few years is that happiness is causal and brings many more benefits than just feeling good. Happy people are healthier, more successful, and more socially engaged, and the causal direction runs both ways (Lyubomirsky, King, & Diener, in press). We look forward to continued research on the correlates and consequences of happiness. The causal efficacy of happiness has focused our research group on one practical matter: interventions that build happiness.

CAN POSITIVE PSYCHOLOGY MAKE PEOPLE LASTINGLY HAPPIER?

From the Buddha, through the human potential movement of the 1960s, through the pioneering work of Michael Fordyce (1977, 1983), through the self-improvement industry of the 1990s, at least 100 "interventions" claiming to increase happiness lastingly have been proposed. We have collected these and have distilled about 40 of them into a form that is replicable and capable of being presented in a manual. Which of these interventions really work, and which are at best placebos?

A royal road of a method for answering questions 20 like these with respect to medication or psychotherapy already exists—the random-assignment, placebo-controlled design (RCT, or randomized controlled trial)—and the very same method can be used to validate what, if anything, builds the positive side of life. We began our work in this area by teaching these exercises first to students in undergraduate and graduate courses and then to a wide variety of mental health professionals in a telephone course. We saw so many powerful case studies (in which the testimonial word *life-changing* kept appearing spontaneously) that we were inspired to try out the interventions in them in RCTs and determine if they worked when subjected to rigorous testing.

We also considered the possibility that there would be no exercises that would make people lastingly happier. Research into the hedonic treadmill, adaptation, and the heritability of positive affectivity has implied that people adapt rapidly to positive changes in their world and soon return to their baseline levels of happiness (Brickman & Campbell, 1971; Kahneman, 1999; Lykken & Tellegen, 1996). But because of the power of the case history anecdotes we encountered, we decided to persist and to put the interventions to the random-assignment, placebo-controlled test.

We now detail the efficacy of five exercises that we have so far put to this test. First, we address two methodological issues: (a) how we measured happiness and depression and (b) how we delivered the intervention and collected outcome data via the Internet.

Measuring Happiness and Depression

Measuring depression was straightforward. We used the Center for Epidemiological Studies-Depression Scale (CES-D) symptom survey (Radloff, 1977). After surveying existing measurements of happiness, however, we could find no parallel symptom survey of all three forms of happiness (positive

emotion, engagement, and meaning). There exist useful measures of general happiness (e.g., Fordyce, 1977; Lyubomirsky & Lepper, 1999), but these do not allow researchers to make finer distinctions in levels of happiness, especially at the upper end of the scale; scores are skewed and thereby impose a low ceiling. Nor do these measures include all of the "symptoms" of the pleasant life, the engaged life, and the meaningful life.

In order to capture the week-by-week upward changes in happiness that we thought might occur following our happiness interventions, we created a new measure, the Steen Happiness Index (SHI). We used as our explicit model the Beck Depression Inventory (BDI; Beck, Ward, Mendelson, Mock, & Erbaugh, 1961). Just as the BDI is sensitive to changes in depressive symptoms, we created the SHI to be sensitive to changes, particularly upward changes, in happiness levels. The SHI contains 20 items and requires participants to read a series of statements and pick the one from each group that describes them at the present time. The items on the SHI reflect the three kinds of happy lives (the pleasant life, the engaged life, and the meaningful life): experiencing and savoring pleasures, losing the self in engaging activities, and participating in meaningful activities. Response choices range from a negative (1) to an extreme positive (5), as in the following example:

A. Most of the time I am bored. (1)
B. Most of the time I am neither bored nor interested in what I am doing. (2)
C. Most of the time I am interested in what I am doing. (3)
D. Most of the time I am quite interested in what I am doing. (4)
E. Most of the time I am fascinated by what I am doing. (5)

Pilot work with several hundred adult respondents 25 showed that scores on this measure converged substantially with scores on other measures of happiness ($r = .79$ with Lyubomirsky & Lepper's [1999] General Happiness Scale, and $r = .74$ with Fordyce's [1977] Happiness Scale), as would be expected, but that they were, as we hoped, more bell-shaped. Furthermore, changes in SHI scores across a one-week period were sensitive to the self-reported occurrence of positive and negative events, even when prior SHI scores were controlled.

Internet-Based Interventions

We used the Internet to recruit participants, to deliver the intervention, and to collect our data (Prochaska, DiClemente, Velicer, & Rossi, 1993). At this stage in our intervention research, this convenience sample served our purposes well, because on average we have 300 new registrants every day to our Web site (www .authentichappiness.org), which contains many of the positive questionnaires for free. But we also believe that this sample may be at least equal to, and perhaps superior to, college sophomores or clinic volunteers in its scientific justification. One small advantage of collecting data via the Internet is that it obviates data entry by the researcher (and associated human error). One larger advantage is substantial cost-effectiveness in large-sample studies. After one pays for Web site development and maintenance, there are virtually no additional costs to data collection for adequately powered studies, and we have offered the use of our Web site to interested researchers.

Much more scientifically important, and controversial, is the possibility of biased sampling. Gosling, Vazire, Srivastava, and John (2004) compared survey data collected via the Internet with survey data collected via traditional methods. They concluded that (a) Internet data are just as diverse as data collected via traditional methods, (b) participants who voluntarily participate in Web-based studies are no more psychologically disturbed than traditional participants, and (c) participants in Internet studies are no less likely to take the study seriously or to provide accurate information than are participants in traditional samples. We believe our sample is biased but in a relevant direction. It is tilted toward those who want to become happier, precisely those who are the ultimate target of our interventions. We would not want to generalize our findings to people who do not want to become happier or to people who have to be coerced into taking psychological tests. On the basis of these considerations, we chose to use the Internet.

Procedure

For our first large RCT, we designed five happiness exercises and one placebo control exercise. Each exercise was delivered via the Internet and could be completed within one week. One of these exercises focused on building gratitude, two focused on increasing awareness of what is most positive about oneself, and two focused on identifying strengths of character. In a randomized, placebo-controlled study, we compared the effects of these exercises with those of what we thought would be a plausible placebo control: journaling for one week about early memories. We followed our participants for six months, periodically measuring symptoms of both depression and happiness.

We recruited a convenience sample from among visitors to the Web site created for Seligman's (2002) book *Authentic Happiness* by creating a link called "Happiness Exercises." The study was described on the site as an opportunity to help test new exercises designed to increase happiness. Over the course of approximately one month, we recruited 577 adult participants, 42% male and 58% female. Almost two-thirds of the participants (64%) were between the ages of 35 and 54 years. Of the participants surveyed, 39% had a degree from a four-year college, and 27% had some graduate school education. Notably, only 4% of the participants did not have education or vocational training after high school, another limit on the generalizability of our findings. Consistent with their reported levels of education, approximately three fourths of the participants classified their income levels as "average" or above. The sample was largely White (77%).

Visitors to the site were told that the exercise they were to receive was not guaranteed to make them happier and that they might receive an inert (placebo) exercise. We did not offer any initial financial incentives for doing the exercises. In order to ensure good follow-up, we did tell participants, however, that upon completion of follow-up tests at one week, one month, three months, and six months after completing the exercise, they would be entered into a lottery. The lottery prizes included one $500 award and three $100 awards.

After participants agreed to the terms presented, they answered a series of basic demographic questions and completed two questionnaires, the SHI and the CES-D, as already described. Then participants received a randomly assigned exercise. Participants were encouraged to print out or write down the instructions for their exercise and to keep them accessible during the week to come. They were instructed to return to the Web site to complete follow-up questionnaires after completing their assigned exercise.

Participants received reminder e-mails. The first reminder, sent early in the week, repeated the instructions for their assigned exercise. They were also given contact information and encouraged to contact the researchers with any questions or concerns. The second reminder e-mail, sent later in the week, reminded participants to return to the Web site for the follow-up questionnaires: "Thank you again for participating in our study. Please remember to return to [url] by [relevant date] to give us feedback about your exercise and to complete follow-up questionnaires."

When participants returned to the Web site after performing their exercise, they completed the same measures of happiness and depression administered at pretest. In addition, participants answered a manipulation check question to assess whether they had in fact completed the exercise as instructed during the relevant time period (scored *yes* or *no*).

Of the 577 participants who completed baseline questionnaires, 411 (71%) completed all five follow-up assessments. Participants who dropped out of the study did not differ from those who remained on their baseline happiness or depression scores, nor was there differential dropout from the six exercises. We include in our analyses only those participants who completed all follow-up questionnaires.[1]

Detailed descriptions of the exercises are available from us upon request. However, the following paragraphs present overviews of each: 35

Placebo control exercise: Early memories. Participants were asked to write about their early memories every night for one week.

Gratitude visit. Participants were given one week to write and then deliver a letter of gratitude in person to someone who had been especially kind to them but had never been properly thanked.

Three good things in life. Participants were asked to write down three things that went well each day and their causes every night for one week. In addition, they were asked to provide a causal explanation for each good thing.

You at your best. Participants were asked to write about a time when they were at their best and then to reflect on the personal strengths displayed in the story. They were told to review their story once every day for a week and to reflect on the strengths they had identified.

Using signature strengths in a new way. Participants 40 were asked to take our inventory of character strengths online at www.authentichappiness.org and to receive individualized feedback about their top five ("signature") strengths (Peterson et al., 2005a). They were then asked to use one of these top strengths in a new and different way every day for one week.

Identifying signature strengths. This exercise was a truncated version of the one just described, without the instruction to use signature strengths in new ways. Participants were asked to take the survey, to note their five highest strengths, and to use them more often during the next week.

Results of the Interventions

Two of the exercises—*using signature strengths in a new way* and *three good things*—increased happiness and decreased depressive symptoms for six months. Another exercise, the *gratitude visit*, caused large positive changes for one month. The two other exercises and the placebo control created positive but transient

[1] Older people were happier ($r = .18$, $p < .001$) and less depressed ($r = -.17$, $p < .001$). Gender and ethnicity were not associated with happiness or depression scores at baseline or at any of the follow-up assessments. In our analyses, we initially controlled for age, but the results were unaffected, so we present only the unadjusted means.

effects on happiness and depressive symptoms. Not surprisingly, the degree to which participants actively continued their assigned exercise on their own and beyond the prescribed one-week period mediated the long-term benefits.

Here are more details. Using analyses of variance (ANOVAs) followed by planned contrasts, we compared the scores of participants across the following time points: pretest, immediate posttest (after doing their exercise for one week), one week after the posttest, one month after the posttest, three months after the posttest, and six months after the posttest. Figures 1 and 2 show the happiness and depression scores of participants by assigned exercise. Sample sizes for each condition are shown in these figures as well as effect sizes associated with statistically significant ($p < .05$) contrasts for the intervention group between baseline scores and those at the different follow-ups.[2]

An overall ANOVA for happiness scores (six conditions $\times$ six time periods) showed significant effects

for time, $F(5, 2025) = 26.38$, $p < .001$, and for the Condition $\times$ Time interaction, $F(25, 2025) = 12.38$, $p < .001$. Similar effects were found for depression scores: a significant effect for time, $F(5, 2025) = 39.77$, $p < .001$, and a significant Condition $\times$ Time interaction, $F(25, 2025) = 5.21$, $p < .001$.

Participants in all conditions (including the placebo control condition) tended to be happier and less depressed at the immediate posttest (after doing their exercise for one week; see Figures 1 and 2). One week later and at every testing period thereafter, however, participants in the placebo control condition were no different than they had been at baseline.

As Figures 1 and 2 show, at the immediate posttest (after one week of doing the assigned exercise), participants in the *gratitude visit* condition were happier and less depressed. In fact, participants in the *gratitude visit* condition showed the largest positive changes in the whole study. This boost in happiness and decrease in depressive symptoms were maintained at follow-up assessments one week and one month later. But by three months, participants in the *gratitude visit* condition were no happier or less depressed than they had been at baseline.

Participants in the *three good things* exercise began to show beneficial effects one month following the posttest. At the one-month follow-up, participants in this exercise were happier and less depressed than they had been at baseline, and they stayed happier and less depressed at the three-month and six-month follow-ups.

A similar long-term improvement occurred for participants in the *using signature strengths in a new way* condition. Immediate effects were less pronounced than for the *three good things* condition, but at the one-month follow-up and beyond, participants in this condition were happier and less depressed than they had been at baseline. In contrast, participants in the truncated *identifying signature strengths* condition showed an effect only at the immediate posttest but not thereafter. Likewise, participants in the *you at your best* condition showed an effect only at the immediate posttest.

---

[2] A closer look with ANOVAs at the individual interventions compared with the placebo condition revealed the following effects. With respect to happiness, there were main effects of time for *gratitude visit*, $F(5, 750) = 39.13$, $p < .001$, *three good things*, $F(5, 645) = 8.76$, $p < .001$, *you at your best*, $F(5, 690) = 26.77$, $p < .001$, *using signature strengths in a new way*, $F(5, 680) = 8.56$, $p < .001$, and *identifying signature strengths*, $F(5, 690) = 24.94$, $p < .001$, and there was a Condition $\times$ Time interaction for *gratitude visit*, $F(5, 750) = 6.88$, $p < .001$, *three good things*, $F(5, 645) = 16.47$, $p < .001$, and *using signature strengths in a new way*, $F(5, 680) = 17.91$, $p < .001$, but not for *you at your best*, $F(5, 690) = 1.75$, *ns*, or *identifying signature strengths*, $F(5, 690) = 0.35$, *ns*. With respect to depressive symptoms, there were main effects of time for *gratitude visit*, $F(5, 750) = 20.91$, $p < .001$, *three good things*, $F(5, 645) = 14.43$, $p < .001$, *you at your best*, $F(5, 690) = 10.37$, $p < .001$, *using signature strengths in a new way*, $F(5, 680) = 13.35$, $p < .001$, and *identifying signature strengths*, $F(5, 690) = 6.59$, $p < .001$, and there was a Condition $\times$ Time interaction for *gratitude visit*, $F(5, 750) = 4.62$, $p < .001$, *three good things*, $F(5, 645) = 5.15$, $p < .001$, *you at your best*, $F(5, 690) = 2.83$, $p < .02$, and *using signature strengths in a new way*, $F(5, 680) = 4.56$, $p < .001$, but not for *identifying signature strengths*, $F(5, 690) = 0.20$, *ns*.

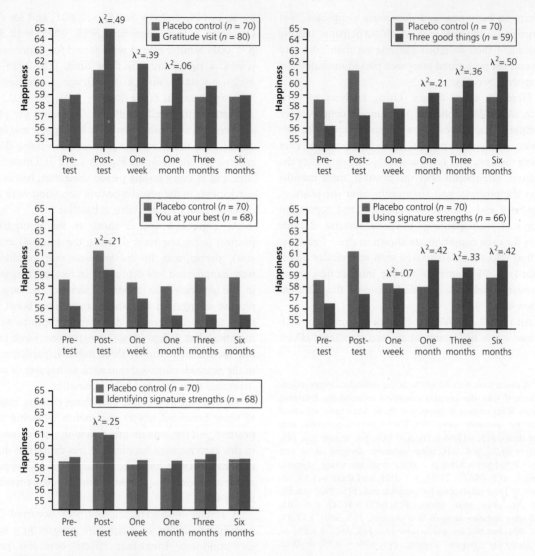

Figure 1 Steen Happiness Index Scores

Note. Figures are effect sizes corresponding to a statistically significant ($p < .05$) difference between the intervention group at that point in time and baseline. If no effect size is shown, the intervention group and the comparison group did not differ.

What caused the long-term benefits? Regardless of their assigned exercise, participants were asked explicitly to perform it for only one week. When we contacted participants for one-week, one-month, three-month, and six-month follow-ups, we asked

them whether they had indeed continued the exercise for more than one week on their own. We hypothesized that continued practice of an intervention would mediate positive outcomes at follow-up. To test this hypothesis, we conducted ANOVAs with reported

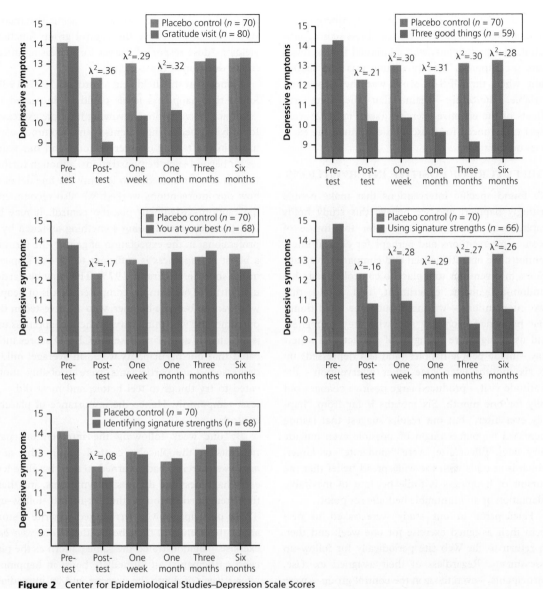

Figure 2 Center for Epidemiological Studies–Depression Scale Scores

Note. Figures are effect sizes corresponding to a statistically significant ($p < .05$) difference between the intervention group at that point in time and baseline. If no effect size is shown, the intervention group and the comparison group did not differ.

adherence to the exercise and continuing the exercise as the independent variables and with the happiness score as the dependent variable. We performed analogous ANOVAs with the depression (CES-D) score as the dependent variable.

The results were straightforward. There was a significant effect for adherence to the exercise on happiness scores at all time periods and a significant effect for adherence to the exercise on depression scores at the one-month follow-up. The interaction between continuing the exercise and adherence to the exercise was significant for happiness scores, indicating that participants who continued the exercises were the happiest. This interaction was also significant when the CES-D score was the dependent variable, indicating—again—that the long-term effects of the effective exercises (see Figure 2) were most pronounced for those who continued the exercises on their own.

THE FUTURE OF POSITIVE INTERVENTIONS

We found specific interventions that make people lastingly happier, and we believe this study holds implications—small and large—for the future of positive interventions and perhaps for clinical interventions. We operationalized and compared five happiness interventions to a placebo control in a sizable random-assignment experiment, and found that two interventions—writing about three good things that happened each day and why they happened, and using signature strengths of character in a new way—made people happier (and less depressed) up to six months later. One other intervention—the gratitude visit—produced large positive changes but only for one month. Six months is far from "happily ever after," but our results suggest that lasting increased happiness might be possible even outside fairy tales. Effect sizes were "moderate" or larger, which is at odds with the widespread belief that the pursuit of happiness is futile because of inevitable adaptation or an immutable hedonic set point.

Participants in our study were asked to perform their assigned exercise for one week and then to return to the Web site periodically for follow-up assessments. Regardless of their assigned exercise, participants—even those in the control group—were on average happier and less depressed at the immediate posttest. This pattern highlights the crucial importance of a longitudinal, placebo-controlled design in research of this nature, particularly with participants who expect to be made happier. As these studies continue and more exercises are explored, more and more inert exercises will be found, and these inert exercises can serve as placebo controls even though they were

intended as active enhancers of well-being. Parametric variation can also serve the control group function, yielding "dose-response" curves for increasing intensity or duration of the exercise.

Pioneers in this field (e.g., Fordyce, 1977, 1983) found that happiness levels could be increased by "shotgun" interventions involving multiple exercises. Identifying specific ingredients is an uncommon early move in the testing of interventions, and our studies go beyond such demonstrations, although further work is of course needed to identify the fine detail of how our interventions worked. We also recommend the random-assignment placebo control. It may be that the mere act of doing something assigned by a professional in the expectation of gain in the form of a boost in happiness is sufficient to lift one's spirits in the short term (Frank, 1973). This may be particularly true of our sample, composed as it is of people who want to become happier, who are invested in the outcome, and who think www.authentichappiness.org is a plausible authority. Baseline CES-D scores indicated that our participants were, on average, mildly depressed. Our participants were probably motivated to try things to feel better, and most did—at least temporarily. Hence the importance of placebo controls.

By one week following the intervention, participants in the placebo control group (the *early memories* exercise) had returned to their baseline levels of happiness and depression symptoms, and there they remained through the six-month follow-up. Those participants who were asked to write a story about themselves at their best—the *you at your best* exercise—demonstrated the same pattern as the placebo participants: an immediate boost in happiness after a week of doing the exercise and an immediate reduction in depressive symptoms as well, with neither effect lasting beyond the posttest. Therefore, we conclude that this exercise is not an effective intervention, at least not in isolation.

We add "in isolation" because in our multiexercise programs (which have not yet been subjected to an RCT), we use this exercise to introduce the signature strengths interventions, and it is possible that telling an introductory story about one's highest strengths, followed by the effective signature strength exercise, may amplify the benefits on happiness and depression. It seems plausible—given that three of the interventions were effective when delivered alone—to suppose that a package of positive interventions, perhaps including ones that were ineffective in isolation, might well exceed the beneficial effects of any single exercise. Such packages—likely containing some moves that are truly inert, some moves that are inert in isolation but effective in a package, and some moves that are always active—are what any therapy consists of. We have designed and are testing such packages.

Further, these single exercises were delivered with "no human hands," that is, electronically on a Web site. Discussions of therapeutic effects often emphasize the power of the relationship with the therapist; only when that relationship is in place do specific interventions work. The finding of beneficial effects with no human therapeutic alliance suggests the operation of powerful specific ingredients in the exercises. We believe that in the hands of a skilled clinician or coach, even more beneficial effects might occur. Our ongoing studies of packages of exercises delivered with human hands find large effect sizes for relieving depression and increasing happiness, in contrast to the mostly moderate effect sizes reported here.

We asked participants to do their assigned exercise for only one week. We did not suggest that they should keep it up thereafter. In retrospect, we believe that one week may not be enough time for participants in the *using signature strengths in a new way* condition and the *three good things* condition to develop sufficient skills and experience. Yet participants in both of these conditions proceeded to benefit from these exercises up to six months later. We found that the participants who continued to benefit from the exercises were those people who spontaneously did them beyond the required one-week period, without our instruction to do so. We believe that these two interventions involve skills that improve with practice, that are fun, and that thus are self-maintaining.

Unlike many therapeutic outcomes, such as weight loss from dieting, these exercises are self-reinforcing. The majority of participants in these conditions answered "yes" to a question about whether they were continuing the exercise on their own.

As we continue to develop and test exercises, we will pay particular attention to the ease with which the exercise can be integrated into an individual's daily schedule and to the processes of self-maintenance. It may not be practical for individuals to schedule a formal gratitude visit on a regular basis, but most people can make time every day to express their appreciation for someone—elaborately and sincerely. In any package of positive interventions, it may be optimal to intersperse exercises that make an immediate impact (e.g., the gratitude visit) with those exercises that are easily integrated into the daily routine.

An important question left unanswered by the current study is whether more is better when it comes to happiness interventions. Given that the *using signature strengths in a new way* exercise, the *three good things* exercise, and the *gratitude visit* exercise were all effective, does it make sense to assign them all to a person who wishes to be happier? And if so, is there an optimal sequence? Is there a personality type for whom some exercises "take" and others do not? We are currently testing the number of exercises both parametrically and in different sequences in an attempt to bolster their effects on happiness and depression.

Measurement of positive states needs more research. Many happiness researchers subscribe to the notion that happiness is necessarily subjective and is essentially whatever the individual defines it to be (e.g., Lyubomirsky, Sheldon, & Schkade, in press). If happiness is in the eye of the beholder, then self-report measures are the only appropriate measures. We do not think that this approach is solid enough: Even though individuals may be the best judge of how happy they are at the moment, they may not be accurate historians with respect to when and in what types of situations they were happy in the past. One challenge for researchers is to develop better behavior-based, domain-specific assessment tools.

We suspect that productivity at work and physical health follow the same patterns as subjective happiness, and we will welcome the day when objective productivity and health measures supplement subjective happiness measures.

Although our study is the most ambitious random-assignment, placebo-controlled test of happiness interventions we know, our interventions were documented only on a convenience sample. This population was largely well-educated, White, and financially comfortable. Furthermore, they were mildly depressed and motivated to become happier. Future research on the efficacy of these exercises for individuals who are either much happier or much more depressed than our current population and who come from other backgrounds may uncover limits on the generality of positive interventions. We are currently asking this question in collaboration with disability counselors whose primary task is to help individuals with disabilities achieve high-quality employment and a high quality of life.

We cannot resist the speculation that happiness exercises may prove therapeutic in depressive disorders. It is important to note that these interventions also reduced depressive symptoms lastingly, and in other studies we are finding that this effect is massive. Typically in the therapeutic endeavor, we tackle disorders head-on: We teach anxious people to relax, depressed people to argue against depressing thoughts, people with conflict to gain insight into the sources of conflict, and people with obsessive-compulsive disorders to find out that disasters do not ensue if they do not perform their rituals. In fact, an unspoken premise of all talk therapy is that it is beneficial to talk about one's troubles and to overcome them by confronting them. We see positive interventions as a supplement to therapy focused on troubles, another arrow in the quiver of the therapist. Psychotherapy as defined now is where you go to talk about your troubles and your weaknesses; perhaps in the future it will also be where you go to build your strengths. Perhaps on the 10th anniversary of the millennial issue of the *American Psychologist*, we will be able to review such developments.

At least since the time of Aristotle, scholars, philosophers, and religious leaders have pondered the question "How can we become lastingly happier?" Yet until recently, the only guiding question in clinical psychology and psychiatry has been "How can we reduce suffering?" We believe that psychology and psychiatry have found some answers to the suffering question and that this is a fine beginning. But even if this question is answered fully, the mission of psychology should not end there. Few people are wholly content just with being less depressed and less anxious and less angry. Psychotherapy has long been where you go to talk about your troubles, a strangely untested assumption. We suggest that psychotherapy of the future may also be where you go to talk about your strengths.

REFERENCES

American Psychiatric Association. (1994). *Diagnostic and statistical manual of mental disorders* (4th ed.). Washington, DC: Author.

Aspinwall, L. G., & Staudinger, U. M. (Eds.). (2003). *A psychology of human strengths: Fundamental questions and future directions for a positive psychology.* Washington, DC: American Psychological Association.

Beck, A. T., Ward, C. H., Mendelson, M. N., Mock, J., & Erbaugh, J. (1961). An inventory for measuring depression. *Archives of General Psychiatry, 4,* 561–571.

Bok, S. (1995). *Common values.* Columbia: University of Missouri Press.

Brickman, P., & Campbell, D. T. (1971). Hedonic relativism and planning the good society. In M. H. Appley (Ed.), *Adaptation-level theory* (pp. 287–305). New York: Academic Press.

Cameron, K. S., Dutton, J. E., & Quinn, R. E. (Eds.). (2003). *Positive organizational scholarship: Foundations of a new discipline.* San Francisco: Berrett-Koehler.

Dahlsgaard, K., Peterson, C., & Seligman, M. E. P. (in press). Shared virtue: The convergence of valued human strengths across culture and history. *Review of General Psychology.*

Deci, E. L., & Ryan, R. M. (1985). *Intrinsic motivation and self-determination in human behavior.* New York: Plenum Press.

Easterbrook (2003). *The progress paradox: How life gets better while people feel worse.* New York: Random House.

Erikson, E. (1963). *Childhood and society* (2nd ed.). New York: Norton.

Erikson, E. (1982). *The life cycle completed.* New York: Norton.

Fordyce, M. W. (1977). Development of a program to increase personal happiness. *Journal of Counseling Psychology, 24,* 511–520.

Fordyce, M.W. (1983). A program to increase happiness: Further studies. *Journal of Counseling Psychology, 30,* 483–498.

Frank, J. (1973). *Persuasion and healing: A comparative study of psychotherapy* (2nd ed.). Baltimore: Johns Hopkins University Press.

Gardner, H., Csikszentmihalyi, M., & Damon, W. (2001). *Good work: When excellence and ethics meet.* New York: Basic Books.

Gosling, S. D., Vazire, S., Srivastava, S., & John, O. P. (2004). Should we trust Web-based studies? A comparative analysis of six preconceptions about Internet questionnaires. *American Psychologist, 59,* 93–104.

Jahoda, M. (1958). *Current concepts of positive mental health.* New York: Basic Books.

Kahneman, D. (1999). Objective happiness. In D. Kahneman, E. Diener, & N. Schwarz (Eds.), *Well-being: The foundations of hedonic psychology* (pp. 3–25). New York: Russell Sage Foundation.

Kahneman, D., Diener, E., & Schwarz, N. (Eds.). (1999). *Well-being: The foundations of hedonic psychology.* New York: Russell Sage Foundation.

Keyes, C. L. M., & Haidt, J. (Eds.). (2003). *Flourishing: Positive psychology and the life well lived.* Washington DC: American Psychological Association.

Linley, P. A., & Joseph, S. (Eds.). (2004). *Positive psychology in practice.* Hoboken, NJ: Wiley.

Lopez, S. J., & Snyder, C. R. (Eds.). (2004). *Positive psychological assessment: A handbook of models and measures.* Washington, DC: American Psychological Association.

Lykken, D., & Tellegen, A. (1996). Happiness is a stochastic phenomenon. *Psychological Science, 7,* 186–189.

Lyubomirsky, S., King, L. A., & Diener, E. (in press). The benefits and costs of frequent positive affect: Does happiness lead to success? *Psychological Bulletin.*

Lyubomirsky, S., & Lepper, H. S. (1999). A measure of subjective happiness: Preliminary reliability and construct validation. *Social Indicators Research, 46,* 137–155.

Lyubomirsky, S., Sheldon, K. M., & Schkade, D. (in press). Pursuing happiness: The architecture of sustainable change. *Review of General Psychology.*

Maslow, A. H. (1954). *Motivation and personality.* New York: Harper & Row.

Maslow, A. H. (1962). *Toward a psychology of being.* Princeton, NJ: Van Nostrand.

Murray, C. (2003). *Human accomplishment: The pursuit of excellence in the arts and sciences, 800 B.C. to 1950.* New York: HarperCollins.

Ong, A. D., & van Dulmen, M. (Eds.). (in press). *Handbook of methods in positive psychology.* New York: Oxford University Press

Park, N., & Peterson, C. (in press-a). Assessing strengths of character among adolescents: The development and validation of the Values in Action Inventory of Strengths for Youth. *Journal of Adolescence.*

Park, N., & Peterson, C. (in press-b). The cultivation of character strengths. In M. Ferrari & G. Poworowski (Eds.), *Teaching for wisdom.* Mahwah, NJ: Erlbaum.

Park, N., Peterson, C., & Seligman, M. E. P. (2004). Strengths of character and well-being. *Journal of Social and Clinical Psychology, 23,* 603–619.

Park, N., Peterson, C., & Seligman, M. E. P. (2005a). *Character strengths in forty nations and fifty states.* Unpublished manuscript, University of Rhode Island.

Park, N., Peterson, C., & Seligman, M. E. P. (2005b). *Strengths of character and well-being among youth.* Unpublished manuscript, University of Rhode Island.

Peterson, C., & Park, N. (2003). Positive psychology as the evenhanded positive psychologist views it. *Psychological Inquiry, 14,* 141–146.

Peterson, C., Park, N., & Seligman, M. E. P. (2005a). Assessment of character strengths. In G. P. Koocher, J. C. Norcross, & S. S. Hill III (Eds.), *Psychologists' desk reference* (2nd ed., pp. 93–98). New York: Oxford University Press.

Peterson, C., Park, N., & Seligman, M. E. (2005b). Orientations to happiness and life satisfaction: The full life versus the empty life. *Journal of Happiness Studies, 6,* 25–41.

Peterson, C., & Seligman, M. E. P. (2004). *Character strengths and virtues: A handbook and classification.* Washington, DC: American Psychological Association.

Prochaska, J. O., DiClemente, C., Velicer, W. F., & Rossi, J. S. (1993). Standardized, individualized, interactive, and personalized self-help programs for smoking cessation. *Health Psychology, 12,* 399–405.

Radloff, L. S. (1977). The CES-D Scale: A self-report depression scale for research in the general population. *Applied Psychological Measurement, 1,* 385–401.

Rogers, C. R. (1951). *Client-centered therapy: Its current practice, implications, and theory.* Boston: Houghton Mifflin.

Ryff, C. D., & Singer, B. (1996). Psychological well-being: Meaning, measurement, and implications for psychotherapy research. *Psychotherapy and Psychosomatics, 65,* 14–23.

Seligman, M. E. P. (2002). *Authentic happiness.* New York: Free Press.

Seligman, M. E. P., & Csikszentmihalyi, M. (Eds.). (2000). Positive psychology [Special issue] *American Psychologist, 55*(1).

Snyder, C. R., & Lopez, S. J. (Eds.). (2002). *Handbook of positive psychology.* New York: Oxford University Press.

Vaillant, G. E. (1977). *Adaptation to life.* Boston: Little, Brown.

Vaillant, G. E. (2000). *Aging well.* Boston: Little, Brown.

Reading Questions

1. In your own words, define *positive psychology*.

2. In research conducted previously, Seligman and his colleagues identified six "overarching virtues" (par. 8) shared among the cultures of the world. What are they?

3. Briefly describe the relationship between "virtues" and "strengths of character."

4. According to the article's authors, what are the "most commonly endorsed strengths" (11), as reported from forty different countries?

5. What are some of the differences in strengths profiles that emerged between U.S. adults and U.S. adolescents?

6. The authors "dissolv[e] the term ['happiness'] into at least three distinct and better-defined routes to 'happiness'" (19). What are the differences between these three routes to happiness?

7. Which two interventions "increased happiness and decreased depressive symptoms" (44) for the longest period of time? Which intervention "showed the largest positive changes in the whole study" (48)?

8. How did the results of the *you at your best* intervention compare with those of the placebo control group? What conclusion do the authors reach about the effectiveness of this intervention as a result?

Rhetoric Questions

9. In the context of their discussion of possible future studies of happiness interventions, the researchers explore a number of limitations of their study. What is the effect of the authors' reporting these limitations on you as a reader? How does this reporting affect the quality of the study overall, in your opinion?

10. One might argue that Seligman and his colleagues work to achieve multiple purposes in their research report, beyond merely describing the results of their study of happiness interventions. How would you describe another possible purpose of their research report? What evidence could you present to support the additional purpose you identify?

11. The central results of this study are reported in the form of two figures, "Steen Happiness Index Scores" and "Center of Epidemiological Studies—Depressive Scale Scores." In your own words, briefly explain the relationship between the two figures. What does the information in each figure contribute to the study overall?

12. Identify an instance in the text of their study when the authors rely on first-person point of view and another instance in which they rely on third person. Offer a rationale that explains why the authors chose to use first or third person when they did.

Response and Research Questions

13. If you were asked to choose one of the happiness interventions to try yourself, which would you select and why?

14. Design a new happiness intervention that you believe would have the potential to both increase levels of happiness and decrease levels of depression in individuals.

15. Make a list of some fields of study, excluding psychology, that could potentially contribute to development of scholarship in the area of happiness studies. As you identify each field, provide a brief explanation for what you believe the field could potentially contribute.

16. Identify one of the limitations the authors of the study outline in the section of their article entitled "The Future of Positive Interventions." In a paragraph, explain what steps you believe researchers could take to overcome the limitation in future studies.

ACADEMIC CASE STUDY • THE SCHOLARSHIP OF WRITING   NATURAL SCIENCES

Meeting the Demands of the Workplace: Science Students and Written Skills

F. ELIZABETH GRAY,[1,3] LISA EMERSON,[1] AND BRUCE MACKAY[2]

F. Elizabeth Gray is a professor and researcher at Massey University in New Zealand. Her research focuses on communication needs in businesses and scientific workplaces, and she is currently engaged in a national study of oral communication skills in accounting graduates. "Meeting the Demands of the Workplace: Science Students and Written Skills" was published in 2005 in the *Journal of Science Education and Technology*. In it, Gray and her co-authors examine the writing skills requirements of employers in scientific fields.

Over the last 15 years, surveys in a range of English-speaking countries, from North America and the United Kingdom, to New Zealand and Australia, have consistently shown that employers rank oral and written communication skills as highly as or more highly than any technical or quantitative skills. However, in New Zealand there has been very little research into determining exactly what is meant by the "written communication skills" employers state they desire. A further issue in this research to date has been a lack of differentiation between employers—no study has specifically targeted the requirements of employers of science graduates. This article reports the findings of ongoing research into the expectations of science students and of employers of science graduates, and centers around several key questions:

- *What do New Zealand employers of science graduates specifically want in terms of their new hires' writing skills?*

- *How can information gained from employers of science graduates be used to motivate science students to take seriously the need to develop their writing skills?*

- *How can writing programs be evaluated and developed to help science students acquire communication skills that are important for their future learning and for their employment and promotion prospects?*

Findings are compared with the findings of the 2004 National Commission on Writing's survey of American businesses.

[1] School of English and Media Studies, Massey University, Palmerston North, New Zealand.
[2] Institute of Natural Resources, Massey University, Palmerston North, New Zealand.
[3] To whom correspondence should be addressed; e-mail; F.E.Gray@massey.ac.nz.

INTRODUCTION

As college instructors working with undergraduate science students, we strive to equip our students with skills that will aid their future learning, their intellectual and social development, and also their pursuit of employment and promotion. Over the last 15 years, surveys in New Zealand and Australia have consistently shown that employers rank oral and written communication skills as highly as or more highly than any professional or technical skills (Higher Education Council, 1992; Australian Association of Graduate Employers, 1993; Victoria University, 1996; Andrews, 1995; Reid, 1997). The workplace's urgent need for employees with strong written skills is also regularly reported in New Zealand's popular press (see for example Hart, 2004; Bland, 2005). A range of studies from North America and the United Kingdom have demonstrated that this demand for graduates with excellent written skills is not confined to New Zealand but is a global concern (see for example Jones, 1994; Jiang *et al*, 1994; Merrick, 1997; Treadwell and Treadwell 1999), and applies to students in all disciplines, from accounting to social work (Park, 1994; Forte and Mathews, 1994; Tanner and Cudd, 1999). The EnterTech Project, a North American educational effort, has been built around the demand for "soft skills" including communication skills coming from the high-tech industry (Nelson *et al*, 2001); a 2002 *Wall Street Journal/ Harris Interactive* survey revealed communication and interpersonal skills were ranked at the top of a list of 24 attributes sought by American corporate recruiters (Alsop, 2002). In 2004, the United States College Board's National Commission on Writing issued a widely-publicized report indicating both how highly employers prize writing skills and how much the lack of those skills may cost both companies and workers themselves. Intensified employer demand, in combination with the speed of technological development and the increasing commercialization of the field of science, has meant that science students at college level must acquire stronger written communication skills than ever before, to be competitive on a global job market.

However, in New Zealand there has until now been very little research that has focused specifically on the needs of employers of science graduates. It is possible that these employers have needs which

are specific to their industry and do not match the profile of the "generic" employer. Furthermore, no research to date has investigated exactly what is meant by the "written communication skills" employers state they desire. Neither have students' (and, in particular, science students') assumptions about the communication skills required of them in the workforce been examined. Consequently, we cannot accurately know whether those universities which teach communication skills to their science students are meeting the requirements and concerns of employers, nor do we know how accurately science students judge their own need to meet those requirements and concerns. This paper reports on ongoing research being undertaken at Massey University, New Zealand, centered around the following key questions:

- What do employers of science graduates specifically want in terms of their new hires' writing skills?

- How can information gained from employers be used to motivate science students to take seriously the need to develop their writing skills?

- How can science-specific writing programs be evaluated and developed to help science students acquire communication skills that are important for their future learning and for their employment and promotion prospects?

Massey University is unique amongst New Zealand universities in requiring that all science majors pass a communication course. The English Department teaches communication and writing classes that serve students majoring in science, applied science, technology, engineering, and several other scientific majors. While located within an English department, the classes are designed and taught by faculty with qualifications and experience in writing across the curriculum, with a specific focus on science writing. Students majoring in science or technology are required to enroll in and pass one of these communication classes as part of their degree, but coalface* experience reveals that these students often express resistance to the idea of "having to take English" and are dismissive of the usefulness of class content to their real-life career aspirations.

In 2004, a long-term project was initiated at Massey, undertaking to survey science students, the faculty who teach science students, and the employers who eventually hire science graduates, in order to find out what these different stakeholder groups perceive as specifically important attributes under the broad heading "communication skills." These data can be used to make recommendations to improve science writing courses at Massey University and elsewhere, and to refine methods and principles of assessment for those engaged in teaching science writing.

METHODOLOGY

In 2004, questionnaires were filled in by approximately 300 science students and 40 science academic faculty members, and mailed to 50 New Zealand employers of science graduates. These comprehensive questionnaires identified specific attributes of written communication, oral communication, and interpersonal communication, and asked respondents to value the importance of each attribute on a 7-point scale, and also to rank the relative importance of each attribute. A rich and complex data set was generated; this article focuses on the data collected from employers concerning writing skills and draws comparisons with the responses of students where these responses highlight important similarities or discrepancies (for a list of the written communication attributes identified by the Massey University questionnaire see Table I). Objectives were to clarify the exact nature of employers' expectations, to ascertain whether students accurately comprehended what their future employers wanted, and to identify and analyze significant discrepancies in expectations, in order to develop and improve the teaching of communication skills in science undergraduate programs.

*coalface: applied.

Of the 50 questionnaires mailed to employers, 23 were returned. The 46% response rate, achieved with no follow-up action or reminders, compares very positively with the response rate from the 2004 National Commission on Writing's survey, in which the initial response rate was just 17%.[4] A range of businesses were represented in those who responded to the survey: 52.38% worked for a national organization; 33.33% for an international organization; 9.52% for a small business employing less than 25 people; and 4.76% for regional organizations. The kind of industries represented also varied widely, including general business firms, agribusiness firms, research institutes, and a variety of others including financial and consulting organizations. Fifteen of the 23 respondents reported hiring employees with an undergraduate degree in science or applied science within the last three years; seven of the remaining eight reported hiring students with postgraduate qualifications in science. The Massey University questionnaire invited interested respondents to volunteer for a follow-up telephone interview, and six did so, a participation rate of 26.1% of respondents. These six employers were then contacted and a semi-structured interview conducted with each one. These interviews provided rich data on the requirements of science employers in New Zealand.

At the same time initial analysis of the results of the Massey University employer survey began, the College Board's National Commission on Writing released the results of a survey of North American employers, investigating employers' requirements concerning written communication skills in university graduates (for a list of the College Board's survey questions on writing skills, see Table II). While the American study is larger in scale, the significant similarities in objectives and findings enable a number of pertinent comparisons to be drawn between the United States and the Massey University studies, allowing conclusions to be drawn on a multi-national basis. It is important, however,

[4]After the lackluster initial response rate, intense follow-up efforts including repeat phone calls produced an eventual response rate of 53%, which the Commission called "very robust."

Table I
Massey University Communication Skills Survey Written Skills Questions

For employers

The purpose of this section is to identify more clearly the written communication skills that you consider important when looking to employ someone with a Bachelors or Masters degree in science.

Please rate, on a scale of 1–7 (where 1 is not at all important and 7 is essential), the importance of the following skills:

For students

The purpose of this section is to identify more clearly the written communication skills that you think will be important for success in your future employment.

Please rate, on a scale of 1–7 (where 1 is not at all important and 7 is essential), how important you think the following skills will be when you are engaged in your career:

1. The ability to spell correctly	☐ 1	☐ 2	☐ 3	☐ 4	☐ 5	☐ 6	☐ 7
2. The ability to use correct punctuation	☐ 1	☐ 2	☐ 3	☐ 4	☐ 5	☐ 6	☐ 7
3. The ability to use correct grammar	☐ 1	☐ 2	☐ 3	☐ 4	☐ 5	☐ 6	☐ 7
4. The ability to express ideas clearly in writing	☐ 1	☐ 2	☐ 3	☐ 4	☐ 5	☐ 6	☐ 7
5. The ability to write in business format (for a non-scientific/non-academic audience)	☐ 1	☐ 2	☐ 3	☐ 4	☐ 5	☐ 6	☐ 7
6. The ability to write a scientific report (for a scientific/academic audience)	☐ 1	☐ 2	☐ 3	☐ 4	☐ 5	☐ 6	☐ 7
7. The ability to write persuasively	☐ 1	☐ 2	☐ 3	☐ 4	☐ 5	☐ 6	☐ 7
8. The ability to convey information accurately	☐ 1	☐ 2	☐ 3	☐ 4	☐ 5	☐ 6	☐ 7
9. The ability to write in styles appropriate to different readers (clients, employees, government agencies)	☐ 1	☐ 2	☐ 3	☐ 4	☐ 5	☐ 6	☐ 7
10. The ability to write logically	☐ 1	☐ 2	☐ 3	☐ 4	☐ 5	☐ 6	☐ 7
11. The ability to collect relevant information from a variety of sources	☐ 1	☐ 2	☐ 3	☐ 4	☐ 5	☐ 6	☐ 7
12. The ability to condense material from a variety of sources and convey it clearly	☐ 1	☐ 2	☐ 3	☐ 4	☐ 5	☐ 6	☐ 7
13. The ability to use a professional writing style	☐ 1	☐ 2	☐ 3	☐ 4	☐ 5	☐ 6	☐ 7
14. The ability to write clear instructions	☐ 1	☐ 2	☐ 3	☐ 4	☐ 5	☐ 6	☐ 7
15. The ability to write a scientific/academic paper (for publication)	☐ 1	☐ 2	☐ 3	☐ 4	☐ 5	☐ 6	☐ 7

Table II

Business Roundtable & National Writing Commission Questionnaire

1. Do you take writing (e.g., of technical reports, memos, annual reports, external communications) into consideration when hiring new employees? *(Please check the box in front of the most appropriate response.)*

   A. Professional   ☐ 1 Almost never   ☐ 2 Occasionally   ☐ 3 Frequently   ☐ 4 Almost always

   B. Hourly   ☐ 1 Almost never   ☐ 2 Occasionally   ☐ 3 Frequently   ☐ 4 Almost always

2. How many employees have some responsibility for writing (either explicit or implicit) in their position descriptions?

   A. Professional   ☐ 1 A few   ☐ 2 About l/3rd   ☐ 3 About 2/3rds   ☐ 4 Almost all

   B. Hourly   ☐ 1 A few   ☐ 2 About l/3rd   ☐ 3 About 2/3rds   ☐ 4 Almost all

3. When a job either explicitly or implicitly requires writing skills, how do you usually assess a job applicant's writing ability? *(Please check all that apply.)*

   ☐ A Writing sample provided by job applicant   ☐ D Impressions based on letter/written application

   ☐ B Writing test taking during the job interview   ☐ E Other (_____)

   ☐ C Review of coursework on resume

4. When you are hiring new employees, how often are samples of written materials or presentations required of the applicant?

   ☐ A. Professional   ☐ 1 Almost never   ☐ 2 Occasionally   ☐ 3 Frequently   ☐ 4 Almost always

   ☐ B. Hourly   ☐ 1 Almost never   ☐ 2 Occasionally   ☐ 3 Frequently   ☐ 4 Almost always

5. If a job applicant's letter or other written materials were poorly composed (i.e., grammatically incorrect or hard to understand) would that count against the applicant in hiring?

   ☐ 1 Almost never   ☐ 2 Occasionally   ☐ 3 Frequently   ☐ 4 Almost always

6. Listed below are several forms of communication that are common in American companies. Please indicate how frequently each form is used in your company by circling the appropriate number.

		Almost never	Occasionally	Frequently	Almost always
A.	E-mail correspondence	1	2	3	4
B.	Other memoranda and correspondence	1	2	3	4
C.	Oral Presentations with slides/visuals (e.g., PowerPoint)	1	2	3	4
D.	Oral Presentations without visuals	1	2	3	4
E.	Formal reports	1	2	3	4
F.	Technical reports	1	2	3	4

7. Effective written communication can have a number of different characteristics. In your company, how important are each of these characteristics?

		Not at all important	Not very important	Important	Extremely important
A.	Accuracy	1	2	3	4
B.	Clarity	1	2	3	4
C.	Conciseness	1	2	3	4

(continued)

Table II

Business Roundtable & National Writing Commission Questionnaire (*continued*)

	Not at all important	Not very important	Important	Extremely important
D. Scientific precision	1	2	3	4
E. Visual appeal	1	2	3	4
F. Spelling, punctuation and grammar	1	2	3	4
G. Other (please specify)......................................	1	2	3	4

8. In your company's <u>current</u> workforce, approximately how many employees have those skills?

☐ 1 A few   ☐ 2 About 1/3rd   ☐ 3 About 2/3rds   ☐ 4 Almost all

9. Approximately how many new employees have the writing skills that your company most values?

☐ 1 A few   ☐ 2 About 1/3rd   ☐ 3 About 2/3rds   ☐ 4 Almost all

10. Does your company take effective writing skills into account when making promotion decisions?

A. Professional	☐ 1 Almost never	☐ 2 Occasionally	☐ 3 Frequently	☐ 4 Almost always
B. Hourly	☐ 1 Almost never	☐ 2 Occasionally	☐ 3 Frequently	☐ 4 Almost always

11. If an employee possesses outstanding technical but poor writing skills, does your company provide writing training?

A. Professional	☐ 1 Almost never	☐ 2 Occasionally	☐ 3 Frequently	☐ 4 Almost always
B. Hourly	☐ 1 Almost never	☐ 2 Occasionally	☐ 3 Frequently	☐ 4 Almost always

12. If your company provides writing training, what is your estimate of the annual cost per trained employee?

Annual estimate per trained employee: [   ]

---

to first note the several differences in the scope and design of the American project. The Commission did not focus on employers of science graduates: it mailed surveys only to Business Roundtable members, surveying businesses in six sectors: mining, construction, manufacturing, transportation and utilities, services, and finance, insurance, and real estate, which means that some areas of science were excluded. While New Zealand has its own Business Roundtable, questionnaires were mailed not exclusively to Roundtable members but rather to companies that had previously hired or directed recruitment efforts at Massey University science students. Also, the American survey did not include small businesses, whereas the Massey University study did (the average number of employees of the American responding firms was over 58,000; in New Zealand, few if any firms have

workforces this large). The Massey University study included questions on oral communication and interpersonal skills not covered by the US survey; conversely, the US survey included several specific written skills questions that were not included in the Massey University study, including questions on the writing of memos, PowerPoint presentations, and e-mails. The Commission's survey also differentiated between the kind of skills needed by salaried and "hourly" or non-professional workers, a distinction that was not made in our study.

RESULTS OF THE MASSEY UNIVERSITY STUDY

At the broadest level, results accorded with expectations raised by previous research. One hundred percent of responding science employers agreed that good communication skills were in the top five qualities they sought in new hires. A slightly lower number, 95.24%, agreed that good interpersonal skills were in their top five desired employee traits. Somewhat less expectedly, results from the science student questionnaire revealed students' agreement with employers' assessments. Despite the appearance of classroom resistance, 97.6% of surveyed students agreed that communication skills were among the five most important attributes for employment in science, and 98.7% stated the same for interpersonal skills. This clearly disproves the assumption that the reason behind student resistance to or disengagement in communication classes is the students' lack of appreciation of the importance of these skills to their future careers. Massey University's science students are aware of the requirements of the workplace, possibly due to the popular media's publicizing of the issue, and they do recognize their need for written, oral, and interpersonal skills in order to succeed in the job market. For this initial measurement, then, the study reveals an unexpected attitude amongst science students, and a striking degree of unanimity between two key stakeholder groups.

Significantly, however, New Zealand employers of science graduates did not find students exhibiting the written skills they required in their employment. About 61.9% of the New Zealand employers surveyed stated that they found the desired level of written communication skills in science graduates only "occasionally" or "sometimes." One employer stated this very bluntly: "we have no expectation they'll come equipped with the skills say to write a proposal instead of an assignment." Similar dissatisfaction was reported by the Commission's study: a majority of employers reported that one-third of workers do not meet the writing requirements of their positions. United States employers, like the employers surveyed in New Zealand, were forthright about the weaknesses they perceived, one stating, "The skills of new college graduates are deplorable—across the board; spelling, grammar, sentence structure . . ." (National Commission, 14).

Additionally, New Zealand students accorded less importance to writing skills across the board than did New Zealand employers. In only one category, "the ability to condense information," did employers and students assign an attribute the same value; in every other category students valued the written skill lower than employers. This finding calls into question the unanimity previously observed: it may be that science students think written skills are important, but not sufficiently important to work on.

A number of employers highlighted as a specific area of dissatisfaction the difference between the academic writing science students were accustomed to produce for college instructors and the "real-world" scientific and business writing that businesses needed their employees to be able to deliver. This conforms to previous studies' identification of "audience awareness" skills as an essential component of effective writing (Jones, 1994; Freedman and Adam, 1996; National Commission, 2004). New Zealand respondents consistently emphasized employees' need to be able to adapt their writing for different situations and end-users, adjusting style, vocabulary, and format to meet differing expectations and differing needs. When asked in a follow-up interview what the employer would choose to tell New Zealand university science students, one respondent stated: "Put yourself in the shoes of the audience you want to reach. Communication is very audience specific and there are lots of audiences out there."

There seems to be clear agreement, crossing national lines, that the demand for strong written skills is growing, not decreasing, with developing technologies; with science's increasing adoption of business modes of operation; and with the ever-intensifying focus on the bottom line. Employers agree that workers who can write clearly can well save their employers money and time: "Writing skills are fundamental in business. It's increasingly important to be able to convey content in a tight, logical, direct manner, particularly in a fast-paced technological environment" (National Commission, 8). Respondents to the Massey University questionnaire were invited to suggest any written communication skills that they considered essential which were not covered by the listed attributes, and the suggestions revealed a concern with writing efficiency. Concision, succinctness,

10

and the ability to write to deadlines were all identified. One respondent placed particular stress on the ability to write efficiently under time constraints, emphasizing the need of prospective employees to be aware that "if you're writing for a busy general manager or minister, [you must] get to the nuts and bolts very succinctly."

HIGHLIGHTS OF THE MASSEY UNIVERSITY STUDY

Fifteen specific attributes were identified under the umbrella of written communication skills, and respondents were asked to rate the importance of each on a 7-point scale on which 7 indicated "*essential*" and 1 indicated "*not important*" (see Table I). While skill in the individually listed areas of punctuation, spelling, and grammar was not rated in the top seven

attributes by either employers or students, employers nonetheless valued each of these foundational skills distinctly more highly than did the students (see Figure 1). One employer wrote in to his questionnaire, "I don't think there is a 'least' important" skill, and general employer agreement with this sentiment is revealed in the consistently high values employers accorded to all 16 individual skills: out of a maximum possible 7.0, the lowest ranked skill was accorded a value of 5.1. A noticeable disparity that appeared in the respective values assigned a specific skill by employers and students appeared with "the ability to use correct grammar." Employers gave grammatical correctness a value of 5.9 compared with the students' assigned value of 5.5. This disparity may reflect students' greater willingness to rely on word-processing tools such as grammar checks, and in the follow-up

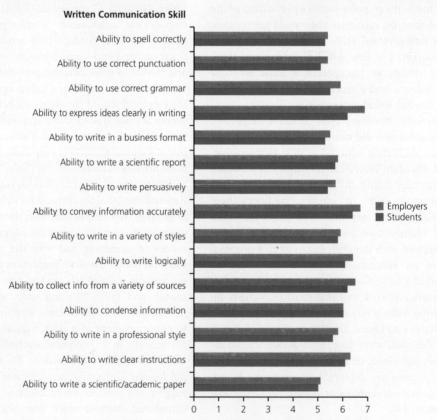

Written Communication Skill

Figure 1 Relative values of specific written skills identified by employers and students.

Table III

Comparative Rankings of the Top Five Written Communication Skills Identified by Employers and Students

Written communication skill	Employers	Students
Ability to express ideas clearly in writing	1	2
Ability to convey information accurately	2	1
Ability to collect info from a variety of sources	3	3
Ability to write logically	4	4
Ability to write clear instructions	5	5

interviews employers were specifically questioned about their perception of the usefulness of the various software tools. Employers uniformly expressed reservations about reliance on spelling and grammar checks. However, one respondent was a keen exponent of a particular software tool, developed for the Australian civil service, which identifies percentage of passive sentences used in a document. He stated that he runs through it all his own presentations, and he has personally conducted an in-house training session for his staff on the importance of primarily using the active voice.

Both spelling and punctuation were accorded a value of 5.4 by employers. Both questionnaire data and information gathered from follow-up interviews firmly underscored New Zealand science employers' demand for these foundational or basic writing skills of punctuation, spelling, and grammar on the part of employees. One described reading badly spelled, ungrammatical documents as giving him "a bad feeling. It doesn't instill confidence. It's symbolic. One takes symbols of quality of writing seriously." Another emphasized the professionalism that can

be conveyed—or undermined—by the grammatical correctness of documents: "It's about giving you credibility . . . [that's] critical. [It's about] giving your work credibility by presenting it to the highest standard possible." The Commission's study grouped "spelling, punctuation, and grammar" skills together as one rankable attribute, but results clearly showed that United States employers, too, see these foundational or basic skills as highly valuable professionally: 58.7% of respondents viewed "spelling, punctuation, and grammar" as "extremely important" and a further 36.5% as "important."

The Massey University study found near total agreement on the central importance of "the ability to express ideas clearly in writing": valued at an average of 6.9, this skill was the clear firstrank choice of employers. Interestingly, while students gave this skill a relatively high score of 6.2, they ranked this attribute second, behind "the ability to present information accurately" (for relative rankings of the five most highly ranked skills, see Table III). Students may be indicating a significant misunderstanding here: even if the information presented in a document is *accurate*, this does not mean the information is *clear*, or well-communicated, and therefore it may not meet the needs of the audience, client, or employer; it may not even be intelligible. Employers valued accuracy highly too, but ranked it second, behind clarity. This data reinforces employers' desire, confirmed by both oral and written feedback to the questionnaire, for a worker in a science-related industry to ascertain the needs of the audience, and adapt the presentation of information to meet those specific needs clearly, accurately, and in timely fashion.

The Massey University study also sought to identify those specific writing tasks in which employers wanted their workers to be proficient. While employers ranked the *general* skill of clear writing extremely highly, they accorded the *specific* skill of report-writing (for a nonspecialist audience) a markedly lower value, 5.8. This was very similar to the value accorded this attribute by students: 5.7. In part, the lower value accorded report-writing by employers can be explained by the diversity of respondents and by the differing needs of the industries represented and of different positions within those industries. However, this lower evaluation does raise an interesting question for educators: a report is a manageable and teachable piece of assessment, useful for college instructors, but arguably may be of less usefulness to potential employers.

However, before dismissing the value of the formal report as a taught assessment, it is important to note that the questionnaire also revealed that employers highly value the ability to collect information from a variety of sources (valued at 6.5), and the ability to condense information from a variety of sources and convey it clearly (valued at 6.0). These skills are both significantly developed in students by the particular tasks involved in researching and structuring a report. Interestingly, students also recognized the value of these two sets of skills, giving them values almost identical to those of employers (6.2 and 6.0, respectively). Thus, there is a strong argument to be made that even if the production of a formal report is not required in every workplace, the array of skills developed by report-writing renders it a tool of ongoing value in college science education. Nevertheless, this finding has implications for the types of reports required by educators, who may also need to consider the literature review as a form of assessment.

The Commission's study interrogated report-writing skill differently. It asked employers to identify what kinds of writing they expect from employees: 62% reported requiring formal reports "frequently" or "almost always." Because of the differing ways the two surveys present this question, it is hard to compare the Commission's findings regarding report-writing with the New Zealand responses, other than to draw the general conclusion that employers in both nations highly value the skills necessary for the production of a written report. The communication tool most often used and/or required in American workplaces, the Commission found, is e-mail.

Other specific results concerning written communication from the Massey University questionnaire are shown in Figure 1.

COSTS OF POOR WRITTEN SKILLS

If, in New Zealand as in the United States, employers are finding desired written communication skills in new graduate employees only infrequently, what steps are they taking to remedy this situation? What do these steps cost them? The follow-up interviews conducted in the Massey study asked employers about the kinds of mentoring and training in writing tasks provided in their organizations. All respondents reported some kind of mandatory or optional training and/or feedback systems on employee writing. This varied considerably, from managerial review of any document going to an external audience, to peer-review sessions of potential publications, which are regularly scheduled at research institutes. The study found a general, and concerning, expectation on the part of New Zealand employers of science graduates that new employees will arrive needing help improving their writing. As one employer reported of new science graduates, "many don't have much in their kitbag."

The Massey University study did not inquire directly into the specific costs incurred by the remedial writing training employees need. However, the costs and benefits of teaching employees basic English skills have recently been debated in New Zealand's leading newspaper (Bland, 2005); the article reports on an employee-literacy initiative at a plastics manufacturing firm in Auckland. Recent reports of British and North American estimates of the business costs of poor written communication have been alarming. Research undertaken by Britain's Royal Mail suggests spelling and grammar mistakes alone cost British businesses over £700 million a year (Royal Mail, 2003). The estimated costs of poor employee writing featured extremely prominently in report of the Commission's findings in the United States: the annual private-sector costs for providing writing training to employees who needed it was calculated at US$3.1 billion annually. It seems incontrovertible, then, that employers and college instructors share a common goal: for students to graduate to employment with greater competence and flexibility in written communication.

Seeking to elicit more information about the diversity of written skills required in the workplace, the Massey University study's follow-up interviews asked employers what they would choose to tell science students about the need for written communication skills in science careers. Such aspects as demonstrating flexibility, writing in plain language, and explaining complex procedures or operations clearly to a lay audience, were all mentioned.

CONCLUSIONS AND FUTURE STEPS

Writing should by no means be regarded merely as a "vocational-skill," and the authors do not recommend that college curricula should be solely shaped by the exigencies of the workplace. It seems inarguable, however, that if science students are to be adequately prepared for rewarding and remunerative work within the science industry, with the opportunity to advance themselves on their chosen career path, colleges should thoughtfully develop programs tailored to improve these students' written skills, based at least partly on the requirements of industry, rather than the expectations of college communication instructors who often have been educated from a non-scientific background. In addition, college science writing programs must take seriously employers' concerns about students' lack of ability to "translate" academic writing skills into practical everyday skills of use in the workplace. What are the specific issues highlighted by this study?

First, the Massey University study shows that science students definitely do perceive the importance of communication skills to their career prospects, although the importance they accord to it is still significantly lower than that accorded by employers. This raises an important question: if students do strongly agree that communication skills will be valuable to them in their future employment, what then are the reasons behind their resistance to communication classes? One reason may be that students perceive a disconnect between class content and actual job requirements. The findings of our study should prove significantly useful in communicating to science students what written skills employers in

their field do specifically demand. Further research into student resistance has already begun, with a new survey and in-depth interviews aiming to assess the range of students' reasons for disengaging from writing classes. This further study should enable the researchers to continue improving the content delivery of written communication skill classes and more fully engaging students, developing a science writing curriculum that is both relevant and popular.

Our study shows that the concerns of employers of science students conform to previous, more generic, studies and confirms employers' demand for strong written communication skills in the college graduates they hire. The majority of employers surveyed feel that science graduates do not usually have an appropriate level of writing skill for entry into the workplace. Clearly, more effort and commitment on the part of colleges is needed to develop students' writing skills, perhaps by integrating these skills into the broader curriculum—it seems that a single class at freshman level may not be sufficient to bring students' skills to a level required by employers.

Employer demand for the foundational writing skills of punctuation, spelling, and grammar, coupled with the general employer perception that graduating students do not always have a reliable grounding in these skills, means all college programs must seriously consider their role in the teaching of these skills. Finding an effective and time-efficient way of doing so will be essential.

The results of the Massey study pose interesting challenges for curriculum development. Scaffolding towards a large piece of writing, the scientific report, is a keystone of the current writing programs; however, employers state that report-writing is not a highly valued skill. Nonetheless, researching and constructing a formal report helps students develop a number of writing skills employers highly prize. It may be possible to retain and adapt this particular writing assignment to increase its relevance to the requirements of the workplace, and to ensure that it requires advanced skills in reviewing and integrating the literature, skills which were clearly prioritized by employers surveyed.

Although this was not investigated in the initial questionnaire, the follow-up interviews showed that employees' use and misuse of electronic communication tools, particularly e-mail, was identified by a number of New Zealand employers as an area of particular concern, which is in line with the findings of the United States National Commission on Writing. As the Massey University study continues, it may be useful to modify the questionnaire to collect more e-mail-specific data. A new or expanded teaching module within science writing courses in electronic communication skills and ethics may be indicated.

Study findings encourage consideration of how college instructors can refine delivery of existing course content to present science students with the real-life application that employers demand. Possible ideas may include collaboration with the private sector: guest speakers from well-known employers might be invited to directly address specific workplace needs, or to reinforce the importance of learning foundational skills.

Finally, it should be noted that the performance 30 expectations and specific skill requirements will vary with employer and also with position, and thus generalizations about the specific demands for written skills should be made cautiously. Nonetheless, the data from this study and those it builds on confirm the vital importance for science students of a communication curriculum that teaches foundational skills of spelling, grammar and punctuation, audience analysis, and clarity, concision, and accuracy in written communication.

REFERENCES

Alsop, R. (September, 2002). The top business schools (A special report)—Playing well with others. *The Wall Street Journal Online*. Retrieved February 3, 2005 from http://online.wsj.com/public/us.

Andrews, R. J. (1995). *A Survey of Employer Perceptions of Graduates of the University of Otago*, University of Otago, Dunedin, New Zealand.

Australian Association of Graduate Employers. (1993). *National Survey of Graduate Employers*, Direct Connection Marketing Consultants, Sydney, Australia.

Bland, V. (January, 2005). Levelling the playing field. *New Zealand Herald Online*. Retrieved February 18, 2005 from http://www.nzherald.co.nz.

Forte, J. A., and Mathews, C. (1994). Potential employers' views of the ideal undergraduate social work curriculum. *Journal of Social Work Education* 30(2): 228–240.

Freedman, A., and Adam, C. (1996). Learning to write professionally: "Situated learning" and the transition from university to professional discourse. *Journal of Business and Technical Communication* 10(4): 395–427.

Hart, S. (October, 2004). Txting's no wy 2 gt a jb. *New Zealand Herald Online*. Retrieved February 18, 2005 from http://www.nzherald.co.nz.

Higher Education Council (1992). *Higher Education: Achieving Quality*, NBEET/AGPS, Canberra, Australia.

Jiang, J. J., Udeh, I. E., and Hayahneh, A. (1994). Employers' expectations of incoming business graduates: From recruiters' views. *Journal of Computer Information Systems*, Summer, 57–59.

Jones, E. A. (1994). Defining essential writing skills for college graduates. *Innovative Higher Education* 19(1): 67–78.

Merrick, N. (1997). Labour set to focus on basic skills. *People Management* 3(15): 11.

National Commission on Writing for America's Families, Schools, and Colleges. (2004). *Writing: A ticket to work or a ticket out. A survey of business leaders.* College Entrance Examination Board. Available http://www.writingcommission_org/prod_downloads/writingcom/writing-ticket-to-work.pdf

Nelson, W. A., Wellings, P., Palumbo, D., and Gupton, C. (2001). *Combining technology and narrative in a learning environment for workplace training.* Paper presented at the Annual Meeting of the American Educational Research Association. ERIC ED453807.

Park, L. J. (1994). Good accounting skills: What more does a successful accountant need? *Journal of Education for Business*, 69: 231–234.

Reid, I. (1997). Disciplinary and cultural perspectives on student literacy. In Golebiowski, Z., and Borland, H. (Eds.), *Selected Proceedings of the First National Conference on Tertiary Literacy: Research and Practice*, vol. 2, Victoria University of Technology, Melbourne, Australia, pp. 1–11.

Royal Mail Group Plc. (March, 2003). Typos cost UK business over £700 million a year. Retrieved February 15, 2005 from http://www.royalmailgroup.com/news/news.asp.

Tanner, J. R., and Cudd, M. (1999). Finance degree programs and the issue of student preparedness. *Journal of Education for Business*, 74: 335–340.

Treadwell, D. F., and Treadwell, J. B. (1999). Employer expectations of newly-hired communication graduates. *Journal of the Association for Communication Administration* 28(2): 87–99.

Victoria University of Wellington, Careers Advisory Service (1996). Skills requested by employers in 1996 employer visit programme. *Student Information Sheet*, Author, Wellington, New Zealand.

Reading Questions

1. What were the researchers trying to learn, and why did they feel that previous research had not adequately answered their questions?

2. What surprises you the most about the results of this study? Did you expect to see the results from students, faculty, and employers that were reported?

3. What was the most highly valued writing skill that employers reported? How did that compare with the most highly valued writing skill that students reported?

Rhetoric Questions

4. Read the first paragraph of the Introduction section, and then read the first paragraph of the Methodology section. What do you notice about the use of first person in the two selections? Why do you think the authors made the choices that they did in those two sections?

5. In the "Highlights of the Massey University Study" section, the authors choose to represent the results from employers and students in a comparative bar graph. Why do you think they made that choice? Why did they not include faculty responses?

6. Go through the article and highlight the parenthetical references (the places where outside sources are cited). Where do most of the references occur? Why do you think they occur where they do?

Response and Research Questions

7. Read the bulleted research questions that are listed in the abstract. Based on these questions, what conclusions would you make about the authors' view of the purpose of a college education? Do you agree or disagree? Why?

8. Take a look at the survey questions asked in Table 1 of the article and write down your answers. Then choose one of those responses and write a paragraph about why you answered the way you did. Why do you believe that skill is more or less important?

9. If you were to distribute the same survey to students, faculty, and employers in your field of study, do you think the responses would be similar to or different from the responses received in the Massey University study? Why?

10. In a democracy, what are potential problems with allowing the workplace to determine what students write and how they think and communicate?

Writing about Nursing Research: A Storytelling Approach

GAVIN FAIRBAIRN AND ALEX CARSON

Gavin Fairbairn is Professor of Health and Social Sciences at Leeds Metropolitan University, UK. He was previously Professor of Education at Liverpool Hope and Professor of Nursing and Midwifery at the University of Glamorgan. His research and publications focus on ethics and academic literacies. The article below, written with Alex Carson, a registered nurse and Senior Lecturer in Sociology and Ethics at North-East Wales Institute of Higher Education, argues in favor of using storytelling as a means of reporting research so that it can be read and understood by "the maximum possible number of people, whether they are nurses, policy makers, or colleagues in other healthcare professions." The article was published in 2002 in the journal *Nurse Researcher*.

> To learn more about nursing as an applied field of inquiry, see pages 296–304.

In this article Gavin Fairbairn and Alex Carson argue that much of what is written by nurses is needlessly difficult, especially when it concerns research they have carried out. The authors make a positive contribution to the ways in which nurses think about what they write and how they write it, suggesting that one way in which things might become better would be for nurses to view their writing as a form of storytelling.

STORYTELLING AS RESEARCH METHODOLOGY

> To learn more about quantitative and qualitative research methods, see pages 191–95.

Stories sometimes feature in the methodology of nursing research, although many prefer to label them as "case studies" or "accounts" (Tilley 1995). However, narrative approaches are often sidelined. We all know why; it has to do with the ascendancy of methods drawn from, and sometimes caricaturing, the physical sciences. This is regrettable since stories have much to offer as a way of understanding. Even when storytelling methods are utilized, the boldness of researchers is often circumscribed by an acknowledgement that narratives can be seen as just another data-collection method (Crepeau 2000, McCance *et al* 2001). Different approaches have been adopted in the attempt to systematize the ways in which stories are gathered and analyzed. For example, Koch (1998) provides a conventional methodological structure for the use of storytelling, in the context of a discussion of whether storytelling is really research.

> Fairbairn and Carson establish the topic of their report: the "problem" of storytelling as a research and reporting method.

In our view it is regrettable that storytelling as a research method is often viewed merely as a way of gathering data to be manipulated in various ways, which probably involves cutting them up into little labelled specimens—themes and sub-themes—that can be sorted and counted and weighed. There is undoubtedly value, at times, in analyzing stories at the level of the concepts or words used. However, to treat stories in this way is to fail to respect the tellers of these stories. It is to fail to listen to their voices. It is to make the assumption that our interpretation of their experience is more valid than their telling of it. Our view of the place of storytelling in nursing research is that it should be viewed less as a method of collecting data, which requires systematic methods for analysis, and more as what it really is—a way of listening to and learning from each other. There are good reasons for this.

> Fairbairn and Carson establish their central claim. Read more about making claims and developing reasons in support of an argument on pages 61–67.

Much of human life is conducted through story. Many of our social institutions are comprised almost entirely of opportunities for telling and retelling stories, for sharing the narratives that constitute our lives. Consider the questions: "How was work today?" and "How is the data collection going?" which invite stories in response, as do the questions: "How did you sleep last night?" "Have your bowels moved yet?" and "How are you feeling now?" Much of nursing involves telling and listening to stories of various kinds. Nurses listen to stories whenever patients tell them what is going on in their lives, and they also tell them every time they pass on information about patients.

Researchers in nursing undertake their work because they want to be able to tell 5 more accurate and more helpful stories about how the world of nursing works. Indeed, there is a sense in which all research, regardless of the methods adopted, is concerned with telling stories about us and about the world. Of course, the stories nurse researchers tell are inhabited not by people, but by ideas, theories, questions, and suggestions about, for example, the ways in which patients can best be cared for and treated, which draw on research results. The plots for those stories develop through the research process—by formulating questions and methods for answering them, by gathering data and by attempting to make sense of it.

In our view, the only real value of nursing research is the contribution it can make to the development of nursing practice: in order that patients can be cared for and treated in more helpful, more beneficial ways. That is why we think that nursing researchers should try to write about their findings in such a way that the maximum possible number of people, whether they are nurses, policy makers or colleagues in other healthcare professions, are able to understand what they have to say.

> Fairbairn and Carson explore a number of reasons to reconsider the place of storytelling in nursing research.

WHY DO NURSING RESEARCHERS WRITE ABOUT THEIR WORK?

You may think that the answer to this question is obvious. For example, you may believe that their principal motivation is the wish to share their research findings and the ideas they have developed about theory and practice. These days, when emphasis is placed on the need to ensure that practice in health care is evidence-based as far as possible, you might even entertain the idea that most nurse researchers write about their findings in order to contribute to the body of available evidence, with the hope and expectation that their work can help to make the world a better place in which to be a patient. Of course, some of them probably do, at least some of the time. However, there are other, arguably less worthy agendas on the horizon. For example, the need to develop and maintain a research profile in order to gain promotion; the need to publish in the highly regarded (usually international, peer-reviewed) journals; and to be considered "Research active" in terms of the Research Assessment Exercise (RAE).

There are other less worthy reasons for academic writing, including the desire to give public displays of familiarity with accepted jargon, and with theories and research methods that are currently in vogue. This is likely to go hand-in-hand with the wish to demonstrate the ability to write in dense, difficult-to-decipher prose (Fairbairn 1996). You may find it hard to believe that there are any researchers in nursing who actually wish to be difficult in their writing. In that case we will have to agree to differ, because we

> To learn more about the use of headings and subheadings in research reports, see pages 200–201.

entertain a significant degree of skepticism about whether much of what gets published in nursing journals is motivated primarily, or even at all, by the wish to communicate with others. Many researchers who in their everyday lives manage to talk in quite ordinary ways seem actively to cultivate a new and less understandable way of speaking, and to adopt a new language when they are writing. It is almost as if they believe that the academic enterprise is about confusing, rather than illuminating, and aimed at obfuscation, rather than clarity. This is just as true in nursing as it is in any other discipline.

SURROUNDING YOURSELF WITH AN AURA OF INTELLECTUAL PROWESS AND ERUDITION: SOME TIPS

Of course, obfuscation and a lack of clarity can be useful. For one thing, if you manage to achieve the right degree of tortured difficulty in the prose you adopt, you can prevent anyone really understanding what you are saying, and thus having the opportunity to criticize you. Not only that, but the more difficult your writing, the more chance you have of convincing your readers that what you have to say is worthwhile, and the more clever you will appear to at least some of them. And so, if you want to look really clever as an author, you may wish to take note of some of the ways in which you can surround yourself with an aura of intellectual prowess and erudition.

1. First, choose your words carefully. For example, it is worth developing the habit 10 of using big words where small ones would do, and difficult words where possible, rather than where necessary; words like *obfuscation and erudition* (which respectively mean, "confusion" or "muddle" and "scholarship" or "sophistication").

In general it is best always to introduce difficult words without any explanation as to their meaning. That way, readers who do not understand what you are talking about will assume that they are at fault and not you. It is particularly helpful to use jargon where ordinary language would convey meaning better. Doing so can see off potential critics, who may think they can detect flaws in what you say or perhaps a lack of rigor in your thinking, but be afraid to say so, because they do not speak the same language as you and fear the dreadful consequences of looking ignorant.

Using jargon from your own area of specialty helps to convey a sense of embeddedness in the tradition and values of your discipline. But it can be even more helpful to use jargon from other fields, for example, sociology or philosophy, in relation to which you can realistically expect that many of those who will read your work will be a little unsure and thus less likely to challenge you.

2. Next, it is worth attending to your use of referencing and citation. Cultivate the habit of making liberal use of references with no real reason for doing so—the more obscure the better. Doing so can help to give the impression of scholarship, because it suggests familiarity, not only with work by others that has actually influenced the way in which you have pursued your own research, but with a wider range of sources. "Dropping" the names of significant nursing researchers and theorists into your writing is especially helpful, because it signals your right to belong to the academic club of which you are a member, or of which you wish to become a member, because you can utter the names of the great and the famous.

Fairbairn and Carson identify writing practices of nursing researchers that they believe obfuscate meaning and detract from their ability to communicate effectively: use of jargon, overuse of citations, and unnecessary references, as well as a lack of structure in reporting.

Notice the rather dramatic shift in tone that occurs here. Fairbairn and Carson are mocking the kind of "erudite" writing that, from their perspective, "obfuscates" meaning.

Within every academic discipline there are authors that it is worth citing if you want to be taken seriously, and nursing is just like other disciplines in this regard. It is always helpful to refer to at least one of the major nurse theorists in your work, whatever it is about. Curiously though, you may do even better by citing a range of famously difficult theorists in, for example, philosophy and sociology, including Heidegger, Hegel, and Husserl, Derrida, Foucault, and Habermas, even if you haven't read them in detail (or even at all) and therefore cannot make substantive use of what they say.

3. Finally, it can be a really good idea if, in reporting your research, you adopt a style   15 that is as devoid of structure as possible, so that your reader never quite knows where she is or where she is going, as she wanders around looking for something to understand. Even better is to confuse things further by avoiding structure while liberally sprinkling your work with apparent structural signposts, which actually mean nothing. For example, you might claim to offer an argument in favor of a conclusion, without actually doing so, or you may refer back to something you said earlier, even though you did not in fact say it. The liberal use of words and phrases that seem to imply an argument or a logical train of thought is especially helpful, like *therefore, however, in contrast, finally*, and *of course*. However, if you adopt this tactic, you must assiduously avoid arguing and you must avoid the temptation to allow logic to enter the picture.

Perhaps we are guilty of painting an over-gloomy picture. Nonetheless, countless academics write in the obfuscatory and opaque style we have been criticizing and unfortunately nursing researchers are not totally blameless in this regard. If you find yourself wanting to argue against our view, a quick browse through a few academic nursing journals should persuade you otherwise, provided you browse with an open mind. Try doing so while bearing in mind questions such as these: Is this as clear and coherent as it might be? Is it well structured and easy to follow? Are all of these references strictly necessary? Do they all add something? Even worse, a quick browse through some of nursing's professional periodicals ought to convince anyone who is willing to be convinced that opaqueness, over-referencing, and stylistic complexity is now acceptable even at the level of professional publication.

ACADEMIC WRITING AS STORYTELLING

How could things become better? Well, one thing that could happen is that nursing could accept that it has no need to emphasize its seriousness as an academic discipline by promoting a style of writing among its writers and researchers that emulates other disciplines. Editors of nursing journals and periodicals could ensure that those who are permitted the privilege of publishing in its professional and academic press are expected to lay aside tortuous, over-referenced prose in favor of a more direct style. Of course, we are not the first authors to attempt to promote a more direct style of writing. For example, Webb (1992) has argued that the first person — in which the author appears as "I"—is appropriate at times. This is to be commended, though we think that use of the first person can be helpful in more contexts than Webb seems to consider appropriate.

Another way in which nurses could improve the ways in which they write about their research is by viewing their task in terms of storytelling. Researchers in nursing

Consider the effect of Fairbairn and Carson acknowledging the severity of their own reactions to "obfuscatory and opaque" writing.

Notice the familiar, conversational tone established here. Consider how it contributes to the substance of the author's argument about the use of storytelling as a response to opaqueness.

In light of the authors' earlier comments on excessive referencing, consider the relevance and appropriateness of this reference. Learn more about paraphrasing on page 96.

have stories to tell. In telling them they share information about how they came to their conclusions, about their methods and hypotheses, about the genealogy into which their work slots, its parentage and forebears and the quarrels it might have with alternative views.

Nursing researchers and different sub-groups within nursing not only have different areas of interest but different ways of telling stories. Some will employ visual means such as graphs and tables to show what they have found. Others will approach their storytelling in ways that do not lend themselves to the use of such visual supports. The stories nursing researchers tell may thus be told in different languages, or in different dialects of the same language. However, thinking of academic writing as a genre of storytelling is helpful in facilitating academic writers in developing their writing, regardless of their level of experience or the research methods they have adopted (Fairbairn 2000).

Certain features of successful storytelling are found in the best academic writing, but are notably missing from the worst. For example, a good narrative writer engages her audience and holds its attention by making her plot and the way she introduces it sufficiently interesting to seduce us into reading further. And she does it by ensuring that the characters that inhabit the world she is creating are sufficiently believable to motivate us to pursue the narrative to find out what happens to them. Good academic writers, including those who write well about nursing research, do similar things, though in general the characters with whom they populate their texts are not people, but hypotheses, methods, results and so on.

CONCLUSION

If nursing researchers want to change the clinical world and the quality of patient care, they must undertake research that is relevant to practice. They must also ensure that they tell their tales as well as they can, because it is only by doing this that they can ensure that those who might be in a position to make use of their findings can understand what they are saying.

If they are to be successful in telling stories, nurse researchers must weave the various elements together in coherent, interesting, and easily understandable narratives, making clear their relationship to the intellectual landscape they inhabit. If they fail to do so they will greatly reduce the possibility that their work can contribute to the development of practice. In our view this will be to fail at the last and perhaps the most important hurdle in the research process.

REFERENCES

Crepeau EB (2000) Reconstructing Gloria: a narrative analysis of team meetings. *Qualitative Health Research.* 10, 6, 766–787.

Fairbairn GJ (1996) Academic writing for publication and public performance: communication or display? *Curriculum.* 17, 3, 188–194.

Fairbairn G (2000) Developing academic storytelling. *Education Today.* 50, 2, 32–38.

Koch T (1998) Story telling: is it really research? *Journal of Advanced Nursing.* 28, 6, 1182–1190.

McCance TV *et al* (2001) Exploring caring using narrative methodology: an analysis of the approach. *Journal of Advanced Nursing.* 33, 3, 350–356.

Consider the ways in which academic writing might be considered a genre of storytelling.

Fairbairn and Carson end with a call to action for nursing researchers. Consider what, specifically, they are calling upon their readers to do.

Tilley S (1995) Accounts, accounting and accountability in psychiatric nursing. In Watson R (Ed) *Accountability in Nursing Practice*. London, Chapman Hall.

Webb C (1992) The use of the first person in academic writing: objectivity, language and gatekeeping. *Journal of Advanced Nursing*. 17, 747–752.

Reading Questions

1. In your own words, explain Fairbairn and Carson's objections to how storytelling is currently viewed as a research method.

2. According to the researchers, what are some of the "less worthy reasons" for nurses to engage in academic writing?

3. Fairbairn and Carson identify three strategies academic writers employ to highlight their "intellectual prowess and erudition" that often result in mere "obfuscation and a lack of clarity" (par. 9). What are they?

4. Identify two reasons Fairbairn and Carson provide to support their contention that nursing research would be improved if researchers saw "their task in terms of storytelling" (18).

Rhetoric Questions

5. Look closely at the headings Fairbairn and Carson use to guide their readers through their argument. Choose two and offer a brief analysis of their effectiveness as headings. Are they appropriate? Why or why not? Could they be improved? If so, how?

6. In what ways do Fairbairn and Carson practice what they preach? In other words, how does their article conform to or deviate from their recommendations for improving research reporting in nursing?

7. Identify three strategies Fairbairn and Carson employ as academic writers to make their research "sufficiently interesting to seduce us into reading further" (19).

Response and Research Questions

8. Fairbairn and Carson call for a reconsideration of the role of storytelling in nursing research. Are there other academic or professional fields of inquiry that you believe might benefit by emphasizing storytelling more? If so, what are they, and how would they benefit from more storytelling? If not, then why not?

9. The researchers suggest that their article may be "painting an over-gloomy picture" of the state of writing in nursing (16). Do you agree or disagree that they paint "an over-gloomy picture"? Why or why not?

10. Choose three paragraphs from an academic study published in a peer-reviewed journal. Read the paragraphs carefully and then rewrite them while trying to avoid the writing strategies Fairbairn and Carson identify as ones that often result in "obfuscation and a lack of clarity" (9).

Writing a Comparative Rhetorical Analysis: Popular and Academic Sources

In this assignment, we invite you to explore rhetorical strategies that writers in this chapter use to address scholarly and popular audiences. Select two pieces from this chapter, and write an essay in which you compare how each writer tailors his or her writing for a specific audience. Choose one piece written for a scholarly audience and one piece written for a popular audience.

Before you begin writing, you might reread each piece carefully, with attention to the following questions:

- Who is the intended audience?

- What are the audience's views on the topic before reading the text? What prior knowledge do they bring to their reading experience?

- What belief systems or values inform the audience's views on the topic?

- What is the author's purpose for writing (i.e., to persuade, to inform)? What does the writer want their audience to do?

- What medium was the piece originally published in?

- What type of evidence does the author rely on? Is this the most persuasive type of evidence for the audience?

- What rhetorical strategies does the author use (i.e., word choice, writing voice, tone, evidence) to write most effectively for the intended audience?

- How might the author have written this piece differently for a new audience?

As you read and engage these questions, mark passages in the text that you might use as supporting evidence for your claims. At the same time, jot down your thoughts in the margins or make a comparison chart with a column for each text as you work toward analysis.

Introduce the two articles, and assert a thesis near the beginning of your analysis. Compare and contrast the two articles' rhetoric in the body of your analysis: what structural, reference, and/or language conventions do they employ? In your conclusion, assess the appropriateness of the articles' construction in light of their intended audiences.

Expressive Writing

For this assignment, begin by recalling a past experience you've had that was difficult or painful but that you would be willing to write about. Then freewrite about that experience for six 20-minute writing sessions over a 2–3 week period (your instructor might give you a different timeline for your writing). Once you have completed writing, reflect on the experience of writing by discussing the following questions:

- What did you learn about yourself?
- What did you learn about the experience you focused on as your topic?
- What challenges did you face in completing the writing task? What was the most difficult part to write?
- How would you write differently if you were solely writing for yourself and not in response to an assignment?
- Do you think that your expressive writing provided any short-term or lasting psychological or physical benefits to you? If so, what were they?
- Were there any negative effects? If so, what were they?

Introduction to Documentation Styles

You've likely had some experience with citing sources in academic writing, both as a reader and as a writer. Many students come to writing classes in college with experience only in MLA format, the citation style of the Modern Language Association. The student research paper at the end of Chapter 5 is written in MLA style, which is the most commonly required citation style in English classes. Although MLA is the citation style with which English and writing teachers are usually most familiar, it is not the only one used in academic writing—not by a long shot.

Some students don't realize that other citation styles exist, and they're often surprised when they encounter different styles in other classes. Our goal in this appendix is to help you understand (1) why and when academic writers cite sources and (2) how different citation styles represent the values and conventions of different academic disciplines. This appendix also provides brief guides to MLA, APA (American Psychological Association), and CSE (Council of Science Editors) styles—three styles that are commonly used in the first three chapters in Part Two of this book. These citation styles are discussed in some detail in Chapter 5 as well. Near the end of this appendix, you'll find a table with other citation styles commonly used in different disciplines, including some of the applied fields discussed in Chapter 10.

Why Cite?

There are several reasons why academic writers cite sources that they draw upon. The first is an ethical reason: academic research and writing privilege the discovery of new knowledge, and it is important to give credit to scholars who discover new ideas and establish important claims in their fields of study. Additionally, academic writers cite sources to provide a "breadcrumb trail" to show how they developed their current research projects. Source citations show what prior work writers are building on and how their research contributes to that body of knowledge. If some of the sources are well respected, that ethos helps to support the writers' research as well. It demonstrates that the writers have done their homework; they know what has already been discovered, and they are contributing to an ongoing conversation.

These two values of academic writing—the necessity of crediting the person or persons who discover new knowledge, and the importance of understanding prior work that has led to a specific research project—shape the choices that academic writers make when citing sources. Anytime you quote, summarize, or paraphrase the work of someone else in academic writing, you must give credit to that person's work. *How* academic writers cite those sources, though, differs according to their academic discipline and writing situation.

Disciplinary Documentation Styles

Citation styles reflect the values of specific disciplines, just like other conventions of academic writing that we've discussed in this book. When you compare the similarities and differences in citation styles, you might notice that some conventions of particular citation styles that seemed random before suddenly have meaning. For example, if we compare the ways that authors and publication dates are listed in MLA, APA, and CSE styles, we'll notice some distinctions that reflect the values of those disciplines:

Author's full name
Year of publication listed near the end

MLA

Greenwell, Amanda M. "Rhetorical Reading Guides, Readerly Experiences, and WID in the Writing Center." *WLN: A Journal of Writing Center Scholarship,* vol. 41, no. 7-8, Mar.-Apr. 2017, pp. 9-16.

Only author's last name included in full

Year included toward the beginning, in a place of importance

APA

Greenwell, A. (March-April 2017). Rhetorical reading guides, readerly experiences, and WID in the writing center. *WLN: A Journal of Writing Center Scholarship, 41*(7–8), 9–16.

Only last name given in full, and first and middle initials are not separated from last name by any punctuation.

Year also has a place of prominence and isn't distinguished from the name at all, emphasizing that timeliness is as important as the name of the author

CSE

Greenwell A. 2017 Mar-Apr. Rhetorical reading guides, readerly experiences, and WID in the writing center. WLN. 41(7-8):9-16.

MLA lists the author's full name at the beginning of the citation, emphasizing the importance of the author. Date of publication is one of the last items in the citation, reflecting that a publication's currency is often not as important in the humanities as it is in other disciplines. By contrast, APA and CSE list the date of publication near the beginning of the citation in a place of prominence. Interestingly, CSE does not use any unique punctuation to distinguish the author from the date other than separating them by a period, reflecting that they are of almost equal importance.

Citation styles reflect the values of the respective disciplines. In a very real sense, citation styles are rhetorically constructed: they are developed, revised, updated, and used in ways that reflect the purpose and audience for citing sources in different disciplines. Some rules in documentation styles don't seem to have a clear reason, though, and this is why it's important to know how to verify the rules of a certain system. Our goal is to help you understand, on a rhetorical level, the way three common citation styles work. Memorizing these styles is not always the most productive endeavor, as the styles change over time. Really understanding how they work will be much more useful to you long term.

Modern Language Association (MLA) Style

WHAT IS UNIQUE ABOUT MLA STYLE?

MLA style is generally followed by researchers in the disciplines of the humanities such as foreign languages and English. One of the unique aspects of MLA style, when compared with other styles, is that the page numbers of quoted, summarized, or paraphrased information are included in in-text citations. While other styles sometimes also include page numbers (especially for exact quotations), the use of page numbers in MLA allows readers to go back to find the original language of the referenced passage. In the disciplines that follow MLA style, the way in which something is phrased is often quite important, and readers might want to review the original source to assess how you are using evidence to support your argument.

We offer some basic guidelines here for using MLA style, but you can learn more about the style guides published by the Modern Language Association, including the *MLA Handbook*, at www.mla.org.

IN-TEXT CITATIONS IN MLA STYLE

When sources are cited in the text, MLA style calls for a parenthetical reference at the end of a sentence or at the end of the information being cited (if in the middle of a sentence). The author's name and the page number(s) of the reference appear in parentheses with no other punctuation, and then the end-of-sentence punctuation appears after the parenthetical reference.

> The frequency with which customers ordered dessert at restaurants can be correlated with the BMI of the waitstaff (Döring and Wansink 198).

1. Paraphrase from article
2. Last name of author
3. Page number where paraphrased material can be found

WORKS CITED CITATIONS IN MLA STYLE

The citations list at the end of an academic paper in MLA style is called a Works Cited page. Citations are listed on the Works Cited page in alphabetical order by the authors' last names.

> Döring, Tim, and Brian Wansink. "The Waiter's Weight." *Environment and Behavior*, vol. 49, no. 2, 2017, pp. 192-214.

1. **Author.**   Author's name is listed first, with the last name preceding the first name and any middle initials. The first name is spelled out and followed by a comma, and then the other authors are listed with the first name preceding the last name.

2. **Title of source.**   Article titles and book chapters are given in quotation marks. All words in the title are capitalized except for articles and prepositions (unless they are the first words). Include a period after the title, inside the last quotation mark.

3. **Title of container where the source was found.**   Book, journal, magazine, and newspaper titles appear in italics. A comma follows the title.

4. **Other contributors.**   If the container has editors, translators, or other contributors, those would be listed directly after the title of the container.

5. **Version.**   If the source is an edition or specific version of a text, that information would be listed next.

6. **Number.**   For a journal, the volume number follows the title of the journal, preceded by the abbreviation "vol." If the journal has an issue number, that would then be listed after the volume number, preceded by the abbreviation "no." Use commas to separate the volume, issue number, and any information that follows.

7. **Publisher.**   If a specific publisher is listed, give the name of the publisher next.

8. **Publication date.**   The year of publication is listed next, followed by a comma. For journals, include the month and/or season before the year.

9. **Location.**   Inclusive page numbers are provided in the MLA citation of a journal article, preceded by "pp." and followed by a period. If you are citing an online source, list the URL as the location.

Citing Different Types of Sources in MLA Style

Comparison of different kinds of sources in MLA style

Type of Source	Example of Works Cited Entry	Notes
Book	Davies, Alice, and Kathryn Tollervey. *The Style of Coworking: Contemporary Shared Workspaces.* Prestel Verlag, 2013.	When more than one author is listed, only the first author's name is reversed in MLA style.
Book chapter	Ludvigsen, Sten, and Hans Christian Arnseth. "Computer-Supported Collaborative Learning." *Technology Enhanced Learning*, edited by Erik Duval, Mike Sharples, and Rosamund Sutherland, Springer International, 2017, pp. 47-58.	Be sure to list both the book chapter and the title of the book when citing a chapter from an edited collection.
Scholarly journal article	Waldock, Jeff, et al. "The Role of Informal Learning Spaces in Enhancing Student Engagement with Mathematical Sciences." *The Journal of Mathematical Education in Science and Technology*, vol. 48, no. 4, 2017, pp. 587-602. *Taylor Francis Online*, www.tandfonline.com/pp/waldock_rowlett_7.pdf.	If more than two authors are listed, write *et al.* after the first author's name. If the source was found in an online database, list the database or website as a second, external, container.
Magazine or newspaper article	Goel, Vindu. "Office Space Is Hard to Find for Newcomers." *The New York Times*, 2 Apr. 2015, p. F2.	Periodical articles can differ in print and online, so be sure to cite the correct version of the article.
Website	Goodloe, Amy. "TIPS—Composing and Framing Video Interviews." *Digital Writing 101*, 2017, digitalwriting101.net/content/composing-and-framing-video-interviews/.	For online sources, include the exact URL for the source as the location, excluding http:// or https://.
Website with no individual author listed	Sage One. "Eight Ideas for Designing a More Collaborative Workspace." *Microsoft for Work*, Microsoft Corporation, 10 Jul. 2014, blogs.microsoft.com/work/2014/07/10/eight-ideas-for-designing-a-more-collaborative-workspace.	When no author is listed, you can begin the citation with the title of the article or site. If an organization or some other entity is sponsoring the article (as in this case), that can be listed as the author.

SAMPLE MLA WORKS CITED PAGE

Works Cited

Davies, Alice, and Kathryn Tollervey. *The Style of Coworking: Contemporary Shared Workspaces*. Prestel Verlag, 2013.

Goel, Vindu. "Office Space Is Hard to Find for Newcomers." *The New York Times*, 2 Apr. 2015, p. F2.

Goodloe, Amy. "TIPS—Composing and Framing Video Interviews." *Digital Writing 101*, 2017, digitalwriting101 .net/content/composing-and-framing-video-interviews/.

Ludvigsen, Sten, and Hans Christian Arnseth. "Computer-Supported Collaborative Learning." *Technology Enhanced Learning*, edited by Erik Duval, Mike Sharples, and Rosamund Sutherland, Springer International, 2017, pp. 47-58.

Sage One. "Eight Ideas for Designing a More Collaborative Workspace." *Microsoft for Work*, Microsoft Corporation, 10 Jul. 2014, blogs.microsoft.com/work/2014/07/10/ eight-ideas-for-designing-a-more-collaborative-workspace.

Waldock, Jeff, et al. "The Role of Informal Learning Spaces in Enhancing Student Engagement with Mathematical Sciences." *The Journal of Mathematical Education in Science and Technology*, vol. 48, no. 4, 2017, pp. 587-602. *Taylor Francis Online*, www.tandfonline.com/pp/waldock _rowlett_7.pdf.

American Psychological Association (APA) Style

WHAT IS UNIQUE ABOUT APA STYLE?

Researchers in many areas of the social sciences and related fields generally follow APA documentation procedures. Although you'll encounter page numbers in the in-text citations for direct quotations in APA documents, you're less likely to find direct quotations overall. Generally, researchers in the social sciences are less interested in the specific language or words used to report research findings than they are in the results or conclusions. Therefore, social science researchers are more likely to paraphrase information from sources than to quote information.

Additionally, in-text documentation in the APA system requires that you include the date of publication for research. This is a striking distinction from the MLA system. Social science research that was conducted fifty years ago may not be as useful as research conducted two years ago, so it's important to cite the date of the source in the text of your argument. Imagine how different the results would be for a study of the effects of violence in video games on youth twenty years ago versus a study conducted last year. Findings from twenty years ago probably have very little bearing on the world of today and would not reflect the same video game content as today's games. Including the date of research publication as part of the in-text citation allows readers to quickly evaluate the currency, and therefore the appropriateness, of the research you reference. Learn more about the *Publication Manual of the American Psychological Association* at www.apastyle.org.

IN-TEXT CITATIONS IN APA STYLE

When sources are cited in the text, APA style calls for a parenthetical reference at the end of a sentence or at the end of the information being cited (if in the middle of a sentence). The author's name and the year of publication are included in parentheses, separated by a comma, and then the end-of-sentence punctuation appears after the parenthetical reference. Page numbers are only included for direct quotations.

> The frequency with which customers ordered dessert at restaurants can be correlated with the BMI of the waitstaff (Döring & Wansink, 2017).

1. Paraphrase from article
2. Last name of author(s)
3. Year of publication

Often, the author's name is mentioned in the sentence, and then the year is listed in parentheses right after the author's name.

> According to Döring and Wansink (2017), the frequency with which customers ordered dessert at restaurants can be correlated with the BMI of the waitstaff.

1. Name of author(s) mentioned in the sentence
2. Year of publication listed in parentheses directly following author's name
3. Paraphrase from article

REFERENCE PAGE CITATIONS IN APA STYLE

The citations list at the end of an academic paper in APA style is called a References page. Citations are listed on the References page in alphabetical order by the authors' last names.

> Döring, T., & Wansink, B. (2017). The waiter's weight. *Environment and Behavior, 49*(2), 192–214.

1. The author's name is listed first, with the last name preceding first and middle initials. Only the last name is spelled out, and the initials are followed by periods.
2. The year directly follows the name, listed in parentheses and followed by a period outside the parentheses.
3. Article titles and book chapters are listed with no punctuation other than a period at the end. Only the first word in the title and any proper nouns are capitalized. If there is a colon in the title, the first word after the colon should also be capitalized.
4. Journal titles appear in italics, and all words are capitalized except articles and prepositions (unless they are the first words). A comma follows a journal title.
5. The volume number follows the title, also in italics. If there is an issue number, it is listed in parentheses immediately following the volume number, but not in italics. This is followed by a comma.
6. Inclusive page numbers appear at the end, followed by a period.

Citing Different Types of Sources in APA Style

Comparison of different kinds of sources in APA style

Type of Source	Example of Reference Page Entry	Notes
Book	Davies, A., & Tollervey, K. (2013). *The style of coworking: Contemporary shared workspaces*. Prestel Verlag.	In APA, multiple authors are linked with an ampersand (&).
Book chapter	Ludvigsen, S., & Arnseth, H. C. (2017). Computer-supported collaborative learning. In E. Duval, M. Sharples, & R. Sutherland (Eds.), *Technology enhanced learning* (pp. 47–58). Springer International Publishing.	Be sure to list both the book chapter and the title of the book when citing a chapter from an edited collection.
Scholarly journal article	Waldock, J., Rowlett, P., Cornock, C., Robinson, M., & Bartholomew, H. (2017). The role of informal learning spaces in enhancing student engagement with mathematical sciences. *The Journal of Mathematical Education in Science and Technology, 48*(4), 587–602.	In APA, the journal number is italicized with the journal title, but the issue number (in parentheses) is not.
Magazine or newspaper article	Goel, V. (2015, April 2). Office space is hard to find for newcomers. *The New York Times*, F2.	Periodical articles can differ in print and online, so be sure to cite where you found your version of the article.
Website	Goodloe, A. (2017). TIPS—composing and framing video interviews. *Digital Writing 101*. digitalwriting101.net/content/composing-and-framing-video-interviews/	
Website with no individual author listed	Sage One. (2014, July 10). Eight ideas for designing a more collaborative workspace [Web log post]. Microsoft. http://blogs.microsoft.com/	When no author is listed for a web-based source, you can begin the citation with the title of the article or site. If an organization or some other entity is sponsoring the article (as in this case), that can be listed as author.

SAMPLE APA REFERENCE PAGE

References

Davies, A., & Tollervey, K. (2013). *The style of coworking: Contemporary shared workspaces*. Prestel Verlag.

Goel, V. (2015, April 2). Office space is hard to find for newcomers. *The New York Times*, F2.

Goodloe, A. (2017). TIPS—composing and framing video interviews. *Digital Writing 101*. digitalwriting101.net /content/composing-and-framing-video-interviews/

Ludvigsen, S., & Arnseth, H. C. (2017). Computer-supported collaborative learning. In E. Duval, M. Sharples, & R. Sutherland (Eds.), *Technology enhanced learning* (pp. 47–58). Springer International Publishing.

Sage One. (2014, July 10). Eight ideas for designing a more collaborative workspace [Web log post]. Microsoft. http://blogs.microsoft.com/

Waldock, J., Rowlett, P., Cornock, C., Robinson, M., & Bartholomew, H. (2017). The role of informal learning spaces in enhancing student engagement with mathematical sciences. *The Journal of Mathematical Education in Science and Technology, 48*(4), 587–602.

Council of Science Editors (CSE) Style

WHAT IS UNIQUE ABOUT CSE STYLE?

As the name suggests, the CSE documentation system is most prevalent among disciplines of the natural sciences, although many of the applied fields of the sciences, like engineering and medicine, rely on their own documentation systems. As with the other systems described here, CSE requires writers to document all materials derived from sources. Unlike MLA or APA, however, CSE allows multiple methods for in-text citations, corresponding to alternative forms of the reference page at the end of research reports. The three styles—**Citation-Sequence**, **Citation-Name**, and **Name-Year**—are used by different publications. In this book, we introduce you to the Name-Year system.

For more detailed information on CSE documentation, you can consult the latest edition of *Scientific Style and Format: The CSE Manual for Authors, Editors, and Publishers*, and you can learn more about the Council of Science Editors at its website: http://www.councilscienceeditors.org.

IN-TEXT CITATIONS IN CSE STYLE

When sources are cited in the text, CSE style calls for a parenthetical reference directly following the relevant information. The author's name and the year of publication are included in parentheses with no other punctuation.

> The frequency with which customers ordered dessert at restaurants can be correlated with the BMI of the waitstaff (Döring and Wansink 2017).

1. Paraphrase from article
2. Last name of author(s)
3. Year of publication

REFERENCE PAGE CITATIONS IN CSE STYLE

The citations list at the end of an academic paper in CSE style is called a References page. Citations are listed on the References page in alphabetical order by the authors' last names.

> Döring T, Wansink B. 2017. The waiter's weight. Envir and Behav. 49:192-214.

1. The author's name is listed first, with the full last name preceding the first and middle initials. No punctuation separates elements of the name.
2. The year directly follows the name, followed by a period.

3. Article titles and book chapters are listed with no punctuation other than a period at the end. Only the first word in the title and any proper nouns are capitalized. If there is a colon in the title, the first word after the colon should not be capitalized.

4. Journal titles are often abbreviated, and all words are capitalized. A period follows the journal title.

5. The volume number follows the title. If there is an issue number, it is listed in parentheses following the volume number, but not in italics. This is followed by a colon. No space appears after the colon.

6. Inclusive page numbers appear at the end, followed by a period.

Citing Different Types of Sources in CSE Style
Comparison of different kinds of sources in CSE style

Type of Source	Example of Reference Page Entry	Notes
Book	Davies A, Tollervey K. 2013. The style of coworking: contemporary shared workspaces. Munich (Germany): Prestel Verlag. 159 p.	Listing the number of pages is optional in CSE, but useful.
Book chapter	Ludvigsen S, Arnseth HC. 2017. Computer-supported collaborative learning. In: Duval E, Sharples M, Sutherland R, editors. Technology enhanced learning. Gewerbestrasse (Switzerland): Springer International Publishing. p. 47-58.	
Scholarly journal article	Waldock J, Rowlett P, Cornock C, Robinson M, Bartholomew, H. 2017. The role of informal learning spaces in enhancing student engagement with mathematical sciences. Journ of Math Ed in Sci and Tech. 48(4):587-602.	Some journal titles in CSE are abbreviated.
Magazine or newspaper article	Goel V. 2015 Apr 2. Office space is hard to find for newcomers. New York Times (National Ed.). Sect. F:2 (col. 1).	
Website	Goodloe A. 2017. Tips — composing and framing video interviews. Digital Writing 101; [accessed 2018 Jan 10]. http://digitalwriting101.net/content/composing-and-framing-video-interviews/.	CSE calls for the exact URL and an access date for web-based sources.
Website with no individual author listed	Sage One. 2014. Eight ideas for designing a more collaborative workspace [blog]. Microsoft at Work. [accessed 2015 Apr 2]. Available from http://blogs.microsoft.com/work/2014/07/10/eight-ideas-for-designing-a-more-collaborative-workspace/.	

SAMPLE CSE REFERENCE PAGE

References

Davies A, Tollervey K. 2013. The style of coworking: contemporary shared workspaces. Munich (Germany): Prestel Verlag. 159 p.

Goel V. 2015 Apr 2. Office space is hard to find for newcomers. New York Times (National Ed.). Sect. F:2 (col. 1).

Goodloe A. 2017. Tips—composing and framing video interviews. Digital Writing 101; [accessed 2018 Jan 10]. http://digitalwriting101.net/content/composing-and-framing -video-interviews/.

Ludvigsen S, Arnseth HC. 2017. Computer-supported collaborative learning. In: Duval E, Sharples M, Sutherland R, editors. Technology enhanced learning. Gewerbestrasse (Switzerland): Springer International Publishing. p. 47-58.

Sage One. 2014. Eight ideas for designing a more collaborative workspace [blog]. Microsoft at Work. [accessed 2015 Apr 2]. Available from http://blogs.microsoft.com/work/2014/07/10 /eight-ideas-for-designing-a-more-collaborative-workspace/.

Waldock J, Rowlett P, Cornock C, Robinson M, Bartholomew H. 2017. The role of informal learning spaces in enhancing student engagement with mathematical sciences. Journ of Math Ed in Sci and Tech. 48(4):587-602.

Other Common Documentation Styles

Many disciplines have their own documentation styles, and some are used more commonly than others. The following chart lists a few of the most popular.

Name of Citation Style	Disciplines	Website
American Chemical Society (ACS)	Chemistry and Physical Sciences	http://pubs.acs.org/series/styleguide
American Institute of Physics (AIP)	Physics	http://publishing.aip.org/authors
American Mathematical Society (AMS)	Mathematics	http://www.ams.org/publications/authors
American Medical Association (AMA)	Medicine	http://www.amamanualofstyle.com/
American Political Science Association (APSA)	Political Science	http://www.apsanet.org/Portals/54/files/APSAStyleManual2006.pdf
American Sociological Association (ASA)	Sociology	http://www.asanet.org/documents/teaching/pdfs/Quick_Tips_for_ASA_Style.pdf
Associated Press Stylebook (AP Style)	Journalism	https://www.apstylebook.com/
Bluebook style	Law, Legal Studies	https://www.legalbluebook.com/
Chicago Manual of Style (CMoS)	History and other humanities disciplines	http://www.chicagomanualofstyle.org/
Institute of Electrical and Electronics Engineers (IEEE)	Engineering	https://www.ieee.org/documents/style_manual.pdf
Linguistic Society of America (LSA)	Linguistics	http://www.linguisticsociety.org/files/style-sheet.pdf
Modern Humanities Research Association (MHRA)	Humanities	http://www.mhra.org.uk/Publications/Books/StyleGuide/StyleGuideV3.pdf

TRACKING RESEARCH

There are many useful, free digital tools online that can help you track your research and sources. Three of the best are personalized research-tracking tools and social applications that enable you to find additional resources through other users of the application:

- **Diigo (https://www.diigo.com/)** Diigo is a social bookmarking application that solves two dilemmas faced by many writers. First, you can access all of the bookmarks that you save in a browser on multiple devices. Additionally, you can tag your sources and share them with others. That means you can search using tags (not very different from searching with key words in a database) and find other sources that users of Diigo have tagged with the same words and phrases that you have chosen.

- **Zotero (https://www.zotero.org/)**   Zotero is a robust research tool that helps you organize, cite, and share sources with others. You can install Zotero into your web browser and quickly save and annotate sources that you're looking at online. Zotero can help you generate citations, annotated bibliographies, and reference lists from the sources that you have saved.

- **Mendeley (http://www.mendeley.com/)**   Similar to Zotero, Mendeley is a free reference manager and academic social network that allows you to read and annotate PDFs on any device.

Your school may also have licenses for proprietary tools such as RefWorks and EndNote, which are also very useful research-tracking applications. Most of these applications can help you generate citations and reference lists as well. However, you need to understand how a documentation style works in order to check what is generated from any citation builder. For example, if you save the title of a journal article as "Increased pizza consumption leads to temporary euphoria but higher long-term cholesterol levels," a citation builder will not automatically change the capitalization if you need to generate a citation in MLA format. You have to be smarter than the application you use.

ACKNOWLEDGMENTS

Text Credits

Barbara L. Allen. "Environmental Justice, Local Knowledge, and After-Disaster Planning in New Orleans." From *Technology in Society,* Volume 29, Issue 2, April 2007, pp. 153–59. Copyright © 2007 Elsevier. Republished with the permission of Elsevier Science and Technology Journals; permission conveyed through Copyright Clearance Center, Inc.

Isabel Allende. "Writing as an Act of Hope." Copyright © 1989 by Isabel Allende. Used with permission.

Gustavo Arellano. "Taco USA: How Mexican Food Became More American Than Apple Pie." From *Reason Magazine,* June 2012. © 2012 Gustavo Arellano. Reproduced with the permission of the author.

Aziz Aris and Samuel Leblanc. "Maternal and Fetal Exposure to Pesticides Associated to Genetically Modified Foods in Eastern Townships of Quebec, Canada." From *Reproductive Toxicology,* Volume 31, Issue 4, May 2011, pp. 528–33. Copyright © 2011 Elsevier. Republished with the permission of Elsevier Science and Technology Journals; permission conveyed through Copyright Clearance Center, Inc.

Jimmy Santiago Baca. "Coming into Language." From PEN America, March 3, 2014, https://pen.org/coming-into-language/.

David Bartholomae. "Writing with Teachers: A Conversation with Peter Elbow." From *College Composition and Communication,* Volume 46, No. 1, February 1995, pp. 62–71. Copyright © 1995 by the National Council of Teachers of English. Reprinted with permission.

Mike Brotherton. Excerpt from "Hubble Space Telescope Spies Galaxy/Black Hole Evolution in Action." From press release on mikebrotherton.com, June 2, 2008. Reproduced with the permission of the author.

Mike Brotherton, Wil van Breugel, S. A. Stanford, R. J. Smith, B. J. Boyle, Lance Miller, T. Shanks, S. M. Croom, and Alexei V. Filippenko. Excerpt from "A Spectacular Poststarburst Quasar." From *Astrophysical Journal,* August 1, 1999. Copyright © 1999 The American Astronomical Society. Reproduced with the permission of the authors.

Nicholas Carr. "Is Google Making Us Stupid?" *Atlantic Magazine,* July/August 2008. Copyright © 2008 The Atlantic Media Co. All rights reserved. Distributed by Tribune Content Agency, LLC. Reprinted by permission.

Wanda Cassidy, Karen Brown, and Margaret Jackson. "'Under the Radar': Educators and Cyberbullying in Schools." From *School Psychology International,* Volume 33, Issue 5, October 2012, pp. 520–32. Copyright © 2012 by the Authors. Reprinted by permission of SAGE Publications, Ltd.

Andrew J. Cherlin. Excerpt from *The Marriage-Go-Round: The State of Marriage and the Family in America Today* by Andrew J. Cherlin. Copyright © 2009 by Andrew J. Cherlin. Reprinted by permission of Alfred A. Knopf, an imprint of the Knopf Doubleday Publishing Group, a division of Penguin Random House LLC. All rights reserved. Any third-party use of this material, outside of this publication, is prohibited. Interested third parties must apply directly to Penguin Random House LLC for permission.

Inimai M. Chettiar. "The Many Causes of America's Decline in Crime." From *Atlantic Magazine,* February 11, 2015. Copyright © 2015 The Atlantic Media Co. All rights reserved. Distributed by Tribune Content Agency, LLC. Reprinted by permission.

Dwight Conquergood. "Lethal Theatre: Performance, Punishment, and the Death Penalty." From *Theatre Journal,* Volume 54, No. 3, October 2002, pp. 339–67. Copyright © 2002 Johns Hopkins University Press. Reprinted with the permission of Johns Hopkins University Press.

EBSCO Health. "Sample Discharge Orders." From www.ebscohost.com. Reproduced with permission from EBSCO Information Services.

Peter Elbow. "Being a Writer vs. Being an Academic: A Conflict in Goals." From *College Composition and Communication,* Volume 46, No. 1, February 1995, pp. 72–83. Copyright © 1995 by the National Council of Teachers of English. Reprinted with permission.

Gavin J. Fairbairn and Alex M. Carson. "Writing about Nursing Research: A Storytelling Approach." From *Nurse Researcher,* Volume 10, No. 1, October 2002, pp. 7–14. Copyright © 2002. Reproduced by permission of R C N Publishing Co. in the format Educational/Instructional Program via Copyright Clearance Center.

F. Elizabeth Gray, Lisa Emerson, and Bruce MacKay. "Meeting the Demands of the Workplace: Science Students and Written Skills." From *Journal of Science Education and Technology,* Volume 14, No. 4, December 2005, pp. 425–35. Copyright © 2005 Springer. Republished with permission of Springer Science and Bus Media BV; permission conveyed through Copyright Clearance Center, Inc.

Daniel Gregorowius, Petra Lindemann-Matthies, and Markus Huppenbauer. "Ethical Discourse on the Use of Genetically Modified Crops: A Review of Academic

Publications in the Fields of Ecology and Environmental Ethics." From *Journal of Agricultural & Environmental Ethics,* Volume 25, Issue 3, June 2012, pp. 265–93. Copyright © 2011 Springer Science and Bus Media BV. Republished with permission of Springer Science and Bus Media BV; permission conveyed through Copyright Clearance Center, Inc.

Arthur L. Greil, Kathleen Slauson-Blevins, and Julia McQuillan. "The Experience of Infertility: A Review of Recent Literature." From *Sociology of Health & Illness,* Volume 32, Issue 1. © 2010 by Blackwell Publishing Ltd. Reproduced with permission of John Wiley and Sons Inc.; permission conveyed through Copyright Clearance Center, Inc.

Barbara Bradley Hagerty. "Inside a Psychopath's Brain: The Sentencing Debate." From NPR news report originally published on NPR.org on June 30, 2010. © 2010 National Public Radio, Inc. Used with the permission of NPR. Any unauthorized duplication is strictly prohibited.

Marissa A. Harrison and Jennifer C. Shortall. "Women and Men in Love: Who Really Feels It and Says It First?" From *Journal of Social Psychology,* Volume 151, No. 6, 2011, pp. 727–36. Copyright © 2011 Routledge. Reprinted by permission of the publisher, Taylor & Francis Ltd., http://www.tandfonline.com.

Dale Jacobs. "More Than Words: Comics as a Means of Teaching Multiple Literacies." From *English Journal,* Volume 96, Issue 3, January 2007. Copyright © 2007 by the National Council of Teachers of English. Reprinted with permission.

Sophia Kerby. "The Top 10 Most Startling Facts about People of Color and Criminal Justice in the United States." Center for American Progress, March 13, 2012. This article was created and published by the Center for American Progress (www.americanprogress.org).

Charles Kerns and Kenneth Ko. "Exploring Happiness and Performance at Work." From *Leadership & Organizational Management Journal.* Copyright © 2009. Reproduced with the permission of the authors.

Patrick J. Kiger. "How Cooking Has Changed Us." *National Geographic,* October 17, 2014, http://channel.nationalgeographic.com/eat-the-story-of-food/articles/how-cooking-has-changed-us/. Copyright © 2014. Reprinted by permission of National Geographic Creative.

Stephen King. "Reading to Write." From *On Writing: A Memoir of the Craft* by Stephen King. Copyright © 2000 by Stephen King. Reprinted with the permission of Scribner, a division of Simon & Schuster, Inc. All rights reserved.

Aimee C. Mapes. "Two Vowels Together: On the Wonderfully Insufferable Experiences of Literacy." From *College Composition and Communication,* Volume 67, No. 4, June 2016, pp. 686–92. Copyright © 2016 by the National Council of Teachers of English. Reprinted with permission.

Donatella Marazziti and Domenico Canale. "Hormonal Changes When Falling in Love." From *Psychoneuroendocrinology,* Volume 29, Issue 7, August 2004, pp. 931–36. Copyright © 2004 Elsevier. Republished with the permission of Elsevier Science and Technology Journals; permission conveyed through Copyright Clearance Center, Inc.

Joshua Marquis. "The Myth of Innocence." From *Journal of Criminal Law & Criminology,* Volume 95, No. 2, Winter 2005, pp. 501–21. Copyright © 2005 by Northwestern University School of Law. Reprinted by permission.

Margaret Shandor Miles, Diane Holditch-Davis, Suzanne Thoyre, and Linda Beeber. "Rural African-American Mothers Parenting Prematurely Born Infants: An Ecological Systems Perspective." From *Newborn and Infant Nursing Reviews,* Volume 5, Issue 3, September 2005, pp. 142–48. Copyright © 2005 Elsevier. Republished with the permission of Elsevier Science and Technology Journals; permission conveyed through Copyright Clearance Center, Inc.

Warren E. Milteer Jr. "The Strategies of Forbidden Love: Family across Racial Boundaries in Nineteenth-Century North Carolina." From *Journal of Social History,* Volume 47, Issue 3, Spring 2014, pp. 612–26, published by George Mason University. Copyright © 2014 Oxford University Press. Republished with permission of Oxford University Press; permission conveyed through Copyright Clearance Center, Inc.

Myra Moses. "IEP" class materials and "Lesson Plan" class materials. Reproduced with permission of the author.

Charles Noussair, Stéphane Robin, and Bernard Ruffieux. "Do Consumers Really Refuse to Buy Genetically Modified Food?" From *Economic Journal,* Volume 114, No. 492, January 2004, pp. 102–20. Copyright © 2004 Royal Economic Society. Reproduced with the permission of John Wiley & Sons, Inc.

Kalervo Oberg. Excerpt from "Cultural Shock: Adjustment to New Cultural Environments." From *Practical Anthropology,* 1960, Volume 7. Copyright © 1960 American Association of Missiology. Reproduced with permission.

Abigail Pesta. "I Survived Prison: What Really Happens behind Bars." From *Marie Claire,* March 19, 2009. © 2009 Hearst Communications. Reproduced with permission.

Cara O. Peters, Jane B. Thomas, and Richard Morris. "Looking for Love on Craigslist: An Examination of

Gender Differences in Self-Marketing Online." From *Journal of Marketing Development and Competitiveness*, Volume 7, No. 3, 2013. © 2013 North American Business Press. Reproduced with permission.

Michael Pollan. "Why Cook?" From *Cooked: A Natural History of Transformation* by Michael Pollan. Copyright © 2013 by Michael Pollan. Reprinted by permission of Penguin Press, an imprint of Penguin Publishing Group, a division of Penguin Random House LLC. All rights reserved. Any third-party use of this material, outside of this publication, is prohibited. Interested third parties must apply directly to Penguin Random House LLC for permission.

Brian Powell and Catherine Bolzendahl. "Counted Out: Same-Sex Relations and Americans' Definitions of Family." Copyright © 2010 by the American Sociological Association. Reproduced by permission of Russell Sage Foundation in the format Educational/Instructional Program via Copyright Clearance Center.

Kevin Rathunde and Mihaly Csikszentmihalyi. "Middle School Students' Motivation and Quality of Experience: A Comparison of Montessori and Traditional School Environments." From *American Journal of Education*, Volume 111, Issue 3, May 2005. Copyright © 2005 University of Chicago Press. Reproduced with permission.

Kevin Rathunde and Mihaly Csikszentmihalyi. "The Social Context of Middle Schools: Teachers, Friends, and Activities in Montessori and Traditional School Environments." From *Elementary School Journal*, Volume 106, No. 1, September 2005, pp. 59–79. Copyright © 2005 by the University of Chicago. Reproduced with permission.

Gary Ritchison. "Hunting Behavior, Territory Quality, and Individual Quality of American Kestrels (*Falco sparverius*)." From Eastern Kentucky University web page. Reproduced by permission of the author.

Michael Ruhlman. "No Food Is Healthy. Not Even Kale." From the *Washington Post*, January 17, 2016. © 2016 The Washington Post. All rights reserved. Reproduced with permission and protected by the copyright laws of the United States. The printing, copying, redistribution, or retransmission of this content without express permission is prohibited.

Susan Saulny. "In Strangers' Glances at Family, Tensions Linger." From the *New York Times*, October 13, 2011.

© 2011 The New York Times. All rights reserved. Reproduced with permission and protected by the copyright laws of the United States. The printing, copying, redistribution, or retransmission of this content without express permission is prohibited.

Sherry Seethaler and Marcia Linn. "Genetically Modified Food in Perspective: An Inquiry-Based Curriculum to Help Middle School Students Make Sense of Tradeoffs." From *International Journal of Science Education*, Volume 26, Issue 14, November 2004. Copyright © 2004. Reprinted by permission of the publisher, Taylor & Francis Ltd. (http://www.tandfonline.com).

Martin E. P. Seligman, Tracy A. Steen, Nansook Park, and Christopher Peterson. "Positive Psychology Progress: Empirical Validation of Interventions." From *American Psychologist*, Volume 60, No. 5, July–August 2005, pp. 410–21. Copyright © 2005 by the American Psychological Association. Reproduced with permission.

Jack Solomon. "Masters of Desire: The Culture of American Advertising." From *The Signs of Our Time: Semiotics, the Hidden Messages of Environments, Objects, and Cultural Images* by Jack Solomon. Copyright © 1988 by Jack Solomon. Reprinted by permission of Tarcher, an imprint of Penguin Publishing Group, a division of Penguin Random House LLC. All rights reserved. Any third-party use of this material, outside of this publication, is prohibited. Interested third parties must apply directly to Penguin Random House LLC for permission.

Benedikt Till and Peter Vitouch. "Capital Punishment in Films: The Impact of Death Penalty Portrayals on Viewers' Mood and Attitude toward Capital Punishment." From *International Journal of Public Opinion Research*, Volume 24, Issue 3, Autumn 2012. © 2012 Oxford University Press. International Journal of Public Opinion Research by World Association for Public Opinion Research. Republished with permission of Oxford University Press; permission conveyed through Copyright Clearance Center, Inc.

Susan K. Whitbourne. "The Myth of the Helicopter Parent." From *Psychology Today, Fulfillment at Any Age* blog, posted February 23, 2013. Reproduced with permission of the author.

WPA Outcomes Statement. Ratified in July 2014. Reproduced with permission by The Council of Writing Program Administrators.

Index

683

Aris, Aziz, and Leblanc, Samuel, "Maternal and Fetal Exposure to Pesticides Associated to Genetically Modified Foods in Eastern Townships of Quebec, Canada," 557–69

Aristotle, 60–61

artistic proofs, 60

artistic texts, 167, 180–81

assumptions, understanding, 67–68

audience
    in the applied fields, 295
    as element of rhetorical contexts, 51–53
    for press release, 124–26
    primary and secondary, 46
    and reading rhetorically, 49
    rhetorical contexts and, 52

author
    as element of rhetorical contexts, 51–53
    reading rhetorically, 49
    and rhetorical context, 46

B

Baca, Jimmy Santiago, "Coming into Language," 599–603

Bahls, Patrick (mathematics), on genres, 27 ○

Bartholomae, David, and Elbow, Peter, "Writing with Teachers: A Conversation with Peter Elbow; Being a Writer vs. Being an Academic: A Conflict in Goals," 611–23

Baumgartner, Jody (political science), on the writing process, 26 ○

Beeber, Linda. See "Rural African-American Mothers Parenting Prematurely Born Infants: An Ecological Systems Perspective" (Miles et al.)

bias, avoiding, 195, 244

bibliography, annotated
    in academic research, 101–2
    in literature review, 214

Bieda, Michaela (student), "My Journey to Writing," 40–43

Bluebook style, 676

Bolzendahl, Catherine. See Powell, Brian; Bolzendahl, Catherine; Geist, Claudia; Steelman, Lala Carr, "Changing Counts, Counting Change: Toward a More Inclusive Definition of Family"

Brotherton, Mike (astronomy)
    on argument and choosing the "right" side, 69 ○
    on audience for a press release, 126
    on how accuracy trumps strong writing, 130
    "Hubble Space Telescope Spies Galaxy/Black Hole Evolution in Action," from, 125–26

"Spectacular Poststarburst Quasar, A" (Brotherton et al.), 129–30
    on writing for different audiences, 123
    on writing in the sciences, 123

Bush, George H. W., "Letter to Saddam Hussein," 53–55

business writing
    business plan, 317–25
    memorandum, 314–16
    plans and proposals, 317

C

Canale, Domenico. See Marazziti, Donatella, and Canale, Domenico, "Hormonal Changes When Falling in Love"

"Capital Punishment in Films: The Impact of Death Penalty Portrayals on Viewers' Mood and Attitude toward Capital Punishment" (Till and Vitouch), 457–68

Carr, Lala. See Powell, Brian; Bolzendahl, Catherine; Geist, Claudia; Steelman, Lala Carr, "Changing Counts, Counting Change: Toward a More Inclusive Definition of Family"

Carr, Nicholas, "Is Google Making Us Stupid?," 604–10

Carson, Alex. See Fairbairn, Gavin, and Carson, Alex, "Writing about Nursing Research: A Storytelling Approach"

Cassidy, K., K. Brown, and M. Jackson, excerpts from "Under the Radar: Educators and Cyberbullying in Schools," 189–90, 199, 201

characters, in student essay, 41

charts, tables, and figures, 202–4, 254

Cherlin, Andrew, "How American Family Life Is Different," 342–46

Chettiar, Inimai, "The Many Causes of America's Decline in Crime: A New Report Finds That Locking Up More Offenders Isn't Making People Any Safer—and May Even Be Counterproductive," 423–28

Chicago Manual of Style (CMS), 170–71, 676

Chopin, Kate, "The Story of an Hour," 155, 157–59

citations, reasons for making, 663–64

claims
    hedging, 168–69, 208
    making, 61–62

close reading
    content/form-response grid, 154–56
    in the humanities, 144–45
    responding to others' interpretations, 159–60
    strategies for, 154–59

college, three stages of transition to, 7

"Genetically Modified Food in Perspective: An Inquiry-Based Curriculum to Help Middle School Students Make Sense of Tradeoffs" (Seethaler and Linn), 570–87

genres
  in the academic disciplines, 120
  analyzing, 121
  choosing, in the applied fields, 295–98
  in the humanities, 172–80
  memoir, 29
  in the natural sciences, 254–79
  of reflective writing, 29
  in the social sciences, 211–38
  understanding, 48–49
Gomperts, Jack (student), "Evaluating Hydration Levels in High School Athletes," 104–13
Google and identifying search terms, 85–88
Gray, F. Elizabeth; Emerson, Lisa; and MacKay, Bruce, "Meeting the Demands of the Workplace: Science Students and Written Skills," 641–52
Gregorowius, Daniel; Lindemann-Matthies, Petra; and Huppenbauer, Markus, "Ethical Discourse on the Use of Genetically Modified Crops: A Review of Academic Publications in the Fields of Ecology and Environmental Ethics," 518–39

H

Hagerty, Barbara Bradley, "Inside a Psychopath's Brain: The Sentencing Debate," 417–19
"Happiness in Everyday Life: The Uses of Experience Sampling," excerpts from (Csikszentmihalyi and Hunter), 205–6, 212–13, 216
Harrison, Marissa A., and Shortall, Jennifer C., "Women and Men in Love: Who Really Feels It and Says It First?," 384–90
health fields
  allied health professions, 296
  in the applied fields, 296–98
  discharge instructions, 300–303
  nursing, 296–97
  scholarly research report, 297–300
  writing for, in the applied fields, 296–98
hedging claims, 168–69, 208
Hemingway, Ernest, *Death in the Afternoon,* 140
higher education, choices of schools, 4–5
Holditch-Davis, Diane. *See* "Rural African-American Mothers Parenting Prematurely Born Infants: An Ecological Systems Perspective" (Miles et al.)
Holtzhauser, Timothy, "Rhetoric of a 1943 War Bonds Ad," 74–78

"How American Family Life Is Different" (Cherlin), 342–46
"How Cooking Has Changed Us" (Kiger), 505–7
"Hubble Space Telescope Spies Galaxy/Black Hole Evolution in Action," from (Brotherton), 125–26
humanities
  American Council of Learned Societies, 139
  asking "why," 162
  conventions of writing
    essays, five-paragraph, 165–66
    learning from peer and others' writings, 160–61
    open-ended questions, 163
    paragraphs and transitions, 167
    research questions, developing, 161–63
    thesis statements, 161–65
    titles and subtitles, 166
    why, what, and *how* questions, 163
  documentation of sources, 170–72
  genres of writing in
    artistic texts, 180–82
    textual interpretation, 172–80
  language conventions
    active voice versus passive voice, 167–68
    descriptive and rhetorical language, 167
    hedging of claims, 168–69
  references conventions
    Chicago Manual of Style (CMS), 170–71
    focus/stance, establishing, 169–70
    introduction and citations in, 169–70
    Modern Language Association (MLA), 170
    other scholars, incorporating works of, 169
    scholarly writing, analyzing, 171–72
  research in
    close reading, 144–59
    content/form-response grid, 154
    images, observing and interpreting, 143–44
    interpretations, responding to, 159–60
    role of theory in, 144
    texts as primary source for, 142–43
  scholars in, 9, 11
  structural conventions, 161, 166–67
  texts and meaning, 140–41
"Hunting Behavior, Territory Quality, and Individual Quality of American Kestrels (*Falco sparverius*)" (Ritchison), 272–79
Huppenbauer, Markus. *See* Gregorowius, Daniel; Lindemann-Matthies, Petra; and Huppenbauer, Markus, "Ethical Discourse on the Use of Genetically Modified Crops: A Review of Academic Publications in the Fields of Ecology and Environmental Ethics"

hypotheses
   defined, 62
   in the natural sciences, 246–47, 255–56
   in the social sciences, 189–90

I

ideas
   discovering through composing, 25–27
   main idea, 31
   mapping, 26
   tools for composing/invention, 25–26
images, observing and interpreting, 143
inartistic proofs in argument, 60, 61
individualized education plan (IEP), 308–13
"Inside a Psychopath's Brain: The Sentencing Debate"
   (Hagerty), 417–19
Institute of Electrical and Electronics Engineers (IEEE),
   676
institutional review boards (IRB), 196, 251
"In Strangers' Glances at Family, Tensions Linger"
   (Saulny), 364–67
interdisciplinary fields, 242
in-text documentation
   American Psychological Association (APA) style, 209,
      669–72
   Council of Science Editors, 673
   documentation in the social sciences, 209
Introduction, Methods, Results, and Discussion
   (IMRaD) format, 122, 197–204, 254, 279
Introduction, Rule, Application, and Conclusion (IRAC)
   format, 328–29
"I" point of view, 30, 32, 40
"Is Google Making Us Stupid?" (Carr), 604–10
issues or topics
   controversial, developing a supported, 102–13
   as element of rhetorical writing, 51–53
   and rhetorical context, 46
"I Survived Prison: What Really Happens behind Bars"
   (Pesta), 430–33
IT industry, writing for, 17–18

J

Jackson, Karen Keaton (writing studies)
   on accidental plagiarism, 99 ◗
   on considering purpose and audience, 46 ◗
   on different kinds of texts, 120 ◗
   on incorporating research to support ideas, 161 ◗
   on transition into college writing, 13 ◗

Jacobs, Dale, "More Than Words: Comics as a Means of
   Teaching Multiple Literacies," 145–53
jargon, in the natural sciences, 254
journals databases, using, 88–91

K

Kapadia, Matt (student), "Evaluation of the Attribution
   Theory," 229–38
Kerby, Sophia, "The Top 10 Most Startling Facts about
   People of Color and Criminal Justice in the United
   States: A Look at the Racial Disparities Inherent
   in Our Nation's Criminal-Justice System," 420–22
Kerns, C., and K. Ko, excerpt from "Exploring
   Happiness and Performance at Work," 190
Kiger, Patrick J., "How Cooking Has Changed Us," 505–7
King, Stephen, "Reading to Write," 592–95
Kish, Zenia (American studies), statement of claim,
   example of, 164
Koniaris, Leonidas G. See Zimmers, Teresa A.; Sheldon,
   Jonathan; Lubarsky, David A.; López-Muñoz,
   Francisco; Waterman, Linda; Weisman, Richard;
   and Koniaris, Leonidas G., "Lethal Injection for
   Execution: Chemical Asphyxiation?"
Kumar, Rubbal (student), "Profile of a Writer: Benu
   Badhan," 16–18

L

lab reports
   IMRaD format, 279–90
   in the natural sciences, 258
Lambrecht, Gena (student), on academic writing, 12 ◗
language, or word choice
   active and passive voices, 167–68
   conventions in different disciplines, 127–28
   descriptive and rhetorical, in the humanities, 167
   humanist views on, 210
   jargon in the natural sciences, 254
language conventions
   in the humanities, 167–69
   in the natural sciences, 254
   in the social sciences, 207–8
LaRue, Michelle (conservation biology), on forming
   study questions, 249–50
law, writing for, 327–28
learning skills and reading rhetorically, 49
Leblanc, Samuel. See Aris, Aziz, and Leblanc, Samuel,
   "Maternal and Fetal Exposure to Pesticides
   Associated to Genetically Modified Foods in
   Eastern Townships of Quebec, Canada"

on thinking about audience, purpose, and form, 122 ⬤

McCurdy, John (history), 139, 140

"Meeting the Demands of the Workplace: Science Students and Written Skills" (Gray et al.), 641–52

Mendeley, online resource manager, 677

metacognition, defined, 28

"Middle School Students' Motivation and Quality of Experience: A Comparison of Montessori and Traditional School Environments," excerpts from (Rathunde and Csikszentmihalyi), 183–84, 193, 194, 195, 200–203, 204, 205–6

Miles, Margaret Shandor, et al., "Rural African-American Mothers Parenting Prematurely Born Infants: An Ecological Systems Perspective," 298–300

Mills, Daniel Chase (student), "The Electricity Monitor Company," 317–25

Milteer, Warren E., Jr., "The Strategies of Forbidden Love: Family across Racial Boundaries in Nineteenth-Century North Carolina," 368–83

mission statements of colleges/universities, 6–7

Modern Humanities Research Association (MHRA), 676

Modern Language Association (MLA), 99–100, 128, 170, 209
    citing different types of sources in, 666
    compared to APA and CSE styles, 664–65
    in-text citations, 665
    sample works cited page, 668
    unique features of, 665
    works cited citations in, 666

"More Than Words: Comics as a Means of Teaching Multiple Literacies" (Jacobs), 145–53

Morris, Jonathan (political science)
    on finding scholarly sources, 92 ⬤
    on the writing process, 26 ⬤

Morris, Richard. *See* Peters, Cara O.; Thomas, Jane B.; and Morris, Richard, "Looking for Love on Craigslist: An Examination of Gender Differences in Self-Marketing Online"

Moses, Myra (educator), lesson plan, 305–8

"Multiple Audiences of George H. W. Bush's Letter to Saddam Hussein, The" (Lopez), 55–57

"My Journey to Writing" (Bieda), 40–43

"Myth of Innocence, The" (Marquis), 481–94

"Myth of the Helicopter Parent, The" (Krauss), 348–49

N

narrative, literacy, 30–32

Natasi, Jonathan (student, translator), "Life May Be Possible on Other Planets," 133–36

natural sciences
    bias, eliminating, 244
    conventions of writing in
        charts and figures, 254
        cooperation and collaboration, 257–58
        detail in writing, 255
        documentation, 256
        jargon in research writing, 254
        objectivity, 253–55
        precision in writing, 256
        recency, 256–57
        replicability, 255–56
    descriptive writing, 245–46
    designing a research study, 249–52
    genres of writing
        Introduction, Methods, Results and Discussion (IMRaD) format, 254
        lab report, 279–90
        observation notebook, 258–70
        research proposal, 271–79
    institutional review board (IRB), 251
    interdisciplinary fields, 242
    language, or word choice, in research papers, 254
    open-ended questions, 248
    other researchers' work, treatment of, 257–58
    references in, 256, 272
    research in
        closed-ended questions, 248
        comparative experiment, 250
        control group, 250
        from description to speculation, 245–49
        designing a research study, 249–52
        hard and soft sciences, 243
        hypotheses, forming, 246–47, 255–56
        institutional review board (IRB), 251
        observation and description, 243–45
        open-ended questions, 248
        publishing, 252
        qualitative data, 244
        replicable and quantifiable methods, 243–44
        results, presenting, 252
        speculative writing, 245–46
        statistical procedures, 249
    scholars in, 9
    scientific method, 241–42
    scientific writing process, 241–42
    structural conventions of research papers, 254
    titles of research papers, 253–54

neutrality, in the social sciences, 195

New Criticism (Formalism) theory, 144

New Historicism theory, 144

newspapers as popular sources, 93

"No Food Is Healthy. Not Even Kale." (Ruhlman), 507–9

Noussair, Charles; Robin, Stéphane; and Ruffieux, Bernard, "Do Consumers Really Refuse to Buy Genetically Modified Food?," 540–55

nursing field, writing for, 296–97

O

Oberg, Kalervo, from "Cultural Shock: Adjustment to New Cultural Environments," 186–89

objectivity, 195, 253–54

O'Brien, William (student), "Effects of Sleep Deprivation: A Literature Review," 218–26

observation
in academic disciplines 121–22
and description, 244
and interpretation, 142
in natural sciences 244–45
notebook, 258–70

open-ended questions, 163, 248

Oquendo, Nichelle (student), peer review feedback of sample rough draft, 23–25

organization of writing, 127

others' experiences, writing about, 228

P

paragraphs and transitions, 167

paraphrasing, 96–97, 210

Park, Nansook. *See* Seligman, Martin E. P.; Steen, Tracy A.; Park, Nansook; and Peterson, Christopher, "Positive Psychology Progress: Empirical Validation of Interventions"

passive voice, 47, 207–8

pathos, appeals to, 60

peer review
in idea mapping stage, 26
of student's literacy narrative, 22–25

peer-reviewed articles, 88

personal experiences, writing about, 65, 227–28

personal investment, in academic research, 82

Pesta, Abigail, "I Survived Prison: What Really Happens behind Bars," 430–33

Peters, Cara O.; Thomas, Jane B.; and Morris, Richard, "Looking for Love on Craigslist: An Examination of Gender Differences in Self-Marketing Online," 391–97, 398–413

Peterson, Christopher. *See* Seligman, Martin E. P.; Steen, Tracy A.; Park, Nansook; and Peterson,

Christopher, "Positive Psychology Progress: Empirical Validation of Interventions"

plagiarism, avoiding, 98–99

Pollan, Michael, "Why Cook?," 510–17

position, qualifying, in argument, 69

Postcolonialism theory, 144

Powell, Brian; Bolzendahl, Catherine; Geist, Claudia; Steelman, Lala Carr, "Changing Counts, Counting Change: Toward a More Inclusive Definition of Family," 350–63

press releases, 125–26

prewriting/invention, 25

primary audience, 46

primary sources for academic research, 83

problems
identifying, in applied fields, 293
posed in an essay, 41

Proctor, Sian (geology), on the different specialties of geological studies, 240–41

"Profile of a Writer: Benu Badhan" (Kumar), 16–18

programming code, 17

proofs in argument, inartistic and artistic, 60

PsycINFO database, 89–90

Publication Manual of the American Psychological Association (APA), 100, 128, 170, 206, 209, 256, 669–72

Q

qualitative research methods, 193–94, 243–44

quantitative research methods, 191–93, 243–44

Queer Theory, 144

questions
developing, 293
why, what, and *how* questions, 163

quoting
in academic research, 97–98
others' interpretations of texts, 160
in the social sciences, 210
summarizing and paraphrasing others' writing, 210

R

Rathunde, Kevin (social sciences), 183
on conditions for well-being and connection, 184
on having multiple perspectives on a question, 192
"Middle School Students' Motivation and Quality of Experience: A Comparison of Montessori and Traditional School Environments," excerpts from (with Csikszentmihalyi), 183–84, 193, 194, 195, 200–203, 204, 205–6

List of "Insider's View" Videos

Insider's View callouts within the book link to a suite of videos where students can hear directly from scholars and students in various academic fields as they explore disciplinary expectations for their writing and reflect on their own writing practices. These videos are available in the LaunchPad for *An Insider's Guide to Academic Writing*.